P9-CMP-585

Maturity *1880-1910*

LEO TOLSTOY

by Ernest J. Simmons

ntage Russian Library R-1001 b *$1.4*

FORSYTH LIBRARY - FHSU
DATE DUE

LEO TOLSTOY

VOLUME

II

VINTAGE *RUSSIAN* LIBRARY

Advisory Committee

Cyril E. Black, PRINCETON UNIVERSITY

Philip E. Mosely, COUNCIL ON FOREIGN RELATIONS

Ernest J. Simmons, COLUMBIA UNIVERSITY

VINTAGE *RUSSIAN* LIBRARY

LEO TOLSTOY

VOLUME

II

The Years of Maturity

1880–1910

BY

ERNEST J. SIMMONS

1 9  6 0

VINTAGE BOOKS : NEW YORK

PUBLISHED BY VINTAGE BOOKS, INC.

Reprinted by arrangement with Little, Brown and Company, the original publisher of the book in association with The Atlantic Monthly Press.

 Manufactured in the United States of America. Published simultaneously in Canada by McClelland & Stewart Ltd.

FIRST VINTAGE EDITION

Contents of Both Volumes

Volume II, 1880–1910

Volume I, 1828–1879

PART FOUR

"And Finally There Is

the Fourth Period . . . in Which

I Now Live

and Hope to Die . . ."

3

XXII

A New Faith

After his long spiritual struggle, Tolstoy reached the conclusion that the problem of life is explained only by religion. But at the end of *Confession* he indicated his distrust of the Orthodox Church and declared his intentions of separating what was true from what was false in the teachings of the Church and in the Bible. Over the next few years he devoted himself to this task. With magnificent arrogance, he swept through centuries of accumulated Biblical scholarship, textual exegesis, commentaries, and historical studies. Like an intellectual titan, he absorbed this mountain of material as he had the "whole libraries" connected with the theme of *War and Peace*. Only now he worked with the spirit of God in his heart and fully conscious of the fact that what he wrote might never see the light of day, in Russia at least. That his attitude toward established religion would be deeply hostile was almost a foregone conclusion: his entire previous intellectual history had been steeped in dissent.

Tolstoy entitled his first important religious work, which he wrote in 1880, *An Examination of Dogmatic Theology*.[1] It is perhaps the least read of all his productions, and undeservedly so, for it is a remarkably fervent and compellingly logical attack on the Russian Orthodox Church. There was nothing of the Voltaire in Tolstoy. He combined with a profoundly religious spirit an unsparing truthfulness. Heedless of personal risk in condemning an all-powerful Church, he sought the truth wherever he might find it.

[1] This work was not published until 1891, and then in a poor edition in Geneva. A better version was printed in England in 1903. The most authoritative edition, with variants, may be found in the Jubilee Edition (Vol. XXI). There is no satisfactory English translation.

In a sense, the anarchistic temper of Tolstoy's mind admirably fitted him for an examination of dogmatic theology: he was not disposed to accept anything that would not stand the test of reason. On the other hand, he had the defect of this virtue, for he was inclined to place too much faith in his own reasoning. After a thorough examination of the dogmas of the Church, he concluded that they were false and an insult to human intelligence. The Church itself, he charged, supported its tenets by deceitful verbal tricks, and sought merely power instead of trying to fulfill its obligation to spread a right understanding of religion on the basis of Christ's teachings. Moreover, he was convinced that nobody really believed the dogmas of the Church, because they meant nothing at all, and a statement must have meaning before it can be believed. To be faithful to a belief, Tolstoy argued, you must have a belief, and a real belief cannot be founded on credulity; it can be achieved only by sincere mental effort.

Tolstoy went still further, for he insisted that Christian dogma deliberately attempts to turn men's minds away from the essential teaching of Christ. Christ had nothing to say about the fall of Adam, the Trinity, or the scheme of the Redemption, but He had a great deal to say about the necessity of love and pity and man's duty to man. The teaching of Christ (about humility, not judging, forgiveness of injuries, self-sacrifice, and love) the Church extolled in words, but in practice it approved of what was incompatible with this teaching. For all human evils—the condemnation of individuals, of whole peoples, of other religions, and the executions and wars that resulted from such condemnations—were all justified by the Church.

After having dismissed the dogmas of the Church and the whole theology in which they were imbedded, Tolstoy turned to an investigation of the Gospels, for he was mystified by what he considered the Church's distortion of the spirit of Christ's teaching. He had observed that those passages in the Gospels on which Church dogmas were based were the most obscure, whereas those from which one derived the practical teaching of Christ were the clearest and most definite. Yet the dogmas and the Christian obligations that resulted from them were defined by the Church in the most precise manner, while mention was made of the practical fulfillment of Christ's teaching only in the most indefinite and mystical manner. Christ, he believed, could not have intended this when He taught his disciples.

At first, Tolstoy's study of the Gospels, particularly the Sermon on the Mount, left him perplexed. The words in the Sermon often were not clear. So complete was the renunciation of everything that life retained little meaning. Nor could he accept the theological explanation that the precepts of the Sermon on the Mount were indications of the perfection toward which one should strive, but that fallen man cannot by his own efforts attain this perfection, and that his safety lies in faith, prayer, and the Sacraments. Would Christ give admirable rules relating to man's salvation and then deny him the possibility of achieving it by his own individual strength of will?

Tolstoy at last found a key to much that had been unclear to him in the Gospels in the passage in Matthew: "Ye have heard that it was said, An eye for an eye and a tooth for a tooth: But I say unto you, Resist not him that is evil." Previously the words "But I say unto you, Resist not him that is evil" had signified nothing to him, and still less the passage that immediately follows: "But whosoever smiteth thee on thy right cheek, turn to him the other also." This latter statement seemed an exaggeration, as though Christ were extolling suffering for the sake of suffering. Then suddenly Tolstoy perceived that all was explained if he accepted literally Christ's injunction: "Resist not him that is evil." For then it would appear that Christ did not command man to present the cheek in order to make him suffer, but He commanded man not to resist him that is evil, and added that this might involve having to suffer.

By accepting the literal meaning of nonresistance to evil with all its implications, much that had been obscure in the Gospels became plain to Tolstoy. For by not resisting him that is evil one will never do violence, will never do an act contrary to love, which Tolstoy felt was the real substance of Christianity. All who would fulfill the law must be prepared to abandon everything and endure all consequences.

Once having decided upon an acceptance of the literal meaning of Christ's words in this instance, Tolstoy applied the principle to many other significant precepts enunciated in the Sermon on the Mount and in the Gospels in general. The results astonished him. He was able to shear away much of the mystical and allegorical interpretation that had distorted the plain meaning of these precepts over the ages. In some instances, by actual study of the earliest Greek texts, he exposed accidental and perhaps deliberate mistranslations. Particularly in the chapters of the Sermon on the Mount, he came to the conclusion that Christ was patently summing up his practical advice by indicating what had been taught in ancient times and then offering an extension or even a direct contradiction to the old precepts. And from this study Tolstoy elucidated five commandments of Christ that he accepted himself, and which if observed by all would alter the whole course of men's lives. Put in brief form they are: *Do not be angry; Do not lust; Do not swear oaths* (by which is meant: "Do not give away the control of your future actions"); *Resist not him that is evil;* and *Love your enemies.*

Tolstoy maintained that these commandments represented the core of Christ's teaching, and if practiced would link religion to our daily lives. He saw clearly all their far-reaching implications. For a man who refuses to swear an oath cannot take any part in the offices of civil government or serve in the army; the complete observance of the commandment *Resist not him that is evil* involves ultimately the entire abolition of compulsory legislation, law courts, police, and prisons, as well as all forcible restraints of man by man; and adherence to *Love your enemies* would mean the end of all wars. He fully realized, of course, that man is weak and incapable of a strict observance of such precepts as *Do not be angry* or *Do not lust,* and to abstain from anger and lust as much as possible, he admitted, was perhaps all that our animal natures would allow.

It would be a mistake to regard Tolstoy as an iconoclast or a mere religious reformer. If there were no God, he might not have invented one, but if his five commandments had not existed in the Gospels, he would very likely have formulated a similar series of rules of life that he would have regarded as his religion. For all these commandments were implicit in much that he had said and written in his diaries, letters, and artistic works before 1880. Unlike the traditional theologian, he was not concerned with the personality of God or the creation and redemption of the world. He simply wanted an explanation of the meaning of life, and he found it in some Higher Power that manifested itself through the workings of reason and conscience. And by experience he became convinced that the existence of that

Power in him constituted a moral force for good which in turn gave a meaning and purpose to life that was not defeated by death. His religion, then, amounted to a series of precepts that made life worth living, and which, if sincerely practiced, would enable him to accomplish the greatest amount of good. He had the courage to preach this religion and to give it force by sincerely attempting to live it. And he proclaimed his faith in the teeth of a powerful and jealous Church that was scandalized by his exposure of its fraudulent dogmas, and in the face of a scornful science and materialistic philosophy that often ignored the existence of moral law.

Immediately after finishing his *Examination of Dogmatic Theology* in 1880, Tolstoy began another book, the *Union and Translation of the Four Gospels,*[2] really a continuation of the first work. With characteristic daring he set out to compile his own version of the Gospels and to justify every change. He rearranged the chapters and verses to suit himself and discarded anything he disapproved of or could not understand. The artist's power of selection, as well as scholarship, is reflected in this undertaking. The result is a version of the four Gospels that presents a remarkably consistent and convincing narrative, and at the same time reveals a new, fresh conception of Christ's personality and teaching. While admitting that an author is often mistaken in judging the comparative worth of his own production, Tolstoy insisted that the *Union and Translation of the Four Gospels* was more important than anything he had ever written. It cost him, he remarked years later, the greatest and happiest effort; it was the turning point of his whole life, and served as a basis for everything that he wrote after it.

As by-products of these two large works in 1880 came two smaller productions. From a few rejected fragments of *An Examination of Dogmatic Theology,* a secretary pieced together an article, "Church and State," that circulated widely in manuscript, since its publication was forbidden.

In his *Union and Translation of the Four Gospels,* he had set down in three parallel columns the Greek text, the Russian version, and finally his own translation. Much of this

[2] This book was finished in 1881, but he continued to work on it until the next year. It was not allowed to be printed in Russia until 1908, and will be published for the first time in complete form in the Jubilee Edition (Vols. XXII-XXIII).

large work is made up of his textual notes and commentaries that cover a vast range of material. The family tutor, V. I. Alekseyev, thought so highly of it that he wished to copy it, in order to make it available to his friends. But his stay in the house was already drawing to a close, so he decided to limit himself to copying only Tolstoy's translation of the four Gospels. Tolstoy looked over the copy and wrote a foreword and conclusion. This smaller work, under the title *A Short Account of the Gospels,* eventually appeared in print and achieved perhaps wider dissemination than any of his formal religious productions.

These writings of 1880–1881 laid the solid foundations of Tolstoy's religious thought, although he was to produce many more works, large and small, in which he elaborated and modified his religious thinking and applied it to nearly every aspect of human endeavor. In the course of time his opinions about Christ changed slightly, and, after having become more thoroughly versed in the religions of the world, he ceased to regard Christ's teaching as unique. For he eventually perceived that what is really vital in life lies at the root of all great religions.

Although Tolstoy came to attach less significance to Christ's personality and to the exact phraseology of the Gospels, he always held to his conviction that the Gospels contain the essential truth and that his interpretation of Christ's teaching was correct. Biblical scholars, like professional pedagogues in the past, resented his intrusion upon their domain. They scornfully pointed out his mistakes, and in some cases he made them, though his scholarly ability was considerable. But he brought to his investigation of the texts of the Gospels a genius never found among scholars and capacities that could not fail to be enlightening in a kind of study that had been feeding on its own substance for generations. His essential contributions have never been refuted. Unusual inventive powers, imagination, and wonderful common sense swept away encrusted traditions and supplied emendations and interpretations in textual exegesis that were beyond the powers of most scholars.

2

In striking contrast to the spiritual suffering Tolstoy had been through was the happiness he now derived from his newly found faith. Experience would soon teach him how difficult it was to conform to his religious precepts. In the meantime, he could not keep quiet about the failure of others to live up to them. In fact, he had scarcely formulated the commandments before he attempted to persuade the Tsar of All the Russias to observe several of them in a situation of grave national consequence.

In the 1860's and 1870's Alexander II had striven to correct the abuses of his predecessor's reign, one of the most reactionary in Russia, by supporting liberal legislation, such as the emancipation act that freed the serfs. These progressive measures by no means satisfied the adherents of a growing revolutionary movement that demanded nothing less than the end of autocratic rule. The activities of the revolutionists were met with severe reprisals and their organizations were forced underground, but they continued to perpetrate violent acts, freely risking their lives to murder those they considered the enemies of the people. On March 1, 1881, a group of terrorists, belonging to the revolutionary organization Peoples' Freedom, blew up the carriage of Alexander II and killed the Tsar. Six of the terrorists were apprehended (including one woman, Sofya Perovski) and were subsequently condemned to death.

The assassination of the Tsar shocked Tolstoy, as it did nearly everyone in Russia, but he was even more distressed over the condemned terrorists. His instinctive repulsion to capital punishment was now intensified by the faith he had adopted, a faith that regarded the taking of human life as a mortal sin. According to the teaching of Christ, he could not absolve himself from responsibility in the execution of these terrorists simply because he himself was not the executioner. This thought obsessed him, depressed his spirits, and convinced him that he must protest. He could not help thinking of the condemned, and of those who would perform the execution, and especially of the new Tsar Alexander III, who, he imagined, would experience a feeling of joy in pardoning the murderers of his father.

One morning Tolstoy, filled with gloom, came down to his coffee and called Alekseyev into the drawing room. He explained to the tutor, a well-educated man and a former participator in revolutionary activity, that in accordance with Christ's teaching he was thinking of writing a letter to the Tsar to beseech him to pardon the condemned terrorists, and he asked Alekseyev's opinion of this step. The tutor, who had become a favorite of Tolstoy and was already partial to his new faith, agreed that in the circumstances this was the least he could do. Sonya, who had overheard the conversation in the next room, suddenly entered, and in an agitated voice declared to the tutor: "Vasili Ivanovich, what are you saying! If my son and daughter had been present instead of Leo Nikolayevich, who does not need your advice, I would at once order you to leave!"

After dinner that day Tolstoy went into his study to rest. He fell asleep and saw in a dream the execution of the slayers of Alexander II, and instead of the executioners designated by the court, it was as though he himself executed them. He awoke in horror and at once wrote a letter to Alexander III.

The letter[3] began in a humble tone: "I, an insignificant, unrecognized, weak, and wretched man, write a letter to the Russian Emperor and advise him how to act in the most complex and difficult circumstances that have ever occurred. I feel how strange, improper, and bold this is, and yet I write." His tone soon changed, however, to that of a tremendously earnest but courageous pleader. He wrote to the Emperor "simply as man to man," he said, and not with the customary "flowers of servile and false eloquence that only obscure both feeling and thought." And at times he boldly assumed the role of prophet that became so characteristic of him in the future.

Tolstoy acknowledged how horrible was the crime that had been committed by the terrorists, and he admitted the possibility that their adherents, "for the sake of the imaginary general good they seek, must wish to kill you too." That the Tsar's soul was filled with a desire for vengeance on his father's murderers, he could well understand. Yet his primary duty was not as Tsar, but as a man, and if he would only follow the teaching of Christ, the temptation of vengeance would be destroyed. Then Tolstoy quoted the passage from Matthew on which he based his commandment: *Love your enemies,* and he implored the Tsar to return good for evil.

Tolstoy then declared that for some twenty years revolutionary organizations had been attempting to destroy the existing order by all manner of crimes against the State. To combat this opposition the government employed two meth-

[3] Only the first draft of this letter exists, and there is evidence that the one sent to the Emperor differed somewhat from the original version. Tolstoy said the original was longer and more heartfelt.

ods: either liberal measures were passed to appease the opposition or else the cruelest repressions were used. Both these methods, he insisted, had failed dismally, for opposition to the government had increased and grew more violent all the time. Why not try a third method—Christian forgiveness—he asked. You stand, he warned the Tsar, at the parting of the ways. If those triumphed who thought that Christian truth was mere talk, and that in political life blood must be spilled, then the Tsar would pass forever from "a blessed condition of purity and life in God, and would enter on the dark path of State-necessity, justifying everything—even the infringement of the law of God and man."

In an eloquent peroration Tolstoy concluded his letter to the Tsar as follows:—

"Forgive! Return good for evil, and from among a hundred evil-doers scores will turn not to you, not to them (this is not important), but they will turn from the devil to God, and the hearts of thousands, of millions, will throb with joy and tenderness at this example of goodness shown from the throne, at a moment so terrible for the son of a murdered father.

"Monarch! If you should do this, if you should summon the condemned, give them money, and send them away somewhere to America, and should write a manifesto headed with the words: 'But I say to you, love your enemies,' I do not know how others would react, but I, a poor subject, would be your dog, your slave. I would weep from tenderness, as I now weep every time I hear your name. But what do I say?—'I do not know how others would react.' I know that at those words goodness and love would pour forth like a flood over Russia. The truths of Christ live in the hearts of people, and they alone live, and we love people only in the name of these truths. . . .

"Who are these revolutionists? They are people who hate the existing order of things; they find it bad, and they have in mind the establishment of a future order that will be better. It is impossible to contend against them by killing and destroying them. Their number is not important, but their thought. To struggle against them one must struggle spiritually. Their ideal is a sufficiency for all, equality, and freedom. To oppose them one must oppose their ideal with one that is superior to theirs and includes it. The French, English, and Germans struggle with them now, and also to no purpose.

"There is only one ideal that can be opposed to them. And that ideal, the one from which they start—though not understanding and blaspheming it—and which includes theirs, is the ideal of love, of forgiveness, and of returning good for evil. Only one word of forgiveness and Christian love, spoken and fulfilled from the height of the throne, and the path of Christian rule which is before you, waiting to be trod, can destroy the evil that is corroding Russia. As wax before the fire, every revolutionary struggle will melt away before the man-tsar who fulfills the law of Christ."

To get such a letter to the Tsar was no easy task. Tolstoy had recourse to his friend Strakhov in Petersburg. He sent him the letter with a covering note, in which he suggested a plan. Strakhov was asked to deliver the letter to K. P. Pobedonostsev, former tutor of Alexander III, and at this time Head of the Holy Synod. Tolstoy hoped Pobedonostsev, who had the confidence of the Tsar, would present the letter to him. In his note to Strakhov, he requested that, if possible, the letter be presented without his name, but he insisted that his name be used if the slightest danger were connected with such a presentation.

Tolstoy's agitated wife complicated matters by insisting upon adding a postscript to this note to Strakhov. Despite all her pleas, she wrote, her husband was determined to send the letter to the Tsar. "Read the letter," she begged, "judge it yourself, and then ask Pobedonostsev's opinion whether or not this letter will arouse in the Emperor any disagreeable feelings or ill-will for Leo Nikolayevich. In that case, for God's sake do not permit the letter to get to the Emperor."

Tolstoy also wrote to Pobedonostsev, explaining his sense of moral responsibility which had obliged him to compose the letter, and soliciting his aid in seeing that it reached the Emperor. But the influential Pobedonostsev, who soon gained the reputation of being the most reactionary force in Russia, flatly refused to transmit Tolstoy's letter to the Emperor.

Strakhov then turned the letter over to Professor K. N. Bestuzhev-Ryumin, who put it in the hands of the Grand Duke Sergei Alexandrovich. Through him it is reported to have reached the Emperor, but his only response, how authentic is uncertain, is recorded by Sonya: "Concerning this letter, Alexander III commanded that Count L. N. Tolstoy be told that if an attempt had been made on his own life, he could pardon it, but he did not have the right to pardon the murderers of his father."

Tolstoy's letter to the Emperor, however, did cause some repercussions which appear to have worried the powerful Pobedonostsev. Fearful that rumors of the intervention of so distinguished an author might create a party opposed to the execution, he wrote the Emperor pleading that nothing be allowed to interfere with the executions. Alexander III reassured him. "Be calm," he replied, "no one will dare to come to me with such proposals; I guarantee that *all six will be hanged*." And so they were.

Three months after Tolstoy had written to him to secure his assistance, and when the terrorists had long been cold in their graves, Pobedonostsev condescended to reply. The letter began with a sniveling excuse for tardiness, but it contained also a veiled warning that boded ill for Tolstoy in the future. "In such an important affair," he wrote in explanation of his unwillingness to accommodate Tolstoy, "everything must be done in accordance with one's faith. And after reading your letter, I saw that your faith is one thing, and mine and that of the Church another, and that our Christ is not your Christ. Mine I know as a man of strength and truth, healing the weak; but in yours I thought I detected the features of one who is feeble and himself needs to be cured."

So Tolstoy had failed in his first major attempt to persuade another to practice the faith he had embraced. In this instance failure was perhaps the only possible result. The letter to the Emperor is a fair sample of the attitude toward public affairs that Tolstoy retained for the rest of his life. And this attitude raises the question of how thorough was his understanding of the processes of government in Russia. In the past, with few exceptions, he had avoided any active participation in political matters. His distrust of civil institutions had been manifested on frequent occasions. Nor can there be any doubt that deeply rooted prejudice, springing from his own aristocratic background, made it difficult for him to have any sympathy for the widespread revolutionary movement. His conviction that the ills of society could be corrected by observing the law of Christ led him into a dangerous oversimplification of political and social problems. He did not see that pardoning a few terrorists, who were quite willing to sacrifice their lives to achieve their ends, would not solve an age-old problem that involved the deprivation of the most elementary human rights for millions of subjects of a despotic government.

The fact is, Tolstoy was seeking for the Kingdom of God on earth. His premise was that men can exist successfully and happily by living according to the precepts of the Sermon on the Mount alone. Human experience, however, does not support the premise. Outside the confines of society, no limit need be placed on an individual's striving for moral perfection. But as a member of organized society, the individual is obliged to submit to forces that are inimical to the teaching of the Sermon on the Mount. Eventually, Tolstoy recognized this fact. His great virtue and largest service to humanity was his insistence that most of the suffering of mankind resulted from failure to abide by moral laws. Implicit in his letter to the Emperor is the clear realization that the failure of both the established government and its revolutionary opponents, in Russia and elsewhere, was caused then, and always will be caused, by the absence of morality in striving for political and social ends.

3

Knowledge of Tolstoy's religious experience and his new faith came as a surprise, and sometimes an unpleasant one, to his close friends. Many of his admirers, to whom he was the famous author of *War and Peace* and *Anna Karenina,* were shocked and bewildered by his abandonment of literature for religion, and idle rumors about this defection quickly went the rounds. "Here in Petersburg," communicated the faithful Strakhov, "all discuss your revolution"; and Dostoyevsky, while on a visit to Moscow, wrote to his wife: "Grigorovich reported that . . . Tolstoy has almost lost his mind and perhaps may have gone completely insane."

Despite sincere efforts to be humble, Tolstoy did not always wear his new religious halo gracefully. Poor Granny, that old and aging friend, was one of the first to fall afoul of his recently acquired beliefs. For years she had been the pious confidante of his religious and philosophical speculations, and in numerous letters she had kindly but persistently attempted to prod him into an acceptance of Russian Orthodoxy. In January 1880, he went to Petersburg to make arrangements for a fourth edition of his collected works, for which he received the munificent sum of 25,000 rubles. While in the city he visited Granny, whom he had not seen for a long time. The meeting ended in a heated discussion on religion. On this subject he was capable at times of forgetting his Christlike humility for the thundering tone of an Old Testament prophet. He parted from Granny profoundly agitated and left the city without saying farewell to her. A letter of apology quickly followed, in which he could not refrain from reminding her that he had torn himself away from the lies that her Church taught. "You have a sincere love for God, for goodness," he concluded, "yet you cannot understand where He is." She dispatched an indignant reply, but followed it up soon after with a letter in which she calmly argued their points of difference. In a long answer he patiently explained why it was impossible for him to accept the religion of the Church. The Christian love they both professed somehow succeeded in alienating them.

Nor did the many years of intimate friendship with Fet mix well with Tolstoy's religious zeal. Their correspondence dwindled, and in May 1881 Tolstoy wrote what appears to have been his last letter to Fet. Fet was a practical man, as well as a poet, and hence Tolstoy's extreme religious views, especially his belief that men should not possess property, seemed like so much nonsense to this large and successful estate owner.

Turgenev could only lament the great loss to Russian literature that would result from Tolstoy's preoccupation with religion. As though he felt that praise might tempt Tolstoy to hew to the literary line, he wrote him from Paris in January 1880 to tell him of his success among the French. He quoted a letter from Flaubert on reading *War and Peace,* in which the great French novelist had declared: "It is of the first rank! What painting and what psychology! . . . It seemed to me that at times there were things worthy of Shakespeare! I uttered cries of admiration during the reading!" And to fill the cup, Turgenev quoted from his own letter to About, printed in a Paris newspaper, concerning the merits of the French translation of *War and Peace*. He had called Tolstoy "the most popular of contemporary Russian authors" and *War and Peace* "one of the most remarkable books of our time."

The glamour of artistic success, however, was something that Tolstoy was now beginning to think of as a positive evil. He wrote to V. V. Stasov, librarian and art critic, a recent fervent worshiper and friend: "Concerning *Anna Karenina:* I assure you that this abomination no longer exists for me, and I'm only vexed because there are people for whom this sort of thing is necessary." For Turgenev, on the other hand, artistic success was nearly life's sweetest happiness. He visited Yasnaya Polyana in May 1880 to execute a literary commission. The eightieth anniversary of Pushkin's birth was to be celebrated in Moscow, and the officials in charge of the affair, aware of Tolstoy's dislike for such public celebrations, had asked Turgenev to persuade him to attend. The visit turned out to be an unusually pleasant one, but when Turgenev, at an opportune moment, made his request, Tolstoy flatly refused.

The next year, in July, Tolstoy visited Turgenev at Spasskoye. He arrived unexpectedly at one o'clock in the morning. The poet Ya. P. Polonski, who was also Turgenev's guest, went down to let Tolstoy in, and at first took him for a peasant, for he was sunburned and dressed in a common blouse with a leather belt. The writers sat up until three in the morning in animated discussion. Polonski had not seen Tolstoy for twenty years, and he was struck by his manner, which seemed to him surprisingly soft and of a winning simplicity. "He appeared to me," said Polonski, "to be reborn, imbued with a different faith, a different love. . . . He did not impose his own views on us and quietly heard out Ivan Sergeyevich's [Turgenev's] objections. In brief, he was no longer the count as I knew him."

On August 22 of the same year Turgenev paid his last visit to Yasnaya Polyana, for he had not long to live. It was Sonya's birthday and merriment reigned in the household. Turgenev entered into the spirit of the occasion and danced a quadrille that the young folks arranged. Then taking off his coat and sticking his thumbs into his waistcoat, he began to perform weird movements with his legs, declaring that this was the way the cancan was performed in Paris. All were immensely amused, but in his diary that day the stern Tolstoy entered: "Turgenev—the cancan. It is sad."

The one Russian author who might have sympathized with Tolstoy's faith in Christ's teaching was Dostoyevsky. And it is an interesting fact that at just about this time he had begun to manifest a lively interest in Dostoyevsky, who had already acclaimed him in print as one of the great writers of the age. Dostoyevsky had been anxious to go to Yasnaya Polyana to meet him, but when he consulted Turgenev on the matter the latter discouraged the visit by telling him how difficult it was to approach Tolstoy. The two never did meet.

Years before (1862) Tolstoy had strongly recommended to Granny Dostoyevsky's *House of the Dead,* and now, in 1880, he wrote to Strakhov, who was close to Dostoyevsky and his future biographer, that he had just reread this work and did not know "of a better book in all modern literature, including Pushkin. Not the tone, but the point of view is surprising—sincere, natural, and Christian. . . . If you see Dostoyevsky, tell him tnat I love him." Strakhov showed the letter to Dostoyevsky, who was immensely pleased with this praise from a man whose literary art he thought supreme.

The next year Dostoyevsky died. Sonya wrote to her sister Tanya: "He [Tolstoy] and all of us have been terribly affected by Dostoyevsky's death. He had only just become known to all people when he died. This led Lyovochka to think of his own death, and he has become still more concentrated and silent." In answer to a letter from Strakhov about the death, Tolstoy wrote: "How I should like to be able to say all that I feel about Dostoyevsky. You, in describing your own feelings, have in part described mine. I never saw this man and never had any direct relations with him, and suddenly, when he died, I understood that he was the closest, dearest, and most necessary man to me. . . . I reckoned him as my friend, and never thought otherwise than that we should meet at one time or another. And suddenly at dinner—I ate alone, was late—I read of the death. What a support has been torn from me. I was at a loss, and then it became clear how precious he was to me, and I wept and weep now."

Tolstoy did not deceive himself. Of all the Russian writers of the time Dostoyevsky was probably closest to him in an ideological sense, however strikingly contrasted their artistic works may be. In their thought and in an insistence upon the importance of morality in life, they had a great deal in common. Dostoyevsky's sweeping doctrine of salvation by suffering and his condemnation of reason as an approach to faith would have repelled Tolstoy. But Christ was their hero. Both men were seekers after God, and in faith in Him they saw the only possibility of salvation. Dostoyevsky, however, attempted to realize the Kingdom of God in his art; Tolstoy sought through his active deeds to establish it on earth.

In his visits to Yasnaya Polyana, Turgenev had noted with dismay that Tolstoy surrounded himself with Bibles and Gospels in nearly all languages, and that he had composed a trunkful of writings on these books. When Tolstoy read some of his religious works to him, he confessed that he simply did not understand them. And he thought with horror of the influence these works might have on younger writers, one of whom, V. M. Garshin, he indicated as already a follower of Tolstoy.

As a matter of fact, the young Garshin, who was then on the verge of a mental breakdown, turned up at Yasnaya Polyana one early spring evening in 1880. He appeared at the door unannounced, and when Tolstoy asked what he wanted, he replied: "The first thing I want is a glass of vodka and the tail of a herring." There was a mad look in his bold bright expression and childish smile that fascinated Tolstoy. Drink and food were provided, and he soon identified himself as the author of the sensational story, *Four Days on the Battlefield,* which Tolstoy had read with great admiration. Soon he held Tolstoy and the children entranced by accounts of his experiences in the Russo-Turkish War in which he had distinguished himself. And then with breathless haste he outlined his plan to bring about universal happiness. Tolstoy was interested, and he must have been struck by Garshin's moral sensitiveness and his condemnation of the horrors of war. There was in Garshin's personality a Dostoyevsky-like sense of infinite compassion and pity that found a ready response in Tolstoy. A few days later this half-mad author was seen riding by on a horse that he had purloined from a Tula cabby, talking to himself and waving his arms wildly.

The one friend from whom Tolstoy could expect a profound sympathetic understanding of his religious transformation was Strakhov. This shy, modest man could be firm to the point of exasperation. He did not tear things with his teeth, Tolstoy wrote him once, but with soft, strong paws. He was interested in everything that Tolstoy did, and since he visited Yasnaya Polyana nearly every summer, he was made a confidant of Tolstoy's developing religious thought. During the entire period of his theological investigations in 1880 and 1881, Tolstoy could always be certain of Strakhov's aid in obtaining material and of his kindly, patient, but independent criticism.

This was more, Tolstoy quickly learned, than he could expect from any of his old friends. Although his new faith obliged him to give no offense and to live in amity with all men, his strenuous nature and emphatic expression often led him into being severe on the conduct and occupations of others. He was soon made to realize that the discoverer of a truth, even though it be old and forgotten, must pay a price in friendship. For his friends and the public, he was a writer of great fiction, and they resented his preaching Christian ethics and donning the prophet's robe. A still greater tragedy brought about by his devotion to the Prince of Peace was that it strained his relations with his family and ultimately left him spiritually alone in his own household.

4

Despite God and religion, fifty-two years of life, and a beard plentifully streaked with gray, the young effects in Tolstoy were not defunct, and for a brief time in 1880 they were sorely tried. Nearly every day on his walks he encountered Domna, the buxom young cook, whose husband was absent on military service. At first he was contented merely to walk behind her, observing, but one day he whistled softly, caught up with her, chatted, and made a rendezvous in a quiet lane for the next day. Conscience struggled with desire as he set out for the appointed spot. On the way he had to pass under the windows of the children's schoolroom. At that critical moment little Ilya poked his head out of the window and reminded his father that it was time for their Greek lesson. Fate was on the side of conscience. He gave the lesson.

Temptation, however, continued. Tolstoy prayed, and strove to overcome his desire for Domna. One day he took the tutor, Alekseyev, aside and excitedly whispered:—

"I'm assailed by temptation of the flesh, and it seems that I'm utterly powerless to resist. I'm afraid I'll give in. Help me!"

And he told the whole story as though deliberately trying to humiliate himself.

"Well, what do you want me to do?" asked the puzzled tutor.

"Come with me on my daily walks. We will walk and talk together, and perhaps this desire will pass off."

Tolstoy seemed able to put Satan behind him by this unique device but, not to tempt the devil too far, he finally managed to have the seductive Domna transferred elsewhere.

Fortunately, Sonya knew nothing of this incident; her immediate worries over the family's future were caused by Tolstoy's new religious beliefs.

Try as he might, he could not adjust his new world of Christ to his old world of family happiness. At first, he did not seem fully aware of his transformation and grew irritated over the inability of his family to understand and sympathize with his changed behavior. The former sinner striving to be a saint found the little domain of Yasnaya Polyana anything but a holy man's hermitage. His new views and religious studies left him little time to devote to farming and the breeding of cattle. His financial affairs went from bad to worse. The income of his three properties of Yasnaya Polyana, Nikolskoye, and the estate in Samara, the capital value of which was some $250,000, shrank to about $2500 a year, a sum far from adequate to meet the mounting expenses of his growing family. More and more he allowed the cares of managing his estate to devolve upon his wife, and Sonya, despite her efforts, was extremely worried over the future.

In her diary at the beginning of 1881, Sonya well described the changed atmosphere of the household. "Every day," she wrote of her husband, "he sits at his work, surrounded by books, and keeps at it until dinner. His health has become very weak, his head aches, and he has grown gray and thin this winter. Obviously, he is not entirely as happy as I should desire, and he has become quiet, self-absorbed, and silent. Almost never does that jolly, lively frame of mind appear which formerly attracted all of us around him. I attribute this weariness to his weighty, strenuous work. It is not as it used to be when he described the hunt or the ball in *War and Peace;* then, happy and excited, he looked as though he had been present and taken part in these amusements. The clarity and calm of the personal state of his soul are undoubted, but suffering over the misfortunes and injustices of people, their poverty and imprisonment, over the evil of people, over oppression—all this acts on his sensitive spirit and consumes his existence."

From the outset Sonya did not agree with her husband's new religious beliefs, but at first she was willing to recognize their value, and in moments of spiritual closeness to him she tried hard to believe in them. Such moments, however, grew increasingly rare. The seeds of discord that had been planted in the early years of marriage had begun to bear fruit, and his religious change hastened the ripening.

In letters to her sister Tanya at this time, Sonya, perhaps with a touch of exaggeration and self-pity, complained of her grief, suffering, and her desire for death, and she hinted darkly of a crisis in her life with her husband. There were two reasons for her fear. The first and most important was an old one—her opposition to having more children. Her protests in the past had been swiftly crushed by Tolstoy's uncompromising attitude. Shortly after the birth of her tenth child,[4] she wrote in an almost hysterical tone to Tanya: "At times I should like to fly away to you, to mama, to Moscow—anywhere, anywhere away from my half-dark bedroom, where bending over the flushed little face of a new boy fourteen times a day I have shrunk away and almost fallen into a faint from the pain in my breasts. I've resolved to be consistent and nurse the last one too." And in succeeding letters to Tanya in 1880, Sonya complained bitterly of the "solitary life" forced on her by childbearing. In October of that year, however, she wrote to her sister: "Misha is always throwing up the little milk that he sucks, and I feel ill. On that score, to my extreme horror, I'm surely pregnant again."

No one would censure Sonya for her protests now, for almost without exception she had spent her whole youth in burdensome pregnancies and painful nursing. Nevertheless, Tolstoy evinced no disposition to take into consideration her physical and psychical limitations. Undoubtedly this vital disagreement aggravated old wounds and intensified the dissension that now arose because of the new demands that his religious life necessitated—the second reason for her fear.

The uncongenial atmosphere at home, for which he was largely, though unwittingly, responsible, no doubt had something to do with Tolstoy's frequent absence from Yasnaya Polyana during 1880 and part of the following year. With

[4] A son, Mikhail, born December 20, 1879.

irritation Sonya wrote to her sister in November 1880: "Lyovochka has plunged into his work, visiting prisons, justices of the peace, district courts, and recruiting stations out of extreme pity for people and for all the oppressed. All this is no doubt fine, great, and lofty, if only to feel the more one's own insignificance and nastiness. But, alas! life has its own rights; it longs for the other side, and the discord is only more painful and powerful." She complained of his sudden contempt for money and of the bountiful way in which he had begun to distribute it to poor peasants, and she lent an attentive ear to her brother, Alexander, who asserted that profound religious and philosophical preoccupation endangered one's mind. For a time relations between husband and wife grew so unpleasant that Sonya confessed to her sister that she even wanted to leave home. "Truly, this is because we have begun to live a Christian life. Formerly, in my opinion, without this Christianity it was much better."

Tolstoy himself was painfully aware of this family dissension. In his diary, amid closely written expressions of horror over the suffering of the poor and the wretched conditions of the prisons he visited, occurred an entry on May 5, 1881: "The family is flesh. To abandon the family is the second temptation—to kill oneself. The family is one body. But do not yield to the third temptation: serve not the family but the one God. The family is an indication of the place one must occupy on the economic ladder. It is flesh; as a weak stomach needs light food, so a pampered family needs more than a family accustomed to privations."

Here was the first recognition of the tragic struggle that had already begun with his family. Some days after the entry just quoted appears another that indicates more pointedly the sharp division of views: "They [members of the family] began a conversation. One must hang, one must flog, one must knock out the teeth of the weak without a witness. Should the masses revolt—it would be terrible. But to beat Jews is all right. . . . Who is insane—they or I?"

On June 10, 1881, Tolstoy, accompanied by one of his servants and a Yasnaya Polyana schoolteacher, set out on foot to make a pilgrimage to Optina Monastery. Perhaps the experience of meeting and talking with the common people on the road, as much as a desire to visit this monastery to converse again with its holy men, lay behind his unusual adventure. For the occasion he disguised himself in shabby peasant clothes.

At his first halting place on the road he wrote Sonya. "You cannot imagine to what degree it is new, important, and useful for the soul (for one's view of life) to see how God's world lives, the real big world and not that one which we have constructed for ourselves."

Tolstoy's efforts to remain incognito were not effective for long. On his fourth day on the road, he spent the night at a large village, where he got into an altercation with a drunken elder who was mistreating a peasant woman. The elder demanded Tolstoy's passport, and at once became quite tractable when he saw the name and title. The party reached the monastery on the fifth day and went for the night to a third-class hotel. Because of their humble appearance, the monk in charge shunted them off into a common night dormitory, disgustingly filthy and insect-ridden. Only a bribe won them a room for themselves. The next day Tolstoy visited the archimandrite of the monastery and the famous Elder Ambrose, with whom he had a long conversation. He left dissatisfied with his talks and returned home by way of Kaluga, where he took the train for Tula.

Two days after his return, Tolstoy jotted down the substance of a conversation about God that he had with his eighteen-year-old son Sergei. "He and they think that to say: I do not know that; it cannot be proved; I don't need it, shows wisdom and education. On the contrary, it shows ignorance. . . . Men have carefully taught them theology and church rites, knowing in advance that these would not stand the test of maturity; they have taught them much totally disconnected knowledge. And they are all left without unity, with disjointed knowledge, and they think this a gain." And he continued: "Seryozha admitted that he loves the life of the flesh and believes in it. I'm glad to have a clear statement of the question. . . . We had an enormous dinner with champagne. The two Tanyas [his sister-in-law and his daughter] were dressed up. Sashes at five rubles on each of the children. While we were at dinner a cart was already starting for the picnic, and passed among peasant carts that were carrying people exhausted by overwork. I went to them but had not the strength to speak out."

Restless and troubled in mind Tolstoy set out again, this time for his Samara estate, and he was accompanied by

Sergei. His attitude toward this distant property, which a few years ago he had regarded as a good financial speculation, had now changed. He could no longer take any pride in this large stud farm nor could he think of his own profits when he saw so much poverty in the surrounding countryside. The prospects for an income from the property that year, he wrote Sonya, were very fine, and then he almost apologetically added: "There are so many poor in the villages that it would be sad if we could not give at least a little help. And it is a timid poverty, unaware of itself."

Sonya did not let the suggestion pass without a comment —her husband's generous and often indiscriminate almsgiving of late alarmed her. She began her letter on an unsympathetic note: "I'm glad that physically you feel fine in Samara. At least, this separation is not in vain. In general, it is more interesting for you there, quieter, and more agreeable than at home. This is sad but so." Then she added: "Even if there will be large profits, the money will reach neither me nor the children if it is given away. In any case, you know my opinion about helping the poor; we cannot feed thousands in Samara and other poor people."

While in Samara Tolstoy saw a good deal of the Molokans and other religious sectarians in whom he was deeply interested. A group of Molokans visited his estate. "I read them fragments from my *Account* [*Short Account of the Gospels*]," he wrote Sonya, "and the seriousness, interest, and healthy clear sense of these half-literate people is surprising." Without any show of condescension he dealt simply and naturally with the Molokans and frankly discussed their spiritual beliefs. In turn, these coarse steppe peasants, with their rugged necks and horny hands, eagerly, trustingly, and touchingly opened up their souls to him. "Obviously, for them as for me," remarked A. S. Prugavin, a student of Russian religious sects who was present at one of these discussions with the Molokans, "it became entirely clear and unquestioned that this noble, this titled aristocrat, not only understood the peasant, but loved him, sincerely loved him with the great and passionate heart of a talented man."

While Tolstoy was discussing theology with the Molokans in the Samara steppes, his wife was engaged in the more prosaic and more burdensome task of house-hunting in Moscow. Sergei wished to enter the university. In the normal course of things he would have been sent along to Moscow to pursue his studies, for he had arrived at the college age when such freedom was considered a necessity. The assassination of Alexander II, however, had stirred up the university students and intensified revolutionary activities among them. Already the government had instituted repressive measures. Sonya feared that her son might become involved in the radical movement if he were freed from parental supervision. Besides, the younger children could obtain better educational facilities in the city, and Tanya, who would soon be seventeen, needed to be brought out into the social life of Moscow.

The decision was largely Sonya's, and it was she who had to hunt down a house in Moscow that would suit their social position and also their dwindling income. It was an onerous task. Further, it had to be undertaken at a time when she was expecting her eleventh child.[5] Her letters to Samara concerning the difficulties she was encountering in finding a suitable house and of all her trials with the children eventually touched her husband and evoked a sudden upsurge of his former sense of duty and devotion to his wife: "You would not believe how troubled I am at the thought that you may be overtaxing your strength," he wrote, "and how I repent of having given you little or no help. . . . My justification is that in order to work with the intensity with which I have worked, and to get something done, one has to forget all else. And I have forgotten you too much, and I now repent. For God's sake and for the sake of our love, take care of yourself as much as possible. Put off as much as you can till my return. I will gladly do everything and will not do it badly, because I will take pains."

Yet Tolstoy did not hurry home, and by the time he arrived the removal to Moscow had been nearly all arranged. In truth, he regarded this event with dark foreboding. Just before he left Yasnaya Polyana, he wrote to friends in Samara: "My disagreement with the life around me is greater and more emphatic than before. All the time I see more clearly and definitely my own role, and I will hold to it: humility and a consciousness that everything to which I am now opposed is the fruit of my own mistakes, and therefore I have only pardon for others and blame for myself. . . . We are leaving on the 15th of September. I cannot imagine how I will live there." He dreaded the life in a

[5] The child, Aleksei, the eighth boy, was born October 31, 1881. In all eleven children had been born to Sonya in nineteen years of married life. Three of them had already died.

great city with all its glaring contrasts of wealth and poverty. What his reactions would be are suggested in a striking entry in his diary shortly before his departure: "An economic revolution not only may but must come. It is extraordinary that it has not come already."

XXIII

A Jeremiah in the Family

On more than one occasion since his marriage Tolstoy had expressed a dislike for city life, but for Sonya it offered the glad promise of a change from the monotony that had bored and fretted her spirit at Yasnaya Polyana. At last she would be able to assume a social position and enjoy the sophisticated pleasures of Moscow.

The family settled in a spacious rented house in Money Lane. Sergei enrolled in Moscow University; Ilya and young Leo entered a *Gymnasium;* and Tanya soon began her studies in an art school. The pattern of their future existence in Moscow was quickly determined. Comings and goings of playmates of the children, relatives and literary friends of Tolstoy, and persistent worshippers of the famous author kept the house as busy as a railway station. "What a quantity and variety of people come to see us," Sonya wrote her sister, "authors and painters . . . *le grand monde,* nihilists, and all sorts!" Sonya, still young, attractive, and elegantly dressed in the latest style, played the charming hostess at the samovar. If her husband was in the mood, he would enter the large drawing room at the tea hour. All conversation ceased upon his appearance, and he would behave with gracious aristocratic politeness to the guests who hung upon his every word. At times, however, something of the real contempt he felt for convention would manifest itself, much to Sonya's chagrin, in a refusal to wear his coat when company was present, because the room was too hot. More often he preferred to desert the large drawing room for the two small chambers that he had appropriated for himself. There, amid clouds of tobacco smoke, he held forth to eager admirers.

Beneath the pleasing surface that confronted their guests, family dissension grew with increasing tempo. The nature of their life together had changed; it had lost its simplicity, its artlessness, its originality. The older children, as well as husband and wife, felt this growing estrangement. The new life according to God that Tolstoy wished to live had nothing in common with the traditional aristocratic city existence that had been instilled into the family. The children felt it was not that they failed to understand their father, but that he had ceased to understand them, and they unconsciously drew away from him in order not to have their own happiness spoiled. Gloomily he walked the streets and grew irritated at the curious eyes that stared at him and at the occasional strangers who, recognizing the author of *War and Peace,* obsequiously bowed. Healthy policemen carrying revolvers annoyed him; and he once angrily remarked to his niece of the hordes of shoppers: "Why are they bustling about? Where are they hurrying? Always business, yet they do not see the principal thing; thus all their life passes and they do not notice that death approaches." When he returned home after such walks, his pent-up feelings often found an outlet in angry criticism of the family.

Before Tolstoy had been long in Moscow, he entered his reactions in his diary: "A month has passed. The most miserable in my life. The move to Moscow. All are busy arranging—when will they begin to live? All is not for the sake of living, but in order to be like other people. Unfortunates! There is no life. Stench, stones, luxury, poverty, debauchery. Malefactors have come together, robbing the people; they have collected soldiers and set up law courts to protect their orgies, and they feast. There is nothing for the people to do except to take advantage of the passions of these others and lure back from them what has been stolen. The peasants are cleverest at this. Their wives remain at home, while they wax our floors, rub our bodies in the bath, and ply as cabmen."

If Tolstoy's reactions to life in Moscow were bitter, his wife's were no less so on the score of his behavior, for she wrote her sister Tanya: "We have been here a month tomorrow and I have not written a word to anyone. During the first two weeks I cried every day, because Lyovochka not only became sad, but even fell into a kind of desperate apathy. He didn't sleep or eat and sometimes literally wept, and I thought I would really go mad. You would be surprised to see how I have changed and how thin I have grown. . . . Now he has arranged to work in a wing of the house, where he has hired two small quiet rooms for himself at six rubles a month; he walks to Maiden Field, makes his way across the river to the Sparrow Hills and there saws and splits wood with some peasants. It is good for his health and cheers him up."

2

Feeling utterly lonely and like an alien in Moscow, Tolstoy visited his friends the Bakunins[1] in the province of Tver. While there he received a letter from Prugavin about an unusual peasant, V. K. Syutayev, who was living in that neighborhood and seemed to share Tolstoy's views. He hastened to hunt him out in a village near by, hoping to assuage his longing for spiritual comradeship. There was nothing striking in the appearance of this peasant—he had a thin, mud-colored beard and wore, indoors and out, a greasy black sheepskin jacket—but he had already acquired a reputation for originality and holiness. In his youth, when he had learned to read, he spent all his spare time with the Bible. The New Testament he had by heart. There was a quiet, simple dignity about him, and in his slow peasant speech one heard an earthy wisdom and a power of conviction that impressed his hearers.

Tolstoy was no less amazed than delighted to find that Syutayev's religious beliefs were so similar to his own. He had rejected the Church and preached brotherhood, love, and life "according to God." Everything is in you, he was fond of saying, for where love is, there is God. Like Tolstoy, he condemned violence and would not allow it even as a means of resisting evil. He refused on principle to pay taxes, and when the authorities eventually dispossessed him of his small property, he accepted the situation without a murmur. His entire family clung to his beliefs. One son had been sent to prison for refusing to serve in the army, for he considered it a sin to take an oath, and would not handle a rifle because it "smelled of blood." Syutayev would allow no priest to officiate at the marriages of his children. When his daughter took

[1] A liberal and artistic family.

a husband, he described how he spoke to the young couple of the way they ought to live, then made their bed, put them to sleep together, extinguished the light, and that was the whole wedding.

What particularly impressed Tolstoy was that Syutayev had the courage to live the life he believed in. Here was a simple peasant who scorned shams and endeavored by hard work and frugality to exist according to his conscience and the teaching of the Gospels. At their first meeting Tolstoy listened with wonderment to his preaching that all things should be held in common, that fields and forests ought not to be divided, and that there should be no locks, no restraints, no war. When Syutayev drove him back to the Bakunins', so absorbed did they become in their discussion of the imminence of the Kingdom of God that the horse strayed off the road and upset their cart in a gully. Fortunately neither disputant was hurt.

Syutayev soon appeared in Moscow, where he gained some fame. Tolstoy frequently entertained him and invited people to hear him expound his views. No doubt Tolstoy obtained a vicarious pleasure from hearing some of his own beliefs put with so much pith and homely wisdom. Sonya wrote her sister that all Moscow was talking of Syutayev and that an article about him had already been published. "Really, he is a remarkable old man," she continued. "The moment he began to preach in the study all rushed there from the drawing room. . . ." While he talked, the celebrated artist Repin and Tolstoy's young daughter Tanya made portrait studies of him. The city authorities grew suspicious over the visits of this strange and heretical peasant at Count Tolstoy's house and made inquiries. But the bewildered gendarme sent to investigate was almost bodily thrown out by the infuriated host. Since Syutayev left the city soon after this incident, the police let the matter drop.

Tolstoy's search for spiritual companionship during these first weeks after the move to Moscow met with further success. V. F. Orlov, a poverty-stricken teacher in a school for children of railway employees, sought him out. He had at one time been imprisoned for revolutionary activities, but now he worked hard, supported a large family on his meager earnings, and tried to live his life according to the teaching of the Gospels. A more interesting fellow traveler of the spirit was N. F. Fyodorov, librarian of the Moscow Rumyantsev Museum. An emaciated little old man and always shabbily dressed, Fyodorov had about him the aspect of a saint. He lived in a garret like an ascetic, sleeping on bare boards and subsisting on scraps of food, for he could not bear to keep a kopek of his own while anyone was in need. A light of inner goodness illuminated his face and shone from penetrating, intelligent eyes. Tolstoy admired his asceticism, and he always listened to Fyodorov with an attentive air. Despite his customary impetuosity in arguing the tenets of his new faith, he never lost his temper with his Christlike librarian.

These new friends inspired Tolstoy with the desire to practice the faith he preached. Yet he was tormented at this time by his inability to break completely with his past and emancipate himself from the old existence. A month after his arrival in the city, he wrote Alekseyev: "I now see that though I knew about all the evil, about all the mass of temptations amid which people live, I did not believe in them and could not realize them, just as you knew from geography that Kansas[2] existed but didn't really know it until you arrived there. And this mass of evil oppresses me, brings me to despair and inspires distrust. I'm amazed that no one sees this. Perhaps I needed to undergo it in order to discover more clearly my own private path in life. At first one of two paths exists: either abandon all and suffer passively, yielding to despair, or make peace with evil, befogging oneself with cards and chatter and bustle. But fortunately, I cannot do the latter, and the former is too painful, so I seek an outlet. The outlet that presents itself to me is preaching and printing, but there stand vanity, pride, and perhaps self-deception, so I fear this outlet. The second outlet is to help others, but here the immensity of the number of unfortunates overwhelms one. . . . The only outlet I see is to live well, always turning one's good side to all. But I have not yet been able to do this as you do it."

3

Although the poverty and evil Tolstoy observed in the city discouraged him, he felt keenly that he must do something to remedy the situation. Such human misery struck deeply

[2] Alekseyev, before he became a tutor in Tolstoy's home, had spent two years (1875–1877) in Kansas, where, with a group of like-minded Russians, he had set up an agricultural community on primitive communist lines. The experiment failed.

at the roots of his new faith and called into question his own way of life. He first felt the need to inform himself fully of the extent and causes of all this suffering. Frequently he stopped and talked with beggars on the streets; their obviously lying accounts gave him some insight into their psychology but little information concerning the true reasons behind their degradation.

Determined to see the worst the city had to offer, one late December afternoon in 1881 Tolstoy made his way to the Khitrov market, a disreputable section of the town. His well-dressed appearance quickly attracted attention among the throng of ragged, shivering, hungry, importunate human derelicts and they crowded around him. He listened to their tales of desperate circumstances, and in an agony of helplessness he bought them hot drinks and distributed money freely. The news of the ministering angel ran through the street. Each upturned begging face seemed to him more pitiful and degraded than the last. The press of people became great; disorder and a crush ensued. Tolstoy took refuge in Lyapin House, a charitable institution that provided free night lodgings. The sight of these tiers of bunks, each with its impoverished occupant in tatters, further sickened him. Feeling terribly ashamed of himself, he hurried away.

Tolstoy reached home that night, ascended the carpeted stairway, took off his fur coat, and sat down to a five-course dinner served by two lackeys in dress clothes with white ties and gloves. And at that moment he understood with his whole being that the existence of tens of thousands of destitute people in Moscow was a crime, not committed once, but again and again; and that he with his luxury not merely tolerated it, but shared in it. He should have given not only hot drinks and small sums of money to those wretched people in the Khitrov market, but the overcoat that he wore and all that he possessed at home. Yet he had not done this, and therefore he felt and would continue to feel that as long as he had any superfluous food, money, and belongings, and someone else had none, then he shared in a constantly repeated crime.

That same evening, after returning from Lyapin House Tolstoy described his impressions to a friend. With some satisfaction the friend began to explain that poverty was a most natural thing in the city and an inevitable condition of civilization. In the argument that followed Tolstoy, quite unconscious of his rising temper, waved his arms at his friend and with tears in his voice shouted: "One cannot live so, one cannot live so! It is impossible!" His alarmed wife ran into the room, and both she and the friend remonstrated with him for his unnecessary ardor and reminded him that the existence of poverty-stricken people did not justify his spoiling the lives of those around him.

Tolstoy agreed that their criticism was just, but in the depths of his heart he felt that he too was right. When he told his experiences to other friends and acquaintances, they approved of his kindheartedness, but insisted that the most that wealthy people could do was to attempt to alleviate the misery of the poor by philanthropy.

Perhaps organized philanthropy, Tolstoy thought, was the only answer to the problem of the poor, and he decided to make use of the approaching decennial census (January 1882) for this purpose. His plan was to persuade the numerous census takers to conduct a canvass of the city's poor in the course of their official duties. On the basis of the detailed information thus obtained, a complete list of the most worthy cases would be compiled along with the relevant data necessary to provide the most effective kind of aid. In order to implement the scheme, he intended to use his influence in setting up a large charitable fund.

Tolstoy began the campaign with a stirring newspaper article, "On the Moscow Census," in which he outlined his plan and made a forthright appeal for aid. Carried away by his own enthusiasm, he declared toward the end of the article: "However little may be done, it will be of importance. But why not hope that everything will be done? Why not hope that we will strive so that in Moscow there will not be one person unclothed, not one hungry, not one human being sold for money, not one unfortunate crushed by fate who does not know where to find brotherly aid? It is not surprising that this has not been done, but it is surprising that these things exist side by side with our superfluity of leisure and wealth, and that we can live untroubled knowing that they exist." He repeated the substance of this plea in the homes of wealthy friends and received promises of financial assistance, but he did not fail to notice among those he solicited the uncomfortable feeling of guilty people and an attitude plainly indicating that his plan was a well-intentioned yet hopeless endeavor.

Tolstoy secured a position as an organizer in the census

and asked to have assigned to him one of the worst sections of the city, where was situated Rzhanov House, a series of cheap lodgings that had the reputation of being a den of extreme poverty and vice. His first reaction was one of pained disillusion. He saw that the majority of wretched inhabitants of these cheap lodgings were not at all exceptional, but just such people as those among whom he lived, and that their unhappiness depended not on external conditions, but on themselves—a kind of unhappiness that money could not remedy. He was amazed at the contentedness and self-sufficiency of many of these poor people and at their charity to each other. Their conditions of life were appalling, but he did not realize then, as he did later, that they could be helped only by changing their outlook on life. To change another man's outlook on life, however, one must oneself have a better outlook and live in accord with it, and Tolstoy was aware that his own view on life had to be altered before he could really assist these unhappy people.

The many loose women who lived in Rzhanov House gave him deep concern. During his rounds he heard of one mother, a prostitute, who had sold her thirteen-year-old daughter. He visited the mother in the hope of saving the girl, for he thought of speaking to ladies of his acquaintance who took a charitable interest in such cases. The mother and daughter he found living in the direst poverty. After talking with the mother, he reflected on the hard sacrifices she had made to rear her child, and later he understood that in selling her daughter she was not doing anything unmoral but only what she considered best for the child. To save the daughter, one ought long ago to have saved the mother—saved her from a view of life approved by nearly everybody in Russia. If he had thought of that then, he wrote later, he would have realized that the fine ladies whose aid he wished to seek themselves lived without work, serving merely to satisfy sensuality, and deliberately educating their own daughters for such a life. "One mother leads her daughter to the tavern," he maintained, "another leads hers to Court or to balls. But both mothers share the same view of life: namely, that a woman must satisfy a man's lust, and for that she must be fed, clothed, and cared for. How, then, will our ladies save this woman and her daughter?"

The more he worked among the poor during the census

and thought of the ultimate causes of all this poverty the more Tolstoy lost heart in the practicality of his grandiose philanthropic scheme. He soon began to wonder whether dispensing money was a remedy. People constantly told him lies to get a few kopeks, and he knew that often the money did them more harm than good. Was not money an evil in itself? Tolstoy described the last night he visited Rzhanov House in the company of census takers and some interested friends: "All the lodgings were full, all the bunks occupied, and not only by one, but often by two people. This crowding was a horrible spectacle in which men and women were mingled together. Women, who were not dead-drunk, slept with men. Many women with children were sleeping with strange men in the narrow bunks. Terrible was the sight of the destitution, filth, raggedness, and fear of these people. And especially terrible was the immense number of people in this condition. One tenement, another the same way, then a third, a tenth, a twentieth, and no end to them. And everywhere the same stench, the same stifling atmosphere, the same overcrowding, the same mingling of the sexes, the same spectacle of men and women drunk to stupefaction, and the same fear, submissiveness, and culpability on all faces; and again I felt pained and ashamed of myself, as I had done at Lyapin House, and I understood that what I had undertaken was horrid, stupid, and therefore impossible."

Perplexed, his nerves frayed, Tolstoy left Moscow for a rest at Yasnaya Polyana at the beginning of February 1882. He also wished to write an article about the reasons for the failure of his philanthropic plan. And it was at this time (February 3) that he began *What Then Must We Do?* Somehow the article did not get on. He had an abundance of material, but he worked under the influence of irritation induced by the discouraging experiences he had just been through. The real cause of the whole matter, which he later discovered to be rooted in himself, evaded him. Shortly before this, that remarkable peasant Syutayev had suggested the reason for his failure. With enthusiasm he had explained to Syutayev the nature of his charitable plan and all that he hoped would be accomplished by it. The peasant listened patiently for some time, his small eyes dim, as though turned inwards.

"It's all useless," said he.

"Why?" asked Tolstoy.

"This whole enterprise of yours is useless and nothing good will come of it," Syutayev said with conviction.

"Why will nothing come of it? Is it useless to help thousands, or even hundreds, of unfortunates? Is it wrong to clothe the naked and feed the hungry, as the Gospel bids us?"

"I know, I know, but not as you are doing it. Can one help in that fashion? You go walking and a man asks you for twenty kopeks. You give it to him. Is that charity? Give him spiritual charity; teach him. But what have you given him? It only means that you have got rid of him."

"No, that is not what we are about. We want to find out a man's needs and help him with money and obtain work for him."

"You won't do anything with these people that way."

"Are they then to die of cold and hunger?"

"Why should they die? Are there so many of them?"

"Many of them?" said Tolstoy, thinking that Syutayev treated the matter lightly because he did not know what an enormous number there were. "Do you know," he said, "that in Moscow alone there are, I suppose, some 20,000 cold and hungry people? And in Petersburg and in other towns?"

Syutayev smiled. "Twenty thousand! And how many homes are there in Russia alone? A million?"

"Well, what of it?"

"What of it?" And his eyes shone and he grew animated. "Well, let us divide them among us. I'm not rich, but I will at once take two. There is that lad you had in your kitchen; I asked him, but he won't come. If there were ten times as many we could place them all. You take one and I'll take one. We could go to work together. He will see how I work and will learn how to live; and we shall sit at one table, and he will hear a word now from me, now from you. That is charity, but your scheme is entirely useless."

Tolstoy was struck by these words of Syutayev at the time, but he did not take in their full implication. And when he started to write *What Then Must We Do?* he still did not fully realize the significance of Syutayev's argument: that the life of the rich consisted in or was inextricably bound up with what separated the rich as far as possible from the poor. Aware that he had not found the solution of the problem of poverty and riches, Tolstoy abandoned his article. After much more reflection he later resumed the work, finally convinced that he had hit upon the truth, and the original article eventually developed into one of his most soul-searching books.

4

Tolstoy dutifully wrote Sonya of his safe arrival in Yasnaya Polyana. The next day he tried to explain to her in another letter why he preferred the country to the city, although he softened this by admitting that his Moscow experiences had been fruitful and that he had learned much from his new spiritual friends, Syutayev, Orlov, and Fyodorov. All this reasoning was wormwood to Sonya. She felt that he had run away, and her own letters struck an entirely new note of bitterness and clearly reflected their sorry existence together in Moscow. After a kind of enraged recital of her manifold domestic duties during his absence, she sarcastically added in her first letter: "My little one [the four-months-old Aleksei] is still unwell, and I'm very tender and pitying. You and Syutayev may not especially love *your own* children, but we simple mortals are neither able nor wish to distort our feelings or to justify our lack of love for *a person* by professing some love or other *for the whole world*." Then, with a suggestion of hysteria, she concluded: "I'm vile, sick, my life is hateful; I cry all day, and if there were poison at hand, it seems as though I would do away with myself."

Letters from Sonya followed in quick succession, filled with a confusing mixture of love and hate, censure, and self-castigation. She wanted him to return and then ordered him to remain away, for she was no longer of any use to him. "How I wish to wound you," she wrote in a pathetic vein, "but if you only knew how I weep every day, when after a day of torment for the *life of the flesh,* as you call it, I remain alone at night with my own thoughts and grief; then my sole happiness is when Andryusha says to me as he did today: 'Mama, who loves you?' I tell him: 'Andryusha, no one loves me; papa has gone away.' And he says: 'I love you, Mama.' " In her very next letter Sonya told her husband that for the first time in her life she did not look forward to his return, for "you will again begin to suffer, be bored, be alive although entirely silent, while censuring my life in Moscow. God, how this wearies me and torments my soul!"

Perhaps Tolstoy took fright over the morbid, almost

ominous, tone of his wife's letters, for he cut short his stay at Yasnaya Polyana. He was also expecting a visit from Granny in Moscow. His new faith was an irresistible challenge to this old friend, whose years—she was now over sixty—had dulled the keen perception and upset the fine intellectual balance that had always distinguished her intercourse with Tolstoy. The Orthodox Church was her weakness, and after their last unpleasant altercation over this subject, she had returned again and again to the charge with more assiduity than good sense. Tolstoy suspected her mission on this occasion, and in writing to accept her request to visit him, he begged her not to attempt "to convert him." They saw a good deal of each other during the ten days of her stay, but the armed religious neutrality they sought to preserve frequently broke out into open warfare. Once he lectured her roundly on what he considered her mistaken views of Christianity. "I have nothing to reply," she remarked coldly, "but I will only say that while you were speaking I saw that you were in the power of someone standing behind your chair." He turned swiftly and almost shouted: "Who is it?" "Lucifer himself, the incarnation of pride," she answered. "Of course," he quickly rejoined, "I'm proud to be the only one who has put his hand on the truth." They parted more hostile than ever to each other's faith. Soon after, Granny wrote to defend once more the Orthodox Church. Her letter seemed insincere and agitated him, and he answered sharply that Orthodoxy was a "loathsome deceit." He recalled the letter and wrote another less provocative, but this too, on second thought, he decided not to send. Like Tolstoy, Granny was an aristocrat, and she found it almost impossible to believe that one of her own class would forsake the faith in which he had been nurtured. Tolstoy was proud, but he never mistook tradition for truth.

5

Tolstoy had been home only a little more than two weeks when he fled again to the refuge of Yasnaya Polyana. Sonya plaintively entered in her diary: "Our life in Moscow would be very fine, if only Lyovochka were not so unhappy in Moscow. He is too impressionable to endure city life, and besides this, his Christian temper doesn't at all harmonize with the conditions of luxury, sloth, and struggle of city life."

Once in the country Tolstoy's disposition mended, as much as it could mend while he was under the constant strain of spiritual obligations he could never seem to fulfill. There was no family to prick his conscience, only familiar country scenes to delight in and servants who loved and appreciated him without criticizing him. He would hold long amusing conversations with Gasha, who tended the dogs. She was an original old woman who had been in the service of his grandmother and hence occupied a privileged position in the household. Her affection for the dogs she cared for was so extreme that she insisted upon living with them in filth and smells. Indeed she loved all animals. So fond was she of sheep that she would never touch mutton. And once when a mouse that she used to feed crumbs to on the table got stuck in the jam pot, she washed the rodent with warm water and set it down on the table again. But she threw away the jam, declaring to the Tolstoy children that a mouse was a heathen beast and hence she wouldn't eat anything a mouse had been at. Prince L. D. Urusov, Vice-Governor of Tula and a cousin of Tolstoy's mathematical friend of the same name, provided almost the only intellectual conversation at Yasnaya Polyana during this visit and others when the family was away. His presence now was not always too welcome, for Tolstoy wished to be alone, but Urusov had become an ardent apostle of his new views and sought enlightenment.

Nearly every day Tolstoy wrote to Sonya, not from a sense of guilt over this second escape from the city, but because it was a long established habit to write her frequently when he was away from home. "In any case," he remarked in one letter, "it is very healthy for me to get away from that mirthful world of the city and get back to myself—to read the thoughts of others on religion, to listen to the chattering of Gasha, and to think not about people but about God."

Sonya answered with restraint and showed concern for his health and mental unrest. She implored him to be happy and jolly. "There is only one thing in the world that I desire, and that is your peace of mind and your happiness." His continual low spirits, however, prompted her to review his position. "Here is my day," she wrote. "The first, most sad mournful thing when I awoke was your letter. It all gets worse and worse. I begin to think that if a happy man suddenly sees in life *only* everything that is terrible and closes his eyes to what is good, then this is the result of illness. You ought to undergo a cure. I say this without any *arrière pensée,* for it seems clear to me. I'm awfully sorry for you, and if you would consider my words and your own position without vexation, you would perhaps find a way out. This grievous condition first befell you long ago; you said then that from 'lack of faith' you wanted to hang yourself. And now? You do not live without faith now, so why are you unhappy? Did you not know before that hungry, sick, unhappy, and evil people existed? Look around you more carefully: there are also jolly, happy, healthy and good people. May God help you, but what can I do in the matter?"

This had its own logic which was irrefutable if one accepted the premise. Sonya could not be expected to see that the elucidation of the moral law was the chief business of humanity. Her proper concern was the future of her family, not the future of humanity, and she expected her husband to devote himself to the same end. Tolstoy always secretly hoped that his wife might share with him the obligation that he felt to society at large, but he was never intentionally ungenerous about her failure to understand or to sympathize with his mission. In a spirit of fairness he replied to her letter: "Do not trouble about me, and above all do not accuse yourself. . . . I long ago ceased to blame you. . . . Life in Moscow has given me very much and has made plain to me my line of activity, if any still lies before me; then it has brought us closer together than before." And in his next he wrote cheerfully and tenderly: "I fear that we may change roles; I shall become healthy and lively and you will be gloomy and run down. You say: 'I love you, but you do not want that now.' It is the one thing I do want. Nothing else can so cheer me, and your letters have cheered me. One's liver counts for something, but one's spiritual life goes its own way. My solitude was very necessary and has refreshed me, and your love gladdens me more than anything in life." Although she had urged him to remain in the country until he got thoroughly bored, he returned to Moscow within ten days.

6

Shortly after his return to the city Tolstoy made the acquaintance of N. N. Ge, one of Russia's most distinguished painters. Curiously enough, Ge had been going through a spiritual crisis not unlike that which Tolstoy had recently experienced. He had ceased to take any interest in art and had retired to his Ukrainian estate in deep dejection, feeling that life was no longer worth living. And again like Tolstoy in his search for truth, he had arrived at a study of the Gospels. His quest had been in vain, however, until Tolstoy's newspaper article, "On the Moscow Census," came to his attention. "In it I found words precious to me," he related in his *Memoirs*. "Tolstoy, visiting cellars and finding miserable people in them, writes: 'Our lack of love for the humblest is the cause of their wretched condition.' As a spark kindles inflammable material, so that word set me aflame . . . I went to Moscow to embrace that great man and work for him."

Ge arrived in the city with canvas and paints and presented himself to the Tolstoys. Long gray curls clustered beneath his bald head, and an eager kindly face illuminated by wide-open clear blue eyes gave him the appearance of a Biblical prophet. With charming naïveté he kissed Tolstoy and at once offered to paint his wife or daughter. Both men understood each other immediately and a friendship began that lasted until Ge's death in 1904. He became literally a member of the family and was loved by all. His devotion to Tolstoy was boundless, and he subscribed to all his doctrines with implicit faith that they gave purpose and meaning to his life. Tolstoy repaid the love and devotion of this apostle by taking a keen and understanding interest in his art. Some of Ge's most remarkable paintings were inspired by the warm friendship of Tolstoy and influenced by his ideas.

Other distinguished men sought Tolstoy out in Moscow to hear him expound his views, for the story of his religious transformation was already widely known. The astute critic N. K. Mikhailovski, who had defended Tolstoy's educational theories in 1875 and had predicted the spiritual crisis toward which he was then drifting, called on him at this time, hoping to get an article for his magazine. On this and subsequent visits Mikhailovski found him very much a man of the world, but simple and sincere, despite his social polish. They often disputed warmly, and Mikhailovski was amazed that Tolstoy could turn his back on all the aristocratic traditions of his life that were so utterly opposed to the conclusions that he had lately reached. Yet he admired him as a powerful thinker and one whom all were bound to respect.

When their discussions grew acrimonious, Tolstoy would say: "Come, we are beginning to get warm; that is not well! Let us each smoke a cigarette and rest a bit." With the well-known philosopher V. S. Solovyov, who was also a frequent visitor, the disputes came dangerously close to quarrels. When Tolstoy was seeing his guest off, however, he would give him his hand with a guilty smile and ask to be forgiven for getting so heated. He regarded Solovyov, as he did many other intellectuals, as a brainy man who lived exclusively on what he could get from books.

7

Admiring friends and the pleasures of social intercourse in the city only served to intensify Tolstoy's feeling of moral dereliction. The year 1882 was one of the most difficult in making adjustments with his new way of life. Repeated trips to Yasnaya Polyana were again a measure of his discontent. Spring in the country revived his drooping spirits. The poet in him responded, and he wrote to Sonya in a lyric strain of the little spikes and tufts of grass pushing up from under the dead leaves and straw in the frost glaze of the footpaths. The buds were swelling on the lilac bushes, "the birds no longer sing at random but have already begun to converse about something, and round the sheltered corners of the house and by the manure heaps bees are humming." In an exultant mood he told her that "everywhere are grass, birds, and honey-bees; no policemen, no pavements, no cabmen, no smells, and it is very pleasant—so pleasant that I grow sorry for you and think that you and the children must certainly come here earlier, and I will remain in Moscow with the boys."

Sonya took his advice and came to Yasnaya Polyana for the summer late in May, and Tolstoy went to Moscow to see the older boys through their examinations. He soon returned to his estate with his sons, and after their first year of discord in Moscow the whole family joyfully resumed the country life that they loved—swimming in the pond, tennis, croquet, picnics, and amateur theatricals. As customary, sister-in-law Tanya and her children were there to add to the general merriment. Every Sunday the Yasnaya Polyana Letter Box was opened with mock solemnity. This had long been a favorite summer amusement. Everyone in the household, young or old, was privileged to drop his unsigned composition into the Letter Box. All the gossip, puppy love affairs, and comic incidents were commemorated in verse or prose. Usually Tolstoy, his wife, or Tanya read the compositions to the assembled family and guests, and there was much giggling and laughter at every good hit or when an anonymous author betrayed himself. Tanya, when in a bad temper, had the habit of sending everyone around her to the devil, and this inspired a composition by Tolstoy, in which he pictured the devil receiving all the unfortunates consigned to him by Tanya. At times a playful malice ran through the offerings, as in the list of Yasnaya Polyana ideals, probably compiled by Tanya. Tolstoy's were set down as "Poverty, peace and concord," and "To burn everything he worshiped, to worship everything he burned."

Tolstoy turned the tables on all the family in an amusing Letter Box composition called "Asylum Bulletin." An insane peasant by the name of Blokhin used to appear frequently at Yasnaya Polyana. He labored under the delusion that, like the gentlefolk, he need not work, but would receive the maintenance due him from the Emperor. When asked if he wished some work, he always replied grandiloquently that work was for the peasants and that he lived simply to pass the time. In the "Asylum Bulletin" Tolstoy compared Blokhin to many of the other "patients" at Yasnaya Polyana, all of whom he described as dangerously insane; Blokhin, however, he considered the only one who could be certified as cured, because he was the only one who reasoned consistently.

The summer domestic harmony that reigned at Yasnaya Polyana was suddenly ruined by one of those painful quarrels between husband and wife that had become so frequent since the move to Moscow. Sonya chronicled the affair in her diary: "Twenty years ago, happy and young, I began writing this book—the whole story of my love for Lyovochka. In it there is hardly anything other than love. And now, after twenty years, I'm sitting up all night reading it and weeping over my love. For the first time in my life Lyovochka has run away from me and is spending the night in his study. We quarreled over trifles. I attacked him for not troubling himself over the children, for not attending to Ilya who is sick, and for not making their jackets. But it is not a matter of jackets, the matter is that he is growing cold toward me and the children. Today he loudly shouted that his most passionate desire is to get away from the family. To my dying day I shall not forget that sincere cry of his, for it was as if he had torn the heart out of me. I pray to God for death. It is terrible to live without his love, and I felt this deeply that his love went from me. I cannot show him how strongly I still love him as of old, with twenty years of love. This would humiliate *me* and annoy *him*. He is imbued with Christianity and thoughts of self-perfection. I am jealous of him. . . . Ilya is ill, lying in the drawing room in a fever; he has typhus, and I keep watch to give him quinine at frequent intervals, which I'm afraid of missing. I will not lie down tonight on the bed my husband has deserted. God help me. I want to take my life; my thoughts are confused. It is striking four.

"I thought—if he doesn't come, then he loves another. He has not come. Duty—I used to know so well what my duty was, but now?

"He came, but we made it up only the next day. We both wept, and I saw with joy that the love I had lamented over on that terrible night had not died. I shall never forget that lovely morning, clear, cold, sparkling with silver dew, when after a sleepless night I went along the leafy path to the bathhouse. It is long since I've seen nature in such triumphant beauty. I sat for some time in the icy water with the idea of catching cold and dying. But I did not catch cold, and I returned home and began nursing little Alyosha, who was glad to see me and smiled."

8

As though reconciled to the fact that the children's education would require years of residence in the city, Tolstoy decided to purchase a home. He found a large wooden one with an attractive garden on Weaver's Lane in a quiet section near the Moscow River, which he quickly purchased for 27,000 rubles (about $13,500). The business of extensive remodeling and furnishing he took upon himself, and throughout most of September he worked industriously at the task in order that Sonya might have a completely equipped home when she returned to the city. He visited furniture shops and bought antique pieces with excellent taste. Christ and the Gospels were now crowded out of the letters he sent to Sonya by elaborate details concerning the redecoration of rooms and the purchase of divans, lamps, and cretonne.

Sonya's reaction to this domestic activity of her husband

was curious in the light of her former complaints. She seemed to resent his successful aid in a sphere in which she dominated. What of the state of his soul, and of what was he thinking?—these were the matters she wanted him to comment on in his letters. "You write only about practical things," she protested, "or do you already think that I have grown entirely stiff? I'm not interested merely in parquet floors and waterclosets. I wanted to copy out for you a whole passage from Seneca[3] so that you could instruct me in it, for it refers to what is alien to the soul, as the city in your case."

Here was a palpable hit. Her husband ignored it and got on with the business of putting the new house into perfect order. When all was ready and Sonya finally arrived on October 8, she displayed a lamentable lack of appreciation. "At Moscow Lyovochka met us with two carriages," she wrote her sister. "At home a dinner was ready, and tea, and there was fruit on the table. But I was so tired from the trip and a week of packing and had become so irritable that nothing pleased me."

The second winter in Moscow brought an improvement in Tolstoy's relations with his family. It was only an external improvement, for he had lost none of his repugnance for the life they were leading. A firmer hold on the humility he strove to impose upon himself made relations in the household more bearable. Sonya heralded the apparent change with pleasure in letters to her sister. He had become quieter and more kind, she wrote, and his tirades against their easy existence briefer and rarer. In months they had quarreled only once, and she added: "Lyovochka is in such fine spirits; it is charming. May God grant that it continue."

Obviously Sonya was also beginning to understand a little more clearly the change that had taken place in her husband's spiritual life and to appreciate the new demands—although she did not sympathize with them. Writing to her sister of his less frequent outbursts against the life of the rich, she remarked: "This pains me, but I know he cannot help it. He is a leader; he goes ahead of the crowd showing the way people should go. But I am *the crowd;* I live in its current. Together with the crowd I see the light of the lantern that every leader carries (and, of course, Lyovochka's also), and I acknowledge it to be *the light,* but I cannot go faster, for I am held back by the crowd, and by my surroundings and my habits."

[3] She had recently taken to reading Seneca.

This household of growing children, constantly swarming with their young friends, recalls the merry Bers family of some twenty years ago, when Tolstoy first courted Sonya. Now, as the mother, seeking the best introduction for her own children into Moscow society, Sonya was in her element. With obvious pleasure, she described in a letter to Tanya the Christmas festivities of 1882: the tree; an evening party at one friend's house; a French play and a large children's gathering at the home of another friend, where young Masha and Leo danced until three in the morning; then the next night a ball at the Shcherbatovs'. Her daughter Tanya was arrayed in the latest style and her mother more conservatively in "a very splendid dress" that cost 250 rubles. Young Tanya danced with the director and was in ecstasies, and she and her mother remained at the ball until six in the morning. "It now seems that we are fully launched in society," she informed her sister, "but the money vanishes terribly!" And she concluded with some scathing remarks on the bad manners of the young cavaliers of this generation who appeared at her regular Thursday receptions.

The gloomy father watched these expensive, empty pleasures, while his recent experiences among the poor at Lyapin and Rzhanov Houses seared his brain. In his diary for December 22, he noted: "Again in Moscow. Again I experience horrible spiritual torments. For more than a month. But they are not unfruitful."

Shortly before this, Alekseyev had written Tolstoy from Samara to complain of his lonely life there. Tolstoy replied, telling him how much he envied his lot. "There has been illness in the family," he wrote, "but now all are fine and more or less as of old. Seryozha is much occupied and believes in the university. Tanya, half-kind, half-serious, and half-wise, does not grow worse—rather better. Ilyusha [Ilya] is lazy and growing, and his soul is not yet strangled by the organic processes. Lyolya [Leo] and Masha seem to me better. They do not possess my harshness, which has taken hold of the older ones, and I think they are growing up under better conditions and are better and kinder than the older ones. The babies are fine little boys and healthy.

"I am fairly quiet, but sad—often because of the triumphant, self-assured insanity of the life around me. Often I do not understand why it has been granted to me to perceive their insanity, while they are quite unable to understand their own madness and mistakes; and so we stand face to face, not comprehending each other, and wondering at and condemning each other. But they are legion and I am alone. They are seemingly gay, and I am seemingly sad."

His only diversion, he told Alekseyev, was a passion for a new language. He had begun to study Hebrew in October 1882, taking lessons from the Moscow Rabbi Minor. He read the Old Testament, but concentrated largely on those parts that were of interest to him in his work. Sonya now objected to the considerable effort he expended on Hebrew as she had earlier complained of his study of Greek.

In December 1882, Tolstoy received a letter from a total stranger, M. A. Engelhardt. This young man—he was only twenty-one at the time—had been exiled to his father's estate for engaging in political activities in the university. Having failed to find a publisher for an article opposing the Orthodox Church, he sent it on to Tolstoy because he had heard of his deep interest in religious questions. Tolstoy's reply so encouraged him that he sent a second letter, in which he attempted to justify the violence of revolutionary struggle for the common good by the teaching of Christ. This drew a lengthy answer.[4]

To this correspondent whom he had never met, Tolstoy began his letter as follows: "You perhaps do not think it, but you cannot imagine to what degree I am alone and to what degree that which is my real 'I' is despised by all around me. I know that he who endures to the end will be saved. I know that only in trifles is it granted man to enjoy the fruit of his own labor or even to see that fruit, and that in the matter of Divine truth, which is eternal, it cannot be given to man to see the fruit of his own work, especially in the short period of his brief life. I know all that and yet I am often sad, and therefore to have encountered you and the hope, almost the assurance, of finding in you a man sincerely traveling the same road to the same goal as myself is a great joy to me."[5]

[4] The letter is really an extensive article, the first of a series of such epistolary articles that he eventually wrote. His reply to Engelhardt, which is on the general theme of nonviolence, contains passages of considerable biographical value.

[5] Engelhardt soon disappointed Tolstoy's hopes. Tolstoy sent a friend to represent him with a manuscript copy of his *Short Account of the Gospels*. The friend, after lengthy discussions with Engelhardt, reported to Tolstoy that he believed more in the violence of revolution than in Christian love.

Sonya, who read the letter, was much offended by these frank comments to a complete stranger, comments that reflected so severely on her and her family, and Tolstoy finally decided not to send it.

In the body of the letter, apart from developing his theory of nonviolence, Tolstoy expressed in concise form some of his principal convictions. "It seems to me now, that if Christ and His teaching had never existed, I myself would have discovered this truth—it now appears to me so simple and clear and convincing. . . . To love God means to love truth; to love one's neighbor as oneself means to recognize the unity of one's soul and life with every other human life, with eternal truth—with God. . . . The significance of Christianity consists of pointing out the possibilities and the happiness of fulfilling the law of love. . . . Only that teaching is true which leads to activity, to a life, which while satisfying the needs of the spirit is at the same time a continual working for the good of others. Such is the teaching of Christ."

In the light of the charge that was repeatedly brought against Tolstoy of not living according to his beliefs, the conclusion of this letter is a remarkably sincere and humble confession of human limitations that goes far to explain his whole present and future struggle with himself, with his family, and with society. "Now another question directly and involuntarily follows from this, 'Well, but you, Leo Nikolayevich, how do you practice what you preach?' That is the most natural question: people always put it to me and always triumphantly shut my mouth with it. 'You preach, but how do you live?' And I answer that I do not preach and cannot preach, although I passionately desire to do so. I can only preach by deeds, and my deeds are bad. What I say is not a sermon; it is only a refutation of a false understanding of Christian teaching and an explanation of its real meaning. Its meaning is not that we should in its name rearrange society by violence; its significance is to find the meaning of life in this world. The fulfillment of Christ's five commands gives that meaning. If you wish to be a Christian, then you must fulfill these commands; if you do not wish to fulfill them, then do not talk about Christianity apart from the fulfillment of these commands. But, people say to me: 'If you find that apart from the fulfillment of Christian teaching there is no reasonable life, and if you love that reasonable life, why do you not fulfill the commands?' I reply that I am at fault and a disgusting creature and deserve scorn for not fulfilling them; but yet not so much in justification as in explanation of my inconsistency, I say: 'Look at my former life and at my life now and you will see that I try to fulfill them. I have not fulfilled one-thousandth part of them, it is true, and I am at fault in this; but it is not because I do not wish to fulfill them, but because I am unable to. Teach me how to escape from the nets of temptations that have ensnared me, help me, and I will fulfill them; but even without help I wish and hope to do so. Blame me—I do that myself—but blame me and not the road I follow, and show it to those who ask me where in my opinion the road lies. If I know the road home and go along it drunk, staggering from side to side, does that make the road by which I go the wrong one? If it be wrong, show me another; if I have lost my way and stagger, help me, support me in the right path as I am ready to support you; and do not confuse me, do not rejoice that I have lost my way; do not cry out with delight: Look at him! He says that he's going home yet he's slipping into the bog! Do not rejoice at that, but help me and support me.'

"So that is my relation to teaching and to its practice. With all my strength I try to practice it, and at every failure I not only repent, but I beg for help in order to be able to practice it, and with joy I meet and listen to anyone who, like myself, is seeking the road."

9

Tolstoy remained in Moscow during 1883 until the end of April, when he went to Yasnaya Polyana. Shortly after his arrival, a disastrous fire broke out in the village, and the huts of twenty-two peasant families were burned down. He took an active part in fighting the conflagration and was amazed at the calm, uncomplaining manner in which the peasants accepted their severe loss and at their faith in their ability to remedy it. To the victims he gave financial aid and grain, and even timber to rebuild their huts.[6]

On May 23, Tolstoy set out for his Samara estate. The ostensible reason was ill health and the desire to take a *kumys* cure. It is curious that on the day of his departure

[6] Tolstoy's aid at the time of the fire is described by Anna Seuron, a volatile French governess in the family at this time, whose published recollections of Tolstoy, however, are not always trustworthy.

he signed over to Sonya rights of attorney on all his property. In one of his earliest letters to her from Samara, he implored: "Please, write me frankly—not in moments of agitation, but when you are calm—how you regard my absence; I must know in order to decide when to return. *Kumys*—this was essentially a fantasy. I'm ready to return at once, and in my heart I wish to, and will be very happy to return immediately."

Sonya's reply was evasive: his health was her first concern, so he must not expect her to summon him back. Let him return when his health and the spirit moved him. There was an undertone of resentment in her letters over the fact that he had once again walked out on her, leaving her with all the domestic cares of the estate and several sick children. More than this, she now excluded a new spirit of emotional independence. He did not seem to need her, well, neither did she particularly need him. "Why do you write that when you return you will be closer to me than before you left?" she coldly asked. "What you do not indicate is: Why? This would be fine if it were again possible. In a letter I did not send, I described to you all my feelings, and then I decided that my sincere feelings were not wanted by you; you have become so careless in your treatment of them that it would be better for you never to know them. It may be that you will become again the same as in years past. But will I be the same?"

Justice seemed to be on Sonya's side in this quarrel, and Tolstoy's answers reflected the fact. Perhaps as a peace offering, he sent her *What I Believe,* the manuscript he was working on, and solicited her opinion. "I read your article, or better, your composition," she wrote. "Of course, it is impossible to say anything against your idea that it would be fine for people to be perfect, and undoubtedly one must remind people that it is necessary to be perfect and what paths they must follow to achieve perfection.[7] Yet I can scarcely refrain from saying that it is *hard* to give up all the toys of life with which one plays, and everyone—and I more than others—keeps a firm grasp on these playthings, and rejoices in the way they glitter, make a noise, and amuse." Without surrendering anything fundamental in his beliefs, Tolstoy was slowly beginning to realize that Sonya's attitude was the natural and prevailing one in a society that would not be saved if it had to sacrifice its toys.

[7] Sonya has somewhat garbled the thesis of *What I Believe.*

The nonchalant air of Sonya's correspondence caused Tolstoy deep concern all the time he was in Samara. He had never for a moment entertained the thought that his new convictions might result in the loss of her love. Finally an unmistakable note of anguish burst forth in his reply to one of her particularly chilly letters. "The further I read, the more I became cold all over. I wanted to send this letter back to you, but it would only annoy you. It was nothing in particular in the letter, but I did not sleep all night, and I have become terribly sad and pained. I have loved you so, and you have reminded me of all the things with which you assiduously kill my love. I wrote to you that it pained me to think that I had too coldly and hurriedly left you. But to this you write me that you will try to live so that I will be unnecessary to you, and that you are very successfully achieving this. Concerning me and what governs my life, you write as though it were a weakness which you hope I will cure by means of *kumys*. About our future meeting, which for me is joyous, a bright point to look forward to, and about which I try not to think so that I might not depart at once, you write as though you anticipated from me censure and unpleasantness. Of yourself you write that you are so calm and contented that there only remains for me to wish not to disturb your contentment and calm by my presence. About V. I.,[8] a pitiful, kind, but entirely uninteresting man to me, you write as though he were an enemy and a trouble-maker between us. Then I vividly recalled these horrible moods of yours, so tormenting to me, and about which I had entirely forgotten. Yet I love you so simply and clearly that it has all hurt me terribly."

Shortly after this troubled letter Tolstoy returned to Yasnaya Polyana. On the whole, his stay in Samara had been unprofitable and disagreeable. One bright spot had been meeting his old friends the Molokans, but this too had its unpleasant aspects, for he was aware that the police were now spying on these meetings and reporting to the authorities. The police reports, which have turned up, would have amused him by their official appraisal of his talks and of his influence over these harmless sectarians. One report describes how he tried to "inspire principles of equality, pointing out that all must share with each other," and that

[8] V. I. Alekseyev, the ex-tutor now on Tolstoy's Samara estate, and a man whom Sonya heartily disliked, largely, perhaps, because she felt that he influenced her husband's religious beliefs.

"to adorn the church is stupid. We gathered from his talk to the peasantry that he rejects authority and government, and on the basis of his conversation we concluded that he is not a sectarian, but simply a socialist." From this time on, the baleful eyes of the Tsar's secret police kept Tolstoy, as so many Russian writers, under continual surveillance.

10

Upon his arrival in Yasnaya Polyana on June 28, Tolstoy received a sorrowful and last letter from Turgenev:—

> Kind and dear Leo Nikolayevich. It is long since I wrote you, for I have been and am, speaking frankly, on my deathbed. I cannot recover—there is no use thinking of it. I am writing to you particularly to tell you how glad I am to have been your contemporary, and to express to you my last, sincere request. My friend, return to literary activity! That gift came to you from whence comes all the rest. Ah, how happy I should be if I could think that my request would have an effect on you!! I am a doomed man—even the doctors do not know what to call my malady, *Névralgie stomacale goutteuse.* I can neither walk, nor eat, nor sleep. It is even wearisome to repeat all this! My friend, great writer of the Russian land, heed my request! Let me know if you receive this bit of paper, and permit me once more to embrace you *heartily,* heartily, and your wife and all yours. I can write no more, I am weary.

To the very end Turgenev could not understand why Tolstoy had forfeited art to solve the riddle of existence. He did not see that for Tolstoy the measure of true greatness was not what we were, but what we strove to be in the ceaseless struggle to achieve moral perfection. Nor did he realize that the same magnificent qualities that made Tolstoy's art immortal—his sincerity and love of truth—were the very qualities that drove him on in his religious and social mission.

After Turgenev's last visit to Tolstoy two years before, they had kept up a desultory correspondence in the friendly spirit of their recent reconciliation. Time had softened without entirely eliminating Tolstoy's reservations on Turgenev, and his new religious feelings induced an attitude of Christian love in his relations. At the first report of Turgenev's illness, he immediately wrote of his concern and of the thought he had entertained of going to Paris to be near him.

The end came for Turgenev on August 22. In a letter to Strakhov after he heard the news, Tolstoy simply remarked: "The death of Turgenev I expected, yet I often think of him now." In September, Tolstoy was asked by the Society of Lovers of Russian Literature to speak at a public memorial meeting in honor of Turgenev. He agreed either to read a paper or to have someone else deliver it.

Although Tolstoy went with the family to Moscow in September for the winter, he quickly returned to the country to work. He also had another purpose that he did not communicate to Sonya—he had been summoned as a juryman in the District Court. The first she heard of it was in a letter, in which he wrote that he had appeared at the court and emphatically refused to serve as a juryman because of his religious convictions. He begged her not to get angry with him, for he had not told her because he feared that his intentions might have needlessly worried her. "It was not necessary to put in an appearance at all," he wrote. "There would have been the same fines, but then I should have been summoned again next time. Now I have told them once and for all that I cannot serve." He was fined a hundred rubles for his refusal to serve as a juryman.

This action was Tolstoy's first defiance of civil authority in an effort to remain true to his religious faith. He regarded his act as a protest against the whole system of public justice. It was a slight act, unostentatiously performed, but it gave him immense satisfaction as his initial attempt to repudiate constituted authority. Sonya's reply to his letter told of her fears that his punishment would not end with a mere fine, and without approving or disapproving his act, she scolded him for not taking her into his confidence.

Tolstoy remained a short time at Yasnaya Polyana to write and to read Turgenev's works in preparation for his address. Delighted with two pleasant letters from Sonya, he answered: "Never have I thought of you so much and so well and so entirely purely as I do now. In every respect you are precious to me. I think about Turgenev always, love him terribly, and wish to read all of his works." When he returned to the city, however, the "strained, even unhappy expression on his face" suggested only too clearly to Sonya that he wished he were back in the country.

Preparing his address on Turgenev had become a labor of love. Sonya wrote her sister that all Moscow was stirred up in anticipation of a public oration by Tolstoy, and that an enormous crowd was expected to attend. Meanwhile, the dark forces of the government were at work. The Minister of the Interior had reported to the Emperor Tolstoy's refusal to serve as a juryman, and gratuitously added in the official jargon of the time that "the dignity of the court having been so offended, the declaration of Count L. N. Tolstoy is subject to a categorically sharp censure on the part of the government, and invokes the necessity of taking measures as a warning against similar objectionable declarations capable of undermining trust in the courts and in arousing indignation among all sincerely believing people."

On top of this the Minister was informed by a Moscow government factotum of the impending public celebration in honor of Turgenev, in which Tolstoy would deliver a speech. But this Tolstoy, he continued, "is a madman, from whom one might expect anything; he may say unbelievable things, and there may be a considerable scandal." And the Minister was advised to take the precaution of reading the speech in advance. The matter was looked into, and the Governor General of Moscow coolly informed the President of the Society of Lovers of Russian Literature to advertise the fact that the meeting in honor of Turgenev "had been postponed for an indefinite time."

The upshot of this whole business, so characteristic of the reactionary reign of Alexander III, is told in a letter from Sonya to her sister: "As you have no doubt seen from the papers and know by rumor, the lecture in memory of Turgenev has been forbidden by your disgusting Petersburg. They say that Tolstoy[9] (the Minister) forbade it. Well, what could you expect from him except tactless and awkward tricks. Only think, the lecture was to have been quite innocent and most peaceful; no one thought of shooting off any liberal squibs. But everyone is terribly surprised. What could have been said? Where could there have been any danger to the government? . . . Everyone without exception is angry about it, except Lyovochka, who is even glad to be excused from appearing in public—a thing he is so unaccustomed to."

[9] The name of the Minister of the Interior was D. A. Tolstoy.

11

Tolstoy's distraught state of mind from September 1881 to the end of 1883 would seem to have precluded any serious writing and reading. It had become his habit not only to read, but to think with pen in hand. Most of his reading had been of the weightier sort—religious works, Epictetus, and Marcus Aurelius. The English novelists, Dickens, Thackeray, and Trollope, who had for so long been his favorites, were now neglected. But he read Balzac "with satisfaction," and reread much of Turgenev and Stendhal's *The Red and the Black*. Of the latter masterpiece, he wrote to Sonya: "I read it some forty years ago, but remembered nothing save my relations to the author: sympathy with his boldness and a feeling of kinship—yet an unsatisfied feeling. And strangely enough I feel the same now, but with a clear consciousness of why and wherefore." He also read Strakhov's biography of Dostoyevsky, a book that altered somewhat his unqualified admiration for this great contemporary.

During this period Tolstoy's literary endeavors were largely of the instructional or didactic genre. In April 1882, he made the first attempt to print his *Confession* in the magazine *Russian Thought*. He offered an introduction to this work and, on the request of the editor, softened some of the phraseology. Nevertheless, the censor banned the production. This was the first of many failures to get his controversial works printed in Russia, but he appears to have accepted such prohibitions calmly, as part of the price he must pay for opposing the accepted order of things.

Some time was spent on polishing the manuscripts of *An Examination of Dogmatic Theology* and his *Union and Translation of the Four Gospels,* although there was virtually no hope of getting them published. The press abroad presented possibilities, for rumors about his new religious views and forbidden theological writings were already causing some stir outside of Russia, and soon an article on the subject was published in a French periodical. And in July 1883, there appeared in the Paris *La Nouvelle Revue* a translation of the introduction to his *Short Account of the Gospels,* the first of many translations of his religious and philosophical works abroad.

During the whole of 1883, Tolstoy devoted himself primarily to writing his remarkable book, *What I Believe*. The distilled essence of virtually everything he had written or thought on the subject of religion and on his personal relation to it up to this time is lucidly and artistically set down in this book. As in *Confession,* the conclusion he reaches is that life is a misfortune for him who seeks only the personal welfare that death inevitably destroys, but a blessing for him who identifies himself with the teaching of Christ and the task of establishing the Kingdom of God on earth, here and now. Despite the didactic nature of the book, it has a profound human quality by virtue of his ability to share with his readers the tremendous inner struggle and intense experience that finally led him to his convictions.

Tolstoy hoped to print *What I Believe,* and when he was putting the finishing touches on it in December 1883, Sonya wrote to her sister: "Lyovochka has finished his work for the press, which they will burn, but I hope that he will now grow calm and no longer write in this vein." In her most charitable moments, Sonya adopted an attitude of resignation toward her husband's religious writings: it was "the will of God," she sighed, and perhaps these works were "for great purposes," the implication being that they were beyond her comprehension. Her real feeling—at this time at least—was one of disgust. She had no natural interest in his religious and didactic works, and she worried over the hostility they might provoke in the authorities. Finally, and perhaps most important for her, such literary efforts were unremunerative.

Sonya on more than one occasion expressed sincere regrets that her husband had turned his back on purely artistic works. She had obtained a lasting pleasure from copying and reading his novels, and the effort had given her a sense of being an integral part of the creative genius that she so much admired in him. In one of those voluntary exiles to Yasnaya Polyana, in March 1882, he wrote her that an idea for a "poetical work" had occurred to him. Her response was immediate and touching. "What a joyous feeling suddenly seized me," she declared in her reply, "when I read that you want to write again in a *poetical vein*. You have sensed what I have long waited for and desired. In that is salvation, happiness; in that, which gives you solace and brightens our life, we will again be united. This is the real kind of work for which you were created, and outside of this sphere there is no peace in your soul."

As a matter of fact, Tolstoy did not entirely abandon imaginative literature over this period. In 1882 he contributed "What Men Live By," to a children's magazine, the first of a series of exquisite stories intended primarily for children and peasants, but which have become popular in many languages among readers of all ages. "What Men Live By" is a simple and beautiful retelling of a story based on the widespread theme of the angel whom God sent to earth, but whose actions men could not understand. There are also fragments of unfinished tales that belong to this period, and it was in 1882 that he probably began his memorable story, *The Death of Ivan Ilyich.*

Immersed in his religious and philosophical studies, however, Tolstoy paid little attention to his wife or to those close friends and admirers who urged him to return to fiction. On occasions he would turn on these well-intentioned critics with some asperity. When his friend, the novelist P. D. Boborykin, remonstrated with him for not employing his artistic powers, he replied: "Why you know, that is just like the former admirers of some ancient French whore repeating to her: 'Oh, how adorably you used to sing chansonettes and flip up your petticoats!' "

In actuality, Tolstoy had not turned his back on art; he had simply rejected his former conception of it, just as he rejected the kind of life he had led before his spiritual conversion. There is a suggestion that he would like to have broken cleanly with art, as with everything else, but art was too much a part of his being. He could not tear it out of himself, and at the same time he recognized that the aesthetic aim that he had formerly entertained could have no place in the new morality and ethics to which he now subscribed.

This dilemma prompted Tolstoy to try to develop a theory of art that would be in accord with his new views of life.[1] He wrote an article in the form of a letter to the editor of a Moscow art magazine, and in it he tried to formulate a definition of art that would satisfy a moral and useful purpose in life. He did not get very far and left the article unfinished, apparently conscious of the fact that he had not thought the problem through. But he had actually begun the

[1] He actually began this attempt in 1882, instead of several years later, as is commonly supposed.

long train of aesthetic speculation that ended fifteen year later with his astounding book, *What Is Art?*

12

Toward the end of 1883 Tolstoy made the acquaintance o V. G. Chertkov, a man who as both guardian angel an evil genius played a most significant role throughout th remaining years of his life. He first heard of Chertkov fror G. A. Rusanov, a young man who suddenly turned up a Yasnaya Polyana in August 1883. He had read a lithograp copy of *Confession*—lithograph, hectograph, and manuscrip copies of Tolstoy's religious works forbidden by the censo had already begun to be disseminated throughout Russia— and had been seized with the desire to see the author an ask him many questions connected with his works. Tolsto received the visitor affably, quickly put him at his ease, an they had a long talk made up mostly of Tolstoy's keen an witty replies to reverent questions on his literary produc tions.[2]

In the course of their conversation, Rusanov told Tolsto of a young Captain of the Guards by the name of Chertkov the son of a rich Adjutant General, who had returned fron the army and settled on his estate, where he spent his tim in performing good deeds for the peasants. Naturally enoug Chertkov's behavior had become a subject of common gos sip, for his family was high in Petersburg social circles an intimate with the royal family. His career in a Guards regi ment subjected him, as he said, to the three classical vice of these aristocratic officers—wine, cards, and women. Bu he soon wearied of debauchery, no doubt much influence by the deeply religious attitude of his mother. He read a great deal and was particularly attracted to the works o Dostoyevsky, which (no doubt) helped to lead him to a study of the Gospels and the teaching of Christ. The con clusions he came to on the wickedness of violence, th necessity of productive work, and the need of humility wer quite similar to those of Tolstoy. Aware that his new con victions would not permit him to continue an army career

[2] Rusanov soon became one of Tolstoy's most devoted and mos valued followers. In his will he paid tribute to the master's tremendou influence on his life by declaring: "Thanks to that greatest of men Leo Tolstoy, I won faith in God and believed in Christ. Tolstoy gave me happiness, and I became a Christian."

: tendered his resignation, much against the wishes of his ırents, in 1881, when he was only twenty-seven. He then tired to his huge estate in the province of Voronezh and ıgaged in all manner of practical activities, aimed at betterg the material existence of the peasants. At the same time : abandoned all luxuries and endeavored to live a life as nple and frugal as that of the peasants.

It was not until 1883, when Chertkov grew agitated over e relation of social questions to the teaching of the Gospels, at he learned from a friend of Tolstoy's concern with this me problem. And it was just about this time that Tolstoy's terest in Chertkov had been aroused by Rusanov. Chertkov gerly desired a meeting, and this was brought about in ctober 1883, when he was passing through Moscow on s way to Petersburg to see his parents.

From Tolstoy's first letter to Chertkov, a little more than month after their meeting, it is clear that he was imensely pleased with his latest disciple. He wrote to thank hertkov for some English books on theological subjects that : had sent, and he flatteringly commented on how Chertɔv's marginal notes had helped him to follow "your inllectual and zealous work." But scenting the breath of :resy because one of the books treated at length the subct of the Resurrection, he sternly reproved his young pupil r concerning himself with such metaphysical nonsense. he relationship had begun auspiciously enough. Tolstoy ıd found a new saint, and Sonya a devil incarnate.

XXIV

Just Plain Leo Nikolayevich

TOLSTOY HAD BEEN slowly coming to the conclusion that th only way to encourage the Christian life he believed in wa by personal example. He realized that the method would b slow, difficult, and indefinite, but at least he would ceas being a parasite living on the back of the working class, a he expressed it.

The initial difficulty was that his life was not his own. A the beginning of 1884 he was the father of eight children with another on the way. Domestic problems were nume ous, and his advice and authority were in constant deman Despite his wife's careful management, the family expense in Moscow mounted. Social caste, tradition, and custo dictated a certain standard of living. No less than five tuto and governesses lived with the family, and as many mo teachers were employed from outside to give lessons to th children. Eleven servants worked in the house, took care o the grounds, and operated a carriage, calash, droshky, an two sledges. Food alone for the twenty-six members of th household was a considerable item in the budget. Sony reckoned her monthly expenses at 910 rubles,[2] a large bu not extravagant amount for so numerous a family.

The income had been derived mostly from Tolstoy estates until his literary earnings had provided a substantia and important addition. Now he not only questioned th

[1] Eleven children had been born to the Tolstoys at this time, bu three had died.

[2] Approximately $455, but the purchasing price of this sum the was several times what it is today.

right of private property, which had troubled him for years, but he believed it immoral to live off the money earned by the toil of others.

It did not occur to Tolstoy to demand that his family should at once repudiate the idle self-indulgent existence they were leading for one of frugality, simplicity, and hard manual work. However unbending he might be about expressing the rightness of his moral principles, he understood human nature too well to expect miracles of self-sacrifice. He placed his hope in an attitude of "sweet reasonableness"—a famous phrase of Matthew Arnold that he admired—and in persuasion by example.

2

Tolstoy began his long struggle to practice what he preached in a mild enough manner. He dropped his title and requested servants to address him as plain "Leo Nikolayevich." In January 1884, after having finished *What I Believe,* he went to Yasnaya Polyana for a short visit. From there he wrote Sonya that he was making a pair of boots for old Gasha, for manual labor he now deemed an absolute necessity. At the same time his letters criticized Sonya's fondness for balls, and the obvious pleasure that she and her oldest daughter derived from the attention paid them by the Governor General at the last dance. And as a moral lesson, he contrasted the well-being of his own children with the poverty of a poor orphan who had appealed to him in the village. Sonya reacted unfavorably: "Moral perfection I will never attain—that is now clear to me. And I cannot enjoy material pleasures because some discerning and stern critic always appears and plunges me into despair at once. That is why I do not love life."

Upon his return to Moscow in February, Tolstoy's behavior baffled his friends and irritated his family. The tasks that servants were accustomed to perform for him, he now dispensed with. Entries such as the following occurred regularly in his diary at this time: "With the children I gaily cleaned up my room. I was ashamed to do what had to be done—empty the chamber pot." But a few days later he recorded his triumph over shame and the chamber pot. Making shoes he now took up in real earnest, employing a workman to teach him the craft. Master and pupil sat at a bench in one of the two little rooms that Tolstoy had reserved for himself in the Moscow house. The smell of leather and tobacco filled the low-roofed, ill-ventilated workshop. As the impatient pupil sat huddled over his task, carefully waxing the thread and splicing the bristles, he groaned over every failure and yet stubbornly refused the attempts of his awed instructor to assist him. When success crowned his efforts, he rejoiced like a triumphant schoolboy. Sometimes he went to his teacher's wretched dwelling for lessons. In his diary he jotted down, after his departure from the humble shoemaker's abode: "How like a light morally splendid in his dirty, dark corner."

In this effort to produce more and consume less, the principle succeeded better than the shoemaking. A pair of shoes which he turned out for one of his sons went unworn, although Tolstoy himself proudly wore hunting boots of his own manufacture. With mock seriousness, Fet, who had renewed his visits, ordered a pair of boots from his old literary friend turned shoemaker. Puzzled callers were obliged to wait until he drove the last peg into the leather sole. Any scoffer who thought the task easy might find himself challenged to a contest of peg-driving; Tolstoy would gleefully win and hand over the money wagered to his poor teacher in the craft. Once, after a long session at his last, he wrote in the diary: "It makes one feel like becoming a worker, for the soul flowers."

At first the family were alternately amused and annoyed by what seemed a bit of proletarian play-acting. Tolstoy was in earnest. Did not the Gospels support his endeavor? He went into raptures over the discovery of the manuscript, *Industry and Idleness,* of a peasant-sectarian, T. M. Bondarev, who had been exiled to Siberia. The author attempted to prove that the evil in men's lives resulted from regarding empty regulations as religious duties while failing to realize the chief duty announced at the beginning of the Holy Scripture: "In the sweat of thy face shalt thou eat bread." Tolstoy sent an enthusiastic letter to Bondarev, in which he admitted his indebtedness to the work, and later he wrote an essay on it. The indebtedness was slight, for Tolstoy had independently reached the same conclusions. He believed that every man should earn his bread with his own hands, understanding by "bread-labor" all heavy, rough work necessary to save man from death by hunger and cold. For he felt it impossible to serve men while consuming what others labor to produce.

The new regime transformed existence at Yasnaya Polyana during the summers. Tolstoy had always enjoyed farm work for the physical exercise and pleasure he got out of it; now he regarded it as a duty sanctified by Holy Scripture. Dressed more like a peasant than a country gentleman, he stood in the hot sun sweating and mowing. He would plow the land of a poor widow, assist at building a hut, or stack and carry grain. Nothing was too menial for him, and he performed all manner of work about the estate with zeal if not always well. One could see him any day carting manure, lugging timber, or sitting astride a top beam of a hut that he was rebuilding, cutting a place for the cross-rafter to fit into; his sleeves would be rolled up, hair disheveled, unbuttoned shirt showing his bare chest, a chisel stuck in his leather girdle, a saw hanging from his waist, and his graying beard shaking at each blow of the ax. It would be a mistake to imagine, however, that all was done merely for the sake of a theory, or to subdue the flesh and elevate the spirit. Like many intellectuals, he sincerely enjoyed manual toil, the physical well-being it provided, the healthy appetite, and the sound, peaceful sleep that followed bodily exhaustion.

The family at first went on with its croquet, visitors, and endless round of summer amusements. They felt sorry that their father should waste his valuable energies on such heavy toil, and perhaps they grew a bit ashamed of their own idle existence. Although he said nothing to them, they knew what he thought, and this made them uncomfortable and spoiled their fun. His proof-by-example began slowly to have an effect on the family. Nineteen-year-old Ilya finally asked his father to assign him some outdoor work. He was at once set to plowing the field of a woman whose husband had deserted her, and he relished the experience. Soon his brothers Sergei and Leo joined him in manual labor, and presently field work became a fashion that swept through the entire household. Young and old, men and women, formed groups and competed in mowing, hacking awkwardly with their scythes, and cheerfully raising blisters in long hours of raking up the hay. Even Sonya in a sophisticated version of a peasant dress did her share, along with the younger children and the governesses.

Nor were visitors immune to this virus of toil. That summer (1885) a young Jew by the name of Isaak Fainerman suddenly turned up at Yasnaya Polyana. Tolstoy's teachings had weaned him away from the revolutionary movement, and he had come to follow humbly in the wake of the prophet. Tolstoy was pleased with his straightforward manner and directed him to work in the village. Fainerman refused to accept money for his labor and almost starved to death. He lived in the most abject poverty, gave away what few good clothes he had, and went around the village in rags. His extreme spirit of self-sacrifice distressed rather than pleased Tolstoy, who always preferred common sense to fanaticism.

Fainerman's success with children suggested the position of teacher in the village school, and he willingly allowed himself to be baptized in the Orthodox faith in order to obtain the post. But the authorities would not permit him to hold the position, and Tolstoy was obliged to give him odd copying jobs. To complicate matters, he confessed that he had a wife and child and asked permission for them to come and live with him at Yasnaya Polyana. His pretty young wife soon revolted against his beggarly existence and deserted him. Army service finally took Fainerman away from the village.[3]

Fainerman was one of the "dark people," as Sonya truculently called them, that growing army of men and women from all walks of life who now began to join up under the new Christian banner of Tolstoy. Two others in the vanguard to appear at Yasnaya Polyana in the summer of 1885 to work in the fields were Marya Alexandrovna Schmidt and Olga Alekseyevna Barshev. In the spring of the preceding year these two mouselike, old-maid schoolteachers in a Moscow institute for girls had stumbled upon Tolstoy's new faith. By chance Marya had heard at a friend's house passages read from a hectograph copy of Tolstoy's *Short Account of the Gospels*. A sincere Orthodox believer, she was both impressed and puzzled by the realistic approach to things holy in this work. With charming naïveté, she and her companion, Olga, went around to various bookshops in an effort to buy this illegal work and were astonished that the production of so famous a novelist was on sale nowhere. They determined to appeal to Tolstoy himself.

The two teachers had heard from students that Tolstoy's

[3] Under the pseudonym of Teneromo, Fainerman wrote a number of works based upon his relations with Tolstoy, but they are extremely untrustworthy.

wife did not agree with his beliefs, and that it was wiser to go to his house early in the morning, while she was still asleep. They set out at eight o'clock. When they rang the bell, however, a servant told them that the count had not yet come down. They departed, walked for a bit, and returned at nine. This time they were admitted to the hall and waited, feeling shy.

Suddenly they heard a light step. Tolstoy entered, very sprightly, and inquired in a harmonious voice:—

"What can I do for you?"

They explained that they wished to obtain a copy of his *Short Account of the Gospels.*

"But what do you wish to do with it?"

Marya told him that twenty-five young girls were entrusted to her care, and hence she must know what the truth is. The chief thing in life for her, she said, was the religious question.

"But I have only one copy."

"Give it to me and we shall make another."

Marya made the copy, and she was soon employed to make copies of other forbidden religious works of Tolstoy. At Yasnaya Polyana the following summer she worked harder than any in the fields, for by now she had decided to abandon her genteel existence for a life devoted to simplicity and rough toil. She soon left Yasnaya Polyana and became a member of a Tolstoyan colony on the shore of the Black Sea.[4] There she cheerfully performed the most difficult kind of physical work and recommended herself to all by her meek, uncomplaining nature. Eventually she returned to Yasnaya Polyana and settled on a small property near by that belonged to one of Tolstoy's daughters. She supported herself by the sale of vegetables from her garden and milk from her cow. The family held her in high esteem and Tolstoy, who said that he had never known a woman so profoundly spiritual, loved her and valued her judgment. In turn, she literally worshipped him, and her nature, fully attuned to selfless service to others, was essentially more Tolstoyan than that of the master.

Even distinguished guests at Yasnaya Polyana were caught up by this strange enthusiasm for toiling in the fields. Ge, whose friendship with Tolstoy had ripened, and

[4] This was one of the first of the agricultural colonies organized by disciples to carry out Tolstoy's teachings in a practical sense. Soon others started in Russia, and the movement spread abroad.

who shared his views on the necessity of physical labor, was one of the visitors who eagerly joined the bands of workers that summer. The previous winter he had come to Moscow to paint Tolstoy, who allowed the artist to observe him while he was writing in his study. And Ge observed him with enraptured eyes, as though anxious not to miss a single detail of his subject. The result was the well-known portrait in which the massive head of Tolstoy resembles that of a Zeus with meditation sitting upon his brow, as though in the very act of formulating great universal truths. The artist saw a quite different Tolstoy at Yasnaya Polyana, when both of them, clad in old clothes, worked industriously together to build a brick oven for a peasant widow.

An unusual man who called himself William Frey visited Tolstoy early in October, shortly before the family left for the city at the conclusion of this unique summer of outdoor work. His real name was V. K. Geins; he was a Russian by birth, but a cosmopolitan by nature. An excellent mathematician and deeply versed in science, he had had an extraordinary career, first serving with distinction in the army, and then, moved by some strong moral impulse, retiring in order to emigrate to America in 1868 where he eventually set up an agricultural communal colony. The experiment failed, and he joined forces with a similar colony in Kansas of which Alekseyev was a member. When this colony also failed, Frey worked for some time as a common laborer in the United States and finally returned to Russia in 1885, after having spent a brief time in England. He heard of Tolstoy's new faith and activities, and upon investigation he realized that they had much in common. A letter to Tolstoy concerning his beliefs brought an invitation to visit him at Yasnaya Polyana.

Tolstoy received Frey with all the delight and ardor he customarily displayed at this time upon discovering anyone who shared his views. He absorbed greedily all that Frey could tell him of existence in Russian communal colonies in America, and he held up as a model to his family and friends the life of moral purity and hard labor led by these idealists, apparently preferring to disregard the obvious conclusion to be drawn from the failure of such social experiments, in which, as one of the colonists expressed it, everyone went crazy in his own way. From Frey, Tolstoy also learned a good deal about the theory and practice of vegetarianism. He was delighted, for he had already been sporadically observing this practice, and now he wholeheartedly embraced it and abstained from meat for the rest of his life.

Frey paid another visit in December (1885), and Tolstoy read to him one of the chapters of *What Then Must We Do?* in which he condemned the positivism of Auguste Comte, a scientific system that he believed usurped the place of religion and abolished the control that moral principles should exercise. This was a mistake. Frey was a fanatical devotee of the philosophy of Comte and fiercely objected to Tolstoy's condemnation of this system. Tolstoy refused to alter his position, and their promising friendship ended abruptly, its only memento a lot of absurd and at times unprintable accusations against Tolstoy in Frey's notebook.

The decision to give up meat was not the only renunciation of Tolstoy during this first vigorous attempt to live the new life at Yasnaya Polyana. He gave up wine; and hunting —the sport that had provided him with so much pleasure and with the material for some of the most brilliant passages of his fiction—was firmly abandoned. The previous fall, after Sonya had returned to Moscow, he wrote in one of his letters to her: "Today I busied myself with the affairs of the estate and then went off on my horse; the dogs stuck to me. . . . I wanted to test my own feeling for hunting. To ride and to pursue game has been a very agreeable habit for forty years. But when a hare jumped out, I wished him luck. Above all, I felt ashamed." Smoking, too, he attempted to give up, having first made the effort in the summer of 1884. He now considered smoking a luxury and declared that, instead of tobacco, grain should be grown to feed the famished. The struggle was hard. He loved to smoke and believed the practice soothed his nerves. Dilating his nostrils, he would eagerly inhale when someone smoked in his presence. The deprivation was a torment and backsliding not infrequent, and not until several years later did he finally conquer the habit.

These renunciations were not thrust upon the family, although Tolstoy always hoped that his example might influence them. In general, they respected his wishes in regard to his own behavior, but they lacked a sympathetic understanding and any spirit of discipleship. When they labored in the fields, they did so not for the reasons impelling him, but because it had become a kind of vogue and furnished them with good healthy exercise. However, Masha, aged fifteen, was beginning to regard her father's views seriously, and so was his oldest daughter, Tanya.

3

After the family had returned to the city at the end of the summer vacation of 1885, Tolstoy lingered on at Yasnaya Polyana to write. Sonya wrote her sister shortly after her return to Moscow on November 1: "He has changed his habits still more. . . . He gets up at seven, when it is still dark. He pumps water for the whole house and lugs it in an enormous tub on a sledge; he saws long logs, chops them for kindling and stacks the wood. He does not eat white bread and positively does not go anywhere."

The "new life" did not permit attendance at those gay social functions that attracted Tolstoy's wife and older children. When he went out, it was usually alone, and in order to probe into the disreputable corners of the city in search of material for his writing. The previous year he had visited Rzhanov House again to inquire about a laundress who had been evicted and died of starvation. On another occasion he went to the police station to ask about a bleary-eyed, drunken, fifteen-year-old prostitute who had been arrested, and he was horrified to be told casually that these girls began their trade at a still tenderer age. After inspecting a stocking factory, in order to acquaint himself with the conditions of the workers, he wrote in his diary: "Sorry factory people—starvelings. Teach me, God, how to serve them."

Although Tolstoy hardly ever went into society now, his house swarmed with people who sought him out for one reason or another. Artists and writers, professors, and men and women of all degree came to ask what they should do to help establish the Kingdom of God on earth. The great painter I. E. Repin, who sympathized with but could never wholly accept Tolstoy's religious views, visited at this time; so did another distinguished painter, V. M. Vasnetsov. And the famous collector of paintings, P. M. Tretyakov, whose artistic taste was considerably influenced by Tolstoy, came to call more than once.

The previous winter, Chertkov had brought to Tolstoy's house his friend P. I. Biryukov, who soon became one of his most devoted disciples and his future biographer. As a young student finishing the naval academy, where he had specialized in astronomy, Biryukov had already decided for himself that nonviolence was the essence of Christianity. His friendship with Chertkov had helped to shape his religious convictions, and his contact with Tolstoy changed the whole course of his life.

Tolstoy's unusual views, which were becoming more and more widely publicized, began to expose him to appeals from a variety of people, some sincere seekers after truth, others religious fanatics or mere mountebanks. This harassment increased through the years as his fame spread far and wide and caused him many unhappy moments. For with a faith based on service to humanity, he felt compelled to lend an ear to every plea. Sometimes he even initiated efforts to help unfortunates, usually the victims of government oppression.

One case that particularly aroused his sympathy in 1884 was that of Natalya Alexandrovna Arnfeldt, a young woman who had been exiled to Siberia for political conspiracy. At the request of the girl's mother, he attempted to persuade the authorities to move her to a prison closer to her mother or to permit the mother to live near her daughter. It was almost inevitable that he should appeal to Granny, as he had on many similar occasions. After nearly two years of silence, he wrote to ask her to intercede through her connection with the Empress, although he did not fail to anticipate further disagreements with his old friend by begging her at the end of his letter: "Only, please, *do not convert* me to the Christian faith." Granny, as always, did not fail him, and managed to have the petition of the exile's mother favorably received. In their correspondence on the matter, their former quarrel came dangerously close to the surface. Granny could not resist hinting once again that it was pride that had led him to abandon Orthodoxy, and his rejoinder amounted to advising her to concentrate her proselyting efforts on those aristocratic "Christians" of her own government set who were so heedless of the precepts of real Christianity that they willingly persecuted poor victims like the Arnfeldt woman.

A different cause for worry was those young men who, influenced by Tolstoy's writings on nonviolence, turned to him for advice on whether or not they ought to refuse to serve in the army. The moral responsibility in such cases weighed upon his conscience and caused him severe mental anguish.

At the end of 1885, A. P. Zalyubovski, a young man who had learned of Tolstoy's convictions through his friend N. L. Ozmidov, who was employed to copy Tolstoy's forbidden works, wrote to Tolstoy for advice. His term of military service was approaching, he explained, and he felt that his religious beliefs would oblige him to refuse to serve, but he feared the effect this decision would have on his mother. After much thought on the matter, Tolstoy decided not to answer. Later, in a letter to Zalyubovski's brother, he gave as a reason: "The teaching of Christ does not dictate anyone's actions; it points out the truth: questions of how one should act in a given occasion must be decided by each person in his own soul according to the degree of clarity and the strength of one's understanding of truth; and they should not be decided as I wish or do not wish to act according to the teaching of Christ, for I cannot act otherwise."

Zalyubovski, not hearing from Tolstoy, refused nevertheless to serve in the army. He was immediately arrested and thrown into a disciplinary battalion for two years and deprived of all legal rights. When Tolstoy learned of this he was deeply moved by the misfortunes of the young man and immediately set in motion every resource at his command to influence high authorities in order to obtain a pardon. His efforts failed. After Zalyubovski had served out his time in the disciplinary battalion, he was excused from further service. The incident left a scar on Tolstoy's conscience, but in no sense weakened his determination to oppose military service and war with all his powers.

A more successful effort to perform a Christian service at about this time was Tolstoy's care of his sick friend and disciple Prince L. D. Urusov. When Urusov's poor health made it necessary for him to go to the Crimea in March 1885, no member of his family was available to accompany him. Tolstoy, although not too well himself and swamped with family difficulties and literary affairs, immediately dropped everything and offered to go with Urusov. The trip had its compensations, for it enabled him to revisit Sevastopol and live again the thrilling scenes of his youth. In a radiant mood he wrote to Sonya: "The flowers bloom and it is hot even in one's shirt. The woods are bare, but in the air, sensitive, springlike, are mixed the smells of dead leaves, human refuse, and violets—all intermingled. We wandered among places that seemed inaccessible, where the enemies' batteries had been, and strangely the remembrance of war was even united with a feeling of liveliness and youth." Just five months after their return from this brief trip, Urusov died, much lamented by Tolstoy and his whole family, particularly by Sonya, who was perhaps more partial to him than to any of her husband's disciples.

4

Chertkov, that newer and younger disciple, whom Sonya had already begun to distrust, was gaining a firm hold on Tolstoy's affections and an important place in his daily affairs. The relations between the two men assumed that peculiar intimacy possible only between master and pupil when they discover that they hate the same things and are willing to compromise on what they love.[5]

At first Sonya's attitude toward Chertkov was variable. She once described him as a "tall, handsome, manly person, a real aristocrat from the first glance." And it is true that Chertkov was an attractive-looking man. Shortly after his first visit, Sonya wrote her husband, who was at Yasnaya Polyana: "I'm sending on to you a letter from Chertkov. Will you always *intentionally* close your eyes to people in whom you do not *wish* to see anything except what is good? Truly this is blindness!" Yet the next year, when Chertkov visited her in Petersburg, she seemed quite flattered and wrote to her husband: "I liked him here very much; he is so simple, affable, and he even seemed jolly."

Indeed, Chertkov could charm when he had a mind to, and at this time he appeared anxious to deserve the good opinion of the Tolstoy family. There was an instability in his nature, however, that led him to offend where he desired most to please. His relations with Tolstoy—in this early period at least—often suffered from this instability. No doubt a morbid attachment to his mother had much to do with his unevenness in human relations. She was a strong-minded woman, and after the death of her husband she concentrated all her affection on her son. A prominent Radstockite, she spent a good deal of her time abroad, par-

[5] Tolstoy's correspondence with Chertkov over this period (1884–1885) has recently been published in full, and it contains many letters that have never before been printed. (See Vol. LXXXV of the Jubilee Edition.) The remaining letters of Tolstoy in this extensive correspondence, almost a thousand in all, are being published in the succeeding volumes of the edition. Two more volumes (LXXXVI-LXXXVII) have already appeared.

ticularly in England, in order to be near V. A. Pashkov,[6] the leader of the Russian Evangelical sect, who had been exiled in 1884.

The mother at first disliked Tolstoy, for she feared his influence over her son. Tolstoy, fully aware of the fact, behaved toward her with delicacy, trying to gain her friendship. "Two letters from Chertkov," Tolstoy noted in his diary in July 1884. "His mother, as is natural, hates me." There were moments when Chertkov appeared to reflect his mother's distrust of Tolstoy. With an exaggerated frankness, he confessed to him in a letter from England in July 1884: "Even while thinking of you, I notice a nasty little devil in my relation to you. A rascally feeling of smugness often takes the place of my sincere friendship when I realize that I am in close, intimate relations with such a 'remarkable' man as you. I feel this is quite like that vain satisfaction I formerly experienced, when the Emperor or even some Grand Duke favored me with special attention in the presence of others."

Chertkov never wearied of admitting to Tolstoy that he was an egoist. This persistent self-criticism may have been an unconscious imitation of a habit common to the master, but in the matter of egoism, Chertkov was abundantly at fault. Tolstoy worried over a lack of warmth in the friendship of his young disciple. With his own ardent nature he often wrote in letters to Chertkov that he "loved him"—as he was accustomed to do in correspondence with people dear to him—and he complained to his friend: "In your letters there is little simple love for me, as for a human being who loves you." Chertkov's answer was curious and deserves to be remembered in the light of his general behavior and future events. "I love you," he wrote, although I love separate personalities very little . . . with the exception of children, and in particular little boys, whom I especially love. But I positively love you, although I'm a little afraid." Shortly before this he excused himself for a poor letter he had written because of low spirits, and then added: "I have now arranged things so that I shall again sleep in the same room with Peter [a young peasant servant]. I do not know why, but when I sleep in the same room with someone, I sleep much better and more quietly in this manner."

Whatever Tolstoy may have thought about Chertkov's

[6] He was married to the sister of Chertkov's mother.

lack of warmth in their friendship, he strongly urged him to marry. Chertkov categorically replied that he was in love with no one; that the wife he took must understand and agree with his views on the significance and purpose of life; and finally that he was convinced that any wife he considered suitable would not please his mother. And he concluded, in answer to Tolstoy's warning concerning the temptations of the flesh in the path of a single man: "It is understandable that I do not wish to marry merely for physical reasons. You correctly refer to a meager life and work. But it seems to me that the principal thing is the will, the internal struggle, and the success of this depends on the internal state of the spirit." Chertkov soon changed his mind; or rather he found the woman he wished to marry not merely for physical reasons.

Although the precious tone of a few of these early letters suggests that their friendship had something in it of the "eternal bond" of a couple of boarding-school misses, when they dealt with doctrinal matters the sharpest kind of criticism resulted. There was more religiosity than religion in Chertkov, and at times a Calvinistic spirit in him annoyed Tolstoy. He sensed a proselyting streak in Chertkov, who adopted a rather stuffy attitude toward the faith of others and felt that he had been ordained to lead man to the fount of his own beliefs. Tolstoy censured him for this failing, mitigating his reproof by freely admitting that he himself had also once burned with the desire to proselyte. But now he felt that he had no right to urge people to accept his own religious convictions, nor did he believe that his path was the only one to the truths he held. Any path was acceptable if it reached the same goal. "I am so firmly convinced," he wrote to Chertkov, "that the truth for me is the truth for all people that the question about when and how people will arrive at that truth does not interest me."

Chertkov's argumentativeness on doctrinal points no doubt represented a sincere desire for knowledge, for in such matters Tolstoy was sometimes inconsistent and not clear in his exposition; yet there is also reason to suppose that the young disciple's proneness to equivocate arose from a desire to preserve some degree of intellectual and spiritual independence in the face of the master. In his letters he raised the question of external aid from God, which Tolstoy dismissed as dangerously metaphysical, and the question of prayer. Prayer to God, Tolstoy explained, was a superstition;

one should pray only for those things that can be fulfilled by people and by oneself. With a large unearned income, Chertkov was disposed to quibble endlessly over Tolstoy's uncompromising stand on the evil of property. It is impossible to be a Christian and possess property, he warned Chertkov. For the important thing in Christianity is not to live so that others will serve you, but to live in order to serve others. Since the possession of unearned money enables one to avoid labor and to exploit the work of others, Tolstoy condemned money.

The aristocratic Chertkov had a distaste for physical toil, if one may believe the report of Tolstoy's son Ilya.[7] Chertkov visited Yasnaya Polyana in the summer of 1885, when the enthusiasm for work in the fields was at its height. After breakfast the whole company went to the stables for their tools and set about their various tasks. Tolstoy's daughter Tanya, who was always lively and fond of fun, seeing that Chertkov was going off with empty hands, called to him:—

> "And where are you going?"
> "To the villa-a-age."
> "What for?"
> "To he-e-lp."
> "Why, how are you going to help? You haven't got any tools. Here, take a rake; it'll do to hand them up the straw."
> "Oh, I shall help them with advi-i-ice," said Mr.——, speaking as he always did, with a drawl like an Englishman, quite unaware of Tanya's irony, and how ridiculous and useless he would be with his advice in "the villa-a-age," where everybody has to work hard, and where people dressed up in baggy English knickerbockers and Norfolk jackets are merely in the way and interfere with other people's work.

There were occasions in these early days of their friendship when the young disciple made bold to question the fundamental truths of the master's faith. Tolstoy would then sternly pull him up and let him understand that if anyone were going to commit heresy, it was he. In a controversy in April 1885 with L. E. Obolenski, a writer and sympathizer, Chertkov supported his views against Tolstoy. The point at issue appears to have been Tolstoy's insistence on the five commandments as the essential basis of Christ's

[7] In this account the author does not name Chertkov, but the person indicated could be no one else.

teaching. In a sharp letter to Chertkov he sarcastically observed that it was Christ and not he who had set the number of commandments. "No, you say, these commandments are insufficient. Well, tell me then what ones are sufficient. Then I will accept yours. Provide another program, your own, or find it in the teaching of Christ. But until you have devised your own commandments, permit me to live better by Christ's, guided by them in life, for to my feeble mind they seem more fully to envision the Kingdom of God."

Such outbursts were rare, and the whole tenor of the extensive correspondence between Tolstoy and Chertkov over these two years emphasizes the deepening bond of friendship and their growing dependence on each other. In the practical matters connected with his literary output and in the propagation of his new faith, Tolstoy began to develop the habit of leaning upon Chertkov, who possessed considerable organizing and financial abilities. In fact, Chertkov was already well on the way toward becoming a sort of self-appointed business manager of Tolstoyism. His crusading zeal was enormous, and he acted as the gadfly in Tolstoy's literary endeavors with consequences of extreme importance.

5

Early in the correspondence of Tolstoy and Chertkov, the necessity for the cheap publication of good literature was discussed. Since the spread of elementary education, the reading public in Russia had grown considerably. Apart from cheap productions of legends, lives of saints, and penny-dreadfuls, no attempt had been made to publish good literature inexpensively enough to be within the reach of the poor. Tolstoy had long recognized this problem. When he had been conducting his school at Yasnaya Polyana, he had been struck by the receptivity of peasants to artistic literature. Now he felt strongly that authors who wrote their books in comfort and consumed what the toil of the poor produced should at least attempt to provide literary food worthy of these people.

In February 1884, Tolstoy read an article that he had written on the necessity of cheap editions of good literature for the masses to a group of people interested in public education. And in October Chertkov proposed the publication of a popular magazine designed for the masses, a proposal that Tolstoy enthusiastically encouraged. By November the project had changed somewhat after Chertkov had had a conference with I. D. Sytin, a Moscow publisher of inexpensive books. An agreement was reached for the printing of cheap booklets and pictures that would bring to the people tales and illustrations in the spirit of Tolstoy's Christian teaching. The stories were to be written by the best Russian authors and the illustrations would be done by the most distinguished artists. Thus the pioneering publishing business, called the *Intermediary,* was founded, one of the most practical and worth-while ventures inspired by Tolstoy's influence, although due credit for its establishment must be given to Chertkov who, along with Biryukov, managed its fortunes for some years. In the first four years of its existence the little *Intermediary* booklets, priced at one and one-half kopeks, sold twelve million copies.

Tolstoy's theory that the masses would read good literature if they could afford to buy it was proved to the hilt. And something of the initial popularity of the publications must be attributed to the fact that three of the first four issues were stories from his pen. Chertkov, mindful of the success of Tolstoy's tale "What Men Live By," written several years before, kept urging him to contribute similar stories for *Intermediary.* And during 1884 and 1885 he wrote no less than fifteen tales and texts describing pictures, most of which were quickly published by *Intermediary.* They include such well-known short stories as "Two Brothers and Gold"; "Ilyas"; "Where Love Is, God Is"; "A Spark Neglected Burns the House"; and "Two Old Men." These stories are mostly retellings of popular folk tales, for which he had a special gift. Their clear religious or moral lesson is never allowed to obtrude upon the narrative interest which is sustained with his usual skill. And the tales are told in that simple language which Tolstoy was beginning to favor more and more as the proper artistic medium for the mass of readers he hoped to reach.

Tolstoy encouraged *Intermediary* not only with contributions of his own, but also with suggestions of works that might be printed. These were all books that he had read and valued highly: Dickens's short stories, *Oliver Twist, Little Dorrit, Bleak House,* and *Edwin Drood,* George Eliot's *Felix Holt* and Kingsley's *Hypatia.* Matthew Arnold's *Literature and Dogma* he also strongly urged upon Chertkov. Tolstoy was enthusiastic about this work. He wrote to a friend that it was "a remarkable production" and contained many of his own thoughts. "He will bring you great satisfaction," he remarked, "because he particularly insists on destroying the notion of God as something outside us, a 'magnified man' as he calls Him." And he requested Chertkov when he was in England to present Arnold with a copy of the French rendering of *What I Believe,* a commission that was fulfilled.[8]

Of the American books that he read at this time, Tolstoy recommended Prescott's *Conquest of Mexico;* and in the works of the noted Unitarian preacher Theodore Parker[9] he "was very happy to find that my own thoughts had been excellently expressed twenty years ago." Emerson's famous essay "Self-Reliance" he found "charming," and the author "profound, bold, but often capricious and muddled." But the books of Henry George—*Progress and Poverty* and *Social Problems*—which he discovered at this time, made a lasting impression on him and influenced his own economic theories. Of *Progress and Poverty* he wrote to Sonya: "This is an important book. It is as important a step on the path of public life as the freeing of the serfs—freedom from private ownership of land. One's view on this subject is the text of a man. It is necessary to read George, who has put this question clearly and definitely. After him it is impossible to prevaricate; one must directly take a stand on his or on the other side. My demands go much further than his; but his are a step on the first rung of the ladder that I'm climbing." Tolstoy urged his friends to read George, and to Chertkov he wrote of *Progress and Poverty:* "The book has not been unnoticed, but not valued because it demolishes that whole scientific web of Spencer-Mill[1]—all that futile nonsense, and appeals directly to the moral consciousness and occupation of people and even defines that occupation. There are weaknesses in it, as in all things human, but in it there is real human thought and heart, and not scientific rubbish." In truth, Henry George's idea of the nationalization of land by means of a single land tax took such a hold on Tolstoy that for the rest of his life he popularized the idea in conversations and in his writings.

[8] Arnold in 1887 wrote a highly interesting article on Tolstoy's literary, religious, and philosophical productions, which is filled with high praise but with certain reservations on his religious views.

[9] *The Transient and Permanent in Christianity* and *Discourse of Matters Pertaining to Religion.*

[1] Herbert Spencer and John Stuart Mill.

The wide reading that Tolstoy did over this period inspired a fruitful idea, for in his diary in March 1884, after a note on his reading of Confucius, he jotted down: "Must compose for myself a Circle of Reading: Epictetus, Marcus Aurelius, Lao-Tse, Buddha, Pascal, the Gospels." For he felt that from these and other great works he could cull thoughts that would best guide man's moral and religious life. More than twenty years later he completed this vast project.

The publication of Tolstoy's own productions at this time was continually encumbered by difficulties with the censor. *What I Believe* was not actually finished until January 22, 1884, after he had lost the first set of proofs when his suitcase was stolen in a Moscow railway station. Convinced by his previous experience with *Confession* that such a religious work would never pass the censor in the ordinary course of events, he attempted a rather familiar dodge. He arranged for an expensive edition of only fifty copies in the hope that the book, obviously not intended for popular circulation, would be certified. The ruse failed. The head of the Moscow Civil Censorship Committee reported that *What I Believe* "must be considered an extremely harmful book as it undermines the foundations of social and governmental institutions and wholly destroys the teaching of the Church." On the basis of this report the spiritual censor Pobedonostsev ordered all copies of the book to be seized and burned.

Actually, not one copy was burned; the whole edition was sent to Petersburg and illegally distributed among high officials and their friends. "That is fine," Tolstoy wrote when he heard of the fate of his book. As so often happens in cases of prohibition, there arose a widespread demand for his banned publications. News of them spread, and he appears to have been unconcerned over the unauthorized reproduction of these works. Secret printing presses and hectograph and lithograph machines were not uncommon in the hands of political revolutionists. And in some cases it is known that they reproduced in quantity Tolstoy's forbidden works, for there was often much in them that revolutionists could use to their own purpose. The situation intensified the hostility of the government toward Tolstoy. A German translation of *What I Believe* appeared in Leipzig in 1884, and the next year in Paris a French version. And in the same year Chertkov published English translations of *Confession,*

What I Believe, and *A Short Account of the Gospels,* none of which works had as yet been printed in Russia.

Like a ghost from the past, there appeared in print, at the end of 1885, several fragments of the beginning of his old projected novel on the Decembrists. He had dug them out at the request of the Society to Aid Needy Authors and Scholars, the organization that he had helped to establish twenty-seven years before. Shortly before these fragments appeared, he received a letter from Granny to tell him that she had uncovered some rich material on the Decembrists. With a nostalgic longing for the literary past of his great novels that she loved, she sadly added that now he probably would not want this material. Although he eschewed a full-length novel, in his spare moments he did work on "The Notes of a Madman" and *The Death of Ivan Ilyich,* which he particularly wished to finish as a surprise for Sonya.

As in the previous year, his major literary concern in 1884 and 1885 was *What Then Must We Do?* In alternate moods of exultation and despair over his progress, he doggedly kept at this work, fully convinced that it would resolve all the problems that had arisen from the clash of his new faith with contemporary economic and social life. As 1885 drew to a close, he saw the end of this long, arduous task in sight.[2] But at just this time a new family crisis arose that utterly ruined his peace of mind and made literary work impossible.

6

When Tolstoy departed suddenly for Yasnaya Polyana in January 1884, he wished a rest after finishing *What I Believe,* but a contributing factor was no doubt his displeasure over the family's indulgence in the social events of the New Year. For Sonya's letters were almost apologetic on the score of the various balls she had been attending, and she expressed regret that she could not enjoy with him the brisk country air and the moral freedom of his solitude. In a letter to her sister Tanya, she revealed a quite different frame of mind over his absence. "Yesterday Sergei Nikolaye-

[2] Tolstoy published three fragments from *What Then Must We Do?* in 1885, and also *The Greek Teacher Socrates,* the work of a friend, A. M. Kalmykov, to which he contributed a large part. In the same year he translated from the Greek *The Teaching of the Twelve Apostles* of Bishop Bryennios.

vich[3] returned from Tula," she wrote. "He had seen Lyovochka at Yasnaya Polyana. He [her husband] sits in a blouse, in filthy woolen socks, disheveled and gloomy; with Mitrofan he stitches boots for Mikhailovna. The schoolteacher reads aloud the lives of the saints. He will not return to Moscow unless I call him back or unless something happens to us. Though he has a swarm of children, he is unable to find in the family any occupation, joy, or duties, and I more and more feel towards him contempt and coldness. We do not dispute at all; I do not even tell him this—do not think so. But it has become so difficult for me with the older children, with a huge family, and with my pregnancy, so that I await with a certain avidity to see if I fall ill or be trampled by horses—if only I could somehow rest and escape this life."

In a few months Sonya would be forty. In twenty-two years of married life she had been pregnant twelve times, and in the last few years she had fought in vain against having more children. Her condition now unquestionably contributed to the mounting hysteria that made living with her a torment for Tolstoy. About two months before the birth of her child, a letter to her sister clearly echoed Sonya's despair: "Sometimes I get wildly despondent. I'm ready to scream and fly into a rage. I will not nurse the child but will get a wet nurse; and I have bought everything at Moscow in cheap shops in order to clothe it."

Meanwhile Tolstoy had returned to the city. He tidied his room, hammered pegs into shoes, read Confucius, and watched Sonya with "silent, critical, and stern" eyes. His diary records the approaching storm. "I remained alone with her," he noted on April 12. "Conversation. I had the misfortune and cruelty to wound her pride, and it began. I did not remain silent. . . . She is seriously, mentally ill. And the point is this pregnancy. And it is a great, great sin and shame."

The behavior of his children intensified Tolstoy's misery. They thought him mad and told him so. "It is very sad in the family," he wrote. "It is said that I cannot sympathize with them. All their joys, examinations, social success, music, furniture, purchases—all this I reckon a misfortune and an evil for them, and I cannot tell them this. I can, I speak, but my words do not affect anyone. They, as it were, do

[3] Tolstoy's brother.

not know the meaning of my words, only that I have a bad habit of speaking thus. In weak moments—such as now—I am astonished at their ruthlessness." And a few days later he exploded: "What for and why do I have such a terrible misunderstanding with the family! I must find a way out of it."

About a month before the birth of the child, relations between Tolstoy and his wife were rapidly reaching a breaking point. The family had moved for the summer to Yasnaya Polyana. He tried to talk to Sonya about the necessity of changing their way of life, but such conversations only infuriated her. "Poor thing," he entered in the diary, "how she hates me. Lord, help me." All his misery, he confessed, was owing to the absence of a loving and beloved wife. And with unusual frankness he wrote a few days later: "The luxury and debauchery of the life that I live is terrible. I have done it myself, I'm depraved, and I cannot reform. I can say that I'm mending myself, but it is so slow. I cannot give over smoking, I cannot find an approach to my wife so as neither to offend nor to indulge her. I search, I try. They do not see and do not know my suffering."

It is a measure of the intimacy that he had already reached with Chertkov that he now felt impelled to make him a confidant of his domestic woes. "On one occasion this year I lay in bed beside my wife," he wrote him. "She was not asleep, nor was I, and I suffered grievously from a consciousness of my own isolation in the family because of my beliefs, and because all of them in my eyes, seeing the truth, turn away from it. I suffered both for them and for myself, and because there was no hope to be seen. At the moment, I do not remember how, but being weighed down and sad, and with tears in my eyes I began to pray to God to open the heart of my wife. She fell asleep. I heard her quiet breathing, and suddenly it came into my head: I suffer because my wife does not share my convictions. When I speak with her under the influence of vexation about her repulsing me, I often speak coldly, even in a hostile manner; never have I entreated her with tears to believe in the truth or told her all simply, lovingly, softly; yet here she lies beside me and I say nothing to her, but what ought to be said to her I say to God."

Sonya was in no condition to listen even to what her husband spoke only to God. He noted that "the estrangement with my wife grows always. She does not see and does not wish to see." If he were only sure of himself, he asserted, he would not continue his present unhappy life. This thought came to him on the eve of the birth of his child. What happened next has sometimes been misrepresented and hence it will be helpful to translate the account of the incident in his diary.

"I went to bathe. I returned cheerful, jolly, and suddenly from my wife came senseless reproaches about the horses, which I had no need of and from which I wish to be released. I said nothing but I fell terribly in the dumps. I left and wanted to go away for good, but her pregnancy compelled me to return when I was halfway to Tula. At home, bearded peasants and my two young sons were playing *vint*. 'She is playing croquet; did you not see her?' said her sister Tanya. 'I do not wish to see her.' I went to the divan to sleep, but I could not from grief. Ach, how sad! Yet, I pity her. However, I cannot believe that she is entirely wooden. I had just fallen asleep at three o'clock when she entered, woke me. 'Forgive me, I'm about to give birth and perhaps I shall die.' We went upstairs. The confinement began. What is the most joyous, happiest event in a family took place as something unnecessary and sad. A wet nurse had been provided to give milk." Under such unhappy circumstance Alexandra was born (June 18, 1884).

The new arrival brought no peace into the household. Tolstoy's diary for the month of July is a poignant record of his sufferings, and his wife must have suffered correspondingly. The problem of the resumption of marital relations widened the breach between them. Of late, after the birth of children that she had not wanted, Sonya had feared this period. Now it was her husband who, still profoundly shaken by their prolonged differences, found it impossible to renew relations. Torn by desire and forgetting that his was the active role, he unfairly blamed his wife for her passivity. He murmured against the unfulfilled "sensual temptation" that he struggled with at night. And less than a month after the birth of Alexandra, he angrily burst forth in his diary: "Cohabitation with a woman alien in spirit, i.e. with her, is terribly disgusting. Just as I wrote this she came to me and began an hysterical scene. There is the thought that it is impossible to change anything, that she is unhappy, and that she must escape somewhere. I was sorry for her, but together with this I recognized that it was hopeless. To my death, she will remain a millstone on my neck and on the children's." Once again the situation became so impossible that he decided to go away. At night he packed his things, awoke Sonya to say farewell, but after a talk with her, he agreed to remain. The next morning he wrote in his diary: "I do not understand how to save myself from suffering or her from the destruction towards which she flies with haste."

Except for fitful bursts of anger, Sonya's hysteria vanished, and the remainder of the summer passed off calmly enough with Tolstoy working in the fields and feeling immensely pleased that his daughters had begun to evince some sympathy for his new way of life. When the family returned to the city, he remained in the country for a short time in the autumn. Letters between husband and wife reveal a marked improvement in their relations over the nightmarish summer. The separation may have contributed, but the deep affection they had for each other was never far below the surface; it flowed freely whenever the dam of spiritual and material obstacles crumbled.

With genuine concern Sonya reproved him for playing the Robinson Crusoe in the country while he neglected that "mental work which I regard as higher than anything in life." And with mingled irony and humor she continued: "So it would have been better and more useful had you stayed with the children. Of course you will say that to live so accords with your convictions, and that you enjoy it. That is another matter, and I can only say, 'Enjoy yourself!' However, I'm distressed that such intellectual powers should be wasted on chopping wood, tending samovars, and stitching boots—all that is fine as a rest or a change of occupation, but not as a special employment. Well, enough of that! Had I not written it, I should have remained vexed, but now it is past, and the thing amuses me, and I have grown calm, saying: 'Let the child amuse itself as it likes, so long as it doesn't cry.' "[4] Then, as though fearful that she had been too severe, she concluded her letter on a touching note of sympathy and understanding that at once revealed the real place he held in her heart: "Farewell, my dear, I kiss you. All at once I vividly pictured you to myself, and a sudden flood of tenderness for you rose in me. There is something

[4] A Russian proverb.

in you so wise, kind, naïve, and stubborn, and it is all lit up by that tender interest for everyone, natural to you alone, and by your look that reaches straight to people's souls."

Tolstoy was grateful. Sonya's criticism he took in good part, and his letters were filled with loving concern over her illness. Her worries over money matters he cheerfully dismissed. "Do not be angry, darling, that I cannot attribute any importance to these money matters. That life should not appear trivial, one must take a wider and deeper view. What our life together is, with our joys and sorrows, will appear to our nine children real life, and therefore it is important to help them acquire what gave us happiness, and to help them to free themselves from what gave us unhappiness; but neither languages, nor diplomas, nor society, and, still less, money performed any part in our happiness or unhappiness. And therefore the question how much our income shrinks cannot occupy me. If one attributes importance to that, it hides what is really important."

During this brief separation, a passionate longing for her husband seems to have banished the ill-feeling in Sonya's heart. "You ask: Why do I not summon you home? Ach, Lyovochka, if I were to write at this moment when I wish to see you, I would write everything that I feel—then I would give vent to such a flood of passionate, tender, demanding words that you would not remain content merely with words. In all relations I am sometimes inexpressibly sad without you; but I have accepted the idea of *fulfilling my duty* in my relation to you as a writer, as a man requiring first of all his freedom, and therefore I demand nothing from you."

This newly won harmony was quickly disrupted by the impact of city life when Tolstoy returned to Moscow at the beginning of November. Scarcely a month passed before he fled again to the solitude of Yasnaya Polyana. The need of quiet to write was his excuse, and his letters were full of the progress he made. Sonya was hurt, disappointed, and the familiar aggravation, caused by his insistence on the new life, reappeared.

7

By this time the struggle had assumed a definite character. Sonya was opposed to every move of her husband that threatened the security of herself and her family. For Tolstoy, it was a necessity to change his manner of life without thought of anyone's security. There were frequent compromises on both sides, for the habits of years of happy married existence were a bulwark against deterioration in their relations. Each suffered for the other in the tragic struggle in which principles warred against love. But their external differences were slowly poisoning the wellspring of this love.

Aroused over what she with some justice considered offensive references to the family in the manuscript of *What Then Must We Do?* Sonya demanded that they be expunged. Tolstoy wrote to Ge's son, of whom he was very fond, that it made him ill to be asked by his family to alter thoughts in an article "about my own life and therefore about theirs." If the thoughts were true, he argued with Sonya, then why must they be altered? In the end he agreed to delete the offensive references, but the controversy drove him to write to Sonya that it was terrible to live without love and still more terrible to die without it.

At the beginning of 1885, Sonya obtained her husband's permission to republish all his works that had appeared before 1881 in a new edition (the fifth). This was not a unique venture for she had the successful precedent of Dostoyevsky's widow, who gave Sonya much helpful advice. Sonya borrowed money to start with and herself did all the work of reading the proofs.[5] While going over the proofs for her edition of his first work, *Childhood,* charming memories were recalled, and she wrote to her husband, who was off to the Crimea at the time: "I went through the chapters of *Childhood* and there arose in me that former girlish feeling that I first experienced when I was eleven, and again my eyes grew dim, and instead of quietly correcting the misprints, I took to weeping. But I know what I loved in you when I was thirteen to fourteen, and I love the same thing now; but that which has been added to it and hardened—that I do not love; that is an addition, an excrescence. Scrape it away, and what is left will be pure gold." Always a bit of a romantic, poor Sonya wanted her girlhood hero to remain a girlhood hero and not a titan dedicated to founding the Kingdom of God on earth.

The business of the edition took her to Petersburg. While she was there, visiting a distant relative high in Court circles, the Empress was suddenly announced. "I frankly

[5] During the first year, Sonya made a gross turnover of some 60,000 rubles (about $30,000).

confess," Sonya wrote to her husband, "that I was very agitated but not embarrassed. She, i.e., the Empress, asked:

" 'Have you been here long?' [6]

" 'No, madame, only since yesterday.' Then we went into the hall. The Empress again turned to me:

" 'How is your husband's health?' I said: 'Your majesty is very kind; he is well.'

" 'I hope that he is writing something.' I said: 'No, madame, not at the moment, but I believe that he intends to write something for the schools in the nature of "What Men Live By." '

"Ekaterina Nikolayevna[7] intervened, saying: 'Countess Alexandra Tolstoy[8] says that he will never write any more novels.'

"The Empress said: 'Surely you do not desire this; it astonishes me.' And having turned to me, I said: 'I hope that your majesty's children have read my husband's books.'

"She inclined her head and said: 'Oh, I surely believe so.' "

In his reply Tolstoy's only comment on this meeting with the Empress was to remark dryly: "Really your joy is surprising. You desired this very much. It was flattering to my vanity but rather disagreeable. Nothing good comes from this sort of thing."

In her edition, Sonya soon fell afoul of Chertkov, who wished certain works for his own publishing venture, *Intermediary*. He grew disagreeable, for he was already developing a proprietary attitude toward the products of Tolstoy's pen, and a long and bitter quarrel was in the making.

So intimate had their friendship become that Tolstoy did not hesitate to write Chertkov at this time a very frank letter concerning his troubles in the family. He complained of "the systematic debauchery" of his children, and continued: "I do not fear death, I even desire it. But this is bad; it means that I have lost the thread granted to me by God for guidance in this life, and for full satisfaction." And as the only means of escape, he revealed an idea that had no doubt been in the back of his mind ever since his spiritual transformation. Must he stay in this "insane, immoral house," he asked Chertkov, "in which I am now forced to suffer every hour," without ever having lived at least a

[6] The conversation was carried on in French.
[7] Sonya's relative and hostess, Mme Shostak.
[8] Granny.

single year in a human way, that is "in a hut with working people, working together with them according to my strength and abilities, bartering my efforts, nourishing and clothing myself as they, and without shame boldly speaking to all the truth of Christ that I know." But he put aside this precious ideal of perfect Christian life that he preached as a temptation, convinced that he must work out his salvation in the milieu where God had placed him.

Chertkov did not hesitate in his reply to offer his own opinion on these intimate personal family difficulties and to advise Tolstoy what course of action he should adopt. "You say that you live in an atmosphere entirely hostile to your faith," he wrote. "And therefore it is entirely natural that from time to time you should have made plans to go away or change the whole family atmosphere. But I cannot agree that this indicates that you are weak and bad." Then citing the example of Christ, he concluded that after Tolstoy had done everything in his power to correct the life of his family and failed, he would then be justified in leaving them in order to live the life he desired.

The summer of 1885, however, was not without its domestic compensations and victories. By his example Tolstoy had inspired the whole household to take up his work in the village and fields. The slightest evidence of interest in his new beliefs on the part of his children gave him great pleasure. And when his oldest daughter, Tanya, confessed to him that her views on things had changed, he hastened to write her: My *one* dream and possible joy, in which I do not dare to hope, is to find in my own family brothers and sisters and not what I have observed up to now—estrangement and deliberate opposition in which I see a certain scorn, not for me, but for truth,—a certain fear before something. . . . It is more important for you to tidy your own room, cook your own soup (it would be fine if you endeavored to see through everything that obstructs this, especially opinion) than it is for you to get married well or badly." Masha followed suit, and even interested herself in vegetarianism. Chertkov, who visited them that summer, also had an influence on Tolstoy's daughters. The hope that the father had secretly entertained of a family living in peace and harmony according to the teaching of Christ took on a fugitive aspect of reality.

Sonya was horrified. All along she had feared the influence of her husband's views on the children, and she was determined to prevent heresy from undermining the foundations of the family. The family, she insisted, needed no reforming; its life, its traditions, and its social and religious views, must remain unchanged.

8

With misgivings Tolstoy returned to Moscow on November 1, fearful that life with his family in the city would again become insupportable. They greeted him with joy, but soon the atmosphere became tense. Sonya wrote to her sister that it was impossible to adjust herself to her husband's convictions. The strain was somewhat relieved when she was obliged to go to Petersburg to try to obtain permission from the censor to include *What I Believe* in the twelfth volume of her edition of Tolstoy's works. Despite all the influence she marshaled up, the permission was not granted.

After her return, Tolstoy's relations with his wife once again reached a crisis. His simmering feelings boiled over. Sonya wrote to her sister: "There happened what has already happened so many times. Lyovochka had fallen into an extremely nervous and gloomy condition. I was sitting, writing; he entered and I looked up—his face was terrifying. Up to that time we had been living excellently, not *one* disagreeable word had been said, none whatsoever. 'I've come to say that I wish to divorce you; I cannot live this way; I'm going to Paris or America.'

"Imagine, Tanya, if the whole house had tumbled down on my head, I would not have been more astonished. I asked in surprise: 'What has happened?' 'Nothing, but if the cart is loaded more and more, the horse stands and does not pull it.' What was loaded on him, I don't know. But he set up a howl, reproaches, rude words, all getting worse and worse. I was patient, was patient but answered almost nothing. I saw that the man was mad, and when he said that where you are the air is poisoned, I finally ordered my trunk to be brought and began to pack. I wanted to go to you if only for a few days.

"The children came running in, wailing. Tanya [daughter] said: 'I'll go with you; what is this?' He began to beg me: 'Remain.' I remained, but suddenly hysterical sobbing started; it was simply frightful. Think: Lyovochka all torn and twitching from sobbing. At this point I became sorry for him." The upshot of all this was that Tolstoy went with his daughter Tanya to the country to stay with the Olsufyevs, family friends.

The reasons for this hysterical outburst Sonya did not tell her sister. Perhaps she did not clearly know, for the scene was the outcome of an accumulation of everything unpleasant in their relations over the last four years. Tolstoy, however, felt it necessary to explain once and for all why their life together had become unbearable. For before he departed for the country, he left behind a long and unusual letter for Sonya which has only recently been published in full. That she read it we know from one Masha sent her sister at the Olsufyevs', in which she wrote: "After dinner today we had quite a disagreeable conversation. Mama attacked vegetarianism. She read a letter that papa left for her, and it obviously upset her."

This long letter of Tolstoy amounts literally to a history of his spiritual development and of the conflict his views had brought about in his relations with his wife. "For the last seven or eight years," he wrote, "all our discussions have ended after much grievous torment in the same thing, on my side at least. I said: there cannot be agreement and a loving life between us until—I said as long as—you do not come to what I have come to, either through love for me, or through that scent given to all of us, or through conviction, and yet you have not gone along with me. I said: as long as you do not agree with me, but I did not say: as long as I do not agree with you, because this is impossible for me. I say impossible, because the way you live is the very way that I have just been saved from, as from a terrible horror, almost leading me to suicide. I cannot return to the way I lived, in which I found destruction, and which I have acknowledged to be the greatest evil and misfortune. But you can attempt to come to what you still do not know about, and which in general features is precisely a life not for one's own satisfaction (I do not speak of your life, but of the children's life), not for one's own ambition but for God and for others—a way of life always accounted the best by everybody, and which your own conscience responds to."

He next begged her to realize that the very illegal works for which she had so zealously been trying to obtain permission to print, he wrote not for the public or as exercises in style, but because his suffering and searching had obliged him to write them. And he asked her to read in these works the reasons why they were written. There she would find also why he could not continue to live the life of the family. He could not now reject the faith that he had found. His faith could not change; nor could he allow it to be a mere matter of words: it must be acted upon. Conscience and intellect demanded it of him, he said, and "I cannot see people, joined to me by love, knowing yet not doing what intellect and conscience demand, and not suffer myself."

Then with passionate earnestness he pointed out that she and the family had always tended to regard his spiritual revelation as an experience suitable perhaps as literary material but not something by which to guide one's life. But only by living according to his new convictions had he been saved from despair and returned to life. Finally, when she began to see that he was serious in his efforts to lead a new life, she condemned it all as a form of mental illness from which she must protect herself and the children.

There followed a long recital of their life over the last few years in both city and country, in which he and the family had steadily drifted apart. At times, he indicated, there seemed only one solution—that he must leave the family. But he had resisted this as a temptation. He had felt it necessary to continue to live as he had lived, struggling with all his power against evil, but always lovingly and meekly. Must this struggle go on, he asked? "It will be sad for me to die with a reproach for all the useless burden of the last years of my life, of which few remain, and it will be sad for you to see me off with the doubt that you ought not to have brought me those grievous sufferings that I experienced in life." And he ended with the ominous warning: "Between us there is a struggle to the death. Either God or no God."

This extraordinary letter from a husband to a wife is a curious mixture of arrant didacticism and the anguished cry of a human soul perplexed in the extreme. But throughout all of it runs an intransigent attitude that gives the lie to Tolstoy's expressed distaste for proselyting. The only justification, or rather excuse, is that he wanted to live with his wife and family and he could not do this with a clear conscience unless they agreed to live according to his beliefs.

It is interesting to observe that at this same time Tolstoy wrote a letter to Chertkov, as the one person who was able "to love in him what was fine," in which he freely expressed all the unhappiness caused by his family. He finally decided not to send this letter, but certain statements in it were revealing. He complained that his children would not read what he wrote concerning the worldly, wasteful life they led, and that when he spoke they did not listen or they answered with irritation. And one of the immediate reasons for the quarrel he had had with his wife was his condemnation of the subscription sale of Sonya's edition of his works, a practice that now outraged his views on property and money and threatened to make him an object of ridicule.

There was little that was new to Sonya in this letter, although for the first time she must have seen their situation in a clearer perspective. Yet the letter does not appear to have changed her attitude in the slightest. She felt offended by his recent treatment, and in her letters to him she did not attempt to justify herself any more; she only reproached him.

Soon after his arrival at the Olsufyevs', Tolstoy wrote Sonya a letter that was intended to be kindly and even apologetic for his behavior. "Ach, my darling," he wrote, "how sorry I am that you torment yourself so, or that the matter [her edition] that you are busy with so torments you. . . . I rejoice that I have now reached such a normal condition that I will not trouble and torment you as I have tormented you lately."

In a reply of mingled sarcasm and seriousness, Sonya made the most of some news she had heard about his young disciples: "Chertkov, in a quarrel with his mother, wished to go away. Fainerman wants to desert his wife; you wish to run away from your family. Truly, if all this were not so, how happy we would be, since in the depths of our souls, we *certainly* love each other. And surely both Chertkov and Fainerman love their own. That is what I will never understand; why the *truth* must bring *evil* and *dissension?* Dissension not with bandits, but with quiet, *loving* people? For the first time in my life I was glad that you departed. How painful and sad this is! But I, of course, will be still more glad when you return."

XXV

"Dark, Dark People!"

THE YEAR 1886 began badly for the Tolstoy family: the youngest son, four-year-old Alyosha, died from croup on January 18. Sonya's grief was intensified by the belief that God had punished her by taking a child she had never wanted. Her husband was sad, but he found solace in his faith. With composure, he wrote Chertkov the day he lost his son: "I know only that the death of a child, which formerly seemed incomprehensible and cruel to me, now appears sensible and good. The death has united us all more lovingly and closely than before."

Shortly after the loss of his son, Tolstoy at last finished, on February 14, his remarkable book, *What Then Must We Do?* For several years he had wrestled with the intricate problems connected with this work, for he felt that upon their solution would depend the justification of his new faith. With overwhelming evidence and irrefutable logic he stated the case of the poor against the rich. Not content with this, he insisted that such economic disparity inevitably resulted in the moral impoverishment of both classes. He did not except himself from the general condemnation of the well-to-do; if anything, he was most severe on what he considered his own guilt.

Tolstoy's experiences and then his reason had convinced him that private or organized charity was not the answer to the problem of the poor. In truth, he observed that the giving of money worked a positive harm and he had come to believe that there was something evil and unmoral in money. His investigation convinced him that money does not usually represent work done by its owner, but rather the power to make others work. That is, money is the modern form of slavery, for it makes the poor the common slaves of all the rich.

In all this theorizing Tolstoy examined his own way of life in the light of his conclusions, and he decided that he ought to consume as little as possible of the work of others in order not to cause suffering and vice. He was convinced that no one possesses any rights or privileges, but only endless duties and obligations, and that man's first duty is to participate in the struggle with nature to support his own life and that of others. When he asked himself the question that his book raised for all mankind, What must I do? he answered in a practical manner that he must attend to his own room, heat his stove, fetch water, mend his clothes, and do everything possible to take care of his own needs. If he had any time and strength left, he must try to serve the needs of others.

The vicious economic contradictions of society, Tolstoy decided, resulted from the exploitation by some of the labors of others, and at the bottom of it all was property. This conclusion was an old one with him, but now he saw it in a new light. Formerly men seized upon the labor of others by violence—slavery; now, it was done by means of property. The division and safeguarding of property, he declared, occupies the whole world. Property is the root of all evil, for it brings about the sufferings of those who possess it or are deprived of it, the reproaches of conscience of those who misuse it, and it causes deadly quarrels between those who have a superfluity of property and those who are in need.

Tolstoy dedicated the last chapter of *What Then Must We Do?* to a subject that had little relevance to the principal theme of the book, but one that had been much on his mind over the last few years—the duty of women. Woman's real work is to bear children, he maintained, and not to shun this law of nature by spending all her time on exercising the charm of her allurements or by imitating the sham work done by men. With uncompromising severity he declared that a woman who refrains from childbirth without refraining from sexual relations is a whore. No doubt he had in mind the common practices of women in his own social set, but behind the indictment lies also a warning to his own wife for her opposition to bearing more children. The book ends with a glorification of the fruitful mother who knows that real life is a matter of danger and effort and self-sacrifice, a tribute that must have left Sonya with a mixed feeling of pride and bitterness.

What Then Must We Do? is a unique work and perhaps did more than any other book up to that time to expose the tremendous problem of poverty in modern society. Tolstoy felt the problem acutely and described its unhappy effects with the skill of a great literary artist, and he condemned the causes of poverty with all the moral indignation of an eloquent preacher. In many respects, however, he may be said to have diagnosed the disease correctly and then prescribed an incantation as a cure. His outlook was circumscribed by the backward conditions of the Russian society of that time, and still more limited by his instinctive devotion to his own class. He was ignorant of the changes that developing industry and commerce were bringing about in the economics of capitalism, and this unawareness was rendered virtually incurable by an ethical arrogance that made him all too ready to condemn achievements remote from his own experience. An enemy of progress in terms of modern technical advancement, he oversimplified the complex phenomena of industrial and economic life. That government in its systematic organization of society might logically strive to achieve righteousness, he emphatically denied. Yet in *What Then Must We Do?* Tolstoy performed a signal service in his frank and fresh treatment of one of the most acute problems of modern times, and his prediction that if the problem were not solved, a "workers' revolution with horrors of destruction and murder" would ensue, was fulfilled in his own country not many years afterwards.

2

Life in the Moscow household of the Tolstoys was rapidly taking on the aspect of a religious revival. Ready-made disciples, who had caught the virus from widely circulated contraband works, called to see the master in the flesh. Or perhaps an old disciple like Ge came to renew his faith at the fountainhead. He arrived early in 1886 to paint more pictures on New Testament themes, and incidentally to do portraits of members of the family and to help young Tanya in her art work. Unlike many of the followers, this gentle artist was always a welcome guest with the family. Tolstoy loved him with a tender and brotherly affection, and for Ge the master was "holy Leo Nikolayevich," whose teaching he yearned to interpret with his immensely talented brush. The author V. G. Korolenko presented himself in February, and shortly after Chertkov, accompanied by Anna K. Diterikhs, who was soon to become his wife, paid a visit. Tolstoy was pleased that Chertkov's proselyting zeal was beginning to have its effect on young Ilya, and even Sergei was not immune to the persistent religious probing of this devoted disciple. As for Sonya, she wrote to her sister that Chertkov frequently irritated her.

And apparently the future bride of Chertkov also irritated Sonya on this occasion of her first visit to the Tolstoys. Anna Diterikhs was presented by Chertkov and Biryukov, who had already inoculated her with the virus of Tolstoyism, and she anticipated her introduction to the master with awe and trembling. Tolstoy greeted her kindly, but he soon left her marooned in the living room with his wife, for he had some business matters to talk over with her escorts. Sonya, after she had ascertained the girl's devotion to her husband's beliefs, vented on her the spleen that she felt for all these disciples.

"Well, I'll tell you frankly," Sonya said, "that you are mistaken, as are many other youths and these shaggy nihilists who come to him from everywhere. He's not at all what you imagine, and I tell you plainly he is not that which he tries to be. What if he does stitch boots and split wood? He was and has remained a Count, and all this simplicity—I speak to you plainly just as I would to him, Leo Nikolayevich—I say that all this is only affectation, simply a pretense, a kind of amusement; he always loved originality. Even in his youth he played various tricks in order to shock people and make them speak about him."

The astonished guest protested that Tolstoy had no need to attempt to be original and that his new faith had brought him blame rather than praise.

"And they blame him justly," Sonya interrupted. "He was a writer, an artist; he wrote novels, tales, and suddenly for no reason he took to philosophy, to religion. Is this his affair?"

At this point Uncle Kostya,[1] a shiftless relative of Sonya's whom Tolstoy sheltered in his home, broke in to add his condemnation of his benefactor's new faith.

The dumfounded visitor was overwhelmed by this criti-

[1] Konstantin Alexandrovich Islavin.

cism of her idol from sources whence she would have expected only adoration. When the question of Tolstoy's novels entered the discussion, Sonya warmly declared:—

"Do you know I copied *War and Peace* seven times, but this rubbish of his, this *Criticism*[2] and things like it I have refused to copy. I will not soil my hands with them. I would burn all these manuscripts with pleasure. Who wants them? Who will read them? . . . He is an artist, and suddenly he becomes a shoemaker! It is plain insanity! He forgets what I meant for him; he sacrifices the interest of his family. I'm convinced that this is madness! It began when he wrote of this Levin of his[3]—in fact, this is he, he described himself. But Kitty—that is I, yes, yes! Are you surprised? . . . In general, all the types of his *best* women he modeled on me. . . ."

In March Tolstoy answered a letter that he had received from Wendell P. Garrison, the son of William Lloyd Garrison. *What I Believe* had found its way to America, and Garrison, struck by the similarity between Tolstoy's views on nonresistance and those of his famous father, had sent him the first two volumes of the biography of William Lloyd Garrison. "To learn of the existence of such a pure Christian being as your father," Tolstoy wrote the son, "was a great joy to me. I have not yet read the books through, but the declarations on nonresistance, in my opinion, really mark an era in the history of humanity." The son's reply mentioned the growing fame of Tolstoy in America.

In April Tolstoy set out on foot from Moscow to Yasnaya Polyana, a distance of a hundred and thirty miles. Not only his dislike of railways and his new desire not to use money prompted this excursion; he thoroughly enjoyed such exercise and the opportunity of meeting peasants on the open road. For companions on this occasion he had two lively young men and fervent admirers, M. A. Stakhovich and the son of Ge. He took with him a linen sack containing food, an extra pair of shoes, a soft shirt, socks, and handkerchiefs. There was also his little notebook with the pencil tied to it for his observations on the road, and stomach drops for his indigestion. Five days later he entered the gates of Yasnaya Polyana, tanned, merry, and exuding satisfaction. A triumphant letter was dispatched to Sonya to announce his arrival: the hike would be "one of the best remembrances" of

[2] Tolstoy's *Criticism of Dogmatic Theology*.
[3] Levin in *Anna Karenina*.

his life; he had slept in a hut with twelve other people, and never had he slept better; he had met an ancient soldier, ninety-five years of age, who told him of army life in the good old days of Tsar Nicholas, when they took down a man's breeches and gave him two or three hundred strokes at a time! The result was "Nicholas Stick," a vivid sketch by Tolstoy that could not pass the censor but was circulated in a hectographed edition and caused the arrest of the man who surreptitiously issued it.

Having reached the conclusion that he must take care of his own personal needs as far as that was possible, Tolstoy did not spare himself. His conscience worried him, but his future way of life seemed clear, and during the summer of 1886 at Yasnaya Polyana he began to lead this way of life in earnest. He worked hard in the fields, plowing, mowing, and carting. Any poor peasant who required assistance was sure to receive his aid. And his example, as in the previous year, was infectious. His older children, especially Masha and Ilya, vied with him.

Meanwhile Tolstoy's fame as a teacher of a new way of life had begun to attract to Yasnaya Polyana all manner of eager seekers for light. The stream started as a trickle, but as the years went on it became a torrent. At first he was pleased with this recognition; later, it became the bane of his existence.

The summer of 1886 brought some unusual devotees and curiosity seekers. A sickly girl from Odessa turned up. She had been attracted by an article; at Yasnaya Polyana she read *What I Believe* and at once declared that the book had changed all her ideas. Tolstoy was puzzled over what to do with her; Sonya was vastly annoyed by these "dark people." A compromise was effected by obtaining a position for the girl on the *Intermediary*.

Déroulède, the French poet-patriot, arrived. His mission was not religion but revenge—a French revenge on Germany for the defeat of 1871. He hoped to prevail upon Tolstoy to use his influence to bring about an alliance of France and Russia to crush Germany. Tolstoy liked the man's striking personality, but as an advocate of nonviolence he gave his warmongering short shrift. He related how he posed Déroulède's theme of *revanche* to one of the wise old peasants of Yasnaya Polyana. The peasant addressed Déroulède with a good-natured smile that showed the stumps of his worn teeth: "You'd better come and work with us and bring the Germans along too, and when we've done our work we'll have some merrymaking together. The Germans are men too, like ourselves."

Another interesting visitor that summer was the American traveler George Kennan, who had just returned from a trip to Siberia, where he had been collecting material for a book on Russian convicts exiled to that region. Tolstoy wrote of him to Chertkov: ". . . he is an agreeable and sincere man, but one with partitions separating his soul from his head—partitions of which we Russians have no understanding, and I am always perplexed upon encountering them." Kennan was equally nonplused by Tolstoy, as he indicated in an article that he wrote about this visit.[4] When he asked Tolstoy if his theory of nonviolence would oblige him to tolerate the persecution of defenseless women, Tolstoy's only reply was to say with tears in his eyes that violence as an answer to violence could never achieve any good purpose. Despite what he considered the heroic fallacies of Tolstoy, Kennan professed warm esteem and love for him.

3

During this busy summer of work in the fields, and of the entertainment of numerous visitors, Tolstoy also maintained a wide correspondence. For now complete strangers began to seek his spiritual guidance through the post and to ask his aid in literary and other matters. He felt a real responsibility toward these new correspondents, although as the years passed their number increased so that to answer them all tried his strength and often his patience.

Poems and stories would arrive from budding authors, who pleaded for his advice and a kind word to a publisher on their behalf. Frequently, he read the manuscripts with care, and if he thought the effort showed talent, he offered sympathetic but uncompromising criticism. To one young author he wrote: "The life of your characters is not apparent, and it is clear that the author relates something that never existed; it is even apparent that it was boring for him to be concerned with this empty matter. . . . Live the lives of the characters described; describe the inner feelings of the characters by images, then the characters themselves will

[4] "A Visit to Count Tolstoi," *The Century Illustrated Monthly Magazine* (1887), No. 34.

do what they must do according to their natures; i.e. the denouement will come of itself." Ashamed now of the commercial uses to which he had put his art in the past, he advised these hopeful authors to forgo writing for money. "If you need money," he wrote to one, "then you will receive it for such work. But for the sake of Christ do not construct your material life on literary work. This is debauchery [*sic*]." And he beseeched them to write for the masses and always with the teachings of Christ in their hearts.

A total stranger wrote for advice on a quarrel with his wife, and like some Biblical lawgiver, Tolstoy handed down judgment. Several girl students of Tiflis, who were dismayed upon reading in one of Tolstoy's articles that woman's mission in life was to bear and raise children, wrote to ask if there were not some other useful tasks they could perform. He replied that they could render a real service if they would correct and improve any of the cheap school texts and moral tales of Moscow publishers that were sold in large quantities to poor people. The great man's letter was published in a Tiflis newspaper, and he was soon deluged with offers from various correspondents to take a hand in correcting and improving these inexpensive schoolbooks.

An unknown admirer in America wrote Tolstoy that one of his books[5] had made disciples for him in that country. He replied gratefully—and in fairly correct English: "In answer to your question, I can state to you that there are 30 or 40 persons known to me who confess with me the Christian principles exposed in my book, and that with every year and month their number increases. We are not organized in a church and never will be. I think that the sole means to get in a true church is not to organize churches or communities, but to seek only after the Kingdom of God and its truth."

Tolstoy was not entirely correct in this statement, for a movement had already got under way to organize Tolstoyan communities or colonies, and at the outset it had the master's encouragement. In 1881, one of his disciples, N. L. Ozmidov, who had hitherto existed on the money he obtained from copying and selling Tolstoy's forbidden works, had started an agricultural colony in the Caucasus. Tolstoy kept in close touch with the project through correspondence, and offered advice and comfort. After about six months of

[5] No doubt *Christ's Christianity,* which included an English translation of *What I Believe, Confession,* and *A Short Account of the Gospels,* which had been published in England in 1884.

effort to live according to Tolstoy's principles, the colonists abandoned the project.

Other colonies soon sprang up in various parts of Russia, and later in England, Holland, and the United States. Without exception, they all eventually failed. Yet somehow these failures did not convince Tolstoy that his Christian-anarchist beliefs were incapable of practical application. The fact that he himself never actively participated in the life of any of these colonies blinded him to their faults. It was not difficult for the colonists to accept his dictum that to love God meant to do the business of God, and that if you loved God, you would unfailingly love people. When the "business of God," however, involved a practical application of nonresistance to evil and a condemnation of property, the services of government, and all the customary aids of modern society, then the business of daily life itself broke down completely. In the struggle for existence man could only be guided by ethical and moral precepts. In trying to adhere rigidly to Tolstoy's principles, the colonists were easily victimized by the first member who manifested a natural desire for economic security. It was human nature to protect oneself against violence or deprivation of the necessities of life. If moral and ethical principles failed to afford this protection, then man would rebel against them. And so ultimately did the Tolstoyan colonists.

Tolstoy's reaction to these efforts of his disciples was a mixed one; later he grew hostile to them. He wished to see his beliefs propagated, for he had a supreme faith in their efficacy, but organized proselyting he deeply distrusted. He was not a dry moralist but at times he fell into arbitrary distinctions, such as his insistence to A. S. Butkevich, who visited him that summer, that to be an army doctor was every bit as bad as to be a soldier. "Tolstoyans," he said, "are the most insupportable people." Yet many of his most radical followers hoped to give the Tolstoyan movement a definite form by attracting masses to it and trying to persuade the master to leave his home, surround himself with disciples, and create a kind of moral Eden. But Tolstoy knew that to tag a movement in the realm of ideas with forms, limitations, and labels meant its destruction—this was the first step in the direction of a church. He said to Butkevich: "To stand aloof, to shut oneself up in a monastery, surrounded by such angels as oneself, amounts to creating a hothouse and those conditions in which it will be easy to be good oneself, but no one else will be warm. Live in the world and be good—that is what is needed."

4

All evil arises from an absence of love, Tolstoy remarked to Chertkov in the summer of 1886. But love flourished with increasing difficulty in the Tolstoy household. Chertkov himself was one of the reasons that the little devil of evil reared its ugly head in the family circle. The hostility between him and Sonya over priorities on Tolstoy's writings grew apace: she wanted them for her edition, he for the *Intermediary*. With some feeling he wrote to Tolstoy: "Sofya Andreyevna told me that when I'm away she is less well disposed towards me than when I'm in her presence. I fear that this arises from the fact that when she hears of my activities concerning the publication of your works, she ascribes motives to me that I do not at all have. I don't know what I would give to settle such misunderstandings." She accused Chertkov of treating her husband's productions as though they were his own. Both disputants appealed to Tolstoy. He made peace between them, but it was an uneasy peace.

Sonya viewed with dismay the growing hold that this chief disciple was obtaining over her husband. The two friends now exchanged diaries. Chertkov wrote that he obtained from Tolstoy's infinite comfort and support on life's journey. Their voluminous correspondence was burdened with intimate confessions, and a frankness prevailed that is possible only when two men possess each other's confidence to the fullest degree. Tolstoy was closer to him, said Chertkov, than any other being, save Christ. The hesitancy that Tolstoy had formerly evinced in confiding in Chertkov his family affairs had entirely disappeared. Indeed, Chertkov now projected himself into the domestic life of Tolstoy with the assurance of a member of the family. In one letter he censured Tolstoy for his irritable behavior toward Sergei, and offered him a little homily on the evils that might result from such thoughtless treatment. Humbly Tolstoy replied: "Your advice on my relations with my son I very much needed. Many thanks to you for this." When Chertkov finally married Anna Diterikhs, a helper with the *Intermediary* and a woman who fully shared his convictions, Tolstoy rejoiced, but perhaps with his own frequently unhappy relations with Sonya in mind, he hastened to write this first bit of advice to the newlyweds: "It is possible that you will quarrel, that you will have your moments of irritation and coolness. May the Lord preserve you. Beware of this sort of thing with all your strength."

Family life at Yasnaya Polyana during the summer of 1886 was complicated by the severe illness of Tolstoy. A neglected sore on his leg resulted in erysipelas that kept him in bed for some nine weeks. Sonya had difficulty in overcoming his scruples against doctors, but when the pain was at its height and his life was in danger, his antipathy vanished and he himself called loudly for a physician. With devotion and an efficiency that was almost aggravating at times, Sonya nursed him back to health. Perhaps with her persistent attentions in mind, he wrote to his son Ilya, who was in Moscow at the time: "General condition good. If anything to complain of it's bad nights, in consequence of which my head is unclear and I cannot work. I lie and listen to women talking; am so lapped in femininity I begin to talk of myself as 'she.'[6] Am peaceful in mind; sometimes a little anxious about some of you, but do not allow myself to worry, and wait and rejoice in the forward course of life. As long as you don't undertake too much, and live without doing evil, all will be well."

However much at peace he was with God, Tolstoy felt it more and more necessary to exercise a degree of restraint in the household. Butkevich noted at this time that among the family he did not display his customary jollity. Sonya was forever screwing up her eyes, scolding, and expressing a dislike for his "dark people." No doubt the sickness and death of her mother (November 11) contributed to Sonya's distraught state of mind over the autumn of this year. She made a few entries in her diary for October, and they reflect the anguish in her heart. She feared she was going mad. Tending Tolstoy in his illness had been sheer joy for her. She was wanted, wanted by the man she loved. Now that he was almost well, she noticed with deep pain that she was no longer wanted . . . "again I'm thrown aside like an unnecessary thing." The children blamed her for her disagreements with their father. In her diary she plaintively wrote, as though taking fright at her morbid thoughts: "If Lyovochka will work in Moscow, I'll become calm. I'll be

[6] Literally: "I begin to say *Ya spalá*," *I slept*, that is, in the feminine, instead of *Ya spal*, in the masculine.

careful with him, attentive, in order to look out for him because of my love for his work."

5

Sonya achieved some degree of calm, for when her husband returned to Moscow that winter he was able to work hard at his writing. In fact, throughout most of 1886 and the next year he found time to write even amid the manifold tasks he imposed upon himself. The practice of a new faith in no sense exhausted his energies, rather it seemed to intensify his mental and moral strength without diminishing his physical powers.

Tolstoy continued to write those legends and moral tales which were designed to exemplify his teaching, and they found wide dissemination in the pages of the *Intermediary*.[7] Indeed he expended much effort on this publishing firm, searching for material among foreign writers for translation and correcting the manuscripts of young authors. *The Death of Ivan Ilyich,* which he had worked on the previous year, was published in 1886. The piece pleased Sonya, for she correctly appraised it as the first purely artistic work he had written since *Anna Karenina*. Although the same wonderful realism of his earlier fiction is recaptured in this tale, it is definitely a problem story, in which he does not so much preach as communicate his own experiences.

Tolstoy was inspired to try his hand at playwriting once again, in 1886, by the request of the well-known actor, P. A. Denisenko, who asked him to rework some of his moral tales into plays for a people's theater. The idea pleased him and he quickly turned out a comedy, *The First Distiller,* a dramatization of his tale, "The Imp and the Crust." It is a highly amusing piece of temperance propaganda. The First Distiller is the Devil, who makes great inroads among the rich and idle, but he succeeds in corrupting the hard-working peasant only by teaching him how to make spirits.

Another request for a play for the people's theater led Tolstoy to write his grim realistic tragedy, *The Power of Darkness* (1886). It is based directly on an account of a crime he had heard several years before: a peasant confessed

[7] In 1886 he wrote "The Repentant Sinner"; "Three Hermits"; "The Grain as Big as a Hen's Egg"; "How Much Land Does a Man Need?"; "The Imp and the Crust"; in 1887 he wrote "Walk in the Light While There Is Light."

to the guests assembled at the marriage of his stepdaughter that he had murdered a child he had had by her and afterwards attempted to kill his own six-year-old daughter. Upon the foundation of this sordid crime Tolstoy built a moving drama that involved the darker aspects of peasant life. A good part of the play he wrote over the autumn of 1886, while he lay ill in bed with his infected leg. Members of the household went about on tiptoe. At times he would drop his pencil, throw his head back on the pillow, and his face took on an expression of pain that arose from his bodily illness mingled with the spiritual suffering he experienced in creating the horrific scenes of his play that dealt with poison, adultery, and infanticide. He admitted that he could never read without tears the scene in the cellar where Nikita crushed his child with a board so that its "bones crunched." The horror of it all is strangely neutralized by a sense of atonement for sin and by the moral message of the terrible evil-begetting power of evil.

The Power of Darkness possessed excellent acting qualities and Tolstoy was anxious to have it staged as well as published. His friend, A. A. Stakhovich, a lover of the theater and a talented dramatic reader, read the play with much success to Petersburg society gatherings at the beginning of 1887. He was asked to give a reading of it before Emperor Alexander III and high Court officials. The Emperor seemed impressed, pronounced the play "a marvelous thing," and suggested that it be staged by the best actors and actresses of both the Moscow and the Petersburg theaters. Preparations went forward rapidly, until the plans were brought to the attention of Pobedonostsev, the Procurator of the Holy Synod, and the archenemy of Tolstoy's new religious beliefs. He read the play and lost no time in writing to the Emperor that the drama filled him with horror and that it represented a "negation of ideals," a "debasing of moral feelings," and "an offense against taste." Alexander III judiciously recanted in his reply. He admitted that the play had made a strong impression on him, but that it had filled him with aversion and that it was his "opinion and conviction that it was impossible to stage the drama, because it was too realistic and frightful in its subject matter." With this fickle royal favor withdrawn, the play could not be acted, although it was published in 1887. A few weeks later the Emperor sent a memorandum to the Ministry of the Interior, in which he used much sharper language about the play and its author: "One ought to put an end to this mischief of L. Tolstoy. He is a downright nihilist and atheist. It would not be bad now to forbid the sale of his drama, *The Power of Darkness,* for he has already succeeded in selling enough of this nastiness and in spreading it among the people." *The Power of Darkness* was not staged in Russia until 1895, but with the aid of Zola it was acted earlier (1888) in Paris, where it at once won a remarkable success.

Purely artistic works, however, Tolstoy regarded as almost a diversion now, and they were indulged in because the creative urge would often give him no rest. The literary effort that really excited him at this time was a lengthy didactic work. In September 1886 he wrote one of his long essays in the form of a letter. It was on the subject of life and death. The theme gripped his attention and he decided to elaborate it. Throughout most of 1887 he could think of little else, and his letters contained frequent enthusiastic references to his progress on the work. He attended meetings of the Moscow Psychological Society, perhaps with the hope that his ideas on life and death would receive some support from such learned men. At one of the meetings he even made bold to read a paper on "Life's Meaning," but his effort was not well received by these disciples of the new materialism. Visitors to Yasnaya Polyana that summer were often treated to readings of the work in progress, and the reactions were not always flattering to the author. Finally, he finished in August of 1887.

Although *On Life*[8] is an important philosophical treatment of Tolstoy's views on the subject, the work is comparatively little known. All the mature wisdom of ten years of meditation on man and his relations to the world is to be found in this treatise, and the beliefs expressed here were little altered during the remainder of his life. Much of what he says had been set down in previous religious and philosophical works, but in one significant respect he seems to have changed his view. In *What I Believe* (1884) he had firmly indicated a disbelief in a personal resurrection and immortality, which had never been asserted by Christ, he maintained; in *On Life,* however, he rather vaguely suggests the possibility of a future life. The teaching of *On Life*

[8] He used this short title because in the final version of the work he devoted little space to the theme of death.

amounts to a complete submergence of the self in a selfless, loving service for the good of others.

6

In the summer of 1887 Tolstoy's favorite brother-in-law, Stepan Bers, whom he had not seen for nine years, visited Yasnaya Polyana. He found Tolstoy considerably altered. Not only did he seem older and grayer, but the prolonged mental and spiritual struggle he had endured had changed his whole personality. There was scarcely a trace of his former liveliness and playfulness. As though guessing the painful shock to Bers of the transformation in him, Tolstoy purposefully reverted to type as it were, played tricks on him, and suddenly jumped upon his back as he walked about the room, as in the old days. But none of this enforced gaiety concealed the calm, sad, serious look in his face.

Tolstoy made no effort to impose his views on the many visitors who sought him out at Yasnaya Polyana that summer. He was willing enough to set forth his doctrines to those who cared to listen, but he left it up to his hearers to exercise their free judgment, fully convinced that his beliefs would prove a blessing to those who adopted them. Some of the visitors who came to hear were distinguished men. T. G. Masaryk, the future President of Czechoslovakia, then a young doctor of philosophy, turned up. He had been preceded by his doctoral dissertation on suicide, and Tolstoy had been attracted by the serious religious views expressed in the study. They liked each other, and their friendship lasted. A result of the visit was Tolstoy's election in 1887 to membership in the Czech Literary Society. The well-known writer, Leskov, who was already partial to Tolstoy's religious views, came. He was a wise and original man, and one consequence of the firm friendship that developed was Leskov's contributions to the *Intermediary*. The brilliant jurist A. F. Koni arrived to make the acquaintance of the man about whom all Russia was talking. Tolstoy's charming behavior attracted him no less than his lofty conversation. On a walk together one fine June evening they came upon a swarm of glowworms in the bushes. With childish joy Tolstoy gathered them up in his hat and carried them home, his triumphant, coarse peasant face intermittently illumined in the dark by the phosphorescent flashes of the glowworms. That striking face was painted during the summer by the amous artist Repin, who came to begin his series of por-raits and studies of Tolstoy.

One visitor whose admiration for his genius did not pre-'ent her from playing the stern critic of his religious views vas his old friend Granny. During her whole stay at Yas-ıaya Polyana, her first, these graying antagonists sparred autiously, afraid to offend each other, yet determined not o relinquish a single conviction. She liked the morning ıours when he would emerge from his room, refreshed by leep and in excellent spirits. Then they conversed calmly, nd he would read her his favorite poetry. If the name of Christ appeared in a line of verse, his voice trembled and ıis eyes filled with tears. She found it difficult to understand uch emotion when she knew that he did not accept the livinity of the Saviour.

When Tolstoy retired to his study to work, he gave Granny all the books, pamphlets, and mail that he had eceived the previous day to peruse. She was appalled at the ıumerous letters from nearly every country in Europe and ven from America. "What fearful pap for your pride, my lear friend," she told him. "I really fear that one day you vill turn into a Nebuchadnezzar before his conversion."

He promptly answered: "Why do you think that this nakes me proud? When I go into the great world [so he alled the huts of the peasants], my glory does not exist for hem; hence, it does not exist at all."

Granny observed in these numerous letters requests for noney, advice, contributions to magazines, and often the xpression of a good deal of nonsense. But if some convert ıppealed to Tolstoy in his own language, he seemed touched. Yet when she pointed out the crudeness of the expressions, ıe rather sheepishly admitted with a smile that what he had oraised was really stupid. He asked her to read a letter of Chertkov, in which this favorite disciple related how he had old a peasant that he did not believe the opening words of he Gospel of Saint John, and how his wife complained that lespite all their efforts they could not convince the peasants o accept them as equals. Granny was infuriated and con-veyed her feelings to Tolstoy. And she observed with some scorn that for all his convictions about the evils of money, Tolstoy still continued to dole out kopeks to the numerous oeggars who applied to him.

Granny and other visitors and members of the family were drafted to take dictation when Tolstoy was suddenly faced with the need to get out some copy in a hurry. Kuzminski, Tolstoy's brother-in-law, was assigned to Granny as a helper. The work before him was *On Life*. "He dictated," she related, "and I wrote. Entirely unexpectedly such awkward phrases began to burst forth that I involuntarily recalled the 'impassable swamp' that Turgenev once mentioned apropos of Tolstoy, and I could not resolve to circumvent the swamp or to set it down for printing in just this form. Kuzminski, although he agreed with me, reckoned it impossible for a simple mortal to dare to correct Tolstoy." Granny had more courage, for she said: "Do you know, my dear, that I am just about to correct your prose to the great scandal of your brother-in-law." Tolstoy instantly replied: "And you would be perfectly right, for I'm concerned only with the idea and pay no attention to my style." Perhaps what Granny did not know was that this piece of writing, both before printing and after it got into proof, would receive numerous, painstaking revisions from an artist who cared infinitely about his style.

Granny took away from Yasnaya Polyana a sense of warm and loving hospitality, but she pitied Sonya and still worried over the husband's unorthodox faith. It was all an amalgamation of truth and darkness, she safely wrote him after she had returned to Petersburg. The hero of his work *On Life* was Reason, but she reminded him that we need something more exalted than reason to subdue our inherently iniquitous tendencies. If he would only regard Christ as a divine personality instead of merely as a moralist, then she would try to harmonize their other points of religious differences. Patiently he replied to her that to lead a true life meant to aspire toward God, drawing nearer to Him with the help of Christ. But why must he see God exactly as she visualized Him? Hers was the traditional faith which he had rejected; if she could advance something new, then she would be right in trying to persuade him to her view. He preferred to arrive at his beliefs rationally, "but you don't," he concluded. "I am fully aware of it; you neither can nor will. It makes you feel at ease. You must follow your own path. All those who make for the same goal will meet there. I love you and embrace you with all my heart."

Among the foreign letters that Granny might have inspected was one from a young French student in the École Normale—Romain Rolland. It was soon followed by another, in which Rolland spoke of a moral crisis in his life that had arisen over his doubts concerning service to science and art as opposed to the demands of physical work and service to one's neighbor. Tolstoy read the letter with tears in his eyes, and in reply sent one of his long epistolary essays on the subject of physical labor and intellectual activity. Rolland became a devoted admirer and a future biographer of Tolstoy, whom he credited with being his first guide in art and life. In truth, Tolstoy was already exercising a powerful influence on the intellectual youth of France.

7

On her visit to Yasnaya Polyana in the summer of 1887 Granny was charmed with the Tolstoy children. There were eight of them. They were kind, simple, gay, and quite gifted. She observed how attached they were to their parents, and how they worshipped their father. Not all of them shared his views, particularly the eldest son, Sergei, a thoughtful man and a talented musician. The second son, Ilya, erratic but warmhearted, strove hard to follow his father's religious and social creed, and his efforts were repaid by a tender solicitude on the part of Tolstoy. His father once suddenly asked Ilya if he ever had anything to do with women, and when he answered in the negative, Tolstoy wept from joy. At about this time Ilya was thinking of marrying, and his father wrote him a long and earnest letter to warn him that he and his future wife must be certain that they both had a useful purpose in life or otherwise they would not be happy together. "Your purpose in life," he counseled, "must not be to enjoy the delight of wedlock but, by your life, to bring more love and truth into the world. The object of marriage is to help one another in the attainment of that purpose."

Although the third son, temperamental Leo, early showed a disposition to subscribe to his father's views, he soon opposed them, and even in print. The younger sons, the ebullient Andrei and stolid Mikhail, had little regard for the teaching of their father, and later they openly displayed their antipathy by voluntarily serving in the army.

Tolstoy once remarked that he had reason to thank God for his daughters, and it is true that they served him with a devotion and sympathy that his sons did not possess. Tatyana, the eldest, while always maintaining certain reservations of her own concerning her father's faith, was much influenced by his teaching and proved a willing helper in his work. But the second daughter, Masha, was a true disciple, and often risked the anger of her mother because of her quiet insistence upon living up to her father's teachings. She worked in the fields, taught the village children, faithfully attended sick peasants, and in her spare time aided her father in his voluminous correspondence and in his literary labors. When these two sisters eventually married, the youngest, Alexandra, took their place as an assiduous disciple, helper, and favorite child of her father.

The deep interest Tolstoy had formerly taken in the education of his children had quite vanished since his preoccupation with religious and moral questions. By now he had lost all respect for the formal education that his children were undergoing, and the matter was already becoming a subject for quarrels with his wife, who insisted that her children should receive the conventional education that would enable them to take their proper place in the class into which they had been born. Tolstoy believed that conventional education was harmful, because its aim was to fit men to rise above their fellow men. The only kind of education he thought worth while was that which taught love and compassion for one's neighbor and service to the masses.

Learning of the temperance movement in America at this time, Tolstoy promptly started a Temperance Society in his own home. Sonya had no objections to his signing the pledge, but she was annoyed by his persuading several members of the household to do likewise and by his preaching to the peasants the evils of tobacco and vodka.

With the financial gain of Sonya's edition of his works in mind, Tolstoy read her a lecture on the evils of money and property, and on her desire to preserve all for her children. Angrily she turned on him with the charge that she asked only eight rubles for the twelve volumes of her edition, whereas he had demanded ten rubles for *War and Peace* alone when he had published it.

Added to Sonya's grief that Tolstoy was voluntarily drawing away from her was her conviction that more and more he was turning to his chief disciple with the confidence and trust he had formerly placed in her. Toward Chertkov she now began to display that jealousy which soon developed into a morbid obsession. "I do not like him," she wrote in her diary (March 6, 1887). "He is unintelligent, crafty, narrow, and unkind. L.N. [Tolstoy] is partial to him because of his adoration." In the next entry she complained: "These so-called new Christian *friends* arouse L.N. against me, and not always without success. I read over again a letter from Chertkov about his happiness in spiritual communion with his wife, and about his sympathy for L.N. because he does not have this happiness, and how sorry he is that he, so worthy of it, is deprived of this communion—hinting at me. I read it again and was hurt. This dull, cunning, and dishonest man, enmeshing L.N. by his flattery, wants (probably by way of being a *Christian*) to destroy that union which now for 25 years has so closely bound us together."

If Sonya had been reading much of the correspondence between her husband and Chertkov at this time—which was probably the case—then it is little wonder that her naturally jealous nature was further provoked. For Tolstoy took a deep interest in all the intimate details of his disciple's married life. When Chertkov's wife was about to have her first child, Tolstoy's advice was sought on whether or not chloroform or gas should be used at the delivery. Sternly he counseled against the use of any drugs and urged that nature be allowed to take its course. And when the infant girl arrived, he rejoiced as though it were his own child, and all agreed that she must be called his "granddaughter."

Of all the disciples that had begun to collect around her husband, Chertkov was only the chief thorn in Sonya's side. "How unsympathetic are all these types that cleave to the teaching of Leo Nikolayevich," she jotted down in her diary. "Not one of them is a normal person. The women also for the most part are hysterical." Each new one added to the fold she regarded with disgust and foreboding. The latest, in 1887, was a Prince D. A. Khilkov. He had abandoned a successful army career, repudiated the Russian Church, and was exiled by the authorities to the Caucasus, where he lived among the Dukhobors. With scorn Sonya wrote to her husband, who was at Yasnaya Polyana, that she had heard that Khilkov was living with a peasant girl, but since he was a Dukhobor, it was unnecessary for him to recognize either the Church or marriage. "All these are very sad manifestations," she added. "Their victims are always the same, i.e. women and children. . . . Dark, dark people! Morally sick and wretched!"

The dark people, however, were only one of the many factors poisoning the relations between husband and wife. On September 23, 1887, Tolstoy and his wife celebrated quietly their twenty-fifth wedding anniversary. In his diary he scribbled that the course of his family life "could have been better." About a month before, in her own diary, the forty-three-year-old Sonya wrote: "Pregnancy both physically and morally tortures me. Lyovochka's health has gone downhill; family life becomes complicated, and my own moral strength diminishes." On March 31, 1888, Sonya gave birth to her thirteenth child, Ivan.

XXVI

"Leave Thy Wife and Follow Me"

MANY PEOPLE in Russia were wondering if the author of *War and Peace* had not lost his mind. For some ten years now, instead of exploiting his great literary success, he had been serving up to readers and listeners religious treatises and moral exhortations. The Church was becoming alarmed over his wholesale condemnation of its dogma and practices, and government officials, long since suspicious, now secretly reported every move of Tolstoy. Because of his wide fame, the police feared to arrest him and granted a kind of extraterritoriality to his estate at Yasnaya Polyana. In January 1888, the Governor General of Moscow sent a confidential report to the Ministry of the Interior, in which he cautiously declared that "every repressive measure taken against Count L. Tolstoy will surround him with an aureole of suffering and will all the more assist in the dissemination of his thought and teaching." Both Church and State were uninterested in his search for the meaning and purpose of life, but the uncompromising Tolstoy failed to understand how anyone could go through life without asking himself: "What the devil does it all mean?" Such satisfied individuals—he might have agreed later with George Bernard Shaw—fell into the category that Calvin predestinately damned.

Of greater consequence to Tolstoy's immediate peace of mind was the fact that his wife's hostility to his views had become more irreconcilable than ever. By 1888, at the age of sixty, he had finally renounced meat, alcohol, and tobacco, and the next year he wrote an article, "Why Do Men Stupefy Themselves?" in which he roundly condemned drinking and smoking as habits employed by mankind to still the voice of conscience. The peasants of Yasnaya Polyana were among his first converts; they reluctantly surrendered their tobacco pouches and took the pledge not to drink, and then broke it by stealth. In two years of effort, after which he gave up his personal crusade, he managed to persuade 741 persons to take the temperance oath, but how many kept it, we are not informed. The five commandments that he had distilled from the Gospels guided his whole existence. Devotion to the Christian ideal as he understood it—a renunciation of one's self in order to serve God and one's neighbor—made of his conscience a watchdog to detect the slightest intrusion of heretical thoughts or actions.

The luxury, frock coats, and singing at the wedding of his son Ilya[1] offended Tolstoy's new sense of proprieties, and he complained of it in a letter to Chertkov. Sonya found her husband's Christian idealism something less than ideal. Having a child at forty-four had placed a terrific strain on her physical powers. Tolstoy wept over her suffering, but it was a joyous compensation for her to see him fondle and kiss the newborn Ivan.

Then, less than three weeks after this event, and in the face of his exhausted wife's bitter protests, Tolstoy, with knapsack on his shoulders, set off from Moscow to Yasnaya Polyana on foot, accompanied by young Ge. He has "again taken the bit in his teeth," the chagrined Sonya wrote her sister Tanya.

Sonya knew that he had gone to plow and sow in the village and to live among his disciples. Even from afar, the very thought of these "dark people" increased her anger over his desertion at this trying time. She jealously rebuked him when she heard that his doting and saintlike follower, Marya Schmidt, actually entered his room at Yasnaya Polyana while he was still in bed. In her irritation she communicated to her sister that "never was Lyovochka so extremely stubborn and obstinate in his lunacies as during the present year." Almost with satisfaction, it seems, she filled her letters to him with details of the terrible pain she endured while nursing Ivan, because of a sore breast and lack of milk, and she suggested the possibility of a wet nurse.

That a mother should nurse her own children had long been one of Tolstoy's most stubborn convictions. In fact, he

[1] Ilya married Sofya Nikolayevna Filosofov on February 28, 1888.

had just terminated an acrimonious controversy on the subject with Chertkov, who had innocently asked his help in finding a working woman to take the place of his wife in nursing their second child. Tolstoy's initial cool rejoinder eventually developed into a forthright scolding of Chertkov for having more faith in doctors, medicine, and wet nurses than in God, and his final advice in the situation was to let nature take its course. After Chertkov's testy reply that simply because he held another view in this matter he ought not to be accused of lack of faith in God, Tolstoy relented and with reluctance agreed to help his disciple find a wet nurse.

Either because she was not a disciple or simply because she was his wife, Tolstoy evinced no disposition to agree with Sonya's justifiable suggestion. He wrote her: "Darling, do not lose heart over Ivan, and do not burden yourself with thoughts, God gave the infant, and God will give it food." The whole question of feeding babies so agitated him that he wanted to write a treatise on the subject. He never got around to doing this, but he did insert a note in a physician's article on the care of children, which he helped to prepare for the press. The note strongly advocated breast-feeding by mothers, and concluded with an extraordinary statement concerning the artificial nipple, dipped in a food preparation, commonly used at this time: "The pacifier has killed in Russia more human beings than the plague and cholera and all illnesses. We must arm ourselves against it and help each other to destroy it."

There was little in the correspondence between husband and wife on this occasion to suggest that Ivan's birth had been anything other than an unnecessary and superfluous event in their lives. All Tolstoy's attempts to change his wife's views and way of life had failed. She simply could not understand his transformed attitude, and was frankly annoyed by the evidence of the Gospels that he quoted to her. Husband and wife had become spiritual and intellectual strangers to each other. The only real bond left was the physical and that too was soon endangered.

2

During the summer of 1888, work—hard physical labor—was part of Tolstoy's daily regimen. The sixty-year-old prophet would return at evening after a full day in the fields, sweaty, grimy, the clay clinging to his boots, a spade on his shoulder and his face happy with the expression of duty well done. He would exclaim: "How fine it is to live in this world!" In letters to protesting friends he took a peculiar delight in telling them that because of his plowing, sowing, and harvesting he had no time to write. If he found a spare hour or two, he worked away at making shoes for his daughters.

With autumn came visitors. Among them was Tolstoy's old friend Fet, who had not appeared at Yasnaya Polyana for a long time. He read to the household selections from his reminiscences, in which was included his extensive correspondence with Tolstoy. Pleasant memories of their early community of thought returned to remind these two old friends how far they had drifted apart.

Upon his return to Moscow in November, Tolstoy resumed his city form of "bread-labor." That is, he made shoes, cared for his room, started the fires in the morning, cut wood, and carted water. He even visited the district school and, appalled by the stupidity of the teaching and the mechanical nature of the discipline, he offered his services, which were politely rejected. His progressive educational ideas were too well known in school circles.

As always, after returning from the country, city life aroused his antagonism as the most uncivilized of existences; it was like some huge monster designed to grind man down, physically and spiritually. In his diary he described one of the large fashionable Moscow stores at this time as "worse than a hospital for syphilitics!" The earnest young men and women who continued to come to his city home to hear the "word" of the master were made to feel like intruders by Sonya. It was a source of constant worry to Tolstoy, and occasionally he vented his anger over his wife's behavior. Among the unusual guests that winter was the American Isabel Hapgood. Earlier she had sent him some of her articles, which he found uninteresting, and soon she undertook to translate his work *On Life*.

Tolstoy's gloomy feelings were momentarily cheered by the news, on the twenty-fourth of December, of the birth of his first grandchild, Anna. He wrote a warm letter of congratulation to Ilya and his daughter-in-law, but he did not neglect to proffer characteristic advice to avoid the mistakes of the times in bringing up their child.

3

The year 1889 in the Moscow household began with some excitement. Tolstoy had written an article for one of the newspapers to deplore the customary carousing and drunkenness on Tatyana's Day, January 12, traditionally celebrated by university students with much merrymaking. The youths did not take kindly to this preaching, and some of them sent him a telegram in which they facetiously "drank to his health." And he was even warned by government officials that a mob of students intended to march on his house and make him eat his words. Fortunately, nothing came of the projected demonstration.

Always glad of an excuse to leave the detested city, Tolstoy accepted an invitation in March to visit his old Sevastopol comrade-in-arms, the brilliant but queer mathematician, Prince S. S. Urusov. His estate was not far from Moscow, near the Troitse-Sergei Monastery. Tolstoy was pursued there by two Americans—an Episcopal minister and a scholar. Sonya had tried to hold them in Moscow until her husband's return on the plea that there was much of interest to see in the city. But they stubbornly insisted that they had come to Russia only to see Count Leo Tolstoy.

They were probably the same two Americans who a short time before had visited Granny in Petersburg. Such visits of foreigners were not uncommon, for they imagined that she, being a relative, would facilitate their access to Tolstoy, a rather needless precaution, for he saw nearly anyone who took the trouble to call on him.

They had come across the ocean, they said, solely to talk with Tolstoy on a very important matter. "You may know," added the theologian, a handsome and still very young man, "that in America we have very many sects and still not the trace of a ruling religion. Therefore, I have conceived the idea of bringing at least a part of these heterogeneous sects under one roof, so to speak, so that they may have some unity of views and faith. But this is not an easy matter, and I must tell you frankly that we definitely do not know how to bring it about."

Despite her fine breeding, Granny could not keep from laughing over this solemn declaration.

"Is it possible," she exclaimed, "that you have made so

long a journey only for this reason? In truth, I'm very sorry for you. Don't you know that Count Tolstoy is the enemy of every church, beginning with his own, and not only does not sympathize with religious ritualism, but accounts as pernicious the worship of God in any form? You will hardly find him a practical and useful director. I can even foresee in part exactly what he will say to your request, and it will not be what you expect."

The poor Americans were not a little dumfounded by this information, but it did not prevent them from going to Moscow to the court of Solomon. "I don't know how this court ended," concluded Granny with cheerful malice, "or what temple was raised as a consequence of their conversation with the universal patriarch. My Americans I saw no more; they apparently, like the Magi, returned by another path."

In his tramps about the neighborhood of the Urusov estate, Tolstoy saw all the evidence of poverty and debauchery among the peasantry and factory workers that always threw him into despair. And he poured out his indignation and sorrow in a letter to Sonya, who had been souring his visit with customary complaints about the family and her illnesses. Nor did she miss this particular opportunity to drive home a moral lesson. "How hopeless is your letter in its views on people and on Russia!" she wrote. "But you are right, entirely right. Not without purpose, although half in jest, have I been always saying lately: 'I suffer from a dislike for everything Russian.' You have always carefully avoided, however, the question of your family obligations. In truth, if it were not for these obligations, which I do not invent but feel in my whole being, I too would dedicate myself to the service of the common good. . . . But I cannot bring up wretched and uneducated children, given to me by God, simply for the sake of the well-being of people alien to me. Perhaps in my old age I will realize this sacred dream."

Shortly after his return to Moscow, Tolstoy visited an exhibit of paintings. He was well acquainted with many artists, and his knowledge of native painting was considerable. Although his judgments were usually well informed, they were often flecked with that cross-grained criticism with which he appreciated so much art. On this occasion he was particularly anxious to see a new canvas of Ge that depicted Christ's departure from Gethsemane. Not long before he had written to this devoted friend and disciple, whose paintings he sometimes inspired, to explain his conviction that what matters most to the artist is not praise, but the feeling that he is saying something new and important, something needed by the people. Here Tolstoy echoed his feeling about his own art: he believed that he saw things that other people did not see, and that he had an imperative duty to make others see them through his writings. Ge's picture impressed him as succeeding in precisely this respect, for it revealed Christ in a new and profound way. He contrasted Ge's canvas with another at the exhibition on a religious subject by Repin; it conveyed nothing new, said Tolstoy, nothing that people did not already envisage in the treatment.

The grown-up members of his family were becoming impatient with the preacher in their father and had lost their enthusiasm for the hard physical labor he still persisted in on the estate. Puzzled peasants were convinced that he plowed, sowed, and cut wood simply because he had nothing else to do. Only his serious daughter Masha still abided by his doctrine of work. "I have a great tenderness for her, for her alone," he wrote in his diary. "It is as though she redeems the others."

One of the most welcome of the several visitors that summer of 1889 was Strakhov, who had not been at Yasnaya Polyana for some time. He found it a "center of spiritual activity," and he saw in the master's calm moral beauty a power of conviction that could afford to dispense with verbal persuasion. To Strakhov, Tolstoy seemed already to have discovered truth, and his serene faith in it required no demonstration beyond his sincere willingness to live what he believed.

The center of spiritual activity, however, was largely in Tolstoy's study, where the "dark people" paid him furtive visits. The rest of Yasnaya Polyana seemed like a palace of pleasure. For the family had decided to remain there for the winter, and they made every effort to keep up their gay social city existence. Sergei had finished the university and had settled down in sedate bachelordom on an estate in the neighboring Chern district, from whence he paid frequent visits to Yasnaya Polyana. Ilya lived with his wife on an estate in the same district. The third son, Leo, a favorite of his mother, had just entered the medical school at Moscow University, but he soon abandoned this and further study in order to try his fortune as a writer. The two younger boys, Andrei and Mikhail, lazy and inattentive pupils, had not even finished the *Gymnasium,* and were now under the charge of a new tutor, A. M. Novikov. Ivan, the baby, was the apple of his parents' eye. The two oldest daughters, Tatyana and Masha, still unmarried, remained with the family in the country, and five-year-old Alexandra was in the charge of an English governess.

As in the city, the entire life of the family at Yasnaya Polyana revolved about the mother. Sonya ran the household, looked after the children's education, edited a new edition of her husband's works, and collected rents from the estate. The numerous children, servants, and peasants turned to her alone for the daily decisions of their lives.

For the most part the father, like a guest in his own house, kept singularly aloof from domestic cares and the affairs of the estate. He serenely led his own existence—a life of the spirit. When the summer work in the fields was over, Tolstoy's daily regimen was fixed, and no one and nothing were permitted to interfere with it. He rose about eight, emptied his chamber pot, swept his room out, and brushed his clothes. If a mouse were caught in the cage—there were many mice in the house that year—he took the cage out to the orchard and carefully released the rodent. No matter what the weather, he went on a solitary walk in the morning and returned about ten for coffee. Then he shut himself up in his study and worked till twelve, when he emerged for a quick lunch and returned to his reading and writing until three or four. It was only now that he grew sociable, for he would invite any member of the family or guests to walk with him, chatting with his companion in lively fashion and questioning peasants on the road. The peasants liked to banter with him and hear his deep, sincere, toothless laugh. Returning for dinner at five, he kept the table in lively conversation and remained until eight, when he retired to his study to write up his diary for the day. He would soon emerge and entertain the family circle with conversation or readings from his own compositions or from French, English, or Russian novels. He read well. Sometimes there would be music or a quiet game of chess, which he played badly but with great seriousness. At about midnight the mail arrived, and after going over his letters, he went to bed.

Sometimes the family's traditional fun-making interrupted the search for God. If the entertainment caught his fancy, he quickly became the life of the party as in the old days. Such an occasion was the performance of his play, *The Fruits of Enlightenment,* at Yasnaya Polyana in December of this year. Tanya and Masha had thought it time to liven up the household, and a play seemed like a good excuse to invite people. They had difficulty in finding a satisfactory piece until Masha remembered seeing the manuscript of a drama among her father's papers. She purloined the manuscript, and with Tanya and the young tutor Novikov read it over with much amusement. It was just the thing—a merry comedy in four acts, in which high society and spiritualism were blisteringly satirized, while some wonderful peasant characters were introduced who provided a combination of farce and genuine distress over their lack of land. To the delight of the readers they at once recognized in the numerous characters members of the family, their friends, and even some of their own peasants. Tolstoy at first remonstrated: staging a play, he said, was simply an amusement of rich and idle people. The young folks stood their ground and soon the author was more deeply involved than his children.

Telegrams were hurried off to Moscow, Tula, and Chern, and in a few days *troikas* dashed up to the house with prospective actors, among them the three Tolstoy sons, Sergei, Ilya, and Leo. Parts were quickly cast and soon rehearsals were being held daily. The author was nearly always present, directing and encouraging the actors, slapping his sides and wagging his head in peasant fashion, and laughing until the tears came when his humorous lines were effectively rendered. With animation he lectured the cast on dramatic art, and during the rehearsals the artist in him was never dormant. He observed attentively the performance of each actor and took notes on the dialogue. At night he collected all the roles, retired to his study, and altered the speeches, sometimes on the basis of the individual abilities of the players. These alterations continued right up to the very performance of the play.

Yasnaya Polyana rang with merriment from morning to night. The guests did not spend all their time at rehearsals. Young people coasted on the hill, skated on the pond, and went on sleigh rides by moonlight along the wooded trails. A well-spread table awaited them upon their return. But decanters of innocuous *kvas* always discouraged the frozen men of the party (intoxicants were not allowed in the house since Tolstoy had taken the pledge), and one by one they stealthily slipped out to a place under the stairs to warm themselves with vodka, which some knowing guest had thoughtfully provided.

On another occasion, when Tolstoy was deep in a conversation with the actors, little Andrei ran in to tell his father that two peasant women urgently wished to see him in the kitchen. Tolstoy went immediately, followed by several of the guests who were aware that something was up. As soon as he entered and asked the women what they wished, they fell on their knees and began to wail. Tolstoy was embarrassed and confused.

"Get up, mother, get up, get up," he said, turning to each in turn, but they did not arise and continued to howl. Tolstoy's features grew stern, his chin trembled, and he helplessly appealed to the women, assuring them that he was not God, and finally, falling on his own knees, he declared:—

"Well, now I shall kneel too. What is it you wish of me?"

But they still remained on their knees lamenting.

"Well, I'm on my own knees, I am, I am! Now, what do you want?" pleaded Tolstoy, bowing to the floor before the women. Suddenly the wailing changed to hysterical laughter, and only then did Tolstoy, looking hard at them, recognize in the disguised women his own daughters. Jumping to his feet, Tolstoy shook with laughter, and finally through his tears he said: "No, this is really impiety," and he went to his study.

The Fruits of Enlightenment was finally performed on December 30 in the big salon room before a large audience and it achieved a triumphant success.[2] It had been a long time since such high spirits and jollity had reigned in the great manor house of Yasnaya Polyana, which now became once again a "center of spiritual activity."

4

Over these two years (1888–1889) Tolstoy's developing social and moral dogma was reflected in his intellectual and artistic interests. His reading consisted chiefly of controversial books and articles on religion, ethics, and political

[2] Shortly after, it was publicly performed for the first time with equal success at Tula. When Tolstoy arrived for one of the rehearsals, the doorman, who did not know him and believed him to be some begging peasant, turned him out.

science. Fiction seemed to be worked in merely as a relief from sterner stuff: Goncharov's *Oblomov* he thought a poor novel; Saltykov-Shchedrin's satirical tales he liked; and the works of a new novelist, A. I. Ertel, especially his *Gardenins,* he praised highly (this novel was much influenced by Tolstoy's art). For the first time he read Chekhov, who was just beginning to publish, and on this occasion his judgment fluctuated between approval and severe criticism. Nor was the fiction of foreign authors neglected—Hugo, Maupassant, Jean Paul Richter, and Mrs. Humphry Ward's *Robert Elsmere*. The comedies of Ibsen, however, he dismissed as bad. It was also in 1889 that Tolstoy read for the first time the verse of Walt Whitman. He jotted down in his diary: "There is much bombast, emptiness, but I have already found something in him that is fine." The next year he described him as the "most original and bold of poets," and recommended him for translation. Tolstoy once wrote to Chertkov that, "after America, the country that is most sympathetic to me is Denmark."

American writers were beginning to appear with greater frequency on his reading list, a fact not unconnected with his growing reputation in the United States. This reputation was amusingly revealed in a visit to Tolstoy, at about this time, by Professor I. I. Yanzhul, a devoted admirer. He found his host stitching shoes and was asked to make himself comfortable in the adjoining study with a bundle of newspapers freshly arrived from America until Tolstoy had completed his task. The first newspaper Yanzhul looked at was a copy of the *Sandusky Times*. Much to his amazement he discovered a full account of a sermon delivered at a Sandusky church on Tolstoy's rendering of the Gospels. The ecstatic praise ascended to a final lyrical outburst over Tolstoy, the "thirteenth Apostle," whose teaching was declared to be as important as that of the other twelve. The contrast between the American newspaper's description of the thirteenth Apostle and Tolstoy in the next room in shirt sleeves and apron sewing away at a pair of shoes sent Yanzhul into gales of laughter, in which the new Apostle heartily joined when the cause was explained to him. A few years later, when Yanzhul had occasion to visit America, he found that letters from Tolstoy, and even the mere fact that he was personally acquainted with the great man, opened any door for him.

For some time now American religious and social thinking had begun to attract Tolstoy. Admirers of his views in the United States sent him periodicals, such as the Swedenborgian organ, the *New Christianity,* and the *World's Advance Thought,* from a reading of which he experienced "a great devotion of spirit." A perusal of the Mormon Bible and a biography of Joseph Smith, however, prompted the following entry in his diary: "Religion proper is a product of deceit—lies for a good purpose." But an American book on the teachings of the Shakers produced a powerful and favorable impression on him, and he thought of writing an article on religious movements in the United States.

At this time (1889) Tolstoy also read the strangely prophetic Utopian romance of Edward Bellamy, *Looking Backward,* which he considered an extraordinary performance. But the American book that now stirred him most and won his spiritual gratitude was Adin Ballou's *Christian Non-Resistance.* Since Tolstoy had declared his own belief in nonresistance in *What I Believe,* it had been a source of joy to discover that American thinkers had long since anticipated his convictions in this respect. To be sure, the doctrine went back to Christ's Sermon on the Mount, and had been repeated for centuries in one form or another by various religious sects, reformers, and moralists. Tolstoy, however, had formulated the doctrine in an uncompromising manner. For him, nonresistance meant that no physical force must be used to compel any man to do what he does not want to do, or to make him desist from doing what he likes. This extreme position has perhaps done more than any of his convictions to damage his reputation as a thinker. For his understanding of nonresistance not only led him to condemn all forms of government that employed any degree of force to compel obedience to its laws, but also to go so far as to maintain that it is wrong even to prevent a madman by force from killing a person. While admitting that compromise with the doctrine of nonresistance was inevitable in practice, he would not admit it in theory, which would be acting, in his opinion, quite contrary to the law of Christ.

Tolstoy's horror of violence led him to accept the request, in 1889, of A. I. Ershov that he write a preface to the author's *Recollections of Sevastopol.* In performing the task he relived again his experiences of thirty-four years ago at the famous siege, and he remembered with loathing the complacency with which he had then accepted the soldier's uty to kill his fellow men. The preface, which the censor anned, is a brief but powerful condemnation of war.

5

'he year 1889 was particularly noteworthy, for it marked e return of Tolstoy to the larger field of creative literature. this year he finished his famous piece, *The Kreutzer onata.* According to Sonya, Tolstoy obtained the initial idea or it from the actor V. N. Andreyev-Burlak. He told the amily of meeting on a train an unfortunate stranger who oured out to him the story of his wife's betrayal. Tolstoy riginally began this tale of "sexual love," as he first called , in 1887, but he put it aside after a mere start. The following year an incident provided him with new inspiration and dded a new motif—that of music. In a gathering at the amily's Moscow house in the spring, the violinist Yuli yasotta, accompanied by young Sergei Tolstoy at the piano, erformed Beethoven's "Kreutzer Sonata." Tolstoy had long een acquainted with the piece, but this performance produced a powerful impression on him. He turned to the distinguished painter Repin and the actor Andreyev-Burlak, 'ho were present, and offered to write a story based on the onata, if the actor would read it publicly in the presence f a canvas, inspired by the same music, that Repin would ngage to paint. Tolstoy once again took up the unfinished le of "sexual love" which now became *The Kreutzer onata,* but of the three artists, he was the only one to fulfill is part of the agreement.

For the rest of 1888 and at various times during the next ear Tolstoy worked away at this strange story of Pozdnyaev, whose violent jealousy over the attention paid his 'ife by a musician drove him to kill her and thereafter to reach the doctrine that sex should be eliminated from uman life as far as possible. Draft followed draft until 'olstoy had accumulated nine of them. Behind this extensive effort was not merely his usual sense of artistic perfection; *The Kreutzer Sonata* had finally taken on a deep personal significance for him. Later, in a letter to his friend lekseyev about the finished story, he declared: "The contents of what I wrote were as new to me as to those who ead them. In this connection an ideal remote from my ctivity was revealed to me so that I at first became horrified nd did not believe it, but then I grew convinced, repented, and rejoiced in what was to me and to others a happy impulse."

The new ideal that had gripped Tolstoy, and for the expression of which his unhappy hero Pozdnyshev became the mouthpiece, was the necessity of absolute chastity not only for unmarried, but even for married people. All his life Tolstoy had advocated marriage as the only normal and moral outlet for sexual satisfaction. And a few years previously, in *What I Believe* (1883), he had roundly condemned a celibate life for those who were ripe for marriage. But the factors compelling him to repudiate his former beliefs and to adopt the ideal of chastity must be studied against the background of his own recent marital difficulties.

"Man survives earthquakes, epidemics, terrible illnesses and every kind of spiritual suffering," said Tolstoy, "but always the most poignant tragedy was, is, and ever will be the tragedy of the bedroom." This new view, ironically enough, he began to express in correspondence with Chertkov, whom only a few years before he had been urging to marry for the good of his health and morals. In several letters to him during 1888, Tolstoy developed his thoughts on marriage and chastity, progressing swiftly from compromise to an extreme position. As so often since his spiritual change, he sought support for his new convictions in the Bible and found it in Matthew (XIX, 11–12): "But he said unto them, All men cannot receive this saying, but they to whom it is given. For there are eunuchs, which were so born from their mother's womb: and there are eunuchs, which were made eunuchs by men: and there are eunuchs, which made themselves eunuchs for the kingdom of heaven's sake. He that is able to receive it, let him receive it."

This new light did not immediately illuminate all the dark corners of Chertkov's mind on this vexed question. Finally, in November, Tolstoy wrote his disciple a rather full and important explanation of his position, which at that very time was being artistically formulated in order to be placed in the mouth of the hero of *The Kreutzer Sonata*.

Tolstoy began his letter by frankly confessing that in his own marriage he had failed utterly to live up to his new convictions, but that in the future he would try to abide by them as the teaching of Christ. Then he outlined his argument. A man and woman fall in love, he wrote, and they marry, and the result is a child. When pregnancy begins, a sexual coolness develops between husband and wife which interrupts relations, as it does among animals. The coolness continues until after the weaning of the child, when once again husband and wife feel sexually attracted to each other. Tolstoy concluded from this that "sexual union when a woman is not ready for childbearing, that is, when she does not have her monthly periods, has no reasonable sense whatever and is only physical enjoyment. . . ." Thus sexual relations can have no physical or moral justification except to produce children. During the time of pregnancy and nursing, husband and wife live like brother and sister, unless the husband, thinking only of his own pleasure, insists on continuing sexual relations. In this abuse, Tolstoy declared, may be found "the key to all the suffering hidden in the enormous majority of families.

"It seems to me," Tolstoy continued, "that when husband and wife live as brother and sister, she quietly, inviolably gives birth, nurses, and in this morally develops, and only in the free periods do they give themselves up once more to love, continuing for weeks, and again there is calm. It seems to me that this amorousness makes for a kind of steam pressure in the course of which the boiler would burst if the safety valve were not opened. The valve opens only during this powerful pressure, but otherwise it is always closed, carefully closed, and our aim ought to be consciously to keep it closed as tightly as possible and to place a weight on it so that it should not open. It is in this sense that I understand: 'He that is able to receive it, let him receive it,' that is, let everyone aspire never to marry, but having married, let him live with his wife as a brother with his sister."

Tolstoy eagerly sought support for his new beliefs in contemporary theory and practice, and he found it mostly in America. At the end of 1888 he received from its American author, Dr. Alice B. Stockham, *Tocology: A Book for Every Woman*. In Chapter XI of this work, on chastity in married life, Tolstoy was delighted to find his own views echoed. In fact, it would be more correct to say that he obtained ideas from the book, for not only his thoughts on the subject of chastity in married life in *The Kreutzer Sonata,* but even the very form of their expression suggest clearly the influence of *Tocology*. He gratefully wrote the author to tell her that her book was not only for women but for all mankind. In October 1889, she visited him at Yasnaya Polyana, and they talked about the religious movements in the Unite States. When her book was translated into Russian, he wro a highly laudatory introduction.

Nor were the Shakers without influence, for in 1889 men bers of this American sect sent Tolstoy some of their liter ture. Soon there appeared an entry in his diary: "I read th Shakers. Excellent. Complete sexual restraint. How strang it is that just now, when I'm concerned with these question I should receive this." He wrote Chertkov of his approv of the Shakers' belief in celibacy and chastity, and later h corresponded with a member of the sect in America and e pressed his agreement with their ideas. His reading Shaker literature served to strengthen his own views o absolute chastity, and it is interesting to observe that in variant of *The Kreutzer Sonata,* he included a bit of di logue (deleted in the final version), where the hero su ported his argument for celibacy by mentioning the examp of the Shakers which, he declared, was based on the fa that Christ had not married.

The original story on sexual love was rapidly turning int a moral treatise on Tolstoy's new faith in celibacy an chastity. But his wonderful artistic sense prevented *Th Kreutzer Sonata* from becoming a mere didactic trac Nothing could be more realistically and psychologicall convincing than the half-mad hero's narative of his mor and spiritual struggle. But Pozdnyshev's presentation of th problems of sex undoubtedly reflects Tolstoy's own opinior at this time, a fact substantiated by the *Afterword* to *Th Kreutzer Sonata,* which he later felt compelled to write i order that there should be no mistake about his own view on sex, for some people actually read into the story an a vocacy of free love. The *Afterword,* however, clearly diffe entiates the idealistic but logically developed thought of To stoy on these matters from the extravagant conviction the deranged Pozdnyshev. In brief, Tolstoy's ultimate pos tion in the *Afterword* is that the Christian ideal is one love of God and of one's fellow man, a love incompatibl with sexual love or marriage which amounts to servin one's self.

Tolstoy finished his story at the end of 1889. At that tim the house was filled with young people rehearsing *Th Fruits of Enlightenment.* Anxious to obtain a reaction *The Kreutzer Sonata,* he had one of the actors, M. Stakhovich, read the tale to the company. Stakhovich soo halted, embarrassed at such outspoken language on the theme of sex in the presence of young ladies. The women were asked to leave, and the reader resumed and finished the story.

"Well, what about it?" asked Tolstoy.

There was a general silence, and one after the other the guests took their leave of the host and went downstairs.

They gathered in the library, closed the door, and began to discuss the story, the idea of which had puzzled them. The consensus was that the tale was weak, the idea too artificial, too pretentious, and the development of the narrative labored. In the middle of the discussion the tutor Novikov opened the door and collided with the eavesdropping Tolstoy. Obviously, he passionately wanted to know whether he had succeeded in conveying his thought clearly, because the new ideas expressed in *The Kreutzer Sonata* were precious to him.

Something of this same bewilderment was evinced by the public at large over the story, which perhaps aroused more popular controversy than any work of Tolstoy. At first there seemed little chance of the censor's permitting its publication. When the story was originally submitted, like so many of Tolstoy's works that had the aura of the forbidden about them, it was eagerly passed around and read by high government and church officials. They of course condemned the tale, the Empress declared herself shocked, and the Emperor categorically forbade its printing.

Sonya, however, very much wished to include *The Kreutzer Sonata* in the thirteenth volume of her husband's works that she was publishing, and much against Tolstoy's will she sought an interview with Alexander III in the hope of obtaining permission to print the story. The interview did not take place until April 1891, after infinite wire-pulling by the stubborn Sonya. When she pointed out that *The Kreutzer Sonata* had been suppressed, the Emperor replied:—

"But then it is written in such a way that I'm sure even you would not give it to your children to read."

Sonya replied: "Unfortunately the story has taken a rather extreme form, but the idea underlying it is this: the ideal is always unattainable; if this ideal is perfect chastity, then people can only be pure in matrimony"—an ignorant or willful misrepresentation on the part of Sonya.

When she boldly asked the Emperor to lift the ban on the story, he answered:—

"Yes, we might allow you to print it in the complete works, because not everyone could afford to buy the full set, and it would not be too widely disseminated."

Sonya won her fight, and in 1891 *The Kreutzer Sonata* appeared for the first time in print in Russia in the thirteenth volume of Tolstoy's collected works. But on her own responsibility Sonya made numerous changes in the text (about two hundred), toning down certain sections and softening the forthright realism of the language.[3]

Long before the first published version, *The Kreutzer Sonata* was known far and wide in Russia and even abroad. Copies of the manuscript (not the final redaction) were sent to friends, who read them to large gatherings in Petersburg and Moscow. Surreptitiously hectograph copies were made and widely distributed in large numbers. So much in demand were they that they sold in bookshops that dared to handle this contraband literature for as high as fifteen rubles. Strakhov told Tolstoy that people, instead of saying "How do you do?" generally asked, "Have you read *The Kreutzer Sonata*?"

An interesting passage in Granny's *Reminiscences* gives some idea of the tremendous impression these illegal works of Tolstoy made upon Russian society. The government never seemed to learn the old truth that repressions increased interest.

> It is difficult to imagine [wrote Granny] what happened when, for example, *The Kreutzer Sonata* and *The Power of Darkness* appeared. Still forbidden to be printed, these works were reproduced in hundreds and thousands of copies; they passed from hand to hand, were translated into all languages, and were read everywhere with incredible passion. It seemed at times that the public, forgetting all its personal cares, lived only for the literature of Count Tolstoy. The most important political events rarely seized everyone with such force and completeness.

Readers of these illegal copies of *The Kreutzer Sonata* deluged Tolstoy with letters. Although the story was eagerly

[3] In fact, until the recent Jubilee Edition, *The Kreutzer Sonata* had never been published in exactly the form in which Tolstoy completed it in his corrected ninth and last redaction. See the Jubilee Edition, Vol. XXVII. This volume also contains the several variants of *The Kreutzer Sonata.*

read, it met with little approval. Some thought it a straight piece of autobiography—as though Tolstoy had murdered his wife—others accused him of preaching immorality, and the Archbishop of Kherson denounced him as a "wolf in sheep's clothing."

Tolstoy's story did not achieve its purpose—to preach a moral ideal through the medium of an artistic narrative. The author was perfectly aware that the didactic purpose obtruded. And discerning critics made this same distinction. The acutely critical but always generous Chekhov praised the design, beauty of execution, and the provocative thought of the story, but he complained that Tolstoy's remarks about syphilis, foundling hospitals, and women's aversion to conception not only were open to dispute, but clearly revealed an ignorant man, who during his long life had not taken the trouble to read a couple of books by specialists. Strakhov wrote Tolstoy of the impressions created by *The Kreutzer Sonata:*—

> Only sensible and reasonable young people and sensitive and reasonable women . . . have recognized the evils you attack, and sympathize with your inculcation of chastity. Even Countess Alexandra Andreyevna Tolstoy amazed me by exclaiming: "How is this? He wants to end the human race!" As if it was someone's business to look after the perpetuation of that race! Or ought we to organize stud-farms for it?

This might also have been Tolstoy's answer to the customary objection that his ideal of chastity, if carried to its logical conclusion, would result in the end of the human race. But he never imagined that his views of complete chastity were anything other than an unattainable ideal. He believed literally the statement in the Bible that "every one that looketh on a woman to lust after her hath committed adultery with her already in his heart." Nor did he believe that sex permitted of any compromises with the devil or with fine words. When the lady in *The Kreutzer Sonata* indignantly declared: "But you are speaking of physical love! Don't you admit the existence of love founded on identity of ideals and on spiritual affinity?" Tolstoy would have heartily seconded Pozdnyshev's incisive answer: "Spiritual affinity! Identity of ideals! But in that case (excuse my rudeness) why do they go to bed together?"

Nor did Tolstoy entertain any illusion that he of all people could achieve his ideal of perfect chastity. Cynical critics, after the appearance of *The Kreutzer Sonata,* slyly suggested that the author was getting old and that the grapes had turned sour. Yet when he was nearly seventy Tolstoy told his biographer, Aylmer Maude: "I was myself a husband last night, but that is no reason for abandoning the struggle. God may grant me not to be so again." In fact, not until he was eighty-one a year before his death, did he admit —again to Maude—that he was no longer troubled by sexual desires.

6

No, when Tolstoy wrote *The Kreutzer Sonata,* the grapes were still very tempting, and this fact has an important connection with the story itself. His wife's plea to the Emperor to be allowed to print the work in no sense indicated her approval of it. Her effort to see the Emperor on behalf of the work has sometimes been represented as an instance of her self-sacrifice for the sake of her husband. In her diary, however, she explained that she sought the Emperor's permission to print the book not so much out of devotion to her husband as a desire to defend her own and her family's reputation, to prove to the world that *The Kreutzer Sonata* had nothing to do with the intimate life between her and her husband.

Despite the many sharp differences in their life, and of late their serious quarrels, Tolstoy had clung firmly to the institution of marriage as an ultimate good. He had remained scrupulously faithful to his wife, and in his writings he had uncompromisingly condemned any violation of the sacred bonds of matrimony. Then, suddenly, toward the end of 1888, his whole attitude changed. He decided that marriage was not one of the forms of service to God, and he concluded by advising bachelors not to marry, and married couples to preserve chastity.

With his usual sincerity, Tolstoy attempted to practice what he preached. It was no easy task. As during the period of his youth, he chronicled in his diary the lapses in his struggle to be chaste. Only now the temptation was not a Caucasian beauty or a bewitching gypsy wench, but a forty-five-year-old wife who had borne him thirteen children. "The devil fell upon me," he wrote. "The next day, the morning of the 30th, I slept badly. It was so loathsome, as after a crime. And on that same day, the 30th, still more powerfully possessed, I fell." In a later conscience-stricken entry, he jotted down: "What if a child should be born? How shameful, especially before the children. They will reckon when it happened, and they will read what I write [*The Kreutzer Sonata*]. It has become shameful, sad. And I considered: not before people, but before God must one be afraid. I asked myself: In this relation how do I stand before God, and I at once grew calmer."

If other evidence were unconvincing, Tolstoy's wife read into *The Kreutzer Sonata* a clear expression of her husband's new ideal. In all their quarrels in the past, they had never once seriously differed about marriage—its sanctity, its duties and privileges. Of late, worn out by constant child-bearing, she had murmured complaints, but she had never once suggested contraceptives, which she knew were morally and physically repugnant to her husband. And in the end, she had always surrendered. Marriage and all it entailed had been the rock on which Sonya had built her happiness, and on which she instinctively felt her future secure no matter how seriously her views may have otherwise differed from those of her husband. Then, suddenly, after twenty-seven years of life together, and without any apparent reason, this rock was smashed to bits. Now she could not help but feel that during all these long years they had been living a cruel lie.

Having constant access to Tolstoy's diary, which she was accustomed to copy, Sonya could hardly fail to relate these new entries concerning his struggle to preserve his chastity to those ancient jottings, which she had read with horror even before her marriage, of his youthful attempts to fight the devil of sex that tempted him in the form of loose women. In his youth he had condemned lust, and now in his old age he condemned all sexual relations. The conclusion was inescapable to Sonya: her husband, even throughout all his married life, had possessed the same aversion to sexual relations that he had expressed as a youth. The possibility had perhaps always existed that she might eventually dwindle into an acceptance of his new way of life. And now the very fabric of their whole married existence together had been torn to shreds. Here there could be no compromise. The family drama had changed from a tragi-comedy to pure tragedy.

What Sonya considered personal allusions to her married life in *The Kreutzer Sonata* deeply offended her and inspired a curious answer in the form of a short story entitled "Whose Fault?" This literary effort was intended to treat the same theme as that of *The Kreutzer Sonata,* only from the point of view of the wife and in her defense. The autobiographical elements are painfully evident. The heroine in the tale is Sonya and the hero her husband. The story tells of a certain Prince Prozorovski who, after a gay youth, marries at the age of thirty-five an eighteen-year-old girl by the name of Anna. In her description of Anna, Sonya spares no virtues or charms. The prince, on the other hand, is portrayed as coarse and brutishly sensual. When walking behind his bride-to-be, Sonya related, the prince hungrily sizes up her hips and mentally disrobes her. In the carriage on their wedding journey, this coarse prince, reeking of tobacco, literally violates his innocent bride, an act that fills her with immeasurable disgust, as no doubt did the incident in the *dormeuse* on Sonya's marriage night. Her husband's sensual love dismays Anna. Then a young artist appears on the scene and manifests a purely platonic affection for her, and the story ends with the husband murdering his pure and innocent wife in a fit of rage over her harmless affair with the artist.

Sonya did not hesitate to read "Whose Fault?" to visitors, and for the guileless who missed the point, she would carefully explain the personal background of the story. She even thought of publishing it, but better sense prevailed. At times, in her anger and self-pity over this latest defection of her husband, she could not refrain from holding him up to ridicule. When Alekseyev visited, he found Sonya alone and had a long talk with her, while she held the baby Vanichka in her arms. The conversation finally turned on *The Kreutzer Sonata.* Sonya, affecting a laugh over Tolstoy's intention in the story, said: "It is fine for Leo Nikolayevich to write and advise others to be chaste, but what of himself?" and with a malignant smile she motioned toward the child.

In these circumstances, relations between husband and wife became terribly strained. Tolstoy's diary mercilessly recalls her reactions. One entry reads: "This morning and last night I thought much and clearly about *The Kreutzer Sonata.* Sonya copies it; it agitates her, and last night she spoke about the disillusionment of the young woman, about the feelings of the man, so strange at first because of his lack of feeling towards the children. She is unjust, and because she wishes to justify herself; but in order to understand and speak the truth, one must repent." Another entry runs: "After dinner Sonya, while looking at an oncoming train, spoke of how she wished to throw herself under it. And I became very sorry for her." And a third note: "Sonya came with the news that she is not pregnant. I said that it is necessary to sleep apart. . . ." "I spoke with Sonya. She says that she is glad. But she does not wish to be apart."

One may date from this time a pronounced development of the hysteria of Tolstoy's wife, traces of which she had exhibited in the first years of their disagreements. This condition was aggravated by his desire to sever the last bond that bound them together. For now, with increasing frequency, extravagant unbalanced declarations began to appear in Sonya's own diary. "He is killing me very systematically . . ." she complained. "I want to kill myself, to run somewhere, to fall in love with someone—anything only not to live with the man whom I have loved all my life. . . ." And shortly after this, she wrote in her diary: "It would be terrible to become pregnant, for all would learn of this shame and would repeat with malicious joy a joke just now invented in Moscow society: 'There is the real *Afterword* of *The Kreutzer Sonata.*' "

XXVII

Money Is the Root of All Evil

IN FEBRUARY 1890, Tolstoy set out with his daughter Masha to visit his sister, now a nun, at the convent of Shamardino. Not finding her there, they went on to Optina Monastery near by, where she was visiting. At this famous hermitage he once again discussed various faiths with the celebrated Elder Ambrose.[1] Shortly after this visit, Tolstoy held forth to company at Yasnaya Polyana on the evils of monasteries. The monks should get rid of their sham ceremonials, he said, of their begging for crusts and kopeks, and earn their own keep.

During this year and part of the next, Tolstoy's health was failing, and at one point he thought he would soon die. At the age of sixty-two, it was becoming more difficult for him to carry out his conviction of service when it involved physical labor. He tried to compensate in other ways. His daughters Tanya and Masha set up a school on the estate for peasant children, and he took an active part in the instruction. A few months later the governor of the province closed the school because it had been opened without permission of the authorities. Permission would hardly have been granted, although the governor was sympathetic to Tolstoy. In fact, this friendliness was soon to result in his being removed to another province.

Peasants came to ask Tolstoy's help for comrades who had fallen afoul of the law, and he always found these requests extremely hard to refuse. Toward the end of 1890 he visited

[1] The model for Dostoyevsky's Father Zosima in *The Brothers Karamazov*.

in the district jail four peasants of Yasnaya Polyana who were on trial for murder. His very presence at the trial brought about a mitigation of the sentence. The court proceedings he condemned as a "shameful comedy." His long hostility to institutions of government had been intensified by his new beliefs, and already he was contemplating an open protest. When a follower at this time wrote him for advice on the project of a newspaper for the lower classes that would reflect Tolstoyan views, he replied that though the idea was a good one it was impossible under the prevailing conditions of censorship, for the government, he declared, "knows that its destruction will follow enlightenment of the masses," and hence it will prevent any sincere attempt to instruct the common people.

Tolstoy's courage in the face of a reactionary government was shown this same year in his answer to the philosopher V. S. Solovyov, who asked for his support in opposing a new anti-Semitic law. Tolstoy permitted his name to be used in a public protest, and he wrote Solovyov: "With all my soul I am glad to take part in this matter, and I know in advance that if you, Vladimir Sergeyevich, express what you think about this objective, that you will also express my thoughts and feelings, for the basis of our abhorrence of oppressing the Hebrew nationality is one and the same—a recognition of the brotherly union of all peoples, and more so with the Hebrews, among whom Christ was born, and who have suffered so much and still suffer from the heathenish ignorance of so-called Christians."

The government quietly took its own measures against Tolstoy, largely through its minion the Church and the reactionary head of the Holy Synod, Pobedonostsev. Even the priests of Yasnaya Polyana were set to spying on Tolstoy, a fact which his wife did not forget to call to the attention of the Emperor when she had her interview with him over the censorship of *The Kreutzer Sonata.* Instances of the close surveillance under which Tolstoy was kept, of the persecution of his followers, and of the censorship directed against his works have already been noted. To this was now added slander. In his annual report to the Tsar on the state of the Church for 1887, Pobedonostsev devoted some space to the harmful views of Tolstoy and the antireligious propaganda he was carrying on among the members of his own family. Three years later in a newspaper account of Tolstoy's heresies, a statement was lifted from Pobedonostsev's report to the effect that Tolstoy "was no longer able to render assistance to the peasants of his estate, and hence his oldest sons have begun to curb his wastefulness." The newspaper was at once requested by the three indignant sons to print a repudiation of this slander.

The next year the Church returned to the charge. A Kharkov priest preached in the cathedral of that city a sermon in which he charged that Tolstoy "more than all others agitates the minds of the educated and uneducated" with his works, possessed of a "destructive power and depraved nature"; that he preached "disbelief, and atheism"; that *The Kreutzer Sonata* was "an incoherent, dirty, and immoral tale"; and that he hoped that "the most pious Emperor will suppress in good time" the subversive activity of Tolstoy.

Shortly after this tirade, the "most pious Emperor" was importuned by Pobedonostsev to do precisely this—suppress the activity of Tolstoy. The attempt came about largely because of *The Kreutzer Sonata.* Tolstoy had disapproved of Sonya's request to the Tsar that he permit its publication. "Her wheedling of the Emperor was disagreeable," he jotted down in his diary. And now he wrote to Chertkov: "There was something nasty in *The Kreutzer Sonata.* It has become terribly revolting to me, every remembrance of it. There was something bad in the motives directing my writing of it, for it has evoked such wickedness." No doubt the distasteful *succès de scandale* that was already connected with the story, as well as the persistent misinterpretation of its meaning and the widespread denunciation, had given him cause to regret. He had recently heard that the post-office authorities in America had banned the work in the mails. Now a new factor had arisen. Although the Emperor had taken pains to qualify his permission to print *The Kreutzer Sonata* by insisting that it should appear only in the thirteenth volume of Sonya's edition of her husband's works, he had not realized that that volume might be sold separately. Nor had this thought been in Sonya's mind. But now the bookstalls were jammed with copies of the thirteenth volume. Pobedonostsev wrote an acrimonious letter to the Emperor, in which he indicated his comprehensive knowledge of Tolstoy's influence and the rising temper of the authorities over his activities:—

"I have decided to write your majesty about unpleasant matters.

"If I had known in advance that the wife of Leo Tolstoy

had requested an audience of your majesty, I would have begged you not to receive her. What has happened is what one might have feared. Countess Tolstoy returned from you with the thought that her husband has in you a defense and justification for all those things in him over which the healthy-minded and religious people of Russia are indignant. You permitted her to print *The Kreutzer Sonata* in the complete collection of the works of Tolstoy. It might have been possible to foresee how they would make use of this permission. This complete collection consists of 13 volumes, which can be placed on sale separately. The 13th volume is a small book, in which has been published, together with *The Kreutzer Sonata,* certain slight articles in the same spirit. They have placed this book on sale separately, and already three separate editions of it have appeared. Now this book is in the hands of *Gymnasium* students and young girls. On the road from Sevastopol, I saw it on sale in the station and being read in the trains. The book market is full of the 13th volume of Tolstoy. . . . Tolstoy is a fanatic in the matter of his own insensate ideas, and unfortunately attracts and leads to madness thousands of giddy people. The amount of harm and ruin he has produced would be difficult to estimate. Unhappily the madmen who believe in Tolstoy are just as possessed as he is of a spirit of untamable propaganda, and they strive to put his teaching into practice and to bring it to the people. There are not a few such examples, but the most striking at present is Prince Khilkov, a Guards officer, who settled in the Sumski district of the Kharkov Province. He has distributed all his land to the peasants, keeping only a farm for himself, and has been preaching to the peasants the Tolstoyan gospel, with its repudiation of the Church and marriage, which is based on the principles of socialism. One may imagine what effect this produces on the ignorant masses. The evil grows and spreads even to the borders of the Kursk Province, in districts where for some time an unquiet spirit has been observed among the people. It is almost five years since I wrote about this matter to the governor and the ministry, but I cannot obtain any resolute measures, and meanwhile Khilkov has already succeeded in corrupting the whole population of the village of Pavlovka and the neighboring countryside. He distributes far and wide harmful pamphlets which the peasants believe. The populace has entirely forsaken the Church; in two parishes the churches stand empty, and the clergy go hungry and are exposed to ridicule and insults. In a parish of 6000 souls, even on the highest feast days there were only 5 old women in the church. Under Khilkov's influence the peasantry refuses to take oaths. Such a situation is pregnant with the greatest danger, and on the basis of the latest information I shall most earnestly request the minister to exile Khilkov, who now boasts before the people: 'They do nothing to me because I teach the truth.' Now, I hope, the ministry will issue an appropriate decree.

"It is impossible to conceal from oneself that in the last few years the intellectual stimulation under the influence of the works of Count Tolstoy has greatly strengthened and threatens to spread strange, perverted notions about faith, the Church, government, and society. The direction is entirely negative, alien not only to the Church, but to nationality. A kind of insanity that is epidemic has taken possession of people's minds."

Alexander III was much displeased by the abuse of his permission to print *The Kreutzer Sonata,* and he is reported to have expressed his chagrin over the behavior of Countess Tolstoy in the matter, although she had acted entirely in good faith. Khilkov was quickly exiled, but Pobedonostsev's letter represented a dire threat not only against the followers of Tolstoy, but against the master himself.

2

The Church struck at Tolstoy's disciples in various ways. Ge was the next to feel its heavy hand. In 1890 his celebrated canvas, "What Is Truth," depicting Christ before Pilate, was quietly removed from the exhibition room in Petersburg by order of the Church authorities. It was a cruel blow, for the sale of the picture meant much to Ge, whose livelihood partly depended on the income from his painting.

Tolstoy at once became his champion. On the way to Petersburg, Ge had made his customary visit to Yasnaya Polyana and had exhibited the picture to the family. Tolstoy was in raptures and for days he could hardly speak of anything else. Ge had omitted the question mark in the title, "What Is Truth," an indication of his interpretation of the famous scene, which agreed with that of Tolstoy in his translation of this account in the Gospel. That is, Pilate utters the phrase ironically, not expecting an answer. When

Christ says that he has come into the world as a witness of truth, Pilate sneeringly throws the words back at him: "What is truth?" Truth is a relative thing which everyone understands as he wishes. The picture clearly suggests this interpretation by its striking contrast of the harried figure of Christ, who during the night had undergone arrest, judgment, and suffering, with the majestic figure of the Roman governor, with his fat, shaven neck, sensual body, and with the arm outstretched in a gesture of contempt.

Tolstoy wrote to his friend, the well-known art connoisseur, P. M. Tretyakov, to persuade him to buy the picture, and he supported his plea by a long critique on why the canvas constituted "an epoch in the history of Christian art." Tretyakov bought the picture, but since he was as yet unable to exhibit it in Russia, he made arrangements for showings abroad. Again Tolstoy lent his aid by writing another long letter to George Kennan, who had visited him at Yasnaya Polyana, to explain the picture and to ask him to sponsor the exhibitions of it in America.

Ge was not the only artist to visit Yasnaya Polyana at this time, an unusual period for the production of art devoted to Tolstoy. In the fall of 1890, Ge did a bust of Tolstoy and also painted a portrait of his daughter Masha, who had endeared herself to the artist. The next summer the more famous painter Repin and the distinguished sculptor I. Ya. Ginsburg visited. On this occasion Repin painted his well-known picture of Tolstoy in his room, with the spade, saw, and scythe standing against the wall; he also executed his less known but excellent study of Tolstoy standing barefoot in the woods, and drawings of Tolstoy reading in the garden and of Sonya with her two youngest children. At the same time he and Ginsburg did busts of Tolstoy. In a letter to Ge, Tolstoy wrote that Ginsburg's bust was bad, Repin's a good likeness, but Ge's was the best of all. On one of their walks, Tolstoy presented Repin to the caretaker of the bees, a peasant by the name of Yermil, who had formerly been educated in Tolstoy's village school. Tolstoy highly valued him for his amazing memory and independent ways. At Tolstoy's request, the peasant treated him quite as an equal and made no attempt to modify his language. During the conversation, however, Yermil suddenly turned on the master and berated him soundly.

"Leo Nikolayevich, I can't understand you! You dress like a beggar, eat no meat, and lead the life of an ascetic. If I were in your place, I should keep a woman—better still, two at a time. . . ."

Tolstoy blushed up to the ears as he broke in: "Fie! You ought to be ashamed to say such things! Think of your soul!"

"You let my soul alone!" said the bee-man, with a cynical laugh. "Who believes in a soul nowadays, I should like to know!"

The shocked Tolstoy trembled all over but made no reply. Yermil, taking advantage of his defenseless position in the presence of a guest, grew still bolder and began to abuse him in the most shameless manner. Tolstoy silently took Repin's arm and walked away.

3

As he grew older, Tolstoy's reading grew more and more eclectic. He was in no sense a bibliophile, for he regarded books as the tools of his craft and collected them largely for use in connection with his writing. Hence the library of some 14,000 volumes that he amassed at Yasnaya Polyana provides striking evidence of the extraordinary variety of his interests, although a considerable number of these volumes were gifts from authors. The broad fields represented by the books, in the order of the number of volumes, are literature and criticism, religion and philosophy, history and biography, pedagogy and children's books, medicine, economics and law, the natural sciences, and geography and travel. Russian books predominate, but there are a great many in English, French, and German, which languages he read with ease. Of the foreign books, English leads with some 3600 titles. His fondness for English and American literature, particularly fiction, has already been indicated. In 1890–1891, we find him reading Thackeray's *The Newcomes,* which he thought poor, and rereading a favorite work, Matthew Arnold's *Literature and Dogma.* Coleridge he read for the first time and jotted down in his diary: "A writer very attractive to me, precise, clear, but unfortunately timid." He made an effort to keep abreast of contemporary literature, both native and foreign,[2] and often surprised young writers who visited him with his acute criticisms of

[2] In 1890 he read works of Minski, Leskov, Sienkiewicz, Björnson, and Ibsen.

their works. The burden of his reading in 1890–1891, however, consisted, as it had during the last few years, of books and articles on religion, ethics, vegetarianism, and temperance.

This same division of interest is reflected in Tolstoy's writing at this time. He began to outline *Resurrection,* and he did some work on two tales, *The Devil* and *Father Sergei.* But the major portion of his efforts was expended on didactic works.[3]

There was at this time a manifest falling off of interest in encouraging others to live a Tolstoyan existence. Individual spiritual growth now seemed to him somehow more important. His emphatic distrust of organized efforts to achieve the good life no doubt contributed to this tendency to shift the emphasis to right thinking and right feeling. First things come first; hence each individual must first seek ways of improving his own spiritual health before worrying about the sick lives of others. He noted in his diary (January 3, 1890): "I read that they told Emerson that the world would soon end. He answered: 'Well, I can get along without it.' Very important." Actually much of the unhappy disagreement with his wife arose not from the fact that she refused to accept his way of life, but that she prevented him from living it.

Though Tolstoy could be dogmatic about the ends of his faith, he was anything but dogmatic about the means of achieving them. He realized that the goal he set was often perfection, and whereas he might be uncompromising about it as a goal, he never expected men, least of all himself, to achieve it. Striving for perfection became the end. An entry in the diary immediately following the one quoted above reads: "We search for mind, powers, goodness, perfection in all this, but perfection is not given to man in anything. . . ."

The expression of certain moral and religious objectives in his major works invited public ridicule that Tolstoy might have been spared had readers gone on to his further treatment of these matters in his lesser known productions. Thus the impractical ideal of complete chastity suggested by *The Kreutzer Sonata* and the *Afterword* is reduced to a

[3] The *Afterword* to *The Kreutzer Sonata,* the article on drink and tobacco, "Why Do Men Stupefy Themselves?" but principally on the longer and more significant work, *The Kingdom of God Is Within You,* which he was not to finish until two years later.

wholly practical rule of life in *Christian Teaching,* where, six years later, he wrote:—

> To overcome the habit of this sin [unchastity] man must first of all refrain from increasing it. If he be chaste, let him not infringe his chastity; if he be married, let him be true to his partner; if he have sexual intercourse with many, let him not invent unnatural forms of vice. Let him refrain from augmenting his sexual sin. If men would do this, many of their sufferings would come to an end. . . . Although only in rare cases are men able to be altogether chaste, still everyone should understand and remember that he can always be more chaste than he formerly was, or can return to the chastity he has lost, and that the nearer he approaches to perfect chastity according to his powers, the more true welfare will he attain, the more earthly welfare will be added to him, and the more will he contribute to the welfare of mankind.

Concentration on his own spiritual development made Tolstoy impatient with those who constantly sought his advice on how to change their way of life and lead a godly existence. These seekers were wearisome, he wrote Ge, but he rarely turned a deaf ear to them. And he did not fail now to censure the Tolstoyans who placed the observance of forms and of ideal communal living isolated from the practical world above individual spiritual betterment in the world of living men. He wrote on this subject to Khilkov, who had sacrificed much in his cause and had now become a special object of persecution by Pobedonostsev. Khilkov had little sympathy for moral precepts that were not actually carried out to the letter in daily existence, and hence he had organized his own Tolstoyan commune. His insistence on action no doubt contributed later to his abandoning Tolstoyism for forthright revolutionary activity. "So I think," Tolstoy wrote to him, "that every organization, every definition, every concentration of the conscience on any condition means the prevalence of anxiety about strengthening love in oneself, self-perfection without good deeds. The most coarse form is standing on a pillar, but every form is more or less such a standing. Every form separates one from the people and consequently from the possibility of good deeds and from invoking love in them. Such are the communes, and this is their insufficiency if we are to recognize them as a permanent form. Standing on a pillar and going into a wilderness to live in a commune may be necessary for people for a time, but as a continual form, it is obviously a sin and foolishness. To live a pure, holy life on a pillar or in a commune is impossible, because man is deprived of one-half of life—communion with the world, without which his life has no sense."

These sudden shifts of Tolstoy, without ever losing sight of his ultimate objectives, disturbed the more literal-minded disciples who lived by dogma. Tolstoy often seemed dogmatic because circumstances had led him to propound a new way of life. Actually no one was more dogmatic than the average man clinging to his traditions and conventions. A rationalist and an acute logician, Tolstoy would not permanently allow dogma to lead him where his common sense could not follow. When his "second thoughts" indicated, as they occasionally did, that his dogma falsified common sense, he did not hesitate to recant. But it was always his own common sense, not common sense dictated by convention. One sometimes suspects that the zest for his new faith was partly sustained by the problems it created and the fresh paths of intellectual and moral speculation which it led him into. To another disciple, V. V. Rakhmanov, who had expressed some dismay over doctrinal differences between an earlier work of the master and what he had been saying of late, Tolstoy cheerfully wrote in March 1891: "Do not imagine that I defend the point of view I formerly expressed in *What I Believe*. Not only do I not defend it, but I am glad we have outlived it. When starting on a new road one cannot help rejoicing at what one first sees before one, and it is excusable to mistake what is at the beginning of the road for the journey's aim."

4

Tolstoy's fame abroad had already begun to bring foreign newspapermen to Yasnaya Polyana. Knowing his hostility to both the government and the Church, the newsmen no doubt hoped for some revealing copy about the Russian enigma. Besides, Tolstoy had now definitely become "news" for all the world. In December 1890, Dr. E. J. Dillon, scholar and correspondent of the London *Daily Telegraph*, visited him, and in March of the next year an editor of the *New York Herald*, Creelman, turned up.

But apart from foreigners and old friends like Ge, Strakhov, and Fet, the most numerous visitors during 1890–1891, much to Sonya's disgust, were Tolstoy's followers. "The *dark ones* have arrived," runs one entry in her diary (December 17, 1890). "There is stupid Popov, an oriental-looking, lazy, weak fellow; and stupid, fat, Khokhlov, a merchant. And these are disciples of the great man! The wretched spawn of human society, chatterers to no purpose, idlers without breeding." She was infuriated when her young son Andrei reported to her that one of the "dark" visitors had stopped him from studying that morning by asking: "Why do you study; you will destroy your soul. Surely your father does not desire this."

Sonya's spleen at this time was particularly directed against the visits of Biryukov, whom she found less difficult to accept, however, than most of the "dark people." But he had fallen in love with Masha, who tended to reciprocate the feeling, and the thought of such a marriage horrified her mother. Sonya's feelings are suggested by an incident that took place in December 1890. During Biryukov's visit, another of the "dark people," Butkevich, arrived, accompanied by a Jewish girl, who (so Sonya decided) was his mistress. Masha and Biryukov at once made a great deal of the Jewish girl, no doubt regarding her as a new convert. "I grew indignant," Sonya noted in her diary, "that a respectable girl, my daughter, should associate with such trash and that her father, as it were, sympathized with this. And I lost my temper, shouted, and remembering in the diary of Leo Nikolayevich[4] . . . everything that tortured me in copying it, I evilly said to him: 'You have been accustomed all your life to associate with such trash, but I have not been accustomed to it and do not wish my daughters to be associated with them.'" Masha did not marry her father's disciple Biryukov.

The heir-apparent of the kingdom of the "dark people," Chertkov, also visited in the winter of 1890. In sharing their spiritual experiences and in conducting the affairs of the new faith, personal meetings of Tolstoy and Chertkov were less essential, for they maintained and even increased their voluminous correspondence over 1890–1891. The letters are concerned with the details of the *Intermediary* publishing venture, moot points of doctrine, Tolstoy's and even Chertkov's writings, and new converts. It is a curious fact that

[4] Four words are deleted in the Russian edition. Words and expressions of a very intimate nature or unprintable are frequently deleted by the editor of Sonya's diaries, her son, Sergei Lyovich Tolstoy.

Tolstoy, at Chertkov's request, returned to him all his letters as soon as possible after reading them. The business of saving souls had now been reduced to something of a routine. Seekers after light would find their way to Yasnaya Polyana. Tolstoy would talk to them and then furnish them with letters of introduction to Chertkov or other well-grounded disciples for further instruction or activity. Such candidates were much discussed in the correspondence of Tolstoy and Chertkov.

The success of the *Intermediary* publications had grown enormously, despite the suspicions of government authorities. Chertkov had attracted another young follower into the business, I. I. Gorbunov-Posadov, and he and Biryukov were occasionally sent to Yasnaya Polyana on matters of the publication. Tolstoy was constantly suggesting books and articles for reprinting by the *Intermediary,* and these suggestions nearly all turned out successfully. Occasionally he read new manuscripts for approval and correction.

Hardly a work of his own was undertaken without writing to Chertkov about it, keeping him posted by mail on progress made, and sometimes sending him early manuscript drafts. Anything that came from Tolstoy's pen, however trifling, had now become sacred for Chertkov. At times he referred to him in his letters as though he were already dead and among the immortals. Since 1889 he had begun a systematic collection of all of Tolstoy's thoughts, which he referred to as his "Vault." He and several Tolstoyans worked at this task, selecting and arranging the thoughts under subject headings with the intention of publishing a work in many volumes.[5] Chertkov's literary detective work got him into difficulties. He had arranged with Tolstoy to have his daughter Masha copy out his diaries and letters and send them to him. Masha soon objected and wrote Chertkov that this copying of her father's intimate papers was distasteful to her. Tolstoy agreed, explaining that it was difficult for him to keep up his diary when he knew that his personal thoughts were to be at someone's disposal. This was probably not the whole reason, for apparently Sonya also objected. Chertkov grudgingly accepted the decision on this occasion, asking only that Masha be allowed to copy sections of Tolstoy's letters, where he developed his

[5] This work was never published and the manuscript is now in the Chertkov archives.

thought or threw new light on old questions for, he added, such material was absolutely essential for his "Vault."

There was little friction now to disturb the harmonious business and spiritual relations between Tolstoy and Chertkov. Occasional matters of doctrine ruffled the disciple, such as the master's extreme position on nonviolence and marriage. Tolstoy patiently but firmly reiterated his stand on both points in letters of 1890, and Chertkov's questioning was silenced. The closeness of the bond between them is reflected in Tolstoy's frequent expressions of concern for the personal existence and health of Chertkov and of his wife and son. His tender solicitude for this invalid wife, who so completely accepted her husband's faith, contrasts ironically with his behavior toward Sonya at this time. In a fit of depression over illness, Chertkov's wife wrote Tolstoy in September 1890: "One thing I desire and only one —complete reconciliation with God—otherwise I do not wish to die. So little remains of life (it seems to me), and yet there is still so much to understand. But you will help me. I am much comforted by this, that always, whatever may happen, you and Dima [Chertkov] will be as one—in complete harmony, as now."

One visitor in July 1891 whom Sonya could now unreservedly accept was Countess Alexandra Tolstoy. Granny brought with her that aroma of the Court that Sonya respected and an intimacy with the imperial family and great personages of state that she secretly hankered after. In Tolstoy's eyes her lofty connections were the least attractive thing about Granny, though he never hesitated to make use of them in times of trouble. Yet he had not lost his affection and admiration for this old friend who neither asked for nor gave quarter in her brilliant conversations and correspondence with him.

"Do you know, Granny," Sonya confessed to her, "you are truly the only person who can talk with him without constraint and without concealing anything of the truth; all the others are afraid and tremble before his greatness."

Mindful of the unpleasant passages of arms in the past, Granny had vowed to herself that on this visit she would avoid any arguments. It was not an easy promise to keep. On the very first day of her visit, Tolstoy trapped her while she was resting in the garden and for two hours assailed her with a reading of parts of his latest manuscript on the abolition of war. "There were many separate, fine, and healthy thoughts expressed there," she recalled in her recollections, "but taken altogether it represented such a bouquet of fantastic, romantic, and ultra-idyllic utopias that only the exalted worshippers of Leo could possibly accept them. I heard him out in silence. Only once or twice did it occur to me to answer with a few words to his questioning glance: 'Yes, it is all very fine on paper. Only what a pity that it should be so unrealizable.' "

The Tolstoy children were awed by the authoritative bearing of Granny in the presence of their father, who seemed to them the last authority on everything, and they secretly sought out her opinion on his articles of faith. One of the daughters asked her what she thought about vegetarianism, and she bluntly dismissed it on the authority of the Apostle Paul. Tolstoy happened to overhear her remarks but said nothing. At the tea table that evening, when she stretched out her hand for a ham sandwich, he sarcastically exclaimed in a loud voice: "My congratulations. You wish to eat a carcass." After this remark she found herself unable to touch the meat. Granny observed that the practice of vegetarianism in the household caused Sonya infinite difficulty. There were two camps, those who ate meat and those who did not. At the table Sonya would triumphantly declare that she would not allow her children—meaning by this the younger ones—to be vegetarians. She worried over her husband's meatless diet, which, she believed, did not agree with his chronic liver trouble. But Granny rejected the rumor that during his illnesses Sonya artfully mixed a meat broth in all his dishes, and that he did not notice this or did not care to notice it.

One day in a gloomy frame of mind, he invited Granny into his study and said to her: "You always say that I breathe and live only for flattery, yet so many people disapprove of me, and quite justly, because my life does not accord with my theories."

"It seems to me," she answered, "that they blame you most of all exactly for your unrealizable theories. In order to fulfill them literally, you would have to begin by going away—is this not true? But you have a family, and you have no right to desert them or to force upon them your inclinations and convictions. You have lived until recently happily and agreeably; they also wish to live so, not experiencing the slightest calling for beggary and work in the fields, or for life in a peasant hut."

Tolstoy listened in silence and a shadow of annoyance passed over his face. Sighing deeply, he said: "You see, I'm doing just this, but it is hard for me."

There was much more that Granny wished to say by way of criticism, but she refrained. Yet she could not resist a parting shot on a matter that deeply concerned her as a Christian and as a relative sincerely fond of him and his family:—

"Still one word more, my dear Leo, instead of mourning over the fantastic, the impossible, and, I might even say, over the useless, have you never thought seriously over your responsibility to your children? All of them produce the effect on me of wandering between heaven and earth. What will you give them in place of the beliefs that you have probably weaned them from? For they love you too much not to attempt to follow you."

Granny was sure that this arrow had struck home. She recalled: "Leo's whole face changed and grew dark. I hastened to leave the room."

Sonya would have blessed her for these words. The arrow struck home all right, but what Granny did not guess (or maybe she did, for Sonya now poured out her complaints to any willing ear) was that for months similar barbs had been launched at the same target with remorseless frequency.

5

Toward the end of 1890 exaggerated stories had appeared in the press of the gay holiday festivities at Yasnaya Polyana and of a ball there in which Tolstoy, advocate of the simple life, had danced, dressed in a frock coat. Incredulous letters from the faithful soon began to arrive. His exasperation over this state of affairs was primarily directed against Sonya and was expressed in his aloofness from the family and in his frequent cold impersonal treatment of her.

As usual, Tolstoy's most intimate thoughts on his tribulations were set down in his diary. During 1890–1891 there are numerous entries on his acute dissatisfaction with his family life. In June 1890, he wrote: ". . . I live tied to a wife's petticoat and subservient to her, leading myself and with all the children a dirty, despicable existence, which they all lyingly excuse by the fact that I cannot transgress love." Another entry in August runs: "The egoism and disoluteness of our life, of ours and of our guests, are horrify-ng. It seems to me that it all goes on, grows stronger. It nust soon end."

Tolstoy's sincerity in wishing to live fully the life he reached can hardly be doubted, nor can his belief that his amily prevented him from doing this. Despite the charges f his wife, he felt keenly his responsibilities to his family. His dilemma was to repudiate those responsibilities and ive the life he yearned after, or accept the responsibilities nd repudiate his own life of the spirit. His situation was urther complicated by the belief that his family's way of ife was morally wrong and would prove harmful to them, nd that he ought therefore to do his utmost to save them, ot by exercising authority, but by his own example. Finally, e always felt that to leave his family in order to live his wn life would amount to evading a moral problem he ught to solve. In this situation his efforts amounted to a ompromise, little understood by his family, and entirely nisunderstood by the public. He endeavored to approach loser and closer to his ideal of life in an atmosphere that vas quite alien and unsympathetic to it.

If Tolstoy felt dissatisfied with the behavior of his chil-dren, he did not absolve himself from blame. "I get angry ver the moral stupidity of the children, except Masha," he vrote in his diary. "But who indeed are they? They are my hildren, my productions from all sides—from the fleshly nd from the spiritual. I made them what they are. They are ny sins, always before me. I have nowhere to go from them, nd that is impossible. They ought to be educated, but I m unable to do this, for I myself am bad. I have often aid to myself: If only I had no wife and children, I would ive a holy life. I have blamed them for preventing this, but fter all they are my doing, as the muzhiks say."

For some time Tolstoy had refused to have anything to lo with his property, for he considered it an evil. He now lecided that the idleness and moral sickness of his family vere in part at least caused by wealth. And this wealth ltimately came from him. In the public press he was being alled a "pharisee," and propertyless Tolstoyans living hriftily in communes wondered why the master remained he possessor of a large estate. To deprive himself and his amily entirely of the property would have fulfilled the letter f his convictions, and this was what he wished to do. Had e attempted such a solution, however, he knew that his wife would appeal to the government, which would hav been only too eager to declare him incapable of managin his affairs. He then tried to persuade Sonya to rid him o this evil by taking over all his property in full ownership "So you wish to hand over that evil to me, the creatur nearest to you," she said in tears. "I do not want it and shall take nothing." His ultimate decision was a compromis —to rid himself of the property by dividing it among hi wife and children, just as though he were dead.

This decision was hastened by an unhappy event in th winter of 1890. The bailiff of Yasnaya Polyana caught sev eral peasants felling trees; they were arrested, sentenced t six weeks in jail, and fined. They had come to Sonya t plead for a pardon, but she refused to do anything for them Her own version in her diary was that she hesitated to ac and in the meantime the peasants were sentenced. The inci dent shocked Tolstoy—here were peasants being punishe for taking from him what he regarded as theirs and a necessary for their existence. He could not sleep at night Stormy scenes with Sonya followed. She noted in her diar that she had "spasms in her throat," wanted to weep all day and that she thought of "saying farewell to all and quietl lying down somewhere on the rails." Finally he told her i the early hours of the morning, after another sleepless nigh over this affair, that he saw only two ways out for him either to leave home or to give all his land to the peasants

After this incident, steps were soon taken to bring abou Tolstoy's compromise decision to divide his estate amon the family. There was no strong opposition to this solution Sonya found something "sad and indelicate" in the whol business and complained about all the details which wer thrust upon her, since her husband would have nothin to do with the matter. Unpleasant quarrels took place be tween the older children and their mother over the division for her main endeavor was to protect the rights of th younger children. And Masha, believing in her father' principles, refused her share and came in for much criticisn from the others. The bickering disgusted Tolstoy. Afte witnessing one scene, he wrote in his diary: "It is terrible I cannot write. I have wept and want to weep again. The say: 'We ourselves would like to do this, but this woul be bad.' My wife says to them: 'Leave me.' They are silent It is horrible! Never have I seen such obvious lying and it motives. It is sad, sad, painfully tormenting."

The official act did not become effective until September 28, 1892. The total evaluation of the property was 580,000 rubles (about $290,000) and it was divided into ten equal parts to be distributed by lot between Sonya and her nine children. Under various conditions, the division gave Nikolskoye to Sergei, Ovsyannikovo to Tatyana, Grinyovka to Ilya, the Moscow house and some land in Samara to young Leo, a larger allotment of Samara land to Mikhail, Andrei, and Alexandra, and Yasnaya Polyana to Ivan and Sonya. Although Masha refused to take her portion (part interest in Yasnaya Polyana and a money allotment), her mother kept it in trust for her. At last, Tolstoy was free of his property.

Tolstoy fully realized that to surrender the ownership of his estate was not a final solution of his dilemma. The struggle between truth and the material welfare of the family continued. A still more vexatious problem, and one that had troubled him for a long time, was the income from his writings. In particular, it pained him to think that the works produced since his change of faith, containing the very thoughts by which he lived, should be sold for money, which in turn was used to support and facilitate the harmful existence of his family. Since he had already given Sonya the right to publish his works written before his religious change, he felt at the time that he could not retract this permission.

His concern is reflected in a number of diary jottings. In one (June 18, 1890), he wrote: "My sons swamp Sonya with requests for money. It will get still worse. Would it not be better if she should reject at least the income from literature. How it would leave her in peace, her sons morally healthful, me joyous, and how useful to people and pleasing to God."

Sonya vigorously opposed this latest "madness" of her husband. The income from his writing was considerable and the expenses of the family were constantly growing. Again stormy scenes, recriminations, weepings, and reconciliations. But he insisted and wanted her to write a letter to the newspapers, in which he would renounce his copyrights. She refused. He entered in his diary after one of these quarrels: "Conversation with my wife, always about the same things: to renounce the copyrights of my works. Again the same misunderstanding of me. 'I'm obligated to the children . . .' She does not understand, and the children do not understand, that in spending the money every ruble squandered by them out of the profits of the books is my suffering and shame."

The matter came to a head in July 1891. Tolstoy declared to his wife that he himself would write a letter to the press, renouncing the copyrights of his latest works. Sonya now felt that such an action would be a public avowal of his disagreement with her and his family. Harsh words followed. According to the account in her diary, he called her a greedy and stupid woman, always out for money, and said that she spoiled the children with it. She retaliated by declaring that he was ambitious and vainglorious, and always endeavoring to humiliate her. He ended by shouting at her and demanding to be left alone.

Sonya then related how she left the house, sat down by a ditch in the orchard, and wrote in her notebook that she was going to Kozlovka (the little railway station near Yasnaya Polyana) to kill herself because she was worn out with the constant trouble with her husband. Her intention apparently was to throw herself under a train, like Anna Karenina. On the way to Kozlovka, she met her brother-in-law, Alexander Kuzminski, who, noticing her distraught state, persuaded her to return to Yasnaya Polyana with him. Tolstoy acted as though nothing had happened, but later that evening when they were alone, he kissed her and made some conciliatory remarks. She now asked him to publish his announcement in the newspapers, but he said that he would not until she understood why it must be done. Sonya replied that she could not understand such an action, and she ended her account in her diary as follows: "I again told him today that I would . . .[6] no longer live with him as his wife. He affirmed that was just what he desired, but I did not believe him. He is now asleep, and I cannot go to him."

Nothing now could change Tolstoy's resolution in this matter. In July 1891, he gave Sonya two statements to publish in the newspapers, one under his name, the other under hers. She did not publish either. In September he sent her a new statement in his own name, directing that it be published in the press. He renounced the copyrights of all his works written since 1881, excepting *The Death of Ivan Ilyich,* which he had personally given to Sonya for her new edition of his works. She was in Moscow at the time, and he

[6] Twenty-nine words are deleted here in the Russian edition.

accompanied his statement with a letter, in which he wrote: "Please, darling, reflect well 'with God' (I say 'with God' as a person thinks before death, in the sight of God), and do this with good feeling, and with the consciousness that for you yourself it is a happy thing, because by this you redeem a man whom you love from a grievous situation. Any loss here, I think, will not be yours, but if that should be the case, then it ought to be more joyous for you, because a good deed is only good when it is done at some sacrifice."

This time Sonya bowed to her husband's will. On September 16, 1891, the announcement appeared in the form of a letter to the editor. In it Tolstoy gave free permission, to all desiring to do so, to publish in Russia and abroad, in Russian and in translation, and also to perform on the stage, all his works written since 1881; and he gave the same permission for any of his works appearing in the future. Although she agreed, Sonya never became reconciled to this step, and even after her husband's death she complained against this act which had deprived a numerous and not rich family of its rightful income.

6

The effort to defend the welfare of her children against what she considered the ruinous demands of their father's faith was only one phase of the emotional struggle that had long been going on between husband and wife. The family quarrels of 1890–1891 aggravated Sonya's growing hysteria, and no doubt another contributory cause was her physiological condition—her approaching "critical age." In these circumstances, her husband's aloofness was regarded by Sonya as a deliberate desire on his part to cast her aside as of no further use. With the lesson of *The Kreutzer Sonata* ever in her mind, she now understood all his attempts at intimacy as sheer physical lust. Her attitude toward him fluctuated between an overpowering desire for pure loving relations and a positive dislike.

A tendency to dwell upon pleasant memories of their married life before the "change" served further to poison Sonya's reactions to her present existence. Expressions of affection for her husband in her diary became less frequent, and criticism of him, not lacking occasional words of contempt for his new faith, noticeably increased. There was now a suggestive concentration on the subject of sex, and the picture she drew of their intimate life together reflected an abnormal state of mind. Although Tolstoy's own diary at this time recorded his struggle with the desires of the flesh, she taunted him for his lapses, and while responding to his passion, she evinced disgust and a conviction that her place in his life had always been that of an instrument for his pleasure.

Feeling ill, Sonya noted in her diary: "The fear seizes me that all these are signs of pregnancy. And it would be no wonder. . . .[7] Lyovochka is tender and always remembers me, where I am and what I'm doing. Ach, if there were only the same relations *without* this! But it rarely happens with him!" After correcting proof of *The Kreutzer Sonata,* she took exception to her husband's views in that work about the passions of young women. A young woman, wrote Sonya, satisfies her husband only because she loves him; her passion does not awake until she is thirty. Then her tender, sentimental love disappears and she becomes like her husband, that is, a seeker after her own sensual satisfaction. Sonya, however, concluded this criticism with a peculiarly Tolstoyan observation: "Happiness exists only where the spirit and the will overcome the body and passions."

Two weeks later she wrote: "Last night I became so angry that I would not talk to him. He kept me awake until two in the morning. To begin with, he was downstairs washing himself for so long that I thought he was ill. For him, washing is an event. He told me that his feet were so calloused with dirt that they had become sore. It quite revolted me. . . .[8] Then he lay down and read for a long time. I am in his way when I am not needed for his satisfaction. These days of aversion to the physical side of my husband's life are terribly depressing to me—but I cannot, I cannot get used to it—I can never get used to the dirt, the smell. . . .[9] I try with all my strength to see only his spiritual side, and I succeed when he is kind to me."

Spitefully she struck at him after a conversation they had on food, luxury, and vegetarianism, for she wrote: "He said that he saw a vegetarian menu in a German paper that consisted of bread and almonds. No doubt the person preaching this regime practices it as much as Lyovochka, preaching chastity in *The Kreutzer Sonata,* practices that."

[7] Eight words deleted in the Russian edition.
[8] Twenty-two words deleted in the Russian edition.
[9] Twelve words deleted in the Russian edition.

In the same vein she noted that he was kind and cheerful again, but she knew the reason, and then she added: "If those who read *The Kreutzer Sonata* with veneration could look for a moment at the erotic life that Lyovochka lives—the one thing that makes him happy and kind—they would cast down this little god from the pedestal on which they have placed him! But I love him when he is normal, weak, and good in his habits. One ought not to be an animal, but then neither should one be a preacher of principles which one is unable to practice."

Although his sensuality was contagious, Sonya admitted, yet her "whole moral being protested against it." And she feared the day "when he will no longer be *amorous,* and then he will cast me out of his life—cynically, cruelly, and coldly." Then she entered in her diary on April 23, 1891: "Tanya has just gone past and said that Lyovochka had asked her to tell me that he had gone to bed and had put out the light. Her innocent lips have brought me a message that is far from innocent. I know what it means, and I'm annoyed."

XXVIII

The Famine

IN THE SUMMER of 1891 Sonya had already begun to plan for a winter in Moscow. It was time for Misha and Andrei to enter a *Gymnasium*. Then she worried for fear young Leo would give up the university if he had to continue to live alone; and Tanya, she felt, would never make a match in the country. But there was the old problem of Tolstoy's loathing of city life. When she put the question to him, he refused to move. Arguments followed. Why didn't she and the children go; he would remain at Yasnaya Polyana and she could make an occasional trip to see him. No, never! she exclaimed in tears. He was throwing her away like an old piece of clothing. In the end, Sonya won; with an aggravating show of resignation, he finally agreed to do whatever she wished.

Before the time of departure, however, there were rumors of an approaching famine because of crop failures in central and southeastern Russia. Millions of peasants faced starvation. Tolstoy's first reaction seemed negative. I. I. Rayevski, a Tula official and an old friend of the family, dropped in at Yasnaya Polyana. He could talk of nothing but the danger of famine. His conversation obviously annoyed Tolstoy, who contradicted him at every turn and kept muttering to himself that it was all nonsense, and that if there were a famine, all one could do was to submit to the will of God. That summer the young family tutor, Novikov, helped Rayevski and his sons to gather statistics on the crops and stores in the neighboring district. Upon his return, he found Tolstoy unpleasantly apathetic about the famine conditions. There are always many who are hungry, he said, but the only way to help a horse to drag its load is to get off its back.

Inwardly, however, he was much concerned, as his diary indicates. The larger question of why there should be a famine at all and of the moral aspects of the customary forms of relief troubled him. "All are talking about the famine, all are worried over the starving and want to help them, to save them. And how repulsive this is. Individuals who have never thought about others, about the people, are suddenly for some reason or other seized with a desire to serve them. In this is expressed either vanity or fear, but not good." He understood that some form of organized aid was necessary, but he had long since taken his stand against conventional philanthropy. For the rich to dole out charity to the poor was an evasion of their moral responsibility. In a letter in July to his friend Leskov, who sought advice on what to do to aid the famine sufferers, he wrote in part: "A good deed does not consist merely of feeding the hungry with bread, but of loving both the hungry and the satisfied. For it is more important to love than to feed, because one may feed and not love, but it is impossible to love and not to feed." Yet he concluded by urging Leskov, a distinguished author, to write that which would touch the hearts of the rich and obtain their aid for the famine-stricken.

Without the permission of either Tolstoy or Leskov, the passage in this letter on the famine appeared in a newspaper in September. The clipping stirred Tolstoy to renewed efforts; he wished to write a long, circumstantial article, for which he needed practical experience in the famine region. For this purpose he visited his brother Sergei at Pirogovo on the edge of one of the famine districts toward the end of September, and shortly thereafter he made several other inspection tours. The conditions of the starving, disease-ridden peasants appalled him. During his travels he again met Rayevski, whom he advised to set up free food kitchens in the villages. Rayevski in turn invited him to settle at his estate, Begichevka, in the Ryazan Province, and help him organize relief in the surrounding regions. Tolstoy agreed.

The news came as a shock to Sonya. It had been such an effort to win his consent to go to Moscow for the winter; now he decided to spend it in a remote district a hundred miles from Yasnaya Polyana, and with his two oldest daughters. What would become of his indigestion and of the girls living in that wilderness? And she would be all alone in Moscow with the young children. He was even asking her for money to help the starving after giving away all his copyrights. Her first reaction was to oppose the whole undertaking. "Sonya is unwell and not in spirits, and I also," he jotted down in his diary. "I hardly slept all night. In the morning I said that this feeding of the hungry is a serious matter. She understood that I did not wish to go to Moscow. A scene began. I said venomous things and behaved badly. . . . Returning home I found her ready for a reconciliation and we made it up."

The cause was a humane one. Sonya's better instincts prevailed. She finally consented, and her husband compromised by agreeing to spend some time in the city. Sonya went to Moscow with the young children, and on October 26 Tolstoy, with his two daughters Tanya and Masha, and his niece, Vera Kuzminski, set out for the village of Begichevka in Ryazan. He was to spend a good deal of the next two years there in humanitarian work that endeared him to the Russian people.

2

Before Tolstoy busied himself with the matter, the famine had remained a kind of state secret. The government did not desire to advertise the country's misery at home or abroad. At a gathering, Alexander III replied to a question on the existence of a famine: "In Russia there is no famine, but there are localities suffering from a failure of crops." And "failure of crops" quickly replaced "famine" in the newspapers. To Tolstoy it was a famine, and he persisted in using the word in his discussions of the subject. In fact, it was partly through his publicizing it that the Russian famine of 1891–1892 became known to the world. His humanitarian efforts strangely increased the hostility of the government, Church, and reactionary individuals.

Although his theories symbolized to many the height of human folly, Tolstoy's famine relief work was undertaken without any illusions and was guided by a keen practical sense. Practicality was a trait of his nature, which manifested itself on various occasions and contributed to the extraordinary plausibility that he often instilled into his more extreme views on life. And this trait is again suggested by the wealth of homely, practical illustrations employed in his moral writings. In Rayevski's unpretentious country residence at Begichevka, a small room ordinarily occupied by the manager of the estate was assigned to Tolstoy. This room, bare of any carpet, curtains, or ornaments, and furnished merely with an iron bed, rough table, chair, and a bookshelf, became his headquarters during all his work in the famine region.

Tolstoy set to work immediately. On the basis of detailed information collected by Rayevski in the district that lay toward the southern part of the provinces of Tula and Ryazan, both men began to organize free food kitchens. They selected a central hut from among one of the poorest families in a village and offered to supply the householder with his food if he would bake bread and cook for the old, the weak, and the children up to the number of thirty or forty persons. Then provisions of flour, bran, potatoes, cabbage, beetroot, peas, lentils, oatmeal, and salt were collected. If one kitchen did not suffice in a village, a second was set up. A list was made of people who ought to be fed, and strict supervision was maintained over those who were admitted to the kitchens and over the quality of the food.

Within a month thirty kitchens were opened in twenty villages, and fifteen hundred people were receiving two meals daily. Although no meat was served, a special effort was made to keep the diet reasonably varied and yet inexpensive. This came as a surprise to the peasants, who firmly believed that rye bread was the most appetizing, wholesome, and cheapest form of food. By serving bread in smaller quantities and accompanying it with dishes such as cabbage soup, porridge, potatoes, peas, and millet broth, it was possible to provide a cheaper meal than by serving bread alone in necessarily larger quantities.

With the varied menus, a peasant could be fed for an average of seventy-five cents a month, but on a straight diet of bread it would cost a dollar and twelve cents a month. The peasants were loud in their praise of the kitchen diet, and declared that they had never eaten better food.

Scarcely had this excellent beginning been made when Rayevski, literally sacrificing his health in relief work, died from influenza. Tolstoy felt the loss greatly, for in their work together he had come to value him highly. Several weeks before his death, Tolstoy had heard from Moscow of another death that grieved him deeply—the friend of his youth, Dyakov. For many years their meetings had been infrequent but always hallowed by memories of youthful pleasures mutually enjoyed and treasured in confidence. He wrote to Sonya that nothing reminded him so much of the nearness of his own death as that of a friend who had been so close to him.

3

Tolstoy did not allow personal sorrows to interfere with the task at hand. As the winter came on, the increasing misery of the peasants and the widening of the famine belt doubled his anxiety. He saw that the job required a great deal more than the efforts of himself and his two daughters. And his was only one small district. Reports of famine conditions were coming in from other regions. His two oldest sons, Sergei and Ilya, were organizing relief in Tula Province, and young Leo had gone to Samara to set up kitchens. Above all, large sums of money were needed to buy up quantities of food for distribution. At this juncture unexpected aid came from Sonya.

Shortly after her arrival in Moscow, Sonya's attitude toward the relief work of the family changed, despite her chagrin at being left alone with the younger children in the city. She wrote her husband on November 1: "I am now entirely reconciled to your activities and I am in sympathy with them." Under this new impulse she indulged in some forthright Tolstoyan self-analysis in her diary: "As I sat down to dinner with the children today, it occurred to me how egotistical, fat, and soporific is our bourgeois city existence, without any contact with the common people, and with its lack of sympathy and help for others! I could hardly eat, so sad did I become over those who were dying from hunger, while my children and I were morally perishing in an atmosphere without any vital activity. But what is the solution?"

Sonya quickly found something to do. She wrote a letter to the editor of the *Russian Gazette,* a letter that her husband might have been proud of, and which seemed to follow his advice to Leskov to write something that would "touch the hearts of the rich." With unconscious art she described the efforts of her family, quoted a passage from a letter of her daughter Tanya about the unbelievable conditions that existed in the famine district, and concluded with a stirring appeal for help. The letter was published. Gifts of money, linen, clothes, and provisions came pouring in. Within a few weeks she collected a sum amounting to over twelve thousand rubles. The letter had been reproduced in all the Russian newspapers, translations appeared in the European and American press, and inquiries and gifts came from abroad. Sonya was in her element talking with tearful donors and listing contributions. Soon she was sending money and materials to her husband and sons, and she busied herself buying up large quantities of foodstuffs for the hungry. Sonya had become a very important part of the relief work of the Tolstoy family.

From the outset Tolstoy himself had fully realized the need of arousing the public. The conspiracy of silence fostered by the government had left the cities partly unaware of the critical situation, and urban dwellers who had some knowledge of it were peculiarly apathetic. As early as September he had sent one article on the famine to a magazine, but as time went on there seemed little chance of getting it approved by the censor. Another article, "A Fearful Problem," he finally managed to get printed in the *Russian Gazette* (November 6, 1891). His main argument in the article was that no positive knowledge existed of the amount of wheat in the country, and that this should be ascertained as soon as possible, for if the quantity were insufficient to tide the population over until the next harvest, then steps should at once be taken to buy food supplies from abroad.

This article served its purpose. The public became alarmed, and energetic measures were demanded. Further, the government's hand was forced, and wheat was supplied to the Zemstvos, the County Councils, in the famine districts for free distribution, but under conditions that limited the effectiveness of this aid. Tolstoy's efforts at publicity also stirred up violent criticism, no doubt encouraged by government officials. For the reactionary newspaper, the *Moscow Gazette,* published four articles in quick succession, attacking Tolstoy and his family for exaggerating the famine situation and for their personal crusade on behalf of the hungry sufferers. And one of the writers added a sinister note by reading into "A Fearful Problem" the political ambitions of Tolstoy as a member of a "new liberal party"; the suggestion, of course, was that the revolutionaries might well regard Tolstoy as one of themselves. This was dangerous. The government had always been hesitant to take positive action against Tolstoy in his guise as a kind of "thirteenth apostle," but as a political revolutionist they could whistle him off down the wind into exile with a clearer conscience.

Tolstoy's enemies did not have long to wait for another

opening. Because of the public stir aroused by "A Fearful Problem," the government warned newspapers not to print anything further on the famine from Tolstoy's pen. Nevertheless, learning at the end of November that the first article he had written on the famine away back in September had been definitely rejected by the censors, he instructed Sonya to send copies to English, French, and Danish admirers for translation and publication in these countries. He hoped by this means to bring the article to the attention of Russian newspapers and thus force them to reproduce it. The English translator was E. J. Dillon, then correspondent in Russia of the London *Daily Telegraph*.

Meanwhile, Tolstoy had succeeded in obtaining the censor's approval for a very abbreviated and much adulterated version of his article, which appeared in the first number of *Books of the Week* in January 1892. Dillon's translation of the original article, with deletions permitted by the author, appeared in the *Daily Telegraph* in London on January 26. Eight days later the "Moscow rats," as Granny called them, devoted the lead article of the *Moscow Gazette* to Tolstoy, a violent attack consisting of an extensive excerpt from his article in the *Daily Telegraph,* translated back into Russian, accompanied by a commentary on the author and his purpose. In one place the commentary declared: "The letters [Tolstoy's article was in the form of letters] of Count Tolstoy do not need a commentary: they are frank propaganda for the overthrow of the whole social and economic structure of the world, which, with a most understandable purpose, the Count thinks of in terms of Russia alone. The Count's propaganda is propaganda of the most unbridled socialism before which even our underground propaganda pales." Tolstoy's device had achieved its purpose, but in a manner he did not expect and did not wish.

The malicious intent of the *Moscow Gazette,* in which Pobedonostsev very likely had an interest, was clear, but there can be no question that Tolstoy provided his enemies with an easy opening. His original article, the publication of which was not permitted in Russia until 1912, contains forceful language and highly provocative ideas, but no more so than *What Then Must We Do?* finished six years before. In "Letters on the Famine," he tried to show the social and moral obligations of all to the starving masses of Russians. After describing the growing danger in the famine district and the precise needs of the peasants, he pointed out that the failure of government attempts at aid resulted from the separation of these officials from the masses. He dwelt on the ineffectiveness of the usual forms of charitable relief among the poor, and on the anomaly of the rich feeding the peasants with the food the peasants grew to feed the rich. "The common people are hungry because we are too full," he wrote. It was not a temporary situation but a permanent one, and the accepted remedy amounted merely to a vicious circle. "All our palaces," he declared, "all our theaters, museums, all this stuff, these riches of ours we owe to the effort of these same hungry people who make these things, which are useless to them, simply because they are fed by this means, that is, they will always be obliged to do this kind of work to save themselves from the death by starvation that constantly hangs over their heads." His conclusion was that help for the needy was not a matter of occasional organized relief but the personal obligation of everybody at all times. And, "The basis of every action that has for its purpose help for one's neighbor must be self-sacrifice and love." This was the kind of material in which the *Moscow Gazette* found evidence of "unbridled socialism." To be sure, the commentator strengthened his position by taking a selection out of its context and by translating Dillon's English version in such a way as to sharpen the phrases and to provide false emphasis. But such adventitious support was hardly required by this newspaper in order to discover revolutionary sentiments in what Tolstoy wrote.

This attack on Tolstoy at once created a public furor. Government and Church circles in Moscow and Petersburg evinced alarm, and high society buzzed with excitement and with a breathless sense of something terrible impending. Conservatives were elated—at last, Tolstoy, the revolutionist, unmasked; the faithful were depressed. Newspapers were categorically forbidden to reprint anything in the *Moscow Gazette* article or to comment on it. The fantastic price of twenty-five rubles was offered for a copy of the issue containing the article.

Of course, the person most alarmed was Sonya. When the safety of the family was threatened, she lost all sense of perspective and was capable of going to any extreme to protect her nest. Her sympathies were naturally on the side of the authorities and high society, and now, fearing the arrest of her husband, she was quite willing to compromise him by protesting publicly, if need be, his usefulness to the government and his loyalty to the Emperor at a time when she knew he was writing a book—*The Kingdom of God Is Within You*—that condemned all governments.

Sonya, however, had genuine cause for alarm. What she did not know at the time was that the Minister of the Interior, I. N. Durnovo, had sent a report to the Emperor on the account in the *Moscow Gazette*. He wrote that the contents of Tolstoy's article "must be considered tantamount to a most shocking revolutionary proclamation," and since this might cause an "undesirable disturbance in certain minds," he advised that Count Tolstoy in the future should be forbidden to publish in the foreign press any article directed against the government. If he refused to agree, the Minister significantly concluded, "then unfortunately it will be necessary to take other means to prevent the harmful consequences of such propaganda." Alexander III scribbled on the report: "No action at this time."

Nevertheless, to Sonya came dark rumors that she could not fail to take seriously. Her sister Tanya in Petersburg had access to government circles through her husband, and shortly after the newspaper article she wrote Sonya: "Did you know that the Council of Ministers had met and that they had already decided to propose exile abroad, but the Emperor stopped it in time. I heard the same thing from various sources. The Emperor is offended. He said that 'I received his wife, which I do not do for everyone.' And that he did not expect that they would betray him to the English, his worst enemies, etc. Of course, these are my own words; I am writing you only the sense. But concerning the proposal to exile abroad, they still tenaciously hold to it and therefore I advise you to act."

That the danger of arrest was real may be gathered from Granny's account of the situation. She was mistakenly convinced that a "son of perfidious Albion," namely Dillon, had published Tolstoy's article in England without his permission. She received anxious letters from abroad, even from America, with requests for information of what would happen to her stubborn relative, for the incident had received wide European publicity. When Granny heard the rumor that the Minister of the Interior designed to incarcerate Tolstoy in the dread dungeons of Suzdal Monastery, that graveyard of forgotten victims of the Church, she at once took action, resolved, she said, "to use all my influence to save him [Tolstoy]." A visit to the Minister[1] brought no results; he was being deluged with denunciations of Tolstoy, he protested, and could no longer keep the matter from the Emperor. Granny next sought an audience with Alexander III. He graciously called on her instead. She immediately came to the point.

"In a few days a report will be made to you about shutting up in a monastery the greatest genius in Russia."

"Tolstoy?" he tersely remarked.

"You have guessed it, Sire," she answered.

"Does that mean he is plotting against my life?" the Emperor asked.

At this Granny inwardly rejoiced, for she realized that the Emperor would not accept the severe punishment suggested by the Minister for the offense that he would charge against Tolstoy. Such turned out to be the case, and she concluded her account by saying that the Emperor answered the report of the Minister by firmly declaring: "I ask you not to touch Tolstoy. I have no intention of making a martyr out of him and thus earning for myself universal indignation. If he is at fault, then so much the worse for him."

Sonya, at the time, did not know of Granny's efforts. In a positive fright she hurried off letters to her husband to inform him of all the dire rumors and threats. Bitterly she blamed him for this new catastrophe: "You will destroy all of us with your rash article. Where, indeed, is that *love and non-resistance?* You do not have the right, with 9 children, to destroy them and me." Tanya, she wrote, had remarked: "How weary I am of being the daughter of a distinguished father," and Sonya concluded: "And how weary I am of being the wife of a distinguished husband." When it was brought to her attention that an article had appeared abroad, declaring that Tolstoy had been imprisoned, she wrote a letter to the foreign press, in which she criticized the enemies of her husband and asserted the good intentions of the government toward him. This letter received wide currency abroad. She also wrote to the Minister of the Interior and visited the Governor General of Moscow to seek advice

[1] In her account, she names the Minister as Count D. A. Tolstoy, instead of I. N. Durnovo. But Count D. A. Tolstoy, who had been Minister of the Interior, had died in 1889, whereas Granny's account refers to January 1892. This was no doubt a slip of the memory on her part, for she wrote the account several years after the events described.

on what could be done to ward off any danger that might be threatening her husband. From these sources, and from the Emperor himself, indirectly through Granny, came the suggestion that what was needed was Tolstoy's public repudiation of his article. She at once turned to her husband, begging him to write the desired letter for publication. "For God's sake, do this, quiet my fears. I'm in a terrible state of mind. What fate has entered my life to destroy it. I neither eat nor sleep, and I'm wearied as never before."

At Begichevka, calmly going about his relief work, Tolstoy was little concerned with the furor his article had caused in Russia or abroad, or with the possible dire consequences that his wife reported. But he was concerned with her extreme worry and the increasingly frantic note of despair that filled her letters as time went on and he failed to write the requested repudiation. Finally, against his better judgment, he agreed. He wrote her on February 25, 1892: "How sorry I am, my dear, that the stupid talk about the article in the *Moscow Gazette* has so troubled you and that you went to Sergei Alexandrovich.[2] Really nothing new has happened. What I wrote in the article on the famine I had said before many times and expressed much more strongly. What, then, is there new in it? All this is a matter of the mob, a hypnotized mob, growing like a ball of snow. I have written the repudiation. But please, my dear, *do not change or add a single word,* and do not even permit it to be changed."

The repudiation was equivocal and hardly did Tolstoy justice. He declared that he did not deliberately write the article in question for an English newspaper; that the selection from it attributed to him in the *Moscow Gazette* had been much altered by virtue of the twofold translation from Russian into English and then back again into Russian; that the article had been originally written for a Moscow magazine and when publication had been refused, he had, according to his custom, released it to foreign translators, and finally that an expression attributed to him by the writer of the *Moscow Gazette* concerning the steps the masses should take in order to save themselves from hunger was a complete fiction, and that his words had been used in a sense entirely opposed to his convictions.

The intention of Sonya had been to publish this repudiation in the official *Government News,* but this organ now

[2] The Governor General of Moscow.

refused to print it on the grounds that it eschewed polemical material; and other Russian newspapers had been forbidden to carry anything on this subject. However, many copies of the statement were made by Sonya and distributed through her and friends to interested people and to editors abroad. Further, when the affair had quieted down a bit, the statement appeared in print in the Russian press. Then the repudiation became generally known.

The chief victim of the repudiation was Dillon, who had originally translated Tolstoy's article for the *Daily Telegraph*. For the statement clearly implied that Dillon had published the article without Tolstoy's permission, and that his translation was faulty. The truth is Dillon had been asked by Tolstoy to translate and publish the article, and his translation is a reasonably faithful version. He visited Tolstoy and appealed to him to set the matter right, for with his honesty questioned, he was in danger of being discharged by his newspaper. Further, mutual friends, Leskov and V. S. Solovyov, protested to Tolstoy over this reflection, however unintentional, on Dillon's good faith. Tolstoy accordingly furnished Dillon with a letter, in which he affirmed the authenticity of his article in the *Daily Telegraph* and explained that mistakes in the selection from it in the *Moscow Gazette* were the result of incorrect translation from the English. Dillon forthwith published in the eager *Moscow Gazette,* and also in the *Citizen,* an explanation, accompanied by Tolstoy's letter mentioned above and an earlier letter which he had written Dillon about the translation of his article. At once, the editors of the *Moscow Gazette* returned to the charge with this new ammunition. They printed in parallel columns the Tolstoy original of their selection from his article, Dillon's English translation of it, and their Russian translation of Dillon's version, and they reached the conclusion that the revolutionary ideas they had ascribed to Tolstoy in their initial article were fully justified.[3]

Tolstoy was saddened by this whole matter, as were some of his close friends and disciples. Even Chertkov was for a moment shaken, but by indulging in sophistical hair-splitting he managed to clear the master of any moral turpitude. He stood on the dubious ground that Tolstoy's repudiation was factually correct: he could not possibly accept the altered

[3] Dillon has given his side of this whole incident in his book, *Count Leo Tolstoy: a New Portrait.*

selection from his article in the *Moscow Gazette* as his own.

However, the talk in high society circles that he had not really meant what he had said in his article on the famine and that hence an explanation to the public was due irritated Tolstoy. He no doubt blamed Sonya for some of this loose talk because of her pathetic eagerness to explain to all that her husband's intentions toward the government and the Emperor were the best in the world. Using a letter of Granny's to Sonya as an excuse, he endeavored to set his wife straight on this score. He wrote: "I see from the tone of dear Alexandra Andreyevna's letter[4] that I have been at fault in something and that I ought to justify myself before someone or other. This tone is unacceptable. For the last 12 years I have been writing what I think, and that which could hardly please either the government or the rich, and I have been writing not simply by chance, but quite consciously, and not only have I no intention of justifying myself, but I hope that those who desire this will not try to justify themselves, but will purify themselves of that which not I, but all life, accuses them. In this particular instance the following has happened: the government has a censorship, absurd and unlawful, which prevents the thoughts of people from appearing in their true light, and it naturally follows that these things appear in a distorted light abroad. The government becomes agitated, and instead of frankly and honestly correcting the situation, it again hides behind the censorship and takes offense over something and permits itself to accuse others but not itself. What I wrote in my article about the famine is part of what I have been writing and saying on all sides for 12 years and will say to my death, and what everyone in the world who is enlightened and honest says with me, what the heart of every uncorrupt person says, and what Christianity says, that very Christianity which is the faith of those who are terrified. . . . Note that my writings are in tens of thousands of copies in various languages, writings in which my views are put forth. And suddenly, because of certain mysterious letters appearing in an English newspaper, all at once understand that I am the guilty one. Truly, it is ridiculous. Only those ignorant, of whom the most ignorant are the people who belong to the Court, could fail to know what I have written, and could actually think that such views as mine could

[4] Granny's letter which Sonya had sent to him.

suddenly change in a single day and become revolutionary. All this is laughable, and for me to reason with such people is degrading and offensive."

4

This last newspaper attack left Tolstoy at Begichevka somewhat disturbed, but he contented himself by writing a few sharp remarks about the press and Dillon to the worried Chertkov. Meanwhile aid from abroad for the famine sufferers increased. Three shiploads of provisions were sent from the United States, and within two months American financial contributions reached the total of some $500,000; in England a special committee was set up to raise funds, and a part of the money was specifically allocated for the use of Tolstoy; and an independent effort of the English Quakers resulted in a contribution of £26,000. The famine, partly through the efforts of Tolstoy, had become world news, and the Russian government could no longer ignore or soft-pedal it. Tolstoy's daughter Tanya tells how a few peasants collected twenty rubles for a trip to Moscow to complain to the Governor General of the plight of their district, and for their efforts, it was said, they were promptly put in jail. But the government now discreetly encouraged private and public aid, and it issued an order that the County Councils were to assist peasants who deserved help but to withhold it from those who refused any work offered them. A kind of boondoggling sprang up, and some of the peasants almost preferred to starve than perform the nonsensical jobs invented for them.

With his understanding of peasant psychology and of their conditions of life, Tolstoy avoided the mistakes of the County Councils in the task of relief. It was not merely the immediate question of the famine; so many of these peasants were constantly undernourished and their diet hopelessly unvaried. They were also in rags: he was shocked at the sight of the children of a widow going around in the winter almost naked. They had little fuel to warm themselves in their damp, wretched, one-room huts, in which the whole family and the livestock lived in the winter. He noted that they literally got inside the ovens of their stoves to keep warm. Then there were drunkenness and laziness to combat, their ignorant opposition to improvements to overcome, and the need to explain, if not justify, the frustrations of those among them who aspired to a better life. In the face of these conditions, he clearly realized that at best all his efforts amounted to a compromise, and he told his co-workers in relief that either the peasants would remain in a state of slavery or else they would revolt, and he prophetically declared that revolt was the more likely.

Tolstoy's guiding principles in his relief activities were two: to provide work for those capable of working, in order that the peasant economy should not break down entirely, and through his kitchens to feed the starving young and old, the weak and the sick. Contrary to the fumbling efforts of government officials, however, he maintained that the work provided should be the kind that the peasants were used to, that the proper conditions for such work should be maintained, and, when required, materials should be furnished.

On the whole, Tolstoy achieved a huge measure of success in abiding by these principles. By March 1892, he and his helpers had organized 187 kitchens in four districts that fed daily some 10,000 people. Huge quantities of wood for fuel had been bought and distributed. By an arrangement with sympathetic people in regions not hit by the famine, peasant horses were sent there to be fed. Large quantities of flax and bast were given free to the peasants for the manufacture of sacking and shoes. Separate kitchens were set up for children from one to three years of age, in which special nutritious foods were provided. Seed was distributed in preparation for the spring sowing. Clothes and material for making clothes were given out to the needy. A few schools were set up in villages, and many small sums of money were supplied as gifts to individuals for debts, funerals, books, and so on. It was a fine record of achievement for the less than six months of effort.

5

Throughout most of the winter and spring of 1892 Tolstoy remained at Begichevka to direct the work of relief. He returned to Moscow during this period for several short visits, at the insistence of his wife. Sonya worried over him and her two daughters, and with reason, for the famine district was ridden with disease. A surprising improvement in the relations between husband and wife may be observed in their correspondence during these months. The reason is obvious. Sonya had identified herself with her husband's work, and her own considerable efforts in raising funds and buying provisions contributed to the success of his enterprise. Here she was closely joined with him in mutual service to others—a Christian ideal of which he had often dreamed.

In the midst of his work at Begichevka, he wrote to Ge's son that for ten years, "I have not been so close to my wife as now, and this is more important than anything else." Lonely in Moscow without him, and weary with her own efforts, she asked him to come home, saying: "What a misfortune at my age to be so attached to and to love a man such as you." And he wrote in turn: "I know only one thing, that I love you with all my soul, and I want to see and calm you."

It is interesting that in a quarrel between Sonya and Chertkov at this time, Tolstoy gently rebuked his chief disciple. Chertkov was engaged in famine relief in his own province of Voronezh, and he wrote Sonya to ask her aid in obtaining certain provisions. In informing him that his request had been fulfilled, she also took the occasion to scold him for urging her husband, "a tired, nervous old man," to hurry and finish a manuscript he was working on in order that he could send it to him as soon as possible. Chertkov, highly indignant, answered that Tolstoy himself anxiously wished to finish the work, and that he ordinarily sent his manuscripts to him, Chertkov, without his having to ask for them. Then he proceeded to lecture Sonya on the score that her husband was less nervous and possessed more spiritual equanimity than all those surrounding him, even those "quite close to him." "I am firmly convinced," he wrote, "that if you survive Leo Nikolayevich, you will in time recognize, as all the sincere friends of your family do now, that by your actions, often contrary to the desires of Leo Nikolayevich, and even though performed with the best of intentions, you not only cause him personally great suffering, but even in the practical, external conditions of life, you do him harm."

Sonya's rejoinder was prompt and tart, and the essence of it may be summed up in one sentence from her letter: "All have seen and still do see our 30 years of happily married life, and if lately it sometimes appeared that there were grievous moments, they have existed only thanks to the interference of people entirely alien to us, who have consciously and unconsciously intruded upon our family life and spoiled it." And in her letter to her husband about this quarrel, she angrily remarked: "What a stupid and one-track mind of a man! I am sorry and vexed that people see so narrowly and so little."

Chertkov sent Sonya's first letter to Tolstoy and a copy of his answer, with a pious justification for writing it and an anxious request for the master's reaction. When it came, it was crisp and edged: "I received your letter with that of my wife and your answer. You are right, but she is not at fault. She does not see in me what you see."

Although Tolstoy's visits to Moscow from Begichevka were made largely to please Sonya, most of the time spent in the city he continued to devote to relief work—writing to influential figures for aid, searching out supplies, and recruiting helpers. During his visit in January 1892, he persuaded the musician, A. G. Rubinstein, to give a concert on behalf of the famine relief. During this same visit, Tolstoy went to see his play, *The Fruits of Enlightenment,* at the Maly Theater, the author's proceeds of which were also spent on relief. According to a newspaper account the following day, he had been taken for some old muzhik at the theater, appearing there in a peasant's jacket, sheepskin hat, and felt boots, and it required some persuasion before he was admitted.

Such visits to the city during the relief work were as brief as Tolstoy could make them. Back at his "general staff headquarters," as the Rayevski house came to be called, he would plunge into manifold activities. There were numerous kitchens to inspect and new ones to set up. Statistics were compiled of the peasants fed and of their further needs, and Tolstoy kept a full account of income and disbursements. Heaps of letters on the famine from all over the world had to be answered. Much of his time was also spent in listening to individual petitions of peasants—125 separate requests, he reckoned, were made on a single day. Many were heart-rending. A peasant and his young son kneeled before him and begged for aid. Tolstoy kneeled himself and with tears in his eyes beseeched this poor muzhik, beaten by want, not to humble himself in this fashion. Another petitioner, a peasant woman, implored him not to let her daughter take food at the kitchen. Surprised, he finally drew from her that she feared her child would lose her soul to the devil if she received food from Antichrist.

This belief was one of the major annoyances that Tolstoy

had to contend with in his relief work. The Church grew alarmed over his activities among the peasants in the famine district, simply because he was Tolstoy. Two priests were sent from Tula to investigate. And, no doubt acting from orders higher up, some local priests carried out an insidious campaign directed against his efforts to help the poor. Playing upon the superstitions of the peasants, they told them: "You think that Antichrist will come to you in an evil guise. No, he will come to you with kindness, with bread at the very time when you will be dying of hunger. But woe to him who is seduced by this bread!"

Such a malicious story was fraught with danger, for gullible peasants were quite capable of taking things into their own hands, and on several occasions co-workers of Tolstoy had reason to fear the hostility of villagers. Under the impetus of the priests, a whole folklore grew up in the region about Tolstoy as Antichrist. "What kind of a Count is this, dressed in peasant fashion, going about the huts?" one of the inhabitants demanded. "Has he no shame! Always on foot, or grubbing about on horseback in storm and blizzard! He's not a human being, he's Antichrist! Where does he get such power? He merely waves one arm—money pours down like rain! He waves the other—a cart with bread rolls right up to him! The bread he gives us comes from the devil . . . !" Tolstoy told with some humor that upon entering one of the villages, a youngster ran after him all the way down the road, shouting: "Antichrist! Antichrist!"

In general, however, the peasants were not deeply influenced by the whisperings of their priests. They were starving and Tolstoy gave them good food, and they blessed him for it. A relief worker overheard two peasants talking. One said: "This Count ought to be destroyed." And the other replied: "You're a jackass to talk of getting rid of such a man. He's the cleverest of men. Just think, if the Tsar himself would actually take time off to spend as many as eighteen minutes with this man's wife . . . and you talk of getting rid of him." Another aid reported to Tolstoy that a sick peasant, who had been tended by the relief workers, kept declaring to visitors: "So you call these children of Antichrist—they are angels of God whom the Lord has sent to us."

The devotion of the peasants to Tolstoy was openly manifested when a government commission for aid in the famine halted at Begichevka. The rumor quickly spread that this imposing, uniformed group intended to arrest Tolstoy. A crowd of angry peasants immediately gathered about the Rayevski house, determined to prevent the arrest, and they were dispersed only with difficulty. When he left Begichevka at the beginning of the harvest, the touching farewell of the grateful peasants, many of whom accompanied him along the road, convinced him that they appreciated his efforts.

Yet stories about the peasant fears of Tolstoy as Antichrist crept into the newspapers, and friends engaged in relief work with him wrote an indignant letter to the press. But as though he were beyond the pale of Christian consideration, it is interesting to note that at the end of 1892, a circular from the Minister of Education requested the members of learned societies connected with Moscow University not to read papers or articles on Tolstoy in their meetings.

6

The much publicized relief work added to the Tolstoy legend throughout Russia and abroad and brought many visitors to the "general staff headquarters" at Begichevka. More important, it brought offers of sorely needed volunteer help.

Among the volunteers were seasoned Tolstoyans, some of whom were rather disillusioned, for they had been members of colonies which for one reason or another had been failing at just this time. They now found an outlet for their zeal in relief work under the direction of the master himself, but for several of them it was not an entirely satisfactory substitute for the unconventional variety of soul-saving that they preferred. Like professional revolutionists, they were never entirely happy unless they were practicing the "dissidence of dissent."

In the evenings, when the varied daily tasks connected with the relief work had ended, the helpers who were living at the Rayevski home or near by gathered at the "general staff headquarters." They sat around a large table and shared their impressions of the day and planned the work for the following day. Tolstoy might play chess, tell anecdotes, or read aloud from the latest periodicals or from the manuscript he was writing at that time—*The Kingdom of God Is Within You.* Such readings often led to serious discussions in which all hung on the words of the master. Not infrequently, however, the young Tolstoyans pressed their teacher hard, for some of them, after the failure of the colonies, were already developing heretical ideas. Their souls ached for something more substantial than the master's advice on relief work. Two disciples, A. V. Alyokhin and M. A. Novoselov, now opposed to his teaching the need of a powerful organization with deeply rooted traditions that had a strong hold on the masses. To his horror, Tolstoy saw that they meant the Church. Then another follower, V. I. Skorokhodov, sharply questioned Tolstoy's advice that he return to his wife and children and work for them. Was he not abiding by the precepts of Christ in abandoning his home and following Him? No, Tolstoy objected, a man has no right to desert his family; he must bear his cross, even though it be a heavy one. Nevertheless, Skorokhodov, taking with him young M. V. Alyokhin (a brother of A. V. Alyokhin), soon set out on foot from Begichevka to search for what he called the "heavenly Jerusalem." The disciples were now accusing Tolstoy of conservatism. "Where do they wish to go?" he sadly asked. "We should be there where we are needed." Yet this same inner demand "to go away" had been troubling his own conscience. Only a few months after these disputes with his disciples, he wrote in his diary: "Not in a moment of irritation, but in a moment most calm, it became clear that I must and should go away from Yasnaya Polyana."

For the non-Tolstoyans among the relief workers, more interesting fare turned up at Begichevka than these dour, "dark people." Repin came to make sketches, and toward the end of January 1892, Tolstoy's wife arrived. Shocked at the dirt and disorderly condition of the "general staff headquarters," she at once took charge of things. She swept through the house, putting everything in order, brought the financial accounts of the relief work up to date, and in her spare time made coats for the ragged village boys. At the end of ten days she swept out of the village, leaving everythink spick-and-span and all the workers quite breathless over her incredible energy.

One day two nameless Americans arrived and pretended to be interested in the views of Tolstoy. He talked with them in English and to his infinite disgust quickly realized that they had no interest at all in his views. They had come all this distance, he declared, simply to be able to say that they had talked with Tolstoy. "It is just as though they had read about me in a Baedeker and had come to confirm it." The local gentry, however, were as zealous in their pursuit of the great as the two Americans. They sought Tolstoy out on every occasion and exaggerated the significance of the slightest attention he paid them. In one house the owner put on exhibition the chair that his guest had used and carved on it: "L. Tolstoy sat here." And another host even treasured in a special trunk the tablecover on which Tolstoy had spilled coffee.

Of the many foreign correspondents who sought him out at Begichevka, Tolstoy was most impressed by a Swede, Jonas Stadling. He arrived in an outlandish Lapland costume, carrying a camera, and speaking no Russian, all of which convinced the peasants that this was really Antichrist who had come to set his fatal seal upon them. Stadling took a deep interest in the relief work and accompanied Tolstoy's son Leo to Samara, where he worked among the famine-stricken and eventually wrote a book about his experiences.

All the relief workers at Begichevka, however, agreed that the most extraordinary visitor was a Swedish Jew by the name of Avram von Bonde. Walking barefoot, he arrived in the village, a man of seventy, with long grayish-yellow hair and beard, clad in rags, and wearing a huge, broad-brimmed hat. As a young man he had given away all his money, having come to the conclusion that one should live according to the laws of nature. He slept on the ground, with his water bottle for a pillow, and was a strict vegetarian, even preferring his food uncooked. After having spent some thirty years in America, he had wandered all over the Far East whence, reading of Tolstoy's beliefs, he had journeyed to Russia to ask this spiritual brother for a bit of land where he could settle down and till the soil with his own hands, without the aid of animals, and thus obtain his sustenance.

Tolstoy could not fail to be touched by this frail old man who, in spiritual sympathy, had found his way to him after wandering thousands of miles. Indeed, he experienced a sense of sinfulness upon discovering another seeker after truth who was able to live up to the letter of his principles, some of which they held in common.

And yet von Bonde must have struck Tolstoy as something of a caricature of his beliefs, for his behavior caused him and the other workers many uneasy moments. Coming upon the group drinking tea around the samovar, he bluntly charged them with making an idol out of the samovar, before which they worshipped. And he insisted that the Chinese starve because they use their land for growing tea for foreign consumption instead of raising wheat. Tolstoy pitied the poor Chinese and for some time found it hard to drink tea. On another occasion von Bonde insisted upon making bread in his own fashion, pounding the unmilled kernels of wheat and mixing them with water. Tolstoy bravely sampled the finished product, and the next morning he was deathly sick. His daughter telegraphed for her mother. Sonya arrived, much agitated, to find the "naturalist" baker sound asleep on the floor, his bare legs and feet rather indecently displayed. When she learned what had happened, she forbade any further concoctions of this "dirty old man" to be fed to her husband.

Tolstoy attempted to persuade Chertkov to take von Bonde in charge. He called himself a practical philosopher, he wrote Chertkov, but "he is more than sincere, a fanatic in his ideas." Chertkov, keen as he was about spiritual oddities, declined, and Tolstoy took von Bonde to Yasnaya Polyana, where he remained for only a short time and then left the country.

7

In July 1892, Tolstoy prepared for the press what he hoped would be a final accounting of his relief efforts. In all he had set up 246 kitchens, feeding 13,000 people daily, and 124 kitchens for children, feeding 3000 daily. Up to April of that year, the contributions that had come to him personally had amounted to 141,000 rubles. He returned to Yasnaya Polyana, feeling weary but curiously empty once he had relieved himself of the huge responsibilities he had shouldered.

But what Tolstoy had feared before he left Begichevka actually happened—a recurrence of the famine. The crops that summer had been very poor, and the stricken region during the past year had not fully recovered from its ordeal. The situation, however, was not so serious in the fall and winter of 1892–1893, although severely complicated by an epidemic of typhus. He felt it his duty to return to the work of relief. But he had not yet recovered from the strain of the previous effort, and besides Sonya's interest and that of the public at large had cooled off considerably. Yet he was about to take up the burden again when his trusted and highly competent disciple Biryukov offered to assume general charge of the work under his direction. Tolstoy gladly accepted. Biryukov worked at Begichevka throughout the winter, and Tolstoy visited a number of times to give his assistant the benefit of his advice. His last visit was at the end of May 1893, and in September he wrote a final report for the press on his famine activities.

This whole experience had morally wrenched Tolstoy. At the outset of his relief work he wrote to Granny that the months spent in feeding the hungry had been the happiest of his life. He liked this practical kind of work which, as he said, was cheering and attractive and provided him with a sense of positive accomplishment. All his helpers testified to his heartiness, good spirits, and wonderful enthusiasm as he directed their efforts.

But it was not in Tolstoy's nature to be satisfied with this kind of positive accomplishment. He was partly convinced that what he was doing was wrong, or perhaps it would be more correct to say that he disapproved of the way that circumstances obliged him to feed the hungry. Had he not long since taken a stand against private charity? And here he himself was distributing the vomit thrown up by the rich, as he expressed it, in order to save the starving. Had he not condemned charity as corroding and debasing the moral nature of the poor? The more you give them, the less they will work, and the less they work, the greater will be their need. With a genuine sense of guilt, he felt it necessary to write disciples and friends to explain that he knew what he was doing was morally wrong and actually harmful to the very peasants he desired to help. After all, he was not a saint, he declared. No, he was only a weak man. The discord between his words and acts might seem to the unthinking a lie or a hypocrisy, but in reality it was only a sign of weakness. What he was trying to be, he pleaded, was a good man, a worthy servant of God. And nearly always these letters of self-condemnation concluded with the firm statement that the starving must be fed, and he could not do otherwise than help. The cold theory that the only way famines could be ended forever was for the well-to-do to change their lives, draw nearer to the common people, and return to them what they had taken from them, he confided to his articles; the hungry he fed by taking money from the well-to-do.

With all his doubts, Tolstoy could not deny his nature. He

ended one of his published reports on the famine as follows:—

"What then? Will there again be a famine? Famine! Kitchens! Famine! Indeed, this is now ancient, and so ancient as to be boring.

"It is boring to you in Moscow, in Petersburg, and here, when from morn to night they stand under the windows or in the doorways, and it is not even possible to go on the streets without hearing the same old phrases: 'We have not eaten for two days, we have killed our last sheep. Must we die?' We are not even ashamed to confess out here that we are so weary of this that we look upon these petitioners as our enemies.

"I arise very early. It is a clear, frosty morning with a red sunrise; the snow crunches underfoot; I go out and hope that I will meet no one. In vain. I have barely opened the door and there are two of them standing: one is a tall, broad muzhik, in a short, ragged overcoat, in torn bast shoes, with an emaciated face and a bag slung over his shoulder (they all have emaciated faces, as though these faces were the special characteristic of muzhiks). With him is a boy of fourteen with no overcoat, wearing a torn jacket, also in bast shoes, and with a bag and a stick. I want to get by them. They begin with the usual bows and speeches. There's nothing for me to do but turn back to the vestibule. They approach.

" 'What is it?'

" 'I've come to your honor.'

" 'What?'

" 'Have pity on us.'

" 'What do you want?'

" 'It's about help.'

" 'What kind of help?'

" 'It's from hunger. Help us to a bite.'

" 'Where are you from?'

" 'From Zatvornoye.'

"I know that this is an impoverished village where we have not yet succeeded in opening a kitchen. Scores of beggars come from there, and I at once size up this man as a professional beggar, and I am vexed that they even lead children about with them and degrade them.

" 'Just what do you wish of me?'

" 'Only consider us somehow.'

" 'But how am I to give you consideration? We can't do anything here.'

" 'We'll go . . .'

"But he does not listen to me. And he again begins what I have heard hundreds of times, addressing me with hypocritical speeches:—

" 'There were no crops, there are eight children in the family, I'm the only worker; my old lady is dead; we ate our cow last summer, last Christmas the horse died. Well, let it go, but the kids beg for food; there's no place to get it; for three days we haven't eaten.'

"This is how it goes, always the same thing. I want to see if he will soon finish. But he keeps saying:—

" 'I thought I would try somehow, but the strength has gone out of me. I've never begged, now God has brought me to it.'

" 'Well, all right, we will go soon and see,' I say and I try to go past him, but my glance by chance falls on the boy. The youngster looks at me pitifully, his beautiful brown eyes filled with tears and hope, and a single tear-drop rolled down his nose at that moment, and fell on the snow-trodden boarded floor of the vestibule. The boy's sweet, worn face, with his flaxen hair curling in a crown round his head, twitched with suppressed sobs. For me the words of his father are an old, customary annoyance. But for him, this recital of the harsh times he has experienced with his father, a recital at just this solemn moment when at last they have made their way to me and to help, unnerves him, weakened as he is by hunger. To me, it is all wearisome, wearisome, and I think only of how to get away quickly for my walk.

"To me it is old, but to him terribly new.

"Yes, it has wearied us. But they still want to eat, to live, to be happy, to love, just as I see by the charming tear-filled eyes of this boy fixed on me that he also desires all this too, good, unhappy lad that he is, tortured by want and full of naïve self-pity."

XXIX

The Kingdom of God

FAME, INSATIABLE FAME, that is what he has always striven for and what he will continue to strive for." This was a theme that Sonya frequently harped upon now in her more hostile moods toward her husband. Tolstoy would have frankly admitted to the temptation of fame, but it was a devil that he constantly guarded himself against. In letters to friends during the famine relief work, he decried the public praise accorded his efforts. Whether he liked it or not, however, he had become a public, in fact an international, celebrity. One after the other the books and articles forbidden by the censor appeared promptly in many foreign countries, both in Russian and in translation, and often the copies found their way back to his native land by illegal means. Admirers pointed to him as not only the conscience of Russia, but the conscience of the world.

In 1893 Tolstoy was elected an honorary member of the Russian-English Literary Society, a distinction that seemed to please him. A letter that he wrote at this time to commemorate the fifty years of literary activity of D. V. Grigorovich provoked such a demonstration when read to the audience that it appeared as though it were Tolstoy instead of Grigorovich who was being feted. In general, he shunned crowds and meetings, and even on the street he hurried along, looking neither left nor right, as though fearing recognition. Yet he was often recognized, for his features had become widely known through published portraits and photographs. On trains he tried to preserve anonymity in order to draw out fellow passengers in conversation, but if recognized he could quickly become stiff and formal. Granny told of meeting him by chance on a train. While chatting she was bothered by a suspicious looking man who fluttered about Tolstoy, interjecting a word here and there, trying desperately to start up a conversation. Granny asked who he was, and Tolstoy replied: "He is someone who desires to prove to the public that he is intimate with me, so do not be surprised at the dry manner in which I answer him." At the end of their talk he asked her if she were not ashamed to be seen with him in public. "Such questions are called in English 'fishing for a compliment,'" she observed. "But surely, my dear, you must know that there are many women who would like to be in my place at this moment." And she concluded with the sarcastic comment: "My compliments were so rare that he was quite satisfied with this one."

At the beginning of January, 1894, the annual conference of Russian scientists took place in Moscow. Young Zinger, son of the distinguished mathematician, gave Tolstoy an interesting account of the learned papers that had been read, and he urged him to attend a session the next day when his father, a good friend of the family, would talk on geometry. "I would go," Tolstoy replied, "but I do not like this sort of parade, and I fear the public, especially when the Grand Duke [the Governor General of Moscow] is present." The next day, however, young Zinger got word to him that the Grand Duke would not be present and that he would arrange it so that the public would not disturb him. Tolstoy appeared at the meeting with his daughter Masha, and young Zinger ushered him through a side entrance to a room off the platform. Unable to hear the elder Zinger's speech clearly, he edged onto the platform. He was recognized at once and a murmur ran through the whole audience. Zinger concluded his address with much difficulty, and at the end the distinguished scientist and chairman of the conference, K. A. Timiryazev, conducted Tolstoy to a place beside him on the platform. There he sat in his characteristic peasant blouse among the learned gentlemen in their frock coats. Bedlam broke loose in the audience and the cry rose: "Hurrah for Tolstoy, hurrah!" The roar grew louder and louder, and at last, frowning and obviously embarrassed, he was obliged to stand and acknowledge the tribute.

"My God, what are you doing to our old gentleman! Aren't you ashamed!" exclaimed Masha, standing at the end of the hall, shutting her eyes and holding her hands over her ears. "It's Leo Nikolayevich's own fault," shouted a friendly scientist at her side. "Why does he appear so rarely in public? Then you'll agree, Marya Lvovna, that there is something fine in all this. Is it not true?" She nodded agreement.

His shyness in public vanished in meetings with the many strangers, seekers after truth, who visited him at Yasnaya Polyana or at the family's Moscow house. On these occasions he was always the genial, considerate host, ready to listen, but he soon took command of the conversation by virtue of his dominant personality. Such visitors were often puzzled by the striking contrast between the notion they had formed of Tolstoy through his writings of an ascetic, plain-living prophet and the first impression they received of his comfortable, well-appointed dwelling. One of these visitors rang the bell of the Moscow house in March 1894. A butler, dressed in a frock coat and wearing a white cravat and gloves, admitted him. To this show of luxury were added the fine furnishings of the entrance hall. The family was just finishing dinner, and Tolstoy soon appeared, straight, broad-shouldered, with grizzled hair, and bits of chopped cabbage still clinging to the vegetarian's long beard. His piercing, deep-set eyes twinkled as he cordially greeted the stranger and asked him to follow. Dashing up a flight of stairs, despite his sixty-six years, he led him through a narrow corridor to his study. This low-ceilinged room, sparsely and simply furnished, at once struck the guest as more in keeping with the man he had read about than the obvious "well-bred" appearance of the rest of the house. Quickly placed at his ease, he was amazed in the ensuing conversation at Tolstoy's memory, for he recalled in detail things that this visitor had written to him eight years previously, and which he himself had entirely forgotten.

At this time Tolstoy also got much pleasure out of visiting the headquarters of the *Intermediary*. Toward the end of 1893 Chertkov had decided to relinquish control of this publishing business. Although he had made a success of it, the problems of censorship had increased, and he wished now to devote more time to his own spiritual development. Further, he had become a kind of literary agent for Tolstoy, managing the translation and publication of his forbidden works abroad. Biryukov agreed to take charge of the *Intermediary* and was assisted by Gorbunov-Posadov. The headquarters were moved from Chertkov's Voronezh estate to Moscow. Besides the huge volume of cheap editions for the masses, two new series were now pushed—various books designed for intellectuals, and a philosophical series. Chertkov offered his services to Biryukov as an occasional editor and translator, in the hope of earning sufficient money to enable him at last to surrender the unearned income from his estates. But this last effort to practice what he preached and live off "bread-labor" failed, for the salary the *Intermediary* could afford to offer him, he decided, was insufficient for his needs.

Tolstoy's interest in the firm under Biryukov's direction did not abate, and he continued to make suggestions for publication, to edit books, and to publish his own works, whenever the censor permitted, under this imprint. The firm also became a kind of refuge for those seekers after truth who appealed to Tolstoy for aid. He occasionally dropped in to the regular Thursday "at home" of the *Intermediary* workers. A special armchair was always ready for him, and these fervent, like-minded young men and women would sit at the master's feet, drinking tea and listening to him pronounce at length on terrorism, socialism, God, and universal love.

2

Tolstoy's enjoyment of this close association with disciples working for the *Intermediary* was mingled with sadness over the persecution now being suffered by his followers. From 1893 both Church and government officials began to intensify their activities against Tolstoyans and others who had been only slightly influenced by his teachings. The refusal of army service was the chief offense in the eyes of the authorities, for this represented a potential danger to a great military power. But pretexts for persecution were not hard to find among government officials who, afraid of making a martyr out of the internationally famous teacher, tried to reach him through his obscure pupils. The police were content now to keep the master under strict surveillance. Tolstoy deliberately made a friend of one of the police spies sent to watch him during the summer of 1894 at Yasnaya Polyana, and his arguments soon reduced the agent to repentance and to abandoning his sleuthing.

Tolstoy and his closest disciples were shocked when they heard, toward the end of 1893, that the exiled Khilkov's two children had been taken from him by the command of the Emperor, baptized against the will of their parents, and put in charge of their grandmother. This action also had the blessing of the Church. All the mother's pleas that her children be returned to her were unavailing. In deep sorrow, Tolstoy wrote to Khilkov to urge him and his wife, whom he pitied most of all, not to abandon the moral and religious principles by which they lived because of this misfortune. And he also wrote to the grandmother in an effort to persuade her to surrender the children to their parents. When this failed, he wrote to the Emperor (January 1894) to plead the cause of the Khilkovs, but his request was silently ignored. The children were never released to their father and mother, and in 1901 Chertkov, when he was safely in England, wrote up the whole story in a pamphlet: *The Kidnapping of the Khilkovs' Children.*

Shortly after this outrage, Tolstoy learned of another tragedy among his followers—the death in prison of his young disciple, E. N. Drozhzhin (January 27, 1894). Tolstoy wrote to a spiritual friend that "the passing of Drozhzhin and the separation of Khilkov's children are two of the most important events which in themselves make great moral demands on all of us." Drozhzhin, a humble village schoolmaster, had refused to take the soldier's oath when called up in 1891, declaring that his religious convictions made it impossible for him to learn to slay his fellow men. He was promptly clapped into solitary confinement for a year and then sent to a disciplinary battalion. When the rigors of this treatment brought about consumption, he was declared unfit for service but sentenced to nine years' imprisonment. Chertkov visited him in prison and reported to Tolstoy about his meekness, unfailing convictions, and cheerful spirits despite the vile treatment he received from his jailors. Finally his health broke down completely under the ordeal and he died. Drozhzhin's fate deeply impressed Tolstoy, and with a feeling of consecration he provided a moving introduction to an account of his life, written by another follower, E. I. Popov. These publications concerning the persecution of Tolstoyans, which of course could only appear abroad, provided highly effective propaganda against the Russian Church and State. The government tried to neutralize this effort in 1894 by forbidding Russian journalists to quote from anything appearing in foreign newspapers about Tolstoy's life or works.

The persecutions mounted. In 1894 Tolstoy's follower M. V. Bulygin was sent to prison, and the next year M. A.

Sopotsko[1] and N. T. Izyumchenko; and the quarters of Biryukov and Popov were searched by the police in the hope of discovering incriminating literature. Tolstoy did what he could to aid these victims. Whenever possible, he visited them in prison, furnished them with material comforts, and wrote encouraging letters, urging them to abide by their convictions. He found himself wishing that he were in the place of these sufferers for the faith. "I understand you," Sopotsko wrote him from his cell, "when you desire to suffer, when you say that you envy me, as you said in the Tula prison." In his letters and diary at this time sounds a persistent note of regret over his freedom, a measure of self-reproach that he was not allowed to share the misery of his persecuted disciples. Apparently he felt humiliated in being a modern Christ without a cross to bear.

Then on a summer stroll he beheld a beautiful sunset and his sadness was dissipated by the eternal miracle of nature. He jotted down in his diary: "No, this world is not a joke, and not a vale of trials or a transition to a better, everlasting world, but this world here is one of the eternal worlds that is beautiful, joyous, which we can and must make more beautiful and more joyous for those living with us and for those who will live in it after us."

Another sorrow that Tolstoy found hard to bear in 1894 was the death of his old friend Ge (June 1). Their admiration for each other's art had been nurtured by a long spiritual partnership. Ge had become the great religious painter of Tolstoyism. He worshipped the master as though he were already canonized, and his ingenuous, transparent nature, filled with gentleness and humility—"a charming, talented, ancient child," as Tolstoy described him—endeared him to all. Several months before his death he had finished his last notable canvas—"The Crucifixion." It depicted Christ on the cross with merciless, almost repugnant, realism, but at the same time suggested something of His heavenly mission on earth. The picture was first hung privately in Moscow, and Ge took Tolstoy to see it.

> Their agitation [wrote Biryukov, who was present] had risen to an extreme point when Leo Nikolayevich entered the studio and halted before the picture, fixing on it his penetrating glance. N. N. Ge, unable to stand the ordeal,

[1] Sopotsko later returned to Orthodoxy and became a violent critic of Tolstoy.

> ran out of the studio into an anteroom. At the end of several minutes, Leo Nikolayevich came out to him and found him humbly awaiting his judgment; he stretched out his hands to him and they threw themselves into each other's arms in an embrace. Soft, restrained sobs were audible. They both wept like children, and through his tears I heard Leo Nikolayevich say: "How could you have accomplished it!"

When the canvas was first exhibited publicly in Peters-urg, the President of the Academy of Art, Grand Duke 'ladimir Alexandrovich, turned away from the picture in isgust, exclaiming: "It is a shambles!" Such a comment rom this lofty personage was sufficient to cause the removal f the canvas. Upon learning of it, Tolstoy wrote a com-orting letter to Ge, in which he said in part: "The removal f your picture and what they said about it are fine and nstructive. In particular the words: 'It is a shambles.' These vords declare to all: in order to depict an execution, that 'ery execution which is now produced, it has to be done so hat they can look at it with pleasure as at some display of lowers. Such is the astonishing fate of Christianity!"

This disappointment, however, as in the case of his pic-ure "What Is Truth," disheartened Ge and no doubt con-ributed to his death a few months later. For weeks Tolstoy's etters and diary were full of his deep grief. He described im as "one of the greatest of artists, and one who had cre-ted an epoch in art." With Tretyakov, who did not have a 'ery high opinion of Ge's work, Tolstoy got into an acri-nonious correspondence at this time in an effort to prove o this connoisseur the immortality of his dead friend's art. \nd in spite of his own ideas about wealth, he was not bove looking around for a "rich man" who would endow museum for the sole purpose of exhibiting all of Ge's aintings.

Ge's son sent him a full account of the death and con-luded: "I have written you all these details because I be-ieve that, although they will pain you, you will want to now fully how your truly sincere and best friend died. 'ather loved you as I never saw anyone love another person. Every day he read your works many times, and one may ven say that his every conversation inevitably hinged on 'ou." Tolstoy replied to thank the son for his thoughtfulness nd added: "I have hardly ever experienced such a great eeling of loss as I experience now. I cannot grow accustomed to it, and several times a day I recall it and for a moment do not believe it, and the next day I again experience a feeling of loss."

Another death in 1894 (October 20), that of Alexander III, left Tolstoy with a quite different feeling. He wrote his friend N. Ya. Grot that he was "very sorry" to hear of the passing of the Tsar, just as he would be for any "man suffering and dying with a soul so grievously burdened," but that this pity did not oblige him to change his opinion about "the deplorable deeds of his reign."

3

The government's intensification of its persecution of Tolstoy's followers may be attributed in part to the publication of his highly significant book, *The Kingdom of God Is Within You,* which first appeared in a Russian edition in Berlin at the beginning of January 1894. He had started it four years before, intending to write merely an article, but as the work assumed greater importance in his eyes, it took on the proportions of a full-length book.

Tolstoy's prolonged activities during the famine considerably interrupted work on *The Kingdom of God,* and more urgent literary tasks, such as the famine articles and reports, interfered. In 1891 he also finished "The First Step," a powerful plea for vegetarianism. The novelist's art employed in the horribly realistic description of the slaughterhouse and its victims, material that he gathered at first hand, makes his argument almost irresistible. To a collection published in 1891 to aid the famine sufferers, he offered his charming folk tale, "The Worker Emelyan and the Empty Drum," written in 1886, and which now proved acceptable to the censor after "Tsar" in the story had been changed to "chieftain"; and in 1892 he published, in a collection of tales and verse about mothers and children, his wonderful *First Recollections,* which though entirely autobiographical possesses the exquisite artistic charm of his first printed work of fiction, *Childhood.* At the beginning of the next year appeared "The Coffee-House of Surat," which he had adapted in 1887 from J. H. Bernardin de Saint-Pierre's tale. And during the famine period he continued to work at odd moments on *Father Sergei, Resurrection,* and other artistic designs.

But *The Kingdom of God* absorbed most of the time he

t free to devote to writing throughout these busy years. ᴇ wrote Chertkov: "Never has any work cost me so much ort, or so it has seemed. I want to finish it, and yet I all be sorry to part with it." Of course there was no hope its being published in Russia. Strakhov wrote Tolstoy that ᴇ censor of foreign books declared, when *The Kingdom God* had been submitted to him in a French translation,[2] at "this is the most harmful of all books that he had ever d an occasion to ban."

In this remarkable work Tolstoy carried his Christian archism to its ultimate development. The core of the book alt with his theory of nonresistance to evil, which he now plied to governments. He reached the conclusion that they re all essentially immoral and existed for the advantage the rich and powerful, persecuting the masses of mankind rough their use of force in wars, in maintaining prisons, d in collecting taxes.

Tolstoy devoted much of the first part of the book to a nsideration of the criticism of the doctrine of nonresistance evil which he had first advocated in *What I Believe* in 84, while at the same time he paid tribute to those who d preceded him in publicly professing this belief. Many these criticisms came from foreign countries, but some longed to native clerical and lay writers, although *What I lieve* had been officially banned in Russia. With some mor he pointed out that even the government encouraged e refutation of a book supposed to be unknown, and argu- ents against it were set as themes for theological essays in ᴇ academies. All the critics, he maintained, had ignored e approach of *What I Believe*—Christ's teaching as a phil- ophical, moral, and social doctrine—and had persisted in garding Christ solely as the founder of a religion of wor- ip and personal salvation. And further, Tolstoy declared, ᴇ critics accused him of preaching moral perfection, hereas he had made it clear that every condition, according Christ's teaching, is merely a stage on the path toward attainable inward and outward perfection and is there- re of no significance itself; blessedness lies only in progress ward perfection. He then condemned Christian churches all denominations for perverting the true teaching of rist in order to maintain their power over the masses

[2] A French translation of the book had appeared in France in 1893, lier than the first Russian edition in Berlin.

upon whom their economic existence depended. Nor c he accept the conviction of many intellectuals of that ti that the real import of Christ's teaching rested in its su posed advocacy of service to all humanity. Christian teac ing, said Tolstoy, had nothing in common with sociali or communists or any preachers of the universal brotherho of man which was based on the advantageousness of su a brotherhood. For true Christian teaching had a firm a clear basis in the individual human soul, while love humanity was only a theoretical deduction from analogy.

Tolstoy also considered the contradictions that exist tween our life and our Christian consciousness. He assert that the chief reason for all the misunderstandings was t belief that Christ's teaching could be accepted withc changing our life. But recognition of this error was beco ing more and more general. "Humanity has outgrown social and governmental stages and has entered upon a n one. It knows the doctrine that should be made the ba of life, but through inertia continues to keep to the c forms of life. From this discord between the new und standing of life and its practice, a series of contradictic and sufferings results, which poisons our life and deman its alteration."

The remainder of the book was concerned with an exar nation of the powers and activities of governments tl enable them to prevent the masses of mankind from reso ing, in favor of Christ's teaching, the contradiction tl exists between their present life and their Christian co sciousness. Force or violence he singled out as the ch instrument that governments employ to maintain themsel in power and the people in subjection to the un-Christi life thrust upon them. Every manifestation of governmen force was treated, but most extensively military conscripti and war. The result was one of the most scathing denun ations of war ever written.

Tolstoy did not accept revolution as a way out. The v lence of revolution he abhorred, and history had taught h that in such forcible changes of government the masses a the sufferers and under the new government oppression no way lessens but sometimes even increases. There is further danger in revolution, he declared. The one sph of human life on which governmental power does not e croach—the domestic, economic sphere—now, "thanks the efforts of communists and socialists, is being gradua encroached upon, so that labor and recreation, housing, dress, and food will all (if the hopes of the reformers are fulfilled) gradually be prescribed and allotted by the governments."

The only escape from the violence and oppression of governments, Tolstoy concluded, was for all mankind to live according to the true precepts of Christ. Man must understand that "his life does not belong to himself or his family or the State but to Him who sent him into the world, and that he must therefore fulfill not the law of his personality or family or State, but the infinite law of Him from Whom he has come—and he will feel himself absolutely free from all human authorities and will even cease to regard them as able to trammel anyone."

Nor did Tolstoy hesitate to blueprint the way of salvation for the man aroused to an understanding of true Christianity. His first precept was to remember that the only guide for a Christian's actions is to be found in the divine principle that dwells within him, which in no sense can be checked or governed by anything else. Man must not suppose that the amelioration of life would come about, as the socialists preached, by some spontaneous, violent reconstruction of society. The freedom of all men could be brought about only by the liberation of individuals separately. Every man, hearkening to the dictates of his conscience and abiding by the teaching of Christ, must quietly refuse to serve the government in any way: he must refuse to take an oath, to pay taxes, or to serve in the army. If he was persecuted for thus violating the law, he must not oppose violence by force. In short, Tolstoy anticipated a growing movement of civil disobedience based on the principle of nonresistance to evil, which he was convinced would eventually undermine the whole structure of government. He believed that such a forward movement of humanity toward a more conscious assimilation of the Christian conception of life already existed. This moral progress, he felt, ultimately would influence public opinion, and once such an informed public opinion gained the ascendancy, it would transform all the activity of men and bring it into accord with Christian consciousness. Then truly would the Kingdom of God on earth be achieved by every man first realizing that the Kingdom was within himself.

It is impossible in a brief analysis to suggest the persuasiveness of Tolstoy's closely reasoned argument, running over almost five hundred pages, and there is also a danger of minimizing its effectiveness, for there is hardly any refutation of the many issues he raised that he himself did not anticipate. The fault he committed in all his didactic works, that of generalizing on the basis of special conditions that existed in Russia, is everywhere in evidence in this book. There was a manifest unfairness in his failure to give credit to the democratic progress of governments of Western Europe and America, although he bluntly declared that the only difference between a despotic government and the republics of France and America was that, in the former, power was concentrated in the hands of a small number of oppressors and the violence was cruder, whereas in the latter, power was divided among a larger number of oppressors and was expressed less crudely.[3]

In his arraignment of the abuses of modern governments—mere Genghis Khans with telegraph wires, he described them, using a phrase of Herzen—and in his condemnation of violence and the folly of war, he struck responsive chords all over the world and exercised a tremendous influence on various reform movements. He saw clearly that the whole history of the last two thousand years had consisted essentially of an alteration of relations between the moral development of the masses and the demoralization of governments. He placed his faith in this moral development of the masses as a final answer to the universal oppression of the many by the few; progressive forces today tend to seek an answer in the organized political and material development of the masses. Tolstoy's critical thought directed against nineteenth-century political, economic, and social institutions was entirely in the tradition of progressive critical thought that came after him. His extreme views on the complete abolition of property, the outlawing of war, the establishment of universal peace, and the economic self-sufficiency of the masses have been reflected in the more temperate thinking later on the need of public ownership of utilities, international disarmament, world peace through a United Nations organization, and universal economic democracy.

[3] The movement today among one or two of the most democratic governments to establish peacetime military conscription would have been regarded by Tolstoy as proof positive of his contention that they have no more essential regard for Christian conscience than the most autocratic governments.

4

The year 1894, which had brought death and persecution to his followers, had begun pleasantly enough for Tolstoy with a merry party at the family's Moscow house. While the grownups were seated around the tea table on the evening of New Year's Day the children suddenly dashed into the room to announce the arrival of masked visitors. Figures made up as Rubinstein, Repin, Solovyov, and other distinguished friends of the family filed in. One of the maskers, the actor Lopatin, perfectly represented Tolstoy, dressed in the dark gray blouse and striking the characteristic pose, with his hands stuck in his belt. When he approached Tolstoy, shaking hands with him and wishing him health, the delighted company roared with laughter, and Tolstoy louder than any.

He was always ready for a frolic of this sort. If only the family did not spend money so and occupy itself with the idle pleasures of the well-to-do—pleasures that any family on the same social level enjoyed. As usual the diary soon testified to his disgust with the "empty, sumptuous, deceitful Moscow life," and before January ended he went off with Tanya to visit the country homes of his sons, Ilya and Sergei. The "slave" labor that Ilya employed on his estate, however, revolted his father, who wrote bitterly about it to his son Leo, who was in France at that time for reasons of health.

At the urgent request of Chertkov, whose wife was severely ill, Tolstoy and his daughter Masha visited them at Rzhevsk during the last week in March. Biryukov also arrived for this occasion. Here was a holy gathering of the faithful. The presence of the master, like a miracle, seemed daily to improve the health of Chertkov's wife. In a radiant mood he wrote to Sonya: "I am very glad that I came; he, indeed they, are so sincerely glad, for we are so close spiritually, have so many interests in common, and see each other so rarely, that it is fine for both of us."

Back in Moscow Tolstoy received a letter, requesting him to express an opinion on Esperanto. He obliged at some length, perceiving in a universal language an instrument for more readily spreading the gospel of God. Whether Esperanto was the desired medium, he modestly declared his incompetence to say, but he did admit to learning to read the language in two hours, testimony that the Esperanto advocates fully exploited.

In the meantime, Tolstoy had resumed his literary activities. In 1893, shortly after concluding his extensive labors on *The Kingdom of God Is Within You,* he wrote an essay, "Non-Acting," inspired by the contrast between a speech delivered by Zola and a letter written to a French newspaper by Dumas. Zola counseled the young generation to put their faith in science. Dumas criticized the youth for their failings and urged them to apply to life the law of brotherly love. Naturally Tolstoy dismissed Zola's advice as dangerous and stupid (he never had any use for his novels either), and supported Dumas's advice by pleading with the young to organize their life in conformity with their consciences. Irritated by an unsatisfactory French rendering of this essay that appeared, he translated it into French himself, rearranging it in the process. He had an excellent command of French and a real feeling for the language.

Tolstoy's last completed work in 1893 had been a long and dry essay, "Religion and Morality," intended as an answer to two questions put to him by a German Ethical Culture Society: What did he understand by the word "religion"; and: Was it possible to have a morality independent of religion in the sense that he understood the word? After an extensive investigation of all aspects of the questions, he provided the following answers: "Religion is a certain relation established by man between his separate personality and the infinite universe or its Source. And morality is the ever-present guide to life which results from that relation." He wrote to his friend Charles A. Salomon, French industrialist and social thinker, who wished to publish a translation of this essay in the *Revue Chrétienne,* to ask him not to do so: "I fear everything that bears the name 'Christian.'" It is interesting to note also that since Tolstoy had publicly renounced the copyrights of his works written after 1881, certain foreign publishers took advantage of this fact to advertise themselves as having exclusive rights to his productions, and he asked Salomon at this time to insert in the French papers his original declaration on the copyrights, and to add that no firm had exclusive rights to his works.

During 1894 Tolstoy worked at a variety of compositions, but the most extensive and best known is a long essay, *Christianity and Patriotism.* In this he set down in condensed form the arguments he had elaborated in *The Kingdom of God Is Within You.* It lacks the spiritual intensity of the longer work, but begins with a keen and often amusing account of the manufactured patriotic enthusiasm that gripped Russia and France on the occasion of the visits of the respective fleets of these countries to Kronstadt and Toulon.

In answer to Baroness A. G. Rosen, who requested light on certain religious questions, Tolstoy wrote another epistolary article, "Reason and Religion." The whole purpose of this essay was to show that man had received direct from God only one instrument wherewith to know himself and his relation to the universe—reason, and that therefore it was entirely proper for man to exert the whole strength of his mind to elucidate for himself the religious foundations on which he rested. Here we have Tolstoy, the rationalist, protesting against mysticism or revelation of any sort, a protest that worried certain of his mystically minded disciples.

A brilliant piece of literary criticism that he completed in 1894 was an introductory essay to a translated collection of Guy de Maupassant's tales, which he had also helped to select. For some time now he had been interested in Maupassant and had translated two of his stories. It was an interest that surprised and even shocked some of his followers. For a time he stoutly defended his judgment, placing Maupassant next to Victor Hugo as one of the best writers of the age. Many judge him wrongly, he declared, for he perfectly understood and explained the whole negative side of the relations of the sexes. Although he admitted that Maupassant approached this theme incorrectly at first, Tolstoy maintained that in his later tales he described the sufferings and spiritual torment born of base relations with women as no other writer had done.

The longer Tolstoy worked at his task, however, the more disillusioned he became with the subject. To his son Leo, who had been joined in Paris by his sister Tanya, he wrote: "I am working over the introduction to Maupassant. The wretches have announced that whoever buys the second volume of Maupassant will have Tolstoy's article on Maupassant,[4] and now I must present the article or be scolded. But Maupassant's moral filth has become repugnant to me, and I have thrown away my first introduction and begun to

[4] The publisher had advertised this fact in the first volume of the tales.

write a new one, in which I wish to say what I think about art, but as yet I have not been able to express it."[5]

5

The summer of 1894 at Yasnaya Polyana was crowded with activity. Tolstoy had scarcely got settled in the country when an American visitor arrived, Ernest H. Crosby. A few days before, he had turned up at the Moscow house, looking for him, and Sonya hurried off a letter to her husband to say: "How did you like Mr. Crosby? I was in raptures over him. Intelligent, refined, educated, and well-bred. Besides, he has a fine appearance and is very serious." This was the kind of disciple she could relish. Tolstoy replied rather dryly: "Crosby, like all Americans, is proper, not stupid, but all show."

As a man of means Crosby had successfully entered New York politics and subsequently had accepted an appointment as judge of the Mixed Courts in Egypt. A French translation of Tolstoy's *On Life* had fallen into his hands at Alexandria and filled him with utter dissatisfaction with his comfortable way of life. After writing Tolstoy, he came, like some prodigal son, seeking advice from the master on how to redeem his past and live in the future according to the teaching of Christ. Tolstoy, doubting his sincerity at first, urged him to support the work of Henry George upon his return to America. Somewhat to Tolstoy's surprise, Crosby followed his advice, lectured up and down America, founded the League for Social Reform, and wrote, among other things, three volumes of poetry dedicated to the Tolstoyan way of life. Tolstoy regretted Crosby's use of verse as a medium of expression, but he soon grew proud of his new disciple and saw to it that the *Intermediary* published his books in Russian translation.

Tolstoy's powerful, far-ranging mind provided family and guests with a liberal education. Since he had become a world figure the press of the world came to his house, and although he had lost none of his contempt for journalism, he

[5] In 1894 Tolstoy also wrote an introduction to the translation of A. F. Amiel's *Journal intime,* and he translated Mazzini's *Letter on Immortality* and a Buddhist tale, *Karma,* to which he wrote a foreword; and he also wrote an introduction for the tales of the peasant writer S. T. Semyonov.

now read a large variety of newspapers. Guests requested his opinions on all manner of daily happenings reported in the press, from a local murder to Chicago labor troubles, and rarely did they find him uninformed. There was never anything hackneyed about his judgments of what he read, but what struck his listeners most was his extraordinary ability to illustrate his points by endless references to scenes and characters in the works and by extensive quotations. He was a born teacher, and the instinct was so strong in him that his replies to questions seemed naturally to take the form of lectures. Though sometimes long, they were never dull, for his intellect moved over the material like a lambent flame, always illuminating the dark corners with original thought. Apparently he made a practice, if he were interested in a writer, of reading and even rereading everything he ever wrote: He had recently reread all of Rousseau and had gone through the whole forty-two volumes of Goethe, whom he did not particularly like.

Often, it seems, his antipathy to running with the herd led him to make quixotic and extravagant statements. He had a horror of conventional judgments, and at times one can detect deliberate wrongheadedness instead of the wisdom of genius in his opinions. In a discussion with Strakhov, who visited that summer, on the poetry of Fet, Tolstoy declared: "I do not understand or like poetry; it is a kind of riddle for which elucidation is always required." In a conversation with the young tutor V. F. Lazurski, he maintained, contrary to all generally accepted opinion, that the Russian poet Tyutchev was greater than Pushkin. The strength of Pushkin, he said, "is in his lyrics and principally in his prose. His longer poems are trash and worth nothing." Perhaps this preference for prose led him to declare to the tutor that "he could not endure" Shakespeare, though he admitted that the English poet had the saving grace of "flying high," and Carlyle he did not like because he knew in advance what he was going to say.

In social and scientific judgments he also startled his guests. He flatly told a couple of medical students who visited him that the newfangled notions about heredity were all nonsense, and he declared that he had compiled statistical tables to prove that inoculation for rabies was not a preventative. Such opinions he formulated a priori. He reasoned thus: "If the fathers sinned, does it therefore follow that the children will pay for them? Obviously, no. Accordingly, it is unreasonable to affirm that the descendants of drunkards will be epileptics, etc."

One evening, while joking with the young ladies about marriage, Tolstoy mildly reproved them for the casualness with which they talked about this subject, although he insisted that he did not condemn the modern girl for her frankness. "But the young people trouble me," he added. "Take even my own sons. When I was a youth, I was in all respects more brilliant than they, but it seemed to me that not a single woman would want to marry me. But my sons so conduct themselves that they have merely to crook a finger and all the women run after them."

In July, Charles E. Turner, lecturer in the English language at the University of Petersburg, visited Tolstoy to talk about translating *Christianity and Patriotism* into English. Besides translating his works, he had lectured in England on Tolstoy as an artist and thinker. He told Lazurski: "Tolstoy has done more to popularize Russian literature among the English than all your writers put together. In his works there is a purposefulness and a religious interest that the English like." A quite different visitor that summer was an American rabbi, Joseph Krauskopf, bearing a letter of recommendation from the American ambassador to Russia, Andrew D. White. He hoped to obtain Tolstoy's aid in establishing a Jewish agricultural colony. As Krauskopf wrote later, after he returned to America, he felt ashamed of his fashionable attire in the presence of this great man dressed so plainly and whom he saw working in the fields like any peasant. (Perhaps with his tongue in his cheek, Tolstoy invited the elegantly attired rabbi to lend a hand with the mowing.) Although Krauskopf sympathized with many of Tolstoy's views, he made it clear that he thought teaching nonresistance to evil a bit unreasonable.

In August, another visitor from America, the widow of a journalist, brought Tolstoy regards from Henry George and a collection of his books and articles. Tolstoy was delighted and eagerly began to read these new works of George.[6] "Once again," he wrote in his diary, "I have become keenly conscious of the sin of possessing land." And the time had come, he noted, to write a new *Uncle Tom's Cabin* on land slavery. A little later he wrote the American woman who

[6] He read at this time George's *The Perplexed Philosopher*, *The Land Question*, and *Free Trade*.

had brought him this literary feast to convey his thanks to Henry George who "has laid a durable foundation for the building of a future economic structure," and whose name "humanity will always remember with gratefulness and esteem."

Tolstoy saw clearly that the land hunger of the peasants was a festering sore in the economic body of Russia. The time will come, he told Lazurski that summer, when "there will be no private property in land." He never regarded Henry George's system of a single tax on land as anything other than a compromise. It found favor in his eyes because it involved no seizure by violence. He entertained the hope that the Tsar by proclamation, as in the case of the emancipation of the serfs, might make the land common property. He wrote to Crosby this year, shortly after the death of Alexander III: "If the new tsar should ask me what I would advise him to do, I would say to him: 'Use your unlimited power to abolish private property in land in Russia and establish a system of single tax, and then renounce your power and give the people freedom to govern themselves.'" One thing that worried him, however, was that the single tax on the land, according to Henry George, would have to be collected by the government, and the government was based on violence. But Tolstoy was willing to accept this ill on the theory that there was no other way out in the existing circumstances, and that in the end the greater good of the greater number would be served.

It is interesting to observe that a small experiment in applying Henry George's solution was tried by Tolstoy. During this summer his daughter Tanya received the first income from the property at Ovsyannikovo that had fallen to her lot in the recent family division. As she watched one of her peasant tenants untie his soiled knotted handkerchief and with gnarled fingers count out the rubles and kopeks, she felt deeply distressed, no doubt under the influence of her father's teaching, at taking this money earned by heavy toil on land that belonged to her. She could not conceal her feelings from her father, and she was much relieved when he proposed to her that the land should be given to the peasants for their use, for which they would agree to pay a nominal rent or tax. This rent should then go into a general fund that the peasants would use for communal purposes on the basis of decisions made at meetings of the commune. Tolstoy and his daughter went to near-by

Ovsyannikovo, and he explained the whole proposal to the peasants.[7] The peasants were much pleased with the arrangement and, as Tanya expressed it, a burden fell from her soul. Things went well for several years, but in the end, when the peasants assured themselves that she was not going to demand the former full rent for the land and did not even attempt to control the sums they paid into the communal fund, they ceased to pay anything and even began to speculate in the land, obtaining it for nothing and leasing it to their neighbors. This experiment ought to have convinced Tolstoy that some form of strict control, governmental or otherwise, was necessary to assure the success of any such reform.

One of the significant changes in life at Yasnaya Polyana during the summer of 1894 was the fact that the Chertkovs had hired a house in the near-by village of Dyomenka. Chertkov had written Tolstoy that spring that he would very much like to be near him during the summer and asked him to locate a desirable place. Tolstoy was delighted, but when Sonya learned of the plan she objected: she feared the competition for her husband's leisure time if Chertkov were close by. Tolstoy frankly wrote him: "If you ask me: does she want you to come, I must say, no; but if you ask: do I think you ought to come, then I think, yes. As I told her and now tell you: if there is any ill-feeling between you, then you both ought to try with all your strength to replace it with love."

Chertkov decided to come, and, as Sonya feared, her husband made frequent trips to the little village, less than four miles away, where his spiritual brother was living. Perhaps Sonya was secretly pleased when Chertkov decided in August that, owing to ill-health, the air of his native province of Voronezh would be more salutary, and he left. After the departure Tolstoy noted in his diary that he was "lonely" without the Chertkovs: "I love them, and him especially, very much."

The "dark" brethren poisoned the air for Sonya that summer. She wrote to her sister who had come to Yasnaya Polyana for only a few days: "Without you, the only visitors, as might have been forseen, are the 'dark' ones. They are so repulsive to me that at times I want to use a pistol

[7] Tolstoy's conversation with the peasants about Henry George on this occasion served as material for Nekhlyudov's conversation with the peasants in *Resurrection*.

on them or feed them arsenic. Pharisees, cheats, dissimulaters with harmful ideas, nothing more!" One of the "pharisees" was Gorbunov-Posadov who proposed that a manuscript periodical be issued, composed of the best things bearing on the new faith to be found in the many letters, articles, and books sent to Tolstoy. And twelve issues of this typed periodical, known as the *Archives of Leo Nikolayevich Tolstoy,* appeared between 1894 and 1896.

A new and important convert who came in August was Dr. Dushan Makovitski, a Slovak. He had read Tolstoy's religious and moral works while still a medical student in Prague, and had become a convinced follower. Tolstoy was pleased to learn from him that members of the Nazarene sect in Austria, believing in nonviolence, refused to serve in the army and were undergoing persecution. A subdued, soft, gentle person, Makovitski endeared himself to Tolstoy.

After the death of Alexander III, Tolstoy shared the hopes of millions in Russia that the new Tsar, Nicholas II, would give the country a constitution, or at least bring about some badly needed reforms. The manifesto he issued upon his accession to the throne, however, reaffirmed all the reactionary traditions of autocracy. Tolstoy indignantly said to Sonya: "In general, in the change of reigns the same old hypocrisy that has existed is still more in evidence; it is painful and terrible to see. The manifesto, however, is exceptionally indecent: 'Mighty Russia is infinitely devoted to us.' " Sonya took alarm and in her next letter begged him not to write anything "for the English, American, or other foreign newspapers concerning the new reign." The Russian press, of course, would have taken nothing critical from him on this subject. Perhaps the only answer he cared to give to this was a note in his diary, written shortly after returning to Moscow for the winter: "What insanity and baseness on the occasion of the death of the old and the accession of the new tsar."

6

At the conclusion of the famine relief work there also ended the happy and reconciling feeling in husband and wife that had resulted from their mutual efforts in this cause. During 1894 nothing occurred to divert the tense undercurrent of unpleasant relations. Every so often, when this undercurrent would come to the surface, the whole family would suffer.

Sonya lived in the fast-fading happiness of their early married life, her husband in the present family existence that prevented him from serving God as he wished. With masculine unfairness he posed the problem to himself in his diary; he wrote that if the views of husband and wife on the world and life did not agree, then it was necessary for the "one who thought less to submit to the one who thought more. How happy I would be to submit to Sonya, but this is really as impossible as for a goose to climb back into its own egg. She ought to submit, but she does not want to—there is no intelligence, no humility, and no love."

About this time Tolstoy began to make Sonya's unhappy mistake of confiding his domestic troubles to outsiders, although he never became as indiscriminate as his wife in this respect. For some time, of course, he had made a confidant of Chertkov, but now the "dark people" were often witnesses of family quarrels, for their very visits provoked Sonya's anger. In August 1894, Tolstoy sent Khilkov in exile a letter that must have been inspired by suffering and great exasperation. "My God!" he wrote. "I say to myself how many times have I thought how glad I would be to submit in order to escape this hell of dissension, and to free the children from it. I am ready for everything, for every torment, humiliation—anything is better than this hell."

An entry in Sonya's diary perhaps reflects the quarrel that provoked Tolstoy's letter. She wrote: "My husband, long since having drifted away from me and having thrown on my shoulders everything, everything without exception: children, the estate, business affairs, the house and books, yet he continues to despise me with his egotistical and critical indifference." She blamed him both for his lack of interest in the children and for the influence of his ideas on them. At times she positively hated Masha, who had completely accepted her father's Christian way of life. And now she began to complain that he and his followers were "tearing" Tanya away from her.

Family cares and her unhappy relations with her husband were severely taxing Sonya's strength. Her diary and letters showed increasing evidence of extravagant grief and a kind of unreasoning excitation that bordered on hysteria, failings that had been latent since youth. And to these difficulties were now added the psychic disturbances that come with a woman's change of life. During the last three years, she had been complaining of what she called a "periodic madness," an abnormal mental and physical condition that occurred every autumn. Toward the end of the summer, 1894, she wrote her sister Tanya: "About myself I can only say that I feel as though a stone pressed on my breast, and this continues day and night. I simply have no strength. I was alone this evening (indeed, Lyovochka is never around; he is either writing, sleeping, walking, or visiting the Chertkovs in the evening), and I was filled with such anguish that I at once remembered you and merely wanted to cry out: 'Tanya, Tanya!' "

XXX

The Death of Vanichka

In January 1895, Tolstoy accepted Prince D. L. Shakhovskoi's invitation to attend a private gathering of Moscow liberals, led by P. N. Milyukov. The purpose was to protest the recent speech of the new Tsar before representatives of the nobility and county councils, in which he had frankly dismissed as "senseless dreams" their hopes for reforms, and at the same time he declared his intention of preserving the autocratic rule of Russia as firmly and uncompromisingly as his father had done. At the meeting, Tolstoy shared the indignation of the liberals, but he hesitated to take part in any organized protest, for he was convinced that his Christian-anarchist views would undermine the effectiveness of such an appeal to the public if his name were attached to it.

In his diary, however, Tolstoy recorded his fear that the Tsar's "arrogant speech" might well hold serious consequences for him. Abroad, the publication of *The Kingdom of God* had already begun to exercise some influence. He heard at this time from Makovitski that another disciple, A. Shkarvan, a Slovak army doctor, had been imprisoned in Hungary for refusing to serve and that the case had aroused much public feeling against the authorities. Tolstoy wrote Makovitski that whenever he learned of such cases, "then I always experience a very powerful mixed feeling of fear, triumph, compassion, and joy." At about the same time he received from America a notification that he had been elected an honorary vice-president of the International Society of Writers; he must have wondered at such a reward to one whose exercise of authorship seemed to be contributing largely to the persecution of people.

While visiting the Olsufyevs in January, Tolstoy finished

a story, "Master and Man," which he had begun the previous year. It struck him as a significant event, for he had not managed to complete a purely artistic work now for some time. He sent the manuscript to Strakhov for his opinion, and asked him, if he found the story satisfactory, to submit it to the periodical, *Northern Messenger*. "It is so long since I have written anything artistic," he declared in the accompanying letter, "that I truly do not know whether it ought to be printed. I wrote it with great satisfaction, but as to its printing—I do not know." Soon Strakhov sent him corrected proofs and a letter in which he wrote: "My God! how splendid, priceless it is, Leo Nikolayevich!" Then followed detailed praise of certain features and some minor criticism. Tolstoy returned the proofs to him so reworked as to be almost unreadable and requested a second set. "In your appreciation," he wrote, "I observe a note of disapproval. Please write more sharply everything you have to say about this tale, just as though you were saying it to someone else. I am interested to know whether or not my powers are slipping. And if they are, then I will not be much afflicted, no more so than I would be to discover that I am unable to run as fast now as I could 40 years ago."

Tolstoy's artistic powers had in no sense diminished, for "Master and Man" is written with his old superb command over his chosen medium. It is a story of the victory of unselfishness over death: The master and his servant are overtaken by a snowstorm and lose their way. Well-clad and fed, the master lies on the almost frozen body of the servant and saves his life. When they are dug out of a snowdrift the next morning, it is the master who is found dead, his last moments gladdened by unselfish sacrifice. "Master and Man" appeared in the March number of the *Northern Messenger,* but its publication caused such a family quarrel that Tolstoy regretted ever having written it.

2

The year 1895 had begun badly with a domestic quarrel over a photograph. Chertkov, while visiting the family in Moscow, persuaded Tolstoy to be photographed with himself and four more close disciples.[1] Sonya was infuriated. "School groups, picnic parties, institutions, etc., have their

[1] P. I. Biryukov, E. I. Popov, I. M. Tregubov, and I. I. Gorbunov-Posadov.

pictures taken," she wrote in her diary. "So now the Tolstoyans have become an *institution*. The public would lap it up and rush to buy *Tolstoy with His Disciples*. What a joke it would be! But I won't have Leo Nikolayevich dragged from his pedestal into the mud like this." She procured the negatives from the photographer, tried unsuccessfully to cut out her husband's face with a diamond earring, and then destroyed the plates.

The disciples were deeply hurt, and insult was added to injury when they learned that Tanya and Masha, whom they regarded almost as spiritual sisters, had supported their mother's protest. The clear implication was that Tolstoy's followers were unworthy of being photographed with the master. Chertkov felt the wound most keenly. Tolstoy entered in his diary: "The story of the photograph is very sad. They are all offended." He tried to make his daughters see their offense, and he wrote Chertkov a humble letter to apologize for the attitude of his family. But that rigidly righteous disciple long remained in an unforgiving mood, especially toward Tolstoy's daughters, although they both tried to make amends. Such a trifling incident, however, served to widen the chasm between the family and the "dark people" and increased the daily anguish of Tolstoy in his search for spiritual harmony.

Sonya had just complaints to make of some of the dark brethren. One of them, P. G. Khokhlov, always shabby and covered with lice, had designs on Tanya and took to rousing the household at four o'clock in the morning to urge his proposal of marriage. Fortunately for all concerned, his pursuit soon ended, for he was committed to an insane asylum. This madman's behavior prompted the following entry in Sonya's diary: "It is strange! Only people morbidly wrenched from ordinary life—weak and stupid people—throw themselves into Leo Nikolayevich's teaching, and they are doomed to perish one way or another. I fear that whenever I begin to write my diary, I fall into the habit of condemning Leo Nikolayevich. But I cannot help complaining, because all the things he preaches for the happiness of people complicate life so much that it becomes more and more difficult for me to live. His vegetarianism means having to cook a double dinner, which causes more expense and more work for people. His sermons on love and the good have resulted in indifference to his family and the intrusion of all kinds of rabble into our circle. His repudiation (verbal) of worldly goods is responsible for this condemnation and criticism."

Throughout January and most of February of 1895 similar criticisms of her husband appeared in Sonya's diary with increasing frequency, obviously leading up to another of her hysterical outbursts. With a curiosity born of morbid jealousy, she read over again the love letters that he had written to Valerya Arsenev almost forty years ago. But among her criticisms are interspersed occasional notes of felicity and love. "My relations with Lyovochka are fine and *passionate*." He brought her "two lovely apples" when she was ill. A feeling of "tenderness and stupid sentimentality" came over her. "I planted the pits to commemorate his unusual kindness to me," she jotted down in her diary. "Will I ever see the pits sprout?" Then the outburst came.

The immediate cause of it all was the publication of "Master and Man." Three years before the attractive editor of the *Northern Messenger,* Lyubov Gurevich—"that scheming, half-Jewess," as Sonya called her—had visited Tolstoy at Yasnaya Polyana. He had liked her and agreed to give her something for her magazine. When he finished "Master and Man," he instructed Strakhov to submit it to the *Northern Messenger* for publication, of course not taking any money for the story. Sonya wanted it for a supplement to the thirteenth volume of her edition. Tolstoy agreed to give her the story, and he also intended to give it to the *Intermediary* for separate publication. But her haste to obtain a copy of the manuscript so that she might publish it before or at least simultaneously with the others angered him.

One evening harsh words were exchanged on this subject, and in a fury Tolstoy ran up to his room, declaring that he would leave the house forever. The thought flashed through Sonya's mind that he wanted to abandon her for Lyubov Gurevich. Determined to leave the house before him, she dashed out into the snow-covered street, although she was clad only in slippers and a dressing gown. With a dressing gown thrown over his drawers and waistcoat, Tolstoy ran after her, begging her to return. She kept screaming: "Let them take me to the police station or a lunatic asylum!" He finally managed to drag her back home.

The next day the quarrel broke out again, and she left the house, determined to lose herself in the woods or in the Sparrow Hills outside of Moscow and freeze to death, like the master in the story that had caused all this anguish.

Masha followed and succeeded in persuading her to return. Another attempt two days later to run away was frustrated by the children. The immediate result of these adventures in the freezing, snowy streets was a severe cold. As she lay ill in her room, weeping bitterly, her husband entered, knelt down, and asked her forgiveness. "If only a drop of the love that was in him then could always remain, I might still be happy," she wrote. Calm descended on the household once again, and "Master and Man" was given to Sonya for her edition. She ended the account of this whole painful incident in her diary by writing: "I'm correcting the proof with joy in my heart and perceive with emotion the artistic greatness of the work. At times my eyes fill with tears of happiness over it."

Two days later (February 23) Sonya set down the following brief entry: "My dear Vanichka died at 11 o'clock at night. By God! to think that I am still alive!" More than two years passed before she resumed her diary.

3

Vanichka, the last child of the Tolstoys, died at the age of seven from scarlet fever. According to many accounts, he was an unusual youngster. Of all the children he looked most like his father: he had the same bright, pensive eyes and the same earnest spirit. His whole appearance conveyed the impression of transparency. The thin little body, pale face, and long curly hair were offset by a radiant nature. His extraordinary sensitivity recalled this quality in Tolstoy as a child. Vanichka was always anxious for everyone's happiness, and he expressed his joy by freely giving away his prized possessions. With an understanding exceptional for his tender years, he would surprise grownups by talking quite intelligently on abstract and spiritual themes. All who came in contact with him were charmed by his joyous nature, a fact reflected in the many tributes sent to the family at his death. He was obviously the apple of his parents' eye.

Sonya's grief over the death of this child of her old age drove her to the edge of madness. Her extreme devotion seemed psychologically unnatural in the light of the many children she had borne and raised. After quarrels with the older children or her husband, she took refuge in her affection for Vanichka, an affection that he always responded to with almost mature understanding and sympathy. There had hardly been an entry in her diary or a letter to her husband over the last few years in which her endless concern for Vanichka had not been expressed. And time and again she sounded a note of foreboding that he would be taken from her, not simply because of his uncertain health, but because of a superstitious fear she nourished that so exceptional a child must inevitably die young. In her more despondent moods, Vanichka seemed to be the only reason for continuing to live. "I stagger from corner to corner and weep like an insane person," she wrote her sister Tanya after the funeral. "Can one live for long with such suffering? Everything, everything has gone out of me, and what is more terrible is the fact that, though eight children still remain, I feel myself entirely alone with my grief and cannot enter into their existence, although they are very kind and affectionate to me. Life seems suddenly to have ended."

The boy's death affected his father in a different way. Tolstoy loved this child. "I somehow dreamed that Vanichka would continue after me the work of God," he told Sonya. And in the letter to her sister, she wrote: "Lyovochka has grown quite stooped and old; he wanders about with a sad look in his bright eyes, and it is clear that the last shining light of his old age has vanished. On the third day after Vanichka's death he sat sobbing and said: 'For the first time in my life I have utterly lost heart.' It was painful to look at him, simply terrible! This sorrow has crushed him." Sonya also described how, on the way to the funeral, he tried to comfort her by recalling that he used to go along this very road to Pokrovskoye to court her as a girl.

Sonya's extreme anguish intensified her husband's grief. But quite characteristically he soon came to accept the death of his favorite child as the will of God and therefore a good. Shortly after the funeral he wrote in his diary: "They have buried Vanichka. It is terrible. No, it is not terrible, it is a great spiritual event. I thank Thee, Father. I thank Thee." He wrote Chertkov and Strakhov that the loss of one so dear to him was compensated by the spiritual ecstasy he experienced, and he compared his reaction to that which he had undergone at the death of his beloved brother Nikolai many years ago. More important for him: he cherished the hope that this family tragedy would reveal the path of truth to his wife and at last unite them spiritually in their declining years.

Their relations became warm and close after Vanichka's death. Like a spiritual father he watched tenderly over Sonya to detect the slightest religious change in her, and he joyously announced these symptoms and his hopes to disciples. "Especially during the first few days," he wrote to Chertkov, "I was blinded by the beauty of her soul revealed as a consequence of this loss." And in his diary he wrote: "The pain of bereavement at once freed her from all that darkened her spirit. It was as if the doors had been rent asunder and laid bare that divine essence of love that exists in our souls."

Shortly after Vanichka's death, Tolstoy wrote a touching letter to Granny about their loss and his wife's grief. He said in part: "Sonya's physical illness, it seems, is not dangerous or severe, but her spiritual illness is very grievous, although it seems to me not only not dangerous, but salutary and happy, as childbirth, or as the resurrection of her spiritual life. Her grief is overwhelming. She had been saved from everything painful, incomprehensible, vaguely disquieting to her in this passionate and reciprocated love for a child whose mind was really endowed with more than ordinary gifts. He was one of those children God sends into this world too early, a world not yet ready to receive them, like swallows that come too soon and are frozen. And now he has been taken from her, and despite her motherhood, nothing seems left to her in this world. In spite of herself, she has to ascend into another and spiritual world where she never lived before. And it is amazing how motherhood has served to keep her pure and receptive to spiritual truth. I am much impressed by her spiritual purity, especially by her humility." And he concluded his letter: "We never before felt so near to each other as now, and never before, neither in Sonya nor in myself, have I felt such a need for love and such a revulsion for every element of disunion and evil. I never loved Sonya as I do now."

4

Despite his eagerness to leave the city for the country when spring came, Tolstoy remained in Moscow longer than usual in 1895 out of consideration for his grieving wife, who was repelled by the thought of Yasnaya Polyana, with every nook and cranny of the place associated with memories of Vanichka. At one point he considered taking Sonya abroad, but there was reason to suppose that the government might not allow him to return to Russia and hence the idea was abandoned. She obtained a brief change of scene in April, however, by going to Kiev with her sister.

Tolstoy idled away the time in Moscow. He listed in his diary no less than nine separate artistic works that he had actually begun or outlined over the last few years and which he now wished to finish, but he was unable to concentrate his efforts on any of them in the city. Was he growing old, he wondered? It is significant that at this time (March 27) he drafted a will in his diary, in which he asked that he be buried in an inexpensive coffin without flowers, speeches, or the presence of priests; that nothing be printed in the newspapers about his death; that his manuscripts be turned over to his wife, Chertkov, and Strakhov, with instructions to select from them and print only those things which would prove useful to people; and finally, he expressed the wish that his heirs should renounce their rights to all his works.

To Chertkov, Tolstoy wrote that he felt he was undergoing a change in life. "Vanichka helps me much, very much in this, and his influence, thank God, has not yet been effaced." And in the same letter he remarked that he was learning to ride a bicycle, a practice in which he became quite proficient.

Tolstoy had hoped that the urge to write would return at Yasnaya Polyana, and he did manage to complete the first draft of *Resurrection,* on which he had been working, off and on, for seven years, but he was thoroughly dissatisfied with it. He found time to write one of his epistolary articles, this one to a Pole, in which he refused to accept his correspondent's contention that the patriotism of an oppressed people was justifiable and laudable, although he sympathized with the cause of Poland. At the end of the summer he also wrote a kind of homily in the form of a long letter to his sixteen-year-old son, Mikhail, whose behavior worried him. In it he pointed out the temptations of youth and tried to lead him into the path of Christian goodness.

Many interruptions that summer interfered with Tolstoy's literary efforts. His eldest son, Sergei, married,[2] a union that he regarded with fear and joy. Of the various visitors, the most distinguished was Chekhov, who met Tolstoy for the

[2] He married (July 10, 1895) Marya Konstantinovna Rachinski, who died in 1900.

first time in August at Yasnaya Polyana. His tales had already made an impression on Tolstoy, and he wrote to his son Leo of the visit: "Chekhov was with us and I liked him very much. He is very talented and he must have a good heart, but so far he has given no evidence of possessing a definite point of view."

The event that now thoroughly stirred Tolstoy and the "dark people" was news of the persecution of the Dukhobors. This sect, like a number of small peasant sects of ancient Russia, had long subscribed to precepts that resembled those of Tolstoy's teaching. Since 1844 the Dukhobors had been settled in the Caucasus. For some time they had paid only lip service to their pure Christian principles and had also developed a theocratic despotism which had resulted in a schism—facts which were not well understood by Tolstoy and his followers at this time. The sect had split over the claim to leadership of Peter Verigin, whom his adherents believed to be the incarnation of the Deity. When these simple people called in government authorities to settle the dispute, they decided in favor of the opponents of Verigin and exiled him to a small town in the province of Archangel in 1887.

While in exile Verigin learned of Tolstoy's teaching and read his writings. Perceiving the similarity of this teaching to the early Dukhobor doctrines, and perhaps seeing that he had a weapon here to use against the government that persecuted him, he instructed his followers, through secret emissaries among them who kept in constant touch with him, to practice nonresistance to violence, to share all things in common, to preserve chastity, to refuse to serve in the army, to abstain from intoxicants, and to become vegetarians. For the Dukhobors who believed in him, this was a command from God, and thousands literally attempted to obey, although many fell by the wayside.

A clash with the authorities was inevitable. This was not the case of an occasional Tolstoyan opposing military conscription, but of whole communities refusing to serve in the army. The government grew alarmed. The Dukhobors even dramatically challenged the government. On the name-day of Peter Verigin (June 29, 1895), three communities of Dukhobors, following the instructions of their exiled leader, ceremoniously burned their weapons as a protest against violence, accompanying the act with much psalm-singing. This was regarded as open rebellion by the authorities. A force of Cossacks descended upon the Dukhobors, beat them cruelly, killed four, imprisoned their chief men, and scattered four thousand of them in remote mountain villages.

Tolstoy soon learned of the persecution of the Dukhobors from his exiled disciple in the Caucasus, Khilkov, and he was deeply shocked. Not knowing much about the sect or its recent trials, he encouraged Biryukov that summer to go to the Caucasus and investigate on the spot. Upon his return he wrote a detailed report, which Tolstoy reworked and to which he added an introduction and a conclusion. The article was at once dispatched to England and appeared (October 23, in the London *Times,* under the title "The Persecution of Christians in Russia in 1895." In it the pure Christian practices of the Dukhobors were emphasized and the cruelty with which they had been treated by the government was exposed.

When the article came to the attention of Church and government officials in Russia, they were vastly annoyed. What they hoped might remain a local Caucasian disturbance had suddenly been given international publicity, and the brutal actions of the Tsar's troops against a peaceful peasant sect had been held up to world censure. Worse still, they saw the hand of Tolstoy in all this and knew that he would not be likely to let the matter rest with a single article. Pobedonostsev at once sent a report on the matter to Nicholas II. It was decided to remove Verigin to Obdorsk in Northern Siberia, a more inaccessible spot, for the authorities discovered that the recent disturbances among the Dukhobors were somehow connected with their contacts with Verigin.

Shortly after Tolstoy's return to Moscow in November, he wrote the first of his long letters to Verigin. Of course Tolstoy was gratified to discover in Russia a religious sect trying to live according to the principles of Christian anarchy that he himself had been preaching. Tolstoyan colonies had seemed somehow to feed on dissension rather than radiate sweet reasonableness. Yet here in the Caucasus was a whole community of simple people germinating the seed sown by Christ 1800 years ago! It was almost as though a miracle had occurred.

Peter Verigin had an earthy, peasant cunning, real courage, and an authoritarian nature that would not permit him to follow whenever he could lead. Although he had perceived the advantage of making use of Tolstoy's name and influence, he had no intention of subordinating his following to any other leader or movement. Nor did he hesitate to push doctrine to absurdity if he felt that by so doing he would better secure his position as the Moses of his fanatical people. Such a case in point prompted Tolstoy's first letter to him. Verigin had written to one of Tolstoy's disciples that books and the printed word in general were unnecessary. Tolstoy, who had already expressed his own ideas about the futility of certain types of literature, candidly replied to Verigin that the right kind of books could do an immense amount of good, and that since there were so many harmful books in the world, a real service could be rendered by writing better books to counteract this evil.

5

The winter of 1895–1896 in Moscow left Tolstoy rather weak in health and sad in mind. At the end of 1895 he wrote a short piece, "Shame!" a scathing denunciation of the flogging of peasants, an old punishment recently reintroduced by the courts.[3] With bitter irony he flayed the "legal" distinction between peasants and the upper classes that the authorities had invented.

Tolstoy was surprised that Nicholas II had certified hi moving drama, *The Power of Darkness,* for performanc on the stage, a step that Alexander III had refused to tak eight years ago. At its first performance in Petersbur (October 16, 1895) a capacity audience acclaimed Tolstoy and realizing the triumph he had won over the censor demanded that a congratulatory telegram be sent to th author. A little more than a month later the play was performed with equal success at the Maly Theater in Moscow At the conclusion, a crowd of students paraded to his hous to pay tribute to him. He listened to the eulogy of th spokesman of the students, and, filled with embarrassmen he was unable for a few moments to say a word in repl

At the end of 1895 Tolstoy received a visit from an earnest English Methodist minister with whom he had bee having some interesting correspondence—J. C. Kenworth This man had accepted Tolstoy's views on life and ha started a Brotherhood Church at Croydon with an appendage, a Brotherhood Publishing Company, for the publicati

[3] The only other work he completed in 1895, apart from tho already mentioned, was "Three Parables."

of his own and other works that subscribed to the new faith. At the request of Chertkov, who had a particular weakness for English disciples, Tolstoy gave Kenworthy the right to publish the first English translation of any of his new works. This move proved to be another contribution to the general confusion arising in connection with foreign editions of Tolstoy's writings since he repudiated his copyrights. And in this particular case the confusion became worse confounded, for Kenworthy soon went out of his mind.

January 1896 brought its toll of deaths, a toll that saddened Tolstoy as the grim Reaper, passing him by, laid low those who were dear to him. The first to go was Gasha, the eighty-three-year-old servant of his long-deceased aunt, Pelageya, and the friend of his childhood, a being who seemed so inseparable a part of Yasnaya Polyana and as deeply rooted there as the ancient gnarled oaks in the park. Then the death of Strakhov, his kind, unwavering friend of years and a most sympathetic critic of his writings and teaching, filled him with a feeling of irreparable loss.

"Always new and full of meaning is death," he entered in his diary at this time. He could not help dwelling on his own old age and on the thought that his turn might soon come. He wrote Sonya from Nikolskoye, where he had again gone in February to his good friends the Olsufyevs to escape the city: "I do not want to admit that I am growing old and am finished, but it has to be. I try to accustom myself to this and not to strain or spoil myself." She replied: "You yourself have said that there was no old age and that you would not give in to it, as though it did not exist." And she implied that the way to forget all this and achieve a proper religious frame of mind was to fast and attend church as she was doing.

Tolstoy's low spirits were not unconnected with the persecution of his followers. A young artist and friend of the family, L. A. Sulerzhitski, was banished to Central Asia for declaring that his Christian conscience would not permit him to serve in the army. Because of his parents' grief, he soon recanted, a weakness considered unforgivable by some of the Tolstoyans. The strait-laced Chertkov condemned such backsliding and roundly scolded Tolstoy, who had expressed sympathy and understanding for his young disciple's lack of fortitude. It was God's will, he replied to the angry Chertkov. He had no right to advise a man to suffer in the struggle with temptation, unless he himself was suffering in this same struggle. If a soldier leaves the trenc to storm the enemy, he wrote, "and has returned to th trench in which I sit and fixes on me a timid, questionin look, I know that I can hardly fail to speak words of com fort to him. . . . If I sat in solitary confinement or if the flogged me and led me to execution, then I could express m grief over the fact that he [Sulerzhitski] did not remai firm, but as long as I indulge myself in all the goods o fleshly existence, I must conceal my grief." Such wisdon and humility of common sense were beyond the tight minded, spiritually truncated Chertkov.

Refusal to serve in the army was not the only offense tha brought the law down on the heads of Tolstoy's followers For example, a Tula woman physician was promptly ar rested for giving a worker a copy of Tolstoy's *What Believe*. In this instance the victim was not really a discipl and had passed on the illegal book at the request of one o Tolstoy's daughters when her father had been unable t supply the worker with a copy. Nevertheless the woman wa tried and sentenced to exile in Orenburg.

This double injustice provoked Tolstoy to write identica letters to the Minister of Justice and the Minister of th Interior. After explaining all the circumstances and insistin upon the woman's innocence, he declared: "I write these books and letters, and through verbal intercourse I dis seminate these thoughts which the government regards as evil, and hence if the government wishes to prevent the diffusion of this evil, it ought to turn against me all the measures it takes against occasional individuals whose only fault is that they have an interest in forbidden books and give them to their acquaintances to read. The governmen ought to do as I request, and all the more so since I not only do not conceal this activity of mine, but, on the contrary, I deliberately declare in this letter that I have written and distributed the very books considered harmful by the govern ment, and I shall continue to write and distribute in books, letters and through conversation the very same thoughts that I have expressed in previous books." There then followed a long and defiant lesson on the beliefs which the government condemned as "evil," and he concluded his letter with a naïve—though possibly ironic—plea to the authorities not to fear to persecute him because of any popularity or social position he might hold. "I not only do not think this, but I am convinced that if the government acted resolutely against me, exiled, imprisoned, or took even sterner measures against me, it would not encounter any special difficulty, and public opinion would not only fail to be agitated by this, but the majority of people would thoroughly applaud such action and would say that it ought to have been done long ago."

The government was too canny to comply with Tolstoy's notion of justice or to crown him with the martyrdom that he perhaps sought. His letters went unanswered. But he was left in no doubt as to the attitude of the authorities. For the Minister of Justice, after receiving the letter, told Tolstoy's close friend, N. V. Davydov, who relayed it to him, that "the government is unable to persecute Leo Nikolayevich himself, but that persecution of people who distribute his works serves as punishment for Leo Nikolayevich."

6

During the summer of 1896 the large manor house at Yasnaya Polyana was treated to an unusual feast of music. The distinguished pianist and composer, S. I. Taneyev, had taken up residence in one of the wings.[4] The excellent pianist A. B. Goldenweizer, who had become acquainted with the family in January, also made lengthy visits. There were solo concerts by both artists and four-hand concerts on two grand pianos. Sometimes Tolstoy played with Taneyev. And now Sonya was taking lessons, for since the death of Vanichka she found relief from her sorrow in a passionate devotion to music. Beethoven and Chopin, she wrote her sister, charmed away her grief, and she just lived from concert to concert.

Sonya's interest in music was tied up closely with her personal interest in the composer Taneyev. Her friendship with him, which dates from this period, grew into a fascination which helped distract her from her grief and her family worries. Tolstoy, as we shall see later, was disturbed by Sonya's feeling for Taneyev, but he did not openly protest.

The Chertkovs, who had again rented a house at Dyomenka, were frequent guests during the summer of 1896. Jane Addams arrived to tell the interested Tolstoy all about Hull House. Two very polite Japanese visitors threw the

[4] Sonya had rented quarters to Taneyev at Yasnaya Polyana during the previous summer.

company into gales of laughter by their weird native sing ing. So would they have laughed, Tolstoy noted in hi diary, if we had sung or played Beethoven to them. Th incident led him to speculate that the ideal of art is it accessibility to all. A visit was also expected from Henr George, a meeting that Tolstoy looked forward to with th greatest anticipation, but unfortunately the American's deat ended this hope.

The married children and their wives gathered at Yasnay Polyana. Only young Leo was away in Sweden, where h married that summer.[5] Goldenweizer related how Tolsto enjoyed luring his guests on walks in the woods. He love to lead them to short cuts along charming leafy paths, bu the "short cut," Goldenweizer added with the ruefulness o a victim, always ended in an extensive hike, in which th sixty-eight-year-old host wore down his companions. T Goldenweizer's amazement, Tolstoy, after watching hi young son Mikhail trying to perform a difficult gymnasti exercise, executed the same stunt with more expertness tha his son. From his conversations with Tolstoy on this visi Goldenweizer recalled two statements: "The ego is th temporary thing that limits our immortal essence. Belief i personal immortality," he said, "always seemed to me a kin of misunderstanding"; and "Materialism is the most mystica of all teachings: fundamentally it places its whole faith in mythical substance which creates everything out of itself, th foundation of everything. This is even more stupid tha belief in the Trinity!"

Neither music nor guests were allowed to interfere wit the long hours Tolstoy spent in his study. His reading thi summer ranged from the works of the English social thinke Edward Carpenter, whom he admired, *Thinking an Reality* of the philosopher A. A. Spier,[6] whose attack o materialism he applauded, to "a charming book of Hind philosophy" by Swami Vivekananda,[7] and six books o prostitution, which he needed for his work on *Resurrection* Tolstoy continued to be dissatisfied with this large novel and put it aside for other writing. He read many literary works that summer, and his diary was filled with observa-

[5] He married Dora Westerlund (May 15, 1896), the daughter of a Swedish physician.

[6] Though Russian born, Spier lived for many years in Germany and wrote his works in German.

[7] Ioga's Philosophy.

tions on aesthetics, for he had at last begun in real earnest the famous work that was to become *What Is Art?*

On July 18 Tolstoy made an unusual note in his diary: "Yesterday I walked along a fallow, replowed field of black earth. As far as the eye could reach, there was nothing but black earth—not one green blade of grass; and there on the edge of the dusty gray road grew a bush of burdock. Of three shoots, one was broken, and its white soiled flower hung down; another was broken, bespattered with black dirt and its stem bent and soiled; the third shoot stuck out from the side, also smeared with black dirt, but still alive and red in the center. It reminded me of Hadji Murad.[8] I want to write. Life asserts itself to the very end, and here in the midst of this whole field it has somehow asserted itself."

This observation, starting a train of associations and ideas in Tolstoy's mind, inspired his remarkable story, *Hadji Murad*. Less than a month later, while visiting his sister at the Shamardino Convent, he made a rough sketch of the tale, but he did not finish it until 1904.[9]

Although Tolstoy was irresistibly drawn to the creation of artistic works, conscience and duty demanded that they be subordinated to his moral and religious writing, and of this much was accomplished in 1896. For some time he had been attempting to set down his understanding of Christ's teaching in a form simple enough to be comprehended even by children. He worked long and hard on this project but remained dissatisfied with both the form and the substance and abandoned it in the autumn of 1896. It was first published in this incomplete form in England in 1898 under the title *Christian Doctrine*. Another religious work was a brief article, "How to Read the Gospels," in which Tolstoy explained his own method of arriving at a correct understanding of the words of Christ.

During 1896 Tolstoy also wrote a series of epistolary articles. He had developed this favorite form to a high degree of literary effectiveness, for it enabled him to combine a personal appeal with skillful argumentation. Further, by one means or another these long letters got into print abroad

[8] The leader of the Caucasian mountaineers who fought the Russians in the 1840's. Tolstoy heard much about him during his army service in the Caucasus.

[9] Two other artistic works that he planned in 1896 were the drama, *The Light Shineth in Darkness*, and the curiously autobiographical tale, "Notes of a Madman."

and achieved wide circulation. One of the best of the epistolary articles in 1896 was addressed to Tolstoy's American disciple, Ernest H. Crosby, on the subject of nonresistance. Crosby had written of the sympathetic reception accorded his efforts to preach Tolstoy's understanding of Christ's teaching in America. The principal objection was the usual one, he reported, that it was impossible to practice such a faith in the modern world, and he quoted the reactions of important American thinkers. Tolstoy's reply is a succinct, tempered restatement of his faith, with particular attention paid to that most contentious of doctrines—nonresistance to violence. To the old argument of whether one should prevent a robber from killing a child, he offered his classic answer, and concluded: "None of us has ever yet met the imaginary robber with the imaginary child, but all the horrors which fill the annals of history of our own times came and come from one thing—that people will believe that they can foresee the results of hypothetical future actions." He faced squarely the fact that so-called Christians honestly believe that there are cases when they have a moral right to deviate from Christ's doctrine not to use violence, such as to defend one's life or the lives of others, to defend one's country, and to save society from lunatics or criminals. There are no moral or practical exceptions, he declared, and the result of making exceptions is that Christ's teaching on the subject of not resisting evil by violence has been completely annulled. "People know it is wrong to use violence, but they are so anxious to continue to live a life secured by 'the strong arm of the law' that—instead of devoting their intellects to the elucidation of the evils which have flowed and are still flowing from admitting that man has a right to use violence to his fellow men—they prefer to exert their mental powers in defense of that error. Do what's right, come what may."

On a different but allied subject is the epistolary article, "Patriotism or Peace," addressed to the English journalist John Manson; it treats the threatened collision between the United States and England over the boundaries of Venezuela. Tolstoy entered the arena of international politics again at this time with a denunciatory article, which he never finished, on the attempted Italian rape of Abyssinia. And not unconnected with political action was an unusual epistolary article—"A Letter to Liberals." This letter was a reply to one from Alexandra Kalmykov, who asked Tolstoy to lend his name to a protest against the government for abolishing the Literature Committee, a voluntary organization of liberal-minded people who were endeavoring to bring good books in cheap editions to the masses. Tolstoy refused to support the protest because he believed it futile, but he used the occasion to administer a verbal spanking to liberals, and at the same time to suggest to them a plan of action which he thought better than their own. After asserting that the government's strength lay in the ignorance of the people, and that therefore it would always oppose true enlightenment, he pointed out that there have been two ways in Russia of opposing the repression of an autocratic government. The first has been the way of violent revolution, the second the way of the liberals, which consisted of carrying on the struggle without violence and within the limits of the law in an effort to gain constitutional rights bit by bit. Revolution has failed, he wrote, and even if it should succeed, history has taught that the advantages gained are lost or perverted by the new power. Further, violence bred violence and was immoral. As for the second method, its failure was evident on every side. Ruthlessly he tore away the veil covering the activities of liberals, and pointed out that with the best intentions they unconsciously played into the hands of an autocratic government. As Alexander II had said, he did not fear liberals because he knew they could all be bought—if not with money, then with honors. The few who stood their ground were suppressed.

No, said Tolstoy, only the people who have something which they would under no circumstances yield could resist a government and curb it. The way out was that which he advised in *The Kingdom of God Is Within You*—passive, civil disobedience to all those demands of government which violated the conscience of man. For only thus would public opinion, the sole power that could subdue governments, be aroused. And only men who lived according to their conscience could exert influence on people, and only activity that accorded with one's conscience could be useful.[1]

A not unimportant part of Tolstoy's literary expression

[1] Other epistolary articles written in 1896 were addressed to M. A. Sopotsko on the deception of the Church; to the German, Eugen Schmidt, on government and Christianity; to Peter Verigin, again on his objections to printing; and to the Irkutsk and Ekaterinograd commanders of disciplinary battalions on behalf of two persecuted objectors to military service.

during 1896 is to be found in the full pages of his diary. Apart from numerous observations on art and aesthetics, there are entries of some length and significance on the philosophic definition of time and space, the problem of error, the use of reason, and the meaning of life. The question of social action occupied him more and more, and hence it is not surprising to find a diary comment on Marx. He wrote: "No undertaking is profitable with a small amount of capital. The more capital the more profits, and the expenses are less. But from this it does not follow, according to Marx, that capitalism will lead to socialism. Perhaps it will lead to it, but to socialism by force. The workers will be compelled to work together, and they will work less and the pay will be more, but there will be the same slavery. It is necessary that people work freely together and that they should learn to work for each other, but capitalism does not teach them that; on the contrary, it teaches them envy, greed, selfishness. Therefore, through a forced uniting brought about by capitalism, the material conditions of the workers can be improved, but their contentment can in no sense be achieved. Contentment can only be achieved through a free union of workers. And for this they must learn how to unite, to perfect themselves morally, to serve others willingly, and not to be offended when they meet with no return. And this cannot be learned under a competitive capitalistic system, but under an entirely different one."

Many of Tolstoy's diary entries over this year, however, are concerned with a searching analysis of his spiritual development or the lack of it. In moments of exaltation, when he achieved a moral victory over some temptation, he experienced a kind of spiritual voluptuousness. More often he felt spiritually debased, and these periods were usually the result of depressing inner conflicts connected with his domestic difficulties.

7

As the months wore on, Tolstoy's hope of a spiritual transformation in his wife after Vanichka's death gradually waned. Sonya's grief was not the kind that finds its outlet or compensation in a profound religious experience; a mother's grief for a lost child rarely does. His first realization that the period of spiritual closeness with Sonya had vanished was recorded in Tolstoy's diary less than a month after Vanichka's death: "She suffers and especially because the object of her love has left her, and it seems to her that her goodness was in this object and not in the love itself. She cannot separate one from the other; she cannot regard life in general or herself from a religious point of view." A little later, in a letter to Strakhov not long before his death, he wrote about Sonya: "Of everything spiritually beautiful that revealed itself immediately after Vanichka's death, and from the manifestation and growth of which I expected so much, there has remained only despondency and egotistical grief."

However deeply Tolstoy regretted the loss of this last hope of real spiritual unity with his wife, it did not lessen his love for her or his concern over her emotional and physical suffering. For her grief continued in an extreme form for months. Five months after her loss, she wrote her sister: "Nothing concerns me, nothing agitates me except one living, burning feeling of anguish, of hopeless grief without Vanichka."

When his grieving wife complained at this time that certain passages in his diaries about her were offensive, he read over all his diaries and dutifully eliminated these statements, for which she lovingly thanked him. "I have never felt myself so guilty and exposed," he wrote at the conclusion of this task. "Oh, if this would only draw us still closer together. If she would only free herself from belief in trifles and would believe in her own soul, in her reason. In going over the diaries I found places—there were several—in which I repudiated *these evil words that I wrote about her. These words were written in moments of irritation. Now I repeat it once again for the benefit of all into whose hands these diaries may fall.* I often grew irritated with her because of her hasty temper, but, as Fet said, for every husband there is one wife who is the right one for him. I already perceived that she was the right wife for me. She was an ideal wife in the pagan sense—in the sense of fidelity, domesticity, self-denial, family love—and in the very pagan in her lies the possibility of a Christian friend. I saw this after Vanichka's death. Will it develop in her? May the Lord help. The events now are joyful to me. She saw and will see the power of love—the power of her love over me."

Relations between husband and wife under the shadow of their mutual sorrow continued to be warm and affectionate.

At the end of 1895, when she was returning to Moscow from Yasnaya Polyana, he took the long ride to the train with her, for he was worried over her health. Shortly after he wrote in his diary: "She was sitting in the carriage and I became terribly sorry for her, not because she was departing, but sorry for her, for her soul. I'm sorry now and I hold my tears back with difficulty. I'm sorry because it is so hard for her, because she is so sad and so alone. She has no one but me, no one else to cling to, and in the depths of her soul she is afraid that I do not love her, do not love her as I can love with all my soul, and that the reason for this is our different views on life. And she thinks that I do not love her because she did not come to me. Do not think this. I love you still more, I understand all, and I know that you could not, *could not* come to me, and for that reason you have remained alone. But you are not alone; I am with you, I love you just as you are, and will love you to the very end as hard as it is possible to love."

Tolstoy hastened to convey his exaltation in a letter to Sonya. He explained it as "an entirely new love." "It is such a holy, fine feeling, that I ought not to speak about it, but I know you will be glad to hear it, and I know from the very fact that I express it that it will not change."

Sonya was grateful. She wrote of her joy over his letter, and she expressed her conviction that their quarrels had not been serious. "The very basis of our relations—an inner feeling for each other—remains serious, firm, and harmonious. We both know what is good and bad, and we both love each other. Thank God for this. And we are both looking in the same direction, towards the exit-door of life, and we don't fear it."

XXXI

What Is Art?

EARLY IN 1897 disaster overtook the inner circle of Tolstoyans. Information had reached them at the end of the previous year that persecution of the Dukhobors, whose fate they were closely following, had reached an intolerable degree. One of the sect had been beaten to death in a disciplinary battalion; numerous families, dispersed among unfriendly villages of Caucasian hill tribes, were perishing from hunger and cold. Of the 4000 exiled in 1896, 400 had already died from various privations. Horror gripped Tolstoy and he at once sent the sufferers a thousand rubles out of his "charity fund."[1]

Chertkov and Biryukov, later joined by the disciple Tregubov, decided on an appeal to the authorities and the public on behalf of the persecuted Dukhobors. Tolstoy encouraged them and associated himself with the project by writing an epilogue. This appeal, entitled "Help!" was sent to many leading citizens, government officials, and the Tsar. The participants fully realized the risk they ran and were prepared to accept the consequences.

They did not have long to wait for repercussions. Shortly after the appeal was circulated, Chertkov and Biryukov were arrested, exiled for five years, and placed under constant police surveillance. Chertkov was allowed to select England as his place of exile; Biryukov was sent to Bausk in Cour-

[1] The fund consisted of royalties from Tolstoy's plays performed by the state theaters. He did not wish to accept this income, after renouncing all financial rights to his works, although these royalties would have reverted to the government, of which he also disapproved. Upon the suggestion of his wife, who managed the affair, he finally agreed to accept money from this source and to use it solely for charitable purposes.

land. Three months later the police arrested Tregubov in Tiflis and also exiled him to Courland for five years.

Tolstoy, as usual, escaped direct punishment. He and Sonya were visiting the Olsufyevs at the beginning of February, when the news reached them. They hurried to Petersburg to bid farewell to Chertkov and Biryukov. An exalted feeling of martyrdom well earned suffused the exiles, who gathered with a little band of the faithful at Chertkov's quarters each evening to hear the master's final words of wisdom. "So radiant, joyous and simple were they," Tolstoy later wrote to Khilkov, "that they did not stir up any apparent feeling of regret."

Fifteen years had passed since Tolstoy had last been in Petersburg, and he made the most of this opportunity to visit old friends. His movements were carefully watched by the police. The report of the slow-witted detective assigned to trail him was a masterpiece of elaborate, patient dullness and inept sleuthing. Every change of clothing was faithfully recorded with an attention to details that would have done justice to a society reporter describing the apparel of the town's latest bride and groom. On February 7, wrote the sleuth, "Count Tolstoy was dressed in an unfinished tan sheepskin coat with several patches, girdled with a gray belt, wore dark-colored trousers outside his boots, and on his head was a dark-gray knitted cap, and a cane in his hand." Each shop Tolstoy went into and what he bought were noted, and every person he stopped to talk with on the street was sketched. A tremor of excitement crept into this dull account only when the sleuth observed that some students, recognizing Tolstoy in a horsecar, engaged him in conversation and eagerly begged him to visit their university. When he agreed, one of the students kissed his hand.

Tolstoy enjoyed pleasant visits with old friends, such as the artist Repin, the librarian Stasov, who for years had diligently fulfilled his endless requests for books, the aging writer Grigorovich, and the famous liberal-minded jurist and member of the Imperial Council, Koni, who was amazed that Tolstoy uttered not a word of bitterness or indignation over the exile of his disciples. He produced on Koni the impression of one of those early Christians who were able to face a terrible death without shrinking and conquered the world with their meekness.

There was little of the early Christian and less of meekness displayed in Tolstoy's visit with Granny, and this was all the more unfortunate since it proved to be the last meeting of these old friends. The armed neutrality that had existed between them ever since he had adopted his new faith now ended in open warfare. Despite his genuine affection for Granny, he could not dissociate from the lady-in-waiting to the Empress the religious hypocrisy that existed in her aristocratic circle, which blandly countenanced cruel persecution of all those who did not subscribe to the Orthodox faith. And undoubtedly this feeling was uppermost in his mind now in the face of the persecution of the honest, hard-working Dukhobors and the exile of his disciples for trying to aid them.

In a gathering of friends, at which Granny was present, Tolstoy rather belligerently declared that a thinking person could achieve his own salvation without the aid of anyone. She understood this "anyone" to mean God, and no doubt he had intended it in this sense for her benefit—that is, a superstitious belief in and dependence on the Christian God she worshipped were superfluous. The next morning when he came to say farewell, she could not resist an allusion to his statement of the previous day, which had shocked her.

He jumped from his seat, his face quivering with anger, and all his meekness vanished. "Permit me to tell you that I know all this a million times better than you! I have studied all these questions and not in a trifling manner, and I have sacrificed my life, happiness, and everything to my conviction, and you think that you can teach me something." When he left, she sadly wondered whether or not his conscience troubled him over this outburst.

If Granny could have looked over Tolstoy's shoulder at the letter he wrote to Chertkov a few days later, she would have understood better the state of his conscience and the real cause of his anger. "Petersburg," he wrote, "gave me a most happy impression. Of course, the high points were the meetings at your house. The unhappiest impression was my conversation with A. A. Tolstoy. The terrible thing was not only the coldness, but the cruelty and forcing a way into your soul, that very thing which has estranged us. What an evil faith is that which makes people so cruel and consequently so insensible to the spiritual condition of others. 'Believe word for word as I do, otherwise if you are not exactly my enemy, still you are a stranger.' "

2

The exile of Chertkov and Biryukov, the two most active of Tolstoy's disciples, caused a stir in various circles. The government's arrows of misfortune were striking closer to the master. Tolstoy's agitation and that of the public were intensified by a sensational event that took place about this time. An attractive, fun-loving girl, Marya Vetrov, who had once visited Tolstoy, had been confined to the dismal Peter-Paul Fortress for alleged revolutionary activity. After being offensively questioned by her jailers and—so it was rumored—violated by them, she poured kerosene over herself in her cell and burned herself to death. The funeral of the girl turned into a public demonstration against the government. Tolstoy wrote to Koni for advice on what he could most effectively do to protest this outrage, but the well-known jurist had nothing to offer on a matter so disturbing to the authorities.

Tolstoy also wrote about the Vetrov case to Chertkov. In fact, he maintained a steady correspondence with his two recently exiled followers, giving them words of advice and comfort, and encouraging them to continue their work in the faith. Exchanges of letters were not always easy because of the vigilance of the police, and various subterfuges were employed. A nostalgic longing to share the fate of his disciples crept into these letters. It seemed to him at times that they had gone out into the world of light and left him sitting in sorrow and alone. "I am not in exile," he concluded one of his letters to Biryukov, "but truly I am now sadder than you. Farewell, my dear, I kiss you."

The private war between Tolstoy and the Russian government and Church was a matter of general public interest. Whatever the issues involved, there was something magnificent in the figure of this old, gray-bearded prophet standing alone against the whole organized force of a reactionary Church and State. At times his was the only voice that spoke aloud and unafraid for the cause of justice in a vast country shackled by an absolute autocratic despotism. His most powerful weapon was moral suasion acting upon Russian public opinion and—what was more feared by the government—on international public opinion. Perhaps as a proof of his effectiveness, causes to fight for were now being laid at his feet in abundance by persecuted individuals and organizations, and if he could see the justice of them in terms of his own religious convictions, he rarely refused to help.

While his defense of the Dukhobors still continued, another sect, the Molokans, appealed to him for aid. At the beginning of summer, two Samara Molokans visited him at Yasnaya Polyana and told him a pathetic tale. In their village, the police, acting on orders from above, had compelled the parents of several Molokan families to surrender their young children. The charge was that the children were not being brought up in the Orthodox faith, and they were ruthlessly carried off to monasteries and convents, put under the care of the Church, and allowed no contact with their parents, who were for a time kept in ignorance of their whereabouts. The parents were finally told that they could see their children in church. When they arrived, however, they found only some other Molokans who were being converted to the Orthodox faith. The Father Superior, unabashed by this cheap and heartless trick, embraced the distracted parents and said: "You are filled with sadness because your children have forsaken you; but so also is the Mother Church because you have forsaken her."

The indignant Tolstoy required no pleas for aid from the Molokans after hearing their story and seeing documentary testimony of the actions of the police. He wrote a detailed and outspoken letter to the Tsar. After stating in full the case of the sectarians, he declared: "Surely this is frightful. Such things were done only at the time of the Inquisition. Nowhere, not even in Turkey, is such a thing possible, and no one in Europe would believe that this could happen in a Christian country in 1897." And he skillfully seized this occasion to plead the cause of the "thousands upon thousands of Russian people" who were persecuted in the name of the Tsar because their religious faith differed from that of the Church or their political convictions from those of the government.

The Molokans were directed to take this letter to Petersburg, and Tolstoy gave them notes to influential friends who were asked to see that the letter got into the hands of the Tsar. In the city, however, the simple sectarians were easily persuaded by an acquaintance that all these letters were dangerous, and they promptly destroyed them and returned to Tolstoy. Disappointed but not discouraged, he again wrote to the Tsar, and this time asked his disciple, P. A.

Boulanger, who was soon exiled from Russia for propagating Tolstoy's ideas, to take it to the city with instructions on how it might be conveyed to the Tsar.

The letter reached Nicholas II, but after months had passed and no action was taken, the Molokans again appealed to Tolstoy. His sympathy for their plight in no sense diminished, he returned to the charge with still a third letter to the Tsar. And he followed this up by a letter on the case to the newspaper, *Russian News,* which refused to print it, but on a second try the *Petersburg News* bravely published it. Still the children were not returned to their parents. At the beginning of 1898 he asked Koni to use his influence. "It is impossible to remain calm," he wrote him, "when such evil actions are committed before your eyes. I am ashamed to belong to a people that stands for such things."

Tolstoy's daughter Tanya was visiting Petersburg at this time and he telegraphed her to do everything she could to aid the Molokans. Against the advice of friends who had stuffy ideas on the proper channels for such a petition, she went directly to the all-powerful Pobedonostsev and stated her case. This irreconcilable enemy of her father received the daughter politely, and after a brief interview promised to rectify the wrong, a promise that he soon fulfilled. Perhaps it was his way of showing his power to the great Tolstoy, who had ignored him in his appeals to the Tsar, newspapers, and highly placed friends, or perhaps it was a none too subtle gesture of amity to a man who seemed outside his all-inclusive sphere of both influence and direct persecution. This sorry incident exemplifies at once the sweeping power of Pobedonostsev and the maddening bureaucracy that oppressed people in Russia. For actually, according to the law, parents who were christened in the Orthodox faith and brought up their children in another belief, as was true of the Molokans, could be legally deprived of their children. Yet Pobedonostsev, the lay head of the Church, could set aside the law of the land on his own responsibility.

3

During the summer of 1897 when Tolstoy was at Yasnaya Polyana, there was no Chertkov at neighboring Dyomenka to consult with daily on the spiritual empire they were building. Tolstoy also missed the frequent visits of the industrious and gentle "Posha" (Biryukov). Even Sonya had a fleeting moment of regret over Chertkov's exile, for he was pleasant company when he forgot his holier-than-thou pose. Yet she resented her husband's going all the way to Tula to send the worried Chertkov a reassuring wire about his feelings toward him. "Leo Nikolayevich simply loves him!" she noted in her diary.

Masha's marriage (June 2) increased her father's sense of loneliness that summer. Pale-faced and sickly as she was, but with a slender and graceful figure, Masha's high forehead, deep, attentive gray eyes, and concentrated expression recalled her father's features. An earnestness and curious inner beauty compensated for a physically unattractive face. She was the only one of his children up to this time to accept unquestioningly his way of life, and she suffered in this large family, particularly from her mother, for this devotion to her father. Masha translated her convictions into service for others. She was tireless in work in the fields, in teaching the village children, caring for the sick, and performing endless tasks for her father. The bond between them went deeper than the love of parent and daughter; it was a spiritual bond.

A handsome young cousin, Prince Nikolai Obolenski, came to stay at the Moscow house of the Tolstoys while he attended the university. He and Masha fell in love and though he was objectionable to both parents as a son-in-law, they married. It was a difficult step for Masha to take. Since her husband had no income and seemed uninterested in a career, she was now obliged to ask for that part of the family estate which had fallen to her lot in the division and which she had renounced according to her convictions. And she knew that her marriage must inevitably weaken if not sever the spiritual bond with her father. For her, it seemed like repudiating holy vows. For her father, Masha's marriage and departure were a severe wrench. Always alone in the family save for Masha, now he was entirely alone.

Despite the absence of dear and familiar faces, summer life at Yasnaya Polyana continued, on the surface at least, as of old, with its hordes of visitors, games, tennis, walks, music, and literary evenings. New disciples made the pilgrimage. Aylmer Maude, ultimately to become the best known English Tolstoyan, translator, and biographer of Tolstoy, arrived, and was promptly set down in Sonya's diary as "ponderous and dull." At the end of a long business career in Russia he accepted Tolstoy's teaching unreservedly for a time and supported the Tolstoyan agricultural colony at Purleigh in Essex. Soon he was to take a leading role in aiding the persecuted Dukhobors. Another Englishman, Arthur St. John, arrived with money from the Quakers to be expended on the Dukhobors. He decided to push on to the Caucasus to investigate these sectarians on the spot, and for his trouble he was arrested and deported.

The usual assortment of accomplished artists—musicians, painters, and sculptors—turned up. Hardly a day passed that twenty or more people—family and guests—did not sit down at the long table for dinner. And nearly all these visitors, as was so often the case, felt their contact with the great Tolstoy worth commemorating in letters, articles, or memoirs which were subsequently published. A peasant from the Caucasus arrived to ask and receive Tolstoy's aid for his fellow Dukhobors; a rich American traveled all the way to Yasnaya Polyana to seek advice on how he might best aid the poor; a friend, a former soldier, anxiously desired to discuss religious questions and to show him a kind of religious catechism he had drawn up; an Englishman wrote to ask how he should educate his children; and a Japanese sent him his book on religion and solicited his opinion. And Tolstoy frequently gathered with poor peasants under the huge oak tree near the house to give them advice or material assistance in their affairs. To no sincere request did he turn a deaf ear.

While Tolstoy posed for a new bust for the sculptor Ginsburg, a servant announced that three girls from Tula had arrived to "look at" the famous writer. "Oh how boring this is," he sadly remarked. "There's no help for it; ask them in. Now you'll see these curiosity seekers. It is terrible how they bother me. Nothing else is essential to them except to look at me." Three awe-struck young ladies were introduced and silently stared. With little success Tolstoy tried to get them to talk, and then sent them on their way, with instructions to the servant to give them copies of his writings.

The incident reminded Tolstoy of an amusing occurrence which he told to Ginsburg. He once received a long telegram from a stranger requesting an interview. Being busy at the time, he refused. One day, several months later, a handsome troika drove up to the Moscow Tolstoy house. A foppishly dressed man jumped out and entered. Tolstoy quickly learned that it was the same person who had sent him the long telegram. The visitor cheerfully announced:—

"I represent the firm of Odol. My principal specialty is advertising. The business is enormous."

"But what do you want from me?" Tolstoy asked.

"Only to meet you, for it is shameful that I, who have met everybody of consequence, have not yet become acquainted with Tolstoy."

Tolstoy brusquely dismissed the man on the score that he was busy. Upon leaving, the visitor presented him with two handsome packages of Odol as a gift for him and his wife. It was a dentifrice.

"Why for me?" Tolstoy asked. "I have no teeth and hence no need to clean them," and he returned the gift. Yet, after this enterprising salesman had left, the two packages of dentifrice were found on the hall table downstairs.

In August of that summer, Tolstoy entered in his diary: "Lombroso was here—a limited, naïve little old man." This was the distinguished Italian anthropologist and psychiatrist —Cesare Lombroso. While attending a medical conference in Moscow, he had expressed a desire to visit Tolstoy. The head of the police suggested that this would be disagreeable to the government, and, making small circles with his finger near his temple, indicated that Tolstoy was not entirely right in his mind. Seizing this lead, the quick-witted Lombroso said that it was precisely in his capacity as a psychiatrist that he wished to see and study Tolstoy. Mollified by such a scientific purpose, the head of the police, with a knowing look, smilingly approved of the visit.

Lombroso had preconceived notions about literary geniuses and their habits of work, but these were all contradicted by this meeting with Tolstoy. On the day of his arrival he watched the sixty-nine-year-old genius play tennis for two hours with his daughter. Tolstoy then invited his guest to go swimming in the Yasnaya Polyana pond and offered to race him. Lombroso almost drowned trying to keep up the pace, and Tolstoy was obliged to help him to the shore. "When I expressed surprise at his strength and endurance," Lombroso related, "he stretched out his hand and lifted me right off the ground, just as easily as though I were a little dog." Later, in one of their discussions, Tolstoy impatiently listened to Lombroso's exposition of his favorite theory concerning innate criminal types and the necessity of protecting society from them. "He remained silent throughout all my arguments," Lombroso wrote, "and finally, knitting his terrifying brow, he turned on me a threatening glance from his deeply sunken eyes and declared: 'All this is nonsense. Every punishment is criminal.'" Despite their disagreement, Lombroso formed a high opinion of the simplicity of Tolstoy's life and his unfailing kindness toward the scores of petitioners who daily sought his aid.

When Lombroso returned to Moscow, the head of the police asked him how he found Tolstoy. "It seems to me," he answered, "that this madman is infinitely cleverer than many of the stupid people here who possess power."

Late in September, a Tula priest, with the permission—and perhaps at the command—of his bishop, visited Tolstoy in the naïve hope of guiding him back to the Orthodox faith. He was treated very politely but firmly, and the only positive impression he made was on Sonya, who worried whether such a visit, actually sponsored by a bishop, did not mean that her husband was regarded as a dangerous heretic.

That summer Tolstoy made a bold bid to obtain international publicity for the plight of the Dukhobors. Learning that candidates for the Nobel Peace Prize were being considered (it was rumored that he was one of them), he hurriedly wrote an article and had it translated into Swedish. In it he made out a strong case for the Dukhobors as the recipients of this large financial award. After pouring scorn on all the would-be claimants who pay only lip service to the cause of peace, he described in detail the terrible sufferings that the Dukhobors had undergone at the hands of the Russian government because, sincerely believing in peace, they had refused to bear arms. People serving the cause of peace, he asserted, serve it only because they serve God. And here were thousands of Dukhobors who said: "We are Christians and therefore we cannot agree to be murderers. You may kill or torture us, but we nevertheless will not be murderers, for this is contrary to the very Christianity that you profess." Tolstoy then eloquently concluded his article by declaring "that no one with greater justice could be more worthy of the money that Nobel desired to give to people who best serve the cause of peace than these Dukhobor families."

Sonya became frightened at the outspoken criticism of the government in this article and had visions of deportation. Tolstoy finally gave in to her weeping and threats to leave the house and softened the criticism, but even in the final version of the article that he sent off to a Stockholm newspaper his attack on the Russian government was still sufficiently harsh to cause his exile if the authorities had been so disposed. Perhaps the Swedish editor thought so too, for he refused to publish the article.

Tolstoy lingered on at Yasnaya Polyana even later than usual that year, until December, and before he left he received a visit from his Slovak disciple, Dr. Dushan Makovitski. It prompted Tolstoy to make in his diary a statement that clarified his attitude toward his followers and their propagation of his beliefs: "I had a talk with Dushan. He said that since he had involuntarily become my representative in Hungary, then how was he to act? I was glad of the occasion to tell him and to clarify it for myself, namely that it is a great and gross mistake to speak about Tolstoyism or to seek my guidance, or to ask my decisions on problems. There is no Tolstoyism or any teaching of mine, and there never has been; there is only one eternal, general, and universal teaching of the truth, which for me, for us, is especially clearly expressed in the Gospels. This teaching calls man to a recognition of his filiality to God and therefore of his freedom or his slavery (call it what you wish); of his freedom from the influence of the world, of his slavery to God, to His will. And as soon as man understands this teaching, he enters freely into direct communication with God, and then he has nothing and no one to ask. . . . People who submit themselves to a guide, who have a faith in him and listen to him, undoubtedly wander in the dark together with their guide."

4

Art is modest, Tolstoy once said, but his theorizing on the subject in *What Is Art?* is perhaps the most immodest contribution to the study of aesthetics that has ever been written. He finished this famous work in 1897 and it marks the culmination point of fifteen years of thought and study, a fact unknown or disregarded by captious critics who treated *What Is Art?* as something that had leaped full-born from Tolstoy's brain at a dyspeptic moment when he had arbitrarily concluded that there shall be no more cakes and ale for the artists of the world.

At the end of the 1870's when Tolstoy took a full reckoning of himself and of his relations to culture, he came to the conclusion that the art he had served for years was a temptation that seduced people from good and led them into evil, and hence he decided to forsake art. Although subsequently he never found it necessary to surrender his fundamental negative position toward other "deceits of culture"—government, law, science, technical progress, and so on—he soon began to doubt his negative attitude toward art. Art was so innate a part of his being that he could not turn his back on it.

However, with his radically new outlook on life, Tolstoy could not be satisfied with the theory of art that he had formerly accepted, and this dissatisfaction inspired his prolonged study of the subject. His main endeavor was to erect a system of aesthetics that would accord with his new understanding of man and his relation to the world. In a real sense, *What Is Art?* may be regarded as the aesthetics of his whole moral philosophy of life. Yet he knew that any system he might set up must be comprehensive enough to justify all sincere works of art.

The problem turned out to be much more complicated than he had anticipated. His first effort in this direction, in 1882, left him entirely unconvinced. And over the next fifteen years, during various periods of time, he struggled with the subject, defining and redefining his position. In the course of this time he read a great many books on aesthetics, philosophy, and many works of belles-lettres, and he studied music, painting, sculpture, attended the theater, and heard opera, always with his projected essay in mind. Apart from a quantity of miscellaneous notes, there exist eight separate articles, fragments of articles, and drafts,[2] which in printed form are almost as extensive as his final effort.

In all his theorizing, however, one can detect a growing emphasis upon the ethical principle as the immanent organizing factor in the artistic process. And this view ultimately became the starting point for the aesthetic theory that he finally elaborated in *What Is Art?* The growing popularity of such movements as Decadence and Symbolism during the last decade of the nineteenth century offended both his artistic and his moral sense and provided him with a new impetus to finish his book on art. He worked almost exclusively on it throughout most of 1897 and finished it in December. It appeared in Russia the next year but was so mutilated, by both the editor and the censor, that Tolstoy

[2] This material has only recently been published in Russian in complete form in *Literary Heritage: L. N. Tolstoy,* No. 37–38 (Moscow, 1939), Vol. II.

disowned this version. At the same time it was published in England in a translation made by Aylmer Maude and supervised by Tolstoy, who declared this English translation to be the first complete and correct edition of *What Is Art?*

In this book, Tolstoy approached the subject as he approached the study of every human endeavor: art is a human activity and hence it must have a clear purpose and aim, discernible by the aid of reason and conscience. And as a human activity, he declared, art cannot exist for its own sake and therefore its value must be weighed in proportion as art is serviceable or harmful to mankind. Again and again in his researches he was confronted with that unholy trinity of the aestheticians—beauty, truth, and goodness, and of these the greatest was beauty. For he found that the commonest definition, repeated in various forms, was that art is an activity that produces beauty. But just what was meant by beauty, no two theorists seemed to agree. The word was used subjectively and according to the variable tastes of the persons who employed it. In general, Tolstoy's study of aesthetics led him to conclude that there was no such science, because it failed to define the qualities and laws of art which in turn could be applied to artistic productions by way of accepting or rejecting them. This chaos has resulted, he maintained, because the conception of art has been erroneously based on the conception of beauty.

Tolstoy, then, propounded his own definition of art:—

> To evoke in oneself a feeling one has once experienced and having evoked it in oneself then by means of movements, lines, colors, sounds, or forms expressed in words, so to transmit that feeling that others experience the same feeling—this is the activity of art.
>
> Art is a human activity consisting in this, that one man consciously by means of certain external signs, hands on to others feelings he has lived through, and that others are infected by these feelings and also experience them.
>
> Art [he declared] is not, as the metaphysicians say, the manifestation of some mysterious Idea of beauty or God; it is not, as the aesthetic physiologists say, a game in which man lets off his excess of stored-up energy; it is not the expression of man's emotions by external signs; it is not the production of pleasing objects; and, above all, it is not pleasure; but it is a means of union among men joining them together in the same feelings, and indispensable for the life and progress towards well-being of individuals and of humanity."

Before Tolstoy applied his definition as a kind of touchstone of true art, he felt it necessary to distinguish between the subject matter and the form of art, for he realized that upon this distinction rested the solution of what was for him the fundamental problem—the relation of art to morality. First he took art apart from its subject matter and pointed out that what distinguished real art from its counterfeit—and much that passed for art he condemned as counterfeit—was the infectiousness of art. If a person who is subjected to an artist's work experiences a mental condition which unites him with the artist and with other people who also partake of that work of art, then the object evoking that condition is a work of art. And the stronger the infection, the better is the art as art. From this point of view, he declared, art has nothing to do with morality, for the feelings transmitted may be good or bad feelings. But the one great quality that makes a work of art truly contagious is its sincerity.

Up to this point Tolstoy had been concerned with an internal test in appraising art. Next he applied an external test in an effort to determine whether a work of art is refined or genteel (the art of the few, the upper classes) or universal (the art of the people). People who admire exclusive art, which is so often considered the only art, do so because they have trained themselves to admire it and not because it is necessarily great art. He pointed out that the majority of the productions of art of the upper classes which were admired by them when first produced were never understood or valued by the great masses of mankind. This refined art is intended only for the pleasure of genteel people and is incomprehensible as a pleasure to the workingman. For almost the only feelings, with their offshoots, that formed the subject matter of the art of his own class, he said, were three insignificant and simple ones—the feeling of pride, the feeling of sexual desire, and the feeling of weariness of life.

Tolstoy next made the point that as soon as the art of the upper classes separated itself from universal art, a conviction arose that art may be art and yet be incomprehensible to the masses. But all great works of art, he insisted, are great because they are accessible and comprehensible to everyone. The majority of people have always had the taste to esteem the highest works of universal art, such as the Epic of Genesis, the Gospel parables, and folk legends, songs, and tales, because they invoke the simple feelings of common life, accessible to everyone, and yet they do not hinder progress toward well-being. Art of this kind, he said, makes us realize to what extent we already are members of the human race and share the feelings of one common human nature.

In applying the touchstone of feeling to art, it is essential to differentiate what are the best feelings and what are evil. Only in this distinction, Tolstoy maintained, will the intimate and inevitable connection between morality and art become apparent. For if art unites men, the better the feelings in which it unites them the better it will be for humanity. He candidly admitted that the definition of the best and highest feelings will differ from age to age. Each age, he pointed out, has possessed a dominant view of life which may be described as its "religious perception." And the true religious perception of the Christian age, he insisted, is Christ's teaching, which permeates the whole life of man today, and if we accept this religious perception, it must inevitably influence our approval or disapproval of the various feelings transmitted by art. The best and highest feelings of art, then, are those which invoke the precepts of Christ—love for God and one's neighbor. When this religious perception is consciously acknowledged by all, said Tolstoy, then the division of art into art for the lower and art for the upper classes will disappear, for art which transmits feelings incompatible with the religious perceptions of our time will be rejected.[3]

Of course, Tolstoy did not limit the subject matter of art to these highest and religious feelings, as some of his critics supposed. There is another division of art, the universal, that he had already described, which conveys feelings of common life accessible to everyone—such as feelings of merriment, of pity, of cheerfulness, of tranquillity, and so forth.[4] The scope of the artist must in no sense be restricted.

[3] As examples of this highest art "flowing from love of God and man (both of the higher, positive, and of the lower, negative kind) in literature," Tolstoy mentioned: Schiller's *The Robbers;* Hugo's *Les Misérables* and *Les Pauvres Gens;* Dickens's *Tale of Two Cities, A Christmas Carol,* and *The Chimes; Uncle Tom's Cabin;* Dostoyevsky's works, especially *The House of the Dead;* and George Eliot's *Adam Bede.*

[4] With qualifications, and only because of their inner content, Tolstoy cited as examples of good universal art produced by the upper classes: *Don Quixote;* Molière's comedies; *David Copperfield* and *Pickwick Papers;* and the tales of Gogol and Pushkin.

The whole world of feelings, Tolstoy wrote, must be the artist's sphere of activity. Yet he did insist that a folk tale, a little song, or a lullaby that delights millions of children or adults is incomparably more important than a novel or symphony that will divert some few members of the wealthy class for a short time and then be forever forgotten. Almost untouched, he said, is this region of art in which the simple feelings are made accessible to all, and this region, like the highest religious art, tends to unite all mankind. He wrote:—

> Sometimes people who are together, if not hostile to one another, are at least estranged in mood and feeling, till perhaps a story, a performance, a picture, or even a building, but oftenest of all music, unites them all as by an electric flash, and in place of their former isolation or even enmity they are conscious of union and mutual love. Each is glad that another feels what he feels; glad of the communion established not only between him and all present, but also with all now living who will yet share the same impression; and, more than that, he feels the mysterious gladness of a communion which, reaching beyond the grave, unites us with all men of the past who have been moved by the same feelings and with all men of the future who will yet be touched by them. And this effect is produced both by religious art which transmits feelings of love of God and one's neighbor, and by universal art transmitting the very simplest feelings common to all men.

The book is rich in learning and in examples drawn from literature and life, and there is not a little fun, however unintentional and ponderous it may have been, at the expense of Wagner's *Ring of the Nibelung* and the opaque poetic effusions of the Decadents and Symbolists. For sheer organization and persuasive argumentation, he never surpassed this achievement in any of his controversial works.

Tolstoy, the great author of *War and Peace* and *Anna Karenina,* whimsically remarked in one place in the book that he knew that his theory of art would be considered an irrational paradox at which one could only be amazed. Nor did he understate the case. The critics quickly belabored it into an undeserved oblivion, although a few reviewers praised it highly, and George Bernard Shaw, with an aesthetic fissure in his brain as deep and wide as that of Tolstoy, hailed the work with delight. Critics might be pardoned for a certain degree of asperity in the face of the sympathy that Tolstoy expressed in his book for the truculent judgment that "critics are the stupid who discuss the wise." For the most part, the critics evaded his altogether excellent definition of art and concentrated their shafts on his withering application of it to certain generally accepted great works of art. For with his stubborn intellectual honesty, he did not shrink from the most extreme consequences of his reasoning. In his selection of examples of good and bad art, he did not claim for himself absolute authority. He humbly admitted that his own taste was probably perverted by false training. And he specifically asserted that he attached no special importance to his selection of examples. His only purpose in mentioning them, he said, was to make his meaning clearer.

With breath-taking execution he consigned all his own artistic productions to the category of bad art, with the exception of two stories, "God Sees the Truth but Waits" and "A Prisoner of the Caucasus." And when he placed Shakespeare's *Hamlet* or Beethoven's Ninth Symphony in this same category of bad art, he did not imply that all the works of these artists are bad. We know from other sources that he ranked some of their works as great art.

Tolstoy never remained satisfied with *What Is Art?* He felt it to be weak in various places, and he returned to the subject often in his diary and in letters. There lurked in his mind a feeling that something in the "mysterious and important" matter of art had never found its proper place in his aesthetic theory. But in this book, as in so many of his controversial works, the current of his thought joined the stream of nineteenth-century liberalism that has flowed down to our own day. He clearly saw and condemned many of the abuses of art that were later condemned by progressive minds, and his blistering attack on the middle-class cult of unintelligibility in art has been echoed many times since.[5]

5

Now, whenever artists gathered in the Tolstoy home, which was often, they were put through the wringer of *What Is Art?* and usually came out very flat and white. For Tolstoy was formidable in argument, though in his old age he

[5] Tolstoy's faith in the innate artistic instincts of people, uniting them in a community of feeling making for the brotherhood of man, was a conviction shared by Lenin, who was a deep student of Tolstoy.

quickly grew impatient with opposition, and, like Dr. Johnson, if he failed to bring his opponent down with a well-aimed shot, he would hit him over the head with the butt end of the gun. At the very beginning of 1898 a group of distinguished artists sat on after dinner. Rimski-Korsakov and his wife were among them. They had come to Moscow to attend a performance of the famous composer's opera, *Sadko*. A discussion on art soon raged. Tolstoy kept thundering away at beauty and its futility as a fundamental touchstone of art. Rimski-Korsakov warmly opposed him. The dispute ended with Tolstoy condemning all the musical views of Rimski-Korsakov. When the frayed and irritated guests finally departed, Tolstoy pointedly and loudly replied to the usual polite amenities of leave-taking uttered by the composer's wife: "No, you've not at all wearied or disturbed me, but today I'm glad that I have seen *obscurity* with my own eyes." The next day, like a repentant drunkard, he jotted down in his diary: "When will I remember that *much talk is much bother*."

Art had to give way to a more pressing practical matter—the Dukhobors. For through the intercession of the Tsar's mother, to whom they had appealed, the government had granted their request to migrate abroad, provided they agreed never to return. This seemed to be the only solution for the persecuted sect, but it raised difficult problems. Permission had to be obtained from a foreign government to accept some twelve thousand Russian peasants and allot them suitable land, and at the same time allow them to live according to their rather extreme convictions. If this problem could be solved, then there was the further one of raising a very large sum of money to finance the mass migration.

During most of 1898, Tolstoy threw himself into this work with his usual ardor, and he also inspired his disciples to render assistance of the utmost importance. Even members of the family caught his enthusiasm and helped, though Sonya grew more and more annoyed with this cause and feared it would all end with their so offending the government that the family would be deported along with the Dukhobors.

The financial campaign was initiated by Tolstoy, who wrote a strong appeal for funds and sent it to English and American newspapers, which were not loath to handle a document that so frankly exposed the harsh treatment meted out to a "harmless" religious sect in darkest Russia. He also wrote a quantity of letters to wealthy fellow countrymen, and the magic of his name and the fervor of his appeal resulted in a rain of rubles, though a few friends, such as Tretyakov, the art collector, coldly refused to make donations. The English Quakers, who never failed to answer the call of oppressed humanity, interested themselves in this cause both financially and in finding a refuge for the Dukhobors.

A place of refuge was the chief difficulty. Initial suggestions, such as the island of Cyprus, Manchuria, Chinese Turkestan, and Texas, were all ruled out for one reason or another, though eventually a small group of Dukhobors went to Cyprus. Tolstoy turned the problem over to his disciples in England. There the thriving Brotherhood Colony had been joined by the exiled Chertkov—or it would be more correct to say that he lived in majestic isolation near by, lending his advice and criticism to the colonists. Maude attached himself to the colony at this time, and Biryukov, who had been allowed to leave Courland, also turned up at Purleigh.

This nest of faithful grappled with the problem of a land of milk and honey for the Dukhobors. They soon quarreled, as was so often the case with Tolstoyans when obliged to cope with a purely practical matter. Chertkov sagely remarked over this disagreement that the disciples had to be convinced by experience that having the same point of view is far from being of one mind. Yet he was one of the chief offenders in this respect. The trusted lieutenant of Tolstoy, he made free and sometimes improper use of the master's name and influence. He possessed authority from Tolstoy to arrange for all first appearances abroad of his works in Russian and in translation, and in 1898 he organized the Free Age Press partly for this purpose. By printing the words "No Rights Reserved" on his editions, he hoped to set a moral example to the publishing world, which seemed rather silly since Tolstoy had already renounced all rights to his works in the original or in translation. He now fully accepted Tolstoy's faith in doctrinal matters, but he lacked his wisdom and common sense in spreading the gospel. Impressive in appearance, highly intelligent, and often charming in manner, he made friends and helpers easily, but he just as easily lost them because of his spiritual arrogance and domineering ways. He quarreled with Maude,[6] who had his own peccadilloes both as a man and as a Tolstoyan, and with other disciples over their mutual efforts to aid the Dukhobors. The news of the disagreements reached Tolstoy and saddened him, though Sonya appeared to derive some comfort from it.

Finally the Canadian government agreed to accept the Dukhobors, and Maude and Khilkov, who had been released from his exile in the Caucasus and had joined the English colony, went to Canada to investigate conditions and help with arrangements for the migration. Their report was very favorable. Canada as a refuge was most acceptable to the leaders of the Dukhobors, but Tolstoy had grave doubts and wrote Chertkov that he foresaw clashes between the sect and the Canadian authorities.

Meanwhile, the Russian authorities, however pleased at getting rid of these industrious but recalcitrant citizens, who had so dismally failed to appreciate the patriotic privilege of serving in the army, did nothing to speed their departure and particularly resented the aid of Tolstoy and his followers in the matter. The Minister of the Interior wrote a confidential memorandum to the civil head in the Caucasus to advise him to prevent any "Tolstoyan agitators" from having dealings with the Dukhobors. And the liberal *Russian News,* which appealed for funds through its columns to aid the Dukhobor migration, was suspended for two months because it had turned over the money to Tolstoy. The government even had an unknown ally in its harassment of Tolstoy. He had received an anonymous letter, no doubt partly inspired by his championing the cause of the Dukhobors, from what purported to be an underground society that called itself the "Second Crusaders." The senders threatened, if he did not reform, to murder him on April 3,

[6] Almost twenty years later Chertkov, still nursing his dislike for Maude, commented on his excellent though excessively subjective biography of Tolstoy as follows: "Unfortunately this most detailed biography of Leo Nikolayevich in English contains, among other things, the most perverted information about Leo Nikolayevich and an entirely incorrect interpretation of his views. Leo Nikolayevich himself, before his death, learning of the contents of certain of these chapters which were sent to Yasnaya Polyana in manuscript, found the account of the relation among people near to him so incorrect that he wrote to Maude about it." (*Diary of Leo Nikolayevich Tolstoy, 1895–1899*), ed. V. G. Chertkov (Moscow, 1916), p. 214.

1898, because he was the "legislator" of sects, had offended "our Lord Jesus Christ," and was an "enemy of the Tsar and fatherland." "I was both uneasy and pleased," Tolstoy wrote in his diary, but Sonya took the threat more seriously. His close friend Dunayev insisted upon remaining with him during the whole of April 3, adopting a clenched-fist pose of defense in preparation for the onslaught. The day passed and the "Second Crusaders" left him in peace and totally unreformed.

At last all arrangements for the migration were made, in which Tolstoy's son Sergei greatly assisted, making long trips to the Caucasus, England, and Canada. Before 1898 had ended, more than seven thousand Dukhobors had sailed for the new world. The largest of these crossings was excellently supervised by L. A. Sulerzhitski, that young disciple whom Chertkov had scorned for failing to abide by his decision not to serve in the army. The life of the Dukhobors in their new home is another story and not always a happy one. But whatever the wisdom of this mass migration of a religious sect from Russia, Tolstoy, as the leading spirit in the undertaking, had acquitted himself magnificently in an extremely difficult task.

6

Tolstoy's efforts on behalf of the Dukhobors did not exhaust his capacity for service to others during 1898. After he had heard from his son Ilya that a famine threatened his neighborhood, he left in April for the village of Grinyovka. With Ilya he rode on horseback throughout the district to observe conditions at first hand. The inspection took them near Spasskoye, Turgenev's former estate, and Tolstoy pushed on to it for he wished to see again this place that he had visited often in the past. He talked with the peasants and eagerly picked up any scraps of information they had to offer about their dead master. Filled with pleasant memories, he wrote the poet, Polonski, who had spent a memorable evening with him and Turgenev many years ago at Spasskoye, to describe his visit and to regret that their old friend no longer lived. Only a month before, he had written a letter to this same Polonski, who had become a bitter critic of his views on religion and art, to plead with him that they remain friends, for it pained him to inspire enmity in any man.

After thoroughly inspecting a number of villages in the district of Mtsensk and Chern, Tolstoy concluded that a real famine did not yet exist, but conditions were so bad that unless help were forthcoming a famine might set in. With the same zeal and practical wisdom he had shown in the famine six years before, he began raising money, attracting helpers, and organizing free food kitchens in the various afflicted villages. The everlastingly suspicious authorities provided the usual opposition. "What would you have me do?" complained one local constable rather shamefacedly, after obstructing the opening of a badly needed kitchen. Did he not have to obey orders from above? "It's very simple," answered Tolstoy, "don't work in a service where you can be made to act against your conscience." His efforts were private charity, Tolstoy argued, and there was no law against that. But not until he had fought the issue right up to the Minister of the Interior were the district minions of the law called off, and even then he was requested not to open any new kitchens. Despite many obstacles, the work was satisfying and highly successful. It undermined his health, however, and after suffering a severe attack of dysentery on the road, he was forced to retire to Yasnaya Polyana to recuperate.

Tolstoy wrote an article on this second attempt to feed the hungry. It is entitled "Famine or No Famine," and in it he described with consummate realism the misery he had encountered among the peasants. In an effort to arouse the conscience of the country he pointed out that their suffering and impoverishment would continue to get worse, no matter what aid was provided in times of crisis. Their poverty, he declared, was not only material, it was spiritual; they had lost all hope. And they must have hope, he asserted; they must be made to realize that life was worth living. One did not have to esteem them. Simply cease to scorn them, he wrote, stop treating them as animals, and give them freedom to learn and to travel. It was reported that even the young Tsar was moved by this eloquent appeal, but when the editor of the *Petersburg News,* to whom Tolstoy had sent the article, asked Nicholas II for permission to print it, he refused. Later it came out in a badly mangled form in a less popular publication.

7

While Tolstoy was resting at Yasnaya Polyana, he received a cable from the *New York World* (August 19) which congratulated him on the results of his struggle for world peace as evidenced by the recent statement of the Tsar's government, and it requested a reply. A week before, the Russian Minister of Foreign Affairs had sent a proposal to all governments for a conference to consider the limitation of armaments in an effort to preserve peace. At that time, international power politics were particularly threatening: America was at war with Spain, Germany was feverishly building up its navy, and a colonial struggle was going on between England and France. Obviously, the American newspaper was merely seeking copy, for it could hardly have been serious in attributing the Russian Minister's proposal for a peace conference to any influence that Tolstoy's ideas may have had on the Tsar, though this naïve possibility exists.

Tolstoy obliged with a characteristic answer which he cabled: "The consequences of the proposal will be words. Universal peace may be achieved only by manifesting self-respect and disobedience to governments that demand taxes and army service for organized violence and murder."

Had the American newspaper been seriously interested in the relations between the Russian government and Tolstoy, it might have received an answer from him that would have made headline copy. Why, for example, were a group of students that summer, who had traveled all the way to Yasnaya Polyana to present Tolstoy with a pitiful gift of a hundred rubles collected among themselves for the poor, prevented by the authorities from spending the money, at his suggestion, on food for starving peasants? Or why, on the occasion of Tolstoy's seventieth birthday that August, did the government send a confidential memorandum to all organs of the press, forbidding them to print any notices or accounts of this event connected with Russia's first citizen?

The celebration took place quietly at Yasnaya Polyana. Nearly all the family gathered and a few close friends. One of the guests made the mistake of toasting Tolstoy, the teetotaler, in wine, but in the ominous silence that followed the offender quickly saved the situation by switching his toast to Sonya, and the general merriment was recaptured. At sunset the whole company, including the children, went for a walk. In the evening the accomplished singer, Marya Muromtseva-Klimentov, sang poorly, according to Sonya, and the brilliant pianist Goldenweizer played very badly. Tolstoy received about a hundred congratulatory telegrams.

On November 28, a "Tolstoy Evening" was organized in his honor at the Moscow Korsh Theater. Tolstoy was not present, but Sonya, who attended, wrote him that it was a failure: "The reading of the fragments in a flat voice was terribly boring. Pravdin, with his German accent, read well 'The Story of Karl Ivanovich.'[7] Klimentov sang badly. The tableaux were repulsive, really shameful in their bareness and lack of taste. Natasha[8] with her hair tousled, all frizzled, and dressed in a cheap riding habit of calico, had a mug that might have been that of an actress or of a chamber maid. And the rest consisted of soldier tableaux: they shot Karatayev[9] (this was a bit better); the Abreks[1] shot. They gave a tremendous ovation to Mikhailovski.[2] Why? Then they recollected and began to shout for Tolstoy. A gentleman appeared and said that he was not in Moscow. They screamed: 'A telegram!' Then they roared: 'Read it!' It was read and you will receive it."

8

If it had not been for the Dukhobors and their troubles, Tolstoy might never have finished *Resurrection,* the theme of which he had first thought of ten years ago. In the course of his efforts to raise money for their mass migration he went over his portfolio of unfinished literary works and decided that he would try to complete *Hadji Murad, Father Sergei,* and *Resurrection,* sell them to Russian and foreign publishers, and give the proceeds to the Dukhobor fund. After a few unsuccessful attempts to continue the first two works, he put them aside and concentrated on *Resurrection.*

Once he got fairly into the composition of the novel, it absorbed him so completely that distractions of any kind, such as the copious letter-writing on behalf of the Dukho-

[7] O. A. Pravdin, an actor in the Maly Theater; "The Story of Karl Ivanovich" in Tolstoy's *Boyhood.*

[8] Natasha in *War and Peace.*

[9] A scene from *War and Peace.*

[1] Chechenian tribesmen in Tolstoy's *The Cossacks.*

[2] N. K. Mikhailovski who helped to organize the affair.

bors, became almost painful. Since *War and Peace,* he told his wife, he had never been so powerfully gripped by the creative urge. He collected information from experts on legal procedure, visited prisons, and talked with prisoners. In fact, the police feared that he was trying to propagandize the prisoners.

Tolstoy early made an arrangement with a publisher to take an advance of twelve thousand rubles on the novel which lent a special urgency to completing the task as soon as possible. With an almost guilty feeling he wrote Chertkov that the novel, though it did not conform to his present ideas of art, especially in form, would not be harmful and might even be useful. Besides, he suggested, the end in this case would surely justify the means—the money would go to the oppressed and unhappy Dukhobors.

Sonya, who wore her eyes out copying his labyrinthine manuscript, cared little about the means, but the end seemed a deliberate affront to her. She was running a private publishing business of her own, getting out editions of her husband's works. Her success rested upon her title to his productions written before 1881, but with those after this date she had to take her chances with all the other publishers, since Tolstoy had renounced his copyrights to these. Her closeness to the source of supply, as it were, gave her a special time advantage, for she could sometimes bring out new works before other publishers, which increased the sale of her editions or the separate supplementary volumes of new works that she published. That her husband loathed all this activity, which was so contrary to his public repudiation of any desire for financial gain from his writings, made no difference to Sonya. For she averaged about twenty thousand rubles a year on her publications, which constituted the largest part of the family income.

Now Tolstoy, without even consulting his wife, had sold the initial publishing rights of a new full-length novel, the first since *Anna Karenina.* Had she been able to bring out *Resurrection* first, she would have reaped a small fortune, but now she must wait until another publisher had skimmed the cream from the initial sale of the book. It was a cruel blow, and it was in no sense softened by the fact that the income from the novel would go to swell the fund that was being raised to send the Dukhobors to Canada. There were his son and daughter, Ilya and Masha, virtually poverty-stricken, she bitterly complained, so why not help them with the money? Who were the Dukhobors anyway, just "proud revolutionists" who refused to serve in the army and thus obliged others to take their places. He mildly replied that it grieved him that they were not in complete harmony in all things. "I have worn myself out with suffering over this disharmony," she wrote in her diary. "But the *whole* life of Leo Nikolayevich has been given over to people and aims alien to me, and *all* my life has been for the family. Neither my heart nor head can accept the fact that Leo Nikolayevich, after renouncing his author's rights and printing it in the newspapers, now finds it necessary to sell this novel for an enormous price to Marx's *Niva*[3] and give the money not to his grandchildren, who have no white bread, and not to his poverty-stricken children,[4] but to the entirely strange Dukhobors whom I can in no sense love more than my own children. But because of this the part that Tolstoy played in aiding the Dukhobors will be known to the whole world, and both the newspapers and history will write about it. Yet his grandchildren and children will eat black bread!"

Sonya's anger over the disposal of *Resurrection* appears to have soured her reactions to the novel itself. She decided that the position of the hero and heroine was extremely false, and one scene in particular deeply offended her. After hearing Tolstoy read a part of the work, she wrote in her diary: "I torment myself over the fact that Leo Nikolayevich, a seventy-year-old man, with the peculiar relish of a gastronome eating something tasty, describes the scene of fornication between the serving girl and the officer. I know, because he himself told me about this in detail, that in this scene Leo Nikolayevich is describing his own intimate relations with the serving girl of his sister at Pirogovo. At that time I saw this very Gasha, now an almost seventy-year-old woman; he pointed her out to me to my deep distress and disgust. I'm tormented over the fact that I see in the hero, Nekhlyudov, portrayed as progressing from his downfall to his moral resurrection, Leo Nikolayevich himself, who thinks this very thing about himself; he has described all these resurrections in books very well, yet he has never practiced them in life. And while describing and relating to people all his fine feelings and becoming sentimental

[3] The magazine *Niva,* edited by A. F. Marx.

[4] Neither Tolstoy's children nor his grandchildren were in any sense "poverty-stricken" at this time.

about himself, he has lived as always, loving sweet food, a bicycle, horseback riding, and lust." In the end, however, Sonya did not exclude *Resurrection* from the praise she accorded nearly all her husband's imaginative works in contrast to her dislike for his controversial writings.[5] Although Tolstoy kept doggedly at work on the novel, he was unable to finish it by the end of 1898.

9

In 1898, as during the previous year, Tolstoy was unusually faithful to his diary, and in it is revealed the richness of his inner spiritual life, as well as the record of literary plans that never reached fruition. In the face of the many volumes he actually produced, it is remarkable that his teeming brain conceived designs for literally scores of novels, plays, stories, and articles, many of which he roughly sketched or even began and then thrust aside. One of the works that he was contemplating at this time, and to which there are many references in the diary, is "The Appeal." It was to be an attack on the existing social order, in which the position of the working class would come in for extensive treatment. For a number of observations in the diary concern the problem of poverty and the panaceas, such as socialism. In one place he noted that there is no sense in the poor man's trying to shame or convince the rich man to share with him, for the latter sees that the poor man wants exactly what the rich man has. Only when the poor man ceases to seek what the rich man also seeks will the latter yield to him.

In another entry Tolstoy wrote: "Socialists will never destroy poverty and the injustice of the inequality of capacities. The strongest and more intelligent will always make use of the weaker and the more stupid. Justice and equality in the good things of life will never be achieved by anything less than Christianity, i.e., by negating oneself and recognizing the meaning of one's life in service to others." And he returned to Marx, whose theories seemed to be much on his mind, in contemplating "An Appeal." "Even if that should happen which Marx predicted," he wrote, "then the only thing that will happen is that despotism will be passed

[5] During 1898 Tolstoy also finished two articles, "Carthago Delenda Est" and "Two Wars," devoted to the subject of war and military service; and an introduction to a translation of Edward Carpenter's *Modern Science*.

on. Now the capitalists are ruling, but then the directors of the working class will rule." The mistake of the Marxists and of the whole materialistic school, he insisted, was in believing that an economic cause was at the root of all problems, whereas the life of humanity was moved by the growth of consciousness and religion. Marx is in error, he concluded, "in the supposition that capital will pass from the hands of private people into the hands of the government, and from the government, representing the people, into the hands of the workers."

Tolstoy confessed in the diary that the intentional or unintentional misunderstandings of his opinions irritated him. People said that he denied God, whereas he had consistently maintained that God is alone the unattainable good, the beginning of everything. Then some accused him of preaching that it was unnecessary to fight evil, but all he had said was that one ought not to resist evil by violence. Nor had he denied marriage or preached the destruction of the human race, as many charged. All he had said, he wrote, was that "one ought to strive towards chastity, and that on this road the highest grade will be virginity, the second a pure marriage, and the third not a pure marriage, i.e., not a monogamous marriage." Finally, he declared that people accused him of saying that all art must be tendentious, whereas what he had written was that art is an infectious activity and that the more infectious art is, the better it is. But whether this activity be good or bad does not depend on how much it satisfies the demands of art, that is, its infectiousness, but rather on how much it satisfies the demands of morality and conscience.

There is much on spirituality and morality in the diary during 1898. In his striving to get nearer to God, Tolstoy seemed able at brief moments to forget his material self and exist in a state of pure spiritual ecstasy. In these rarefied moments he saw the connection between cause and effect only in the spiritual world. The trouble with the materialists, he pointed out, is that they take as a guide for their acts the physical causal connection which one can never fully know, because every effect is an effect of an effect. On the other hand, he condemned those who live for spiritual ends alone, just as he would those who live solely for worldly ends. "There is peace only," he wrote in the diary, "when a man lives for the service of God among people."

The tendency to replace moral progress by technical progress he regarded as one of the main calamities of modern life.

Relentlessly searching his daily thoughts and actions, Tolstoy set down meticulously in his diary any infractions of the spiritual life he was struggling to live. For admissions of guilt had their moral compensations. Nothing softens the heart, he remarked, as the consciousness of one's guilt, and nothing hardens it so much as the consciousness of one's right. The fear of death he seemed to regard as a guilty feeling, and there are a number of observations on this subject in the diary during 1898. Illnesses were frequent this year, and he had at last accepted the fact that he was getting old and weak and must cease the physical exercise he loved. All this meant to him that he was getting closer to death. But he shunned any fear of it. Fear of death is a horrible superstition, he entered in the diary. For death is a joyous event standing at the end of each life. Whatever may have been his subconscious, unuttered feelings on the subject, he appears to have had no fear of death. Indeed, he now looked forward to it.

After returning from an inspection tour during his work in the famine region that summer, he wrote Sonya: "I rode back through the woods of Turgenev—Spasskoye; it was twilight: the fresh green of the forest under my feet, the stars in the heavens, the smell of the flowering osier, of the drooping birch leaves, the sounds of nightingales, the noise of cockchafers, cuckoos—the cuckoo and solitude— the pleasant, cheerful motion of the horse under me, and physical and spiritual health. And I thought, as I think constantly, about death. It became clear to me that it will be as fine on the other side where death is as it is on this side, but only different, and I then understood why the Hebrews have described paradise as a garden. The most pure joy—the joy of nature. It became clear to me that there it will be just as fine—even better."

XXXII

Soupe Printanière and Fugues

After vanichka's death in 1895 Sonya had acquired passion for music as a kind of escape from her grief. Eve her husband hoped that this new interest would help he regain her emotional equilibrium. The distinguished pianis and composer S. I. Taneyev, who had rented a wing o Yasnaya Polyana during the summers of 1895–1896, als became a frequent visitor at the family's Moscow house Sonya could not see enough of Taneyev, and her partialit soon became clear to everyone except Taneyev, who seeme unaware of the deep feeling behind Sonya's pursuit of him In general the musician was indifferent to women.

With growing anxiety Tolstoy watched the unbelievabl behavior of his wife—her repeated invitations to Taneyev the agitated way in which she pursued him with question on the musical world, their frequent meetings at the home of acquaintances and at concerts from which she would accompany him to his carriage. Her husband knew that this was an extreme manifestation of her hysteria, that it was simply the case of an ill woman transferring a love for music to a representative of the art. Yet at times he wondered, and then he could not suppress a feeling of jealousy. It was a mere whim, he comforted himself, and would soon pass.

The children also were distressed over their mother's actions; servants, friends, and even strangers were beginning to gossip. Rumor-mongers were maliciously whispering of the ironic fate of Tolstoy, placed in the terrible position of the betrayed hero of *The Kreutzer Sonata,* whose wife had fallen in love with a musician. But the hero in real life was sixty-eight and the heroine fifty-two, and they had been married thirty-four years! It all seemed like a monstrous practical joke.

This intimacy, which had first become noticeable during Taneyev's stay at Yasnaya Polyana in the summer of 1896 increased during the next two years. Sonya defined her feeling as love. As far back as 1890, in a moment of boredom with life, but before her intimacy with Taneyev, she had written in her diary: "Would it not be better to have memories of love—of even a sinful love—than this present emptiness, this spotless conscience?" And not long after she wrote: "I'm tormented by sinful thoughts."

The bachelor Taneyev, carefully watched over by his old nurse, hardly looked or acted one of the masculine sides of an eternal love triangle, nor would one have imagined him capable of inspiring sinful thoughts in any woman. He was twelve years younger than Sonya. He was not attractive, having a small head with small eyes set in a red face trimmed with a small beard, the whole mounted on a fat body. And his thin piping laugh only served to accentuate a naturally cold and stiff personality. He no doubt valued his associations with the Tolstoys and this fact perhaps encouraged the attentions he paid Sonya, whose endless adulation he also relished.

Though there is no concrete evidence that Sonya possessed sinful thoughts about Taneyev, she continued to give every indication that she was in love with him. She had been complaining for some time of weariness and the approach of old age, and now she suddenly felt a new "zest for life." With evident satisfaction she recorded in her diary the surprised comments of people on her youthfulness. She walked more lightly, her body felt healthier, and she found a renewed joy in gay evening parties or in skating with one of Taneyev's pupils. She noted in her diary her annoyance at the presence of other people when Taneyev visited, and then with the poetic mystery of a young girl in love for the first time she added: "S.I. [Taneyev] and I had no chance to talk to each other, but we exchanged a few phrases comprehensible to ourselves alone." When Taneyev was absent, she was inconsolable, and she contrived every imaginable pretext to call on him. Her whole being was transformed when he played. "His playing made my heart bleed," she wrote in the diary. "As he came to the end of the Polonaise, my eyes filled with tears and I nearly burst out sobbing." Here was love transforming with its magic touch a woman of fifty-three into an irrational girl of eighteen.

"Even the purest love finally leads to the desire for intimacy and possession," Sonya once observed in her diary. But nowhere in the records of her attachment to Taneyev is there any clear indication that she nourished such a desire. Besides, Taneyev at best was but a passive receptacle for her ardent feelings. Of the more than sixty letters that she wrote him, only one or two trespass the bounds of commonplace civilities of invitations or polite inquiries about his health. She never ventured to become more personal than to say: "How vexatious, Sergei Ivanovich, that we do not see each other! Will you not come tonight instead of taking your walk? I will be home and alone; I would be infinitely more gay with you than with myself. If possible, come, for I have a present for you—very fine photographs."

Despite a pathetic attempt to observe all the proprieties in an attachment that she wished to represent as a sincere friendship and nothing more, her older children saw something deeper and soon resented the frequent visits of Taneyev. Their outspoken criticism of their mother's behavior pained and angered her. Even fourteen-year-old Sasha (Alexandra) sensed that there was something wrong in her mother's relations with Taneyev. Her pleasant feeling for him as a friend of the family quickly turned into one of positive dislike. She recalled that on shopping tours her mother would casually direct the driver of their carriage to stop at Taneyev's house, and turning to Sasha she would say: "We must see how Sergei Ivanovich's old nurse is getting along." Young Sasha would keep silent and set her teeth, for she knew it was not the old nurse whom her mother wished to see.

Perhaps Sonya's unrequited passion deserved pity and understanding from her family rather than censure and harsh words. Though undoubtedly she was emotionally and psychologically ill, her temperament and extreme actions, like the failings of many sick people, constantly irritated those who most wanted to aid her. Her love for Taneyev clearly helped to fill the gaping void left in her emotional life by the death of Vanichka, a void that her husband could not satisfactorily fill because of their spiritual disharmony. Taneyev and Vanichka morbidly fused in her mind. She related in her diary how she talked with her dead son and asked him if there was anything evil in her feelings for Taneyev. "Today Vanichka seemed to turn me away from him. He must have felt sorry for his father; but I know he does not blame me, for it is he who sent me Taneyev, and he will not wish to take him away from me." The two were coupled in her dreams—Vanichka and Taneyev stretching their arms out to her, and in another dream she saw her dear son sitting on Taneyev's knee. Years later, when her passion for Taneyev was only a memory, Sonya was able to write of it in her autobiography[1] with a detachment that belied her actions, yet she did significantly recognize her exceptional emotional condition at that time. Relating what a soothing effect music had on her after the death of Vanichka, she added: "But the music that affected me more powerfully than any was that of Taneyev, who was the first to teach me by his own superb execution to listen to music and to love it. . . . At times I had only to meet Sergei Ivanovich, to hear his unimpassioned, quiet voice, and I grew calm. . . . My state of mind was abnormal. It coincided with my critical period. The personality of Taneyev had almost nothing to do with my condition. Externally he was uninteresting, always equable, extremely secretive, and to the end a man quite incomprehensible to me."

During the course of this abnormal relationship, Sonya could not resist comparing her husband and Taneyev. The fact that Tolstoy's jealousy interfered with her free intercourse with Taneyev unconsciously sharpened her asperity toward him and at the same time fed a feeling of guilt that she strongly resented. When Tolstoy was away during much of 1898, she cautiously refrained from mentioning in her letters the frequent visits of Taneyev, although she meticulously listed all the other callers. And of course she said nothing of her visits to the composer. Her diary during 1897–1898 is filled with cruel comments on her husband and rather shameless observations on the intimate side of their life together.

With a suggestion of elation, she noted in her diary on June 10, 1897: "I've knocked over Leo Nikolayevich as my idol." She was still devoted to him, yes, but he could no longer bring her "real happiness." Had he been displaced by another idol? She did not say, but she made it clear how

[1] This work is still unpublished.

keenly she was missing the company of Taneyev that summer. In her loneliness, her thoughts turned to suicide, and she almost wept over the letter she composed in her mind to explain her untimely end to friends: "I don't wish to suffer any longer," she exploded, "and I can't, I can't, I can't, I can't, I can't! I must either live without suffering, or die—and dying is the better course!" Then immediately following this outburst is a declaration that is pathetic in contrast. "And now I've got to write the menus again: *soupe printanière*— Oh, how I hate it! *Every* day for thirty-five years it has been *soupe printanière!* I don't want to hear any more of *soupe printanière;* I want to hear the most difficult fugue or symphony."

Her husband's criticisms of her attachment provoked Sonya into making extravagant statements about him in her diary. She imagined *What Is Art?* to be a deliberate attack on Taneyev. Unconsciously she contrasted the composer's pure relations to her with the physical passion of her husband. Although she reproached Tolstoy for writing unkind things about her in his diary, she did not hesitate to record his failings in hers. His cheerfulness during the day merely forewarned her to expect a night of passion, and, obsessed with her own pure desires, she wrote: "It has an entirely different effect on me; I feel ashamed and sad, and I yearn for a poetic, spiritual, even a sentimental relationship with someone—only to get away from this eternal sex." Then in another entry she deliberately drew a comparison: "He needs me only at night, not during the daytime; I grow sad and cannot help longing for last year's dear and friendly companion [Taneyev]." Sonya's concentration on the subject of sex in her diary during this period was no doubt a manifestation of her abnormal condition.

Though criticism of her husband appeared frequently in Sonya's diary during these two years of her attachment to Taneyev, there were also many expressions of devotion to him. Never did she question the supreme position he occupied in her heart. Even though she had knocked him over as her idol, she still worshipped at his shrine. Between the extremes of condemnation and fervent devotion, her judgment on Tolstoy and her relations to him at this time may be summed up in the statement she entered in her diary on May 20, 1898: "I've had at times both a passionate lover and stern judge in the person of my husband, but I've never had a friend in him, and now less so than ever."

2

In Tolstoy's eyes marriage was a relationship that united people for life and in complete fidelity to each other. Accordingly Sonya's feeling for Taneyev seemed to him an expression of infidelity. He tried hard to regard the affair in its proper perspective and to accept it as an affliction that he must bear in accordance with the moral and spiritual philosophy he professed. At times Sonya was puzzled by his polite and considerate behavior toward Taneyev, when she knew how intensely he disliked the composer. But she did not know the effort of will it had cost him to achieve this "love for one's enemies," an ineffable sweetness, he mentioned in his diary, "greater in proportion as the love is unattractive to you." Only once in the diary did he permit himself a direct criticism of Taneyev by name, and this occurred in the summer of 1895 before Sonya had evinced any partiality for him: "At home there were . . . Taneyev, who disgusts me with his self-satisfied moral and (though it seems ridiculous to say so) aesthetic (genuine, not superficial) stolidity, and his position of *coq de village* in our house."

Over these two years 1897–1898, Tolstoy's struggle against jealousy continued to find expression in his diary, but in guarded statements in which no names are mentioned. On January 12, 1897, he wrote: "Early morning. I cannot sleep for anguish. And neither choler nor selfishness nor sensuality is to blame, but this tormenting life. . . . Here there are nothing but pastimes of all kinds and guzzling and senile flirtation or still worse; it is abominable. I'm writing this down so that people may at least know after my death. Now it must not be said. Worse than those who are deaf are those who shout. She is sick, it is true, but it is the kind of sickness, that is taken for health. She receives encouragement instead of treatment. What will come of it, how will it end? I pray without ceasing. I blame myself and pray. Help me as Thou alone knowest." He went on in this vein, listing the sacrifices he had made—giving up his life to God's service, distributing his estates, and separating from his family—in order that he might experience real spiritual love, but now he had to witness this "degrading madness." Then, ashamed of his outburst, he humbly added that this sorrow had been sent to him, that he must bear it, and that there had been too little of suffering in his life of service to God. Finally, he tore out this page of his diary and sent it to Chertkov to be read and destroyed.[2]

That no measures were being taken to "heal" the sick passion of Sonya deeply disturbed her husband. Shortly after he went to visit the Olsufyevs in January 1897, Sonya left for Petersburg, ostensibly to visit her sister. Tolstoy knew that her real reason was to attend a symphony concert in which Taneyev was to perform. He took this occasion to write her a letter on her feeling for Taneyev.[3] After confronting her with the fact that she had misrepresented to him the real purpose of her trip, he wrote: "But you are doing this unintentionally. It is terribly painful and humiliating to think that a complete outsider, an unnecessary person, and in no sense of the word an interesting one, rules our lives. . . . It is humiliating and tormenting to think that one must find out where he is going, at what rehearsals he is playing, and when. It is frightfully, frightfully disgusting and shameful. And it is taking place just at the end of our life—a good life lived cleanly together—just at the time when we were coming closer and closer, in spite of all that might have divided us. This union of ours began long ago, before Vanichka's death, and grew closer and closer, especially of late. And now suddenly, instead of the natural, good, and cheerful conclusion of thirty-five years of life together, here is this vile abomination that leaves its horrible stamp on everything. I know that it is hard for you and that you too are suffering because you love me, and you want to be good, but up to now you have been unable to be, and I am terribly sorry for you, for I love you with the best love of all—not of the flesh and not of the mind, but of the soul."

During the remainder of the winter and spring of 1897, Tolstoy suffered intensely. Even the spiritual comfort on which he depended was failing him. Lilliputian hairs seemed to bind him, he wrote in his diary, and he felt "physically, intellectually and morally weak." While at Yasnaya Polyana, after receiving more news of Taneyev's

[2] But before destroying it, Chertkov photographed it.

[3] In the edition of Tolstoy's letters to her, Sonya did not include this one. It was published for the first time in Russian in a valuable article by N. N. Gusev, whose discovery of hitherto unpublished material on the family tragedy of the Tolstoys has been of great service. See "On the History of the Family Tragedy of Tolstoy," *Literary Heritage,* No. 37–38 (Moscow, 1939), II, 675–697.

visits to Sonya in Moscow, he entered in his diary on May 16: "Things are just the same, I didn't sleep all night. Never have my sufferings reached such a pitch." That same day he wrote to Chertkov. After informing him of his extreme unhappiness and vaguely hinting at the cause, without mentioning any names, he concluded: "I have tried everything: anger, prayers, expostulations, and lately, forbearance and kindness. Yet things get worse. I suffer from humiliation and cruelty, though I am ashamed to admit it." The letter struck him as too indiscreet and he did not send it. The next day he wrote in his diary: "My heart aches terribly. Tears rise in my throat." Finally, on the following day, he entered:[4] "It is just the same, my heart not ceasing to ache. For three nights I haven't slept, and I feel that I will not sleep tonight. I have, I think, come to a decision. It will be hard to carry out, but I cannot and ought not to do otherwise."

The decision was to go away, the temptation that he had firmly resisted for a number of years. On the night of May 18, he wrote his wife a letter, but deciding that it was too harsh, he destroyed it and drafted another. "Your intimacy with T. disgusts me and I cannot tolerate it calmly. If I go on living with you on these terms, I shall only be shortening and poisoning my own life. For a year now I have not been living at all. You know this. I have told it to you in exasperation and with prayers. Lately I have tried silence. I have tried everything, and nothing is of any use: the intimacy goes on and I can see that it may well go on like this to the end. I cannot stand it any longer. It is obvious that you cannot give it up; only one thing remains—to part. I have firmly made up my mind to this. But I must consider the best way of doing it. I think the very best thing would be for me to go abroad. We shall think out what would be for the best. One thing is certain—we cannot go on like this."

Still dissatisfied, and apparently feeling that his decision to go away had been too rashly taken, Tolstoy wrote a third letter, much longer and more tempered.[5] Repeating the story

[4] Apparently fearing to compromise his wife, Tolstoy tore out the pages containing the last four diary entries mentioned, and gave them, along with the unsent letter to Chertkov, to his trusted disciple, P. A. Boulanger, who was aware of Sonya's feeling for Taneyev, to read and destroy. Boulanger, however, preserved the documents and they have recently been uncovered and published.

[5] Both these letters were published by Gusev for the first time in the article mentioned above.

of his suffering and its cause, he wrote that he had decided to go away, "but when I thought of you—not of how painful it would be for me to part with you, no matter how painful it would be—but of how it would grieve you, torment you, of how you would suffer, I realized that I could not do it, that I could not go away from you without your consent." Then he proposed several solutions. The first and best, he wrote, was to break off all relations with Taneyev at once; the second, difficult for him, but "a thousand times better for me than to continue the life we have been living this year," was for him to go abroad and part with her forever; a third was to break off intimacy with Taneyev and go abroad with her husband; the fourth, "the most dreadful course, of which I cannot think without horror and despair," was to go on as they had been living: "for you to go on seeking—without being actually aware of it—every opportunity for intimacy, and for me to look on, observe, conjecture, and be tormented, not with jealousy, although perhaps there is something of jealousy in it, jealousy is not the principal thing. The principal thing I feel, as I have told you, is shame; I am ashamed both of you and of myself." He admitted there was a fifth course, which she had suggested: "to give up looking at this the way I do and wait for it to pass of itself." But he had tried and he simply could not accept this way. "Sonya, my love, you are a good, kind, fair-minded woman. Put yourself in my place and try to realize that I cannot feel otherwise than I do, that is, I cannot help but suffer tormenting pain and shame; try to think of the best way, love, not so much to relieve me of this as to relieve yourself of still worse sufferings which are bound to come in one form or another unless you change your attitude to all this and make an effort."

Expecting Sonya to arrive at Yasnaya Polyana the next day, he left both these letters for her, begging her to think the whole matter over calmly. Then, worn out with mental anguish and sleepless nights, he left for Pirogovo to visit his brother.[6]

[6] This may not have been the only correspondence that Tolstoy addressed to his wife on the theme of Taneyev. Sonya tells in her diary (June 21, 1899) how she came across a forgotten letter in one of her husband's books. On the envelope he had written that ". . . he had resolved to kill himself because he saw that I loved another. . . ." When she started to open the envelope to read the letter inside, Tolstoy snatched it from her and tore it into bits.

3

Far from being deterred by his remonstrances, Sonya invited Taneyev to visit at Yasnaya Polyana only a couple of weeks after reading her husband's plea that she break off her relations with the composer. The visit resulted in another quarrel, although Tolstoy, to her surprise, behaved toward the guest with the utmost civility. Either misled by this or incapable of resisting the desire to see Taneyev, she invited him again about a month later. "I haven't told Leo Nikolayevich yet, in case it upsets him," she noted in her diary. "My God, will he be jealous again! . . . Wouldn't Sergei Ivanovich be surprised if he knew! But I can't help being delighted at the thought that there will be music and pleasant conversation with such a cheerful, decent man."

One of the children at dinner dropped a hint of Taneyev's impending arrival. Tolstoy's anger frightened Sonya, though there is just the suspicion, as she tried to calm him, that she secretly enjoyed what she interpreted as a jealous rage. On July 8 he wrote a letter in which he informed his wife that he was leaving her. But he did not give her the letter nor did he leave. "He has suddenly quieted down," she entered in her diary, "he has softened; he went riding yesterday on his horse and on his bicycle, and he is not angry with me." Apparently he was able to conquer once again the impulse to go away in the belief that he must bear the shame and humiliation that God had sent him.

Tolstoy did not destroy this letter. He kept it, not among his papers, but hidden under the upholstery of one of the armchairs in his study. On the envelope he had written: "To be opened fifty years after my death." Several years later (May 1907) when he heard that Sonya was going to have the furniture newly upholstered, he rescued the letter, put it in another envelope, on which he wrote: "To be given to Sofya Andreyevna after my death," and he handed it over for safekeeping to his son-in-law. When the envelope was opened by Sonya after his death, there were two letters in it. After reading one of them, she remarked: "More foolishness and jealousy and reproaches," and she tore it into small bits. The other letter, dated July 8, 1897, she at once gave to the press. In order to save his wife from public censure over the real reason for his desire to leave her, Tolstoy had written two letters, one intended for his wife alone and the other for the world, if she cared to make it public.

In the letter that Sonya published, he wrote:—

"I have long been tormented by the incongruity between my life and my beliefs. To oblige you to change your way of life, your habits, which I taught you myself, was impossible; to leave you has also been impossible up to this time, for I thought that I should be depriving the children, while they were still young, of the influence, however small, which I might have over them, and should be causing you pain. But to continue to live as I have been living these sixteen years, at one time struggling and harassing you, at another yielding to those influences and temptations to which I was accustomed and by which I was surrounded, has also been impossible for me at last; and I have now made up my mind to do what I have long wished to do, to go away; first, because with my advancing years this life grows more and more burdensome to me and I long more and more for solitude; and secondly, because the children have now grown up, and my influence is no longer necessary and all of you have livelier interests, which will make you notice my absence less.

"But the principal reason is, just as the Hindus when they near their sixties retire into the forest, as every religious old man desires to dedicate the last years of his life to God and not to jokes, puns, gossip, and lawn tennis, so I, who am now entering upon my seventieth year, yearn with all the strength of my spirit for that tranquillity and solitude and, though not perfect accord, still something better than this crying disharmony between my life and my beliefs and conscience.

"If I did this openly, I should be met with entreaties, reproaches, and arguments, and perhaps I should hesitate and fail to carry out my decision, and it has got to be carried out. Please forgive me then if this step that I am about to take causes you pain; and in your heart, Sonya, and above all, let me go of your own free will; do not seek for me, do not find fault with me, do not condemn me.

"My leaving does not mean that I am dissatisfied with you. I know that you could not, literally *could not,* and cannot, see and feel as I do, and hence you could not and cannot alter your life and make sacrifices for the sake of what you do not believe in. I do not find fault with you;

on the contrary, I recall, with love and gratitude, the long thirty-five years of our life together, especially the first half of it, when, with maternal self-abnegation which is characteristic of you, you bore so zealously and patiently with what you thought was your appointed burden. You gave me and the world what you were able to give. You gave much maternal love and self-sacrifice, and I cannot fail to esteem you for that. But during the latter period of our life, during the last fifteen years, we have fallen away from each other. I can believe that I am to blame, because I know that I have changed, not for my own sake or for the sake of other people's opinion, but because I could not help it. And I cannot blame you for not having followed me, but I thank you and I lovingly recall and ever shall recall all that you have given me. Good-bye, dear Sonya."

If Sonya had known the contents of this letter in July 1897, it is doubtful if she would have, or even could have, given up Taneyev. When she returned to Moscow at the beginning of the autumn, Tolstoy lingered on in the country until almost the end of the year. Dislike for city life and a desire for the quiet of Yasnaya Polyana to work on *What Is Art?* contributed to this decision, but he also loathed the thought of being subjected to the frequent visits of Taneyev at their Moscow home. Shortly before her departure Sonya wrote in her diary: "I shall soon go to Moscow, where I shall hire a piano and play; and I hope Taneyev will come and play to me. The very thought of it gives me a new lease of life." He soon called and she was "terribly excited." When he failed to turn up for a brief period because of illness, she impatiently scribbled: "Oh what a terrible, violent, hopeless desire to hear that man play again! Will I *never* hear him?"

As Tolstoy continued to delay his return to Moscow, Sonya grew more and more irritated and began to suspect his real reason for not coming. "Is writing one article more or less of greater consequence to you than the happiness of your wife?" she wrote. Then her daughter Tanya, who had arrived from Yasnaya Polyana, passed on her father's remark that his life in Moscow was sheer suicide. With bitter scorn she wrote him at the end of November: "As you put the matter, you will come for my sake, for this would not be *self*-murder, which I suppose means that it is I who will then murder you, so I hasten to write you to say, for God's sake do not come; your painful arrival will deprive us both of calm and freedom. You will imagine yourself always as being murdered, and I will regard myself as the murderess. What a fine life in the name of love!" And she pointedly concluded: "Well, good-bye, now I shall wait for you no longer. Every spiritual strain has become unendurable to me. I will spend the evenings at concerts as much as possible."

The stage was being set for another quarrel, and the cause was already in the making. On December 17, Tolstoy wrote his disciple Dushan Makovitski: "Concerning the foreword to Carpenter, it has been the cause of great unpleasantness for me. And you were the unwitting reason for it. My wife suffers from some strange hatred and jealousy of Gurevich. It began at the time of the printing of 'Master and Man.' I thought it had passed, and I did not imagine that the foreword would produce such an effect, but I intended to tell her of this. It so happened that this information, received from you, had a terrible effect on her, so that I have had a bad time of it and have canceled the article with the *Northern Messenger* and will not print the foreword at all." And he cautiously added in a postscript: "Please do not answer me on this subject, for she reads my letters and every remembrance about this is a torment to her."

The reference is to an introduction that Tolstoy had written for a translation of Edward Carpenter's *"Modern Science,"* and he had sent the piece to the attractive editor, Lyubov Gurevich, of the *Northern Messenger*. When Sonya learned this bit of news from Makovitski, who visited her in Moscow, she became hysterical. "For a moment I wanted to take my life," she wrote in her diary, "then to go somewhere, then I played the piano for five hours, ate nothing all day, and slept in the parlor as only those sleep who are in great grief or agitation; I dropped down like a stone." That he should again send an article to Gurevich was a clear indication to her that he must be in love with the woman.

Sonya could think of no better way to express her grief than to leave home and go to the Trinity Monastery, a few miles from Moscow, a visit timed for the day when her husband had promised to return from Yasnaya Polyana. A telegram brought her back. "Leo Nikolayevich met me at the entrance with tears in his eyes," she wrote in her diary. "We threw ourselves into each other's arms. He agreed . . . not to print the article in the *Northern Messenger*, and

I promised him quite sincerely, not intentionally to see Sergei Ivanovich, to serve Leo Nikolayevich, to take care of him, and to do everything for his happiness and peace of mind. We talked so pleasantly that it was easy for me to promise him everything, for I strongly and warmly loved him and am ready to love. But today he has written in his diary that I *recognized my fault* for the first time and that this is joyous! My God! Help me to endure this! Again, before future generations, he must make himself out to be the *martyr* and me the one who is *at fault.* But in what am I to blame?"

A few months later Sonya calmly announced to her husband that she did not mind if he published his introduction to Carpenter in the *Northern Messenger,* for she would also like to use his piece in the supplementary volume of her edition of his works.

4

Sonya could not abide by her promise; she continued to see Taneyev, and "intentionally," through the early months of 1898. Nor could she resist the temptation to go all the way to Petersburg again to hear his music—she wanted to attend the Wagnerian operas there, she lied to her husband, a reason for her visit that was equally unintelligible to him. There were fewer of those veiled references to his sufferings in his diary this year. His grief and anger, however, were reflected in a series of sharp judgments on women, which were obviously inspired by his wife's behavior. "Women do not use words to express their thoughts, but to attain their ends. . . ." When falling in love "breaks out in the life of people after marriage," he observed, "it is out of place and disgusting." And in another entry he wrote: "Woman—and so also runs the legend—is the tool of the devil. She is generally stupid, but the devil lends her brains when she works for him. Then she accomplishes miracles of thinking, farsightedness, constancy, in order to do something nasty." And again: "It is impossible to demand from a woman that she evaluate the feeling of her exclusive love on the basis of moral feeling. She cannot do it, because she does not possess real moral feeling, i.e., one that stands higher than everything."

Such harsh judgments give a distorted impression of Tolstoy's opinion on women; they are the passing observations of a man profoundly hurt and perplexed by the actions of one woman—his wife. Scattered through his literary works are portraits of the highest types of womanhood, and in his controversial writings and in conversation Tolstoy frequently paid tribute to women as the better half of the human race.

When the opportunity came in April to help the famine-stricken in the district of his son Ilya, Tolstoy eagerly seized it. His desire to use the experience he had accumulated in this kind of work was sincere enough, but he also guiltily confessed in his diary at this time: "I accepted money and undertook to use it simply to have a reason for going away from Moscow, and hence I acted badly." Sonya and Taneyev had again become too much for him.

Tolstoy's work among the hungry peasants left no time for his personal worries. But when he returned to Yasnaya Polyana that summer, ill and in need of a rest, he found his domestic situation unchanged. Much against his wishes, Sonya went off to visit her friends the Maslovs at their country estate Selishche on July 12. She knew that Taneyev would be staying there at the same time. Overwhelmed by this new overt act, Tolstoy once more thought of going away from home, for he wrote letters to his Finnish disciple, Arvid Järnfeldt, the well-known author, and to Chertkov, in which he suggested such a move. Apparently his plan was to go to Finland, but again he overcame the temptation of taking a step that might so easily prove to be irreparable.

Sonya returned by way of Kiev, stopped there with her sister Tanya, and finally persuaded her to come to Yasnaya Polyana for a brief visit. It had been a "pure delight" to listen to Taneyev's playing at Selishche, but now at home Sonya experienced a feeling of guilt, which was increased by her sister's unsparing criticism of her pursuit of the composer. A few days after her return, she entered in her diary: "I walked through the woods alone and bathed and wept. At night the same talk of jealousy began again; and again there were shouting, abuse, and reproaches. My nerves could not stand it; something that kept the balance in my brain gave way and I lost my self-command. I had a terrible attack of nerves. I trembled all over, sobbed, raved, and kept starting up in fright. I do not well remember what happened to me, but it ended in a kind of numbness."

The conversation that brought about Sonya's violent attack of nerves that night was actually written down by Tolstoy in the form of a letter which he intended for her sister but never sent. He called it "A Dialogue." Tolstoy began by saying that he had gone to bed with his wife that night in a "good and pleasant frame of mind," consoled by what his sister-in-law had told him during the day and by her belief that all this unhappiness would soon end. As they lay in bed together, Sonya soon began to accuse him of talking about her and Taneyev to her sister. He begged her to drop the matter since he did not wish to discuss it and hoped that it would finally quiet down and be done with. Then he continued the dialogue:—

"*She:* I cannot stop speaking of it, for it is difficult for me to live in constant fear and trembling. If he should happen to come here, it will start all over again. He did not say anything, but he may come.

"The news that he may come—as always it was put as if he 'should happen,' when in reality he was certain to come —upset me very much. Just as I was trying not to think of it, here was this annoying visit again. I said nothing, but I could not sleep and finally could hold out no longer.

"*I:* Just as I was hoping to get some peace you begin to prepare me again for a disagreeable happening.

"*She:* What am I to do? It may happen. He told Tanya. I didn't ask him. Perhaps he will come.

"*I:* It is of no importance whether he comes or doesn't come, and even your trip is of no importance; what is important, as I told you two years ago, is the attitude you take to your feeling for him. If you had acknowledged this feeling to be a bad one, then you would not have even troubled to mention whether he was coming or not.

"*She:* Well, what am I to do now?

"*I:* Repent of your feeling in your soul.

"*She:* I don't know how to repent and don't understand what it means.

"*I:* It means that you have to judge for yourself whether your feeling for this man is right or wrong.

"*She:* I haven't any feeling, either right or wrong.

"*I:* That is not true.

"*She:* It is such an unimportant, insignificant feeling.

"*I:* All feelings, and therefore even the least significant, are always either right or wrong in our own eyes, and hence you must decide whether this is a right or a wrong feeling.

"*She:* There is nothing to decide. This feeling is so unim portant that it cannot be bad. And I am sure there is noth ing bad in it.

"*I:* No, the exceptional feeling of an old married woma for a strange man is a wrong feeling.

"*She:* It is not a feeling for him as a man but as a huma being.

"*I:* But this human being is a man.

"*She:* For me he is not a man. It is not an exceptiona feeling. There is only this—that after all my grief I found consolation in his music, but I have no particular feeling for the man.

"*I:* Why do you speak an untruth?

"*She:* Oh, very well then. Let us leave it that way. I did wrong to go and it hurt you. But now it is all over with. I will do everything possible in order not to hurt your feelings.

"*I:* You cannot do so, because the whole point is that whatever you do—go to him or not, receive him or not—the whole point lies in the attitude you take to this feeling of yours. You must decide for yourself whether it is a right feeling or a wrong one.

"*She:* There isn't any at all.

"*I:* That is not true, and this is what is bad for you. You want to hide this feeling, in order to keep it in check. But until you make up your mind whether it is a good or bad feeling and acknowledge it to be wrong, you will not be able to avoid hurting me. If you acknowledge, as you are doing, that this is a good feeling, you will never be strong enough not to wish to gratify it, that is, to see each other. And if you wish it, then you will certainly do everything you can to see him. And if you avoid seeing him, you will only be sad and always yearning to see him. So it follows that everything turns on your decision as to whether it is a good feeling or a bad one.

"*She:* I have done nothing wrong. What I did wrong was to give you pain, and I am sincerely sorry for it.

"*I:* That is just what is bad about it; you repent of your actions but not of the feeling that guided those actions.

"*She:* I know that I have never loved anyone, nor do I love anyone more than I love you. I should like to know then what your conception of my feeling for you is? How could I love you if I loved someone else?

"*I:* This inner conflict is the result of your not having explained to yourself the meaning of your feeling. A drunkard or a gambler may love his wife dearly and yet be incapable of keeping away from cards or wine; and he never will be able to keep away from them as long as he does not decide in his heart whether his love of cards and wine is a right feeling or not. Only when this is decided will he be able to free himself."

The argument continued. Tolstoy kept insisting that she recognize her feeling for Taneyev for what it was, until Sonya, with some justification, exclaimed in desperation: "The same thing over and over again. It is simply torture!" All she wanted, she declared, was "that *he* should come once a month and sit awhile and play for me, as any good acquaintance might."

"Yes," he replied, "and by those words you are proving that you have a particular feeling for this man. There is, after all, no other person whose monthly visits could give you joy. If this one visit a month would be pleasant, how much pleasanter would be a weekly or a daily visit. You have confessed involuntarily to your particular feeling. And unless you settle the question of whether it is good or bad, nothing can be altered."

Recriminations followed over instances of her chasing after Taneyev, and Tolstoy scornfully described her "as one of those ladies who never miss a concert at the conservatory." This appeared to be the last straw for Sonya and she became hysterical.

A long silence ensued, and Tolstoy continued: "Then I remember God; I pray and think to myself: *she cannot renounce her feeling,* she cannot bring the influence of her mind to bear on her feeling. With her, as with all women, feeling dominates, and any change that takes place in her feeling will perhaps do so independently of her mind. Perhaps Tanya is right, and this will take place gradually in its own peculiar feminine way, incomprehensible to me. I ought to tell her this, I think to myself, and, full of pity and a desire to soothe her, I tell her that perhaps I am mistaken in putting the question in my own way. Perhaps she will arrive at the same thing after her own fashion, and that this is what I am hoping for."

At that moment, however, her irritation reached an extraordinary pitch and she poured out a torrent of harsh words and wild threats, ending in a fit of hysterics. He concluded: "Sobbing, laughing, and whispering meaningless, and alas, feigned protests, such as 'My head is ready to split . . . just here at the parting . . . cut a vein in my neck. Oh, this is the one. . . .' She tried to frighten me with this and a great deal more rubbish. I held her. I know that always helps. I kissed her brows. She could not get her breath for a long time. Then she began to yawn and sigh, and at last she fell asleep and is still sleeping.

"I do not know how this madness can end. I cannot see any way out. It is evident that she values this feeling as much as her life and does not want to acknowledge it as wrong. And without acknowledging it as wrong, she cannot get rid of it and will continue to do the things the feeling demands, things that are tormenting and shameless for the children to witness, if not for me."

5

Sonya's feeling for Taneyev did change "gradually in its own peculiar feminine way," but not through any effort of her own will or because she finally recognized it as a "bad feeling." Taneyev put an end to the affair. For several more years she kept up the chase, attending concerts in order to sit with him, and making summer pilgrimages to Selishche to be near him. She observed that he began to avoid her, and she imagined that he had heard of her husband's jealousy or that he had received a letter from him, but Tolstoy never once uttered a word to Taneyev about his wife's attitude toward him. Finally came an affront too obvious for her to ignore: he left her box at a concert and went to sit in the gallery. This took place in April 1904. She wrote him to demand an explanation. He evaded the issue. She wept, grew melancholy, and could not sleep. Painful exchanges of letters took place, she hoping for a favorable explanation of his behavior, he cautiously avoiding one. Eventually he offered her a silly explanation, which she gratefuly accepted, that he had left her at the concert because his thoughts kept turning on her but he valued the music of Tchaikovsky more. But something had snapped in her feeling for him; her happiness was gone and only memories remained. The man who at one time seemed to her to possess all the possible virtues, she could now describe as "thick-skinned and gross, both in body and spirit."

Through the concluding months of 1898 Tolstoy again shunned the city as long as he could, immersed in the business of the Dukhobors and in work on *Resurrection.* With him in the country and Sonya in Moscow, peaceful relations were more easily maintained. She wrote him less frequently than was her custom, for she was extremely busy with music and concerts. But of these matters and of Taneyev she now made little mention. The debauchery of young Misha and the broken engagement of Andrei to a Georgian lady, who in despair shot herself, were the subjects of her letters. And she complained of her strange "autumn grief" and the "smell of a corpse," a hallucination that had obsessed her since Vanichka's death. Tolstoy wrote her sympathetic, loving replies. Chafing at his continued absence, she went to Yasnaya Polyana to spend a few days with him. So happy were they that she wept on parting. Though he failed to arrive in Moscow in time for their thirty-sixth wedding anniversary, she paid him an unusual tribute in her diary: "I do not complain, and it is fine that he cares about me, so jealously guards me, and is so afraid to lose me. But he need not. Whomever I might love, there is no one else in the world I would even *compare* with my husband. He has held too great a place in my whole life and in my heart."

XXXIII

Resurrection

ALL COPIED the manuscript of *Resurrection*—members of the family and their guests. Duplicate sets of corrected proof had to be prepared for translators. Anguished telegrams arrived from the editor of *Niva* to beg for final copy for the next weekly issue of the magazine. Cablegrams and letters from abroad offered huge sums for the first publication rights. Racing against time, but always the exacting artist, Tolstoy kept to his study for days on end, mangling successive sets of proof, repeatedly rewriting whole sections, and hurrying off last-minute changes to the editor in an installment just about to go to press. He deserted the family, often took his meals alone at odd hours, and saw few visitors. The atmosphere of the household was tense and strained by the mighty effort. Finally, on December 18, 1899, he wrote in his diary: "Completed *Resurrection*. Not good, uncorrected, hurried, but it is done with and I am no longer interested."

Twelve years before, the eminent jurist, A. F. Koni, while visiting Yasnaya Polyana, had planted in Tolstoy's mind the seed of this novel by relating an incident connected with his law practice. One day an agitated young man had come to his office to ask aid in conveying a letter to a girl who had been sent to prison, for the jail official had refused to do this unless he were permitted to censor the letter. Koni agreed to help him and subsequently learned the details of the case. As an orphan child the girl had been taken in by a wealthy lady who owned the farm her dead parents had rented. Although given some education, she was eventually relegated to the position of a servant in the family. When she had reached the age of sixteen, a pretty, well-formed girl, a relative of her benefactor happened to visit the estate. This visitor, the same young man who had appealed to Koni, seduced the girl, and when her benefactor observed her pregnant condition, she drove her from the house. Abandoned by her seducer, she placed her newborn child in an asylum, and after a hopeless attempt to earn an honest livelihood, she became a prostitute and sank lower and lower. Detected in stealing a sum of money from one of her drunken "guests" in a brothel, she was arrested. On the jury that tried the case fate placed the young man who had seduced her. Their meeting in such circumstances produced a powerful impression on him and awakened his conscience to the injustice of his behavior. He decided to marry the girl, who had been sentenced to four months in prison. Koni concluded the tale by relating that they were actually married, but shortly after her sentence expired the girl died from typhus.

The story deeply moved Tolstoy and he urged Koni, an extremely talented person, to write it for the *Intermediary*. Koni promised to do this. When a year had passed and he failed to fulfill his promise, Tolstoy asked to be allowed to make use of the story. For the next ten years he worked at it by fits and starts, but only when the need for money arose in 1898 to aid the Dukhobors to emigrate to Canada did he turn to the novel with renewed determination and zest.[1]

Koni's slender tale served as the foundation of a novel of some five hundred pages. As in Tolstoy's other long novels, the development of the story element was a protracted, tortuous process. There were several quite different beginnings, and again and again he deleted themes and introduced entirely new ones. Even small details such as the description of the external appearance of the heroine Katya Maslov exist in as many as twenty variants. There are six separate redactions of *Resurrection,* and before he had finished his laborious revision he had piled up enough rejected material to fill a volume almost as large as the novel itself.

Again as in Tolstoy's previous full-length novels, there is a great deal of autobiographical matter. The original hero, Valerian Yushkin, was inspired by Tolstoy's brother Sergei, but in later redactions the hero became Dmitri Nekhlyu-

[1] Tolstoy worked on the novel, more or less consistently, during the following years: 1889–1890, 1895–1896, 1898–1899.

dov,[2] and now he curiously resembled Tolstoy himself and also Chertkov in some aspects of his spiritual development. Many of the characters are plainly modeled on people Tolstoy knew. Toporov, it is interesting to observe, is a thinly disguised and unflattering portrait of Pobedonostsev.

Before the serial publication of *Resurrection* had got well under way, Tolstoy began to regard his compact with *Niva* as one with the devil—he had sold his soul for that advance of twelve thousand rubles, even though the money went to the Dukhobor fund. This sole instance of violating his previous repudiation of all copyright privileges to the extent of accepting money for the initial publication of a novel caused him endless trouble. *Niva* at first attempted to run the novel in weekly installments. With his painstaking correction of proof and the constant introduction of new matter, Tolstoy found it extremely difficult to keep up this pace. Finally his health broke down and he virtually decided to end the novel with Part II, omitting the brilliant third part. Only the willingness of the editor to forgo his demand for weekly installments persuaded Tolstoy to continue. Then newspapers and magazines pirated the chapters as they came out, so that Tolstoy had to make a public request that *Niva* be permitted to publish the whole novel before others availed themselves of the right he had long since given them to produce his works free. On the whole, this request was observed in Russia.

Abroad, arrangements went forward, largely under Chertkov's direction, for the simultaneous publication of translations in England, France, Germany, and America. Foreign editors were eager to buy first rights, this money also going to the Dukhobor fund. As soon as Tolstoy finished a final batch of corrected proof in duplicate, a set was sent to Chertkov in England. It was not so easy to prevent foreign firms from pirating, a fact that caused Tolstoy much embarrassment. Twelve different translations appeared in Germany alone in 1900. In 1899 and 1900, fifteen editions were published in France. Obtaining faithful translations was difficult, a misfortune Tolstoy's works had nearly always suffered abroad. The extreme liberties taken with *Resurrection* were of the order of those in a German translation of

[2] Characters by the name of Nekhlyudov turn up persistently in previous fictional works of Tolstoy, in *Boyhood, Youth, A Landlord's Morning,* and "Lucerne," and in the last two, Nekhlyudov is clearly autobiographical.

Anna Karenina, in which the motto of that book, "Vengeance is mine; I will repay," was altered to "Revenge is sweet; I play the ace!" While the French version of *Resurrection* was appearing in the *Echo de Paris,* Parisian readers characteristically complained that the love scenes of the hero and heroine, which they relished, were too infrequent. The businesslike editor had no scruples about omitting the next regular installment and substituting for it one in which the hero and heroine are again occupied with each other. In America, on the other hand, the editor of the *Cosmopolitan,* who had bought the first serial rights, did not hesitate to tone down or delete love passages that he thought might offend that magazine's respectable middle-class readers. Chertkov promptly broke this contract and a lawsuit was threatened which naturally added to Tolstoy's worries. In the end he was happy at the thought of reverting to his rule of taking no money for his writings, unwilling perhaps to realize that the rule itself had been the cause of all his troubles.

Not the least of Tolstoy's worries was the censor. This high executioner of words could hardly be expected to tolerate the author's blasphemous handling of the Church and religion or his exposure of the way prisoners were treated in Siberia. And much was struck out. Only 25 chapters of the 129 in *Resurrection* entirely escaped the censor's red pencil.[3] Tolstoy protested in some instances, but in general he shared the surprise of many people that the book was allowed to be published at all in Russia. It had always been thought that the Russian edition of *Resurrection* issued in England by Chertkov, and which subsequently became the source of many foreign translations, was entirely unexpurgated. However, in sending Chertkov the corrected proof sheets, Tolstoy inadvertently included a number of the censor's deletions and alterations. Not until 1936 was the complete and unaltered text of *Resurrection* published in Russia.[4]

Tolstoy was seventy-one when he finished *Resurrection,* the last of his great novels. At this age he had a right to expect some diminution of his creative powers, and it is clear that the work falls short of the artistic eminence of *War and Peace* and *Anna Karenina.* Further, the concluding

[3] It has been estimated that 497 separate deletions or alterations were made in the text of *Resurrection* by the censor.

[4] See the Jubilee Edition, Vols. XXXII-XXXIII.

parts suffered from obvious haste in composition. Though written in his former manner, *Resurrection* is unlike his previous novels in several respects. Although there is the same fresh and realistic treatment of his own gentry class, this kind of life, which he knew so well, is brilliantly contrasted with a new element—the life of the protesting, revolutionary intelligentsia. And the struggle between the moralist and the artist that had been reflected in its initial stages in the last pages of *Anna Karenina* is everywhere in evidence in *Resurrection*. Rarely does the moralizing element appear unadorned with the rich, variegated garments of real life. The essence of all that Tolstoy had thought and suffered since his spiritual change is condensed in the pages of the book. It is unashamedly a purpose novel, but then so are nearly all great novels. The principal purpose of *Resurrection* is to reveal the evil consequences of the violence of government and the hypocrisy of the Church.

Tolstoy's own sins and passions, his manifold struggle with life, are reflected in the nature and actions of Nekhlyudov. And the hero is also imbued with his creator's instinct to discover the purpose of life. He found it, like Tolstoy, in the Sermon on the Mount. "From that night," the novel concludes, "there began for Nekhlyudov an entirely new life, not so much because he had entered into a new condition of life, but because everything that happened to him since then assumed a significance utterly different from that which he had formerly experienced. How this new period of his life ends, the future will show."

This struck many readers as a lame conclusion. Throughout the novel Nekhlyudov had been portrayed as a man of action, and this transformation into an intellectual Tolstoyan seemed false to his nature. The end of the book, however, hints at a sequel that will tell the story of Nekhlyudov in his new life. What form of activity that will take is suggested in Tolstoy's diary shortly after he had finished the novel: "I want terribly to write an artistic, not a dramatic, but an epic continuation of *Resurrection:* the peasant life of Nekhlyudov." Apparently in his new existence the hero was to play the part of a peasant, perhaps a successful Tolstoyan peasant, which would have been unique in either fiction or life.

Any appraisal of the novel according to the new standards that Tolstoy had announced in *What Is Art?* does not discredit him as an artist or as a theorist on art. To be sure, such an appraisal inevitably contains a large element of subjective judgment, but the popular judgment of time and posterity lends its increment of support. According to Tolstoy's principal criterion of real art—infectiousness—*Resurrection* holds up extraordinarily well. The novel deals with feelings profoundly experienced by the author and re-created so that they infect readers and cause them to share these feelings with him and with each other. And the novel also abundantly possesses those other aspects of real art which Tolstoy had listed in his treatise—sincerity, individuality, and clarity. Yet he would have been the first to admit, and perhaps sadly, that the book is not popular art, not art for the masses. It belongs to the exclusive art of the leisured and cultured classes. With this limitation, *Resurrection* is real art. But does it belong to the category of the best art, according to Tolstoy's definition? That is, do the feelings it conveys make for the highest perception attainable by man—positive feelings of love of God and of one's neighbor? In this respect, too, Tolstoy can claim a large measure of success. More than any of his novels, *Resurrection* evokes in us feelings of brotherly love and of the common purpose of the life of all humanity—a striving to achieve spiritual and moral perfection through service to others.

Curiously enough, it did not occur to critics to use Tolstoy's recently published artistic criteria in judging his novel. The book was enthusiastically received, and in England and America it enjoyed a larger sale than any other work of Tolstoy up to that time. Though a few conservative native critics shouted "Propaganda!" the more progressive showered praises, for they admired almost the only man in Russia who could so boldly and courageously expose in fiction the evils that beset their country. For Russia, the publication of *Resurrection* was an event transcending its artistic significance or the fact that Tolstoy was the author. Some of the widespread excitement aroused by the novel is conveyed in a letter from Stasov in Petersburg while the chapters were appearing in *Niva:* "Leo Nikolayevich, how all of us here rejoiced when we learned that the chapters of *Resurrection* will not be 60 or 80 but 100 or more. Without exception all are saying on every side: 'Ah, there will be more, more will be added! May God grant that there will be still more and more!' And not only the people here, but I think throughout all of Russia from one end to the other, they wait solely for that day, Friday morning, when the bell rings and the boy brings the latest *Niva.* Friday everywhere is turned into Sunday.[5] . . . Oh, what an amazing miracle is your *Resurrection!* How all of Russia now lives and is nourished by it."

2

Tolstoy's absorption in *Resurrection* during 1899 left him little time to devote to his spiritual empire. At the beginning of the year, however, he dropped everything to turn his attention to a cause close to his heart. The *New York World,* dissatisfied with his answer of the previous year on the international conference for disarmament, again turned to him for his reactions, for it was now certain that a meeting would be held at The Hague that summer. This time his statement provided the kind of copy the American newspaper was eager to print. He wrote: "My answer to your question is that peace can never be achieved by conferences or be decided by people who not only jabber, but who themselves go to war. This question was decided 1900 years ago in the teaching of Christ as this teaching was understood by Him and not as it has been perverted by the churches. All conferences can be summed up in a single dictum: All people are sons of God and brothers, and therefore they ought to love and not kill each other. Forgive my sharpness, but all these conferences invoke in me a strong feeling of disgust over the hypocrisy that is so obvious in them."

Meanwhile, a group of distinguished Swedish intellectuals had sent Tolstoy an unusual proposal. In their letter they summarized the history of peoples and groups in various lands who had refused army service on religious grounds. They proposed that this matter be placed on the agenda of the forthcoming Hague Conference, and that citizens of all countries should be allowed to reject army service because of religious beliefs provided they agreed to accept service for an equivalent period of time in some peaceful and socially useful occupation for the State. The hope of the Swedish intellectuals was that if such a proposal were accepted by the nations at the Hague Conference, it would eventually prove a deathblow to the maintenance of large armies and would thus ensure world peace. And they respectfully requested Tolstoy to use his great influence to bring this proposal to

[5] A pun on the title of the novel, *Voskreseniye,* which means in Russian both "Resurrection" and "Sunday."

the attention of the Tsar or his ministers and of the public.

Tolstoy replied in a letter (January 9, 1899) that he eventually elaborated in the form of an epistolary article which Chertkov published in England. He paid a sincere tribute to the good intentions of the Swedish intellectuals, but their proposal was "entirely irrelevant." "Such a proposal can have only one good consequence, namely, that it will evidently unmask the emptiness, idleness, and hypocrisy of the Conference. The Conference cannot refer itself other than negatively to such a proposal, for it will never permit people to go unpunished for refusing to accept military service, because such refusal undermines the foundations of governmental power and even the very reason for its existence."

Tolstoy's position was realistic: after two months of deliberation and diplomatic shuffling, the only tangible result of the Hague Conference of 1899 was a series of conventions on the more "humane" conduct of war. The question of total disarmament or the limitation of armaments, which had originally inspired this meeting of nations, did not interest the conferees at all. The representatives had barely had time to return to their several countries when one of the participants in the Conference, England, plunged into a bloody war with the Boers. Tolstoy wrote in his diary: "It is necessary to point out that the present state of affairs, especially the Hague Conference, has shown that nothing is to be expected from the higher powers, and that the resolution of this horribly destructive situation, if at all possible, will depend solely on the efforts of private individuals."

In general, Tolstoy had no faith in the customary organized efforts to achieve world peace. He rigidly adhered to his belief that only the widespread refusal of individuals to participate in violence of any kind could end wars. It was largely for this reason that he also refused an invitation in 1900 to serve on the committee of the Tenth International Peace Congress at Paris.

There was something positively indecent, as Tolstoy pointed out later, in the fact that the proposal for the Hague Conference should have come from the Russian government and at a time when it was secretly giving orders to increase the size of its army, and through oppressive measures was quelling every manifestation of liberal thought at home. Before its delegates left for The Hague, a nationwide strike of college students took place, in February 1899. Students of Petersburg University, indignant over a brutal threat of reprisals by the authorities if any disorder occurred during one of their traditional holidays, decided not to attend classes. At an outdoor protest meeting the students were charged by Cossacks with swinging whips, and some of the ringleaders were arrested. They then organized and demanded redress of their wrongs and freedom from arbitrary persecution by the government. On a platform that included an agreement to commit no acts of violence, whatever the provocation, the movement quickly spread, and soon students and even some professors in higher institutions throughout the country went out on strike in sympathy with the Petersburg group.

The students sent a delegate to Tolstoy to persuade him to write an open letter in their defense. He had long been interested in student movements and had faith in the progressive thinking of these young men and women. On this occasion he expressed his sympathy for their cause, which the students made more than free use of in their publications, but he declined to write an open letter, probably because he felt it would do them more harm than good. The matter obviously worried him, for a couple of months later he began an article in which he considered the student strike, but he never finished it. He sent his material to Chertkov who used it for an article on the subject which he published in England. Tolstoy was pleased with the article and wrote Chertkov that he had expressed "the very thoughts that I have had on this theme."

3

Tolstoy's preoccupation with *Resurrection* during 1899 did not deter visitors, though he saw less of them. Both in Moscow and at Yasnaya Polyana the family had for some time been leading a kind of public existence and gradually they had become conditioned to it. Mere curiosity-seekers annoyed them, but distinguished writers, musicians, painters, and sculptors turned the Tolstoy house into a palace of art. If Sonya was flattered by the attention of social lions, she grew exasperated with the many nonentities who sought out her husband. He, on the other hand, regarded it as a duty to meet and talk with all these nondescript people who timidly rang his bell hoping to enter the portals of truth. Many of them were deeply religious, but now they were citing Tolstoy's forbidden texts as they used to cite the Bible. And they yearned for nothing more than to be admitted to his sanctuary, where each sat patiently, like Moses, hearing the voice of God on Mt. Sinai. Some were already convinced Tolstoyans, but these green disciples often annoyed Tolstoy, for they were everlastingly asking him how they could change their lives when he believed that they should be doing their own work, provided it did not clash with their convictions. "He is a Tolstoyan," he remarked to Goldenweizer of one of his callers, "that is, a man with convictions utterly opposed to mine."

For obvious reasons the unknown, down-at-the-heel seekers after truth were not mixed with the social celebrities in the Tolstoy household. On this score a tacit understanding seemed to exist between husband and wife. Perhaps Sonya was a bit ashamed of exposing her aristocratic guests to these shabby seekers, who came furtively but often in a state of elation.

This double standard of hospitality is illustrated by the account Sofya Shil gives of her visit to the Tolstoys in Moscow on Easter Eve, 1899. A cultured person and a worker on the *Intermediary,* she was not regarded as one of the "dark people" and was not even a disciple of Tolstoy. She was ushered into the upstairs living room by a lackey in white gloves and found it filled with guests and members of the family engaged in the usual polite conversation of society. While seated at a round table, one of the young hostesses pointed out to her that the cloth cover had been embroidered with the names of visitors. They wrote their names in chalk, and one of the girls in the family embroidered over the signatures. Sofya Shil noticed that many of the names were preceded by "Prince" or "Count." No one suggested that she sign her name. Obviously, this was a tablecloth for *comme il faut* people.

Soon Tolstoy entered with his brisk step and kindly greeted and chatted with each of the guests. Sofya Shil was surprised at his aged appearance. Deep furrows lined his bronzed, weather-beaten face. The skin lay about the back of his scrawny neck in folds, and she involuntarily thought of the coarse, baggy skin of a hippopotamus. But his eyes were bright and full of life. The black trousers and dark blue peasant blouse made of fine material seemed the natural attire for such a man. He was tired, he remarked, for he had just returned from the railroad station where he had been observing the departure of exiles to Siberia.

As he vividly described these unhappy victims and expressed sympathy for them, he seemed to be formulating in his mind a new chapter for *Resurrection,* for he had gone to the station in order to obtain material for his novel.

Meanwhile guests continued to arrive and leave. The lackey passed visiting cards on a silver tray to Tolstoy. Presently two tall, refined, and distinguished-looking gentlemen entered. They were S. P. Dyagilev, editor of the well-known periodical, the *World of Art,* and future ballet producer, and D. V. Filosofov, his chief collaborator. Greetings were warm and gay. Conversation took on a new life—politics, art, the doings of important people in the government. Finally the two guests, who had come all the way from Petersburg, got around to the real purpose of their visit. They were organizing a celebration in honor of the hundredth anniversary of the birth of the great poet Pushkin. Would Tolstoy lend his aid by contributing an article to the issue of their magazine commemorating the event? The name of the poet was enough to set Tolstoy off on a brilliant exposition of what he admired and condemned of Pushkin's works. Though he felt deeply about some of these productions and praised generously, it was clear that he did not share the reverential attitude of his two visitors toward Russia's illustrious poet. But the visitors brought him back to the point—would he aid in the celebration? Frowning and immediately dropping his agreeable manner, he flatly refused. With an intolerance that often took the form of paradox when his opposition was aroused, he brusquely declared that such celebrations were superfluous, that there were no immortals, and that each man lived for his own age alone. A writer, he said, is like a potato that is absorbed by the organism, digested, and then discarded. His contemporaries assimilate all that is of value in his creations, rework all that is precious in this spiritual food, and then when it is of no further use they cast it aside, consign it to complete oblivion. Sofya Shil wondered if the two visitors were not saying to themselves at this moment: "Well, what about yourself? Would you want to be gulped down like a potato and quickly discarded?" Dyagilev and Filosofov soon departed, plainly annoyed by Tolstoy's refusal to aid their project and offended by the manner in which he expressed his disagreement.

While the general conversation in the room continued

on the subject of Pushkin, the ubiquitous lackey entered and whispered something in Tolstoy's ear. He immediately left the company. And Sofya Shil remarks at this point: "There were two entrances to the house. People who were *comme il faut* or those with some position in society entered by the front door. But there existed a rear flight of steps for those seekers after truth who came to Tolstoy the moralist. They went up directly to him without disturbing anyone."

The interruption on this occasion, however, was not caused by a seeker after truth. For Tolstoy soon returned carrying a palm branch and a note in his hand, and he laughingly explained to the guests that several theological students had just visited him, coming directly from vespers, and they had thrust in his hand the palm leaf and note and fled. The note was read aloud and it contained a naïve but sincerely written prayer expressing the hope that Tolstoy would return to the Orthodox Church.

Among the many young writers who came to burn incense, Chekhov and Gorky were regarded by Tolstoy as the most talented. Their fiction was taking the country by storm at the time *Resurrection* began to appear. As early as 1889 Gorky, utterly unknown then, had turned up at Yasnaya Polyana, looking much the worse for wear after a long tramp, only to discover that Tolstoy was in Moscow. He pushed on to the city and tried to see him there. But Sonya informed him that her husband was ill and could receive no one. (Tolstoy was not ill at the time of this visit. Sonya used this excuse to visitors she felt were undesirable.) She took him to the kitchen like some tramp and gave him a cup of coffee and a roll, and while he ate she made pointed remarks about the hordes of loafers who sought out her husband. Shortly after this unpleasant encounter, Gorky wrote a letter to Tolstoy, in which he solicited his aid in setting up an agricultural colony, but he received no answer.

Some ten years later (January 16, 1900) Gorky, now a famous writer, again visited Tolstoy and was made most welcome. In his account of this first meeting Gorky remarks that he was put through a kind of examination, for Tolstoy wanted to know all the facts in his life. Then he got around to Gorky's writings. Some he praised, others he severely criticized. *Foma Gordeyev* he simply could not finish—"everything in it was invented." Varenka Olesova in Gorky's story of that name Tolstoy condemned as not true to life. "If a girl is over fifteen and healthy," he admonished, "she likes to be embraced and touched. Her mind is fearful of what is unknown and of what she does not yet understand—that is what is called modesty and bashfulness. But her body is already aware that the unknown is inevitable and legitimate, and despite the mind, demands the fulfillment of its law. In your work you have described this Varenka Olesova as healthy, but she feels anemically—which is not true to life." Next he turned on the heroine in the short story "Twenty-six and One," and spoke of her in such improper language that Gorky, who had spent much of his life with "creatures who once were men," felt embarrassed and a bit offended, though later he decided that Tolstoy used coarse words in this instance only because he found them more precise and pointed. All through the examination, however, Tolstoy was kind and full of attention. Embracing Gorky as he was about to leave, he declared, "You are a real muzhik! You will have a hard time among the writers, but fear nothing, and speak always as you feel no matter if it comes out coarsely. Wise people will understand." And in his diary on that day, he entered: "Gorky was here. We talked very well. I liked him. A real man of the people."

Gorky felt a bit like a wrung-out dishcloth after this first encounter. For a time he did not know whether to be pleased or hurt by the thorough inquisition and criticism he had been subject to. In the end he decided that Tolstoy's intentions had been sincere and good, and a few days after the visit he wrote him: "I thank you, warmly thank you, for all that you told me, Leo Nikolayevich! I am glad that I saw you and am very proud of this. In general, I knew that you treated people simply and sincerely, but I did not expect, I confess, that you would treat me quite so well." Tolstoy answered: "I was very, very glad to make your acquaintance, and I am glad that I have become fond of you. Aksakov said . . . that people were either better or worse than their books. I have liked your writings, but I found you better than your writings. I pay you this compliment, the worth of which consists chiefly in the fact that it is sincere."

Gorky obviously bore Tolstoy no malice because of the severe criticism of his writings, for he paid another visit that year (October 8), this time at Yasnaya Polyana. The young writer, whose works were being acclaimed in many circles, aroused considerable interest among the other guests. One of them thought that he looked more like a factory worker than a literary artist. In truth, there was a proletarian aspect about his appearance—very tall and thin, with an unhealthy face, a broad, turned-up nose, small blue eyes sunk deeply in his head, and long hair combed back. He was simply dressed in a black blouse with a broad leather belt. Nor did he make the slightest attempt to affect polite airs. At dinner he sprawled, put his elbows on the table, and maintained a stubborn silence. When Tolstoy offered to read to the guests an article that he had just finished, Gorky frankly declared that he did not like to hear things read aloud. And through most of the reading he sat noisily turning the pages of a book. Perhaps he was saved a scolding by the sudden entrance of Sonya, who interrupted the reading of her husband with comments about her children and with a surprising declaration that she very much wanted to write a book entitled "The History of a Mother." In summing up in his diary his impressions of the guests that day, Tolstoy wrote that Gorky was "less agreeable" than the others. Sonya showed her esteem for Gorky on this occasion by photographing him and her husband together.

Chekhov, whose literary star had risen earlier than Gorky's, had already endeared himself to Tolstoy, who took delight in reading favorite stories by him to the family and guests. If Tolstoy regretted Chekhov's lack of any real focus in life and art, he could not fail to appreciate his warm, sympathetic nature and artistic humility. Although Gorky at this time was forcing comparison with Chekhov among literary critics, there can be no question that Tolstoy preferred Chekhov's writing. "Gorky lacks a sense of proportion," he told Goldenweizer. "He has a familiar style which is unpleasant." But of Chekhov, all of whose stories he had recently reread, he declared: "His mastery is of the highest order."

Yet Tolstoy left Chekhov under no illusions about his opinion on his plays: he emphatically did not like them. He saw a performance of *Uncle Vanya* at the beginning of 1900 and it shocked him. Chekhov, in his own charming, guileless manner, related to a friend what Tolstoy had told him about his play: "You know, he does not like my dramas. He swears that I'm not a playwright. There is only one thing that comforts me. . . . He said to me: 'You know, I cannot abide Shakespeare, but your plays are even worse. Shakespeare, however, grabs the reader by the scruff of the neck and leads him to a definite objective, not permitting him to wander off the road. But where are you going with your heroines? From the divan where they lie to the closet and back.'" At this point in his account Chekhov laughed so hard that his pince-nez fell off his nose. "But, really, Leo Nikolayevich is serious," Chekhov continued. "He was ill. I sat with him at his bedside. When I began to get ready to leave, he took my hand, looked me in the eye, and said: 'Anton Pavlovich, you are a fine man.' Then, smiling, he let my hand go and added: 'But your plays are altogether vile.'"

Chekhov's self-effacement and his unfailing sense of humor would never have allowed him to be offended by this perverse yet thoroughly understandable reaction of Tolstoy to his dramas. Besides, he worshipped the man and sensed his true significance as few were able to in Russia. When Tolstoy became so dangerously ill at the end of 1899 that thousands of people anxiously read the newspaper bulletins on his condition, Chekhov wrote to a mutual friend:—

> His illness terrified me and held me in suspense. I fear the death of Tolstoy. If he should die, then a great gaping void would exist in my life. In the first place, I have never loved a man as I do him. I am an unbelieving person, but of all faiths I think his is the nearest to mine and most suitable for me. In the second place, when there is a Tolstoy in literature, then it is easy and pleasant to be a writer; even to recognize that one has not done or will not do anything is not so terrible, for Tolstoy does it for all. His achievement serves as a justification for those hopes and expectations that we possess in literature. In the third place, Tolstoy stands firm, his authority is enormous, and while he lives bad taste in literature, every vulgarity, insolent or tearful, all crude, exasperating ambitions will be kept at a distance, deep in the shadow. His moral authority alone is capable of holding the so-called literary spirit and trends on a definite plane. Without him it would be like a shepherdless herd, or a muddle in which it would be difficult to discriminate.

Not only young Russian writers visited Tolstoy in 1899–1900. In April of both these years the German poet Rainer-

Maria Rilke made the pilgrimage to Tolstoy. Rilke was tremendously impressed by him on his first visit. When he returned to Germany, he enthusiastically studied Russian and read Tolstoy's works in the original. On his second visit a year later, he was delighted that he could understand his host in his own language. He sent Tolstoy a copy of his works along with some other books he had shown an interest in, and his accompanying letter was politely answered by Tolstoy. But it appears that Rilke produced no particular impression on him.

Another young artist whose star was just rising, Fyodor Chaliapin, visited Tolstoy in January 1900 and sang for his host with that magnificent voice which was just then electrifying Russian audiences. But Tolstoy was strangely unmoved, which Goldenweizer, who was present, charitably ascribed to the fact that he was in a bad mood.

4

The task of revising *Resurrection* and correcting proof during 1899 left Tolstoy little time for any other writing, but he felt called upon to send an epistolary article on the Boer War to G. M. Volkonski. The struggle in South Africa horrified him, and coming as it did so shortly after the Hague Conference he felt that it revealed all the cynicism of such organized efforts to maintain peace. The causes of war, he pointed out in his letter, were the unequal distribution of property, the existence of a military class, and false religious teaching. As long as we made use of privileged wealth while the mass of people were crushed by toil, he wrote, there would always be wars for markets and for gold mines, and the like, which we needed to maintain privileged wealth. Shortly after writing this letter, he remarked to Goldenweizer in the course of a discussion on the Boer War: "I always consider that moral motives are effective and decisive in the historical process. And now, when the universal dislike of the English is so clearly expressed, though I shall not live to see it, it seems to me that the power of England will be much shaken."

Several months before Tolstoy finished *Resurrection,* he wrote Biryukov that he wished to "free himself" from artistic work, for his "fingers fairly itched" to write articles. This struggle between the urge to create and the moral duty to reform society by his pen he had been waging for some years. In a sense, *Resurrection* represented a compromise between the two. When he finished the novel, he turned to purely "moral" writing again with a feeling of relief.

The first work Tolstoy undertook in 1900 was an article or pamphlet called "The Slavery of Our Times." An interesting incident inspired it. At the end of 1899 a peasant friend from a village near Yasnaya Polyana, who was then working as a weigher at the Moscow-Kazan railroad station, visited Tolstoy. In the general conversation about his occupation, he mentioned that the men who loaded and unloaded freight worked thirty-six hours at a stretch. Tolstoy was incredulous and decided to investigate. He spent several hours at the station talking with his friend and the peasant workers and in going into all the details connected with their jobs and living conditions. Not only did he learn that they worked thirty-six hours at a stretch, often hauling individual loads of three hundred pounds, but he also learned that they received a mere thirty rubles a month for this labor, bolted their wretched meals in the few minutes allowed them, and lived in filthy, overcrowded barracks.

This experience filled Tolstoy with mingled despair, hopelessness, and moral indignation. Beasts of burden, he said, were better protected by the State than these workers. It would seem, he wrote in his article, that members of the leisured classes who called themselves liberals and humanitarians, and who were sensitive to the sufferings not only of people, but of animals, could not remain silent for one moment in the face of this human slavery. The purpose of his article, he noted in his diary, was to show that the peasants, after their emancipation, had merely exchanged the chains of serfdom for those of industrial slavery. Supporting this evil, he maintained, was the systematic use of organized violence. The intention of the article was to show that progress in human well-being could only be achieved by relying more on reason and conscience and less on man-made laws; that we must be ready to sacrifice even material progress rather than accept the injustice and inequality so flagrant in the case of these railroad workers and millions of others.

Though "nonresistance" had become Tolstoy's invariable answer to all such problems, this ideal anarchistic answer was not offered without a canny awareness of the real economic and political forces at work in the class struggle. He told Goldenweizer that he wanted to take for the motto of "The Slavery of Our Times" Marx's saying that since capitalists had made themselves the masters of the working class, European governments had lost all shame. And he was convinced that socialist ideas, such as that everyone should have the right to enjoy the fruits of his labor, had already become truisms. Yet he maintained that the slavery of the workers could not be alleviated by their own efforts or by the efforts of the socialists, whose doctrines had not dispensed with compulsion.

It is only when the privileged classes, guided by the true teaching of Christ, cease to exploit the working class that their slavery will end. It will cease, he declared to Goldenweizer, "when everyone is free to choose his work and the time needed for it." As for what the emancipated workers would do with their freedom, that did not concern him. Let them arrange things for themselves, was his answer. The authorities among the privileged class in Russia, however, were unwilling to see "The Slavery of Our Times" printed there and threatened to suspend the magazine that requested permission to publish it. So Chertkov brought it out in England.

Much the same line of reasoning, though applied to a different problem, runs through Tolstoy's article "Patriotism and Government" (1900). The cynicism of the peaceful professions of the great powers shocked him in the face of such immediate conflicts as the Spanish-American War and the Boer War. As usual, his diagnosis of the factors that promote war is convincing, but the remedy he offers appears to defy the logic of civilization's development. To deliver mankind from the ever-increasing evils of armaments and war, he argued, neither congresses nor conferences nor courts of arbitration will do; simply destroy those instruments of violence which are called governments, from which humanity's greatest evils flow. And to eliminate the violence of governments, he insists, only one thing is needed: people should be made to realize that the feeling of patriotism, which alone supports this instrument of violence, is a bad feeling, and, above all, is immoral. It can be eradicated only when men are educated through Christ's teaching that it is wrong to kill.

Somewhat the same approach is employed in a shorter article in 1900, "Thou Shalt Not Kill," inspired by the assassination of King Humbert of Italy. Here Tolstoy's tone becomes shrill, and his customary moral earnestness gives way to harsh criticism of the mighty. Kaiser Wilhelm, who told his soldiers that they must be willing to kill their own fathers if he commanded them to, is in Tolstoy's eyes "a narrow-minded, ill-educated, vain man, with the ideals of a German *Junker*"; and Nicholas II of Russia, he wrote, can propose a "childish, silly, hypocritical project of universal peace" while he gives orders to increase his army and mercilessly insults and oppresses a whole nation, the Finns, and still the press and his people praise him. But there is no point in killing these rulers, as Humbert was murdered, Tolstoy argues. Such violence is not only terrible, it is also utterly unreasonable. The thing to do, he wrote, is to withdraw support from that order of society which places rulers in the position of arbiters over the lives of their fellow men. Naturally, this article could not appear in Russia, but it was widely printed abroad, though in Germany all copies were ordered destroyed because of the insult to the Kaiser.

Tolstoy wrote other articles and several epistolary articles and introductions to books during 1900,[6] but the only artistic work to his credit that year is the drama *The Live Corpse*. In 1897 his friend N. V. Davydov, head of the Moscow District Court, had related to him the details of a curious case. A married couple in the city had separated, for the husband was a weak individual and addicted to drink, and the wife was in love with another man. In order to enable his wife to marry her lover, and apparently with her connivance, the husband simulated suicide by leaving his clothes and identification papers on the bank of the Moscow River. He then disappeared and the wife married her lover. But later, through an indiscretion of the husband, the whole story came out and the couple were arrested and sentenced to a term of deportation.

Tolstoy used these facts in a very general way in *The Live Corpse*, though the protagonists have little in common

[6] He wrote the articles: "Where Is the Outlet?" and "Is This Really Necessary?" (both drafted in 1897–1898, finished in 1900, and published that year by Chertkov in England); two epistolary articles, one to the Dukhobors in Canada, and a second to a retired German soldier; and introductions to the following books: Tentjaro Macato, *Japanese Notions of European Political Economy;* J. C. Kenworthy, *Anatomy of Misery;* Wilhelm von Polenz, *Büttnerbauer* (to the Russian translation); and L. P. Nikiforov, *John Ruskin* (in Russian).

with the real husband and wife, and the husband in the play actually commits suicide.

Tolstoy did not get to work on the subject until 1900 and he never entirely finished it to his own satisfaction. When the theatrical director V. I. Nemirovich-Danchenko eagerly requested permission to produce the play, he refused. Several reasons have been given for his not finishing this excellent drama. Maude related that Tolstoy told him that he did not wish the play to be produced while he lived, lest he should be drawn into expending time on revising it to the detriment of other tasks he considered more important. Another reason was that an account of *The Live Corpse* got into the press and was read by the real husband, N. S. Gimer, who appealed to Tolstoy not to publish the play since he feared to be compromised by it. Even the wife, through her son, is reported to have made a similar request, and Tolstoy willingly agreed, saying that "a human life is more precious than any piece of writing." It is known for certain that Gimer did visit Tolstoy, who aided him in obtaining work and exacted a promise from him never to touch liquor, which he kept. At any event, the play was never produced or published during Tolstoy's lifetime.

The Live Corpse is one of the most interesting of Tolstoy's dramas and has had considerable success on the stage. It was almost inevitable that he should turn this rather sordid court case into a criticism of the harm that law—government's organized instrument of violence—may do when it thrusts itself into the delicate relations of men and women. In the spirit of his theories in *What Is Art?* he quickly infects us with his feelings over the marital difficulties of Fedya and Lisa. With marvelous economy of effort, each of the characters is revealed in a few simple, psychologically searching lines. But in the end, though living, they lack warmth and fail to inspire deep human sympathy. They seem rather to infect us with their creator's cold moral interest in them.

In 1899 Tolstoy read S. G. Verus's book on the Gospels,[7] which denied the existence of Christ as a historical person. Such a conclusion did not dismay Tolstoy. "All this is very interesting and even valuable," he said, "for it makes it unnecessary to wrangle any further over refuting the authenticity of the Gospel stories about miracles, and it

[7] *Vergleichende Uebersicht der vier Evangelien* (Leipzig, 1897).

proves the teaching of the Gospels to be the words of not one superman, but the sum of the wisdom of all the best moral teaching expressed by many peoples at various times."

Tolstoy favored this idea, for he preferred to think that his own moral and religious philosophy, for which he claimed no originality, had been the inevitable conclusion of all the great thinkers of the world. For example, during the next year, when he had more leisure, he steeped himself in the Chinese classics,[8] which he had begun years before, and also Buddhist writings. In this Eastern wisdom, he found his own moral convictions mirrored. Compared to Confucius, he wrote in his diary, "all the others seem insignificant." He also reread that year the favorite work, *Parerga und Paralipomena,* of his favorite German philosopher, Schopenhauer, and the *Also sprach Zarathustra* of Nietzsche, whom he considered half mad.

There were less formidable books on his reading list that year—works of George Eliot and Ruskin, both of whom he admired, and the *Annals of Toil* of J. Morrison Davidson, to whom he wrote to express agreement with his Marxian belief that "history must be the history of the working masses," and to hope that this thought "will soon be recognized by all." He read "The Man with the Hoe" and wrote Edward Markham a letter to tell him how much he liked the poem. Contemporary Russian writers he kept up with, as always, and he ironically praised their technical perfection. But what of their content? Where was the connecting inner link in their writing? "The most important thing in a work of art," he told Goldenweizer on the subject of contemporary authors, "is that it should have a kind of focus, that is, some place where all the rays meet or from which they issue. And this focus ought not to be fully explicable in words. This indeed is one of the significant facts about a work of art—that its content in its entirety can be expressed only by itself." Very few of the modern authors, he felt, were able to achieve this.

At the end of the nineteenth century there began a thin stream of productions in Western Europe and America on every conceivable phase of Tolstoy's life and works, a stream that soon reached the proportions of a raging torrent of both valuable and misplaced human endeavor. In 1900 he had the privilege of reading one of these early efforts, P. Elzbacher's *Der Anarchismus.* Tolstoy was one of the

[8] He read them in the translations of James Legge.

seven anarchists treated in the book. The work pleased him, perhaps not so much because of the part he played in it, but because anarchism, so often crudely identified with bomb throwing, had at last achieved the dignity of scholarly investigation by a learned professor. He hastened to write the author to indicate his satisfaction at not having been treated as an anarchist in the sense of a political reformer, for in the index the word "force" had not been attributed to his doctrines, whereas the names of the six other anarchists had been listed under this hateful designation. "Is this not an indication," he triumphantly asked the author, "that the teaching you ascribe to me, but which is in very fact only the teaching of Christ, is not a political but a religious teaching?"

That same year (1900) Tolstoy was made an honorary member of the French Ethnographical Society, and in Breslau he received that final and most fatal accolade of the prophet—the founding of an International Tolstoy Society for the propagation of his doctrines.

5

The family life of the Tolstoys continued to revolve in the customary domestic pattern of marriages, births, and deaths. Twenty-two-year-old Andrei, shortly after his miscue with the Georgian lady, married Chertkov's sister-in-law, Olga Konstantinova Diterikhs, on January 8, 1899. The family gathered in Tula for the event. Sonya forebodingly wrote in her diary that she was sad and agitated. "Andryusha, as in a dream, is deeply moved but does not understand why he is marrying and what this will mean. I understand Olga still less. Marriage is always terrible, mysterious, and touching. I wanted all the time to weep."

A departure from the family circle that affected Tolstoy and his wife incomparably more than that of Andrei was Tanya's, who married ten months later (November 14, 1899). With her bright, artistic spirit, Tanya was the general favorite in the house. She was partial to her father's views, and after Masha's marriage he no doubt cherished the hope that Tanya would remain with him, a faithful and understanding helper in his work. After all, he had reason to hope, for she had reached the age of thirty-five without marriage, though she had had many suitors of whom he had been a bit jealous.

Then Tanya decided to marry Mikhail Sergeyevich Sukhotin, a man much older than she and with six grown children left him by his first wife. No one in the household favored the marriage. Sonya was deeply chagrined. She had entertained hopes of a brilliant match for Tanya. She wrote her sister after the wedding: "You cannot imagine how grief-stricken and sick at heart Lyovochka and I were while accompanying Tanya. . . . It was all so gloomy, just like a funeral and not a wedding. When Tanya came to say good-bye to Lyovochka, he wept so that it was painful to look at him." A few days later Tolstoy wrote in his diary with unaccustomed bitterness: "Tanya has departed with Sukhotin, and why? It is sad and offensive. For 70 years I have been lowering and lowering my opinion about women, and still it has to be lowered more. The woman question! How can there help being a woman question? But it bears no relation to the fact that women should begin to direct life, but to the fact that they should stop ruining it."

The large house that for so long had echoed loudly and merrily to the voices of children was now almost denuded of them. Only Alexandra and, as his exasperated mother called him, "wild Misha" remained. And less than two years later the troublesome Misha married a childhood sweetheart.[9] With the fledglings, all but one, grown and departed from the nest, their father could now look back, perhaps not without a twinge of remorse, on time and effort not well spent. They had received the customary education of children in their circle of society, but their father, after his spiritual change, distrusted and even scorned this worldly education. He continually cast a shadow over the social life they enjoyed. Pleasures that their companions took for granted would suddenly be poisoned for them by an instinctive feeling of guilt induced by the silent disapproval of their father. Tolstoy always hoped his children would perceive that there was another life, and he eagerly and constantly searched their behavior for indications of any change. In this respect, his two older daughters had gladdened his heart, but their marriage, though it did not ultimately lessen his love for them, interposed a real obstacle in their future relations. No one of his sons took up the challenge of a new life for very long, and their actions often caused him grief and suffering. If he nourished a

[9] He married Alexandra Vladimirovna Glebov on January 31, 1901.

hope that any one of his sons would become his spiritual heir, that hope had died with little Vanichka.

Sonya did her best to control the unruly instincts of her younger boys. One of her misfortunes was an inability to bring to her daily household cares a saving sense of humor, a lack in her nature that she herself recognized. "I do not like humor," she wrote in her diary, "I'm not able to laugh—this is a deficiency in me." She was everlastingly blaming her failure with the children on her husband's lack of interest in them. Yet he was deeply interested in them. His attitude was that an ounce of moral prevention was worth a pound of the conventional practical cure in these matters. When his wife once wrote him to deplore his absence from the city at a time when Andrei and Misha were misbehaving, he replied: "My presence in Moscow, as you very well know, will not prevent Andryusha or Misha from living evilly if they want to do this. The sternest father in the world cannot prevent people with sprouting beards from living in a manner that they think is good."

The implication was that the youthful waywardness of her sons was a result of the kind of social existence with which she surrounded them. They must feel in their hearts and conscience that this existence was wrong before they would be able to change it. Tolstoy tried in conversations and in long earnest letters to effect this moral transformation.

Such moral suasion had little success. None of the sons became a Tolstoyan. Andrei and Mikhail accepted their service in the army, and Leo, who at one time favored his father's beliefs, weakened in the end and was ready to serve but was rejected by an army physician. As the father of a large family that had now grown to maturity, Tolstoy came to the rather pathetic conclusion, which he noted in his diary in 1900: "My position in the family is strange. They perhaps even love me, but they do not need me; rather I encumber them."

Sonya's diary during 1899–1900 reflects a marked improvement in her relations with her husband compared to the anguished trials of the preceding three years. She was mortally afraid of going down to posterity as the despised scold in her husband's life. "They always distort the private life of famous men in their biographies," she said to Goldenweizer. "I'm sure they will make me out a Xantippe. You must defend me, Alexander Borisovich." There was little scolding in her diary over this period, no hysterical outbursts, and her morbid concern with the subject of sex almost vanished. At times, she remarked, women like to play at romance in a sentimental fashion with their husbands. On such occasions she felt a "spiritual tenderness" for him. "But he is affectionate," she sadly concluded, "only when in him tenderness awakens, and then, alas, it is not the same kind!"

Husband and wife were growing old together, perhaps not always gracefully, but with an apparently new determination to respect each other's domain of activity. Only the interjection of some external stress or strain into their intimate life could now disturb this equanimity. She tended to her book business and the cares of the household, he to his writing and spiritual world. And together they grieved over the death of a grandchild and the stillborn babies of their two daughters. He visited his brother and married children while she remained at home in Moscow or Yasnaya Polyana. But now she did not complain bitterly over these separations. Their letters on such occasions were friendly, even loving. She had begun to treat him like an old man; she begged him to eat the proper food, wear warm clothes, and she wanted to know whether she should send him his boots and the new galoshes he had forgotten to take, for his weak health worried her. He was just as anxious over her health, for she too had been sick, and he warned her not to overdo things and to watch out for her failing eyesight. If unmarried women live in the future, married ones often dwell in the past, but only rarely now did Sonya strike a nostalgic note over the happiness that she persisted in regarding as a memory. On their thirty-eighth wedding anniversary Tolstoy was in Yasnaya Polyana, Sonya in Moscow. She wrote him: "I just got up, and the first thing I wanted to do was to write you, dear Lyovochka, and to recall the day that united us through these many years of life together. I grew sad that we were not together today, but then I turned my heart to you and to the infinitely deeper, tenderer, and better memories of our life, and then I wanted to thank you for the former happiness you gave me and to regret that it did not continue so strongly, fully, and calmly throughout our whole life." And she concluded by saying that she hoped before the day was over to sit for a moment in the church where they had been married thirty-eight years ago.

XXXIV

Excommunication

THE YEAR 1901 was eventful for Leo Tolstoy. It began with two epistolary articles on faith and prayer in answer to the questions of an unknown worker who had renounced the Orthodox Church.[1] Meanwhile, the Church's patience with Tolstoy had run out. Such articles were disseminated throughout the country in hectograph copies and also in published form, for Chertkov saw to their printing in England from whence they found their way back to Russia through various illegal channels. Then, too, *Resurrection* had shocked and embittered ecclesiastic officialdom. The mutilating government censor of that novel had not hacked vigorously enough, for he had left a damning residue of ridicule of church ritual and of the Procurator of the Holy Synod, Pobedonostsev.

As early as 1888 action against Tolstoy had been discussed in Church circles. In November 1899, when *Resurrection* was appearing in the issues of *Niva,* the Kharkov Archbishop, Ambrosius, proposed to the Holy Synod that Tolstoy be excommunicated, but no action was taken. The next year the Metropolitan of Kiev suggested to the Synod that in the event of Tolstoy's death prayers for the repose of his soul be forbidden in all churches, unless he had previously repented of his heretical beliefs.

The Church was merely an arm of the government—Pobedonostsev, a lay figure and close to the throne, was the connecting link—and its hostility toward Tolstoy reflected in a real sense the attitude of secular authorities. The temper of dissatisfaction, which had been rising throughout

[1] These letters and one other were addressed to V. K. Zavolokin and were published by Chertkov in England in a single article under the title, "On Reason, Faith, and Prayer" (1901).

the nation for a long time, had recently been accelerated by repressive measures. Tolstoy had become a national symbol of this popular dissatisfaction. As a contemporary figure put it, Russia had two tsars, Nicholas II and Leo Tolstoy, and in the public mind a struggle was being waged between them to see which of the two would prove the more powerful. It made little difference that Tolstoy had no sympathy with either the hopes of the liberals for legislative reforms or the violence of the revolutionists. All knew that he was an open, courageous, and irreconcilable critic of the whole political and social order. Unrest existed everywhere. Progressive-minded students were again on the march, but this time the government issued regulations that they should be sent to serve as soldiers if arrested for participating in disorders. And when a large number of Kiev students were actually sentenced to the ranks, a public clamor arose. Students in other cities went out on strike, and for the first time they won for their cause the active support of all layers of the population. Tolstoy again sympathized with the students. The situation in Moscow and Petersburg grew ominous.

It was at this juncture that the Church decided to act against Tolstoy, and unquestionably with government sanction. The blow they struck was no doubt intended to deflate his tremendous popularity, for the ecclesiastical hierarchy could reasonably suppose that in the sacred matter of religious faith the vast masses of the people would support their holy judgment. The Church could enter where the government feared to tread, and not only Russia, but the whole Christian world would condemn the sinner and iconoclast.

On the initiative of Anthony, Metropolitan of Kiev and Ladoga, the Holy Synod agreed to a formal announcement separating Tolstoy from the Church. Pobedonostsev drafted the edict, and it was published in the Synod's journal, the *Church Gazette*, on February 24, 1901, signed by seven of Russia's leading ecclesiastics. The edict began with a reminder that the efforts of heretics, false teachers, and all the powers of hell have never prevailed against the Holy Church. "But in our days," the document continued, "God has permitted a new false teacher to appear—Count Leo Tolstoy. Well known to the world as a writer, Russian by birth, Orthodox by baptism and education, Count Tolstoy, seduced by intellectual pride, has arrogantly risen against the Lord and His Christ and His holy heritage, and has plainly in the sight of all repudiated his Orthodox Mother Church which reared and educated him, and has dedicated his literary activity and the talent given to him by God to disseminating among the people teachings opposed to Christ and the Church, and to destroying in the minds and hearts of people their national faith, that Orthodox faith which has been confirmed by the universe and in which our forefathers lived and were saved, and to which Holy Russia till now has clung, and in which it has been strong. In his works and letters, distributed in great numbers by him and his followers throughout the whole world, and particularly within the borders of our dear land, he preaches with zealous fanaticism the overthrow of all the dogmas of the Orthodox Church and the very essence of the Christian faith." There then followed an itemized listing of his heresies: that he denied God worshipped in the Holy Trinity, Christ as a God-man who was raised from the dead, the immaculate conception of the Lord Christ, and the virginity of Mary; that he did not acknowledge a life and retribution beyond the grave; that he rejected all the Sacraments; and that in particular he subjected to derision the greatest of Sacraments, the Holy Eucharist. "Therefore," the edict concluded, "the Church does not beckon him as its member and cannot so reckon him until he repents and resumes his communion with her."

The edict is not in canonical language, whatever it may be in intent, a formal excommunication, for at the end it appears to leave the door open for reconciliation. But Tolstoy regarded it as a statement of excommunication, and so did the public. The day following its publication in the *Church Gazette*, it appeared in nearly every Russian newspaper, and the telegraph wires carried the astounding news to the four corners of the globe. The government, however, had first taken the precaution to forbid the Russian press to print any comment on the edict of the Holy Synod.

2

The edict created a sensation, but not the kind the Synod had anticipated. To a people in a rebellious mood, the excommunication of one of their champions served only as another and greater indictment of oppressive authority. The day on which the edict first appeared was a Sunday.

People swarmed the streets of Moscow, for the student unrest was at its height. Tolstoy had gone with his friend Dunayev to Lubyanskaya Square. A crowd of several thousand had assembled there. Sonya related in her diary that someone recognized Tolstoy and ironically shouted: "There goes the devil in human form!" All eyes were turned on him and a cheer roared from hundreds of throats: "Hurrah for Leo Nikolayevich! Long live Leo Nikolayevich! Hail to the great! Hurrah!" Only with the aid of mounted police did Tolstoy extricate himself from the turbulent, acclaiming crowd.

Quantities of sympathetic letters and telegrams poured in from people in Russia and abroad; many statements came expressing indignation over the action of the Synod, often bearing hundreds of signatures, and in one case over a thousand. Deputations, sometimes bearing flowers and gifts, waited on him to convey their regrets. Messages of protest, sent to both Tolstoy and the ecclesiastics who signed the edict, represented all groups, from aristocrats and intellectuals to simple factory workers. Before one of Repin's canvases of Tolstoy, hung at a Petersburg exhibition, demonstrations took place. Crowds gathered before the portrait, adorned it with garlands of flowers, and shouted, "Down with Pobedonostsev!" and "Hurrah for Leo Nikolayevich!" One of these gatherings dispatched a laudatory telegram, and then afraid that this would not reach him, for it soon became known that the authorities were intercepting such telegraphic messages, they also sent a letter, signed by 397 persons, which described the nature of the demonstration. The portrait became so persistent a focus for public manifestations of feeling on behalf of Tolstoy that the authorities had it withdrawn from the exhibit. This was the famous canvas, entitled "Tolstoy at Prayer," portraying him standing barefoot in the woods. He jokingly remarked to Goldenweizer: "Repin painted me décolleté, barefoot in a shirt! I have to thank him for not having taken off my trousers too. And he never even asked me if I liked it. But I have long since got used to being treated as if I were dead." Perhaps with no little personal satisfaction and a certain amount of cheerful irony, he finally sent a letter to the press "to thank all those people, from high officials to simple workers," for the sympathetic messages they had sent him because of the action of the Holy Synod.

The daily mail brought not only letters of sympathy or congratulation. There were anonymous threats of murder and angry epistles, scolding him as a heretic and praising the Synod's edict. Postal and telegraph officials did not interfere with these messages of condemnation. Such charges were relatively few, but in some conservative circles of rigid Orthodox believers the excommunication brought him abuse and persecution. His books were banned in a number of public libraries, sermons were preached against him in churches, and perhaps the unkindest cut, with a comic touch about it, was his exclusion from the Moscow Temperance Society against the vigorous protests of some of its more enlightened members.

The excommunication shocked members of the Tolstoy family and aroused some of them to indignant protest. Although a nun, Tolstoy's sister Marya declared her exasperation with the Synod, for she knew that her brother "had God in his heart." Even young Alexandra, who had been strictly brought up in the Orthodox faith by her mother, wished to break away from the Church at this time. Tolstoy persuaded her to attend services in order to spare the feelings of her mother, who was inclined to blame him for influencing her daughter to abandon her faith. Alexandra tells in her account of the excommunication that she and young Misha Sukhotin, her sister's stepson, dropped their studies and devoted themselves to distributing forbidden literature by way of protest. They secretly procured a hectograph set and printed, among other things, copies of two satiric fables then going the rounds, "The Victorious Pigeons" and "The Lion and the Asses," which ridiculed the government and the Church. But this truly hazardous business was stopped when Sonya discovered their illegal activities.

The excommunication deeply disturbed Sonya, and she rushed to the defense of her husband with perhaps more indignation than judgment. She straightway dispatched identical letters to Pobedonostsev and the three Metropolitans, who had signed the edict. Asserting her own unalterable faith in the Church, she declared that this public separation of her husband from it had inexpressibly shocked her. She then rubbed it in a bit by describing the numerous expressions of sympathy and love from all over the world that this act had evoked. And she ended with a barbed statement that there were many outside the Church who led a more truly Christian life than certain high ecclesiastics "wearing diamonded miters and stars."

Sonya was pleased with this effort and saw to it that copies got abroad. "No manuscript of Leo Nikolayevich," she wrote in her diary, "ever had such swift and wide dissemination as this letter. It has been translated into all the foreign languages. This rejoiced me, but I did not become proud, thank God! I wrote it at once, swiftly, ardently. God commanded me to do this and not my will." The Metropolitan Anthony eventually wrote a reply, which was published, along with Sonya's letter, in the *Church Gazette*. The answer, filled with pious platitudes and labored evasions, left Sonya utterly cold. "It is entirely proper and entirely soulless," she noted in her diary. Tolstoy was perhaps more surprised than pleased by his wife's courageous defense of him, for he knew how stubbornly she adhered to her Orthodox faith and what little tolerance she had for many of the people on whose side she now found herself in this cause. Rather puzzled, he wrote to his daughter Masha: "Your mother's letter has had a very good effect on her. It is impossible to foresee anything. With us men, thought influences action, but with women, especially feminine women, actions influence thought. She [Sonya] now judges otherwise, and she accepts many judgments differently."

3

Tolstoy's first reaction was rather scornful, like that of the lady who sent him a piece of holy bread and a letter, in which she wrote that she had just received the Sacrament and had taken the Host for his benefit, and she concluded: "Eat it in health and pay no attention to these stupid priests." The numerous callers who came to see him he laughingly greeted at the door with the words that he positively declined to accept congratulations.

On the other hand, Tolstoy saw clearly that the excommunication was an attempt on the part of the Church and government to combat his influence among the people. In reality the Synod's act increased his influence, made his home in Moscow a center of inspiration to the downtrodden and persecuted, and prompted him to intensify his agitation against the political, social, and religious abuses in a State run by police. Shortly after the excommunication, Cossacks beat the people in a street gathering in front of the Kazan Cathedral in Petersburg. The distinguished Prince L. D. Vyazemski, a member of the Council of State, was on the spot and tried to halt the brutality of the Cossacks. He was roughly handled for his efforts and later received a public reprimand from the Tsar and was banished from the capital. Defiantly Tolstoy wrote Vyazemski a letter, signed by a number of people, in which he informed him that his courageous and humane action at the time of the demonstration had aroused the esteem and gratitude of all. Since the letter could not be printed in Russia, he sent it to Chertkov in England for publication. And when the Minister of the Interior closed the Writers' Union because it protested the actions of the Cossacks, Tolstoy, among others, signed a letter commending the Union's leaders for their stand.

Some three weeks after his excommunication, Tolstoy returned good for evil. Disturbed by the news of various demonstrations aimed at the government, he wrote an article, "An Appeal to the Tsar and His Officials," which was delivered to them. With frankness and admirable clarity, he stated the case of the people against the government. Tranquillity would not be achieved, he said, by following the recent naïve order of the Minister of the Interior to the police to disperse the crowds promptly, and to fire at them if they did not disperse. The time might well come, he warned, when soldiers and police would refuse to commit the terrible crime of fratricide. Thousands of people had been unjustly persecuted by a despotic regime which had for years not only stood still but receded and separated itself more and more from the people and their demands. What was needed, he declared, was not for the rulers to defend themselves against those who really did not wish to injure them, but to seek out the causes of social discontent and remove them. He then formulated the four principal demands of the people: To grant the peasants equal rights with all other citizens; to abolish special enactments that would permit the Common Law to be disregarded; to remove all barriers to education; and to abolish all limitations of religious liberty. After itemizing in some detail the various abuses perpetrated by the government and Church, he concluded by stating that the removal of the causes of complaint would pacify the majority of the people and free them from those terrible sufferings and (what was worse than sufferings) crimes which would inevitably be committed on both sides if the government continued to concern itself solely with the suppression of disturbances, leaving the causes of these disturbances untouched.

If Nicholas II had given heed to this simple bill of rights, he might have anticipated the revolt that took place four years later or even the 1917 Revolution that swept him and all his family into oblivion. The article is interesting from another point of view, for it illustrates Tolstoy's practical wisdom and good judgment. Clearly foreseeing a bloody revolt, he put aside his own maximum program of Christian anarchism and offered to a government that he felt had no right to exist at all the minimum terms that might prevent its total destruction.

But the government of the Tsar could learn nothing, and it certainly could not forget that in Leo Tolstoy it had a subject more to be feared than to be accepted as a guide. He received no acknowledgment of his article, and no attempt was made to follow his advice. With no little chagrin the arch-villain in the piece, Pobedonostsev, confessed in a letter to the editor of the *Church Gazette:* "Indeed, what a heap of anger has already been aroused over the epistle" [the edict of excommunication].

Tolstoy finally decided to reply to the Synod's official statement separating him from the Church. His answer, dated April 4, 1901, was actually published by the *Church Gazette* and by two other unofficial Church periodicals, but with significant deletions which the censor found impossible to print "without offending the religious feelings of the faithful." Reprinting even this censored version was forbidden in Russia, and the answer was published in complete form at this time only in England.

Having made clear what he considered to be true and what untrue in the Synod's statement, he admitted that he did not believe in what the Church said it believed in, but insisted that he believed in much that the Church had attempted to persuade people that he did no believe. "I believe in this," he wrote. "I believe in God, whom I understand as Spirit, as love, as the Source of all. I believe that He is in me and I in Him. I believe that the will of God is most clearly and intelligibly expressed in the teaching of the man Jesus, whom to consider as God and pray to, I esteem the greatest blasphemy. I believe that man's true welfare lies in fulfilling God's will, and His will is that men should love one another and should consequently do to others as they wish others to do to them—of which it is said in the Gospels that in this is the law and the prophets. I believe therefore that the meaning of the life of every man is to be found only in increasing the love that is in him; that this increase of love leads man, even in this life, to ever greater and greater blessedness, and after death gives him the more blessedness the more love he has, and helps more than anything else towards the establishment of the Kingdom of God on earth: that is, to the establishment of an order of life in which the discord, deception and violence that now rule will be replaced by free accord, by truth, and by the brotherly love of one for another."

After this confession of faith, Tolstoy rose to heights of noble sincerity in the conclusion of his answer to the Synod. "Whether or not these beliefs of mine offend, grieve, or prove a stumbling block to anyone, or hinder anything, or give displeasure to anybody, I can as little change them as I can change my body. I must myself live my own life, and I must myself alone meet death (and that very soon), and therefore I cannot believe otherwise than as I—preparing to go to that God from whom I came—do believe. I do not believe my faith to be the one indubitable truth for all time, but I see no other that is plainer, clearer, or answers better to all the demands of my reason and my heart; should I find such a one I shall at once accept it; for God requires nothing but the truth. But I can no more return to that from which with such suffering I have escaped, than a flying bird can re-enter the eggshell from which it has emerged."

4

Tolstoy left for Yasnaya Polyana early in May, 1901. Over the next couple of months he wrote three short articles. Two of them, "A Soldier's Leaflet" and "An Officer's Leaflet," received wide distribution abroad and were well known in Russia in quantities of hectograph copies, largely put out by revolutionary organizations. These articles were on the familiar subject of the relation of Christians to military service and were inspired by the manuals for soldiers compiled by the War Department.

Boulanger related that Tolstoy burned with indignation over the way these manuals would couple texts of the Gospels with cold-blooded instructions on how to kill. Tolstoy handed him one of the manuals, Boulanger wrote, and "with peculiar agitation and a characteristic spasm in his throat, as though sobbing, he said: "No, look at this! Is it possible to write and distribute it along with the appealing words of Christ about love and brotherhood? Read this passage." And Tolstoy pointed out a place in the soldier's manual. " 'Always strike, never cease to strike. Having struck with the bayonet, club with the butt; if the butt won't do, beat with the fists; if the fists fail, sink your teeth in.' No, this is frightful," he said. "This is too incredibly animal-like—'sink your teeth in.' "

"The Only Means," the third article, attempted to answer the question: What can free the laborers from their ills? The answer—faith in God and His law as expressed in the Gospels—adds nothing new to Tolstoy's panacea for the world's ills. His tendency to solve all social, political, and economic problems by the application of a simple moral formula had by now become characteristic. Persons of deep and abiding faith oversimplify life's complexities and are often unwilling to accept the fact that many human problems do not admit of an absolute wrong or right solution but may be resolved with justice to all only through compromise. To be sure, such persons avoid the tragedy of the equivocators who drown themselves in a spoon of water in their efforts to get to the bottom, but they risk the greater tragedy of effortless infallibility.

Senator Andrew D. White, at one time American Minister to Russia, in an account of his visit to Tolstoy remarked that his host, like certain other Russian thinkers, having given birth to striking ideas, coddled and petted them, could see neither spot nor blemish in them, and at last virtually believed himself infallible. This observation was not without its point with reference to Tolstoy in his old age, though he might have been surprised at its coming from White. For after one of the latter's visits, Tolstoy asked the family if they knew how the United States was governed. They admitted their ignorance. "Well," he said, "each state elects its wisest and best men to govern it, but the two very wisest and very best men from each state are sent to Washington to make the laws for the whole country. I have had one of those men with me today. He has learned all the sciences, and knows all the languages, and has read all the books—the only pity is that he has not yet begun to think."

However, Tolstoy honestly tried to avoid the sin of intellectual pride. He observed in his diary that summer: "Those people are terrible who always want to be right. In order that they should be perfectly right, they are ready to blame the innocent, the holy, and God Himself." Becoming convinced that faith was entirely a matter between God and the individual, he tended more and more to discourage intermediaries or any organized effort to propagate his beliefs. He wasted little sympathy on the failure of the English colony at Purleigh, in which Chertkov and Maude were interested. And when Percy Redfern, head of the Manchester Tolstoy Society, wrote him at this time for support, he bluntly replied: "I have always been of the conviction—and it cannot be changed—that to be a member of the ancient society founded by God at the beginning of the conscious life of humanity is more productive for myself and mankind than to be a member of any restricted society organized by us for the achievement of those aims which we in substance recognize. . . . Apart from this, a man belonging to the great society of God fulfills also many other Christian actions which have been neither foreseen nor defined by Tolstoyan Societies nor by any others whatever they may be." In general, he now urged all who shared his faith to devote their time to ordering their own inner spiritual being rather than to promoting his beliefs.

During this summer Tolstoy secretly asked his daughter Masha to make a copy of the will he had written in his diary in 1895, perhaps because he distrusted the intentions of his wife, who kept these old diaries under lock and key. He had obtained this particular diary from Sonya with difficulty and returned it at once. Masha visited Yasnaya Polyana toward the end of June, 1901. The next morning, surprised that her father did not appear, she entered his bedroom and found him ill. Sonya had left that morning for the estate of her son Sergei. Masha asked him why he had not told her mother of his condition. "He burst out with a flood of complaints, a thing very rare with him, and said that it was difficult for him to get along with mother, that there was no person in the world more alien and further from him than she, and how terrible this was since she was the one who stood closer to him than anyone. At this he pointed at their beds, standing side by side."

Masha comforted him and then presently asked why, if he felt that way about her mother, he had designated her as one of the executors of his writings. (Masha was referring to one of the conditions of his will which she had recently copied, namely, that Chertkov, Strakhov—now dead—and Sonya should take charge of all his papers. The other two important conditions were that he should not be buried by the Church and that his heirs should not attempt to profit financially from his literary works.) Tolstoy had actually forgotten that he had designated Sonya, and he asked Masha to bring him the copy of the will and said he would change this place and then sign it. She had left the copy at her home, but she promised to bring it to him soon.

On another visit, in August of that year, Masha gave her father the copy of the will to sign and reminded him of his expressed wish to change it. "You mean about mother?" he asked. "No, I shall not change it. It is unnecessary. Let it remain as it is. It was written at a time of good relations with her and it ought not to be changed." After he had signed the will, she asked if she should send the copy to Chertkov or give it to her mother. He directed her to keep it.

Though at first only Tolstoy, Masha, and her husband knew of this matter, it was revealed by chance in a family gathering a few weeks later. Sonya's wrath was colossal. It appears that the worst fears of Masha and her husband were justified, for Obolenski wrote to Chertkov about the whole incident and reported Sonya as saying that upon the death of her husband she intended to request the Tsar for permission to bury Tolstoy with full rites of the Church. And in her diary Sonya wrote of the will in Masha's possession: "It was extremely disagreeable to me when I learned about this by chance. To make the works of Leo Nikolayevich *common* property I regard as wrong and senseless. I love my own family and desire for it the best kind of prosperity, but by turning these works into public property, we shall only enrich the wealthy publishing houses. . . . I told Leo Nikolayevich that if he died before I did, I would not fulfill his desire and renounce my right to his works; and if I had regarded it as a good and just thing, I would have granted him this pleasure of renouncing the right during his lifetime,[2] but after his death this would have no meaning for him."

Sonya at once broke with Masha and her husband over this matter and they left Yasnaya Polyana, but the breach was healed later. She kept after her husband, demanding the signed copy of the will. Finally, in the autumn of 1902, Masha related that one evening her father came to her "and gently and shamefacedly asked me to give him this document. He said that mother tormented him with tales . . . that for the sake of the greatest good it was necessary to give her this will. . . ." Sonya got the will and preserved it with the following note: "This is not a *will*, and my husband never asked my daughter Masha to copy it; she did it at her own discretion and kept it secret from the whole family, and today my husband gave it to me to destroy at my desire. SOFYA TOLSTOY." This was only the beginning of the long battle of the will.

That summer at Yasnaya Polyana Tolstoy's health began seriously to decline. Toward the end of June he came down with a severe attack of malaria. Doctors were summoned from Tula and Moscow, and at one point it seemed that he had reached the end. Attentively watching his wife apply a compress to him, he wept. " 'Thanks, Sonya. Don't think I'm not grateful and don't love you,' " she quoted him in her diary. And weeping herself, they embraced. "Now my Lyovochka sleeps," she jotted down later. "He's still alive, I can see and hear him and care for him. And later? My God, how unbearable my grief would be, how terrible my life without him. . . ."

Tolstoy recovered, but the reports of his closeness to death had been so persistent that even the cautious government sent confidential telegrams to the various proper authorities with instructions that, in the event of his dying, care should be taken "to prevent any demonstrative speeches, activities, or public manifestations." Messages of sympathy and concern from all over Russia and abroad deluged Yasnaya Polyana, including one from the very literary Queen of Romania. A member of the family was reading some of

[2] It will be recalled that Sonya had refused to agree to his desire to renounce the rights to all his works during his lifetime; she agreed only in the case of those written after 1881. This will of 1895 was not legally binding, for it had not been drawn up according to statutory requirements.

these letters to him while he was convalescing and he laugh ingly interrupted to remark: "Now, should I begin to d again, I really must bring it off; there can be no jokin next time. All will swallow it, correspondents will com letters and telegrams, and suddenly it will all turn out t be not so. No, this is impossible, it is simply indecent."

Another severe illness at the end of July convinced th doctors that the seventy-three-year-old Tolstoy could n stand the fall and winter climate of Yasnaya Polyana an Moscow in his weakened condition, and they advised hi to go south. Hearing of this decision, the wealthy Petersbur Countess S. V. Panin generously placed at the disposal c the family her estate at Gaspra on the southern shore c the Crimea. On the night of September 5, Tolstoy, Sony Alexandra, and Masha and her husband set out fror Yasnaya Polyana.

5

P. A. Boulanger, Tolstoy's devoted friend and discipl made the arrangements for the trip and accompanied th family. As a railway official, he persuaded his superiors t make available the luxurious private car of the director c the road. The twelve cold miles to the Tula station wer made in a carriage drawn by a team through a sea of mu the inky excuse for a road being illuminated by a groor riding on ahead with a torch. This painful drive brought o a sinking spell in the sick man, and for a moment the cor pany considered taking Tolstoy back to Yasnaya Polyan The decision to push on was eventually rewarded by th warm drawing room of the private car with its elegan upholstered furniture and piano, and its individual sleepin compartments.

The next morning the train passed through Kursk an the travelers could already feel the warm breath of th south which revived their spirits and even inspired Tolsto to do a bit of writing. At the next stop, Kharkov, the hoped to have time to dine at the station restaurant. As th train pulled in Boulanger noticed that the platform wa thronged with people, and some youths were even astrid the crossbeams of the roof, peering with expectant face at each car. There could be no doubt: the crowd was waitin the arrival of Tolstoy. Though government authorities ha expressly forbidden the press to print any mention of his journey the news had already got to the public.

"Tolstoy! Tolstoy!" the cry went up, mostly from the students in the throng. A look of mingled fear and agitation came over the face of the sick man, and he ordered all the blinds to be drawn. The car was swallowed up in a crowd of some three thousand people. Students pressed forward, begging that Tolstoy receive their deputies. Sonya appeared to tell them that her husband was ill. The students pleaded and she finally let in a committee of them. Their ardor momentarily lost in embarrassment, they mumbled greetings and good wishes. The suffering Tolstoy mumbled a few words in reply and they withdrew, only to have their places taken by another delegation that had forced its way in. At last the third bell rang; the train started. A roar went up from the crowd and shouts for him to appear at the window. He did. Hundreds of voices yelled "Hurrah! Get well! Come back healthy! God protect you!" Handkerchiefs waved, hats were thrown in the air, but finally those running beside the train were left behind. The members of the family settled back quietly in their seats, but the excitement lingered. This spontaneous public demonstration in honor of the great writer touched them all, and even Tolstoy was visibly affected. Goldenweizer, determined not to be separated from his idol, had managed to join the party at Kharkov.

At Sevastopol another ovation took place. But because the exact time of arrival had been unknown, only a few of the more persistent of those who had been waiting for several days were on hand when the train pulled in. The party decided to remain in Sevastopol until the next day. They were all in good spirits and Tolstoy's condition improved.

Tolstoy and Boulanger went for a walk around the town. Forty-five years ago he had been one of thousands of Russian soldiers engaged in that bloody, heroic, but futile defense of this city. How it had changed! They went into a museum dedicated to the memory of the defenders. Excitedly Tolstoy inspected the various objects of the siege collected there and strained at his memory to recall the events with which they were associated. But suddenly he came upon a picture of himself which evoked different and unpleasant recollections and thought. They left the museum and on the way back to the hotel he said to Boulanger: "How sad it is. What sense is there in that expensive building, that elaborate collection of all those old buttons and shell fragments. All this horror ought to be forgotten. . . . It is terrible, terrible!"

The next morning the party set out for Gaspra in two carriages. As they left the environs of Sevastopol behind them, Tolstoy eagerly searched the topography for memorable sights of battlefields and earthworks, and especially for the celebrated Fourth Bastion where he had so often risked his life during the siege. But he could identify nothing and sadly kept commenting on how things had changed.

When they reached the famous Baidar Pass, they left the carriages and proceeded on foot till they suddenly came upon the breath-taking view of the towering cliffs and the vast expanse of the Black Sea sparkling in the sun away beneath them. At the next stop Tolstoy walked ahead with Boulanger while the horses were being changed. He turned at one point to a passing youth to ask for some details about the locality. Obviously a bit contemptuous of this poorly clad, peasant-looking old man, the youth answered his questions condescendingly and with reluctance. Presently the first carriage overtook them and Tolstoy, politely thanking the stranger, got in and drove off. As Boulanger waited for the second carriage the youth asked him if he knew the old man.

"He is Count Tolstoy," answered Boulanger.

"What!" exclaimed the youth. "The real Count Tolstoy, the writer?"

"The very one."

"Oh, my God, my God!" the youth moaned, and tearing his hat from his head he flung it on the ground. "And I spoke to him in that way! I would have given all I possessed merely to see him, and now, like a fool, I spoke to him like that, thinking he was just some old man!"

Late that evening the party arrived at Gaspra and drove up to the imposing mansion of Countess Panin, whose servants came out to welcome them. All the evidence of wealth, luxury, and bad taste made a disagreeable impression on the Tolstoys—the cold, formal, high-ceilinged rooms, the marble work, and the heavy expensive furniture. But on closer inspection they were delighted with the spacious lower veranda screened by thick, grape-bearing vines and the upper veranda that looked right out to the open sea.

Here they settled down, scarcely realizing at the time that they were to remain for almost a year.

6

During these months at Gaspra death knocked more than once at the door of Tolstoy's sickroom. All members of the family gathered around on several occasions, prepared for the end. Doctors summoned from Yalta, Moscow, and Petersburg were in constant attendance, and at times their professionally grave faces signaled that hope was running out. But the wonderful constitution of Tolstoy, who as a youth had dreamed of being the strongest man in the world, triumphed over successive attacks of angina pectoris, inflammation of the lungs, and typhoid fever, complicated by rheumatism, liver complaints, and a weakened heart.

All these afflictions Tolstoy bore with patience and humble spiritual resignation. He cheerfully tried to obey the regimen prescribed by his physicians, despite his distrust of medicine, and he accepted the endless care of his family and devoted followers with a sense of embarrassment over the trouble he was causing them. His thoughts were fixed on death and any fear he may have had of it he had conquered. Spiritually he prepared himself for the end and calmly anticipated the moment when the spark of life in his pain-racked body would be extinguished. Sickness he regarded as a positive virtue. "One must suffer a severe illness," he dictated for his diary at this time, "in order to convince oneself of what life consists: the weaker the body, the stronger becomes one's spiritual development." And he also entered in his diary a few lines of a folk poem which had captured his fancy:—

The dear old man has begun to groan,
The dear old man has begun to cough,
It's time for him to be under his shroud,
Under his shroud and in his grave.

He liked to repeat these lines to his doctors and members of the family, and on one such occasion Sonya noticed tears in his eyes. "I'm crying," he explained, "not because I'm dying, but because of the artistic beauty of the thought." Upon recovering from this illness, he wearily entered in his diary: "It's boring to be alive again."

Both the Church and the government were almost as much concerned as the family, though for different reasons, with the course of Tolstoy's illness. The authorities kept informed of events at Gaspra through spies. Alexandra gives an amusing account of being trailed by one and then suddenly turning the tables and tracking the tracker so assiduously that in confusion and humiliation he was obliged to desert the field. There was real point in Tolstoy's observation at the time that the only sensible place of residence for a Christian in Russia was prison.

In January 1902, when it seemed that there was little chance for Tolstoy's recovery, the government took the most elaborate precautions. The telegraph company was forbidden to accept wires with requests about his health, and the press was instructed, "in the event of the death of Count Tolstoy," not to make any references to the excommunication of the Synod and in all reports of the event to observe "the necessary objectivity and circumspection." Confidential memoranda were even prepared by the Synod and the Ministry of the Interior, forbidding church services, public demonstrations, and detailing the formalities and conditions to be observed in transporting the body from the Crimea to Yasnaya Polyana.

At this same time Pobedonostsev fathered a plot that did credit to his reputation as the most reactionary and Machiavellian influence in the government. He secretly instructed the head of the local clergy, which had free access to the Panin estate because of the presence there of a private chapel, to have one of its members in the house when Tolstoy neared the end. As soon as he had died, the priest was to leave the house and at once declare to all that Tolstoy had recanted his beliefs and passed away a true son of the Orthodox faith. The government would then see to it that these glad tidings were immediately spread throughout the world. Members of the family got wind of this base business and were indignant. They planned to circumvent the plot by concealing the news of Tolstoy's death long enough to send telegrams to the press abroad with the message that he had died true to his convictions.

The Church was obviously interested in reclaiming Tolstoy either by fair or by foul means. For shortly after this incident, Sonya received a letter from Metropolitan Anthony, exhorting her to persuade her husband to return to the faith and die a Christian. "A quiet death under the influence of the rites of the Church," Tolstoy observed, "is like death under morphine." Though Sonya knew how hopeless it was, she told him of the Metropolitan's request. Write Anthony, he instructed her, that this is my last prayer: "From Thee I have come, and to Thee I shall return. Thy will be done." When she remonstrated about his attitude toward the Church, he continued: "Let there be no talk of reconciliation. I die without any enmity or evil. But what is the Church anyway? How can there be a reconciliation with such an indefinite thing?" And he ended by asking her not to answer the Metropolitan.

7

There were periods of convalescence between the various illnesses when the desire to live thrust aside thoughts of death. Kind attendants carefully swathed Tolstoy's feeble and emaciated body until he looked like a bearded Egyptian mummy, and carried him to a wheelchair which was pushed along the gravel paths. On one of these outings the cheery Boulanger suggested they take a sail. Tolstoy was carried to the deck of a Turkish felucca moored near by. The slender boat sped effortlessly over the smooth blue water and this new sensation filled the weak old man with a wonderful feeling of exhilaration. Only the thought of what his wife would say when she learned of this escapade dampened his high spirits.

When the weather was fine, Tolstoy held his little court on the broad lower veranda of the Panin house just as he had been accustomed to do on the terrace at Yasnaya Polyana. For almost as many visitors made their way to Gaspra to see and talk with Russia's first citizen. Revolutionists and sectarians, devoted followers such as Makovitski and Sulerzhitski, and local inhabitants called. One day, much to his surprise, he received a request from Grand Duke Nikolai Mikhailovich, first cousin once removed of the Tsar, asking permission to visit him. He had a huge estate near by. In the royal family Grand Duke Nikolai Mikhailovich had achieved some distinction for his intellectual interests as a historian, publishing a series of studies, especially on the period of Alexander I.

Tolstoy invited the Grand Duke to call. They conversed politely about inconsequential things, though it seems that the Grand Duke requested advice concerning his love for a certain lady. He asked if he could be of help in any way and entreated Tolstoy to make use of the heavily guarded grounds of his huge estate to stroll in. After he had left, Alexandra reports her father as saying: "Strange, what does he expect of me? He told me of his personal life and asked permission to come again. But he is a simple, unpretentious man and seems intelligent." To Chertkov he wrote less favorably of the Grand Duke's visit: "What does he want? I don't know. He is of little interest. A too familiar type."

Upon the Grand Duke's second visit, Tolstoy greeted him as follows: "I'm very glad to see you. As I awaited you my conscience tormented me and I wish to ask whether you considered what you were doing when you first called. For I'm in quarantine, like a person with scarlet fever; I'm excommunicated, people fear me, and here you come to see me. I repeat, I have scarlet fever. I'm contagious, and because of me you can experience misfortune; they will look on you with suspicion because you have visited a politically unreliable person."

Whether or not Tolstoy was joking—less important people had become suspect in the eyes of the authorities merely because they visited him—there is little doubt that the Grand Duke had carefully considered his visits. He was close to the Tsar, and it is not likely that he would have sought an acquaintanceship with Tolstoy without royal approval. It is even possible, in the light of their later relations, that the Grand Duke was acting on instructions to cultivate Tolstoy in the hope either of persuading him of the fallacy of his attitude toward Church and State, or at least of acting as an intermediary in making his peace with the Tsar. For a long correspondence developed between them in which Tolstoy, rather naïvely at first, attempted to persuade the Grand Duke to use his influence by way of getting the government to adopt Henry George's single-tax system. Since members of the royal family were among the largest landowners in Russia and stood to lose heavily by the adoption of such a system, the Grand Duke evaded the issue in his letters and gently suggested that Tolstoy was a bit of an idealist. In his reply, Tolstoy very firmly put the Grand Duke in his place and pointed out that he was hardly in a position to judge the efficacy of the plan, since he had obviously never read any of Henry George's works, which was true. After this Tolstoy soon grew cold toward his would-be royal patron.

Tolstoy felt much more at home with the literary visitors at Gaspra, among whom were new younger writers of distinction—Balmont, Korolenko, and Skitalits. The latter recalled the majesty and goodness impressed on the worn, ancient face of the sick man, and how he felt like a five-year-old child ready to burst into tears from shyness in the presence of the "great Leo." Balmont he greeted with the sentence of condemnation: "Aren't you the one who writes all those decadent verses?" He disliked the Symbolist poets and had pilloried them for their literary trifling and unintelligibility in *What Is Art?* When Goldenweizer had told him that Maeterlinck, another of the Symbolists he detested, had recently declared in print that Tolstoy's drama, *The Power of Darkness,* was one of the greatest of plays, he replied with mingled humor and scorn: "Then why doesn't he imitate it?" Tolstoy promptly asked Balmont to recite some of his verses. He recited one of his symbolic poems, "The Fragrance of the Sun." At the end, Balmont relates how Tolstoy rocked back and forth in his chair, laughing soundlessly, and then said: "Oh, what nonsense! Fragrance of the sun! Oh, what nonsense!" Apparently undiscouraged, the young author defended his verses and recited another poem. Tolstoy suddenly broke in with his customary question to newcomers: "Tell me, who are you?" Balmont then related his life history, and Tolstoy listened with rapt attention, occasionally interrupting to ask the most pointed questions. "Perhaps never in my life," wrote Balmont later, "has any man listened to me in that way. For this one capacity of an alien soul to enter so completely into another alien soul, one may endlessly love Leo Tolstoy, and I love him."

The literary visitors who gave Tolstoy most pleasure at Gaspra and with whom he now felt on entirely familiar terms were Chekhov and Gorky. Chekhov was living at near-by Yalta, having come to this warm climate in a vain effort to improve his tuberculous condition which in a few short years brought about his death. A slightly bent figure, carrying a cane, he resembled the conventional image of the absent-minded college professor with his pointed beard, spectacles, and shy, serious expression. Red, sunken cheeks and a constant muffled cough signaled his dread disease. He came several times to see Tolstoy at Gaspra. Their admiration for each other and sympathetic understanding had deepened, so much that one suspects Tolstoy keenly regretted Chekhov's failure to accept his moral and spiritual views. He loved Chekhov, Gorky said, and when he looked at him his eyes were tender.

Gorky, too, lived near Gaspra. He had recently been imprisoned for political activities, and was now under police surveillance, but the authorities had permitted him to come there for his health (he had weak lungs). On the occasion of his arrest, Tolstoy had written a warm defense of his character to the Minister of the Interior. Gorky was a frequent visitor to Tolstoy, who wrote to Chertkov at this time that he had grown much fonder of this strangely timid and somewhat uncouth young author. Perhaps Gorky was right in believing that Tolstoy's interest in him was ethnological, so to speak, as though he belonged to a species not familiar to him. On the other hand, Tolstoy fascinated Gorky not only as a man and an artist, but as the human material for psychological literary study. There was much about Tolstoy that baffled him and yet much that his keen insight into human nature penetrated and interpreted with remarkable clarity. It was during these visits at Gaspra that he wrote the often brilliant notes and observations that make up the larger part of his reminiscences of Tolstoy.

Gorky saw in Tolstoy a god, not a Jehovah or an Olympian, but a kind of Russian folk god who "is perhaps more cunning than all the other gods." At times he seemed to Gorky to be a man who knew everything, one who had settled every question. Gorky observed how continually the thought of God gnawed at Tolstoy, and he was inclined to attribute it to his "exquisite human pride." But his relations with God, said Gorky, were suspicious and sometimes reminded him of the relations of two bears in one den. He also noted that Tolstoy talked much of women and always with the coarseness of a Russian peasant. He quoted him as asking Chekhov one day: "You whored a great deal when you were young?" In embarrassment Chekhov muttered something inaudible. "I was an indefatigable . . ." And Gorky added: "He said this penitently, using at the end of the sentence a salty peasant word. And I noticed for the first time how simply he used these words, as though he knew no more fitting ones to use. Coming from his shaggy lips, they sounded simple and natural and lost their soldierly coarseness and filth."

8

During his illness, Tolstoy's mind worked with all its accustomed vigor and clarity. Though reconciled to surrendering his body to death, he seemed determined to wring out of his brain the last thought, the last bit of writing. Perhaps force of habit kept him at these tasks, but there was also the conviction that what he had to say was of importance to posterity. One of the attending physicians related that when death was hovering over Tolstoy and he thought he was lying unconscious on the bed, the sick man suddenly opened his eyes and demanded pencil and paper. When the pencil fell from his trembling hand, he called for his daughter Masha and dictated to her corrections to an article he had been writing.

Thus thoughts for the diary and notebooks were entered and letters and articles were written through these months of alternating illness and convalescence. When too weak to write himself, he dictated to willing attendants. Death stood still while the seemingly endless process of literary composition continued. At the end of 1901 he wrote an article, "On Toleration,"[3] inspired by a speech delivered by his friend M. A. Stakhovich, at the Orël Missionary Congress. To the amazement of his religious audience, Stakhovich, a distinguished local official, condemned them roundly for never once mentioning in all their deliberations the old-fashioned words "freedom of conscience." Lack of this freedom in Russia he blamed on the civil authorities, and he urged the Church to demand the abolition of all legal punishments for those who leave the Orthodox faith for another. As official business of the Congress, the speech was published in the Church paper and created a stir. To have his own position in this matter so ably and publicly argued by another gladdened Tolstoy, and he hastened to write his article to support the stand of Stakhovich.

In February 1902, after partially recovering from a severe case of inflammation of the lungs, Tolstoy put the finishing touches on an extensive article that he had been writing for some time, *What Is Religion and Wherein Lies Its Essence?* No essentially new arguments on this old subject were advanced in the work, but it is his most succinct, persuasive, and best tempered treatment of religion. He ap-

[3] This was published by Chertkov in England in 1902.

proached the subject historically and arrived at the following definition: "True religion is a relation, accordant with reason and knowledge, which man establishes with the infinite life surrounding him, and it is such as binds his life to that infinity and guides his conduct." Whereas faith, he asserted, is neither hope nor credulity, but a special state of the soul that obliges man to do certain things.

In January 1902, feeling that he might die soon, Tolstoy decided to write the Tsar what he believed to be a final letter of advice on the fate that threatened the country if conditions were not radically altered. He wrote: "Dear Brother.—I consider this form of address most suitable, because in this letter I address you as a brother-man rather than as a Tsar, and also because, awaiting the approach of death, I write as it were from the other world. I should not wish to die without telling you what I think of your present activity, of what it might be, what good it might bring to millions of people and to yourself, and what evil it can bring to people and to yourself if it continues in the same direction as now."

Tolstoy then itemized the various abuses under which the whole country groaned. The land is run by an army of police and the people have been driven by the cruelties of both Church and government to a point of open rebellion. Do not imagine, he warned the Tsar, that popular expressions of enthusiasm in public places are sincere. These demonstrations are organized by the authorities.

"Autocracy," he continued, "is an outmoded form of government which may suit the demands of a people somewhere in Central Africa, far removed from the world, but not the demands of the Russian people, who are becoming ever more enlightened through the common enlightenment of the whole world, and therefore that form of government and the Orthodoxy bound up with it can only be upheld, as is now being done, by means of every kind of violence. . . ."

Tolstoy next reviewed the specific acts of the Tsar's reign which he felt contributed to the misery of the people and the shame of Russia abroad. "Measures of coercion make it possible to oppress a people but not to govern them. In our time the only means of governing a people is by placing oneself at the head of their movement from evil to good, from darkness to light, and by leading them to achieve the goals nearest to that end. In order to do that it is first of all necessary to let them express their wishes and needs, and once having heard them, to fulfill those which answer to the demands not of one class or section, but of the majority —the mass of the working people." He finally listed the demands of the vast majority of the working people, which are similar to those he set down in his "Appeal to the Tsar and His Officials."

Once again, as in his earlier appeal, Tolstoy put aside his own ultimate convictions to plead for what amounted to a compromise, for he saw the bloody handwriting on the wall if conditions were not soon remedied. He persuaded the Grand Duke Nikolai Mikhailovich to deliver this letter to the Tsar. And convinced of the harmful influence of government ministers, he asked the Grand Duke to convey his wish to the sovereign that the letter should not be revealed to them. Somehow he felt that if the Tsar were left to his own reasoning and conscience, he might react favorably. The letter was delivered and the only acknowledgment Tolstoy received from Nicholas II was the comically ironic message "that he should not worry for he would not show it to anybody." When Tolstoy realized that this was all the answer he would get, he dictated to Boulanger the following note: "Every thinking person of our time cannot fail to see that there are only two ways out of the oppressive and menacing situation with which we are now confronted: one, though very difficult, is bloody revolution; the second is recognition by the governments of their obligation not to oppose the law of progress, not to defend the old or, as we have done, return to the past, but rather to understand the direction in which humanity is moving and to lead the people in that direction. I have tried to point out the way in my two letters to Nicholas II. . . . Up to now no hope has been given me that this attempt would achieve its purpose or even gain a hearing. Therefore, in view of the inevitability of the first way out, that is, revolution, I now offer these two documents for distribution[4] in the hope that the thoughts contained in them will lesson the fratricidal strife to which the government at present leads its people." Within three years Tolstoy's prophecy of bloody revolution was fulfilled.

[4] "An Appeal to the Tsar and His Officials" was published in England in 1901 and the "Letter to the Emperor" in 1904.

9

Tolstoy's illness and closeness to death drew the children together and brought out their devotion to their father. The public concern of the world over his health impressed upon them the sacredness of their own obligations. On several occasions, when the end seemed near, they all hurried to Gaspra. The married daughters took turns nursing him, and young Alexandra, now seventeen, was a constant attendant and at this time even assumed the difficult task of copying his nearly illegible manuscripts. The sons too shared the duty of ministering to the sick man, especially Sergei and Ilya. Big, strong Sergei carried the wasted form of his father in his arms up and down stairs. Only his son Leo caused him distress. For Leo's novel was receiving a good deal of popular attention at this time because of its ridiculing of Tolstoyans, and the fact pained his father. Thinking he was about to die, he wrote a final touching letter to Leo, who angrily tore it up in the presence of the family. Tolstoy apparently discovered none of his own talent in Leo's literary efforts, which he described to his brother as "stupid, untalented, and tactless."

Sonya's position during her husband's prolonged illness became an extremely difficult one. In her diary she confessed annoyance with the ancient notion that geniuses are invariably misunderstood by their wives. "When between a wife and a genius there exists real love, as there did between Leo Nikolayevich and me, then the wife does not need a great mind to understand; all that is needed is the *instinct of the heart,* the scent of love, and all will be understandable and both will be happy as we were."

However onerous the fate of being the wife of a genius, Sonya tried hard to accept it dutifully and graciously. But the first principle of success in this situation—to love your genius husband without criticizing him—she could never accept. She thoroughly enjoyed the warmth of Tolstoy's reflected glory, and thoughts of his approaching death sometimes frightened her with the dreary expectation of a cold and cheerless future. During his long sickness she was indefatigable in her devotion, even to the extent of worrying him by her prodigies of nursing. And her task was not an easy one, for though he was unusually considerate to those who ministered to him, simply because she was his wife and closest to him Sonya bore the brunt of a sick man's impatience with pain and weariness of being ill.

At one point, when it seemed that Tolstoy could not possibly recover, she entered in her diary the following striking confession: "I do not know why I write, for this is a conversation between me and my soul. My Lyovochka is dying. And I understand now that my life cannot go on without him. I have lived with him for forty years. For everyone else he is a celebrity, for me he is all my being. Our lives were lived for each other, but, my God, how much blame and remorse . . . have accumulated! How much love and tenderness I gave him, but how much have my frailties grieved him! Lord, forgive me! My dear, dear, sweet husband, forgive me!"

Yet Sonya's frailties were not conquered even during her husband's severe illness at Gaspra. It seemed that everything about this spot on the Crimean coast annoyed her. But her complaints against the strange house, the people, the food, and the climate had another significance. She yearned for familiar scenes, friends, and pleasures. When her husband was still in a grave condition, she wrote in her diary: "Various advertisements of concerts, about the playing of certain compositions of S. I. [Taneyev], have agitated my tiny soul, and just as a famished person desires food, I suddenly and passionately want music, and the music of Taneyev, which with its depths acts so powerfully on me."

Apparently unable to resist this desire any longer, she left Gaspra for a visit to Yasnaya Polyana and Moscow in April 1902. She spent only a day in the country, and the rest of her trip she remained at Moscow seeing art exhibits, plays, and attending concerts. She gathered together her close friends for an evening of entertainment, and among them, of course, was Taneyev. In her diary she mentioned that he "played for me the slight things of Arenski, Schumann's sonata, and his own charming symphony, which more than anything else gave me satisfaction."

Contented, Sonya returned to Gaspra, only to find Tolstoy deathly ill again, this time with typhoid fever. He knew the real purpose of her leaving him, for he thoroughly understood the yearning that still troubled her soul. Gorky, after one of his talks with Tolstoy at Gaspra, set down in his notes: "Women, in my opinion, he regards with implacable hostility. . . ."

10

This illness was the last that Tolstoy suffered at Gaspra, and considering all the sickness he had been through, his recovery was little short of miraculous. By the middle of May he was in a wheelchair, seeing guests and working away at his writing. And finally the doctors agreed, to the rejoicing of all the family, that he was strong enough to return to Yasnaya Polyana.

On June 25 the party left for Yalta where they boarded a boat for Sevastopol. At Yalta the young writer Alexander Kuprin met Tolstoy for the first time. He related how Tolstoy got out of a carriage, looking small and feeble, and wearing high boots, a short overcoat that fell in folds over his wasted body, and a bowler hat. In this array and with his long white beard, he created a laughable and pathetic impression, wrote Kuprin, like some old Jew selling rags. He boarded the boat and went up to the prow, his weak bowed form looking nothing like the Moses of Michelangelo that Kuprin had expected. A group of new acquaintances approached him and suddenly he became a changed man, his voice firm, his tired eyes bright, and his manner that of the worldly aristocrat. With vivid expressiveness he related to the newcomers an anecdote: "You know, some days ago I was ill. A certain deputation, apparently from Tambov Province, arrived, and since I could not receive them in my room, they were presented to me outside my window. Perhaps you remember in my *Fruits of Enlightenment* the stout lady? Maybe you have read it? Well, just such a lady comes up and says: 'Deeply esteemed Leo Nikolayevich, permit me to thank you for those immortal productions with which you have rejoiced Russian literature.' I saw by her eyes that she had read nothing of mine. I asked: 'What in particular have you liked?' At that point she was at a loss because obviously she had read nothing. Someone behind her whispered: '*War and Peace, Childhood,* and *Boyhood.*' She grew red, her glance wandered in embarrassment, and finally in utter confusion she murmured: 'Oh, yes! *The Childhood of a Boy . . . Warlike Peace* . . . and others.' "

After listening to Tolstoy's conversation and observing the reverence with which he was regarded by all the passengers, Kuprin concluded his account: "When I went ashore, I met the captain of the steamer. I asked him: 'Do you know whom you have for a passenger?' And I was surprised when his face at once lit up in a broad, happy smile, and swiftly taking my hand (since he was in a hurry), he shouted: 'Of course I do! Tolstoy!' This name was, it seemed, a kind of magic, unifying word, equally understandable to all throughout the length and breadth of the world."

At Sevastopol a special car awaited Tolstoy, which had been secured again through the efforts of Boulanger. As on his trip to Gaspra, he was once more, despite all police precautions, hailed by hundreds of people at the station stops. They brought him flowers and shouted congratulations on his recovery to health. At the Kursk station a particularly large crowd awaited his arrival, for at that time a congress of schoolteachers was meeting in the city. They appointed a group of delegates, headed by Prince P. D. Dolgorukov, to see Tolstoy at the station and convey their greetings. For his leading part in what the authorities considered an illegal "demonstration," Dolgorukov was summoned before the local police head. At the interrogation he fearlessly replied that the teachers were unable to regard Tolstoy "exclusively from the police point of view," and he admitted that they had waved their handkerchiefs to Tolstoy standing at the car window and had shouted "Hurrah!" If anybody was guilty of disturbing the peace, Dolgorukov angrily concluded, then it was the police themselves, who shoved the crowd about, shouting: "Who commanded you to yell 'Hurrah!' It is forbidden to shout 'Hurrah!' without an official order."

XXXV

Spirit *versus* Matter

THE ANGEL OF DEATH had been pursuing him again, Tolstoy wrote his daughter Masha in the summer of 1902, but God had found other business for His dread messenger. He continued to accept his poor health with cheerful resignation and laughingly told his friends that he had gained so much from sickness that for their own good he wished them all bad health. The newspapers, however, were a constant annoyance. If they would only cease treating him as a kind of subject for actuarial speculation. He finally wrote a letter to the press. Many people, he agreed, were no doubt much concerned, though for entirely different reasons, about his approaching demise, but he begged the editors to stop printing bulletins on the state of his health.

The doctors decided that Tolstoy should not risk another winter in Moscow. At last, precarious health and feeble old age had gained him that respite from living in the accursed city when all else had failed. Sonya this time offered no objections, for the alternative to Yasnaya Polyana was the Crimea, which she abominated. Nor did she oppose the decision on separate bedrooms. After forty years of sharing one, he was moved to two sunny rooms on the second floor of the large manor house, one for sleeping and the other for a study.

That summer, after Tolstoy's return from Gaspra, Marya came from her convent of Shamardino and Sergei from near-by Pirogovo to visit the brother they had thought never to see again. When Sergei arrived, he was not recognized by the servants so long had it been since his last visit to Yasnaya Polyana. Tolstoy had lost none of his affection for his older brother. Sergei, now a misanthropic old man, lived the life of a recluse with his socially unacceptable gypsy wife and three swarthy daughters, whose Tolstoyan views had been blamed for the unhappy marriages of two of them. At this unexpected meeting with his famous brother, Sergei's customary grimness gave way to restrained joy. The two old men, behaving toward each other with the fine aristocratic manners that came so naturally to them when together, sat in the study and talked of former days. Tolstoy spoke of his literary work but carefully avoided views that he knew his brother frowned upon. He was tenderly solicitous about Sergei's health and comfort, and he offered him apples, trying to pick the softer ones to suit his poor teeth. During lapses in the conversation loud prolonged yawns, as though someone were in dire pain, would come from the study, startling everybody in the house.

Some six weeks later an entirely different type of person visited Yasnaya Polyana for the first time—Peter Verigin, leader of the Dukhobors. He had been in exile for fifteen years and had at last received permission from the authorities to join his followers in Canada, where many of them at this time were making things extremely uncomfortable for their Canadian hosts by staging naked parades to protest what they considered infringements of their religious prerogatives. Tolstoy's correspondence with Verigin and the many stories he had heard about him made him eager to meet this leader of the sect he had done so much to help. In one respect he was not disappointed—the calm but strong personality of Verigin suggested the tremendous force and authority of a man born to lead. But in their conversation he was annoyed by Verigin's Messiah-like behavior and by his exasperating habit of carrying Tolstoyan beliefs just one step further to logical absurdity. It is all right, Verigin would argue, to make boots for oneself, but one must not use metal tools in the process, since men had to slave in mines to obtain metal; or if men should not be enslaved, then why not free all living things, horses and cattle, from slavery? Why not cease to spoil the earth by tillage—that is, go about naked, live off fruits and nuts that ripen of themselves in warm climates—and thus man would be free to spend his time in contemplation? All this, solemnly argued, gave Tolstoy the unpleasant feeling of having his leg pulled and forced him into the awkward position of devil's advocate of his own beliefs. In the end he was obliged to conclude that Verigin, though an intelligent and highly moral person, had by some trick of fate become the leader of a religious community while being himself not yet religiously born.

Though Tolstoy was confined to his bed for much of the remainder of 1902, he managed to peck away at several writing tasks. One article he finished was "An Appeal to the Clergy" (published in England in 1903). The edict of excommunication was by no means the Church's last word against Tolstoy. Since their public denunciation of his heresy had, if anything, boomeranged, they continued to attack his beliefs in various articles, which were often sent to his wife, either with the naïve intention of supplying her with theological arguments to help her convert him anew, or to protect her own orthodoxy from his wicked convictions. With these attacks of the clergy in mind, he entered in his diary on August 8: "Why do they hate me? I must write lovingly to them." "An Appeal to the Clergy," however, is hardly suffused with a spirit of brotherly love. In fact, the piece is one of the most vigorous attacks ever written on the Church and organized religion. The essence of the reasoning and the flavor of the language of the article may be gauged by his resounding charge that the Christianity preached by the Church "is an inoculation of false Christianity resembling the inoculation for smallpox or diphtheria, and has the effect of making those who are inoculated immune to true Christianity." After this there could be no turning back, and the Church at last recognized that Tolstoy was a hopeless heretic everlastingly damned.

As a kind of illustration of his argument in "An Appeal to the Clergy," Tolstoy wrote at about the same time a semiliterary piece in the form of a legend, "The Destruction of Hell and Its Restoration." With transparent symbolism the legend describes how hell (the kingdom of sin) is destroyed by Christ, revealing the truth to people, and is then restored by the devil after he has modified Christ's teaching so that it conveniently guides people who are bent on evil.[1] When Sonya heard Tolstoy read this aloud to a group, she flew into a rage over the obvious attack on the Church and its priests, and, to the horror of one of the visitors present, assailed him "in indelicate, unceremonious, and even vulgar" language.

In October, Tolstoy worked for the last time on his play,

[1] This legend was published in England by Chertkov in 1903.

The Light Shineth in Darkness, but he still did not finish it. He had conceived this drama away back in the 1880's and obviously regarded it as a significant work. "It will contain my own experiences," he wrote to a friend, "my struggle, my faith, my sufferings—all that is close to my heart." In fact, the play reflects his personal experience more deliberately than any other creative effort of Tolstoy, and, quite fittingly as a piece of autobiography, he never wrote the last act.

The play reveals him in an unpleasant light, and perhaps for the curious reason that his artistic sincerity and conscience obliged him to portray things as they are and not as he wished and believed them to be. He attempted to dramatize the essential domestic tragedy of his life—to show how his wife, family, relations, friends, and social surroundings prevented him from really living according to his convictions. The hero, representing Tolstoy, is a kind of Pippa in reverse; he passes through the world and everything he touches he blights.

One cannot blame the "darkness" in the play for not comprehending, for the spiritual light that shines is hardly a blazing beacon but at best a dim flickering candle that sputters and goes out at the end. Though a dramatic failure, the play is a tribute to Tolstoy, for only a morally great man would employ the sincerity of his art to depict himself so unmercifully. He could not sympathetically dramatize his heroic spiritual struggle, but with devastating reality he did show the harmful effects of this struggle on those who surrounded him, to whom he often appeared in the play as a most aggravating husband and father.

In September 1902 the Russian periodical press celebrated the fiftieth anniversary of Tolstoy's literary activity, his first work, *Childhood,* having appeared in 1852. There were many laudatory articles, and a few not so flattering. He received a telegram signed by Nemirovich-Danchenko, Stanislavski, Chaliapin, Gorky, and Leonid Andreyev, hailing him as one of the "greatest men whose spirit will continue to direct human thought for centuries." Most of the articles stressed the millions of copies of his works distributed and the fact that he was not only a national, but an international celebrity of the utmost social significance. Whatever personal gratification he may have obtained from all this public praise, he characteristically ignored the whole celebration.

2

Tolstoy's health improved during 1903, though he suffered periods of weakness and illness. With returning strength he resumed his practice of long walks and rides. On Délire, a spirited young horse that had belonged to his daughter Alexandra, he would ride along the narrow trails in the Zakaz woods that he knew so well, and in the summer he brought back bouquets of wild flowers that he loved or a hatful of firm mushrooms with rose-tan stems, carefully placed on large fresh leaves.

Now that the decision had been taken to remain at Yasnaya Polyana, some phases of the customary Moscow winter life of the Tolstoys were transplanted to the country. The comparative remoteness of the estate and wretched traveling conditions did little to discourage the usual stream of petitioners and visitors who used to make their way to the city house. Like the Sistine Madonna or the Winged Victory of Samothrace, the ancient gray-bearded Tolstoy had become Russia's most famous museum piece which foreign visitors felt they must inspect before leaving the country.

At the beginning of January two English youths, Tom Ferris and Bertie Rowe, turned up at Yasnaya Polyana bent on converting Tolstoy to spiritualism. They belonged to a "Non-Money Group," and had somehow made their way to Russia without a penny. Their proselyting only annoyed him, but their half-starved, ragged condition aroused his pity, and after having them fed and clothed, he bought them return tickets to Moscow and sent them packing.

Of a different order of queerness was A. M. Dobrolyubov, who visited Tolstoy in September. A decadent poet and religious thinker, he produced the impression of a saint on some people and a madman on most of those to whom he preached his strangely mystical and anarchistic beliefs. Though a man of education, he wandered over Russia, identifying himself with the peasantry in work and appearance. So thoroughly had he assimilated peasant ways that after two hours of conversation Tolstoy became convinced that he had been talking to a genuine peasant and refused to believe that he was one of the decadent poets whom he despised. Tolstoy had esteem for his Christian life and shared the basic position of his teaching but rejected its mystical direction.

An interesting sequel to the visit was a letter from Dobrolyubov, in which "in a spirit of love" he pointed out to Tolstoy his failure to abide by his convictions and leave his large estate and seek his livelihood by physical labor. Nor did this uncompromising taskmaster think that old age and poor health should prevent such a sacrifice. Now, as always, such charges, and they were frequent, preyed on Tolstoy's mind.

Less challenging and much more flattering was the visit of William Jennings Bryan, who arrived at Yasnaya Polyana in the early hours of a December morning. He brought his son with him. Shortly before this visit Tolstoy had remarked to Goldenweizer that the materialism of the majority of Americans and their complete incapacity for understanding the true spiritual life shocked him. And he told of a certain American millionaire who "donated five million dollars to a university and at the same time increased the price of kerosene by one cent a kilogram and continued the increase until he had regained his five million." Apparently Tolstoy did not include the Great Commoner among the materialistic Americans. Bryan was charmed with his hospitality, and gave up an audience with Nicholas II the next day in order to remain longer at Yasnaya Polyana. Tolstoy questioned him closely in a long conversation, employing an interpreter only on the rare occasions when he was at a loss for a precise English word. After lunch they went off on horseback, the huge Bryan garbed in a stylish fur coat, girdled with a leather strap, and a cap with earmuffs, cutting an odd figure on his light bay mare whose back seemed to sag under the heavy load.

Tolstoy apparently found qualities in Bryan that he admired, for he wrote one of his disciples that he was "an intelligent and religious American." Bryan, on his part, asked Tolstoy pointed questions on his beliefs, such as why he valued physical labor so highly, and how he explained his strange doctrine of nonresistance to evil. At that time Tolstoy was writing a brief introduction to a condensed biography of William Lloyd Garrison.[2] In it he related how Bryan, "a remarkably wise and progressive American," with the obvious intention of pointing out to him wherein he erred, posed the stock argument of what he would do if he saw a bandit murdering or assaulting a child. And

[2] It was published in England in 1904.

Tolstoy replied with his stock answer that in all his seventy-five years he had never met anywhere this fantastic brigand who would murder or outrage a child before his eyes, whereas in war millions of brigands kill with complete license. "When I said this," Tolstoy concluded, "my dear companion, with his characteristically quick understanding, did not let me finish, laughed, and agreed that my argument was satisfactory."

It would have been most interesting if Tolstoy had confronted Bryan with a more pertinent question that he raised in this same essay—violence against Negroes: "The nature of this question has remained insoluble, and the same question, only in a new form, now stands before the people of the United States. Then [in Garrison's time] the question was how to free the Negroes from the violence of slave-owners; now the question is how to free the Negroes from the violence of all the whites and the whites from the violence of all the blacks. And the solution of the question in its new forms consists not of lynching the Negroes and not of any of the dexterous or liberal measures of American politicians, but only of an application to life of those very principles which were advocated a half-century ago by Garrison." Perhaps he did not trouble to confront Bryan with this terrible problem of his own country because he realized that his answer would be that of the politician. He remarked to the company after the American had departed: "Byran is a broad-minded, sensitive man. Strange that he can give his heart to political activity."

Violence was much on Tolstoy's mind. Some eight months before Bryan's visit a terrible pogrom against the Jews had occurred in Kishinyov. Horrified by this event, Tolstoy readily lent his name to a protest signed by a group of distinguished scholars. More clearly than most, he recognized that the pogrom was not simply the result of the traditional hatred of gentiles for the Jews, but had been deliberately fomented by reactionary police authorities in order to divert the public mind from the threatening activities of revolutionists. And with his characteristic courage, he did not hesitate to proclaim publicly the bloodguilt of the Russian government. For when the *North American Newspaper* cabled him for a statement that would place the blame for the frightful massacre, he answered: "The fault is that of the government, in the first place for excluding the Hebrews, as a separate caste, from the common law, and in the second place for forcefully inspiring the Russian people to substitute idolatry for Christianity." When the well-known Jewish writer, Sholom Aleikhem (the pseudonym of S. N. Rabinovich) requested him to contribute something to a literary collection to be published to aid the pogrom sufferers, Tolstoy willingly responded by writing three short tales.[8]

The endless stream of letters that poured into Yasnaya Polyana from all over the world was becoming a constant trial to Tolstoy and consumed a great deal of his time. Though his daughters and hired secretaries aided with the correspondence, he felt it a duty to devote his personal attention to the vast bulk of it, often writing as many as twenty-five letters in reply in a single day. The nearly illiterate letters of unknown peasants and workers asking his advice on problems ranging from intimate domestic difficulties to naïve matters of faith aroused his most sympathetic attention. And sometimes his answers turned into extensive efforts, taking the form of epistolary articles.

Always good newspaper copy, Tolstoy was continually receiving letters and telegrams from foreign journalists, who solicited his opinion on events in the news. Occasionally these requests were deftly baited or contrived to obtain the maximum sensation out of the anticipated unorthodox reaction of Tolstoy. Such was the letter of an English journalist in January 1903, concerning the scandalous behavior of Louisa, Crown Princess of Saxony. She had deserted her husband and family and fled to Switzerland, where she openly lived with the former tutor of her children. In an interview with this English correspondent, Michael A. Morrison, she breezily asserted that her philosophy of life had been profoundly influenced by her reading of Tolstoy's works. And now Morrison, in his letter, wished to know if Tolstoy's teaching would justify Louisa's unconventional conduct which was being loudly condemned on all sides. Tolstoy promptly replied that not one word of his writings would justify such behavior, which he deplored. Being dissatisfied with his answer, he intended to rewrite it or not send it at all, but unfortunately it got mixed up with letters that were going to the post that day and was dispatched. Morrison at once sent the letter to a correspondent of the

[8] The titles of these tales, translated in Yiddish by Sholom Aleikhem and first published in Warsaw in 1903, are "The Assyrian King Esarhaddon," "Three Questions," and "Toil. Death and Disease."

New York World in which it was immediately printed and quickly picked up by the foreign and Russian press. Even before the letter was published, Tolstoy, perceiving his mistake, wrote a second time to Morrison, asking that his first letter should not be printed, and at the same time he wrote Chertkov in England, directing him to publish the present letter if his first one to Morrison should appear. And in this letter to Chertkov, after expressing regret for his hasty judgment, and explaining the reasons for it, he wrote: "I not only do not condemn her, but with all my soul I sympathize with her sufferings, and I wish that she may be delivered from the fallacy that has possessed her, and that she may achieve the calm that is always possible for believers in God and turn to Him for help."

Unhappily, it was too late to undo what he had done, and soon he was deluged with letters berating him as a believer in God's mercy for passing such cruel judgment on one of His erring children. Wearily he answered these charges, frankly admitting his fault and trying to make amends for it. The incident sharpened his hostility toward the press, but it also indicates how easily he could revert to the puritanical morality of the end of *Anna Karenina* in a matter that touched the sacredness of marital relations, even though his new faith taught him that he was a sinning mortal and had no right to cast a stone.

On August 28 of this year Tolstoy reached his seventy-fifth milestone. Messages of congratulations arrived from all over the world, even from Manchuria. He was particularly touched by the greetings of peasants and of a group of Kharkov workers, who acclaimed him as a fighter against all prejudices, slavery, and inequality in human relations. A delegation from the *Intermediary* publishing firm presented him with the initial copy of *Thoughts of Wise People,* the first of several volumes of selected quotations drawn from his vast reading which he hoped would present to the world the fundamental unity of thought underlying the religious perceptions of the sages and teachers of East and West. He also received greetings from a Moscow group of Social Revolutionists, accompanied by a long and remarkable statement which he must have read with mixed feelings. It began:—

> On this day when the whole world honors the seventy-fifth year of life of the great humanist, the herald of

> universal brotherhood, permit us, Social Revolutionists, to unite our voices to those coming to you from the ends of the earth with greetings, and to express our profound and warm thanks for all that you have done for the triumph of the ideas of socialism. Though our paths have diverged in achieving this purpose, yet the purpose itself—establishing the "Kingdom of God" on earth . . . with its ideals of the happiest future, of love and brotherhood, this purpose we hold in common, and the efforts you have made with your mind and talent to bring about the realization of these ideals make you infinitely close and dear to us.

Tolstoy did not allow the festivities to interfere much with his customary day of labor in his study. And the only notice he took of the occasion in his diary is the rather acid observation: "The 28th passed wearily. The congratulations were truly grievous and unpleasant—insincerely the *Russian land*[4] and every stupidity. The tickling of my vanity, thank God, is unnecessary."

3

Biryukov, who was then working on his biography, asked Tolstoy to contribute reminiscences of his life. The suggestion both attracted and repelled him. "To write about all my nastiness, stupidity, depravity, and meanness," he told Biryukov, "entirely truthfully, even more truthfully than Rousseau, would make an alluring book or article. People would say: Behold the man whom many place on a lofty pedestal, but what a scoundrel he was. . . ." He began his reminiscences and intermittently worked on the manuscript till 1906, but he never reached the period of his youth and early manhood, the period of "nastiness, stupidity, depravity, and meanness." The fragment he left is an account of his childhood miraculously recovered from the deep well of memory and told with the wonderful charm and freshness of his early artistic works.

There is an autobiographical aspect in the fine story, "After the Ball," which he wrote in the summer of this year. In it he returns to his student days in Kazan, to a beautiful girl with whom he may have been in love, and to her

[4] A reference to Turgenev's famous praise of Tolstoy as the "great writer of the Russian land" which was frequently quoted in the many laudatory greetings and articles that appeared in the press.

devoted military father who the morning after a ball, in which he had gaily danced a mazurka with his daughter, unconcernedly officiated at the execution of a Tatar soldier who was brutally beaten to death in running the gauntlet.

A much longer artistic work, the last such extensive effort in Tolstoy's lifetime, was *Hadji Murad* which he did not finish until 1904 and left unpublished. At times the life of this colorful patriot-robber entirely absorbed his attention, and he read all the books he could lay his hands on concerning the Caucasus and the war that Shamil and his mountaineers waged against the Russians. As was usual with him now, he felt that he was wasting time on a mere work of art, and he was by no means pleased with his efforts. When a guest at Yasnaya Polyana was reading parts of the novel to a group, Tolstoy kept popping in and out of the room to listen. Once he broke in to declare the work uninteresting, and finally, with some irritation, he asked the reader to stop bothering with such rubbish. "If that is so," one of the listeners demanded, "why did you write it?" "But it is not finished yet," he replied. "You came into my kitchen and no wonder it stinks with the smell of cooking."

Hadji Murad is anything but rubbish; it is a masterpiece of its kind, almost a perfect example of the "good universal art" that Tolstoy had acclaimed. It is the story of the mountaineer chieftain, Hadji, who out of vengeance and personal ambition deserts his leader Shamil and goes over to the Russians. An irresistible desire to see his son, who is held as a hostage by Shamil, leads him to escape into the mountains where he is run down and killed. Hadji is vividly characterized—a shrewd, brave fighter, endowed with all the vices and virtues of his half-wild people. His story is simply told, revealing the tragic irony of misunderstanding between men of different orders of civilization. The last scene—the death of Hadji and his four followers at the hands of a horde of pursuers—rises to sublime heights.

One of Tolstoy's characteristically cross-grained efforts at literary criticism—"On Shakespeare and the Drama"—vied with this brilliant Caucasian story for his attention in 1903. This work at first was designed as a preface to *Shakespeare and the Working Classes,* an essay by his American disciple, Crosby. But it soon took the shape of a formal critique and assumed the proportions of a small book. Tolstoy seized upon this opportunity to feed fat an ancient grudge he had for the Bard of Avon. Even as a young man he had expressed his dislike for Shakespeare's dramas, and after his religious conversion this dislike was intensified by the new demands he made upon literature in matters of morality and art. He had always experienced feelings of repulsion, weariness, and bewilderment on reading these plays. "Now," he declared, "before writing this article, as an old man of seventy-five, wishing once more to check my conclusions, I have again read the whole of Shakespeare . . . and have experienced the same feelings still more strongly, no longer with perplexity but with a firm and unshakable conviction that the undisputed fame Shakespeare enjoys as a great genius—which makes writers of our time imitate him, and readers and spectators, distorting their aesthetic and ethical sense, seek nonexistent qualities in him—is a great evil, as every falsehood is." He then frankly anticipated that the majority of people would not even admit the possibility of his views being correct, but he firmly declared that he would try as best he could "to show why I think Shakespeare cannot be admitted to be either a writer of great genius or even an average one."

To prove his point, Tolstoy elected, with perhaps some malice prepense, to make a detailed analysis of *King Lear*. Here he was able to prove to his own satisfaction that the play did not fulfill the most elementary and generally recognized demands of art; that the characters speak not a language of their own, but an unnatural, affected Shakespearean language which no real people could ever have spoken anywhere; that the play lacks a sense of proportion; that its contents reflect a vulgar view of life which regards the external elevation of the great ones of the earth as a genuine superiority while despising the common man and repudiating not only religious, but even any humanitarian, efforts directed toward the alteration of the existing order of society; and finally, that the play lacks sincerity. Generalizing on these faults, he found them present more or less in most of Shakespeare's plays.

It appears that Tolstoy did not intend to publish this long article during his lifetime, and he did so in 1906 only upon the urging of Chertkov. The printing of it resulted in an interesting exchange of letters between George Bernard Shaw and Chertkov. Shaw, who was an admirer of Tolstoy, found himself in agreement with his condemnation of social and religious evils and with his conviction that civilization would not improve without an internal moral and intellectual change in man. Although they differed on the means of bringing about this change, it is not surprising that both men, in certain respects, had reached the same position on Shakespeare. Hence, when Chertkov was translating Tolstoy's article in England, he wrote Shaw for advice on some points and also gave him a general idea of the conclusions of the article. Shaw replied, enthusiastically embracing Tolstoy's views as Chertkov described them. He agreed that Shakespeare possessed no real philosophy of life, and that his plays revealed no religious, moral, or social thought worthy of consideration. "After the criticism of Tolstoy," he wrote, "Shakespeare as a *thinker* must be discarded, for under the scrutiny of such a gigantic, bold critic and realist as Tolstoy, he will in no sense pass the test."

Encouraged by Shaw's attitude, Chertkov finally sent him a complete translation of Tolstoy's article. Upon reading it he at once realized that he had far overshot the mark in identifying himself with Tolstoy's views on Shakespeare. He hastened to write Chertkov a long letter, soon followed by another, which contain a brilliant criticism of Tolstoy's article and, in passing, some of Shaw's best observations on Shakespeare and his plays.[5] Unlike Tolstoy, Shaw made a sharp distinction between Shakespeare the thinker and Shakespeare the artist. He could go along with Tolstoy in dismissing Shakespeare the thinker as inconsequential, but as an artist, he stoutly maintained, Shakespeare was irresistible. In his own criticism of the dramatist, Shaw wrote in one of the letters that "he had endeavored in no small degree to open the eyes of Englishmen to the emptiness of Shakspeare's philosophy, to the superficiality and unoriginality of his moral views, to his weakness and confusion as a thinker, to his snobbery, to his vulgar prejudices, to his ignorance, to every aspect of his undeserved reputation as a great philosopher." But, he continued, "No one would listen to me if I took it into my head to support my protest by denying his humor, his gaiety, his capacity to create characters more real for us than actual living people, his tenderness, but chiefly his unusual power as a musician of words." The trouble, he said, was that Tolstoy attempted to judge Shakespeare from the point of view of abstract logic.

[5] The three letters of Shaw to Chertkov (August 2, November 3 and 19, 1905) are to be found in the Chertkov Archives in Moscow. Citations from them are from Russian translations.

"Life is not logical," he cautioned, "and it is not for Tolstoy, writing his productions as a poet, to condemn Shakespeare for not writing his as a jurist." In the end he asserted that Tolstoy's position on Shakespeare was to a certain extent a healthy one, but that the article as a whole was very bad.[6]

4

Throughout this year Tolstoy revealed in his diary and letters to close friends and adherents his continued efforts to achieve spiritual peace through a rational comprehension of the precise balance between matter and spirit, between the tribulations of this world and the promise of the next world. Many pages of his diary are filled with inconclusive speculations on the meaning of life as he struggled to arrive at a satisfactory definition. He seemed to be planning a philosophical work on this theme, but the subject stubbornly defied his persistent attempts at clarification.

Though Tolstoy clearly recognized the significance of the materialistic sphere of knowledge, he naturally tended to discount its contribution to the solution of the eternal problem of the meaning of life. He would not admit that the progress of humanity may be measured by its technical and scientific achievements, or that modern civilization in general was moving toward the greater good. Progress, he insisted, did not consist in an increase in knowledge or in the material improvement of life. "There is progress only in a greater and greater understanding of the answers to the fundamental questions of life." A popular worship of scientific progress in a society still incapable of distinguishing between right and wrong represented a terrible danger to him. "When the life of people is unmoral," he entered in his diary at this time, "and their relations are not based on love, but on egoism, then all technical improvements, the increase of man's power over nature, steam, electricity, the telegraph, every machine, gunpowder, and dynamite produce the impression of dangerous toys placed in the hands of children."

There was never any danger that the spiritual life Tolstoy sought would remove him from the immediate, sentient,

[6] The only other piece Tolstoy wrote for publication in 1903 was an article, "To Political Activists" (printed in England, 1903), which concerned the activities of the revolutionists.

throbbing life around him. In fact, his problem was how to lead a spiritual life without ceasing to be a vital, active participant in the world's joys and sorrows. "The true spiritual life," he told Goldenweizer, "is liberated in a man when he neither rejoices in his own happiness, nor suffers from his own suffering, but suffers and rejoices with others and fuses with them into a common life."

What was beginning to distress Tolstoy more than anything else was the feeling expressed on many sides that he had reached his position of destructive criticism of modern civilization merely out of a willful spirit of contradiction, out of a desire simply to be different. This charge was as offensive to him as the occasional glorification he received from adherents who hailed him as another Messiah. At the beginning of 1903 he wrote to one of his French critics: "All my critics, and it is with regret that I must say that you are not an exception, reproach me for my attacks on churches, or on science, or on art, or especially on all sorts of violence employed by governments. And some of them call this simply stupidity or madness, others inconsistence or mere exaggeration. I am given all kinds of flattering titles: genius, reformer, a great man, etc., and at the same time I am not accorded the simple commonsense of seeing that the churches, science, art, and governments are indispensable for societies in their present state. This strange contradiction proves only that my critics in judging me do not wish for the moment to abandon their point of view and put themselves in my position, which is really a very simple one. I am neither a reformer nor a philosopher, and least of all am I an apostle. I am only a man who, having lived a very bad life, has learned that the true life consists only in fulfilling the will of the One Who has put me in this world, a man who, after having found in the Gospels the true principles of life, abandoned his life of illusion and has lived and lives only according to these principles. From this point of view it is clear that when I combat the churches, governments, science and art, it is not for the mere pleasure of combating them, or because I do not understand the importance that men attach to them, but precisely because, having found these things most often contrary to the accomplishment of the will of God, which is the establishment of the Kingdom of God on earth, I cannot help but reject them. For those who judge these things objectively and according to observation and reason, the existence of churches, science, art, and especially governments, must appear to them indispensable and even inevitable. But for a person like myself, who recognizes an inner truth derived from a religious conscience, all these reasons and observations have not the least weight when they contradict the truth of a religious conscience. I am not a reformer or a philosopher or an apostle, but the least of the merits which may be attributed to me, and which I attribute to myself, is that of being logical and consistent."

5

The family still remained an obstruction to Tolstoy's effort to liberate the true spiritual life in himself. He could not fuse his existence with theirs, because their joys and sorrows depended upon a worship of the material things of life which he was struggling to surrender. The apparent literary jealousy of his son Leo, and Andrei's desertion of his wife and two children, hurt him deeply but seemed also the inevitable price that must be exacted from people leading their kind of life. He was equally distressed by the constant pressure from his wife to give her first publication rights of new artistic productions for her collected edition of his works. These editions had been an everlasting torment to him, although he refused to have anything to do with the profits. He knew that he could not justify her activities, though her position was theoretically that of any other publisher who had free access to his uncopyrighted works. And now Sonya listened avidly to the offer of a million rubles for a permanent copyright of his writings and to one from another publisher of a hundred thousand rubles for a copyright limited to two years. Her efforts to persuade him resulted in a firm determination not to publish henceforth any new artistic works, and with minor exceptions he abided by this decision.

The accusations of such people as Dobrolyubov and others that he was living in physical idleness and comparative luxury now cut Tolstoy more deeply than ever. He wrote to a disciple, M. S. Dudchenko: "However strange and bad it may seem that I, while living in luxury, permit myself to advise you to continue to live in want, I boldly do this because I cannot doubt for a moment that your life is a fine life before your conscience and God, and therefore very necessary and useful to people, but my activity, however useful it may seem to some, fails, not entirely, I hope, but surely in the greatest part of its significance, as a consequence of the unfulfillment of this chief token of the sincerity of what I profess."

The cross Tolstoy bore was perhaps a light one, and at times there might be a suspicion that the cross was bearing him. But if he considered it a moral duty to accept his life of comparative comfort as a cross which he had no right to abandon, his position was not made any easier by those who actually practiced the beliefs he advocated and even suffered in their cause. Their example always inspired a kind of reverential admiration and his own failures an unsparing self-condemnation. Thus, he wrote to a disciple who had been exiled in 1903 for eighteen years for refusing to serve in the army: "When I learn of such people as you and about what has happened to you, I always experience a feeling of shame, envy, and a guilty conscience. I envy you because I have lived my life without ever once having succeeded or even dared to put my faith into deeds. I am ashamed of myself that at a time when you sit with so-called criminals in a foul prison, I live in sumptuous fashion with criminals not so-called, availing myself of the material comforts of life. I have a guilty conscience because through the works that I write, risking nothing, I may well have been the cause of your behavior and its grievous material consequences. The most powerful feeling that I experience towards such as you is love and gratitude for all those millions of people who will be benefited by your act. I know how your situation is complicated and made more difficult because of family ties, but if you acted not for the sake of people, but for God and your conscience, I think that the burden you bear will grow lighter, that you will find a way out and triumph in the matter. May God help you."

And Tolstoy himself tried to continue his spiritual pilgrimage "for God," and not "for the sake of people," but the people in the form of most of his family stood athwart his path to Nirvana and his wife kept them anchored there. Sonya herself was quite capable of accusing her husband of hypocrisy for his failure to abide by the precepts she scorned. Her concern for the external comforts of his existence grew excessive and seemed, psychologically, a compensation for the inner moral suffering she caused him. The inexhaustible energy that had formerly been largely expended on her young children now found an outlet in fleeting enthusiasms for photography, painting, and writing. She felt impelled to publish a long, naïvely critical letter in the press, protesting the filth and immorality in the stories of Andreyev, and she embarrassed Tolstoy by contrasting the beauties of "that great production *War and Peace*" with the improprieties in the works of the younger writer. For her pains she received many letters from readers who blamed her husband for beginning this tradition of "filthy literature" with such productions as *The Kreutzer Sonata* and *Resurrection*. Neither did Tolstoy relish the pornographical and sensationally macabre aspects of Andreyev's writings, but with a sense of humor which his wife never possessed, he amusingly dismissed the matter by recalling the story about a boy who, unable to pronounce the letter "r," said to his chum: "I went for a walk and suddenly I saw a wolf. . . . Are you fwightened? Are you fwightened?" "So Andreyev," continued Tolstoy, "also keeps on asking me: 'Are you fwightened?' And I am not in the least frightened."

Since neither husband nor wife had encouraged the pious practice of discreet dissimulation and the little white lies unconsciously designed to lessen the emotional wear and tear of marital discord, each suffered from a full knowledge of the other's private griefs and unspoken censure. Of late, however, Sonya had been falling into the habit of concealing things from her husband, especially in her relations with Taneyev.

After years of happy life at Yasnaya Polyana, Sonya began to complain that this existence among landed gentry and rural folk was unnatural. "We have nothing in common with these people," she wrote in her diary. "It is false not to try to be with the cultured class on our own level." Yet visitors from that cultured class were so numerous at Yasnaya Polyana that Sonya with some justice protested in a letter to her sister: "There is a constant commotion and mass of people here. The longer you live in the world, the more you accumulate various relations, obligations, acquaintances, and trials. I positively do not invite anybody, but there are guests here all the time, guests without end, and sometimes I simply want to cry from weariness." Three months later, capriciously enough, Sonya was writing to Stasov to complain that she and her husband were all alone: "The quiet in the house is terrible."

Perhaps the real reason behind Sonya's inconsistent complaints at this time was that her duties at Yasnaya Polyana prevented her from making as many visits to Moscow as she would have liked in order to attend concerts and to see her own cultured set, especially Taneyev, who was now trying to end this strange intimacy. As it was, her trips to the city were frequent enough, and noticeably and painfully so to her husband. His illness occasionally interfered with her visits, and this annoyed her. "In general," she wrote in her diary, "I do not like men; they are always physically alien and offensive to me, and I have had to love in a man his soul and talent before he could become dear to me and attractive in every respect. In all my fifty-eight years of life, there have been only three such; and of course the chief one was my husband."

Though Sonya did not indicate who the other two were, Taneyev was certainly one of them, and she continued to contrast this pure relationship with the sensual one of her husband. On nearly every trip to Moscow from the second half of 1902 through the next year she contrived to be with Taneyev, to talk to him and listen to his music. Her agitation increased with the dawning knowledge that this precious musician was now politely trying to evade her, and her sense of guilt grew with the intensity of her pursuit. In a striking passage in her diary, Sonya related that, while correcting the proofs of a new edition of *Anna Karenina,* "I followed step by step the state of her soul and I understood myself and felt terribly. But people do not deprive themselves of life in order to *avenge themselves* on someone; no, they commit suicide because they *no longer have the strength to live*. At first a struggle, then prayer, then submissiveness, then despair and, at last, helplessness and death. And then I suddenly imagined Leo Nikolayevich weeping an old man's tears and saying that no one saw what had taken place in me and that no one had helped me. But what help is there? Let S. I. [Taneyev] come or invite him, and help me establish the friendly, calm relations of old age with him. So that the fault of my feeling should not weigh on me and should be *forgiven* me."

As perhaps never before in all this strange and confused passion for Taneyev, Sonya was compelled to confess to herself a kind of mental infidelity to her husband. She told in her diary how her joy over his recovery from another sick spell "does not heal the illness of my heart. When I enter his room, that evil secret of the inner state of my soul again takes possession of me, and I want to weep and to see that man who is now the very central point of my madness, of my shameful, untimely madness; but let no one raise a hand against me, because I have grievously suffered and I fear for myself. I *must* live, take care of my husband and children; I must not betray and show my madness, and I must not see that man with whom I am morbidly in love."

Sonya, however, betrayed her madness at every turn, and her husband continued to watch its progress with dismay, hoping as always that it would eventually disappear. Only the most cryptic references in his diary still hinted of his moral anguish over Sonya's conduct. Angry thoughts were incompatible with the spiritual peace he sought, and he tried, though not always successfully, to maintain an attitude of love and kindness toward his guilt-obsessed wife. "Tonight," she noted in her diary, "when I had covered him up and bade him good night, he tenderly stroked my cheek, as though I were a child, and I rejoiced at his paternal love." She treasured this chaste love, and gloried now in her solitary room where she could dream "pure, maidenly dreams." But at times, contemplating their separateness and the curtain he had drawn between their intimate life and his retreat into his spiritual self, a sudden wave of mingled fear and sadness would come over her. She entered his bedroom at night and he asked her to massage his stomach. "His thin, ancient limbs look pitiful," she observed. And she reflected that never did she hear a word of comfort from him now. "There has come to pass that which I have foreseen," she wrote. "My *passionate* husband is dead, a husband-friend there never was. . . . Happy wives live to the end in friendship and sympathy with their husbands! But the unhappy, lonely wives of egoists, of great men, are the wives of whom posterity makes future Xantippes."

XXXVI

War and Revolution

At the beginning of 1904, Sonya wrote in her diary: "On January 8 three students from the Petersburg Institute of Mines arrived with a message. I talked a great deal with them; they are intelligent people, but as with all our youths nowadays, they do not know where to apply their strength."

The three visitors were a delegation on behalf of a circle of students who sat at the feet of the distinguished revolutionary author V. G. Korolenko, and they carried a message containing formal greetings and a request for information on several matters under discussion by the group. At Tula a talkative coachman, smelling a fare, boldly thrust himself forward as a "Tolstoyan" and offered to drive them cheaply to Yasnaya Polyana. On the way he cheerfully regaled his passengers with lies and legends about Tolstoy. Pausing for breath at one point, he drew a bottle of vodka from his coat and, throwing his head back, did not so much drink the fiery liquor as decant it from one vessel to another. One of the students twitted him, as a "Tolstoyan," on his fondness for vodka. The coachman slyly replied that Tolstoy, an educated man, did not demand the impossible from his adherents and hence had given him a special dispensation to drink.

Tolstoy received the awed students coldly, glanced through the message they presented to him, and at once launched forth on a dry, moral sermon. "In your letter," he declared, "you praise me, as is usual, for some revolutionary service or other. But there is no point to your praise. I'm not at all a revolutionist in the sense in which you understand this word. My political convictions are a consequence of and part of my religious convictions, which you probably do not know, and if you know them, you do not share them."

The old man continued his sermonizing, glancing severely at the resentful students from beneath his bushy eyebrows. He spoke of the necessity of self-perfection and of educating the masses in the spirit of true Christianity. These are not new ideas, he declared, but the thoughts of the foremost minds throughout the ages. And he added that he had been collecting such wise sayings for a calendar of reading for every day. "Let us see what I've selected for today," he said, turning to the bookcase. Behind his back the crestfallen students exchanged glances that plainly said: "We're wasting our time here. Let's go."

Suddenly Tolstoy turned to them with an open book in his hand, his whole body and long beard shaking with noiseless laughter. "Oh how wonderful! How splendidly put!" he exclaimed, wiping the tears from his eyes with his fist like a child. "And most of all, how precisely it fits me! 'A man standing on his tiptoes, cannot stand long,'" he read. "How neat that is! I read this book every day and I always find something useful in it. I very much recommend it to you! Very much! One must stand on the earth—there you have it!" And still laughing, he stood firmly on the ground and crouched, as though ready to leap. Herding the visitors into a corner, he began nudging them in the back, gaily repeating: "Let's eat! Then we'll talk! Come on, you must be famished after your trip." The ice was broken. As he courteously showed them to the door leading to the dining room, he blew through his mustache and made a face at the last one to enter, whispering: "Now, now, how angry you are! Were you offended by the old man!"

After the meal the students were turned over to Sonya while Tolstoy took his nap. With the air of a professional museum guide, she showed them through the house:—

"Here you have Prince Volkonski's portrait. The grandfather of Leo Nikolayevich. Described by him in *War and Peace*.

"Leo Nikolayevich's writing table. Notice how low the chair is. This is to save Leo Nikolayevich from bending over. He's very nearsighted.

"The divan on which several generations of Tolstoys were born. I also gave birth to children on it.

"The bedroom of Leo Nikolayevich. Observe how simple everything is. Leo Nikolayevich doesn't like luxury.

"Leo Nikolayevich's washbasin. Leo Nikolayevich empties out his own slop pail."

The students soon grew bored with the tour and two of them escaped to play chess. Sonya carried off the third to her own room. "You've probably heard various rumors about me," she began. "I imagine what horrible things people say. I have many enemies. And many envy me, which is natural, being the wife of Leo Tolstoy!" Then she poured forth a long series of complaints about her domestic lot and the difficulties of life with her husband. "If I were not religious," she concluded, "I would long since have killed myself. Do you want tea?" she asked without pausing.

The transition from suicide to tea was so sudden that the startled guest stumbled over the polite answer. Over the teacups Sonya continued her self-revelation on a less painful level. She spoke at first of her love for music and painting. Then boasting a bit and becoming coquettish, she announced: "I write! Not long ago I composed a little poem in prose, in the manner of Turgenev. When it is printed, read it. The title is 'Moans,' and my pseudonym is 'The Weary One.'" Pointing to her diary on the table, she significantly remarked: "When I die people will read this and learn that I also in my way was a 'lioness'!" After a good deal more of this sort of monologuing, she finally reverted to domestic quarrels, her son Andrei's separation from his wife, and the death of Vanichka, a memory that always drew tears from her. The bewildered student was eventually happy to be released to join the family at dinner.

With the meal out of the way, Tolstoy took the students aside for the conversation they had been eagerly anticipating. Leaning his elbows on the table, he thrust his gnarled fingers through his long beard up to his ears, and fixing the students with his piercing glance, he began: "Well, do you go to the girls in the brothel?"

Observing their shamefaced confusion, he laughingly continued:—

"Of course I know that you go. I myself, when young, went."

His joking tone swiftly turned serious.

"You regard yourselves as socialists, yet you make use of prostitution. It's bad! You agitate against the government, yet you prepare yourselves for the position of civil officials. You sit on your parents' neck, read books, emancipate snub-nosed girl students, think yourselves better than all, and that you have the right to direct not only people, but a whole government. But has any one of you worked with the peasants in the fields or with laborers in a factory? Do you know what the peasant thinks and wants? I mean the real peasant in bast shoes and shirt. This is not the peasant you read about in books. I'm sure that you do not know! Why, then, do you dare to speak and write in their name? To encourage them to strikes and to murders? Who among you has sat in prison? Then what kind of revolutionists are you?"

With such arguments Tolstoy harried the idealistic beliefs of his young radical guests. Vividly he portrayed the bloody course of revolution. For the sake of the so-called "common good," thousands will be destroyed. A new order will be established. But what then? The form may be new, but the content will be the old one. The people will remain as formerly, as they did after the French Revolution. Yes, he agreed, it is necessary to change the whole structure of society. But it must be done by ideas, not by bombs. And the most destructive idea of all is the Christian idea of nonresistance to evil. Only stupid people call it a weak idea. For have not all the powerful oppressors of the earth feared this idea more than any revolution and persecuted its adherents as the most dangerous of enemies? "Revolutionists trim the branches of the tree, Christianity destroys the tree at its roots."

The students forgot their arguments in this flood of eloquence. They felt like Lilliputians at the mercy of a giant. But he was now a good-natured giant in his triumphant wisdom, and having beaten them over the head with his club of nonviolence he mercifully dismissed them with a Christian socialist fillip: "I'm not for the government and not for the revolutionists—I'm for the people!"

When the students left that night, Tolstoy politely lighted their way to the outer door with a candle. They looked back to see him standing at the head of the stairs, majestic, like a statue, his huge lionlike head with its massive brow and silvery beard thrown into relief by the dim light. He cheerily called after them: "Thanks for the visit. Don't forget the old man. We've had a good talk together. My respects to your comrades and to Korolenko for the message. Only don't write anything for the newspapers. Will you? However, if anyone asks you, say: 'There's nothing to report. Tolstoy still lives!' "

2

Yes, the old man still lived, but the shadow of death was remorselessly closing in on the intimate friends of his own generation. "We must prepare ourselves. A pleasant end soon awaits us," Tolstoy remarked to the eighty-one-year-old Stasov when he was visiting him at Yasnaya Polyana in 1904. "What end?" Stasov queried, still full of the joy of life in spite of his age.

"Death, of course. I'm sure that even you expect it."

"To hell with it!" Stasov exclaimed. "An abomination, a filthy thing to prepare oneself for! I often sleep badly and toss about in bed when I think that death will come."

"But don't you feel your old age and that the end is near?" asked Tolstoy.

"I feel nothing of the kind, nor do I deny myself anything as formerly, and I hope that you, Leo Nikolayevich, don't give up anything. You still ride horseback and play lawn tennis."

When the irrepressible Stasov was departing, however, he had a presentiment that it would be the last time he would see his revered hero, and this actually turned out to be the case. Now, in a flood of emotion, he seized Tolstoy's hand and kissed it as he said farewell. Less than two years later he died.

In April of this same year Tolstoy entered in his diary: "Alexandra Andreyevna has died. How simple and fine this is." Thus briefly did he chronicle the passing of Granny, the adored woman of his early manhood, his unfailing aristocratic friend at Court, and the ancient confidante and unyielding critic of his religious views. But death's visitations now came swiftly and often and won scant space in his record of passing phenomena. Their last quarrel during his visit to Petersburg in 1896 had soon been forgotten, for it saddened him to spoil a friendship. For her part, though Granny possessed little Christian humility, she was not lacking in a spirit of forgiveness. A year before her death he had asked her to send him certain information on Nicholas I that he needed in his writing. As always, she obliged, and in his letter of thanks, the last but one in their brilliant correspondence of more than forty years, he struck again the note of profound affection and esteem that had characterized their troubled but enduring relations.

"The older I grow, the more I wish to turn to you with greater and greater tenderness. . . . It may be that we shall not see each other again in this world; if this pleases God, then it is well. Nor do I think that we shall meet in the other world, as we understand the meaning of 'meeting'; but I do think and am fully convinced that in the after-life all the kind, loving, and fine things that you have given me in this life will remain with me, and perhaps some crumbs that have come from me will stick with you. . . . Farewell, dear, dear friend; I give you a tender brotherly kiss and thank you for all your love."

A few months later (August 23, 1904) Tolstoy's brother Sergei died at Pirogovo, after a long, painful illness, of cancer of the tongue. To the end Tolstoy had been solicitous, visiting him and trying to comfort him. The misanthropic Sergei had always been secretly proud of his famous brother, though he had little sympathy with his religious and social views. Tolstoy deplored his lack of faith and unwillingness to reconcile himself with death. Three days after the end, he cryptically wrote in his diary: "Seryozha is dead. Quietly, without consciousness, without any pronounced consciousness that he was dying. That is the mystery. It is impossible to say whether it is better or worse this way. A real religious feeling was inaccessible to him. (Perhaps I deceive myself, but so it seemed.) But it was even good for him. Something new and better was revealed to him, just as for me. The road—an important measure of enlightenment. As for what it leads to in the endless circle—that is of no consequence."

Dmitri, Nikolai, and now Sergei. He was the last of the four Tolstoy brothers. The living go on dying, he reflected. But were the dead forever dead? An immortal something, the manifestation of God in man, lived on. Of that he was certain. As more and more of those near to him left this earth for the world of light, his own mind, curious but unafraid, embraced the concept of death with a new sense of urgency.

3

For Tolstoy, however, these personal bereavements lost their significance in the face of the terrible impersonal deaths of thousands now being slain in battle. For in January 1904, the Russo-Japanese War had begun when units of Japan's fleet attacked Russian ships without warning in the outer harbor of Port Arthur.

The news shocked Tolstoy. At the outset he rode horseback all the way to Tula on four separate days to obtain the latest information on hostilities. The merits of the issue did not concern him, except as they substantiated his long-held and frequently expressed convictions concerning the moral bankruptcy of governments and the conspiracy of their rulers to send thousands of subjects to destruction for the sake of a bit of land, national honor, or the capture of world markets. What did concern him was that two peoples who professed religions that forbade killing were now slaying and maiming each other solely because they had been ordered to do so. Then there were the daily tragedies that came under his own observation in the village: peasants unwillingly torn from essential work by the draft, and the womenfolk of these impoverished families appealing to him for aid. And his burden of sorrow was increased when his son Andrei decided to volunteer for the fighting in the Far East. That Andrei became an aide-de-camp gave his father some comfort, for in this position he would have no occasion to kill Japanese.

Tolstoy frankly admitted that the Japanese were incomprehensible and unknown to him. He had heard only of their wonderful capacity for adapting and surpassing in some respects the superficial side of European culture. That they could duplicate in a few decades what had taken a thousand years to build only served to support his negative regard for the accomplishments of European civilization. The government-sponsored hate-the-Japanese campaign, however, he condemned as opposed to all his instincts and convictions.

Though the world knew well Tolstoy's attitude toward war, the foreign press now hounded him to commit himself on a struggle in which his own country was immediately engaged. To a cable from the *North American Newspaper* as to whether he favored Russia or Japan or neither, he replied with his usual courage: "I am neither for Russia nor Japan, but for the working people of both countries, who have been deceived by their governments and forced to go to war against their own good, their conscience, and their religion."

Despite his previous writings on the subject of war, Tolstoy felt it essential to speak out once more. His many followers expected it, and his moral conscience obliged him to state his position at length on the present conflict. This work, an extensive pamphlet, entitled *Bethink Yourselves!* was published in England by Chertkov in 1904. Two years later an attempt was made to print it in Russia, but the whole issue was confiscated. Translations appeared quickly in various European languages. Even the staid London *Times* opened its columns to a rendering.

As though weary of his own arguments on the subject, Tolstoy introduced the chapters of his pamphlet with quotations condemning war, drawn from the works of various distinguished writers and thinkers, which lent a suggestion of universal authority to his position. If he had little to offer on his own that was entirely new, the whole work gained in nobility, eloquence, and effectiveness by virtue of the fact that he had an immediate and horrible war to point his moral at every turn, and a war that was peculiarly purposeless and widely unpopular. With masterly polemical skill, he supported his arguments by introducing the direct evidence of conscientious objectors and the nearly illiterate letter of a doubting Russian seaman at Port Arthur, who, after hearing a priest speak of the "Christ-loving army," naïvely implored Tolstoy to answer his question: "Is it true or not that God loves war?"

At such a perilous time in Russia, it took a great deal of personal fortitude to oppose his country's so-called patriotic war and to denounce—as Tolstoy did in the pamphlet—the Tsar and Aleksei Kuropatkin, commander-in-chief, for condemning thousands of peasants to futile slaughter. When the Grand Duke Nikolai Mikhailovich, whose persistent attempts at friendship Tolstoy now found unnatural, mentioned that he would like to visit Yasnaya Polyana, Tolstoy hastened to write him: "Though it would be agreeable for me to see you here, I think that I have become so disliked by the government, and especially now since my article on the war, that your visit to me might well have disagreeable consequences for you, and hence I feel it necessary to forewarn you of this." The Grand Duke decided to forgo his projected visit.

While Russian priests warned their congregations against the devil-inspired antiwar views of Tolstoy, the foreign press for the most part acclaimed his pamphlet, *Bethink Yourselves!* Some criticism appeared in English newspapers, especially in the London *Times*, but the general level of appreciation was reflected in the rapturous encomiums of the *Daily News,* which hailed the pamphlet in the following words: "Yesterday Tolstoy released one of those great messages to humanity which leads us back to the first fundamental truth and at the same time impresses us with its surprising simplicity." Such reactions irked the Russian government which had good reason to suspect England's maneuverings in the war with Japan.

It is difficult to estimate the influence of *Bethink Yourselves!* in Russia during the time of the war. Copies had to be smuggled from abroad, and the strict censorship prevented any mention of the pamphlet in the press. For various reasons the conflict was unpopular; wives and mothers at Kharkov lay across the rails to halt the trains taking their menfolk to the Far East. But if one may judge from the flood of mail Tolstoy received and from the testimony of the swelling number of conscientious objectors, his past and present antiwar agitation contributed in some measure to the popular discontent. To be sure, letters from patriotic intellectuals fiercely attacked him for betraying his country. One aristocratic Russian lady, having heard the reading of a French translation of *Bethink Yourselves!* wrote him in flaming anger: "Everything that is sacred and precious to us, everything that has constituted and still constitutes the power of Russia—its Holy Church, love for the Tsar, and love for our native land—all this you tread under your feet and cover with filth!" Humbly he turned the other cheek in his answer, begging forgiveness if his work had revealed harsh indignation or an unchristian spirit, but still firmly insisting upon the sincerity and justice of his opposition to war.

Did Tolstoy hate the violence of war more than he loved his country? On a less abstract level: Had this former hero of Caucasian fighting and of the famous Fourth Bastion at Sevastopol entirely freed himself from the pride of patriotism in the glorious tradition of Russian arms? The answer is "No!" He excitedly followed the course of the struggle with the Japanese, and each victory of the enemy brought him chagrin and anguish. "I cannot get rid of a feeling of grief when I hear that the Russians are getting beaten," his daughter Alexandra reports him as saying. In our time, he proudly told his son-in-law Obolenski, the fall of such a fortress as Port Arthur, possessing sufficient stores and forty thousand men, would have been regarded as a shame and an impossibility. And he frankly confessed in his diary: "The surrender of Port Arthur distressed me; I felt badly. This is patriotism. I was brought up in it and am not free from it, just as I am not free from personal egoism, from a family and even an aristocratic egoism, and from patriotism. All these egoisms live in me, but also in me is a consciousness of a divine law, and this consciousness holds these egoisms in check so that I am free not to serve them. And little by little these egoisms become atrophied."

Later, after the crushing of the Russian fleet at Tsushima, Tolstoy adopted a curious attitude of rationalization toward his country's defeats. It is now clear, he wrote in his diary, that it could not be otherwise. In the past, Christian nations had prevailed in wars with non-Christian peoples solely because of their technical proficiency. When non-Christian nations, the highest ideals of which are love for the fatherland and heroism in war, catch up in technological skills, then Christian nations will never be a match for them in armed conflict. This was precisely the case with Japan, he argued, for the country had already equaled and even surpassed the technical progress of the West, a gloomy reflection on the so-called materialistic culture of Europe. The lesson we must learn from this, he declared, was to forsake this culture and return to the true Christian life of purity, brotherhood, and love. However, he quickly added, "I do not say this to comfort myself for the defeats we have suffered from the Japanese. The shame and disgrace remain. And they remain not only because we have been beaten by the Japanese, but because we undertook to do something which we were unable to do well, and which was bad in itself." Of course the flaw in the argument was his ignorance of the fact that Russia lagged far behind the West and even somewhat behind Japan in the technical proficiency that contributes to successful modern warfare.

In the conflict, however, it was some small comfort to learn from a letter, addressed to him by Iso Abe, editor of a Japanese socialist magazine, that in Japan he had highly moral and religious friends and followers who opposed the present conflict. He hastened to grasp this straw in the wind, but in his reply he did not neglect to tell Iso Abe that he had no sympathy for his socialistic teaching. This teaching was now much on his mind. Fully aware that the unpopular war had increased the rising tide of social revolt in Russia, he feared the bloody consequences.

4

The revolt that Tolstoy had warned the young Tsar would take place if social and political changes were not forthcoming broke out in 1904–1905. It required no prophet to foretell it. Though an unpopular and disastrous war hastened the outbreak, decades of reactionary rule and black oppression in a European time-scheme of relative progress had made an uprising of the Russian people inevitable. In so far as political parties existed at all, such as the Social Democrats, the Social Revolutionaries, and the Constitutional Democrats, they had to function underground. Each of these parties had its own specific panacea for solving the ills of the country, but they were obliged to work on an ineffective conspiratorial level. Despite their differing programs and special appeals to the several social classes, they were all united in demanding the end of autocracy and the introduction of a representative government elected by universal ballot.

The fatal indecision of the Tsar to meet any of the demands resulted in a series of disturbances, ranging from bold political speeches by intellectuals to student riots, peasant uprisings, disaffection in the army, and the assassination by terrorists of Plehve, Minister of the Interior. This first revolutionary wave reached its culmination on January 9, 1905, when an organization of Petersburg workers, led by the priest Gapon, made their way to the Winter Palace to appeal to Nicholas II. Though their intentions were clearly peaceful and their cause a just one, the troops were ordered to fire, and several hundred workers were killed or wounded. This "Bloody Sunday" marked a turning point in the history of the Russian revolutionary movement, for it resulted in an alliance of the socialist working-class parties and made of the workers a decisive force in bringing about political and economic changes.

Frightened by the roar of protest throughout the country, the government made a feeble concession—the calling of a national congress or Imperial Duma, which was to have solely a deliberative function. The workers' answer to this half-measure was a general strike. Electricity and the water supply of cities were cut off and railroads came to a standstill. At first, the core of this proletarian resistance was the Petersburg Soviet of Workers' Deputies, which was also to play a significant part in the later revolutionary events of 1917. Made up of representatives of the two socialist parties, it was actually under the control of the Mensheviks, the moderate right wing of the Social Democrats, and their leader Trotsky. Similar soviets of workers were formed in other cities, but before they could effectively combine in revolt, the government, upon the initiative of Count Witte, issued a manifesto (October 17, 1905) which promised the fundamental principles of civil liberty, a democratic franchise, and legislative powers to the Duma. And the liberal Count Witte became Prime Minister, with a mandate to form a coalition cabinet of the various opposition parties.

These concessions failed to stem the tide of revolt; the socialist parties insisted upon carrying through their revolutionary doctrines, maintaining that the government was not sincere in its promises. It was now the Bolsheviks, the radical left wing of the Social Democrats, with their leader Lenin, who became the powerful opponents of the government's conciliatory policy. The strikes went on and an insurrection broke out in Moscow in December. But the masses, impressed by the government's concessions, were not yet ready for the extreme measures of the Bolsheviks. Accordingly, the government was able to resume control of the situation. The soviets were forced to disband, riots were suppressed, and reactionary "Black Hundred" organizations, such as the so-called "Union of the Russian People," engaged in pogroms among the Jews and in other diversionist activities, with the tacit consent of the Tsar's police. In the end, governmental measures partly succeeded in drawing the support of workers and peasants away from the opposition. Certain real gains were made over the hopelessly reactionary situation that had existed, but the revolutionary movement was crushed for the time being.

This violent national activity had its repercussions in isolated Yasnaya Polyana. Alarms ran through the village. In remote districts the houses of landowners had been burned down and their owners, in some cases, murdered by the peasants. Serious strikes occurred at near-by Tula. Fears swept through the Tolstoy household. English, American, French, Spanish, and Hungarian correspondents rushed to Yasnaya Polyana to obtain the reactions to these significant events of Russia's first citizen. He received them with gracious politeness, though not untinged with the suspicion that he felt for all journalists. More often than not they found themselves talking about God and immortality rather than about the burning political events in Russia. Instead of interviewing, they were themselves interviewed on their personal lives and the political and social customs of their countries. He told them frankly that he found it hard to understand why anyone would want to be a journalist. Meanwhile, intellectuals hoped he would head a petition to the Tsar for a constitutional government; others asked him to write an open letter to the Tsar's soldiers, pleading with them not to shoot down their brothers.

The acts of violence throughout Russia grieved him as deeply as the carnage of war in the Far East. After the shooting on "Bloody Sunday," he fulminated against the agitators: "Those who arouse the workers imagine that they will influence the government by such a course. But this is a mistake. . . . The Tsar is not free. He talks now to one now to another. He listens to his uncles, his mother, Pobedonostsev. He is a pitiful, insignificant, even an unkind person." In his diary he gloomily entered in October: "The revolution is in full swing. There will be killings on both sides."

When Tolstoy read the manifesto of Nicholas II, promising civil liberties and an elected Duma, he brusquely dismissed the move: "There is nothing in it for the people." In fact, the argument over whether or not a constitutional government was the answer to the problem facing the country became a matter of bitter controversy in the household, with Tolstoy firmly supporting the negative. With his son Sergei the argument ended in a quarrel. Tolstoy flatly declared that 90 per cent of the people did not want a constitutional government. Why change one form of violence for another, he asked? "A man living under a despotic government, such as Turkey or Russia," he wrote in his notebook, "may be more or less free, though he will be exposed to the violence of a rule in which he has no say, but a subject in a constitutional government, while always recognizing the lawfulness of the rule under which he finds himself, is always a slave."

It was characteristic of Tolstoy that at a time of great crisis in his country he refused to throw his tremendous influence on the side of any of the contending parties. He had repeatedly condemned the abuses of tsardom, and he had no less uncompromisingly denounced the extremes of the radicals. The proponents of the middle way—the constitutional reformers—had some reason to hope for his support in their efforts to establish a government based on the democratic franchise and public opinion. If for no other reason, however, his instinctive dislike for all organized effort to solve the ills of mankind obliged him to go his lonely way. When the *North American Newspaper* cabled him for his reaction to Zemstvo[1] agitation for representative government, he categorically replied that these efforts would only delay true social amelioration, which, he added, "can be attained only by the religious and moral perfection of all individuals."

This statement was reprinted, in the usual garbled form, in a Russian newspaper, and soon Tolstoy was receiving quantities of letters, some asking him for further information on his position, others berating him for his fence-sitting at such a time of national distress. It is all right for you to sit comfortably at Yasnaya Polyana perfecting yourself, wrote one correspondent, but how would you feel if the government starved you or threw you into prison? In the light of such criticism, Tolstoy believed it necessary to state his position on the issues of the day at some length in an article, "On the Social Movement in Russia."[2] Scornfully he turned on those who imagined they could achieve a kind of utopia by substituting a constitutional government for the present despotic rule. "In England, America, France, and Germany," he boldly asserted, "the perniciousness of government is so masked that these people, pointing at the events in Russia, naïvely imagine that what takes place there could happen only in Russia, and that they possess complete freedom and do not require any improvement in their situation; that is, they find themselves in the most hopeless condition of slavery—the slavery of slaves who do not realize they are slaves, and they are proud to be slaves."

At least, Tolstoy's position in this national crisis had the dubious virtue of consistency. For years he had warned his country of the danger of revolution, and on several occasions he had made direct appeals to the Tsar to correct what he considered to be the abuses that were leading to social

[1] The Zemstvos, elected representatives of the counties, had provided, since their reform in 1864, almost the only progressive form of local self-government in Russia.

[2] This was published by Chertkov in England in 1905 and was printed in translation in various European countries.

revolt. He did this not because he had any love for autocracy, for he condemned all governments. But he was willing to compromise with his own ultimate ideals, for he feared the violence of revolution and what he believed to be the illusory hopes it offered the people more than he hated the abuses of autocracy. His warnings had been ignored, and now that revolution had come, he felt it necessary to revert to his original Christian anarchist position. In his eyes all governments were ultimately despotic, and he saw no point in changing one for another. He was willing to admit in private that if the Tsar asked his advice he would urge the adoption of constitutional rule, but he hastened to add that the majority of the people—the peasants—did not understand it and did not want it. America, he scornfully declared, had reached an impasse. "In that country you will find trusts, multimillionaires, an army of 10,000, and, side by side with these, men and women without sufficient food and clothing, or a decent roof over their heads." As for the English, they obeyed laws made by their representatives and all the time imagined they were free men. But in Russia, Tolstoy countered, I do not make the laws and consequently I am not bound to obey them—I am a free man. Nicholas II, he admitted, "can gore us to death, but that is just a matter of chance—whether one is killed by an ox or by a tile falling on one's head." When one of his questioners pushed him to tell what he thought of parliamentary government, he answered: "To ask me what I think about parliamentary government is just like asking—I won't say the Pope—but some monk his opinion as to how prostitution ought to be regulated."

With some justice Tolstoy's critics among the liberals charged him with evading the principal issue that the country had to face—autocratic rule or constitutional rule. In a period of emergency they considered the antithesis he set up between politics on the one hand and individual religious and moral regeneration on the other as highly unrealistic. But he doggedly adhered to the one unchangeable conviction that he had been advocating for the last twenty years—nonresistance to evil by force. This was the axiom by which all political, social, and economic questions were to be solved. It made no difference to him what the motive for the use of physical force might be, or that constitutional governments might employ it in the interests of the good of the greater number. All governments owed their very existence to the use of physical force, therefore all governments were evil.

Baffled friends among the Social Revolutionaries pointed out to Tolstoy that individual self-perfection was a long and arduous process. In the meantime, the Russian masses were suffering from very real wrongs that required practical remedies. Yes, he knew, but the chief wrong could be corrected by a practical remedy that he had been advocating for years—the prohibition of private property in land. The land hunger of the peasants was driving them on to kill landowners. They did not care a fig about who governed them, provided they obtained as much land as they could work. So vital a factor did Tolstoy believe this to be in the present revolutionary disturbances that he wrote an article, "The Great Sin," in which he once more proposed the single-tax solution of Henry George. But the peasants of Yasnaya Polyana, who could not understand that he had deeded all his land to his family, wondered why their "squire," who told them of the evils of owning land, did not give his away to them. Worse still, they wondered why his daughter Alexandra actually bought and sold land contrary to her father's convictions. Whatever his own failings in the matter, Tolstoy was a true prophet. Twelve years later the slogan "All land to the peasants" virtually won a revolution.

Both radicals and liberals were disgusted with Tolstoy's stand. They understood little about his ideological consistency; they knew only that the doctrine of the moral self-perfection of man became ridiculously quixotic in a time of grave revolutionary crisis. In particular, the Marxian Social Democrats, who had wooed him for some time, because more effectively than any of their members he had widely exposed the evils of the Russian government, Church, and capitalism, now turned on him with fierce criticism. In his writings he had repeatedly made clear his objection to materialism as a philosophy of life. "Socialism," he once said, "is unconscious Christianity," and he frankly accepted the fact that some of the aims of the socialists were his own. In a sense, he and the Marxian socialists might be said to have shared the same ultimate ideal—the withering away of the State. But for Tolstoy, this ideal could be realized only by man's moral self-perfection and not by an organized communistic process of material development. "Economic ideals," he wrote, "are not ideals."

In July 1905, Tolstoy entered in his diary: "Only that revolution which is impossible to stop is a fruitful revolution." That is, he was not opposed to revolution provided the process was a constant change through peaceful means in man's existence from something worse to something better. Even in the present revolution he could see something good, and he made a strikingly prophetic statement on it to Goldenweizer: "The present movement in Russia is a world movement, the importance of which is little understood. This movement, like the French Revolution formerly, may perhaps, through its ideas, provide an impetus for hundreds of years to come. The Russian people have in the highest degree a capacity for organization and self-government. They gave up their power to the government once and waited for the liberation of the land, as they formerly did for the liberation of the serfs. They have not been given the land, and they themselves will carry out that great reform. Our revolutionists do not at all know the people and do not understand this movement. They might help it, but they only hamper it. In the Russian people, it seems to me, and I do not think I am biased, there is more of the Christian spirit than in other peoples." What Tolstoy criticized in the Marxian socialists, apart from their materialistic philosophy of life, was that they did not thoroughly understand the masses and their real needs; that their conception of revolution was change by violence; and that hence their leaders would be content to seize power, which they would retain by force and thus revert to the very oppression of the masses that they had set out to destroy.

From the Marxian point of view, perhaps the fairest and most understanding appraisal of Tolstoy's contribution to the Russian revolutionary movement was by Lenin himself in a series of seven articles. In his first article, "Leo Tolstoy as a Mirror of the Russian Revolution," written in 1908, he summed up the contradictions in his doctrines as follows: "On the one hand, an artist of genius, contributing not only incomparable pictures of Russian life, but literary productions of the first rank that belong to world literature. On the other hand, a landowner, wearing the martyr's crown in the name of Christ. On the one hand, an extraordinarily powerful, direct and sincere protest against social lies and hypocrisy; on the other, a Tolstoyan, that is, a worn-out, historical sniveler called the Russian intellectual, who, publicly beating his breast, cries: 'I am bad, I am vile, but I am striving after moral self-perfection; I no longer eat meat and now live on rice cutlets.' On the one hand, relentless criticism of capitalist exploitation, the exposure of governmental violence and of the comedy of justice and governmental administration, revelations of all the depths of contradictions between the growth of wealth and the achievements of civilization, and the growth of poverty, the brutalization and suffering of the working masses. On the other hand, weak-minded preaching of 'nonresistance to evil' by force. On the one hand the soberest realism, the tearing away of all masks of whatever kind. On the other hand, advocacy of one of the most corrupt things existing in the world, that is, religion—an attempt to replace the official state clergy with priests by moral conviction, that is, cultivating a clericalism of the most refined and hence most loathsome kind."

Lenin maintained that Tolstoy had thoroughly identified himself with the peasants, with their moods, hopes, and aspirations. In fact, he declared that Tolstoy's contradictory views were a veritable mirror of the contradictory conditions surrounding the historical activities of the peasantry in the revolutionary movement, which in turn accounted for their failure as a class in the 1905 Revolution. Tolstoy, like the peasants, concluded Lenin, was unable to realize that the old order which all abhorred could be destroyed only by a class-conscious socialist proletariat. While recognizing the great debt of the revolution to Tolstoy's writings, Lenin flatly declared that "Tolstoyan nonresistance to evil [was] the most serious cause of the defeat of the first revolutionary campaign."

Lenin, however, did not give sufficient weight to the significant part played in Tolstoy's thinking by his utter repudiation of violence in any form. It was the keystone of his whole doctrine. Had he been inclined to compromise with it, he might have met the radicals halfway on certain levels of activity. Many of his friends among the Social Democrats also detested violence, but they were inclined to forgive it if the motive in their opinion was a good one, such as the killing of those in power who opposed the revolution. When this proposition was put up to Tolstoy by one of his socialist-minded friends who asked: "Is there not a difference between the killing that a revolutionist does and that which a policeman does?" Tolstoy answered:

"There is as much difference as between cat-shit and dog-shit. But I don't like the smell of either one or the other."

5

With the bloody events of 1904–1905, the power of Tolstoy's pen over the Russian people began to wane. Widespread violence seemed to break the magic spell of his doctrine of nonresistance, and thousands of the little people, whose hopes were lost in the ultimate failure of the rebellion, licked their wounds in no spirit of Tolstoyan Christian charity. They had learned from bitter experience the physical law that when two forces meet the greater will prevail. Next time the greater force would be on their side. Passive resistance in the face of bayonets or bullets took more moral courage than they possessed. As for peacefully waiting for change—well, time flies and death also waits. Tolstoyans quietly began to join the ranks of radical revolutionists. Even so fervent a disciple as Biryukov admitted to Tolstoy that his religious-philosophical works were being ignored by the people. Society will be attracted to such articles, he advised, only if you give it fresh artistic productions, and then the people will remember "that it is Tolstoy who speaks to them."

But Tolstoy was serving God, not the leaders of the revolution. He was passionately concerned with all the unfinished business of world thought—those insoluble questions about God, life, death, violence, and poverty which the leaders of mankind, like bored parliamentarians, always lay on the table for future consideration. He once related, by way of illustrating the fact that even geniuses err, a conversation he had had with the skeptical and pessimistic old butler of the Olsufyevs. It was in the country and he remarked to the servant, referring to the weather and the gathering of the harvest: "God knows what He does." To this the butler replied: "Yes, but He too makes mistakes!" Whatever God's failings, Tolstoy refused to admit any mistake in the doctrine he preached in His name. And in the midst of the turmoil of 1904–1905, he doggedly continued to belabor the public with his polemical articles, though they could reach the Russian people only in contraband copies.

Apart from the writings of this nature already mentioned, Tolstoy published two more lengthy pamphlets in 1905,

The One Thing Needed and *The End of an Age.*[3] The first was an arraignment of the whole institution of government, a kind of warning to both the constitutionalists and the socialists that any rule either might establish was doomed to end in the autocratic abuses they condemned. Apart from his argument from history, he had nothing new to offer in either the evils of government that he attacked or the remedy he offered. One detects a mounting critical asperity, however, and an impatience with those who will not see the light. Even Chertkov, when he first read the manuscript, expressed some dismay over the harsh epithets applied to Russian tsars, especially to the one still occupying the throne, and he persuaded Tolstoy to moderate his language a bit. Later Tolstoy regretfully remarked to a friend about this decision to soften various expressions in the work: "I only wish now that as many as possible had read them. One cannot write sharply enough about Nicholas and people like him. A saintly person, Nicholas! One would have to be a fool or a vile man or insane to do what he does."

In order to avoid quarrels with his wife, Tolstoy had decided not to publish any further purely artistic works,[4] but he continued to write them. Though seventy-seven, his head swarmed with literary designs, and at this chaotic time of war and revolution he actually revived his plan of some forty years ago—a huge novel on the Decembrist. "*Ars longa, vita brevis,*" he now mournfully jotted down in his diary. "Sometimes I am sorry. There is so much I wish to say." The design for a last great novel had to be dropped, this time forever. It gave way to a long short story, "The False Coupon," which he had planned in the late 1880's and now finished. It is a brilliantly constructed tale, told in his new simple and rapid narrative manner, and it concerns a succession of evil deeds that grow out of an initial evil act—the counterfeiting of a ruble note—which in turn are contrasted to a series of good actions that lead to the salvation of all concerned.

"Alyosha Gorshok," another short story, in this case less than five pages in length, was written in 1905. It is a little masterpiece, a rare and perfect sublimation in artistic form

[3] Both works were published by Chertkov in London in 1905 and appeared widely in translations shortly thereafter.

[4] Tolstoy published one other article during 1904, a foreword to an article of V. G. Chertkov, "On Revolution."

of one of Tolstoy's spiritual convictions. The peasant boy Alyosha, who is everyone's drudge, achieves through his simplicity of soul and unquestioning submissiveness to all that harsh fate throws his way the inner light and perfect peace that his creator strove for in vain.[5]

During 1904 and part of 1905 the literary work that Tolstoy labored on most, as did the whole household and any willing guests at Yasnaya Polyana, was the *Circle of Reading*. This production was an outgrowth of *Thoughts of Wise People for Every Day* (1903), and was continued in succeeding years in a modified form. Almost medieval in conception, the *Circle of Reading* was designed to reflect in a broad sense Tolstoy's religious philosophy through the medium of a great number of quotations drawn from numerous thinkers and partly from his own works. Thirty-one themes were decided upon, such as "Faith," "The Soul," "One Soul in All," "God," and "Love," one for each day of the month, and a series of quotations, bearing on each theme, was set down for each day throughout the whole twelve months. He made no pretense at faithfully translating the selections from the various foreign authors, for he often modified the sense to suit his own purpose.

Like an old man bored with his own wisdom, Tolstoy now sat among heaps of books, scanning their dusty pages for forgotten gems of thought. The work became a passion with him, and the more he dwelt with these famous authors of the past, the greater grew his disgust with those of the present and with people's ignorance of their heritage of wisdom. "During all this time," he wrote an admirer, "having read not only Marcus Aurelius, Epictetus, Xenophon, Socrates, and Brahmin, Chinese, and Buddhist wisdom, Seneca, Plutarch, Cicero, but also the later ones: Montaigne, Rousseau, Voltaire, Lessing, Kant, Lichtenberg, Schopenhauer, Emerson, Channing, Parker, Ruskin, Amiel, and others (for two months now I've stopped reading newspapers and magazines), I become more and more surprised and horrified at the ignorance, at the 'cultured' barbarism in which our society is steeped. In truth, enlightenment, education is the way we make use of and assimilate the cultural inheritance that our ancestors bequeathed to us, but we read the newspapers, Zola, Maeterlinck, Ibsen, Rozanov, etc."

[5] The only other artistic work finished in 1905 was "The Posthumous Notes of the Elder, Fyodor Kuzmich."

While the family and guests sat around the big table, copying his manuscript or translating and transcribing selected quotations, he would dash from his study to try out on them another "beautiful" thought he had just discovered in some ancient tome. The work enabled him to refresh his memory with many favorite authors, and of these, Dickens gave him the purest delight. Time and again he read passages to the family from Dickens or retold his stories. He recalled having heard him at a literary evening in London during his visit there. "He read excellently, and with his sere, powerful figure he produced a vital impression. But I had no contact with him. At that time I was interested in educational problems." One of the guests on this occasion asked him if Dickens had influenced his literary work. He replied affirmatively, but added, "Stendhal's influence on me, as I have already said, has been greater than all."

In the tremendous amount of reviewing of imaginative literature that he did for the *Circle of Reading*, the zest and joy of the explorer in great art never deserted him. And always his test was that which he applied to his own writing, that the highest art should be clear, simple, and accessible to all. Despite his own enormous production, he could never regard writing as a profession. "One ought only to write," he told Goldenweizer at this time, "when one leaves a piece of one's flesh in the inkpot each time one dips one's pen in."

6

Almost the only widely applauded act of Nicholas II during these two years of strife was the amnesty he granted to many political prisoners and exiles in August 1904, on the occasion of his becoming father of an heir to the throne. The action gave Tolstoy special cause for rejoicing, for it permitted the return to Russia of one of the most faithful of exiled disciples—Biryukov. After eight years of separation the reunion was a happy event. Biryukov had hurried to Yasnaya Polyana at the end of 1904, and much to his surprise he found that Tolstoy was not the feeble old man he had expected to see after his long illness, but still the same cheerful, indefatigable worker.

Chertkov's release came later, and he did not arrive at Yasnaya Polyana until May of the next year. Tolstoy mentioned in his diary that the visit had been "very fine, even beyond expectation." For some time now Chertkov had assumed a proprietary interest in Tolstoy's writings. While in England he had been playing the part of critic-editor of the numerous articles Tolstoy sent him, and he had set up the Free Age Press to publish these. Besides, he arranged for various translations and was engaged in getting out an edition of all of Tolstoy's works forbidden in Russia. In fact, he had apparently already begun to think of himself as future literary executor, for the year previous, while still in England, he had sent an emissary to Yasnaya Polyana to learn of Tolstoy's intentions concerning the rights to his productions after his death.

Sonya resented more and more Chertkov's privileged position, for she fully understood the tremendous financial possibilities of her husband's works after his death, and she naturally wished to protect them in the interests of herself and her family. She had long formed the practice of sending his manuscripts for safekeeping to the Moscow Rumyantsev Museum. In January 1904, she had all these manuscripts moved to the Historical Museum in Moscow. "It is necessary," she wrote in her diary at this time, "to save everything possible from senseless plundering by the children and grandchildren." She had in mind here principally her daughters, who worked closely with Chertkov on matters relating to their father's manuscripts.

A new force for peace and order in the family was the Slovak, Dr. Dushan Makovitski. After Tolstoy's illness in the Crimea, it was thought essential to have a physician attached permanently to the household. Several had already filled this position and left, but at the end of 1904 Makovitski was employed and remained until Tolstoy's death. One of the conditions was that he should also run a dispensary to take care of the village sick.

Though Makovitski left much to be desired as a physician, from nearly every other point of view his selection for this position was ideal. For some years now a devoted follower of Tolstoy, this pale, mousy, anemic-looking, little bald-headed man had a profound reverence for him and a keen sense of his historical position among the world's great artists and moral thinkers. Meek, humble, and self-effacing, he unobtrusively went about his various duties like one consecrated. So gentle was his nature that he could not bear to hear people quarreling. His medical care of Tolstoy was almost his least important service, but he became invaluable as a kind of secretary and literary assistant and won his master's complete devotion. When he took a month's vacation to visit his native land, Tolstoy complained to a friend: "But how am I to live without Dushan? . . . I'll tell you frankly, I don't need his medicine, but when I do not see his hat there for a day or two, I somehow or other feel lost. Holy Dushan!"

For Makovitski, as for many of Tolstoy's disciples, everything the master said seemed worth preserving. He constantly carried in his coat pocket a tiny block of paper and short stubs of pencils, and daily copied Tolstoy's conversation in a shorthand system of his own and without taking his hand out of his pocket so that his activity remained unnoticed. Every night, when all had gone to bed, he would sit up to the small hours of the morning transcribing these notes and adding accounts of the various happenings of the day. The result was a journal, with few interruptions, of daily life at Yasnaya Polyana from the end of 1904 to Tolstoy's death. Intimate friends of Tolstoy and members of the family agreed on the remarkable accuracy with which Makovitski reported Tolstoy's talk.[6]

Makovitski in his notes makes the interesting point that there were no secrets in the household. What Tolstoy could not say to all, he did not tell even to those most intimate with him. Sonya, he added, "told to everyone—servants, guests, and chance visitors—what she confided to her intimates." Obviously Makovitski sided with Tolstoy in the quarrels that still fitfully broke out between husband and wife. As a doctor, he often grew annoyed with Sonya's attempts to heal her husband when he was ill. She continually fussed over him, denying him the rest and quiet he needed. When it was better for him not to eat, she insisted on his partaking of dishes that she had specially prepared, and she often applied homemade nostrums that had no curative effect. Wearied with protesting against her ministrations, he would finally submit if for no reason other than to calm her agitation. Sonya said to her husband once that he did not know how to take care of himself. He replied "that if he followed her advice, he would have been dead long ago." Rather harshly Makovitski summed up his judgment on Sonya as follows: "[She] did not

[6] Up to the present, only a very small part of this material has been published.

esteem Leo Nikolayevich, did not desire his advice and friendship, and only valued his life as a source of income (the editions of his works). She was entirely alien to his thoughts though she boasted of her husband's fame. On the whole, she loved him as she would have loved any husband and the father of her children."

Tolstoy once said that marriage was either paradise or hell, that there was no purgatory. However, his marriage, which had long ceased to be a paradise, now teetered on the edge of purgatory and would occasionally slip over into it when a quarrel flared up about money matters, the children, or the wasteful life at Yasnaya Polyana. And always there was present the latent danger that his marriage would plunge down to the lowermost circle of hell. But he was an old, old man for whom marriage had long since become a way of life that he was trying to slough off as an encumbrance in his search for God. "We sit outdoors and eat 10 dishes," he disgustedly entered in his diary in July 1905. "Ice cream, lackeys, silver service, and beggars pass, yet kind people continue quietly to eat ice cream. Amazing!!!!" Still he had lived this life for almost half a century. Could he turn his back on it now? Did he have a right to? "The struggle of light and darkness, of good and evil takes place in me, but I think, so it seems, that I am wrestling with it," he wrote in his diary. It was a struggle that had begun in his youth. When darkness and evil threatened to prevail, he often visited Marya Schmidt, the former schoolteacher, grown old and worn in devotion to his ideals, tending her cow, tilling the little plot of ground allotted to her at near-by Ovsyannikovo, and selflessly serving all who asked her aid. As he drew strength from the saintly Marya's example, he ruminated: "How easy it would be for all to live like this. Oh, if only to participate in it just a little!"

XXXVII

Life Is Beyond Space and Time

SONYA BEGAN 1906 by inviting Taneyev to Yasnaya Polyana, where he had not been for nine years. She had been contenting herself with meeting this musician during her trips to Moscow or, in summer, at the estate of their mutual friends, the Maslovs. Though for some time Taneyev's complete indifference had chilled her passion considerably, she had sublimated it in an irresistible desire to hear him play. So music was the professed reason for the invitation now, and as though to indicate her impartiality, she also invited Goldenweizer to lend his talents for the occasion. And much delightful music was played by these masters of the piano. As always, when Taneyev was a guest, Tolstoy conducted himself with precise hospitality. He entered into the spirit of the affair and even played a waltz he had composed in his youth. In his diary that day, however, he mysteriously jotted down: "There were several examinations." An "examination" was his word for a difficult situation in his personal life that called for careful scrutiny of his moral behavior. Two weeks later Sonya was in Moscow, and she entered in her daily diary: "This morning I was at Sergei Ivanovich's [Taneyev's]; I gave him the album of photographs. We were both restrained and unnatural."

Actually, the lone position Tolstoy had taken in the bitter social and political struggle served to increase his loneliness in the family circle. The spirit of revolt against authority in the country in general seemed to have invaded the household. During the summer of 1906, for example, the wrangling became almost unbearable for him. Leo and Andrei gave their allegiance to the most reactionary political thought and treated their father's sincerest beliefs with scant respect; and Sonya insisted upon her property rights in utter disregard of her husband's feelings.

No doubt Tolstoy's agitation over the misery, assassinations, and executions throughout the country had increased his sensitivity to the comfortable life at Yasnaya Polyana. One day that summer his secretary was walking with old Marya Schmidt near the tennis court where members of the family were playing and others watching. Suddenly Tolstoy appeared in the path, an expression of suffering on his face. "It's terrible, unbearable!" he said in a quiet but trembling voice. "Formerly, when people did not notice this, it may have been more endurable. But now, when this is plain to all of us, such an existence is unendurable! I must get out! it's beyond my strength." That evening the secretary entered Tolstoy's study and found him deep in thought. He abruptly declared, referring to his statement earlier in the day: "It's so patent to me that wherever I might go, within a couple of days Sofya Andreyevna would appear by my side again with servants and doctors, and everything would go on as before!"

Overt acts on the part of members of the family threw Tolstoy into deeper despair and drew from him tortured entries in his diary. "Today all my sons, and it is especially painful. There is a distressing unnaturalness in this conventional closeness to me and the greatest spiritual separation. At times, as today, I want to run away, to disappear." A letter arrived from a peasant youth, expressing Christian views close to his own. After tea, he began to read it to the family. Andrei noisily jumped up from the table and brusquely announced that he was not interested in the letter. And his brother Leo demonstratively arose and followed him out of the room.

While members of the family were sitting on the veranda, two of the younger sons complained about the laxity of the courts, that the masses had got entirely out of hand, and that the old traditions were being trampled upon.

"All these misfortunes are not so great that it is impossible to endure them," their father quietly observed. "Every generation has its terrible calamities. Our grandfathers had Napoleon, before that Pugachyov, or cholera, floods, earthquakes. Each generation has its own experiences which it must bear."

"Yes, it's fine for you to talk in this way," interrupted one of the sons. "You go off, shut yourself up in your study, and you know nothing."

"It's so fine for me," his father retorted with sudden agitation, "that I pack my suitcase every week! That is what I've borne up till now!" And he left the company.

These incidents were not casual quarrels. They mark an intensification in the development of the family tragedy, in which certain of the sons openly identified themselves with their mother's cause in the struggle with her husband. They were on the side of property; they aimed to protect their interests in the estate and to defend established law and order against their father's "anarchism." When he expressed his horror over the news that the Slavophiles in the Duma had advocated the death penalty, Andrei and Leo literally drove him to tears with their loud denunciations of his most hallowed doctrine of nonviolence. And that summer these two sons sympathized with their mother's intention of having several peasants arrested for cutting oak trees in the forest of the estate. Stubbornly she refused to listen to the pleas of all to pardon the peasants as they stood guiltily before her, caps in hand, bowing and begging forgiveness for stealing trees which Tolstoy felt they had a perfect right to if they needed them.

Relations in the household were taxing the furthest limits of his spiritual resources. Gloomily he wrote to the one person in the family, his daughter Masha, who would be certain to understand and sympathize with his trials: "It has been very distressing. Now it has become better. It even went so far that two days ago I lost my temper because of a conversation with Andryusha and Lyova,[1] who argued with me that the death penalty is good. . . . I told them that they do not esteem me, that they hate me, and I left the room, slamming the door, and for two days I could not recover. Today, thanks to the prayer of Francis of Assisi and John: 'one not loving his brother does not know God,' I regained control of myself and resolved to tell them that I regard myself very much at fault . . . and ask their pardon. Andrei left for somewhere that night, so I could not tell him, but, meeting Leo, I told him that I had been

[1] His sons Andrei and Leo.

to blame and asked his forgiveness. He did not answer an went off to read a newspaper and to argue gaily, acceptin my words as a duty on my part. It is difficult. But the mor difficult it is, the better for me."

2

A danger affecting the existence of all members of th household suddenly cleared the atmosphere of strife. A the beginning of September, an illness that Sonya had bee complaining of for some time took a critical turn. A phy sician from Tula and Dr. Makovitski diagnosed a tumo of the womb. An operation was essential. The distinguishe surgeon V. F. Snegiryov was hurriedly summoned and soon arrived with assistants, a nurse, and even an operating table.

Telegrams brought absent members of the family to Yasnaya Polyana. The house filled up and took on the aspect of a medical clinic. Tenseness gripped everyone. Father, sons, and daughters forgot their differences in the presence of imminent danger to a beloved wife and mother. Sonya's behavior acted like an alembic, refining the feelings of all. She bore her agony uncomplainingly. In the face of death she seemed transformed, sloughing off all earthly dross, and humbly composing herself to meet the end. Believing that she would die, she said farewell to each member of the household, offering them the affection and spiritual comfort that they had intended to bring to her.

Tolstoy rejoiced over this sudden change in his wife, and there arose in him once again, as at the time of Vanichka's death, the hope that she was undergoing a spiritual rebirth. The fussing of the doctors, the thoughts of the operation, all these efforts to frustrate one of life's greatest experiences disgusted him. He entered in his diary on September 1: "I have not written for 6 days. Sonya's illness is still worse. Today I felt especially sorry. But she is touchingly sensible, truthful, and kind. I do not want to write of anything else. Three sons, Seryozha, Andryusha, and Misha, and two daughters, Masha and Sasha, are here. The house is full of doctors. This is distressing. Instead of devotion to the will of God and a solemn religious atmosphere, it is petty, unruly, and egotistical. My thoughts and feelings were good. I thank God. I am not living nor does the whole world live in time: an immutable universe in time, formerly unattainable to me, now unfolds itself. How much easier and more understandable this way! And from such a point of view how clearly is death not an end of something but its full unfolding."

"While dying," he noted in another entry, "Sonya unfolds herself to us," and he instinctively rebelled against any mundane interference with this spiritual process. Death was the great conciliator, he told himself, invoking love in all, and was not the evil that people believed. He did, however, consent to a priest's coming to confess Sonya. "There are people," he wrote, apropos of her request, "to whom a pure, abstract, spiritual relation to the principle of life is inaccessible. For them a crude form is necessary. But this form is also spiritual. And it is fine that it is so, even though in a crude form."

Although still another well-known physician had been summoned from Petersburg for the operation, Dr. Snegiryov decided not to wait any longer, for he feared that peritonitis might set in. He asked Tolstoy's permission, saying that it was a matter of life or death. Tolstoy was reluctant to give his consent. If her time had come, then an operation seemed to him like an unholy interference with the will of God. In the end, he evaded the issue, declaring that the decision must rest with his wife and children. Preparations were made. Tolstoy went to Chepyzh, a forest adjoining the estate, to be alone and pray. He left directions to ring the big bell outside the house twice if the operation were successful, if not . . . well, he would come anyway.

The operating table was set up in the middle of the room; physicians in white coats talked in whispers and moved about softly; then Sonya, moaning in pain, was carried in and the door was shut. Soon all was silent. Only Dr. Snegiryov's loud voice could be heard, at first severe, then nervous and irritated. Suddenly Alexandra heard him burst into vile and indecent swearing. ". . . you German mug . . . son of a ——, accursed German! . . ." The catgut which a German dealer had supplied for stitching the wound turned out to be poor in quality and tore in Snegiryov's hands. Finally, the door flew open and the doctor, hot and purple in the face, dashed out. Someone threw a wrap over him and led him downstairs, and someone else followed with a bottle of champagne for the exhausted physician. The operation was pronounced a success.

Alexandra ran off to Chepyzh to tell the glad news to

her father. So did Ilya and Masha. They saw him at the edge of the woods.

"Successful! Successful!" they shouted.

"Good, go back, I'll come in a minute," he replied with suppressed emotion, and turned back into the woods again to pray.

Later, when he emerged from his wife's room, after she had recovered from the anesthetic, Ilya recalled that he was choking with indignation and declared: "My God, what a horrible thing! A human being cannot even be left to die in peace! A woman lies with a slit stomach, tied to a bed, without pillows, and she groans more than before the operation. There's torture for you!"

When the shroud is entirely removed, then life ends, Tolstoy had thought as he watched over the agony of his wife. But Sonya's "unfolding" had ceased. She now lay convalescent, securely wrapped again in the shroud of life. Her recovery was rapid. She wrote her sister of her feelings in the presence of death. All the vanity of people seemed so strange and insignificant to her then, and she wanted to advise everyone to abandon it. Even the children and all that she loved she was prepared to leave without any deep regret. "I felt sorry only when I said farewell to Lyovochka for the last time, as he began weeping and went to the door, his thin shoulders hunched with sobbing, crying and blowing his nose. But even then I only made the sign of the cross and did not weep."

These feelings and memories quickly vanished with the return of health. A little more than a month after the operation, Masha wrote of her mother's condition to a friend of the family: "Now her health is so good that she has begun to go about with a brisk step, talks in a loud voice, and again enters into things, and though one rejoices over this return to life, yet along with it goes a withdrawal from that serious, touching frame of mind, which exists at the moment of greatest physical weakness, and which appeared in mother when she was dying. I am sorry to part with this and to lose it."

Perhaps because he was expecting it, Tolstoy detected Sonya's reversion to type sooner than his daughter. Only two days after the operation he entered in his diary: "It's terribly sad. I'm sorry for her. Great sufferings and virtually in vain. I don't know. It's sad, sad, but very good." For him spiritual harmony had become more desirable than life itself. Perhaps his deepest yearning had been to find in this woman whom he had once so passionately loved the perfect spiritual mate of his old age. That hope now seemed lost forever.

And now, after Sonya's peculiarly delicate operation, her seventy-eight-year-old husband at last repudiated that sensual intimacy with her that had meant so much to him in the past. He told Makovitski: "I've been in love many times, but I can say that I never remember about love. . . . Perhaps this is not an important matter." And in his diary, before Sonya had fully recovered, he wrote the following passage which may well have come under her own eye: "What can be more vile than sexual intercourse. One need only describe this act with preciseness in order to invoke the most terrible repulsion. Therefore, among all people who have emerged from an animal condition and entered a spiritual life, shame has always manifested itself among its members in connection with the sexual act."

Meanwhile, with Sonya's return to health and retreat from spiritual grace, the war on Tolstoy's beliefs was renewed, and existence in the household seemed more irreconcilable than ever with his dreams of spiritual peace. Angrily he wrote in his diary several weeks after the operation: "Our life is again very disgusting. They sport, doctor themselves, go hither and yon, take part in this or that, dispute, concern themselves with what is not their business, but they have no life because they have no obligations. It is frightful!!! I feel this more and more often."

3

"Masha greatly alarms me. I love her very, very much." Tolstoy wrote in his diary on November 23, 1906. His favorite daughter had fallen ill with pneumonia. Confronted with this new danger, once again the family ranks closed.

Masha had achieved a singular position in the household. A "Tolstoyan" in the best sense of the word, she exerted a constructive influence on members of the family by her practical kind deeds and quiet, self-effacing efforts to live her beliefs, an influence denied her father with his dogmatic theorizing and spiritual self-concentration. Masha "served" in a practical sense. She soothed away family misunderstandings, tended the sick, defended those at fault, and won the affection and confidence of all, though her mother could never in her heart forgive her for espousing her father's beliefs. Not only the family, but most of the villagers, who were indebted to her for numerous kindnesses, loved Masha. Tolstoy early found in her a spiritual child, searching with him for the unattainable. Though their intimate communion had suffered because of her marriage, she had never lost her place as his chief confidante and comforter in the family. Awe before his genius had no place in her reverence for him. Her simple, sincere nature enveloped him in its affection and warmth as naturally as it did everyone. When he was troubled in mind and spirit, she would stroke his hand, caress him, say something endearing, and a happy smile would quickly brighten his face.

Now he sat in the sickroom, holding Masha's clammy hand as the dread disease took its course. He wept and kept murmuring to her: "Be patient." He kissed her hand and she drew it weakly to her breast and whispered, "I'm dying." Shortly after, she passed away (November 27, 1906).

Though the passing of no one in the family could have left Tolstoy with a greater sense of personal loss, Masha's going did not shake his conviction that death was an unfolding, the beginning of life. His attitude and comments about the event differ little from those at the time when he thought his wife was dying. "I did not experience either terror, or fear, or the consciousness that anything exceptional had taken place—not even pity or sorrow," he wrote in his diary the night that Masha died. "It seems that I rather felt it necessary to invoke in myself a particular feeling of tenderness and grief, and I did so; but in the depths of my heart, I was more serene than I would be if I were confronted by a bad or improper act of someone alien to me, not to speak of such an act of my own. Yes, this is an event in the bodily domain and therefore indifferent. I looked at her all the time that she was dying—surprisingly quietly. For me she was a being who had unfolded before my own unfolding. I watched this unfolding, and I rejoiced."

Obviously, Tolstoy's prolonged concentration on things of the spirit was making it difficult for him to contemplate life's deepest personal joys and sorrows in the ordinary terms of human experience. Nothing could provide a more striking contrast to his spiritualized reactions to Masha's death than those of Sonya in a letter to her sister about the event. After telling of the "polite notes of thanks" she had sent to friends who had aided, she launched forth on a long detailed description of her daughter's illness, death, and burial. There was no suggestion of the hysterical grief she had suffered at the time of Vanichka's death. She concluded prosaically: "Of all the children, Masha loved *him* [Tolstoy] more than all, and in her we lose that zealous supporter, who was always ready to help and to sympathize with everyone, and more so with that which concerned her father."

Death had lost all its terror for Tolstoy. It was natural and necessary, not an antithesis of life, but rather a continuation of it. What distressed him most was the transiency of people's feelings and their trivial, unthinking attitude before life's greatest mystery. He had continued the diary passage quoted above on Masha's death with much philosophizing on life and spiritual love, and then he ended: "In serious moments, as now, when there lies the still unburied body of a beloved person, how clearly apparent is the immorality, the fallibility, and burden of the life of the rich. The best remedy for grief is work. But they have no need to work; there is only gaiety. Yet gaiety is out of place and involuntarily takes on the aspect of false, sentimental twaddle. Just as I received some hypocritically sympathetic letters and telegrams, I met the idiot Kynya.[2] She knew Masha. I said:—

" 'Have you heard of our affliction?'

" 'I've heard.' And she immediately followed up with: 'Give me a kopek.' How much better and easier this is."

4

The family griefs and quarrels of 1906 and also of 1907 must be viewed against the thunder-and-lightning background of national strife, for, as in the preceding two years, the tension that continued to exist everywhere was still reflected in the Tolstoy household. Though the revolution had been crushed, the government's bungling attempts to introduce reforms merely succeeded in stirring up further social opposition without being able either to control or to satisfy it. The first Duma, elected in March 1906, was dissolved by the Tsar four months later, largely because he did not like its proposed solution of the agrarian problem.

[2] A half-demented Yasnaya Polyana peasant.

Disgruntled members of the defunct Duma showed their teeth to the government at this point by adopting a Tolstoyan policy, though from different motives: they issued an appeal to the people to resist the government by refusing to pay taxes or to submit to military conscription. Tolstoy would have predicted the utter failure that actually overtook this move, for the appeal was made on political, not on moral and religious grounds.

The life of the second Duma, which gathered in March 1907, was even shorter than that of the first. But now the new Prime Minister, P. A. Stolypin, had his own program of agrarian reforms. It amounted to abolishing the age-old communal ownership of land and encouraging the peasants, with the aid of loans, to purchase individual farms. Stolypin's hope was to set up a new class of small landowners to form the basis for a new state economy. The second Duma, with a larger left-wing element than the first, and one that was strongly influenced by Lenin's political strategy, supported the agrarian bill introduced in the first Duma—the expropriation of nearly all the land in the interests of the peasants. The conflict between government and Duma became acute. Finally, on a trumped-up charge that a group of socialist deputies had organized a plot against the Tsar, the Duma was dissolved. The third Duma, elected in November 1907, on a modified electoral law that enabled the right wing to obtain a majority, gave Stolypin and the moderate parties complete control.

This struggle in high places had its counterpart in continued disturbances throughout the country, though there was little of the large-scale violence of the revolutionary years 1905–1906. The peasants, who had been hard hit by the recently concluded Russo-Japanese War, were further impoverished by a severe drought in many regions. A famine condition existed in the Samara district. As in former years Tolstoy once again aided, this time by expending, through an agent, five thousand dollars placed at his disposal by the now thriving Dukhobors of Canada, who had not forgotten his help during their own sufferings. A widespread epidemic of thievery and thuggery broke out, and the revolutionists still kept up their activities with strikes and political assassinations. Stolypin's countermeasures were ruthless, and with a sinking heart Tolstoy daily read in the newspapers the mounting list of executions.

In various ways this misery and galloping unrest were

brought home to him personally. Suspicious characters roamed about the neighborhood of Yasnaya Polyana and robbery and several murders were committed. During his customary walks on the highroad, he talked with burning revolutionary zealots. One asked him for money to buy a revolver. Strange young men in workers' clothes sought him out and freely argued with him, using in hit-and-miss fashion such words as "proletariat," "exploitation of the masses," and "Social Democrat." To his earnest arguments one worker fearlessly replied: "Does the law of God say the proletariat is to be exploited? People used to think so, but now they know better, and it can't go on. . . ." In May 1907, he was shocked to learn that his engineer brother-in-law, V. A. Bers, had been murdered by terrorists in the course of a strike.

Each new levy of recruits for the army brought to Tolstoy reports of increasing numbers of conscientious objectors and sometimes personal pleas for aid in the often severe punishment meted out to these unfortunates. And he never failed them. In 1906 he wrote a supporting note, which was published, to a plea of his disciple, I. M. Tregubov, on behalf of those Christians who were persecuted by the government for refusing to serve in the army.[3] For a mere unknown youth, who had been denounced to the authorities for calling the Tsar "a drunken fool," he drafted a petition requesting the monarch's pardon for the boy.

Such personal experiences and his observation of the state of affairs in the nation distressed Tolstoy more than the severer disturbances of the previous two years. He had hoped then that the flame of the revolution would consume all impurities in the Russian people and would light the way for a moral and spiritual rebirth. He recognized that there could be no life without sin, but he saw no logical reason why mankind should persist in sin. Even now the hope still persisted, for he wrote in English to his American disciple Crosby in April 1906:[4] "As to the disturbances that are going on now, they are only precursors of the great revolution which I hope will begin at once everywhere and will consist in the annihilation of state powers." In this spirit he had written a stirring article during the tortured

[3] This piece, entitled "A Note to the Manifesto of I. M. Tregubov," was published in a Russian newspaper, 1906.

[4] Ernest Crosby died at the end of this year and Tolstoy paid him a glowing tribute.

years 1904–1905, with the added intention of directing the revolutionary forces toward the great good he championed.

Now, in retrospect, Tolstoy had begun to wonder whether he had not been wasting his time. The revolutionary flame was burning out and only the dross remained. He had no illusions about the power of his influence, for he was fully aware that many people regarded him as queer, as a strange kind of anarchist, and that it did little good to tell them that his anarchy consisted only in the application of true Christianity to the relations of people. And he was even less sanguine about how the future would regard him, for he prophetically wrote in his diary: "I know that these simple and clear truths about life which I now write will undoubtedly be defined by learned readers of the future as mysticism or even by some other title, thus enabling them, while not understanding these truths, to remain in their calm self-satisfied ignorance." In fact, he had once said in *War and Peace,* partly in jest, that the dissemination of books was the most powerful means of spreading ignorance, but now, on the basis of more extensive experience, he was coming to believe that it was a sad and terrible truth.

Radical intellectuals condemned Tolstoy's egoism in his recent writings. But he cared little for intellectuals and was ashamed to think that he was one of them. Tolstoy had faith in the common people of Russia, and it discouraged him to see how easily they succumbed to the blandishments of so-called reforms. Nearly everybody was talking about the Duma, and great things were expected from it. Tolstoy heard much about its activities from his son-in-law, M. S. Sukhotin, who was a delegate to the first Duma. Tolstoy's only regret was that the members were intelligent and educated. "It would be infinitely less of a sin if they had been stupid and illiterate." After all, the Duma was merely an imitation of Western European democratic institutions, and that would have been enough to damn it in his eyes. He was pleased to find this opinion shared by Morrison Davidson, an English social thinker with anarchist leanings whose books he had long admired. Davidson now wrote him of the faults of British and American parliamentary systems and added: "We, the people of Europe, expect from Russia at the present time not imitation, but guidance." Gratefully Tolstoy replied in English: "Your opinion of our Duma, is, I regret to say, quite true. I hope that the fallacy of all this will soon be clear to everybody, and that we Russians will travel another road." If the Russians were barbarians, as many in the West imagined, then they still had a future. But the people of the West, Tolstoy observed, were civilized barbarians and hence could expect no future.

Tolstoy told a correspondent that he found something comical about the Duma, as though the deputies were children playing at being grown-up. In their eagerness to copy European parliamentary practices, they took a naïve delight in speaking about their "lobbies" and "blocs." It all reminded him of provincial fashions in Russia. For when gowns and hats ceased to be worn in the capital, they were taken up by the provincial dames who imagined they were in the height of fashion. So the Duma, he said, was our provincial hat. The words of Herbert Spencer, he told the correspondent, applied precisely to the Russian deputies—all members of parliament stand lower than the average level of their own society; and yet they take upon themselves the problem of resolving the fate of a hundred million people. And in conclusion, he rapped out, the Duma was "abominable because of its coarseness, of the incorrectness of the motives it exhibited, because of its frightful bumptiousness, but chiefly because of its wrathfulness."

He realized that one of the most difficult things for man to do is to change his pattern of thought, especially when it has been sanctioned by time and experience. "It is a shame not to change it, because the very sense of life consists of a greater and greater understanding of oneself in the world." To this fact he attributed the unwillingness of people to contemplate the new idea that they could live without government, just as at one time people thought that they could not live without slaves. People in the government were always telling him how necessary and useful government was, just as the owners of pubs and keepers of brothels consider their establishments necessary.

In dismay Tolstoy watched while the revolution, instead of replacing a bad old idea with a good new one, strove merely to sugar-coat the old conception of governmental power with glittering promises. The reformers were beginning to loom in his eyes as a graver danger than the defenders of tsarist bureaucracy. Both sides justified the killing of each other in the struggle for power by the same argument—they killed for the common good. The fine-sounding words used by all the parties in opposition to the

Tsar's rule—"freedom of the people," "democracy," and "constitution"—he set down as mere masks to conceal their own desire for power, and the consequence of such false intentions would be the struggle of all against all, the substitution of hatred for love, and the destruction of national morality.

5

In the present struggle Tolstoy saw the dilemma of his country as an obligation to select one of two paths of social existence: either to limit the power of government by transferring more of it into the hands of the people, or to eliminate all power on the basis of the dominance of one religious-moral law in the hearts of people. His own choice was clear; it involved one of those new ideas which mankind found so difficult to accept in place of the old idea of rule that for centuries had dominated the mind. Though he was discouraged with his previous efforts, and somewhat skeptical of the value of the printed word, his conscience obliged him to continue to appeal to the people in another series of articles and pamphlets during 1906–1907. Perhaps he did this with greater hope now because of the partial relaxation of the censorship, a reform of the new government which was already making possible the printing of a number of his works hitherto banned in Russia. To be sure, one could never be certain to what extent these murderers of words would tolerate free expression, even under the new dispensation. In 1907 a publisher, N. E. Felten, was promptly jailed for printing Tolstoy's article "Do Not Kill," written in 1900. Indignant, Tolstoy retaliated by writing another article, "Do Not Kill Anyone," an elaboration of the same theme, but he managed to get it published only after the censors had considerably lacerated it.

During this period the three principal articles that deal in one form or another with Tolstoy's solution of the country's political dilemma are "A Letter to a Chinese"; "An Address to the Russian People: to the Government, to the Revolutionists, and to the Masses"; and "The Significance of the Russian Revolution."[5] The inspiration for the first article was two books sent to him by the Chinese writer Ku-Hung Ming.[6] Tolstoy's letter of acknowledg-

[5] All three were written and published in Russia in 1906.

[6] The books were *The Moral Causes of the Russo-Japanese War* and *Papers from a Viceroy's Yamen.*

ment turned into an epistolary article. He began by prophesying a great future for the peoples of the Eastern world, except the Japanese, whose imitation of Western civilization, he said, would bring about their undoing. "I think," he wrote, "that in our time a great revolution in the life of humanity will be accomplished, and in this revolution China ought to play a tremendous role at the head of the Eastern peoples." But he sternly warned them, in their reform movement, to avoid the present mistakes of Russia in trafficking with Western ideas of democracy as substitutes for despotic power. "Everything that the Western peoples do," he wrote, "can and ought to be an example for the peoples of the East, not as an example of what should be done, but of what ought not to be done in any circumstances. To pursue the path of the Western nations means to pursue a direct path of destruction." And he concluded by suggesting to the Chinese his own panacea of civil disobedience and nonviolence in the spirit of their revered religious teachers, Confucius, Buddha, and Lao-tse.

Tolstoy's "Address to the Russian People" contains nothing new, as he himself admitted. He had written it because he had felt "an obligation before God" to do so. It amounts again to calling down a plague on both the houses—the radical reformers and the constituted government—and to appealing to the masses to heed his own nostrums. The real interest of the article lies in the passages that he finally deleted. When he sent the first draft to Chertkov in England, this spiritual twin felt moved to reply with a sharp criticism, particularly of his handling of the revolutionary element. For some years Tolstoy had valued and often followed Chertkov's advice on his writings and frequently accepted his suggestions for changes. Now he stubbornly refused to delete offending passages, for his feeling about the violence of the revolutionists had reached a high pitch of indignation. He could not accept even the possibility that the motives of these men and women might be entirely selfless, and that they reluctantly engaged in violence in the sincere belief that it was the only means of achieving what they considered to be a lofty human goal.

It was not until Chertkov returned to Russia and talked the matter over with Tolstoy that he was able to persuade him to make the suggested changes, and in this revised form the article was finally published. But from all the variants which have recently appeared in print,[7] one can gather how severe had been the criticism of the revolutionists in the original article. He addressed the revolutionists in one of the variants as follows: "If you will only look within yourselves seriously and ask yourselves about the sincere inner motives that arouse you to this activity, you can hardly fail to see that these motives are either the most insignificant, trifling, vain, almost physiological—an idle life demands some display of activity—or they are the most low, disgusting motives: vanity, self-love, envy, even cupidity." And in another passage, questioning again the motives of the revolutionists, he wrote: "You say that you do all this for the sake of the masses. But truly you yourselves know that this is a lie, that your business is no concern of the masses. You do not know and do not love them." There is much more of this sort of harsh treatment in the variants, and enough of it was left in the printed version to arouse the revolutionists to furious anger against him.

"The Significance of the Russian Revolution," the most extensive of the three articles, is Tolstoy's last formal treatment of this theme, a final effort to point out clearly to mankind the two roads to the future from which it must choose—one leading to the destruction of civilization, the other to salvation on earth. Fully aware that despotism, like Russian autocracy, was bound sooner or later to give way before the progressive forces of the world, he now recognized as the principal danger to the world the democratic conception of government of Western Europe and America. Accordingly, much of the article is devoted to a destructive criticism of this form of government, in which he tried to prove that democracy would turn out to be more ruinous than Russian autocracy. Part of his argument was based on what he considered the fallacy of a concentration on industry and trade in the democracies at the expense of agriculture, which made these nations more and more dependent on outside sources for their chief means of subsistence. He next turned to his own people, whom he now, curiously enough, designated as "Eastern," and warned them of the pitfalls of Western democracy and of any form of governmental power. Stick to the land and avoid the industrial civilization of the West, he advised.

All this was to be accomplished by nonresistance to evil

[7] See the Jubilee Edition, Vol. XXXVI.

by force. In this article, however, Tolstoy attempted to meet the obvious practical objections to his doctrines. Will not the armed forces of the government kill people who passively resist it? Yes, some will suffer and die, he answered, but only a fraction compared to the millions killed in revolutions and wars. But if the protection of the government is removed, will there not be unbridled robbing and slaying? The government, with its courts, police, jails, and executions, does not restrain people from crime, he answered; rather, it increases crime by degrading the moral level of society. People by nature are good and law-abiding, and the moral consciousness of the majority expressed through social opinion will eventually prevent crime. Will all the advantages of civilization, industry, and science have to be abandoned if the nation becomes one primarily of agriculturalists? No, he answered, for all these advantages that are really essential and good for the people will be retained, but those that are harmful or superfluous will be abandoned. But if government is done away with, will there be no organization to take care of the common needs of any community? Nothing more, he replied, than would be necessary in taking care of the communal needs of a Russian village.

In conclusion, he pleaded with his readers not to imagine that he was offering them a utopia if they would only free themselves from the law of man. In life under the law of God, he wrote, people will not be "some new sort of beings—virtuous angels. People will remain exactly as they are now, with all their attributes, weaknesses, and passions; they will even sin, perhaps quarrel, commit adultery, walk off with property, and even murder, but all these things will be exceptions and not the rule as now. Their life will be entirely different by virtue of the one fact that they will not accept organized violence as a good and necessary condition of life; they will not be brought up on the evil deeds of governments that are represented as good deeds."

6

The importance Tolstoy attached to agriculture as man's chief occupation and sacred duty is emphasized in "The Significance of the Russian Revolution." Now, when the Duma made the nation's agrarian problem its principal concern, he hastened to renew his appeal of previous years that Henry George's single-tax solution to the land question be seriously considered. At a newspaper interview in the summer of 1906, he gave the correspondent a brief prepared statement on the agrarian problem. This was subsequently published in the interview under the title, "The Only Possible Solution of the Land Question." And that year he wrote an introduction on the same theme for a Russian translation of Henry George's *Social Problems.*

Tolstoy, however, had little hope that the deputies of the Duma, these "children playing at being grown-up," would be influenced in any way by what he had printed on this vital problem. He boldly decided to appeal directly to the Prime Minister, whose father had been his comrade-in-arms at the siege of Sevastopol. On July 26, 1907, he wrote Stolypin a long letter, "not as the son of my friend, but as a brother, a human being. . . ." The direction of his appeal is interesting: he seemed to take the position of a person in the government confronted with the problem of how best to put an end to the violence of the revolution. "The reasons for these revolutionary horrors that are now taking place in Russia have very deep foundations, but one, the most pertinent of them, is the people's dissatisfaction with the unjust distribution of the land." He then went on to outline his proposal, suggesting that the Prime Minister acquaint himself with Henry George's works, and offering to send to him his friend, S. D. Nikolayev, foremost Russian expert on these matters, for consultation. Propose this solution to the Duma, he concluded, and the weight of your influence will carry it; "and thus the revolutionists will be deprived of one of their principal means for justly arousing the exasperation of the people."

Once again, Tolstoy was willing to compromise with the governmental power that he condemned in order to abolish private property in land and at the same time provide all the peasants with the possibility of cultivating as much land as they needed. The Prime Minister did not answer. Tolstoy wrote again, this time to request Stolypin's aid on behalf of a man who had been imprisoned for distributing religious literature, but he took the occasion to express regret that his previous letter had gone unnoticed. When Stolypin did reply, it was a coldly polite refusal to accept the solution of Henry George. "Nature has placed in man certain innate instincts, such as the feeling of hunger, sex, etc., and one of the most powerful feelings of this kind is the feeling for property." And he hinted at his own solution of developing a class of small private landowners among the peasantry. Tolstoy answered, expressing his dismay over this solution which, he said, would destroy the village commune, the ancient basis of peasant life, and at the same time increase the element of violence that was rooted in private property in land. Stolypin's reaction was no more than he expected, he comforted himself, but in his heart he felt sad over this final failure to achieve a cherished ideal. His opinion of the Prime Minister's capacities had not been high; it now swiftly deteriorated, for he held him largely responsible for the many executions of the government's revolutionary enemies. Toward the end of his life Tolstoy was heard to remark in a private conversation: "That son-of-a-bitch Stolypin is in love with the gallows."

It never occurred to Tolstoy that in the realm of political and social thought life had outstripped him, and the wave of history had carried far beyond him. Politics, for example, which he loathed, and which his own generation mostly ignored, had become the passion of an aroused nation. It was a dirty but necessary business, in which the end justified the means. Born an aristocratic landowner, he had lived most of his life in a little village in the middle of Russia, isolated from the new developments and thoughts that were filling men's minds. His own class, and the peasantry among whom he lived, he understood from long experience, and with his rare powers of observation and psychological penetration he made scores of representatives of these classes live in his fiction with a wonderful truthfulness to life. And even in his controversial works, his arguments carry a convincing authenticity when based upon a knowledge of those layers of society with which he was entirely familiar.

But neither in his fiction nor in his controversial writings does Tolstoy evince any deep knowledge or understanding of the rising middle class and the proletariat which were beginning to dominate the future destiny of his country. Lenin put his finger on precisely this fault in Tolstoy's relation to the revolutionary movement. How little he grasped the thought, temper, and desires of the young members of the proletariat who were to forge the successful revolution of 1917 is strikingly illustrated by an incident that took place in the summer of 1907. In a village near

Yasnaya Polyana, he engaged in a discussion with several youths on the theme of how the workers might best free themselves. He first made the point that the workers had confirmed their own slavery by serving the rich and the government, and that they would free themselves only when they refused such servitude and lived according to the law of God, of love. Then he asked the lads:—

"What do you think about the present position of Russia, that is, what we call the revolution? Do you expect success from it, and improvement in the situation of the people, and if you expect it, what will the improvement be?"

After some hesitation one of the youths answered:—

"The eyes of all of us are fixed on the revolution and we expect success and improvement from it. This is the only way out. At least, such is my opinion."

Tolstoy objected that the violence of the revolutionists was no different from that of the government, to which the same lad replied:—

"One must use a wedge to drive out a wedge."

Tolstoy maintained that such means would only serve to strengthen the government's hand, and that in the ensuing conflict many sins would be committed and much misery caused.

"Yes, but take the government, it doesn't own up to any sins," shot back one of the lads.

"The government is the most to blame," agreed Tolstoy, "because it accustoms the people to the idea that murder is possible. The people have learned from this: if the government murders, then we also may murder. The teachers are bad and the pupils do wrong to accept this kind of instruction."

"The people are taught by life, not by teachers," solemnly returned one of the youths, who seemed more revolutionary-minded. "Life's conditions force one to grab a revolver and shoot."

"No," objected Tolstoy, "people live together and unfailingly learn from the best, the wisest men who have bequeathed to us their precepts, and we must make use of them. What you call life is an animal existence. Human life is intelligent."

"The people will sooner accept revolutionary propaganda," replied the same youth, and with an ironical smile he added: "If I had money, then I would be one of your followers."

Restraining himself with an effort, Tolstoy quietly answered: "On the contrary, in the Gospel the opposite is said: the poor are blessed and the rich are unhappy."

"That's an old song!" the same youth protested with some heat. "The priests have been singing it to us for ages. We are being destroyed by pauperism and ignorance. Ignorance thrives on poverty."

An impasse had been reached. Tolstoy skillfully continued to emphasize the fallacy of believing that wealth has any connection with real happiness, and he tried to implant in the souls of these young men a sense of humility and a belief in service to others and in love for their neighbors. But they had experienced hunger, they had been kicked around, they had read revolutionary pamphlets, they knew what they wanted from life, and it had little relation to what Tolstoy wanted. Yet these were the youths who in ten short years would destroy the whole flimsy superstructure of the old Russia he knew and build on its foundations a new civilization. And they were fully aware then, in 1907, that you could not win a revolution on Tolstoy's slogan of "God's law, humility, and love," instead of *liberté, égalité,* and *fraternité.*

Like some sage whose wisdom is timeless, however, Tolstoy would have been no more convinced by the successes of the 1917 Russian Revolution than he had been by the accounts he had read of the French Revolution. He knew only that power corrupts and that this was just as true of a democracy or a socialist state as of an absolute monarchy. For him political progress could not be measured in terms of democratic or socialist progress, for he saw both the hypocrisy behind universal suffrage and the ever-present danger of power, even though held by the few elected by the many. His writings are full of prophecies of democratic and socialist states turning into monstrous dictatorships; of non-military democracies becoming powerful military states; of civilized countries championing fiendish theories of racial superiority; of all the wonderful advances of science being turned into frightful instruments of war to kill most expeditiously millions of peoples. All this, he foretold, will be achieved in the name of political, social, and scientific progress. And there will be no end of such "progress," he warned, while humanity continues to worship the law of man as higher than the law of God.

There was strength in Tolstoy's unworldliness, for it

enabled him to stand above the turmoil of everyday life and to reach beyond history, beyond time itself, to find a universal answer to the problem of living that would not be conditioned by materialistic factors of human existence. If this process had its limitations, he would have answered that God needs our limitations also. Toward the end of "The Significance of the Russian Revolution" he argued for his conception of progress:—

> Why presuppose that the progress, of which people are proud, will always be in increasing the population, in preserving life, and not in the moral perfecting of life; that it will always be in these pitiful mechanical inventions, thanks to which people will produce more and more unnecessary, harmful, and corrupting objects, and that it will not be in greater and greater unity of one another and in the subjugation of one's lusts which is so necessary for this unity; why not suppose that people will rejoice in and compete not for riches or luxury, but for simplicity, moderation, and kindness to one another? Why not think that people will see progress not in obtaining more and more, but in taking less and less from others and in giving more and more to others; not in increasing their own power, not in waging war more and more successfully, but in humbling themselves more and more and in living together more and more closely—people with people, nations with nations?

7

In 1906 Tolstoy remarked that he was becoming deaf and stupid from old age. That Easter he heard the bells of the village church, and he recalled that so he had heard them fifty years ago, only those who had rung them then were now old or dead. Youngsters had displaced them. Soon he too would be displaced. This year and next he had frequent periods of illness and he sadly observed that his memory was weakening. Old friends noticed an increasing gentleness and tenderness in his behavior to all.

Despite his seventy-eight years, Tolstoy still began the day with a brief walk, and upon his return he met outside the house the usual petitioners, whose tales of woe always depressed him, and the beggars whom he could never pass without distributing copper coins. Usually, after going over his mail, he read the thoughts for that day set down in his *Circle of Reading,* and then retired to his study for work, during which time absolute quiet had to be preserved in the household. After lunch at two or three, he set out for his long walk or ride on horseback. Sonya, now always fearful about his health, usually asked where he was going, a question that annoyed him since he never knew where he was going. He finally compromised by allowing a servant or secretary to follow some paces behind, for on these walks or rides he wished to be alone to concentrate on ideas, on characters and images for his writing. He carried in his pocket a notebook for such jottings. This daily routine, however, was frequently interrupted by visitors who now taxed his waning strength. They were particularly numerous over 1907, and he regretted, as he put it, that visiting him seemed to have become a fashion. They ranged from the Japanese writer Kenjiro Tokutomi and sundry Americans, including Stephen Bonsal of the *New York Times,* to throngs of Russians of all political and religious beliefs, of whom one was a mad student firmly convinced that he was Christ and Tolstoy God.

At the end of 1906 and during part of 1907 Tolstoy took up again an occupation that had absorbed him more than forty years before—the teaching of children. The practice began gradually, growing out of conversations on various matters with Dorik Sukhotin, the stepson of his daughter Tanya, and with little peasant boys from the village who came to borrow books or just to chat. Soon a class was formed, then two classes, according to age, and regular sessions were held in the library after dinner.

Though Tolstoy's ideas on how children should be taught had not changed much in all these years, he had a different conception of subject matter. The chief thing, he felt now, was not the three R's, but religious and moral education. "This is my university," he remarked about his classes to M. A. Stakhovich. "I simply expound to them, as I understand it, the law of God. And how difficult this is!" He took the teaching very seriously, prepared his lessons beforehand, and the reactions of his young students were always his chief criteria of success, which he duly noted in his diary. With the deft hand of an old master, he avoided dull theology and taught the story of Christ through simple appealing narratives that he made up. Nor did he restrict himself to the Bible. His aim was to teach these youngsters moral behavior and the rules of right living, and he ransacked his mind and printed material for effective illustrations. He might retell the story of the temptation of Christ or how the former family servant Gasha showed her pity for dogs, cats, mice, and cockroaches.

The class of ten or twelve children would gather, their eyes merry, their laughing voices sounding gaily through the house. The kindly smiling face of the silvery-haired master of seventy-nine responded to their merriment. After the lesson was read, a warm discussion took place on the meaning of the story. Questions and answers flew back and forth, and when everybody got to talking at once the teacher beamed his satisfaction. When he failed to stimulate such general interest, he blamed himself. Out of these lessons came his work, *The Teaching of Christ Told for Children*.[8]

Tolstoy derived deep satisfaction from his teaching. He wrote in his diary at this time: "Only old people and children, free from sexual lusts, live a true life. The rest are only a factory for the continuation of animals. That is why debauchery is so repulsive in old people and children. Yet people think that all poetry may be found only in sexual life. All true poetry is always outside it. His wife, however, did not see things this way. She looked upon his teaching children as just another new hobby and crossly observed: "He drills some Christian truths into youngsters' heads. They repeat them by heart, like parrots, and he feels assured that something will remain in their heads." And on one occasion when he was delightedly commenting on the children's progress to members of the family, Sonya testily interrupted: "It won't make any difference, they will grow up drunkards and thieves anyway." Tolstoy fell silent.

On the whole Tolstoy had grown used to schoolchildren. They came from far and near, many perhaps for no better reason than that of the girl, a gold-medal student, whose proud father had offered her the choice of a bicycle, a watch, or a trip to see Tolstoy. These shy young visitors, who came individually or in small groups, were a contrast to his own merry and familiar Yasnaya Polyana students. They stood around awkwardly, in embarrassed silence, and their gaping parents or teachers looked as though they expected their charges to be infected with wisdom before their very eyes

[8] Published in 1908. Other pieces written at this time, such as "Believe Yourself," "Conversations with Children on Moral Questions," and several tales are connected with Tolstoy's interest in teaching children.

by being exposed to the great man. In the summer of 1907 some 850 boys and girls from Tula, in the care of teachers, descended upon Yasnaya Polyana, an excursion that had received Tolstoy's permission. He and his family and guests greeted the children warmly. The boys were taken to bathe in the Voronka, while Tolstoy anxiously watched along the bank for fear of accident. He helped the smallest with their dressing, showed them gymnastic exercises, and soon had them all at their ease. Later Sonya supervised the girls while they bathed. Refreshments were served, games were played, and upon departing the children lustily cheered their hosts.

Tolstoy's teaching and close association with children in 1907 prompted the idea of compiling a "Children's Cycle of Reading." Though he did much work for this, he finally decided to merge the material with a new edition of the *Circle of Reading*. Two volumes had appeared in 1906–1907. Apart from the other writings mentioned during this period, much of his time was spent on this compilation, for he had enlarged the design so that the selections would mirror his philosophy of life. Besides the more difficult task of choosing the great thoughts to conform to his new plan, he busied himself with writing brief introductions on many of the authors of the passages, and he also composed for it a number of moral tales illustrating the various themes.[9] The more he worked on this compilation the more significance it took on in his eyes, and he finally drafted a brief introduction for it, in which he tried to explain systematically his whole outlook on life. Over the next three years, according to his secretary, he recast this introduction more than a hundred times.

8

The news that most excited Tolstoy in the summar of 1907 was that Chertkov planned to spend a couple of months in the neighborhood of Yasnaya Polyana. Save for two brief visits, Chertkov had remained in England to take care of his publishing and other business since receiving permission to return to Russia. He now felt it necessary to be close to his

[9] Some of the better known tales that he included in this work, which finally appeared under the title, *For Every Day,* are "Divine and Human"; "Prayer"; "Kornei Vasilyev"; "Father Vasili"; "For What?" and "Strawberries."

spiritual father for a longer period of time and made arrangements to rent a house for the summer near Yasenki, a village about three miles from Yasnaya Polyana.

Since his daughter Masha's death and the family's increased hostility to his views, Tolstoy, in his spiritual loneliness, tended to turn more and more to the masterful comfort of Chertkov. Though perhaps inevitable in the circumstances, it was a fatal tendency for all concerned, except Chertkov. For this huge, handsome man with the suffering eyes of a saint and the iron will and temperament of a Savonarola had the habit of quarreling with those whom he could not dominate and of absorbing utterly those who submitted to his powerful personality. Few were more capable of unintentional wrong in the name of righteousness. Friendship with Tolstoy had been his life's work, and Tolstoy was perhaps inclined to exaggerate in generous fashion the sacrifices Chertkov had made for his sake—a rich Court life, exile, and unstinting labor over the publication of his writings. In the long history of their relationship, one can observe the slow but steady growth of the influence of the pupil on the master in material matters if not in spiritual doctrine.

The previous year, for example, Tolstoy's Slovak disciple, Albert Shkarvan, had translated into German some new tales of Tolstoy. He promptly received a letter from Chertkov to the effect that he had no authority to publish the stories since he, Chertkov, had sold the first translation rights to the English firm, William Heinemann. Shkarvan appealed to Tolstoy, who regretfully but firmly informed him that he had given Chertkov exclusive permission to arrange these matters and hence he could not interfere. Chertkov apparently used the profits of such enterprises to finance his own publishing ventures, which enabled him to print Tolstoy's works free.

When Tolstoy received a telegram announcing the arrival of Chertkov, his wife and son, he was agitated to tears and rode horseback to Tula to meet them. They remained at Yasnaya Polyana until their own house was put in order.

It had been a long time since so much "Tolstoyan" atmosphere hung over the neighborhood. Besides the Chertkovs, sympathizers or fervent followers such as Goldenweizer, Gorbunov-Posadov, director of the *Intermediary,* and the Henry George specialist Nikolayev settled down for the summer in houses near by. Visits were exchanged between Tolstoy and Chertkov nearly every day. There were long serious discussions on doctrine and publications. Tolstoy inspected the prodigious and still growing manuscript of the "Vault" of his thoughts that Chertkov had been compiling for years, and tears came to his eyes as he viewed this huge labor of love. The devoted friends had a spiritual feast, and frequent were the notations on "joyous meetings with Chertkov" in Tolstoy's diary.

As was his custom, Chertkov gathered around him a following of young novices at Yasenki, and the master and his star pupil held forth to them on the faith. One of these youths, N. N. Gusev, who was to become a distinguished scholar on Tolstoy's life and works, was hardly a Tolstoyan novice. He had become a devoted follower several years before and had already met and recommended himself to the attention of Tolstoy. Before Chertkov departed that summer, he persuaded Tolstoy to accept Gusev's services as a secretary, which would also allow him to keep a doctrinal eye on the Yasenki peasants whom the zealous Chertkov had already proselyted. Tolstoy agreed, but the young secretary had hardly worked a month when he was arrested, having been denounced for his propaganda work among the peasants. The incident distressed Tolstoy, who felt himself to blame. He visited Gusev in prison, brought him warm clothes, food, and money, and after strenuous efforts with the authorities he procured his release. Gusev continued his task as secretary and proved an invaluable assistant and recorder of life at Yasnaya Polyana.

This wonderful summer of faithful followers and spiritual communion came to an end. Chertkov left on September 15 to return to England. Tolstoy's daughter Alexandra, his remaining sympathizer in the family circle, was also away at this time. He felt lonely. "I am very sad without Chertkov and Sasha," he wrote in his diary. But the next day his spirits rose. He had received a "joyous letter" from Chertkov, in which that careful man wrote of their "joyous communion" that summer, and signed himself, "loving you so that, if I could love everybody in this fashion, it would be a paradise on earth for me."

9

Yasnaya Polyana had been "no paradise on earth" for Sonya that summer. The "dark people" seemed to have taken over the estate and she resented them more than ever. She could not fail to notice her husband's changed disposition and new interest in life when surrounded by his followers, as though he had been starved for their kind of Tolstoyan affection and activity. Nor could she fail to notice and be jealous of these almost daily visits to Chertkov by a husband who seemed to have so little time to spare for her.

Sonya resented Chertkov's attitude toward her husband and his assumption of privileges, such as interrupting Tolstoy in his study, which not even members of the family dared to do. In fact, Chertkov's whole behavior was arousing her suspicions of his ulterior motives. Their ancient quarrel over the publishing rights of her husband's works still smoldered, and she suspected that Chertkov was trying to procure for his own future private use all the manuscripts of Tolstoy that he could lay his hands on. In April of 1907 she wrote him a sharp note to ask if he did not have in his possession certain diaries of her husband that had disappeared from Yasnaya Polyana. This action irritated Tolstoy, who was finding it increasingly difficult to keep peace between Chertkov and Sonya.

Nor was this the only situation that now arose to disturb Tolstoy's peace of mind. The storm clouds of family dissension that had been dissipated by Masha's death gathered again during the latter half of 1907. In vain he recalled the excesses of his own youth in an effort to temper his severe judgment of those of his sons. Yet he now found it difficult to understand or accept the behavior of Andrei, who, having abandoned his wife and two children, ran off with the wife of the governor of Tula, the mother of six children. The governor resigned and appealed to the agitated Tolstoy for his help. Though he pleaded with the lovers, Andrei persisted and finally married the woman. And now Leo culminated a long period of what Tolstoy frankly described as "envy of me, leading to hatred," by publishing an article, "Negation or Self-Protection?" which fiercely attacked his father's views. Taking the position of defender of the monarchy and the social system under it, he condemned his father as an enemy of the government and organized society, a "baneful influence on Russia," and as the person largely responsible for the revolutionary fervor throughout the nation. Though Tolstoy called upon all his spiritual resources to quell the anger that stirred in him, he could not forbear applying to Leo the scathing epithet *chernoso-*

tenets—that is, a man belonging to or sharing the reactionary views of the Black Hundred, the secret organizers of pogroms and repressions in the interests of the Tsar's government.

At the beginning of the fall the storm clouds broke in fury. For some time tension had been growing between the Yasnaya Polyana peasants and the stewards of the estate. In order to increase profits, the stewards had raised the peasants' rent, fined them heavily for spoiled crops, and impounded their animals for wandering in the estate gardens. One night in early September a caretaker surprised several peasants attempting to steal cabbages from the Tolstoy garden. Some shots were fired, whether by the peasants or the caretaker was not definitely proved. This incident, along with other misdeeds of the peasants, prompted Sonya, with the support of Andrei, to appeal to the governor of Tula for protection. The authorities, only too happy to render such assistance in this particular instance, promptly arrived, investigated, arrested several peasants, and left two armed policemen on the estate to keep order.

A report of the affair got out to the public. Newspapers printed sensational accounts under such headlines as "Home of L. N. Tolstoy Attacked!" And conservative and religious periodicals ran articles, in which they maliciously pointed out that the great teacher of nonresistance to evil by force had cried to the police for help the moment his own skin was in danger.

Tolstoy cared little for the ridicule of the newspapers—he had long since got used to it—but he was profoundly disturbed over Sonya's action and the arrest of the peasants. Their parents pleaded with him to intercede. "They cannot admit," he wrote in his diary, "that I, especially since I live with her, am not the owner, and therefore all blame me. This is grievous, very much so, but also good, for by making it impossible for people to have a fine opinion about me, it will drive me into that region where the opinion of people carries no weight. These last couple of days I have been unable to overcome a bad feeling." He had moments, however, when he thought of leaving for the estate of his daughter Tanya.

In the end Tolstoy did take the part of the peasants and wrote the governor, requesting their release. That official refused, expressing surprise at such a request since he had the letter of Tolstoy's wife asking him to protect the estate from the depredations of the peasants. Unpleasant conversations with Sonya followed. He wanted her to have the police guard removed, for it distressed him to have armed men around, threatening the peasants and demanding passports from anyone who entered the grounds of the estate. When he protested to them because of their behavior, they answered offensively and indicated that he was interfering with their duties. He replied: "It would be fine to die. No letters, no petitioners, no policemen." The guards stayed. And to make matters worse, shortly after this Sonya had several more peasants arrested for stealing lumber, a charge she could not prove.

In the family only Alexandra sympathized with his suffering over this situation. She argued with her mother and Andrei about the guards. "Must papa be watched over by guards?" she demanded. "How distressing it is for him! If it were not for papa, I would leave right now."

The skirmishing that had been going on in the family for years on this question of property was now ended and the lines had been formed for the final battle. Tolstoy believed that property was the root of all evil, and it had now become the chief evil in his relations with his family. His position was anomalous. He had legally signed away all his rights to his estate to the family and had publicly renounced the copyrights of his works. Yet old Yasnaya Polyana peasants, whom he had known as boys, often took him to task for not giving away his land; disciples sometimes reproached him for continuing to live on a wealthy estate when he had repudiated property; and there was constant bickering going on over the rights to his books.

Tolstoy realized that his anomalous position had resulted from the compromises he had made with his own convictions. There were two reasons why he had remained on his estate. He had always nourished the hope that his family, and particularly his wife, would finally accept his views, divide the estate among the peasants, and live on it on equal terms with them. He had entirely failed in this. If anything, the family had become more hostile to his views as the years went on. This failure he blamed on himself for living the life of a Pharisee, as he expressed it, and not fulfilling his own teaching. The other reason was that, however severe the trials he had to endure from them, he considered it his duty to remain with his family. Anything else would be an evasion of this duty, an attempt to follow the line of least spiritual resistance.

When V. A. Sheerman, a man sympathetic to Tolstoy's beliefs, gave away his huge estate in 1906 to the peasants and offered to live on it simply as one of them, Tolstoy applauded his act. Yet when a Tolstoyan, who found life difficult in his own village, wished to leave it and join the fortunate peasants on Sheerman's estate, Tolstoy said to him: "It is very improper for me to speak about myself, but I will say it anyway. The life I lead is a hundred thousand times more offensive to me than yours is to you, but I cannot desert it." Gusev reports him as declaring at this time: "I ought to have gone into a monastery. In truth, if I had had no wife, I would have entered a monastery."

No doubt the accumulation of vexations, and the harassment of family quarrels over the question of property during 1907, prompted Tolstoy to make a public statement. He wanted to put an end to the interminable requests he received from all over the world for gifts of money. Though he had publicly renounced all property and income, hardly a day passed that he was not asked for financial aid from mere pittances to amounts running into thousands of rubles. Behind his attempt to stop this practice was the larger purpose of restating to the public his personal position with reference to the whole question of property. He sent to the newspapers, where it was widely publicized, the following letter: "More than 20 years ago, because of certain personal considerations, I renounced the possession of property. Real estate belonging to me I transferred to my heirs, just as though I had died. I also renounced property rights in my productions, and those written after 1881 became public property." He then added that he sometimes received money from abroad and from people in Russia for charitable purposes, and this he distributed to the poor, as the need arose, to the best of his ability. And after requesting people not to turn to him for material aid, he concluded: "I less than anyone am able to fulfill such requests, for if I have really acted as I here testify, i.e., I have ceased to possess property, then I cannot help with money those who appeal to me. If, however, I am deceiving people in saying that I have repudiated property and really possess it, then it is even less likely that they should expect aid from such a person."

Public reaction to this attempt to clarify his position was

hardly an anodyne to his painful feelings on the subject. He received malicious and ridiculing letters. From Moscow one person wrote: "Count, you write in the *Moscow Journal* that you have died, and that like a corpse you have nothing. But when you print new productions do you receive an honorarium? You ought not to since you are dead; and how awkward it is for the Countess to fleece a corpse (she thoroughly flayed you when alive) of the money, which according to your will, should certainly go to the poor. This is the voice of very, very many." Newspaper reactions were equally scurrilous, playing largely on the theme: Was the great man being simply naïve or hypocritical? One newspaper ran a caricature under the description: "The honored Tit Titych, having read L. N. Tolstoy's recent letter, immediately declared himself a Tolstoyan." The drawing depicts a fat muzhik with a face similar to Tolstoy's. He sits at a table and firmly grasps a bowl with fruit, various viands, and a bottle with a printed label: "Pigeon's Milk." On the bowl, chair, table, and nearly every object in the drawing, is the sign: "Property of My Wife." And around the table press famished, skeletonlike creatures.

Tolstoy had made his point at the expense of public ridicule. In some respects the effort was intended as much for his wife and sons as for the public. In the diary where, as he said, he conversed with his soul, he wrote shortly before he sent this letter to the newspapers: "More and more I suffer almost physically from inequality—from the wealth and luxury of our life in the midst of beggary. And I cannot lessen this inequality. In this is the secret tragedy of my life."

Yet Sonya, when her husband had renounced his estate, had assumed all the responsibility for it in the interests of the family. But the more faithfully she tried to fulfill her duties in this respect, the wider grew the rift between her and her husband. What was she to do? Only that which duty obliged her to do—fulfill her responsibilities to herself and family. They had been the responsibilities of her whole married life. She had not changed. Only her husband had changed, and because of it she seemed to him always at fault. Yet every new resolute step she took to resolve the problems of the family's existence caused him moral suffering, undermined her own spiritual equilibrium, and served to aggravate her tendency to hysteria.

XXXVIII

The Jubilee Year

The company sat chatting around the tea table at Yasnaya Polyana. It was the evening of New Year's Day, 1908. Tolstoy finally got up to retire to his study. He lingered for a few more words of conversation. Guests and members of the family surrounded him in a half circle. A twinkle came into his eye.

"Well, let's have a song. What do you say?"

Andrei led off with a folk melody that delighted his father. All joined hands, united in the spirit of jollity and comradeship that Tolstoy naturally inspired. No consecration to a religious doctrine could destroy his love of life and people. If he now yearned, like some old Buddhist, for an ascetic existence in his declining years, it was a wish alien to his instinctive fondness for communion with people.

Yet in the ceaseless struggle between the spiritual and the earthly, between good and evil, Tolstoy was approaching the ideal of perfection which he knew could never be achieved. He dreamed that he had written a drama about Christ, and he imagined himself taking the various parts, including that of the Saviour—the absolutely good man. "For the first time, and with an unusual new clarity, I was conscious of my own spirituality," he wrote in his diary in January. He distinctly felt that the center of gravity of his life was moving away from the corporeal into the region of the spirit. Though he wished to free himself from the body, as he philosophically expressed it, he did not hanker after the disembodied condition of the hero of a tale that he had read. So far removed from everything material had the hero become that he failed to recognize his wife and at moments was uncertain of his own earthly existence. Yet Tolstoy did tell his wife at this time that the first concern in life must be for the things of the soul, "and if household duties interfere with that, then damn household duties."

There was little likelihood that Sonya would slight her household duties for anything so insubstantial as "things of the soul." She did admit this year, however, that a remarkable change had come over her husband. "It is noticeable," she wrote in her diary, "that the spiritual life predominates" in him, and though he still likes to ride, enjoys tasty food and plays cards and chess, "yet his body lives a separate existence, and his spirit remains indifferent to earthly life, somewhere aloft, more independent of the body." And she sadly added that "something new, strange, and far away is being experienced by Leo Nikolayevich, and I'm often unbearably grieved and sorry over the loss of something in him, in his life, and in his relations to me and to everything surrounding him."

Emotionally hypersensitive, Tolstoy fought the anger that arose in him because of frequent daily annoyances. "Rejoice when they scold and revile you," he kept telling himself. If he did not exactly achieve perfection in this Christlike behavior pattern, he had by now learned to turn the other cheek with extraordinary docility for a man of his temperament. Each such action he reckoned a victory for the spirit. "Though your Christianity is higher than that of the priests, yet it is a lie," screamed a blind peasant who made periodic trips to Yasnaya Polyana to roast Tolstoy. "Your disciples are bandits and you are the chief of the bandits. They are all scoundrels and you are the first among them!" Tolstoy stood in the rain, humbly, quietly trying to reason with him until Sonya ordered the offender to be off.

Such encounters were not uncommon, but always Tolstoy tried to preserve an attitude of loving humility toward those who abused or hated him. Even when passing some mild stricture on a person's behavior, he usually prefaced it by declaring that he had no right to judge. When his old friend and former sympathizer, the writer M. O. Menshikov, published two scathing articles on Tolstoy, even going so far as to accuse him in print of hypocrisy, the infuriated Sonya wrote a stinging reply. Tolstoy answered with a letter of love, expressing the hope that it would inspire a similar feeling in Menshikov. To the scolding, often vituperative, letters he received—and there were many—he now replied in this same spirit of meekness. Those that most tried his patience were letters from religious people who fiercely condemned his beliefs with no apparent understanding of them. An enraged member of the Old Believers, a woman, wrote to curse his works and to express an obviously sincere desire to shoot him and execute all his followers, if it were only in her power to do so. In his answer, he told of his "great delight" in hearing from her, for as a religious woman he felt that a spiritual communion between them was possible. But he ended with a mild rebuke: "You seem to think that you and those who taught you are the only people who know the truth and that all the rest are lost. I do not think I am the only person who knows the truth and that everyone else is in darkness. I am eighty years old and I am still searching for truth. Your teachers have led you into the sin of pride and condemnation. Every man in the depths of his soul has something he alone comprehends, namely his attitude towards God. And this sphere is sacred. We must not attempt to invade it or to imagine that we know all that lies hidden in its depths."

These remarks were characteristic of both Tolstoy's humility, achieved with so much difficulty, and his final attitude towards the religious beliefs of others. Turning the other cheek was not instinctive in a nature essentially proud and aristocratic, and in this practice he feared above all to appear either ridiculous or insincere. Out of the same wise humility came a still greater degree of tolerance for the religious convictions of others. He wrote in his diary in February: "One cannot suggest or convey to another a religious creed. Each has his own. If each did not have his own special kind, then there would be no reason for each person to exist. One can give only the materials out of which one's own conception of the world is formed, and the individual himself will take from these only what he needs." Nor did he escape moments of doubt in his convictions after all these years of striving for a faith he could accept, for we now find him freely confessing in his diary: "This morning while lying in bed I experienced what I have not experienced for a long time—a feeling of doubt in everything. But in the last analysis one thing however remains: good, love—that goodness which no one can take away."

In March Tolstoy had just finished translating a tale of Victor Hugo and was walking about the room when his secretary suddenly saw him slipping to the floor. After he revived, his memory completely failed him. All was jumbled in his mind—relatives, friends, the names of well-known places. Though this soon passed, leaving him simply in a weakened condition, his remarkable memory began to give evidence of slow deterioration. This was the first of recurring fainting spells.

In his poor state of health, Tolstoy was now glad to avail himself, as a time-saver in the ever-increasing stream of correspondence, of a dictaphone, one of the marvels of that science he so often ridiculed for producing superfluous mechanisms. The previous year, Stephen Bonsal of the *New York Times* on his visit to Tolstoy had kindly offered to have a dictaphone sent to him. Thomas Edison, whom Tolstoy had once slightingly referred to in an article because of a statement attributed to him that he would invent projectiles that would kill more people in an hour than Attila had slain in all his wars, willingly agreed to make him a present of one. It was perhaps good advertising. After all, Tolstoy probably had the largest personal mail of any man in the world.

The machine finally arrived at Yasnaya Polyana. Tolstoy hastened to try it out. At the end of the first letter he was in a state of exhaustion. "Oh, I'm so tired!" he told his daughter Alexandra. "I don't see how people can use this thing! It's all very well for the well-balanced Americans, perhaps, but for us Russians it's no good." Yet he soon learned to use it with comfort and appreciated the immense saving in time.

Some months after the arrival of the dictaphone, Tolstoy received a letter from Edison, containing a characteristic request of an American businessman. "Can I prevail upon you," Edison wrote in part, "to make for me one or two phonograph records in English or French, preferably both, of short messages not longer than four minutes in duration, conveying to the people of the world some thoughts that would tend to their moral and social advancement? My phonographs have now been distributed throughout all of the civilized countries, and in the United States alone upwards of one million are in use. Your fame is world-wide, and I am sure that a message from you would be eagerly received by millions of people who could not help from being impressed with the intimate personality of your own words, which through this medium would be preserved for all time."

The grateful Tolstoy willingly complied. For several days before the arrival of two Englishmen with a special recording apparatus, he was agitated over the anticipated performance. The French piece, which he composed specially for the occasion, went off well, but he stumbled over several words of the English reading—a selection from *The Kingdom of God Is Within You.*[1] On a second try he succeeded to the satisfaction of all. He asked the technicians many questions about Edison and rejoiced to learn, so the account runs, that he had been a vegetarian for thirty years.[2]

So accustomed did Tolstoy become to the dictaphone that he began to use it in his literary work, which was a blessing for those who had had the task of copying the barely decipherable first drafts of his manuscripts. The well of creative literature, however, was at last drying up. Various designs for stories and dramas still continued to flash through his mind, but, with few exceptions, the urge to employ his pen in the interests of his religious and moral beliefs predominated. Nor did he see much hope in contemporary literature, either native or foreign. Its decadence, he declared, was a natural resultant of the decadence of modern civilization.

But a contemporary writer who proved a mixed blessing to Tolstoy at this time was George Bernard Shaw, who had sent him some of his works[3] and even marked the passages on which he desired his reactions. Shaw's previous criticism of Tolstoy's study of Shakespeare had revealed both the similarities and the differences in the thinking of the two men. While he admired Shaw's great talents, Tolstoy decided, using a line from *Man and Superman,* that "he has got more brains than is good for him." He did not relish the serious business of life flavored with the salt and pepper of Shavian wit, and he now wrote a letter to tell him, among other things: "Dear Mr. Shaw, life is a great and

[1] Another account describes the English piece as a selection from Tolstoy's work *On Life.*

[2] Later, through Chertkov, Tolstoy requested Edison to employ in his factory a young Russian who had been stranded in America and had appealed to him for aid.

[3] Among the works of Shaw that Tolstoy read were *Man and Superman, John Bull's Other Island, Major Barbara,* and *The Impossibilities of Anarchism.*

serious business, and all of us, in the brief interval allotted us, must try to find our own appointed destiny and to fulfill it as best we can. This applies to all people and especially to you with your great gift of original thought and your penetration into the essence of every question." In his diary, he was much less polite: "I read Shaw. His triviality is astounding. Not only is he devoid of a single thought of his own that elevates him above the banality of the city mob, but he does not understand a single great thought of the thinkers of the past. His whole attraction rests in the fact that he is able to express artistically the most stale trivialities in a most perverted modern way, as though he were saying something his own, something novel. His chief characteristic is this—a tremendous self-confidence equaled only by his complete philosophical ignorance."

A literary giant of the past, Tolstoy now looked back to the old writers with nostalgia whenever contemplating the new. He still fully agreed, he told Goldenweizer, with his own ideas about art that he had written years ago. Everywhere he saw the commercial instinct dominating modern writers. "He lives by literature," he severely said of one of them. "And this, in my opinion, is like prostitution."

2

Tolstoy's efforts at spiritual concentration were somehow incompatible with the activities of the Russian government; the humility he felt toward his personal detractors he could not apply to the enemies of the people. By 1908 the Stolypin forces, apparently fully entrenched in power, felt safe in reverting to many of the repressive measures practiced before the revolution. The civil liberties promised the people were now curtailed, and any infringement of law and order was punished, often with severity. Opposition was outlawed, and it seemed that the radicals' distrust of the liberal promises of the Tsar's government had been fully justified.

Tolstoy now became a special object of attack by reactionary authorities who once again felt secure in their power. Still afraid to strike a person of his international renown, they continued their old policy of wounding him by striking at his followers and all who deliberately or unwittingly furthered his beliefs. Those caught publishing, possessing, lending, or distributing his antigovernment or antimilitary works were prosecuted. As always, nothing could be calculated to wound him more deeply, and each such case threw him into a turmoil of moral agitation. He wrote again and again to government officials and influential friends to ask their assistance for these victims. Driven to extremes, he threatened, in the case of one of his disciples, V. A. Molochnikov, arrested for distributing his works, to attend the trial at Petersburg and plead the prisoner's cause. A legal friend advised against such a procedure. Then he wrote a public letter, followed by an article, in which he demanded that the authorities punish him instead, the real culprit, as the author of the works in question. Nothing availed; Molochnikov was sentenced to a year in jail. And others were similarly treated, despite all his protests.

Those final acts of violence—executions—distressed Tolstoy even more. With moral horror he continued to follow the brief accounts in the daily press. "Merely to think of what is now happening throughout Russia!" he said to Goldenweizer with a sigh. "My God, my God, these executions, these prisons, these jails, these exiles! And they imagine that they will improve something or other!"

"Today, May 9," Tolstoy read in a newspaper, "on the Strelbitski field at Kherson, twenty peasants[4] were executed by hanging for a bandit attack on the estate of a landowner in the Elizavetgrad district." He remarked in a shocked tone to his secretary Gusev: "There it is. Yes, how well we have arranged life. I would have been convinced that there did not exist in Russia a man so cruel as to kill 20 people. But here it is done unnoticed: one subscribes, another reads, this wretched executioner hangs."

This was more than Tolstoy could bear. The thoughtless revolutionists had been objectionable to him, he said, but they now seemed holy in comparison to these official government murderers. For some time he had been considering writing on the subject and had started collecting material; the hanging of the peasants now inspired him to immediate action. He begin his famous article, *I Cannot Be Silent*. A weight fell from his shoulders as he set to work. The self-assurance and satisfaction of an effective participant in a noble cause took possession of him. He gathered information from legal friends and read accounts of executions, such as the recently published book, *Russian Women on the Scaffold*. As his stormy emotions took compelling

[4] It later turned out that twelve were executed.

shape on paper he became tearfully happy. Perhaps with his tongue in his cheek he remarked that if Sonya had been a revolutionist—no doubt he had in mind the account he had just read of Sofya Perovski, who had been executed for her part in the assassination of Alexander II—"she would have been a terrific revolutionist. For this business a certain narrowness and terrible energy are needed which women customarily direct into motherhood." In a little more than two weeks he finished *I Cannot Be Silent* and sent it off to Chertkov with the plea that it be published at once.

On July 3 several leading Russian newspapers dared to print selections from the article, and for weeks it continued to appear in fragmentary form in the provincial press. At Tula a complete version was issued by an illegal press. Owners of nearly all the newspapers that handled the article in any form were either fined or imprisoned. Abroad, it appeared in translation in hundreds of newspapers and periodicals in various countries.

The immediacy of the theme and the emotional intensity and high seriousness with which it was handled contributed to the tremendous success of *I Cannot Be Silent*. Tolstoy's great literary talent, his sense of drama, of vivid description, of human psychology, made doubly impressive this anguished outcry against man's inhumanity. He struck a note that won a response from all thinking people. The crimes of the revolutionists are terrible, he declared, but they do not compare with the criminality and stupidity of the legalized violence of the government. The delusion, however, is the same on both sides. And the excuse, he added, "is that an evil deed committed for the benefit of many, ceases to be immoral; and that therefore, without offending against the moral law, one may lie, rob, and kill whenever this tends to the realization of that supposed good condition for the many which we imagine that we know and can foresee, and which we wish to establish."

Since the government claimed that all these executions were done for the general welfare of the Russian people, then, as one of the people, Tolstoy insisted that he could not escape the feeling that he was an unconscious participator in these terrible deeds, that his personal safety and chattels were protected by the horrors being perpetrated by the government.

"And being conscious of this I can no longer endure it, but must free myself from this intolerable position!

"It is impossible to live so! I, at any rate, cannot and will not live so.

"That is why I write this and will circulate it by all means in my power both in Russia and abroad—that one of two things may happen: either that these inhuman deeds may be stopped, or that my connection with them may be snapped and I put in prison, where I may be clearly conscious that these horrors are not committed on my behalf; or still better (so good that I dare not even dream of such happiness) that they may put on me, as on those twelve or twenty peasants, a shroud and a cap and may push me also off a bench, so that by my own weight I may tighten the well-soaped noose around my old throat."

The article created an uproar. As the famous painter Repin put it, in a statement for the newspapers, Tolstoy voiced the things which had been boiling in the hearts of all Russians. A stream of letters poured in to Yasnaya Polyana, by far the majority of which acclaimed his courage and applauded his uncompromising condemnation of the government's executions. The sentiments of most of them are reflected in the words of one humble correspondent from Moscow who wrote: "You have removed a stone from our hearts, as it were, for you seem to speak as a symbol of faith and we repeat your words in our hearts, because we are unable to speak so and can only feel."

A few of the letters, most of them anonymous, abused Tolstoy and his article. A neat box arrived which contained, if not a "well-soaped noose," a stout coil of rope with an accompanying message: "Count. An answer to your article. Without troubling the government you may do it yourself; it is not difficult. In this way you will do good to both our country and our youth. A RUSSIAN MOTHER." He humbly replied, regretting any unhappiness he had caused, and beseeching her to write him and explain the cause of her unkind feeling toward him.[5]

3

Preparations for celebrating Tolstoy's eightieth birthday on August 28 had already got under way as early as January 7, when an Initiating Committee was set up in Petersburg.

[5] During 1908 Tolstoy also wrote two other articles connected with the theme of violence and executions: "The Law of Violence and the Law of Love" and "Christianity and the Death Penalty."

The idea caught like wildfire and spread throughout the country. The progressive press responded enthusiastically and organized a large meeting with delegates from various newspapers and periodicals. A "colossal" and "super" celebration was planned, something far surpassing the celebration in honor of Pushkin in 1880. Tolstoy was not merely a national but an international figure, and members of the press waxed lyrical over the publicity possibilities. Soon there began to appear in the newspapers nearly every day, under such headings as "Tolstoy Jubilee," "A National Holiday," and "Grandiose Celebration," accounts of preliminary plans and interviews with celebrities on the significance of Tolstoy.

Meanwhile, at Yasnaya Polyana, these widely advertised plans for a mammoth celebration were viewed with mixed feelings of alarm and elation. Sonya had already prepared a little statement to welcome the committee members on the day of the Jubilee. She intended to say: "All my life I have worshipped before the strength of talent and mind of Leo Nikolayevich, and I have tried to understand him. And if I have not succeeded in raising myself to his level, then at least I have tried to make his life easier with my love." And she added that it would please her very much if the committee would present her with flowers and testimonies of their esteem.

On the other hand, Tolstoy wrote in his diary in March: "They have decided upon a celebration and this is doubly painful to me, in the first place because it is stupid and disagreeable flattery, and in the second place because I long ago fell into the habit of seeing in this not satisfaction but interest. It is offensive to me." One of his disciples, A. M. Bodyanski, who had been convicted for the crime of distributing Tolstoy's works, wrote to the newspapers that nothing would give Tolstoy more moral satisfaction than to be put in prison on the day of his Jubilee, in accordance with what is accepted as justice in Russia. The newspapers refused to print the statement, but Tolstoy was delighted with the suggestion and wrote Bodyanski: "Actually nothing would satisfy me so completely and give me such joy as to be put in a prison, in a real good stinking prison—cold and hungry."

This was a birthday present that Tolstoy would never receive; he early set about, however, to forestall those that were designed for him. In February, he wrote his close friend, M. A. Stakhovich, a member of the Initiating Committee, to do everything in his power to cancel the celebration and set him free. But the preparations went on. Committees to honor him on his eightieth birthday sprang up all over Russia, in most of the capitals in the West, in America, India, and Japan. The prospects grew terrifying to him.

In the meantime, bitter letters from faithful Orthodox believers began to appear in the press, and some were sent to Tolstoy, complaining of the extraordinary honor Russia was preparing for a man who had been excommunicated. And an acquaintance of the family wrote to Sonya to point out that every loyal member of the Church would be offended by the celebration. Such an argument left him no recourse. In March he published a letter in the press, in which he frankly explained his intense objections to the proposed celebration. Apart from his personal dislike for such an honor, he added, "it was stirring up among people—and quite justly—a feeling for him that was the very opposite of love. And this grieves me extremely." His whole desire, he said, was to gain the love of people and to inspire love in them, and that he would willingly forgo any praise or honor if by so doing he could prevent an unfriendly feeling in a single person. And he concluded: "I will not say that I quite sincerely do not regard myself as undeserving of these honors that are being prepared: that would take on the aspect of false coquetry. But I cannot fail to say what I think, namely, that I would be happy if people would abandon this business and would do nothing in this direction."

Confronted with this public request, the Initiating Committee had no alternative other than to desist. It did so in a long published statement that ruefully reviewed all the enormous preparations that were under way in Russia and abroad, and concluded:—

> The great artist puts an end not only to a most deserved but a most impressive honor, an undertaking delighting all. The greetings and adoration of the whole world do not comfort the great soul of the wise old man if they can arouse irritation, malice, and an offensive feeling in other people. He himself is his own highest tribunal. Every thoughtful person will reverently accept his decision, and the Initiating Committee and the Bureau of the Press regard it as their duty to abandon their activity.

In all this agitation the government had adopted, for it at least, a very correct attitude. The Minister of the Interior had circularized all police heads with a sheaf of instructions on how to behave in this "crisis": they were not to interfere with individuals or organizations that desired to honor Tolstoy as a famous artist, but they were to prevent any groups from attempting to exploit the occasion for demonstrations against the government. High officials of the Church were less discreet. The Holy Synod published a statement requesting the faithful "to refrain from participating in any honoring of Count L. N. Tolstoy" as "an unyielding opponent of the Orthodox belief." Less dignified was the printed address of Germogen, Bishop of Saratov, on "the morally unlawful undertaking of certain parts of the population . . . to celebrate the jubilee day of the anathematized atheist and anarchist revolutionist Leo Tolstoy." And he was described in this address as "an accursed and most disdained Russian Judas," as "a despicable debaucher and slayer" of youth, as "a damned blasphemer of God," and sundry other uncomplimentary things. Tolstoy replied in his humble manner, pointing out that only God could know which of them was right in their understanding of the teaching of Christ, but that if he had erred, then as a human being and brother of the bishop he merited his loving correction and not his contempt. And he signed himself: "Your loving brother, Leo Tolstoy."

In July, Tolstoy developed an embolism of the veins in his leg and became seriously ill. For a time it seemed that he might be confined to his bed on his eightieth birthday. But the leg mended sufficiently for him to get around in a wheelchair. Though a formal celebration had been definitely abandoned, there were many indications that he would not escape the homage of a world eager to honor him. *I Cannot Be Silent,* which had just been published, had suddenly raised popular enthusiasm for him to a fever pitch.

On August 27, operators with a moving picture apparatus arrived at Yasnaya Polyana and persuaded Tolstoy to let them take some sequences of him sitting on the veranda, as well as scenes depicting life on the estate. Under the title of *The Eightieth Birthday of Count L. N. Tolstoy,* the film was soon shown in many Russian cities. He later manifested a lively interest in the cinema and thought of writing for it. Grasping the possibilities of this infant art, he remarked: "It is necessary that the cinema should represent Russian reality in its most varied manifestations. For this purpose Russian life ought to be reproduced as it is by the cinema; it is not necessary to go running after invented subjects." He little realized then how much of Russian life would be revealed to the world on the screen through the medium of his own great works of art.[6]

August 28 brought a flood of greetings from Russia and all over the world, and they continued to arrive for days. Some two thousand telegrams alone were received. They came from institutions and organizations, from all manner of individuals—titled nobility, great public figures, and even members of the Church, and convicts in prison. An Englishman presented in person a message of greetings and lofty praise signed by hundreds of his countrymen, including such figures as Meredith, Hardy, Wells, and Shaw. From America came a fulsome tribute and one from Australia, and from most of the countries of Western Europe. Ironically enough, his old Sevastopol battery sent congratulations to this man who now loathed war, and from the students of the University of Kazan came greetings to one of its dismal failures as a student but now its most illustrious alumnus. Then there were numerous greetings from factory workers and humble peasants; one of whom wrote simply: "Do not be silent, old man, inspired by God, and live for many years."

Many gifts arrived: quantities of candy from an enterprising manufacturer who placed Tolstoy's picture on the boxes and wrapper; a magnificent album containing original paintings by famous Russian artists; twenty bottles of San Rafael wine, "the best friend of the stomach," from France; a handsome samovar from the waiters of a well-known Petersburg restaurant with a towel on which were embroidered the titles of Tolstoy's stories for the people; and a case of cigarettes from another advertising-minded but dull-witted manufacturer who placed Tolstoy's picture on the package. He promptly sent them back with a letter of warning on the harm of smoking. But one package was saved for Sonya's collection, for all messages and gifts received she gathered up for her collection of Tolstoyana at the Historical Museum.

It seemed as though the whole world had united in honoring this man, not simply as the author of universally

[6] In 1912 a film on the last years of Tolstoy's life was made in Russia, but it was never shown because of the objections of his wife.

loved novels, but as a great moral teacher, the articulate conscience of humanity, the symbol of mankind's ceaseless striving for moral improvement. The thousands of messages clearly indicated that those beliefs closest to his heart, which he had advocated untiringly for almost thirty years—the purifying of religion, nonresistance to evil by force, and the freeing of the soil from private ownership—had found a response in the hearts of people all over the world.

Tolstoy could not help but be affected, even to tears, as he read communication after communication expressing sympathy for his ideas and admiration and love for him. Unlike most great moral teachers, he had received visible evidence before his death that his teaching had won a world audience. He remarked to Goldenweizer: "I believe I am right in saying that I now have no vanity, but I cannot help being touched involuntarily. And yet, at my age, I live so far away from all this, and it is all so unnecessary and so humiliating. Only one thing is necessary, the inner life of the spirit." And on another occasion he said to him: "But one thing is pleasant: in nearly all these letters, congratulations, and addresses, the same thing is repeated—it has simply become a truism—that I have destroyed religious delusions and opened the way for the search after truth. If it is true, it is just what I have wanted and tried to do all my life, and this is very dear to me."

Since it was impossible to answer the tremendous number of messages, Tolstoy sent a letter to the newspapers in which he wrote: "I cordially thank all who congratulated me, and especially those (the majority of those who addressed me) who quite unexpectedly and to my great joy expressed in their messages their complete agreement, not with me, but with those eternal truths that I have tried, as well as I could, to express in my writings. Among these persons, and this was especially gratifying, the greater number were peasants and workers."

The birthday party was restricted to the family, relatives, and close friends. But they made up a large enough gathering. There was much gaiety, with popping of champagne bottles and drinking of toasts. Only the birthday child seemed unhappy, but this was probably because of fatigue and his painful leg, which was propped up as he sat at a separate table. After dinner he was glad to retire to a quiet game of chess. Later he asked Goldenweizer to play, and the musician complied with several pieces, including Chopin, one of Tolstoy's favorite composers. Much moved by the music, Tolstoy left the company. Later Goldenweizer went to his room and found him lying on the bed. He pressed the pianist's hand and thanked him. There were tears in his eyes. Goldenweizer kissed his hand and left. That night, before she retired, Alexandra entered his room.

"Well, Sasha, how is everything?"

She looked hard at him, trying to guess what he was thinking.

"Depressing!" he said.

"What—the fun—the people?"

"Yes—rather the people. It's chiefly that there is so much insincerity and falseness."

Later, however, when Sonya entered, as was her custom, to tuck at his back a warm comforter made by her, he said apropos of the celebration: "How splendid! How fine everything was! If only along with all this there were no grief."

A few weeks after the celebration Tolstoy wrote in his diary: "Only now is there real work, only now, at 80 years of age does life begin. And this is not a joke if one understands that life is measured not by time."

4

Chertkov, having finally cleared up his affairs in England, settled near Yasnaya Polyana in June 1908, for what seemed a permanent stay. Sonya must have regarded this move with foreboding. He bought part of Alexandra's Telyatinki farm and set about building a large house that would accommodate his numerous entourage. Tolstoy viewed the project with misgiving and the considerable expenditure of money with dissatisfaction. Wryly he remarked to his secretary: "Chertkov is building next to me, but my abode will soon be far away."

Chertkov now went into the business of Tolstoyism on a big scale. As heir apparent, he had to have his own little court. He made converts easily out of the local peasantry, for he paid quite well for their services, and few served him on the farm without finding it personally advantageous to adopt the outward aspect of the conventional Tolstoyan, however deficient they were in the spiritual observance of the doctrine. His household soon contained more than thirty people, from farm workers and domestics to typists and secretaries, who were always mysteriously busy with copying Tolstoy's manuscripts and working on the seemingly endless "Vault" of his thoughts, the usefulness of which the master was now beginning to doubt. His family and all these helpers—Chertkov called no one servant—ate together at a long table directly from huge pots, bowls, and frying pans. Tolstoyan equality and brotherhood were the rule, which lacked much, however, in the observance. For Chertkov sat at the head of the table, flanked by his semi-invalid wife and F. A. Strakhov, a devoted follower and "director" under Chertkov of the compilation of the "Vault." The middle section of the table was occupied by the skilled assistants, and the lower end by the common laborers. This social division was defined by the youngsters in the group, said Alexandra, who visited the Chertkovs, as "first, second, and third class." And she once overheard Tishka, a lively boy who watched the horses, exclaim to his companion:—

"Look, look, Alyosha is trying to squeeze into the first class."

"Well, he likes rice cakes and jam and stewed fruit! I guess he's tired of boiled potatoes and sunflower oil."

The wellspring of all wisdom for Chertkov was only two miles from Telyatinki, and he felt the urge to imbibe almost daily, especially since Tolstoy's health at this time prevented him from visiting his friend. He is "virtually living in our house and hardly ever leaves Leo Nikolayevich alone," Sonya complained in her diary. Often he came shepherding a barefoot brigade of novices to meet the master. If Sonya happened to enter the room when her husband was talking to these converts, "he grew silent, looked at me questioningly, so that I, understanding his desire that I should not be present, felt it necessary to leave." Chertkov sometimes brought an English photographer to snap Tolstoy in various aspects for his collection of pictures of the master.

Chertkov read every word from Tolstoy's pen, often suggesting changes with an unctuous insistence that forced compliance. And he followed him around with a notebook in hand, taking down any of his conversation that he thought significant. Visitors to Yasnaya Polyana, who did not evince commendable respect for Tolstoyan principles, would sometimes provoke his displeasure. Gusev tells of the visit of a neighbor, Mme A. E. Zvegintsev, whose company Sonya enjoyed as one of her own social set. Because of the disturbances in the neighborhood at this time, she came well protected by guards and carrying a small revolver, which she deposited on a shelf in the entrance hall. Chertkov, arriving after her, spied the revolver with horror.

"What effrontery to visit Leo Nikolayevich with a revolver!" he exclaimed to Gusev. "Have you a copy of 'Do Not Kill'? Bring it here, please." And he wrapped the pamphlet about the handle of the revolver, and copies of more forbidden literature of Tolstoy were stuck into the pockets of the unsuspecting lady's coat.

"What a limited creature is Chertkov and what a narrow point of view he has in everything!" Sonya wrote in her diary, after she had overheard him warn her husband that his habit of occasionally making the sign of the cross might lead people to think he had returned to the Orthodox faith. "All Chertkov has to do is to take notes, to collect, and to photograph, and that only."

5

With Chertkov as a permanent neighbor virtually living at Yasnaya Polyana, the customary life of the household was altered. The change was extremely distasteful to Sonya. In September she noted in her diary: "I have reached that time of age when two paths stretch out before me: either to elevate myself spiritually and travel the path to self-perfection or to find satisfaction in eating, in rest, in every kind of enjoyment, from music and books to the society of people. I fear the latter path." She knew the path that her husband wished her to follow. On it there were no resting places to satisfy her unfulfilled desire for achievement in art and music. Now even these desires were lessening. "And so all my life," she wrote, "unsatisfied passions and the stern fulfillment of duty. Now the passions grow calm; before me that wall has been lowered, the limit of human life, which checks these life-giving passions, this artistic agitation. . . . Only prayer remains, but even that grows cold before this weary, worldly, material life. Get rid of it, throw it all over. But to whom?"

Yes, to whom? There was no one to take up Sonya's burden. And a petrified sense of duty would not permit her to drop the burden anyway and lead her husband's life of prayer and self-perfecting. But this was all mere speculation. If she could see the tragic flaws in her existence, she lacked the strength to mend them. There was no hope of change. All that was left was to save what she could from the debacle of her life for herself and her family. Self-preservation seemed more logical to her than self-perfection. And her emotional instability, increased by the steady accumulation of adverse circumstances in the struggle, led her from one indiscretion to another.

Duty and necessity had governed Sonya's existence. Now with a mixed feeling of envy and criticism, she commented on her husband: "He always worked according to his own choice and not by necessity. He desired to, and he wrote, he wanted to plow and he plowed. He took it into his head to stitch boots, and he stubbornly stitched them. He planned to teach the children and taught them. He grew bored and threw it up."

With the frequent presence of Chertkov and his novices in the house, Sonya felt as though she were being abandoned. "I am sad at heart and lonely," she wrote in the diary. "No one loves me. It is obvious that I am unworthy." The transition from such a state of mind to resentment and even to quarrelsomeness was natural and inevitable. And as might be expected, there was often not much point in her irritation save to hurt her husband. The charming sister of M. A. Stakhovich was reading poetry to the family group. She read excellently, and about one of her selections, Tyutchev's "Last Love," Tolstoy casually remarked:—

"In it the very lowest feeling is represented as an elevated one."

"There he goes!" Sonya broke in, not raising her head from her sewing. "I always say that he doesn't understand love and never has loved anyone."

A heavy silence followed, and since no one of the company cared to rise to this fighting declaration, Sonya continued to worry the theme:—

"No, really, how have I lived with him for forty-six years if he imagines that love is a low feeling! Love is the best thing in life; if there had been no love, I would long ago have hanged myself from grief."

All this time Tolstoy had been silently turning the pages of Tyutchev, and at the conclusion of his wife's outburst he himself read a poem, "The Decembrists," and remarked that he did not like the first two strophes.

"A low feeling!" Sonya indignantly repeated.

"What is the matter with you?" Tolstoy finally felt obliged to ask.

"I'm referring to your statement that love is a low feeling. Take Chertkov, how does he love and protect his wife? For some time now she has not been his wife. Is that also a low feeling?"

"Really, I said nothing," he quietly replied. "There is nothing bad in it; it is only bad when people exalt it."

When Stakhovich's sister remarked at this point that there was some justice on Sonya's side, the latter triumphantly rapped out:—

"This is a lack in Leo Nikolayevich. However, it's impossible for a man to have everything."

"They have sung the burial service for me here," Tolstoy laughingly admitted, and hurried out of the room in order to halt this embarrassing argument.

These verbal exchanges did not always end so peaceably. There were deeper reasons for quarrels than whether love was a low feeling. Most chronic was the rights to his literary productions, and in 1908, with Chertkov as a constant irritant in the matter, this old cause of strife took a serious turn. During his illness in August, Tolstoy, thinking that he might die, dictated several wishes to Gusev for his diary, among which was the hope that his heirs would make all his writings public property. If this wish were carried out, of course, it would mean that Sonya would have to surrender the rights he had given her to his works written before 1881. That all his productions should become public property had long been one of his fondest desires.

Sonya had no intention of doing anything of the kind. More than ever she jealously guarded her rights to the early works. When a family friend came to Yasnaya Polyana to discuss the possibility of publishing a children's anthology of tales taken from Tolstoy's early works, in honor of his eightieth birthday, Sonya roundly berated him and threatened to go to a lawyer and write to the newspapers. It was as if he stole her silver spoons, she hotly declared. Tolstoy, frowning, listened in silence to her tirade. Sonya actually did write to the newspapers to threaten prosecution for anyone who published without her permission the material in her husband's early books for children. To his mortification Tolstoy received a letter from a friend, in which he regretted that these *Readers*, because of the monopoly of the family, were now priced too high for peasant children. "It is exactly the same," wrote the friend, "as though the heirs of Moses traded in the Bible or the heirs of the Apostles in the New Testament."

Now, with the death of her husband an ever-present possibility, Sonya began to press him for the rights to all his works after he died, or even to those which would remain unpublished. A fresh consideration drove her to hysterical outbursts in this demand. The assiduity with which Chertkov almost daily carried off in his mysterious little bag folders of manuscript or copies increased her old suspicion that he intended to defraud her of publishing rights. She knew he possessed copies of virtually everything her husband had written for years, including such highly salable fiction as *Hadji Murad*, which Tolstoy had refused to print, along with other purely creative pieces, in order to avoid any controversy with his wife. Sonya wondered: Would not Chertkov publish these works after her husband's death and reap the profit for himself? The thought was maddening. Her position, she felt, was unassailable—she wanted only to protect the interest of her children and the increasing number of grandchildren.

The quarrels over this subject between husband and wife during 1908 were frequent and bitter in the extreme. Often all present were drawn in, including Chertkov, who customarily took out his little notebook and jotted down bits of the argument for his diary. He recorded one such quarrel on December 4: "Sofya Andreyevna, turning to Leo Nikolayevich, irately asserts that the property rights of all his written, unpublished works belong to the family. Leo Nikolayevich objects. She runs to her room and fetches a pocket diary written in her hand and reads her own record to the effect that Leo Nikolayevich had given as public property only those writings which had appeared after 1881, but not those which had not appeared in print during his lifetime. Leo Nikolayevich again begins to object. She shouts him down. Finally, in a resolute, authoritative tone, he obliges her to hear him. (She had just said that she was not concerned about herself, but that her children would assert their own claims.) Leo Nikolayevich: 'You imagine that our children are like rogues who want me to do something opposed to that which is most dear to me.' Sofya Andreyevna: 'Well, as for being rogues, I do not know, but . . .' Leo Nikolayevich (firmly): 'No, let me finish speaking. According to you it appears that the children will play the dirtiest trick possible on me. And a dirtier trick it is impossible to play. You know the principles for which I've renounced these rights—the principles of my faith, and what do you wish, that these principles should be turned into hypocrisy? I gave you my fortune, I gave you my earlier writings, it now seems that I ought to give my own life—that for which I live. Yet I daily receive abusive letters, accusing me of hypocrisy. And now you desire that in very fact I should become a hypocrite and a scoundrel. It is astonishing how you torment yourself without any need.' And he left the room, firmly closing the door behind him."

6

Tolstoy closed the door firmly behind him many times in the course of this Jubilee Year. Besides the sore point of the rights to his works, there were the offensive guards with revolvers on their hips whom Sonya still retained in spite of his objections; there were further arrests of peasants for stealing timber; and there were the complaints about the "dark people" and about Chertkov on the score of his visits and persistent photographing and note-taking. Wistfully he wrote in his diary: "How strange and true is the saying that husband and wife (if they live spiritually) are not two, but a single being." And curiously enough now, at the age of eighty, he dwelt upon the memory of his mother, "who has remained for me a holy ideal," a woman who existed only in his imagination, since she had died when he was two years old. The women he really knew were something less than ideal and naked of ideas. Women bear children and not thoughts, he said. And he cynically wrote in his diary: "If men knew all women as husbands know their wives, they would never dispute with them or value their opinions." It is little wonder that he agreed with one of his young disciples that it was a mistake for men, believing as they did, to marry.

Beneath the exciting surface of events at Yasnaya Polyana this year, Tolstoy experienced such intense dissatisfaction with his private life that by July he was almost ready to make a radical change. It was at this time (July 2) that he began his "Secret Diary." For some years now Chertkov had obtained from Tolstoy a reluctant promise that he would have access to his diaries. Masha and later Alexandra had copied out for him passages that might be used for his compilation of Tolstoy's thoughts. These copyings had grown more and more extensive, and now, with Chertkov near by, having direct access to the diary, he made no scruples about copying all the entries. Tolstoy disliked this practice, for it hindered the free flow of his intimate thinking and writing. However, he felt that he could not deny this privilege to his closest friend and disciple. Now, in his anguished state of mind, when he wished to pour out his most heartfelt thoughts for himself alone, he began this Secret Diary which he intended should come under the eye of no one.[7]

The Secret Diary clearly reveals some of the causes of Tolstoy's extreme moral suffering at this time.

"*July 2, 1908.* If I had heard about myself, as about a man who lived in luxury with guards, squeezed what he could from the peasants and put them in prison, professed and preached Christianity while he gave away five-kopek pieces, and in all odious affairs concealed himself behind a dear wife, I would no doubt have called him a scoundrel! But I even need this very thing in order to free myself from personal glory and live for my soul.

"When I ask myself: What must I do? Go away from all of this. Where? To God, to die. I criminally desire death.

"*July 6.* Painfully hard is the test or payment for lust. The reckoning is terribly hard. Chertkov just related a former conversation with her: 'He lives, avails himself of luxury and speaks . . . all pharisaism . . . etc. I, I sacrifice myself.'

"Help me, Lord. I again want to leave. I do not decide. But I do not reject it. The chief thing is: if I go, do I do it for myself? In remaining, I know I do not do it for myself.

"*July 7.* The evening was very painful, I reckoned the money and took thought how to go away. I cannot see her without ill feelings. Today it is better.

"How apparent in her is the whole horror of love of the

[7] It is interesting that in August of this year, when he thought he might die, faithful to the end to Chertkov's desires he sent him the Secret Diary with instructions to copy what he felt would be useful and then to destroy the manuscript. Chertkov copied the entries entirely and destroyed the original manuscript.

body, of self-love conducing to the loss of spiritual obligations.

"*July 9.* I thought of writing her a letter. Thank God there is no unkind feeling. One thing is always more and more distressing: the falsehood of senseless luxury in the midst of the undeserved poverty and want in which I live. It all grows worse and worse, more and more grievous. I cannot forget it or fail to see it.

"All are writing my biography, and in my whole biography there will be nothing about my connection with the 7th commandment. Nor will there be all the terrible filth of masturbation and worse, from my 13th, 14th year to the 15th, 16th (I do not remember when I began my debauchery in the brothels). And so up to my union with the peasant girl Aksinya—she is alive. Then marriage, in which once more, though I never betrayed my wife, there was lust in my relations with her—nasty and criminal lust. There will be none of this and there is none in the biographies of me. And this is very important, and all the more important, since at least of all the vices this is the one of which I am the most conscious, the vice which more than all others compels recovery.

"*July 18.* The bad feeling has ended."

This final entry in the Secret Diary indicates that the crisis which inspired it had passed. His relations with Sonya did improve, but only for a brief time. There was no balm for this disease. "My illness," he told Goldenweizer, "is Sofya Andreyevna." In truth, the knowledge of a domestic feud dividing members of the family had by now become common property among friends, disciples, and hangers-on. Sonya talked of her troubles with anyone who would listen. Tolstoy was now placed in the embarrassing position of receiving letters from followers who offered advice or censure in the matter. And since their remarks usually turned on the very solution—leaving Yasnaya Polyana—which had become an aching moral problem with him, he felt it necessary to explain and justify his failure to take this step.

To the letter of his disciple M. S. Dudchenko, he replied: "I can only say that the reasons restraining me from making the change in my life that you advise, the absence of which is torment for me, are that the reasons obstructing this change flow from that very foundation of love in the name of which this change is desired both by you and me.

It is most likely that I do not know, am not able to, or simply that I possess evil attributes which prevent me from doing what you advise. But what then am I to do? With all the strength of my mind and heart, I cannot take this course."

To the more truculent and critical advice of his follower E. I. Popov, Tolstoy answered: "I attentively read your letter and I entirely agree with you that I have not acted and do not act as I should like to, i.e., according to the ideal of perfection. Nevertheless, with every desire to act according to what seem to be the highest demands, I cannot do this, and not because I desire tasty food, a soft bed, a saddle horse, and other things; I cannot cause grief and unhappiness or provoke exasperation and evil in a woman who in her own mind fulfills everything that falls to her lot as a wife, and as a consequence of her union with me fulfills entirely and well her obligations according to her own ideal. . . . You have told me directly what you think of me, and I am sincerely thankful to you, though I cannot, however I may wish to, profit from your guidance, because I have been a sinner and am a sinner, and if I wish to lessen my sins, I shall try to lessen them in my present existence, for I can on no account change my situation without committing new sins now."

Before the world Tolstoy would have it that his wife was more sinned against than sinning. All that mattered was the life of the spirit, and he had not yet fathomed its human limits.

XXXIX

Conspiracy

THE PUBLIC PROTEST evoked by *I Cannot Be Silent* had no effect on the government's harsh policy toward those who opposed its power. And Tolstoy's followers and those who published or distributed his banned works continued to suffer and be humiliated, for such persecutions mounted during 1909. The police, on directions from above, were obviously conducting a planned campaign against the spread of his influence. His letter to a judge trying the case of one of these publishers demanded that he be allowed to take the place of the accused, because the writings in question had been published at his request. The judge simply ruled that the petition be ignored, since Tolstoy lived in another legal district. In general, his protesting letters to the authorities were now left unanswered, and those to the victims offered the wholly sincere but cold comfort that he would like nothing better than to serve their term in prison. In connection with an article that he had recently finished, "The Death Penalty and Christianity," he noted in his diary: "Today I wrote just a small addition to the article . . . about the Tsar, with the secret purpose of provoking persecution of myself." The addition is a bitter denunciation of the Tsar as the chief accomplice in all these executions. But Nicholas II, like his father, had no intention of drawing down upon himself the indignation of the world by making a martyr of Leo Tolstoy. If His Majesty wished to manifest his displeasure in this matter, there were plenty of Tolstoyans to martyrize.

The Church, emboldened by the government's crusade against Tolstoy, intensified its own criticism of him. Though still an uncompromising opponent of the Church, he had long since ceased to think of religion in the narrow terms of Christian Orthodoxy, a fact that the ecclesiastics did not fully understand. Years of study of religious thinkers had convinced him that the simple truths of his faith had guided all the great religions of the world. He merely believed that Christ had best formulated and expressed these universal truths. "Each of us," he now declared, "must find in his faith that which is common to all faiths, and while rejecting what is exceptional in his own, support what is common to all." This position inspired deep respect even among those members of the Church who, like his sister Marya, a nun, sincerely believed without demanding that others believe as she did. He saw in all Russians an instinct for religious faith, which had vanished in the West, he said, because of the influence of Catholicism, an opinion that he shared with Dostoyevsky. Even Russian socialism, he admitted, advocated the economic side of Christianity.

"Ah, Mashenka," he half jokingly exclaimed to his sister one day, "how I regret not being a member of the Orthodox Church!"

"But, why?" she asked in amazement.

"Because I could now go off to some monastery or other. How fine for the Buddhist when he grows old—he goes off to the desert."

"And what about the family?" Sonya broke in.

"Well, at such an age all obligations end."

In January, Parfeni, Bishop of Tula, visited Tolstoy. It was hardly a social call at a time when the clergy was attacking him as an atheist in the ecclesiastical press. He treated the bishop with kind caution. Brushing aside the charge that he corrupted people's faith, he went on to tell the clergyman that he inspired faith even in those who had none. And at the end of the visit he presented the bishop with an autographed copy of the *Circle of Reading*. When a notice of this meeting mysteriously appeared in the newspapers, Tolstoy, fearing some sort of ecclesiastical snare, hastened to grant an interview to a correspondent, in which he gave a full account of all that was said in their conversation, and this was published. His kindly feeling over the bishop's seeking him out turned into one of annoyance when he learned of the clergyman's talk with his wife. He wrote in his diary: "It was especially disagreeable that he asked Sonya to let him know when I die. It is as though they were planning something to convince people that I 'repented' before death. Therefore I declare that . . . anything they may say about my repentance and communion before death is a lie. . . . I repeat on this occasion also that I ask to be buried without divine services, and that my body be laid in the earth so that it won't stink."

At the beginning of March the police struck their hardest blow—Chertkov was given three days to clear out of the province of Tula. The vague charge of "pernicious activities" was lodged against him; it was also rumored that a neighboring landowner had complained to the authorities of his proselyting among the peasants of the district and of his urging them not to pay taxes. Any reason would have been sufficient for the police if they had decided that it was desirable to prevent the chief disciple from being so accessible to the master. It is perhaps significant that at about the same time the police raided the house of Biryukov, another of the principal followers of Tolstoy. Protests over the removal of Chertkov were made. Even Sonya, despite her dislike for this man, wrote a letter to the press. His mother, with influential contacts at Court, brought the case right up to the Tsar, but the only favor she received for her son was a short delay until his health—he was ailing at the time—should enable him to travel. So great was Tolstoy's indignation that he actually refused to shake hands with the officer who came to arrange for Chertkov's departure, for him an unforgivable act of impoliteness that made him groan at night when he woke up and recalled it. Chertkov and his numerous menage moved to Kryokshino, the estate of his relatives, the Pashkovs, situated in the Moscow district.

2

Among the visitors at Yasnaya Polyana that summer the most eminent was the Russian scientist I. I. Mechnikov, at that time Director of the Pasteur Institute at Paris. He had written a rather friendly article on Tolstoy, who in turn had been severely critical of several of Mechnikov's scientific-philosophical works, Since Tolstoy's opposition to science was widely known, though generally misunderstood, the press and photographers were on hand for this meeting of mighty opposites. But the anticipated verbal battle did not take place. Mechnikov turned out to be a kind, amiable man who preferred to talk—and he talked well—about literature and music. His scientific "prejudices" were revealed only in the dismay he evinced over the family's eating uncooked vegetables and drinking unboiled water. Smilingly Tolstoy expressed the hope that God would allow this cautious pundit to live to be a hundred, and Mechnikov, no doubt placing his faith in science rather than God, solemnly volunteered that he might even live longer. Evidently science failed him since he died at seventy-one.

Dissatisfied with his failure to draw Mechnikov out in company on spiritual questions, Tolstoy took him for a drive. The conversation did not begin auspiciously, for Tolstoy complained of those people who charged him with being hostile to science. "I highly value true science, that which interests itself in man, in his happiness and fate, but I'm an enemy of that false science which imagines that it has done something unusually important and useful when it has determined the weight of Saturn's satellites or something of this sort. True science is entirely in harmony with true religion." The discussion got nowhere. "I made an effort," Tolstoy told Goldenweizer later, "but he became silent. He believes in his own science as in some holy scriptures, but religious and moral questions resulting from a simply moral feeling are entirely alien to him." Mechnikov, the scientist, who liked to dabble in literature, valued Tolstoy more as a writer of great fiction than as a moral and religious thinker. Coming as it did from a man of learning, it was the kind of evaluation that now particularly disgusted Tolstoy. It was as though someone said to Edison, he remarked of a similar admirer of *War and Peace* and *Anna Karenina:* "I deeply esteem you because you dance the mazurka so well." The trouble with these scientists, he complained, was their preoccupation with the nonessentials of life. "You wouldn't believe me," he announced to some guests, "but I became interested and looked it up in the encyclopedia. How many different kinds of flies do you think the scientists have already accounted for? Seven thousand! How can they find any time for spiritual problems!"

Mechnikov's visit helped to inspire the substance of an epistolary article, "On Science," in answer to the request of a peasant youth on whether or not science was harmful. Modern science, Tolstoy defined as "knowledge of *every-*

thing, of everything in the world, except that one thing which every man must know in order to live a good life." Hence modern science, he declared, was false science, for whatever its benefits to the few, it increased rather than lessened the human misery of the many. However much science had improved the material lot of mankind, he maintained, it had impoverished it spiritually. There is only one true science, he wrote: *"the knowledge of what every man must do in order that he may live out as well as possible in this world the brief span of life which has been allotted to him by God, fate, or the laws of nature. . . ."*

A less distinguished but perhaps a more welcome visitor that summer was the son of Henry George, who made his way from America to Yasnaya Polyana, the unrealized "sacred dream" of his father. Tolstoy eagerly received him and exploited the occasion to give an interviewing reporter a brief article on Henry George's solution of the land question. His convictions on this score had somewhat weakened, but in the article he used George's single tax as a club to beat the Stolypin land reforms that he utterly detested. In fact, that very year he had, with no success, urged several members of the Duma, friends of his, to raise the question of adopting Henry George's solution.

When his guest was leaving, Tolstoy said, with an attitude of complacency about his death that had now become habitual:—

"We shall not see each other again. What message do you give me for your father in the other world?"

"Tell him that I am continuing his work," replied the son.

Tolstoy could not restrain his tears at these words.

Early in June he set out to visit his daughter Tanya at Kochety, her husband's estate. He undertook this tiring trip of almost a hundred miles partly because with the coming of summer the domestic atmosphere at Yasnaya Polyana had again grown troubled. He went to escape this and to see Chertkov. For Kochety was on the edge of Tula Province, and by renting a hut just inside the boundary of the neighboring Orlov Province, he was able to have two of those "joyous meetings" with his devoted disciple without breaking the law.

Tolstoy prolonged his stay at Kochety, much to Sonya's annoyance. She had accompanied him on his journey but returned alone, and now the big house seemed dismal and empty without him. All the glory and excitement had vanished. With this grim foretaste of what his death or going away would mean to her, she sadly wrote him: "Dear Lyovochka, we live without you at Yasnaya Polyana like a body without a soul." She now missed the many "tiresome" visitors, told him of her loneliness, and complained of burdensome household tasks, of Andrei's demands for money to pay his debts, and of Leo's angrily smashing to bits a bust of his father, who had not hurried back to pose for him—his artistic urges had led him from writing to sculpturing—and of his going off in a huff to Sweden, bemoaning his fate as the son of a great man. "I repeat my advice," Tolstoy coldly comforted her in his reply, "not to attach importance to household tasks, but rather to that about which you correctly write: to do good. This and this only is necessary."

Tolstoy remained almost a month at Kochety. The change seemed to improve his health, but the conditions of life that he observed in the district, the peasants and workers he talked to, and the contrasting comfortable existence of his son-in-law's family depressed him spiritually. He wrote in his diary at this time: "The principal thing is the painful feeling of poverty—not poverty but the debasement, the oppression of the masses. The crulty and insanity of the revolutionists are pardonable. Then after dinner . . . talking French, and tennis, and along with all this slaves, hungry, naked, and oppressed by drudgery. I cannot endure it and want to run away."

3

With Tolstoy's return, life began again at Yasnaya Polyana—and so did the family bickering. The unpleasant feeling over the police guards, of whom two still remained, broke out in an open quarrel. One of them had caught a peasant fishing on the family side of the pond. Alexandra came upon them in the office just as the guard was cursing the apprehended peasant and seemed on the point of striking him. Calling him a "villain," she demanded that he release the peasant at once. The guard informed his superior that he had been insulted in the performance of his duty, and a complaint was prepared against Tolstoy's daughter. Her mother supported the guard, criticized Alexandra's behavior, and wished to have the peasant arrested. When the district police officer appeared at the house with his complaint, Alexandra shouted at her mother: "If they had behaved so with my daughter, I would have put the officer out of the house! I'll pack my things at once and leave!" To all of which Sonya replied: "And good riddance!"

The next day Alexandra saw the Vice-Governor at Tula to make her own complaint about the guards, whose presence on the estate she knew deeply offended her father. To her demand that they be removed, he sardonically answered that since the disturbances growing out of the revolution Yasnaya Polyana was the only estate at which guards were still stationed; that he had wished to remove them but her mother had requested that they remain, and he cheerfully showed her the Countess's letter. Upset by this startling news in the face of her father's repeated requests that the guards be withdrawn, Alexandra returned to have another unpleasant talk with her mother. The guards were soon removed. Sonya expressed her fears that thefts on the estate would be renewed and hired a mounted Circassian to protect the property.

Whenever it was possible, Tolstoy kept out of such quarrels and brooded in silence. With misgivings he had noticed his wife's growing nervousness this year and her hypercritical attitude to much that went on in the house. While copying the manuscript of a story that he had just begun, all the ancient jealousy of her husband flared up in this woman of sixty-five as she read the description of one of the peasant characters. She at once wrote in her diary: "His delight in the *strong* body of a woman with the tanned legs of a girl that once so powerfully tempted him; it is that same *Aksinya* with the shining eyes who now quite unconsciously, in his eightieth year, emerges from the depths of his memories and sensations of former years. Aksinya was a Yasnaya Polyana wench, the last lover of Leo Nikolayevich before his marriage, and now still living in the village. All this invokes in me a painful feeling."

In one respect Sonya may have been correct, for during this year Tolstoy wrote a new ending for the tale, *The Devil,* which he had kept concealed from Sonya for years, no doubt because its autobiographical subject would have aroused her jealousy. The theme concerns his passion for this same village wench, Aksinya, and perhaps her image, becoming bright and fresh in his mind again from working over a long forgotten tale, inspired the features of the new heroine of the unfinished story that Sonya copied. These forbidden but pleasurable "memories and sensations of former years" may well have provided the old man with fleeting moments of escape from a gloomy domestic situation.

This situation became still gloomier shortly after Tolstoy's return from Kochety at the beginning of July. He received an invitation to participate in the Eighteenth International Congress of Peace at Stockholm in August. Though he had always declined such offers in the past, he now felt it his duty to accept this opportunity to present his views on peace at a world forum. And with a feeling of elation he eagerly set to work on his speech.

It appears that the organizers of the Congress were more surprised than pleased by Tolstoy's acceptance. They had hardly expected a feeble old man of eighty to come all the way to Stockholm, for it seems that they desired his name and moral support more than his physical presence and spoken views, with which they were already too familiar. And their surprise turned into embarrassment when the news leaked to the press that he planned to attend and challenge the Congress to be honest for once and demand the abolition of all armies as the only sincere and effective means of achieving world peace. The news created a sensation in Russia and Europe. Mixed feelings of alarm and joy stirred interested groups in Stockholm. Elaborate preparations got under way to welcome the great Russian writer, and there were various rumors that he would receive the Nobel Peace Award. However, concern and even fear gripped officials of the Congress that Tolstoy's presence and speech might affect the customarily smooth-running sessions.

Meanwhile, Tolstoy's decision had caused almost as much agitation in his family as in Stockholm. When he first told Sonya of his intention, she at once strenuously opposed the trip and raised all sorts of objections, such as his extreme age, the dangers of a sea voyage, and the cholera in Petersburg through which he must travel. When he remained adamant she became hysterical, locked herself in her room, would admit no one, and threatened to poison herself.

Scenes such as this became daily occurrences. Tolstoy found it impossible to talk with Sonya about the proposed trip. On July 26 he wrote: "After dinner I discussed the journey to Sweden, and it provoked terrible hysterical exasperation. She wanted to poison herself with morphine; I snatched it out of her hand and threw it under the stairs. I struggled with myself. But when I lay down and quietly thought it all over, I decided to give up the trip. I went and told her. She was a sorry sight and I sincerely pitied her."

The reasons for Sonya's intense objections were no doubt mixed in her mind. With some justification, and particularly after the scenes she had caused, she may well have believed that he would use this opportunity to stay away for good. Though she was perhaps quite sincere in her worry over his health on such a long journey, she promptly forgot all these objections, for she finally agreed to the trip if he would allow her to accompany him. A few days after he had informed her that he would not go, he entered in his diary: "S. A. [Sonya] came in and declared that she would make the trip, but 'all this will unquestionably end in the death of one or the other of us and in innumerable difficulties.' Under such conditions I would not think of going." Three days later he wrote: "S. A. is preparing herself for Stockholm, and as soon as she speaks about it, she falls into despair. She pays no attention at all to my proposal not to go. There is one salvation: to live in the present, and silence."

At one point Sonya seemed determined to go, even without her husband if necessary, and she actually offered to read his address at the session. He ironically remarked that at least they would not reply to her in an unmannerly fashion, "for to whom would they be more polite than to her, the wife?" Sonya said that "for this one occasion one must be well dressed." And that very night she sent a friend to Moscow to buy new clothes for the journey.

How this family tragicomedy would have ended it is hard to say; the last act was avoided by the news that a workers' strike in Sweden had caused the Congress to be postponed until the next year. Some newspapers flatly declared that the real reason was the fear that Tolstoy would actually appear and give his address, a reason that he himself was inclined to accept. A Berlin concert entrepreneur offered to arrange for ten readings of his speech at five thousand francs a reading, the proceeds to go to charity. Tolstoy, still anxious to get his views on peace before the public through the spoken word, agreed provided he could nominate the reader. The German police, however, intervened and refused to allow the readings to take place unless the speech was heavily censored, Tolstoy would not permit this and there the matter ended.

The trip to Stockholm was only a contributing factor tc the wretched relations between husband and wife during this summer. The real cause was the old one of the rights to Tolstoy's works. Sonya, angered over the publication of an anthology that included certain of her husband's early writings, threatened to sue the publisher who hac not bothered to ask her permission or to pay her for the pieces. The prospect of a suit on such a matter agitatec Tolstoy. "Last night," he wrote in his diary, "was distressing because of a conversation with Sofya Andreyevna over the printing and prosecution. If she only knew anc understood how she alone was poisoning the last hours days, months of my life!" And he even talked over witl Alexandra and Makovitski the possibility of depriving hi wife of the power of attorney he had given her years ag if she brought suit against the publisher.

In this situation Sonya, taking advantage of the visit o a relative and a judge, I. V. Denisenko, showed him he power of attorney over her husband's estate, issued in 188 and asked whether this document would permit her to sel Tolstoy's works without his consent and to prosecute thos who infringed upon her rights in this respect. Knowin full well Tolstoy's feelings in the matter, Denisenko wa shocked and gave Sonya a negative answer. He eve pointed out that her power of attorney did not actuall give her legal title to the works published before 188 as she had always believed and as the public in general ha taken for granted. Frantic at the thought that she woul have no control over his writings after his death, sh appealed to Tolstoy to grant her this right, or at least t give her power of attorney to prosecute people who pul lished his works without permission. He resolutely refuse She again threatened to kill herself and had a fit of hysteric

This quarrel, aggravated by their violent differences ov the trip to Stockholm, so frayed Tolstoy's nerves that h could not eat, sleep, or work. He wrote in his diary c July 21: "I'm tired and cannot stand it any more. I fe quite ill. I feel the impossibility of facing it all reasonab and lovingly, the complete impossibility. For the time beir

I wish only to get far away and take no part in anything. I can do nothing else, and I have already seriously thought of running away. Well, now show your Christianity. *C'est le moment ou jamais.* And yet I wish so much to go away. My presence here is hardly necessary to anyone in anything. A hard sacrifice and harmful to all. Help me, God, teach me. One thing I want—to do Thy will and not mine."

He even went so far as to confide this desire to leave Yasnaya Polyana to his faithful followers, Marya Schmidt and Makovitski. Could he go abroad without a passport, he asked the much traveled Makovitski. "You know how one can get across the border. I want remoteness, to get far away from worldly vanity as the old Buddhists do. I tell this only to you."

One thing Tolstoy decided in the course of these quarrels—to make his works public property after his death by drawing up a legal will. Whether this crucial idea was first proposed to him by one of his friends or disciples will never be known for certainty, though it appears likely. For as early as June 23 of this year he wrote to Chertkov, who had apparently already broached the idea, that it was repugnant to him, and that he would rather send all his writings to the devil if it would prevent any hard feelings. But shortly after this he appears to have come to the conclusion, because of the many discussions and quarrels on the subject, that he could not fully trust his heirs to carry out his wishes concerning the disposal of his literary property. Ordinarily he would have instinctively rebelled at calling to his aid the law, an arm of the government. But he had compromised with the government before on issues that seemed to make for the greater good of the greater number, and insuring that his works would become public property after his death would appear to be such an issue. He would use the law not to protect private property but to safeguard his works as public property. At any rate on July 22 he approached the same Denisenko, whom Sonya had shocked by her legal queries, with the request to draw up a will, in which he would deed the rights to his works to the public and his land to the peasants, forgetting for the moment that he long ago had given the land to his family. This will was not executed, but a train of events had been set in motion that was to torment the last few months of his life.

The sorrows of this unhappy summer, however, had not yet ended. Now it was the government that on August 5 once again struck at Tolstoy. The family had just finished dinner. He and Goldenweizer had begun a game of chess. The bell rang. It was the local police who had received an order to arrest Gusev. The secretary was given only a few minutes to collect his belongings. Stunned members of the family went downstairs to say farewell to this man who had endeared himself to all of them. Tolstoy's sister Marya, who was visiting them, could not restrain her indignation which she expressed in good Russian fashion by spitting after the police as they carried off their prisoner. Tolstoy was silent and pale, and tears stood in his eyes.

Gusev had been arrested for distributing "revolutionary books," which could mean nothing other than Tolstoy's works. And since his arrest was by administrative order, he received no trial and was condemned to banishment for two years to the distant province of Perm. Tolstoy at once sent to the newspapers a flaming denunciation of this action, again claiming that he was the guilty one, and he even tried to persuade a member of the Duma to raise the matter there as an indefensible act of the government. But the government had no favors to offer Leo Tolstoy. He had lost a most valuable and devoted assistant who never saw him in life again.

4

At the height of the family strife that summer over the copyrights of Tolstoy's works, Alexandra had written his sister-in-law, Olga Tolstoy,[1] on July 24 that she hoped to visit Chertkov at Kryokshino to discuss her father's will. Tolstoy had come to the conclusion, though still with some misgivings, that a will should be legally drawn up, and his inner circle of followers were also urging it. And it is clear that their intention, for the time being at least, was to keep the matter a secret from Sonya.

It was partly with this purpose in mind that Tolstoy set out to visit Chertkov at Kryokshino on September 3. With him went Alexandra, Dr. Makovitski, and a family servant. Tolstoy, in excellent spirits, was as excited as a child over the trip, which would take him to Moscow for the first time in eight years. Persistent movie photographers pestered him at the station, and so did numerous people on the train who recognized him.

[1] The divorced wife of Andrei and sister of Chertkov's wife.

At the Moscow terminal Chertkov and a delegation from the *Intermediary* welcomed him. A murmur of "Tolstoy!" ran from person to person on the platform, and only with difficulty did the carriage make its way through the crowd shouting greetings to him. That night he stayed at the family's old Moscow house. The next morning, at Goldenweizer's suggestion, he went to Zimmerman's music store to see the latest in mechanical inventions—a player piano! On the way, the swarming streets and city din filled him with horror and confirmed his disgust for modern civilization.

At Zimmerman's the enterprising manager, who had been forewarned of the visit of the great writer and his party, was prepared with a bouquet of flowers for Alexandra and a photographer to immortalize the occasion. Tolstoy listened intently to the player piano and was delighted with the pieces rendered by Paderewski. The flattered manager ordered a mechanical piano to be sent to Kryokshino for as long as Tolstoy remained there.

On the way to the station Chertkov suggested that they inspect the recent monument of Gogol, whose hundredth anniversary was being celebrated. With certain reservations, Tolstoy admired Gogol, and in March of this year, at the request of a magazine editor, he had written a brief article on him. He also found something to admire in the statue, which was then the object of much criticism, but he remarked: "In general, I don't like monuments. It is something very difficult to do. The artist has to convey the man's soul, yet he must also model his behind." At the station, the party boarded a third-class carriage and was soon at Kryokshino, only some twenty miles distant.

A marked English influence was apparent in the attractive house and landscaping of the park with its pond at Kryokshino. Here the Chertkovs lived in the "Tolstoyan" fashion that had prevailed in their establishment at Telyatinki. A host of assistants, laborers, and servants dined with the family, a custom that much embarrassed the old Tolstoy retainer who kept leaping to his feet every time any of the gentlefolk came near his chair.

In this atmosphere, saturated with his own moral and religious influence, the low spirits that had depressed Tolstoy during recent months vanished. He was surrounded by loyal followers who accepted his every word as law and reverenced him as a living saint among sinning mankind.

Visitors from near-by Moscow, who had learned of his presence there, were endless. He sometimes avoided them in long solitary walks through the countryside, though usually followed at a respectful distance by the devoted and devious Chertkov. During the evenings, there were concerts of live music by artists from Moscow or of the canned variety by Zimmerman's player piano, which had not yet lost its novelty for Tolstoy.

One day about forty schoolteachers arrived. In preparation for this visit Tolstoy had written a brief article[2] on the problems of the teacher, and after it was read he conducted a kind of seminar for the group. From his article and a complete transcript of the discussion that followed, one gathers that these village teachers were baffled by his extreme simplification of their problems. To his advice that they should ignore the required subjects if necessary in order to place all emphasis on moral problems and clean living, they objected that the authorities would not permit this. His only answer was to disobey the authorities and be willing to suffer for their moral convictions. Tolstoy's deference to Chertkov's occasional interruptions and explanations during the discussion left no doubt in the minds of his listeners that he regarded this chief disciple as the authoritative interpreter of his doctrine.

When Tolstoy had been at Kryokshino about ten days, Sonya arrived, having been delayed by an ailing leg. Her nervous presence introduced an alien element into the harmonious Tolstoyan atmosphere. Though everything was done to mollify her, an unpleasant scene took place. She insisted that they go home on the eighteenth and stay overnight in Moscow. Tolstoy wished to remain until the nineteenth and return directly to Yasnaya Polyana in order to avoid any possible demonstration that his appearance in the city might cause. A fit of hysteria on Sonya's part decided the matter.

Before he left, however, Tolstoy planned to finish up the business of the will, which he had discussed with Chertkov. He drafted the contents himself and a clean copy was made by Alexandra. In it he stated that all his published or unpublished works, written after January 1, 1881, and all

[2] This article, "The Chief Problem of the Teacher," was subsequently published. During 1909 he also wrote "On Education" and published two other longer articles: "The Inevitable Revolution," and "The Sole Commandment."

unpublished works written before that date, "constitute, after my death, no person's private property, but to be freely publishable and republishable by all who may desire so to use them." He further requested that all his manuscripts and documents extant at the time of his death be handed over to Chertkov, "to the end that, after my decease, he may dispose of them as heretofore, and that they may be freely accessible to all who may desire to make use of them for publication." And he finally requested Chertkov to select a person or persons who, in the event of his own death, would carry out Tolstoy's behests.

The principal differences between this will and the informal one that he had drawn up in his diary in 1895, the substance of which he had repeated in various forms in his diary later, are striking. In the first will, apart from directions about his burial and the publication of his diary, he merely requested his heirs, though he did not bind them to it, to surrender to the community their property rights in his works published before 1881. He said nothing about his works written or published after 1881, apparently taking it for granted, since he had publicly renounced his rights to these, that his heirs would respect this fact. Now, in the second will, which he intended should be legal, he tacitly agreed that Sonya should retain the copyrights he had granted her on his works published before 1881, but he legally bequeathed to the public all those written after that date. Further, in the first will, he had named as literary executors his wife, Chertkov, and his old friend Strakhov, who had since died; in the second will Sonya is pointedly dropped in favor of Chertkov.

On the day of departure from Kryokshino, Tolstoy and the witnesses gathered in a small room. He was agitated, partly perhaps from a fear that Sonya would enter and surprise them at his business. He read over the text of the will, signed it, and so did three witnesses, friends and followers—A. B. Goldenweizer, A. V. Kalachev, and A. P. Sergeyenko. Tolstoy believed that he had executed a legal document.

The time had come for leaving. At the little station a small crowd had gathered and several movie photographers. Sonya asked her husband to walk up and down the platform so that they might be photographed together, and he complied unwillingly. A larger crowd and more photographers awaited them on their arrival at Moscow. At home the telephone rang continually and utter strangers kept inquiring about Tolstoy, for this time the news had spread all over the city that he was there. In fact, the newspapers announced the time of departure of the party on the morrow. Old Moscow friends crowded the house. Tolstoy grew excited, talked brilliantly with some, joked with others. A. N. Dunayev tried to interest him in a new German booklet on Christ.

"You see, my dear Alexander Nikoforovich," Tolstoy countered, "I'm a bit afraid of these little books. Yesterday, for example, I went for a moment to the water closet. I pulled the chain but I really didn't pull it hard enough and the water kept running. Then I suspected that I had not pulled it far enough and when I did the water stopped. That's the way it is with these questions: you've either got to tell nothing at all or tell the whole truth."

That evening Tolstoy, feeling particularly gay, wanted to go to the theater. Someone lightly suggested the ballet and added how surprised people would be to see him there. Why not go, he said, recalling some former male ballet acquaintances whom he had admired. But the ballet was not performing and the party went to a motion picture instead. The audience recognized him at once, twisted in their seats, and craned their necks. The picture was a stupid melodrama, and the monotonous music from a piano out of tune shredded his nerves. At the end of the first part he walked out, expressing his disgust at the prostitution of this new art and his wonderment that the public could enjoy such tripe.

The next morning, the day of departure, crowds began to gather outside the house, among them the ubiquitous motion-picture photographers. Tolstoy with Sonya, Alexandra, and Chertkov left in a carriage. People in the crowd bared their heads. Tolstoy kept bowing. One old woman ran up and begged for a word with him. The photographers in another carriage dashed ahead, grinding away on their mounted camera.

At the station a crowd had long since assembled and kept growing by the minute. All classes of the city's population were represented. As the carriage approached, the cry went up: "He's coming! He's coming!" Several hundred dashed forward and surrounded the carriage. All hats came off and a loud "Hurrah!" roared from thousands of voices of people who had jammed the square and station. Tolstoy took his hat off and bowed.

In making its way to the train the little party was in danger of being crushed by the press of people until someone shouted to form a chain by linking hands, and through this human corridor the group were able to proceed to the train. Tolstoy appeared at the window of his compartment as the throng seethed in front of it. Voices called for a speech and a hush at once fell over the multitude.

"I never expected such joy, such a manifestation of sympathy from all sides," he said in a halting voice from the open window. "Thanks. . . ." And tears prevented him from continuing.

"Thanks to you!" the crowd roared.

The third bell rang, and the train began slowly to move out. The throng moved with it.

"Thanks, friend, thanks!" Tolstoy said as the train gathered speed.

"Live to a hundred! Keep on helping us! Till we meet again!" hundreds of voices shouted.

"Till we meet again, if God grants it," were his last words which were answered by a final roaring "Hurrah!"

5

The Moscow triumph almost proved fatal, for the excitement and strain on Tolstoy's feeble strength had been too much for him. Soon after the train pulled out he slipped into unconsciousness. They thought he was dying. When they got him home Dr. Makovitski and Alexandra worked frantically to bring him to, while Sonya hovered over him, begging him to tell her where the keys to his drawer were for she feared he would die and the manuscripts would be stolen.

With his still remarkable recuperative powers, however, Tolstoy quickly recovered and again plunged into his literary labors, beginning several articles and a short story. Toward the end of September he wrote Chertkov: "A letter from a Transvaal Hindu moved me." The unknown correspondent was none other than M. K. Gandhi. He had been deeply impressed and influenced by Tolstoy's writings, especially *The Kingdom of God Is Within You,* and, in a subsequent letter to Tolstoy, he called himself "a humble follower of yours." His civil-disobedience campaign and passive-resistance doctrine owe much to Tolstoy, though the master would no doubt have disapproved of Gandhi's later political activities and dealings with the British government.

Tolstoy had long been interested in Indian philosophy and the lot of that country under English rule. In 1908 he had written an epistolary article, "A letter to a Hindu," addressed to Tarakuatta Das, in which he opposed Das's policy of violent resistance to aggression that had resulted, he said, in the extraordinary paradox of the enslavement of hundreds of millions of Indians by a handful of English. If the people of India are enslaved by violence, he wrote, it is only because they themselves live and have lived by violence and do not recognize the eternal law inherent in humanity.

This article was widely publicized and attracted Gandhi, who understood correctly its implicit message of civil disobedience and passive resistance. And when he first wrote Tolstoy, it was to inform him of the passive-resistance campaign that he was leading among the Hindus in the Transvaal, aimed against the discriminatory laws of the British. Tolstoy hastened to reply that the letter gave him great joy, and he encouraged Gandhi's activities. Several more letters were exchanged. Gandhi sent him his book, *Indian Home Rule,* which Tolstoy read and warmly praised. "This book is interesting in the highest degree," he told Makovitski. "It is a profound condemnation, from the point of view of a religious Hindu, of all European civilization." Obviously Tolstoy regarded Gandhi as one of his followers, and after his death Gandhi often referred to him as the "Russian titan" and "the highest moral authority."

The tense feeling in the household, however, was not conducive to the peace of mind Tolstoy required for his literary work. If anything, since his return from Kryokshino, the domestic situation had deteriorated. Sonya's nervous habits increased, her criticism of her husband and his disciples grew more bitter. Taking a visiting journalist, G. K. Gradovski, aside, she read her diary to him and poured out complaints about her life while he busily took notes. When her sons Andrei, Mikhail, and Leo visited, she tried to rally them to her side, to urge them to protect their inheritance, and they listened sympathetically. On October 21 Tolstoy noted in his diary: "I have just talked with Sasha. She told me of the avarice of the children,[3] and of their calculation of

[3] Here Tolstoy has in mind the younger sons, for Sergei, Ilya, and his daughters were inclined to respect his wishes in the matter of their inheritance.

the sums from my writings that will come to them after my death, that is, they are counting upon my death. How sorry I am for them. During my life I have given them all my substance so that they should not be tempted to desire my death, and yet my death is wished for by them."

Now this question of inheritance rose once again to plague him. Before Alexandra left Moscow, on the return from Kryokshino, she had taken the precaution to submit the will drawn up at Chertkov's estate to a lawyer, N. K. Muravyov, to determine its legality. After examining the document, he decided that it would not be accepted by the courts for various reasons, but principally because, according to Russian law, you could not leave property to "no one"; it had to be left to some definite legal person who would dispose of it as Tolstoy wished. Subsequently several consultations were held in his office by Chertkov, his close friend and assistant, F. A. Strakhov, and Goldenweizer, and several drafts of a model will were drawn up by the lawyer to be submitted to Tolstoy. He was to be asked to select one or reject them all if they did not meet with his approval.

Strakhov arrived at Yasnaya Polyana on October 26 when, according to information he had received, he believed that Tolstoy's wife would be in Moscow. By chance, she was returning home on the same train that brought him there. He managed to fulfill his commission, however, without revealing to Sonya the purpose of his visit. Alone with Tolstoy, he explained in detail the legal objections to the previous will and presented the drafts of the model text.

Tolstoy read over the drafts, selected one, and wrote at the bottom that he agreed with this form. But after thinking a little, he said: "The whole affair is very painful to me. And it is all unnecessary—to secure the spread of my ideas by such measures. Now Christ—although it is strange that I should compare myself with him—did not trouble about anyone appropriating his ideas as his personal property, nor did he record his ideas in writing, but expressed them courageously and went on the cross for them. His ideas have not been lost. Indeed, no word can be completely lost, if it expresses the truth and if the person uttering it profoundly believes in its truth. But all these external measures for security come only from our non-belief in what we are uttering." And with this statement he left the room.

Strakhov was in a quandary. He felt that Tolstoy now

wished to drop the whole matter of a will. Before he reported to Chertkov that his mission had been unsuccessful, he decided as a last resort to present fully the views of the little group of friends on this subject. When he could get Tolstoy alone again, he brought up his previous statement. You mentioned Christ, he argued with him. He did not have to trouble about the dissemination of his ideas because he did not write and received no payment for his ideas. But you write, he continued, and now your family receives payment for your works. And if you do not secure the public use of your writings, you will be indirectly furthering the rights of private property in them on the part of your family. It has been painful to your friends, said Strakhov, to hear you blamed because you transferred your estate to your wife, in spite of your denial of private property. Now it will be even more painful to them to hear people say that in spite of his knowledge that the public repudiation of his copyright had no legal validity, Tolstoy took no steps to ensure that his wish would be carried out, and thus assisted the transference of his literary property to his family.

Tolstoy admitted the strength of Strakhov's arguments and asked for some time to think the matter over. After several hours he called Strakhov and Alexandra into his study and said to them: "I shall surprise you by my final decision. . . . I want, Sasha, to leave everything to you, understand, everything, not even excepting what I reserved in the declaration in the newspapers." Did this mean that his wife would have to forfeit the income from those works which she had been accustomed to regard as her own, the astonished Strakhov asked. Tolstoy hastily added: "All this Sasha will arrange for her [Sonya] during her lifetime in accordance with my desire, in short, arrange things so that my will does not bring about any change in relation to her."

Strakhov hurriedly telegraphed the triumphant news to Chertkov. The friends were delighted with this new decision. It meant that Tolstoy would leave all his works, not even excepting those published before 1881, which he had formerly assigned to his wife, to his daughter Alexandra, who, with Chertkov as a literary executor, would faithfully fulfill Tolstoy's determination to make all his writings the property of the public.

Muravyov drew up a new will with these specifications. On November 1 Strakhov and Goldenweizer went to Yasnaya Polyana with the document. All felt uneasy, even guilty, about the unsuspecting Sonya. Tolstoy carefully locked the two doors of his study, and after reading over the text signed it and the two witnesses signed.

In a household where there had never been any secrecy, especially between husband and wife, there now existed a kind of conspiracy. Sonya quickly sensed this fact, even if she could not at first understand all its reasons and implications. And it completed her isolation in the family. She felt desperately lonely. Her husband was surrounded by devoted followers who now regarded her with open hostility, the wife who was "poisoning" the last days of her saintlike husband. With a pain in her heart, she saw how happy he was in their company, how gloomy in hers. When she entered the room the conversation stopped among these disciples, the cheerful expressions on their faces turned sour. Her pathetic attempts to bridge the gap that separated them were coldly received. She felt hopelessly alone in the family, for her younger sons were more of a hindrance than a help in her struggle against these followers of her husband, who, she believed, had designs on her property and that of her children. When she took complaints of this sort to her husband, he would grow furiously angry and threaten to shoot himself, and then she was terrified that he might do it. His own efforts to be kind and considerate—and there were some—were now fumbling and inadequate. Forty-seven years of married life seemed to her a dismal failure, yet her only comfort now was to dwell upon the happy early part of that union.

In these circumstances Sonya's behavior grew more and more irrational as her nervous forces were exhausted by factors that she could neither control nor understand.

XL

Escape

EVENTS OF FAMILY life, like those of history, go on repeating themselves to the delight of the young and the boredom of the old. The traditional New Year's celebration at the beginning of 1910 at Yasnaya Polyana was a happy time for many of the "twenty-three grandchildren," a sweeping figure that Sonya was fond of repeating and in which were included her own children. There were a Christmas tree, a masquerade in which Sonya appeared dressed as an old witch, dancing for the youngsters, and cards for the grown-ups. Later a cinema expert came to take moving pictures of the family, and at night he showed a film of Tolstoy's recent trip to Kryokshino and Moscow.

Tolstoy thought the film dull and in general he felt sad in the midst of this merriment. So many of the guests were alien to him in thought and he could not enter into spiritual intercourse with them. Besides, all these servants slaving for members of the family while they played left a bad taste in his mouth. It was not that he had lost, at the age of eighty-one, his wonderful capacity for enjoying the simple pleasures of life. Music still moved him to tears. He could not resist the gypsy songs and balalaika playing organized by Alexandra and the young people who came to the house. He took two Japanese visitors, "savage people in a tender rapture over European civilization," to the new village library founded in his honor by the Moscow Committee on Literacy and treated them to peasant singing and dancing. His little granddaughter, Tanichka, sat round-eyed on his knee, fascinated by the tales he made up for her. And when Sonya devised a puppet show for her grandchildren, he attended, peering at the small figures with his nearsighted eyes through grotesquely large marine binoculars. Though this year he tried to give up cards as a waste of time and riding because he grew ashamed of appearing before the peasants on a fine horse like Délire, he soon slipped back into these habits. And despite his age he still led family and close friends in the traditional spirit-reviving "Numidian cavalry" charge, boisterously dashing around the room when a boring guest had finally taken his leave.

But time and human energy were running out. Tolstoy's increasing feebleness and spiritual concentration led him to withdraw more and more within himself. The usual daily tasks now taxed his failing strength. Though conscience and duty demanded the last measure of attention, he sometimes grew more annoyed than formerly with the never-ending stream of petitioners, visitors, and letters. A feeling of dejection and hopelessness crept into his reactions to their unreasonable requests: a youth asked funds for a camera; a girl begged eighty rubles for a sewing machine; another lightly asked a hundred rubles for a trousseau; and scores of begging letters came from young people asking help in paying for their education. In despair he once again wrote out a statement to the newspapers on his inability to satisfy these demands. Worse were the heaps of manuscripts from budding authors, mostly poets, that he was asked to read and place with publishers. Nearly every problem in life, from incest to the chaste fears of puppy love, was offered for his solution by these many correspondents. Young people who could not forbear to communicate to him the eternal secrets of existence that they had unearthed asked his advice on their palpitating discoveries. Often they felt that their questions would be answered more fully if they appeared in person at Yasnaya Polyana, like the well-dressed young lady who wanted to share her views with him on education, and when these met with a cold reception was willing to leave contentedly if he would only give her a lock of his hair; or the half-mad peasant who insisted on making an incomprehensible speech into the dictaphone on the Apocalypse, the law of inertia, and electricity, ending with some resounding profanity on Tolstoy and Chertkov, and could only be silenced by the offer of a meal by the wise and gentle Dr. Makovitski. The spirit of God lives in everything, remarked Tolstoy about some of his silly petitioners, but so does the spirit of stupidity.

So numerous were the indigent who now came to Yasnaya Polyana that Chertkov made a public appeal for funds to build a hostel in the village to take care of them. Many, however, sought not alms but the truth, and to these Tolstoy talked earnestly and eagerly, and usually sent them away with a copy of one of his pamphlets dealing with the subject discussed. Most were impressed with his kindness and gentleness which became so marked in his old age. He felt still more responsible for those disciples of his who languished in prison, and besides the long encouraging letters he sent, he often distributed small sums of money among them from his "charity fund." Of late, such direct efforts to aid followers and workers and peasants had grown considerably. On a bitter January day this year he went all the way to Tula to be present at the trial of several peasants whom he believed had been unjustly accused of robbing the post, and for whose defense he had arranged. They were acquitted, and the press agreed that his very presence in the courtroom had acted as a moral influence on the jurors. The political or religious beliefs of those who sought his aid made no difference provided he was convinced of their need and sincerity. A hairy-chested revolutionary sailor turned up at Yasnaya Polyana in February in the course of dodging the police. He needed money to get abroad. Though he shocked some of the visiting Tolstoyans, their master admired the sailor's frankness and collected the necessary funds from among the family.

The revolutionists on the other hand did not hesitate to return his good with evil, especially in the matter of political doctrine. One of them, S. I. Muntyanov, exiled to Siberia, wrote him in January, after having read one of his articles, that he "was obviously badly acquainted with the working class." Its enemies, he declared, must be wiped out "even though the whole world be bathed in blood. In short, kill until not a single one of the wretches remains, not even pitying their little children." I am sorry, he concluded, "that you, perhaps, will not live till then. Well, I wish you a happy death."

Much disturbed by this apostle of violence, Tolstoy wrote him of the futility and unmorality of his convictions, and supported his arguments by sending more of his printed pamphlets. But the only concession he could obtain from this revolutionist was stated in his answering letter: "It is difficult, Leo Nikolayevich, to remake me. This socialism is my faith and my god. Of course, you profess almost the same thing, but you use the tactic of 'love,' and we use that of 'violence,' as you express it."

This was a pithy summing up, in Marxian terminology, of the essential difference between the doctrine of Tolstoy and that of the revolutionists. Curiously enough, future history seemed to be on the side of both, for if the "tactic of violence" brought about a positive good in the 1917 Revolution, it resulted in a negative evil in the terrible Second World War that followed, which Tolstoy prophesied in January 1910, when he wrote in his diary: "Anarchism is not the teaching by which I live. Rather it is the fulfillment of the eternal law, not permitting violence or participation in it. Will the consequences be either anarchism or, on the contrary, slavery under the yoke of the Japanese or the Germans?"

Violence creates violence and there is no end save universal destruction, and the only alternative to this, Tolstoy said, is the eternal law, the "tactic of love."

2

Tolstoy wrote little in 1910 but considerable effort went into completing *For Every Day,* the compilation of quotations from great authors arranged so as to illustrate the development of his own philosophy of life, a task that he had worked on for three years. With true insight he now began to see "a certain pedantry and dogmatism" in this huge effort, but before he had even finished it he began to rework it in the form of a systematic exposition of his thought on the basis of separate subjects under individual titles. The result was still another compilation, entitled *The Path of Life*. Obviously these attempts were a poor substitute for the original systematic philosophy that he had long wished to write. But he derived a deep satisfaction in finding that his own convictions on many fundamental problems of life were shared by great thinkers of the past, and he daily read the appropriate passages from the *Circle of Reading* and *For Every Day* as though these books were his Bible.

No doubt such compilations were more congenial to an old man whose literary imagination and invention were flagging. He was now fond of applying to his literary work the expression of a servant who, when invited to bathe, replied: "No, I won't go. I've already bathed myself out."

Tolstoy felt that he had written himself out. Occasionally vast themes for fiction would occur to him. He wanted to treat them in the spirit of the new demand that he made on art, which he now phrased: "As soon as art ceases to be art for all the people and becomes art for a small class of wealthy people, it ceases to be necessary and important and becomes an empty amusement." Instead of vast designs, however, there emerged during the early part of this year only slight unfinished sketches and a mediocre play, *The Cause of It All,* which he wrote for the amateur theatricals of Dima, Chertkov's son, and his peasant lads at Telyatinki. After completing two brief bits in a series, "Three Days in the Country," revealing the miseries of peasant life, he wearily entered in his diary: "On the whole, I must stop writing and caring about writing."

Other more important matters were haunting his brain—approaching death and the spiritual calm with which he longed to meet it. But existence at Yasnaya Polyana was daily becoming less compatible with the serenity he sought. His wife's nervous energy kept the household in a state of constant activity. Things often went badly with the management of the estate. Two of the sons, in financial difficulties, were pressing her for loans. "I'm terribly nervous, am short of breath, and keep wanting to cry. I've too many different things to do," Sonya pathetically noted in her diary in April. Yet she had now begun a new edition of her husband's works, the twelfth, and in twenty volumes, a huge task, but the income from this source had become a vital factor in the family budget. As always, this endeavor was hateful to Tolstoy, and more so now since he had just been pleading unsuccessfully with Sonya to lower the price of his early children's *Readers,* about which he had been receiving more complaints from teachers. In her free moments she busily wrote her memoirs, posted her diary, and copied her portrait in oils that had been painted by the artist V. A. Serov.

A strange calm, not unpleasing to Tolstoy, settled over the household on Sonya's periodic trips to Moscow on business, to see her friends and attend concerts. On a visit at the end of March she heard a lecture on her husband by the family friend, M. A. Stakhovich, at the Tolstoy Museum House. "He mentioned me with reference to my services," she wrote in her diary, "and when he pronounced my name the whole assembly in that literary-artistic society rose and unanimously applauded loud and long. I got up, bowed to the lecturer and then to the public, and felt terribly confused." Sonya liked this.

In April Alexandra fell ill and the doctors detected symptoms of tuberculosis. It was felt advisable to send her to the Crimea for a time, and a young student, V. F. Bulgakov, who had already taken Gusev's place as Tolstoy's secretary upon Chertkov's recommendation, now assumed Alexandra's tasks as her father's helper. The parting was hard for Tolstoy. Over the last couple of years they had grown very close. She was the one person in the family on whom he felt that he could implicitly depend. When she left he noted in his diary: "She is sad. I had a good talk with her. We both burst into sobs."

Every small circumstance seemed to increase the old, gnawing dissatisfaction that Tolstoy felt over the disparity between the life around him and that which he wanted to lead. One day he came to tea, looking gloomy and muttering that life was a burden.

"Why is it a burden to you?" asked Sonya. "Everyone loves you."

"Yet, it is a burden," he replied. "Why should it not be a burden? Simply because the food here is fine?"

"Why no, I merely said that all love you."

"I imagine that everyone is thinking: The damned old fellow says one thing and does another; it is time for you to die before you become an utter Pharisee! And this is entirely just. I often receive such letters, even from my friends, who write me in this vein. And they are correct. Every day I go out on the road and there stand five tattered beggars, while I ride a horse and after me a coachman."

Frequent entries in the diary over the early months of 1910 testify to Tolstoy's acute moral suffering and shame over this problem. "I did not dine," he wrote on April 12. "Tormenting pangs from the consciousness of the vileness of my life in the midst of working people hardly able to keep themselves and their families from death by cold and starvation. Yesterday 15 persons gorged themselves on pancakes, while 5 or 6 servants with families of their own ran about scarcely able to prepare and serve up what we devoured. I'm tormented and terribly ashamed. Yesterday I rode past some stone-breakers and felt as if I were running the gauntlet."

The need of a change of scene and perhaps the added hope of seeing Chertkov led Tolstoy to visit his daughter

Tanya at Kochety early in May. To his "great joy" Chertkov arrived a few days later. He had received special permission from the authorities to make the trip. This first meeting after some eight months was a happy occasion, and the two friends at once secluded themselves for a long conversation on many matters that intimately concerned them. Tolstoy was a little annoyed that Chertkov had brought along his English photographer, who persisted in snapping pictures of him even without asking permission. You see, Chertkov unctuously explained, posterity will treasure photographs of you. Tolstoy did not agree, but then he could not deny his friend this slight favor.

The friends had the field to themselves for only a short time, for soon Sonya and her son Andrei arrived. When she saw Chertkov, Sonya decided that he had been the reason why her husband had been "in such a hurry to leave home." Tolstoy chronicled their coming in his diary as follows: "The insanity of our life becomes clearer and clearer. Sonya arrived with Andrei. With Andrei I was not good—sharp. For the first time I expressed to Sonya part of what weighs on me. And then, in order to soften what I had said, I silently kissed her—she quite understands this language."

Despite the pleasant calm and well-ordered existence of Kochety, Tolstoy soon began to feel oppressed by the burden of the moderate luxury of the Sukhotins' estate and the idleness of their landowners' life. "Everyone is working except me," he complained. He departed on May 20, but before he left, Chertkov invited him to Meshcherskoye, where he had now moved in order to be closer to Tolstoy. Come, he said, "if it does not displease you to be away from Yasnaya Polyana so much." Tolstoy smiled bitterly at this sally and agreed to make the visit.

3

Tolstoy returned to a houseful of summer visitors at Yasnaya Polyana. They gave him no peace and exhausted Sonya's incredible store of nervous energy. A few of the guests were pleasant and relaxing, like the brilliant sculptor Paoli Trubetskoi, who executed an equestrian statue of him. He enjoyed this vegetarian artist with his long, horselike face and strong hands who bluntly replied to Sonya's question as to whether he had read *War and Peace:* "I never read anything." Tolstoy roared and envied the original mind of a man like this, unpolluted by the printed word. But he did not approve of the naked bathing in the Voronka of Trubetskoi and his wife.

There were few such congenial guests, however, and added to the strain of many visitors was an unpleasant domestic situation. Peasants protested to Tolstoy that the sullen Circassian whom Sonya had hired to protect her wooded land took his duties so literally that he drove them off the estate grounds on their way to work, forcing them to take a much longer route. He pleaded with Sonya to remedy the situation and she promised. In turn she complained to him of her hard lot and said that she could no longer continue to manage the estate.

"I don't understand you, Sonya," he answered. "Who forces you to do this? Give it up."

"But what will become of me?"

"Go off somewhere."

"Where?"

"Wherever you wish. To Odoyev,[1] to . . ."

"You are driving me away; you want to get rid of me!"

A hysterical scene followed and Sonya left the house. When she did not return, the agitated Tolstoy sent out searchers and they found her sitting in a ditch and brought her home.

He tried to make amends and treated her with extra kindness and consideration. But shortly after this incident he was returning from a ride and met the Circassian roughly handling a peasant who had been one of his pupils years ago. The guard had caught him carting off part of a tree. "I felt terribly depressed," Tolstoy wrote in his diary, "and at once wanted to get away from here." There were further scenes and bitter words over the Circassian and the distraught life at Yasnaya Polyana, all of which no doubt contributed to another of Tolstoy's fainting spells followed by extreme debility and temporary loss of memory. Sonya set it all down to his liver and unfeelingly wondered why the activity of this organ could not be controlled by Christian ideas.

Alexandra had recently returned from the Crimea quite cured. Worried over her father's illness and its probable causes, she wrote a detailed letter to her sister Tanya, who was already partly aware of the situation, since she had been at Yasnaya Polyana on a brief visit that summer. Devoted to both her parents and thoroughly aware of the nature of

[1] A small provincial town.

the struggle going on between them, Tanya sent her mother a frank letter. She pointed out to her that in spite of her advancing age she still refused to relinquish any of her many tasks and even needlessly added to them while always complaining that she was an overworked jade. Tanya advised her, in her old age, to take life more simply, thoughtfully, and calmly, and cease surrounding her husband with the turmoil and worries of insignificant household cares. "You say," she wrote, "that he is very contented and that he demands only his horse, Ilya Vasilyevich,[2] and Dushan.[3] However, why do you not ask him what is dearer to him: all the external good things of life, or your nearness to his soul and your aid in saving him from suffering and witnessing various acts of violence of no use to anybody? There is no point in your ascribing his sufferings to his stomach, his liver, or in general to any external causes. Standing on the threshold of death, he finds it more and more burdensome to live under conditions that allow a strange savage young Circassian to hunt down an old acquaintance of papa's, a muzhik dear to him, simply because he has carted away the limb of a tree without asking permission. Principally, papa, loving you, suffers because you are able to do such things and allow them to take place before his eyes. You suffer when he eats badly; you try to save him from boring and difficult visitors; you sew blouses for him; in short, you surround his material life with every possible care, but that which is dearer than all to him you somehow lose sight of. How touched he would be and how he would return a hundredfold your efforts if you had as much concern for his inner life."

But the wise Tanya had made her appeal too late. Her unfortunate mother had drifted beyond the reach of rational argument.

Though obviously against Sonya's wishes, Tolstoy decided to escape again from his trying existence at Yasnaya Polyana and visit Chertkov. He left June 12, accompanied by Alexandra, his secretary Bulgakov, and Dr. Makovitski, and he represented the visit to his anxious wife as a brief one. However much he yearned to leave permanently, he could not take this step. That year an earnest Kiev student and disciple had enthusiastically written him: "Abandon your estate, give your property to your relations and the poor, leave your-

[2] A servant in the household.

[3] Dr. Makovitski.

self without a kopek, and as a mendicant go from town to town." Tolstoy answered: "Your letter has profoundly moved me. What you advise me has been my sacred dream, but up to this time I have been unable to do it. There are many reasons . . . but the chief reason is that my doing this must not affect others." And he wrote one of his followers in jail at this time: "I'm not in prison, unfortunately, but my prison without bars sometimes seems to me, in weak moments, worse than yours."

4

As at Kryokshino, Tolstoy's spirits rose as he settled into the pleasantly familiar atmosphere of Chertkov's household at Meshcherskoye. Here was the calm and discriminating solicitude he needed for spiritual concentration, and that prayerful expectancy of great thoughts aborning that naturally encouraged his writing. He could even overlook the unique annoyance perpetrated by Chertkov's semi-invalid wife: a ladder from Tolstoy's second-story window to the ground which had to be used by his visitors during the invalid's rest hours for fear of disturbing her by going up and down the stairs. In fact, despite his age, he longed to try the ladder himself. His recovered gaiety served to remind the severe sectarians surrounding the host that they ought not to live by Tolstoyism alone. He soon had them laughing at his sallies and singing cheerful songs of an evening, led by Bulgakov's strong tenor and to the accompaniment of Alexandra.

In the immediate neighborhood was a large hospital center accommodating mostly mental cases. Long keenly interested in insanity, Tolstoy paid several visits to the hospitals and talked with a number of patients. The more he observed the more convinced he became that all people were abnormal and that it was only a question of degree between those in and outside asylums. He was impressed by one mad patient who fiercely insisted that he had not stolen but merely taken things. Tolstoy talked with him about death, and he solemnly replied: "Why die? Live!" Upon taking his leave Tolstoy politely remarked that he hoped they would see each other again in this world. "Why this world?" asked the puzzled madman. "There is only one world." Tolstoy saw more logic than insanity in this reply.

Inspired by the many fresh impressions he had received,

and enjoying ideal conditions for writing, Tolstoy happily plunged into work at Meshcherskoye. He worked at *For Every Day* and *The Path of Life* and on a couple of articles.[4] Even the urge to attempt fiction took hold of him again, and he wrote two short pieces.[5]

With the recent flare-ups at Yasnaya Polyana in mind, Tolstoy's sunny disposition was occasionally shadowed by sad thoughts of Sonya. She had been invited to come to Meshcherskoye, and her refusal no doubt made him suspicious. As though to disarm her anger over his absence, he wrote her chatty and kind letters. He was living as at Yasnaya Polyana, he cautiously remarked in the first one, except that there were no visitors and petitioners, which was very pleasant. Then he told her all about the lunatic asylum and his observations there. And at the end he pointedly wrote: "However fine it is to visit, home is better. And I shall return as I intended, certainly not later than the 24th, if all goes well with you and me. How are you and your affairs getting on —both the editing and the household? Aren't you worried too much about them? To have a tranquil mind is the principal thing—more important than all material considerations. . . . Good-bye, my dear old wife. I kiss you." Five days later he wrote another chatty letter, said that he had now decided to leave on the twenty-fifth, and rather pathetically and obviously repeated: "It is fine to visit, but it is better at home."

At home Sonya's rage was mounting. She had the house filled with painters and plasterers, was rearranging all the furniture, and staying up till the small hours of the morning working on her edition. Her answer to Tanya's plea for understanding had been: "You refer to your father's imaginary unhappiness too tragically. Such a fuss over a Circassian." And anyway, she reminded Tanya, if her father ceased to live materially, how and where would his spirit live? She, for one, was not capable of arranging a new life, she concluded.

Nor were Tolstoy's kind letters from Meshcherskoye any palliative. Her brief answers gave no hint of the coming storm, which apparently burst in full fury over the bit of information he unsuspectingly wrote her in his letter of June 19. He had just received "the welcome news," he said,

[4] These were an epistolary article to the Slav Congress at Sofia, and an article entitled "On Insanity."

[5] "Unexpectedly" and "Grateful Soil."

that the authorities had permitted Chertkov to be at Telyatinki during the period of his mother's visit there, which was to begin on June 27.

Something snapped in Sonya after receiving this news. She reacted in a violent manner, physically and emotionally. On June 22 Tolstoy received a telegram: "Sofya Andreyevna intensely nervous attack, insomnia, weeping, pulse hundred. Asked me to telegraph. Varya." This telegram had been dictated by Sonya to Varya M. Feokritov, her typist and a close friend of Alexandra, but Varya added the last four words on her own as a hint that the message was really Sonya's. Detecting this hint, Alexandra pointed it out to her father, and after talking it over and deciding that Sonya was in all probability simulating illness, he sent a wire to the effect that it would be more convenient to come on the twenty-fourth.

According to Varya, when Sonya received this telegram she cried: "Don't you see that this is Chertkov's expression, that he won't let him go. They want to kill me, but I have some opium. . . ." And she ran to the cupboard, seized a vial of opium and spirits of ammonia, and declared that she would poison herself if her husband did not come back. Meanwhile, she had sent another telegram: "Implore you to come quickly, on the 23rd." And since Varya had by now become thoroughly alarmed over her threats of suicide, she agreed to send in her own name a third telegram, also dictated by Sonya: "I think it necessary."

When he received this message, Tolstoy decided to leave at once and reached Yasnaya Polyana late at night on the twenty-third. He wrote in his diary: "Found things worse than I expected. It is impossible to describe the hysteria and exasperation. I restrained myself pretty well, but was not gentle enough."

5

Sonya's behavior was not merely the result of Tolstoy's failure to return immediately. A complex of psychotic wounds combined with adverse material factors over the whole course of her married life had brought an inherently unstable nature to the point of mental and emotional collapse. A morbid purity fixation had been outraged before marriage by reading in her future husband's diary of his youthful debauchery, and this condition had been further aggravated by the events of the wedding night and the nature of subsequent sexual relations. Tolstoy's virtual repudiation, after his religious experience, of the kind of existence they had been living for years tremendously widened the rift between them and increased Sonya's feeling of material insecurity, just as his struggle at that time to cease sexual intimacy increased her sense of emotional insecurity. With the coming of old age, the severance of the sexual bond, and his desire to withdraw within himself spiritually, Sonya's isolation from her husband was complete. Since she could not share his spiritual life, she was denied the usual compensations that old married couples enjoy. And now, on top of all this, the fear that he would leave her had entirely undermined what little stability she had left. In a frenzy of desperation she sought for a symbol of her failure and found it in Chertkov.

While waiting for Tolstoy to return on the night of June 23, Sonya wrote a "Memorandum before Death" in her diary which she correctly described as "a sick woman's ravings." She told of her condition: spasm in the throat, pain in her heart, aching head, and continued sobbing. She wondered what was the matter with her. Was it hysteria, a nervous stroke, or the beginnings of insanity? Then she lucidly wrote: "Let me confess the truth. I was wretched because of this long, unaccustomed separation from Leo Nikolayevich. He has a repulsive, senile love for Chertkov (in his youth he used to fall in love with men), and he is completely subject to his will. . . .[6] I am insanely jealous of Leo Nikolayevich's intimacy with Chertkov; I feel that he has taken from me all that I have lived for during 48 years."

The rest of this extraordinary document contains an incoherent account of the events of the last few days. "The worse I feel the better," she revealingly remarked of her distraught state. Then she wrote of her plans for suicide, a description of her coffin with its rounded lid covered with rose-colored or white brocade, and of how enormous her nose would seem as it stuck up in death. "Quicker! Quicker!" she concluded. "It will be too late. . . . I have drunk the opium. . . . He is coming."

Tolstoy found her very much alive, however, when he entered the room, but he did not succeed in calming her

[6] This is followed by a partly erased phrase which is unprintable. In her diary during this year unprintable words, usually referring to Chertkov, are rather frequent.

until the early hours of the morning. Three days later another outburst occurred. Sonya had read an entry in his diary made recently at Meshcherskoye: "I want to try consciously to struggle with Sonya by kindness and love." "Am I a wretch that he must 'struggle' with me?" she shrieked, entirely missing the implication of the word in his entry. She demanded the last diary notebook he had completed, for she wished to find out if he had any other remarks about her. Chertkov had it. Then she remembered. Where were his diary notebooks for the last ten years? These, too, he finally had to admit were in Chertkov's possession, but he had put them in a Moscow bank for safekeeping. Sonya scented a plot: Chertkov and his friends could read the things her husband wrote about her in his diary and might publicize them. All day she followed her husband around pleading for the diaries. Lightly clad, she ran out in the rain, returned, and then moaned on the balcony outside his window, preventing him from sleeping. Her hysterical condition continued far into the morning.

Tolstoy had no thought of publishing his diaries. For years, though rather reluctantly, he had given Chertkov access to these little notebooks to aid him in compiling the "Vault," and he had even asked him to delete anything that seemed harmful to other people. To recover these notebooks and prevent Chertkov from using them now became another fixed idea with Sonya and the cause of infinite misery in the family. This desire was connected, as Tolstoy recognized, with her mortal terror that she would one day be represented to the world as a shrew and the poisoner of her husband's life. With a new fear that anything pertinent she now found in his manuscripts might be made the occasion of a quarrel, he hastened to change the description of the external appearance—vaguely resembling that of Sonya—of an unsympathetic character in a recent tale from ". . . his wife, a handsome, energetic brunette with shining eyes" to ". . . his wife, not very tall, plump, a blonde, with tender, kind blue eyes."

The next day, June 27, the mere announcement by Bulgakov that Chertkov had arrived in near-by Telyatinki sent Sonya running out of the room shouting that she hated the man. To Goldenweizer, who was present, she admitted that she might be out of her mind but simply could not control herself. In an effort to avoid Chertkov's visit, she hurried off Tolstoy and herself to the estate of her son

Sergei, a tedious trip. But they returned after a day's stay, perhaps because she received a severe scolding from Sergei and his sister Tanya, who was also visiting, when she tried to gain their sympathy. Both these older children were extremely worried over the effect of her hysterical actions on their father's feeble health.

The almost daily visits of Chertkov, however, could not be avoided. On his first call she fiercely assailed him on the question of the diary notebooks. In such a situation Chertkov was not the man to stand on ceremony or politeness, and besides he had long entertained a feeling of hostility toward Sonya for interfering in what he considered his private affairs with Tolstoy. In her diary she reported part of his remarks to her on this occasion with some regard for truth. He said to me, she wrote: "Are you afraid that I will *expose* you by means of the diaries of Leo Nikolayevich? I have had it in my power for a long time, and I have sufficient influence to *smirch* you and your family, and if I did not do this, it is only out of affection for Leo Nikolayevich. . . . If I had such a wife, I should long ago have shot myself or run away to America."

For two weeks the battle of the diaries continued, with all and sundry in the house, servants, children, and visitors, being initiated into the various issues of the controversy. Every visit of Chertkov—and he persisted in making them, though with less frequency—was a provocation to Sonya and often resulted in a hysterical scene. And Tolstoy's visits to his friend were no less inexcusable in her eyes. A stuffy written apology from Chertkov, conditioned by many subtle phrases, for his harsh statements to Sonya availed him nothing. Tolstoy tried by alternate kindness and firmness to reason with her and control her outbursts, but a day of comparative peace thus gained was followed the next by bitter words, wailing, and extravagant actions that robbed him of his sleep and further undermined his precarious health. He and Chertkov feared that if the diaries were surrendered, she might destroy them. There was also the further worry that in the most recent diaries she might uncover references to his will. But as she tragically put it, either she got the diaries or she would commit suicide. And now her son Leo had come and he supported her demand that the diaries be returned.

On the evening of July 10 another quarrel took place over Chertkov and the diaries. She went on the balcony outside his room late at night, moved about and groaned. As she wrote in her own diary, she lay down on the bare boards in the hopes of finding death on the very spot where forty-eight years ago she had first experienced her husband's love. Now, however, he asked her to go away and let him sleep. Loudly accusing him of driving her out of the house, and shouting that she would kill Chertkov, she rushed out into the dark garden in a thin dress. When she did not return, the distracted Tolstoy woke up his son Leo and Dr. Makovitski and asked them to search for her. They found her lying on the wet grass, threatening to kill herself unless her husband, who had put her out like a dog, as she exaggerated, came to get her. Leo rushed back to his father, apparently used harsh language, and demanded that he go out and persuade her to return, which he did.

Tolstoy wrote in his diary: "Barely alive. A terrible night. Up till four. And more terrible than all was L. L. [his son Leo]. He scolded me like a child and ordered me to go to the garden after S. A." He felt utterly beaten and had about made up his mind that the diaries, which had already been brought back to Chertkov's from the Moscow bank, would have to be taken from him. Meanwhile Sergei and Tanya had been summoned in the hope that they might have a calming influence on their mother.

Another hysterical night on the thirteenth brought Tolstoy to a decision. The next day he wrote a letter to Sonya and gave it to her. It reads:—

"1. My present diary I will not give to anyone; I will keep it myself.

"2. The old diaries I will take back from Chertkov and will keep myself, probably in a bank.

"3. If you are troubled by the thought that certain passages in my diaries that I wrote, under impressions of the moment, about our disagreements and conflicts will be used by future biographers ill-disposed towards you, I want first of all to point out that such transitory expressions of feelings, both mine and those in your diary, can in no sense give a correct understanding of our true relations. If you fear this,[7] then I will gladly take an opportunity to express

[7] Sonya annotated this letter in her diary. Opposite this phrase she wrote: "It is precisely this that I do not at all fear . . . I was simply hurt that the diaries—the holy of holies of my husband—were accessible to Chertkov, an outsider, and not to me, his wife, from whom they have been concealed and are concealed in all sorts of ways."

in my diary or simply in a letter my relations with you and my appreciation of your life.

"My relations with you and my appreciation of you are: as I loved you when you were young, so I have loved you increasingly and still love you, despite various causes of coolness between us. The causes of that coolness (I do not speak of the cessation of marital relations;[8] such a cessation could only remove deceptive expressions of a love not real) were:

"First, my ever-increasing alienation from the interests of worldly life and the revulsion I felt for them, whereas you did not wish to and could not part with them, not having in your soul the principles that led me to my convictions, which was quite natural, and I cannot reproach you for this. That is the first thing.

"Second (forgive me if what I am going to say is disagreeable to you, but what now is happening between us is so important that one must not fear to speak and to hear the whole truth), secondly, then, your character over these last years has become more and more irritable, despotic and unrestrained. The manifestation of these traits could not fail to chill, not my feeling itself, but its expression. That is the second thing.

"Third, the chief and fatal cause, for which neither you nor I are to blame, is our entirely opposite conception of the meaning and purpose of life."

Tolstoy went on to elaborate this third point at some length, stressing their different attitudes toward property, people, and the proper way to live. Then he returned to further conditions:—

"4. If my relations with Chertkov at this time distress you, I am ready to forgo seeing him, though I am bound to say that I should find this trying, not so much on my own account as on his, knowing how unpleasant it would be for him. But if you wish me to, I will do it.

"Now 5. If you do not accept these conditions of mine for a kindly and peaceful life, then I shall take back my promise not to leave you. I shall go away. But I shall certainly not go to Chertkov. I will even make it an unfailing condition that he should not come to live near me. But I shall

[8] Sonya comments: "Of course the coolness resulted entirely because of the cessation of marital relations, owing to the illness and age of Leo Nikolayevich. Who should know that better than a wife."

certainly go away, for it is impossible to go on living as we now do.

"I could continue to live this way if I could calmly endure your sufferings, but I cannot. Yesterday you went away agitated and suffering. I wanted to go to sleep, but I began, not so much to think of you, as to feel you, and I could not sleep. I listened till one o'clock and then two, and again woke up and listened, and in a dream, or almost in a dream, I saw you.

"Try to think quietly, dear friend, try to listen to the response of your heart, and you will resolve it all in the right way. As for me, I will say that I have already resolved it, and I *cannot, cannot* decide otherwise. My darling, stop torturing, not others, but yourself—yourself, for you are suffering a hundred times more than all the others."

True to his word, Tolstoy sent Alexandra that day to Telyatinki for the diaries. Chertkov and his assistants kept her waiting for a long time while they busily copied out passages that might compromise Sonya, and which they felt she might suppress. Then, wrapping up the diaries, and making the threefold sign of the cross with the package over her head in mock solemnity, Chertkov surrendered them with regret. Sonya pounced upon the package when Alexandra returned, but Tolstoy had them locked up in a deposit box in a Tula bank and he kept the key.

In her own diary that day Sonya wrote: "The diaries have been returned, but at what a cost!"

6

The situation that had developed at Yasnaya Polyana would probably have been rejected by Tolstoy, the novelist, as "too sensational," "untrue to the experience of life." Here was a woman of sixty-six who, after being married for forty-eight years, was accusing her husband of almost eighty-two of homosexual relations with a man of fifty-six! Sonya was willing to go to almost any lengths to drive the hated Chertkov out of her husband's life. In her moments of mental derangement, often accompanied by physical illness, she unquestionably suffered terribly. In her calmer moments, however, she was overwhelmed with remorse and pity for her husband. Some in the household were convinced that her ravings and absurd actions were cunning dissimulation, practiced to gain her own ends, not realizing that dissimulation was a symptom of her peculiar illnes Desperately she tried to enlist all on her side, freely pourin forth her woes even to complete strangers. But the onl real supporters she had were her two sons, Leo and Andre and motives other than those of devotion to their mothe played a part in their defense of her cause.

However exaggerated were Sonya's fears of Chertkov, sh had real reasons to dislike and distrust him. She had onc told him that he was the "best friend" of her family, bu that was at a moment when he exuded the personal charn of which he had much. In general, he was a difficult perso and quarreled with his friends, even with those who wer disciples of Tolstoy—with Maude in England, Gorbunov Posadov, director of the *Intermediary,* and at one time o another with all of Tolstoy's daughters. His overbearin manner, pomposity, and holier-than-thou attitude wer hardly compensated by his moral rectitude and willingnes to suffer for his convictions.

Though his relations with Tolstoy were by now most unusual, only the overwrought mind of Sonya could hav detected anything perverted in them. Tolstoy once wrote i a light vein: "If there were not a Chertkov, it would b necessary to invent one; for me, at least, for my happiness." Chertkov was his special defender before the world, and n man knew so intimately the master's teaching or could interpret it so successfully. So thoroughly did he understan Tolstoy's thought and moral feeling that he was able t justify his own actions, as well as Tolstoy's, in these term with uncanny ability. When a Tolstoyan sympathizer Christo Dosev, wrote Chertkov in the course of this yea to protest Tolstoy's slavery to "a stupid, vulgar woman," h answered in a long letter which in its doctrinal aspect might well have been written by Tolstoy. When Tolsto read a copy of the letter, he commented that it was salutary elucidating the past and present, and a program for him that he was still far from carrying out. In this instance, however, Chertkov betrayed a tactlessness that was one of his worst faults and often resented by Tolstoy. He was unable to understand how offensive it was to Tolstoy to pass on to him Dosev's crude comments on his wife, or his own still cruder comments on Sonya in his letter, or to quote to a comparative stranger—as he did in his answer—passages from Tolstoy's private diary. In his hostility to Sonya in the present struggle, Chertkov often forgot that she was

Tolstoy's wife whom he loved, and to whom he had special obligations sanctified by many years of married life.

At times Tolstoy also grew annoyed with Chertkov for making his manuscripts accessible to his own friends and for some of his critical strictures on his works. But over the years of their association he had come to value highly Chertkov's innumerable services in connection with the editing and publishing of his writings. Loyalty was a strong quality of Tolstoy's nature, and he probably felt it doubly necessary now to defend Chertkov in the light of the mounting criticism of him. As he said many times, this disciple was his best and closest friend.

Chertkov seemed to be the principal irritant in the unhappy domestic strife at Yasnaya Polyana. But the assumption that peace would reign if he removed himself from the scene, as a gentleman normally would in a quarrel between husband and wife, was altogether too simple. The causes of the dissension went much deeper. Besides, he had a spiritual vested interest in Tolstoy and his teaching. He had given up the best years of his life to this cause, and now he had no intention of allowing "the crazy will of a woman," as he expressed it, to endanger his favored position at the right hand of the master. As the chief editor of Tolstoy's enormous literary heritage and the continuator of his teaching after his death, Chertkov looked forward to occupying the remaining years of his own life with a most congenial and sacred trust. And he was prepared to exert himself to the utmost to defend these prerogatives against Sonya and any members of her family—even against Tolstoy himself.

Chertkov had helpers at Yasnaya Polyana in this struggle. Alexandra took his side and did all in her power to carry out his plans. Painful childhood memories lingered in her mind: the old nurse's cruel story of how Sonya, when pregnant with her, had done everything possible to bring about an abortion since she loathed having this child; of hearing her mother sobbing of God's injustice at the time of Vanichka's death in taking her son and not Sasha. The feeling between mother and daughter now was often one of hatred. Alexandra believed that there was more cold-blooded selfishness than sickness in her mother's behavior toward her husband, and Tolstoy was often obliged to beg her to show more consideration for her mother's suffering. Alexandra's close friend, Varya Feokritov, helped Sonya with her edition but conspired against her in the family quarrel. The accomplished Goldenweizer's reverence for Tolstoy made him a willing helper in the interests of Chertkov, and while staying at Telyatinki he visited Yasnaya Polyana nearly every day, faithfully reporting back to Chertkov the events there. Bulgakov, Tolstoy's secretary, tried to be neutral, but he too was somewhat committed to Chertkov as the man who had recommended him. And finally, gentle Dr. Dushan Makovitski, though disinclined to quarrels of any sort, was often filled with hatred for Sonya, whose neurotic condition he felt was all nonsense, because of her tormenting the man he worshipped.

The household was a beehive of conspiratorial activity—eavesdropping, concealing documents, secret messages going back and forth between Yasnaya Polyana and Telyatinki, copies of Tolstoy's letters being smuggled out of the house, and mysterious meetings in the environs. Visitors, like Korolenko, that summer, were taken aside by each party and told the real "truth" about the family crisis. All the participants in these events, save Tolstoy, gave the impression of being favored witnesses to an international scandal rather than to a sorrowful quarrel between a husband and wife in their old age. All of them wrote diaries—eight daily records were being kept simultaneously of the events taking place in this unhappy household. No family quarrel has ever been so fully documented.

In this turmoil of misdirected human effort, Tolstoy, the central figure, often appeared like a weary umpire arbitrating between two sweaty, fiercely struggling teams. In a sense, he was now suffering the martyrdom, though in a form he had never expected or wished, that had been inflicted upon many of his followers by the authorities. If he had any doubt as to the course he ought to pursue, his rule was to do that which required most self-sacrifice. This meant to remain at Yasnaya Polyana however severe the trials he had to bear. But torn this way and that by the conflicting demands made upon him by both sides in the struggle, he often lost courage. "It is very hard for me," he wrote in his diary, "in this house of insane people."

7

Tolstoy's hope that by recovering the diaries from Chertkov and depositing them in a strongbox in the Tula bank he would appease his wife proved to be a vain one. The very next day, Sonya fell on her knees in the corridor before her husband's bedroom, seized his legs and screamed: "This is my last request! Give me the key or write me out an authorization to obtain the diaries. I do not believe that you won't give them back to Chertkov."

"Get up. Please get up! For God's sake stop this and leave me alone!" he shouted in a trembling voice.

She jumped up, ran to her room, and then cried out: "I've drunk the whole phial. I've poisoned myself."

He rushed to her, but she answered in a calm voice: "I deliberately deceived you. I didn't drink it. . . ."

Tolstoy went into the garden, his weak heart pounding, and asked Alexandra to tell her mother that she seemed to be doing everything she could to force him to leave the house. In her diary Sonya wrote: "I basely deceived Leo Nikolayevich into thinking that I had taken it [opium], but immediately confessed the deceit and wept bitterly, but I made an effort to control myself."

For days a feeling of tension gripped all in the family in expectation of another mad scene as Sonya continued in a highly nervous state. Now she shifted her ground a bit. The diaries were kept in the background while she concentrated her attacks on Chertkov. Apparently with Tolstoy's promise in mind, made in his letter of July 13, that he would cease meeting with Chertkov if she desired, she strove to bring this about by her behavior without actually demanding it. She turned every visit of Chertkov into a painful experience for all. Whenever a carriage drove up, she began to tremble, fearing her "enemy" had arrived again. She shadowed him and her husband through the house, refusing to let them talk alone for a moment. To preserve peace Tolstoy felt obliged to ask Chertkov not to mention the diaries in conversation and not to try to see him in private. And before visiting Chertkov, he would ask Sonya's permission. If Chertkov delayed his departure of an evening, she would ostentatiously arise and loudly announce: "It's time to go to bed!"

This campaign did not daunt Chertkov, though it kept Tolstoy in a continual state of worry. But Sonya failed to stop with these tactics. She shouted threats against Chertkov, that she wanted to kill him, to drive a knife into his fat body. Losing all sense of discretion, she plotted with her neighbor, Anna E. Zvegintsev, who disliked Chertkov, to denounce him to the authorities and have him again removed from the district. And a police search was actually made at Telyatinki that summer. Still more disturbing, she read aloud to members of the family and guests a passage in Tolstoy's diary, which he wrote at the age of twenty-three of his love for men, and she openly accused him and Chertkov of unnatural relations. Her shocking threats and accusations provoked a stern letter of reproof from Chertkov's mother, who was then staying with him.

Tolstoy and the older children thought the time had come to call in a physician to examine Sonya. On July 19 the family friend, Dr. D. V. Nikitin, and the neuropathist, Dr. G. I. Rossolimo, arrived. Dr. Rossolimo's diagnosis of the illness was: "A degenerative dual constitution: paranoial and hysterical, with a predominance of the former. At the present time there is an episodic aggravation." Separation from her husband for a period, and baths and walking, were prescribed.

Sonya was outraged. Such cures for one "who has been morally wounded" by the fact that her husband has fallen in love with a man! She went to the Voronka "to measure its depths to see if it were possible to drown herself." Various ways of suicide were imagined, but she favored Anna Karenina's cruelly vindictive method of throwing herself under the train that would carry off her husband in the separation the doctors advised, and thus inflict on him a totally useless but irrevocable remorse.

A crescendo of scenes culminated in Sonya's leaving home on July 25, because her husband, she said, had driven her out of the house and her daughter had spat at her. She wept at departing, forgave Alexandra, and took some poison with her. Behind her she left a letter for Tolstoy, in which she thanked him for her former happiness and declared that, since the doctors had advised separation, she was going away to leave him free to have all the secrets and meetings with Chertkov that he desired. To the press she also left a letter about the "extraordinary event" that had happened at "peaceful Yasnaya Polyana"—her leaving "with despair in her soul," because she could no longer endure the presence of Chertkov.

But Sonya was careful to depart in the carriage that was being sent to Tula to meet Andrei, and in a few hours she duly arrived back at Yasnaya Polyana with her son. She feared her husband's derision, but he came to her, she wrote in her diary, kind and touched, and thanked her with tears in his eyes for having returned. Then she immediately brought up the question of Chertkov again and he grew angry.

Sonya, however, had won out once more, for the next day Tolstoy wrote Chertkov to say that, though it pained him, he felt that they ought not to meet as long as his wife's sickly condition lasted. His friend accepted the blow with bad grace, and took the occasion, in replying, to sermonize Tolstoy in Tolstoyan accents on the danger of abandoning the freedom of action necessary to accomplish, not his own will, but the will of Him who sent him.

Earlier in July Tolstoy had decided to alter the will he had executed the previous year. He wished to designate his daughter Tanya as the alternate heir of all his literary productions in the event that Alexandra should die before him. This alteration, he felt, was necessary not only as a legal safeguard, but also as a kind of moral protection for Alexandra in the family. Besides, he did not want to hurt the feelings of his oldest daughter who he knew could be trusted to carry out his wish that his works become public property in the manner he desired. He signed this new will on July 17 during his last visit to Chertkov at Telyatinki. By mistake the words "being of sound mind and memory" were omitted. He had to make a fresh draft which he wrote out in the woods near Yasnaya Polyana on July 22, and he signed it along with the three witnesses, A. B. Goldenweizer, A. P. Sergeyenko, and A. D. Radynski. This was Tolstoy's last will and testament. A few days later he also signed a separate document which explained why he had felt obliged to make a formal will, and he left specific directions in it for the surrender after his death of all his papers and manuscripts to Chertkov, who was empowered to edit and publish them according to the principles on which he had published Tolstoy's writings during his lifetime.

During Chertkov's visit to Yasnaya Polyana, the day before their meetings ceased, the wary Sonya overheard a snatch of conversation in which Tolstoy asked him if he agreed to the changes he had made, meaning changes in the supplementary note to the will. Her suspicions at once aroused, she demanded of her husband that he tell her what agreement he had been talking about. He refused to answer. She jumped to the conclusion that a secret will had been the subject of their conversation, and from that time on she daily pestered her husband, Alexandra, Bulgakov, and others on this score.

The subject of the will was now added to Sonya's collection of fixed ideas provoking her hysterical outbursts. Tolstoy's patent evasion on this theme naturally increased her suspicions and agitation. And his situation was rendered doubly painful by the fact that the existence of a will was a matter in which Leo and Andrei could entirely support their mother's demands, though with perhaps more self-interest than filial devotion. For they were keenly conscious of the vast financial possibilities of a literary inheritance from their father. They conducted an unsuccessful inquisition of their own on Alexandra, and Andrei put the question of the existence of a will directly to his father, who firmly refused to give him any satisfaction.

Of course Chertkov and his friends at near-by Telyatinki quickly heard of this new trial of Tolstoy, and they grew alarmed. Chertkov at once wrote him. All this was a deliberate plot, he said. His wife's supposed illness or "fatiguing dissimulation" had first been used to separate them. Now the persistent and united pressure of his wife and two sons was being used to extort from him or to learn from his diaries or papers whether he had made a will depriving them of a literary inheritance. "If they decide that you have not executed a will," he continued, "then they hope to prevent you from doing so by watching over you incessantly until your death. On the other hand, if they learn that you have written a will, they will try to keep you from going anywhere until they can get a physician, in their pay, to pronounce you feeble-minded and thus invalidate the will." Goldenweizer and A. P. Sergeyenko wrote in the same vein to Tolstoy, and all urged him to escape at once to Kochety. Obviously the friends feared more than anything else the defeat of all their plans in the matter of the will.

Tolstoy was annoyed by this concerted and gratuitous advice, and he sharply told Goldenweizer that he entirely disagreed with the sentiments expressed in these letters. "All of you exaggerate. What is said at a moment of irritation, you explain as a deliberate plan. But if it should turn out that you are right, then so much the better; it would give me freedom of action." Though Tolstoy had understandable moments of wavering in his belief, he had little sympathy for the idea that Sonya's hysterical behavior was merely a cunning device to achieve well-planned objectives. He said to Bulgakov on one occasion: "Sofya Andreyevna is not well. . . . If Vladimir Grigoryevich [Chertkov] could only see her as she is today! It is impossible not to feel sorry for her sufferings, and impossible to be so hard on her as he and many others are, and as I often am. And she has no reason for her behavior. If she had any reason, she could not refrain from expressing it. It is simply that she is stifled here and cannot breathe. I cannot fail to pity her, and I rejoice when I am able to do so."

The conspiratorial atmosphere surrounding the will was not to Tolstoy's taste. By nature he was open and frank, and during many years of married life he had had no secrets from his wife. At times he now felt compelled to justify the secrecy to himself. For if he dismissed Chertkov's notion of a deliberate plan on the part of his wife and two sons, he admitted that they had given him much reason to believe that they would make every effort to violate his frequently expressed wishes concerning the disposition of his writings after his death. It is significant that at this time he began "A Diary for Myself Alone," one that would come under the eye of no one, not even Chertkov. And the first entry in this on July 29 reads: "Today I must note one thing: if the suspicions of some of my friends are just, then an attempt has now begun to obtain her ends by affection. For some days now she has been kissing my hand, which she never did before, and there are no scenes nor any despair. May God and good people forgive me if I am mistaken. It is not easy for me to be mistaken in what is kind and loving. I can love her quite sincerely, but I cannot do this in my relations with Leo. Andrei is simply one of those in whom it is difficult to think the spirit of God exists (but remember that it does). I will try not to get irritated, and abide by my primary resolution—silence. I cannot deprive millions of people of what they perhaps need for their souls. I repeat 'perhaps.' But if there is even the smallest probability that what I write is needed by men's souls, I cannot deprive them of that spiritual food in order that Andrei may drink and indulge in debauchery, or that Leo may smear and . . . But heaven help them. Do your own duty and do not judge."

Tolstoy's lurking discontent over the secret nature of his will was suddenly intensified by a conversation with Biryukov. His biographer came for a visit at the beginning of August and was at once informed by both sides of all the unpleasant details of the family quarrel. Since he was close to the Chertkovs, he also heard about the will from them. To their dismay, however, he took a contrary position on the whole question, and he humbly advised Tolstoy to summon the family and even several friends as witnesses and simply announce his wishes concerning the disposal of his writings after his death. This advice once more aroused in Tolstoy the feeling that he had acted wrongly. In fact, several days before he had entered in his secret diary: "Chertkov has drawn me into strife, and that strife is very hard and repulsive to me." And now he wrote him a letter: "I talked yesterday with Posha [Biryukov] and he very correctly told me that I was at fault in having made my will secretly. I should have done it openly, informing those whom it concerned, or I should have left things as they were and not have done anything. He is quite right that I acted badly, and I now regret it. It was bad to do it secretly, thereby assuming ill-will in my heirs. Above all, it was certainly wrong to avail myself of an institution of the government that I reject by drawing up a will in legal form. The circulation of my writings will hardly atone for the distrust evoked by the inconsistency of my conduct. . . . But I think that for the present it is best to leave things as they are. Yet it is hard."

Panic seized the little group at Telyatinki. A council of war was held, and Chertkov hurried a letter off to Tolstoy to discredit Biryukov on the score that he knew nothing of the facts that had obliged him to write a will and keep it from the knowledge of his family. Tolstoy then asked Chertkov to provide him with the history of these facts. He did in a very long and extraordinary letter that reviewed in detail over many years the attitude of Sonya and certain members of her family to property rights and to Tolstoy's rejection of them. Though the picture is distorted here and there and the interpretation occasionally malicious, Chertkov stuck fairly close to the facts and they invoked the most painful memories in Tolstoy. He capitulated to the triumphant Chertkov and once again agreed with him that the will and the secrecy attendant upon it were necessary, though he still insisted that he was dissatisfied with his own conduct in the whole affair but that he did not know how to act more wisely in this instance.

Meanwhile, Tolstoy's misery continued, though the cessation of Chertkov's visits lessened the frequency of his wife's outbursts. She lived for the hope that he must soon leave Telyatinki, for the police had permitted him to stay only till the termination of his mother's visit in September. Now convinced that there was a will, Sonya blamed her sufferings on Tolstoy's nonobservance of his principles, whereas formerly she had ascribed them to his adherence to his convictions. He sometimes caught her rummaging among his papers looking for his diary which he now had to keep locked up. When he took his daily walk or ride, she shadowed him for fear he might be having a rendezvous with Chertkov. At times she wondered whether it would not be better to have Chertkov visit the house if it would put an end to their letter-writing. "You are always carrying on a secret amatory correspondence," she furiously objected. And she sent him a mad letter containing the passage from his youthful diary on his love for men and her comments on it.

The strain was telling on Tolstoy. His sleep was disturbed by worry and Sonya's frequent visits at all hours of the night. It was impossible to work. His attempt to treat her tirades with silence only exasperated her the more. He began to feel that there was something ridiculous, humiliating, and shameful in allowing himself to be cut off from Chertkov. Death would seem to him like a welcome relief, he wrote in his diary. For some days he had been thinking about trying to get away from her and go to Kochety for a rest, and Tanya, who was visiting Yasnaya Polyana, strongly encouraged this step. But every time it was mentioned Sonya had hysterics, and she loudly threatened, if he went, to go to her friends the Maslovs where Taneyev was vacationing.

On August 14 Tolstoy wrote in his secret diary: "Always worse and worse. She did not sleep last night. She jumped up in the morning. 'With whom are you talking?' Then she told me horrible things: sexual irritation. Terrible to say. . . . Terrible, but thank God she is pitiful and I can pity her. I will endure. God help me. She has worn everybody out, and herself most of all." Shortly after this Tanya entered her father's room and found him with his face in his hands, sobbing. He repeated to his daughter some of

[9] Tolstoy struck out three words here.

the things Sonya had said to him. She had demanded that they resume what had long since ceased—marital relations!

This last experience was too much for Tolstoy, and he firmly decided to leave for Kochety the next day.

8

Sonya did not carry out her threat to go to the Maslovs and Taneyev. Instead, to the dismay of the whole party, she insisted on accompanying her husband to Kochety. Tanya, feeling that the whole purpose of her father's visit to her estate would be frustrated, sternly warned her mother that she expected her to be on her best behavior.

For several days relations between husband and wife improved in the cheery surroundings of Kochety, until Sonya read a news account to the effect that the government's ban on Chertkov's living at Telyatinki had been entirely removed. It almost seemed as though the authorities, aware that Chertkov's presence near Yasnaya Polyana was a vital factor in a scandalous family feud, had decided to let him remain there as a part of their indirect campaign against Tolstoy. He and his daughters had known of this news for nearly a week, but had feared to tell Sonya. Now her despair was terrible. "I will kill him!" she shrieked at her husband, and she even drafted a letter to Stolypin, head of the government, demanding that he remove Chertkov from her neighborhood. Only by reaffirming his promises not to see Chertkov at all and not to give his diaries to anyone, and by agreeing to a new promise she demanded not to allow Chertkov to take photographs of him, could Tolstoy reduce her to some semblance of calm.

Sonya's diary at this time contains shameless expressions concerning the "passionate relations" between her husband and Chertkov. She crazily imagined licentious scenes of perverted intimacies that they wrote to each other in their letters, and the very sight of a photograph of her husband and his friend together caused a hysterical explosion. Fully aware of the horrible thoughts that were filling her mind, it is little wonder that Tolstoy, forgetting his former passionate professions of love for Sonya, should now write in his secret diary at Kochety: "Today, remembering my wedding, I thought that it was a fatal step. I was never even in love. But I could not avoid marrying."

For some time Sonya had been an eager reader of critical

attacks on her husband's teaching, and she often appropriated such views and repeated them as her own original observations. Now she tried to draw him into argument so that she could ridicule his convictions before the company at Kochety. Her diary contains the substance of one such discussion on chastity, in which she maliciously parroted ignorant opinions of critics who disregarded Tolstoy's contention that chastity was an unrealizable Christian ideal toward which all should strive even though they could never achieve it. She fulminated that it was all very well for her husband to preach chastity. "But at his wish," she declared, "I've been pregnant sixteen times: thirteen children born and three miscarriages. In those days he suggested to me, a young woman, that he could not work or write or be healthy if I refused to cohabit with him."

Tolstoy continued "to struggle with Sonya by kindness and love." And when that failed, he observed silence. At times, however, all his good intentions were forgotten in the face of her mad unreasonableness, and then angry words would fly. After such an exchange, he bitterly wrote in his secret diary on August 28: "It is continually harder and harder with Sofya Andreyevna. Not love, but a demand for love that is close to hate and changes into hate. Yes, such egoism is insanity. Having children formerly saved her—an animal love, but all the same a self-sacrificing one. When that ended there remained only a terrible egotism. It is egotism of a most abnormal character—insanity."

Whatever harsh sentiments about his wife Tolstoy permitted to himself in the privacy of his secret diary, he did not lightly tolerate them from anyone else. In this respect he continued to rebuke the indignation of Alexandra and the offensive asperity of the little group of friends. Hardly a letter to Chertkov, chafing in his isolation and wounded pride, failed to carry a plea for greater understanding of Sonya's wretched condition. "I know it appears strange to you," Tolstoy wrote in one of these letters, "but she often seems to me terribly pitiable. When I consider what it must be like for her alone at nights, more than half of which she spends sleepless, with a dim yet painful consciousness that she is not loved and is a burden to everyone, except the children, I cannot help pitying her."

After another unpleasant scene, Sonya left for home on August 29 to comfort her favorite son Leo, who was involved in a court case. Husband and wife parted in loving fashion, kissing and weeping, and begging each other's forgiveness for all that had passed. At last Tolstoy was able to settle back to enjoy the quiet and rest which had been the purpose of his visit to Kochety. He wrote her kind letters, describing his daily occupations, inquiring about her health, and drawing an alluring picture of how fine their life could be together if she could only master the feelings that tormented her.

Sonya's replies were complaining, suspicious, and her true state of mind she described in a letter to Tanya, in which she declared that her husband must definitely make a choice between her and Chertkov, "the man he now loves so insanely." Soon Tolstoy received an alarming report from Alexandra of the goings-on at Yasnaya Polyana—Sonya's agitated condition continued. She had called in a priest, shocked him with her lengthy tale of misery, and had him sprinkle holy water over her husband's room in order to drive out Chertkov's evil spirit. A few days later Sonya arrived back at Kochety, refusing to be separated any longer from her husband.

On the urging of Tanya and Alexandra, Chertkov at this time wrote Sonya a long letter in an effort to effect a reconciliation. In encyclopedic fashion he reviewed the whole troubled course of their relations, tried to explain away his harsh words to her as having been the result of an occasional loss of "spiritual equilibrium," and made an earnest plea at the end that she throw off the burden of hostility and hatred of him that oppressed her and tormented others. Her answer was equally detailed, going over all the old scores she had to settle with him. But her attitude was utterly unforgiving: he was an obnoxious intruder in her family, had caused all her suffering, and she demanded that he leave them in peace.

Tolstoy's brief period of quiet was abruptly terminated by Sonya's return to Kochety. Her nervous irritation continued, and the climaxing hysterical outbursts now exhausted his patience. "Today, the 10th, everything is still the same," he wrote in his secret diary. "She eats nothing. I went to her. . . . In the morning I thought I could stand it no longer, and that I should have to leave her. There is no living with her, only torment, as I told her. My trouble is that I cannot remain indifferent. Towards evening the scenes began again: dashes into the garden, tears, screams. When I went after her to the garden, she cried out: 'He's a beast, a murderer! I can't endure the sight of him!' She ran to hire a cart with the intention of leaving at once. So it went on all evening."

Tolstoy's despair and shame were increased by the rumors and first-hand reports passed on to him by the sleuthing friends at Yasnaya Polyana, who found his family life such a fruitful field for their personal diaries. Varya Feokritov took down verbatim Sonya's remarks, when she had returned from Kochety, concerning her plans for Tolstoy's works after his death. If he left no legal will, she intended to publish his writings for her own profit. However, if he willed all to Chertkov or to the public, she said, then she would simply refuse to surrender his unpublished pieces, which she would insist had all been written before 1881. And anyway, she declared, she and her sons would contest a will, maintaining that it was made under duress when he was feeble-minded. Varya Feokritov gave a copy of these remarks to Goldenweizer, who promptly sent it on to Tolstoy after using it for his own diary. Tolstoy could hardly doubt the truth of this unpleasant report, but he was in no sense grateful to those who made it available to him, for he curtly wrote Goldenweizer: "Though it is hard for me to know all this and to know that so many outsiders know about it, it is salutary for me. However, in what Varvara Mikhailovna [Varya Feokritov] writes, and in what you think about this, there is much and bad exaggeration, a disregard of her sickly condition, and a confusion of good sentiments with those that are not good."

With a new firmness Tolstoy resisted all Sonya's hysterical attempts to get him to return to Yasnaya Polyana with her or even to name a definite date. Finally, "insanely sobbing," as she described herself, she left without him on September 12. He did not join her until September 22, in time to be on hand for the next day, their forty-eighth wedding anniversary. Terror seized him, he wrote in his secret diary before leaving, at the thought of what awaited him there. His fears were justified. She greeted him with bitter reproaches.

9

Dressed in a white silk gown, Sonya stood with her husband before a screen on the day of their forty-eighth wedding anniversary. Bulgakov nervously clicked the shutter. But the picture did not turn out well, and the next day she insisted that another be taken. His dislike for this business made no difference to her. Had he not let Chertkov take scores of pictures of him? Besides, a newspaper, she heard, had published a rumor that they were divorced. She would send this photograph to the press and prove to the world that Tolstoy still loved her. "She needs only one thing," he had written in his diary a week before, "that people should think that *I love her*. That is what is so terrible." She clung to his arm, turned her face full toward him, and tried to elicit with her faded smile an answering smile from him. But he stared stonily ahead, profound discontent frozen forever on his careworn face.

Alexandra raged, scolded her father. Why had he allowed himself to be photographed with his wife when she had forced him to promise not to let Chertkov take him? Besides, he had done nothing about the fact that her mother, while he was at Kochety, had removed from their favored position over his desk a large photograph of Chertkov and his nephew and one of her and himself and replaced them by her own photograph and one of his father. Tolstoy, feeling harassed and gloomy over this criticism from his daughter, shook his head and sorrowfully remarked that she was becoming like her mother. Shortly after he rang for her to come to his study and take dictation. She refused. He sent Bulgakov for her. She entered, sat in silence, her pencil poised. He tried to begin, but his old head fell on the arm of the chair and he burst into sobs.

"I don't need your stenography!" he cried through his tears. She rushed to him and asked his forgiveness, and they both wept.

The unpleasantness over the photographs did not end there. Perhaps to please Alexandra, and because he felt that he must be firm, Tolstoy put back in their original places the pictures that Sonya had removed. She indulged in another hysterical fit when she discovered the change. So her husband, forbidden to see Chertkov, could not part with his picture, she fumed. She ripped it from the wall and tore it up. Weeping and raving about the house, she threatened suicide. Going to her room, she began shooting a toy pistol, hoping that her husband would hear and run to her rescue. But he sat gloomily in his study. Instead, old Marya Schmidt, who was calling at the time, grew terrified over the shots, and hurried off a message to Alexandra, who was visiting her sister-in-law with Varya, to return at once. When they arrived late that night a stormy scene ensued, with Sonya shouting that she would drive Varya away as she had driven away Chertkov. Alexandra went to her father and declared her intention of leaving the house. "It all leads to one end," he wearily replied. In the morning, Alexandra, taking Varya with her, moved to her little house at Telyatinki, near the Chertkovs. She came to Yasnaya Polyana a few hours every day to work for her father.

Sonya was somewhat humbled by this unexpected turn of events and made a serious effort to control her more extreme actions. In her anxiety now to please Tolstoy, she often amazed him with nervous, endless, and frequently senseless chatter. And he found something unpleasantly incongruous in an old woman's explosive acts of tender love. Grateful for this degree of relief, however, he tried to repay her affection. "Today I realized for the first time a possibility of overcoming her by love and kindness," he hopefully wrote in his secret diary.

But the tension was still there, as Sonya's own diary at this time indicates. She continued to trail him around, to require an accounting of his every movement, to snoop among his papers, and to demand that he read his mail to her. When he objected to this surveillance, to being a rag under his wife's slipper, she ironically accused him in turn with having fixed ideas. He wants to be free, she wrote in her diary. "But is he not free now, except for intercourse with Chertkov and a mad desire to see him?"

At this moment, however, Chertkov at near-by Telyatinki, sulking like Achilles in his tent, was indignant over Sonya's blistering rejection of his letter of reconciliation. He testily wrote Tolstoy that he had made a big mistake in allowing "a spiritually alien person" to interfere in their relations. Depressed by reproaches and accusations from this quarter too, Tolstoy entered in his secret diary: "They tear me to pieces. I sometimes think I ought to get away from them all." Though he recognized some justice in Chertkov's complaints, he frankly replied: "I fully agree that I have made a mistake and that it ought to be corrected. But the whole matter seems to me much more complicated and difficult to resolve than it can possibly appear even to such a close friend as yourself. I must solve it alone in my soul, before God, and I am trying to do so, and every interference makes this task more difficult. Your letter pained me. I felt that I was being torn in two—no doubt because, rightly or wrongly, I detected a personal note in what you wrote." There were moments when, in his sense of the word, Tolstoy wondered whether his friend was a truly religious man. Chertkov realized that he had overshot the mark, and he immediately replied, humbly begging the master's forgiveness.

Badgered on every side. Tolstoy found little time or inclination for his dwindling literary work. Not to be writing saddened his spirits all the more and made his existence seem peculiarly futile. A rich artistic design had flashed into his mind and cried out for realization. On October 2 he entered in his diary: "I have written nothing, but at night I thought well and clearly about how fine it would be to depict artistically the triviality of the life of the rich and civil-official classes, and of the peasants and workers, and then portray among these and others a single spiritually living person in each class. It could be a woman or a man. Oh, how wonderful this could be! And how it attracts me! What a superb thing it could be!"

But art had now to give way to his moral struggle over his wife as he stood on the edge of the grave. For on the same day he made the following entry in his secret diary: "Today I felt a strong desire for artistic work, but I realized the impossibility of concentrating on it because of her, of this persistent feeling about her, and because of the struggle within me. But of course that struggle, and the possibility of victory in it, are more important than any possible work of art."

The next day, Tolstoy, worn out with the emotional strain of the past months, fell dangerously ill. He had convulsions and a prolonged period of unconsciousness. Sonya, in a frenzy of despair, clasped her husband's twitching legs and softly whispered: "Lord, only not this time, only not this time!" And she said to Alexandra, who had been hurriedly called: "I suffer more than you. You will lose a father, but I will lose a husband for whose death I am to blame!" For all her sincere and terrible grief, she could not resist the desire to purloin Tolstoy's portfolio, containing papers; she hid it in her cupboard. The children observed her in this act and hastened to secure from her his secret diary and the key of his desk. When Tanya demanded the portfolio, she returned it, saying that she did not want Chertkov to get it.

Tolstoy made a quick recovery. But Sergei, Tanya, and Alexandra held a council, and Sergei warned his mother that if she did not come to herself, the family would place her under the control of doctors and separate her from her husband. For if he died, said Sergei, the whole world would believe that it was her doing. Thoroughly contrite now, Sonya begged forgiveness of Alexandra and Varya and asked them to return to the house, which they did.

A few days after Tolstoy's illness, the now thoroughly shaken Sonya melted to the point of inviting Chertkov to call. Once the invitation was tendered, she longed to revoke it. Terrible palpitations seized her, she wrote in her diary, as she heard the sound of his approaching carriage. She had begged her husband not to embrace him in the customary fashion of intimate Russian male friends, and she had purposely ordered an early bath for him so that the visit would be cut short. Though she avoided Chertkov when he came, she peered through her husband's window with opera glasses to see how they met after their long separation. Victimized by her extreme agitation all that day, Tolstoy decided that he would seek no more visits from Chertkov.

Any hope of tranquillity Tolstoy expected from this decision was blasted, for Sonya found a misplaced copybook containing the entries, running from July 29 to September 22, of his "Diary for Myself Alone." She came upon this little book which he had tucked away in one of his boots. Of course, she did not scruple to read it, despite the plain statement on the first page that it was intended only for himself. In it were various frank reflections on the family strife and also plain allusions to his will and to some of its terms.

The hysterical scenes began all over again. Sonya's discovery confirmed not only her suspicion about the will, but all her other suspicions, which was a typical reaction for a person with her mania. For days, she wrote in her diary, she went about with only one thought—suicide. Her husband would give all his works to the public and thus would take "the bread from the mouths" of her twenty-three children and grandchildren. He was holding a threatening dagger over her—if he should die before her edition of his works was published, she might well lose all the income. Of course, that "wicked Pharisee," Chertkov, was the cause of it all. "I must end these tortures more quickly," she wrote, "or tomorrow Mr. Chertkov will be carrying away not manuscripts, but *me* to a lunatic asylum!"

Sonya left a letter on her husband's desk, in which she argued the family's rights to his literary inheritance with considerable skill from her point of view, and she must have stung his conscience to the quick by heaping scorn on him for repudiating his principles in making a legal will. And she even offered to renounce her own rights to his works in favor of her children and grandchildren. "I am seized by horror," she prophetically concluded about the will, "at the thought that I may survive you and see the evil that will spring up around your grave. . . ."

Tolstoy answered her objections about the will with silence or a plea that she refrain from mixing into his affairs. But in his secret diary he wrote: "A letter with reproaches because of some document about rights, as if the question about money were the most important thing. Yet this is better, clearer, but when she exaggeratedly speaks about her love for me and goes on her knees and kisses my hand, it is very hard."

Sonya's spying on his movements continued. She followed him for miles in a carriage, fearful that he would try to meet Chertkov, and from concealment she watched him in the distance with opera glasses. One day, with an air of determination, he firmly announced that he was going to Telyatinki, for he had heard that Chertkov's wife was ill. Despite a hysterical scene, he left. She followed soon after, running nearly all the way to Telyatinki, and hid in a ditch to await the meeting. But Tolstoy did not arrive, for he had decided that the visit would be unwise. She returned hours later, numb with cold, and took her place at the dinner table, sitting there silent, accusing, without eating, fully clothed in her coat, hat, and galoshes.

At last Tolstoy had begun to feel the futility of continuing this seemingly endless struggle with Sonya by love and kindness. He wondered whether his very presence was not actually hindering her recovery from her sick abnormality.

On October 20, an old peasant friend, M. P. Novikov, close to Tolstoy in spirit, visited Yasnaya Polyana. They talked a great deal together. When Novikov reminded Tolstoy of his former unfulfilled promise to visit him, he replied that he could now keep his promise, for he was superfluous at Yasnaya Polyana and might come one day to die in his hut. Late that night, when Novikov was about to retire, Tolstoy softly entered his room and said with some agitation: "I didn't want to speak to you about my affairs, but I've only just understood and felt, without explaining it to you, why I've always been unable to visit you. I'll not conceal from you the fact that in this house I'm roasted as though I were in hell. I've always thought and desired to go off somewhere—to the woods, to a watchman's hut, or to some poor peasant in the village where we could help each other, but God did not give me the strength to tear myself away from my family—my weakness, my sin. For my own satisfaction I could not oblige others to suffer—even my family. . . . I couldn't run away secretly without causing an uproar and bringing grief to my family, and my wife would on no account agree to my going to you or to anyone else. If I insisted, there would at once be the scenes customary in our circle—tears, hysterics, fainting fits—and I would not be able to endure them."

The surprised Novikov did not know what to make of this unexpected declaration, and he timidly offered a true story about a peasant friend whose wife was a chronic drunkard. For years her husband had done everything to cure her—he had ordered special prayers from the priest, bought miracle-working icons, and had gone on a holy pilgrimage. But last summer, concluded Novikov, he flogged his drunken wife a couple of times and it acted better than all the saints. She was cured.

Tolstoy liked this story and laughed. But growing serious again, he said: "I've endured more than your friend. For thirty years I've borne this cross and bear it still. . . . They value me here in rubles and say that I'm ruining the family. True, they have taken loving care of me physically; they see to it that my food does not grow cold, and that I have a clean blouse and breeches. . . . But no one, except Sasha, has any interest in my spiritual life. I will go away, I will unfailingly go away," he ended in a toneless voice. And at parting, he said once more: "We shall soon see each other, perhaps even sooner than I expect."

Three days later Tolstoy actually wrote Novikov a letter, recalling their conversation and asking him to search out in his village a warm hut should he decide to come.

Sonya relentlessly, fatally, pursued her mad course—peeping from behind doors at her husband, dashing into his bedroom in the dead of night to demand his diaries or that he burn his will. A firm was again tempting her with an offer of a million rubles for the publishing rights of all her husband's works. The very thought was repulsive to him. The whip of Novikov's peasant friend dangled perilously before him. He planned a statement to the newspapers, aimed at preventing Sonya from selling the rights to his works to anyone.

He had begun to make secret plans, to tell Alexandra and to ask her to inform Chertkov. Should he go, each of them would use a pseudonym in all communications. A feeling of tense expectancy took possession of him. Habit, duty, and love for Sonya demanded that he stay. When he whispered his intention to dear old Marya Schmidt, this frightened worshipper exclaimed softly: "Darling Leo Nikolayevich, this will pass; it is only a momentary weakness." And he replied: "Yes, yes, I know that it is a weakness, and I hope that it will pass." He sincerely hoped. But at the same time he waited for a real reason for leaving Yasnaya Polyana forever, and he knew in his heart of hearts that he would take advantage of it. And the unfortunate, tragic Sonya soon gave him that reason.

On October 28 Tolstoy wrote in his diary what had happened in the early hours of that morning:—

"I lay down at half-past eleven. Slept till three o'clock. I awoke, and again, as on previous nights, I heard the opening of doors and footsteps. On other occasions I had not looked at my door, but now I glanced at it and saw through the crack a bright light in the study and heard a rustling. That was Sofya Andreyevna searching, probably reading. The day before she had asked, insisted, that I should not close my doors. Both her doors were open so that she could hear my slightest movement. Day and night my every word and movement must be known to her and under her control. Again footsteps and a cautious opening of doors, and she went out.

"I don't know why this aroused in me an unrestrainable aversion and indignation. I tried to go to sleep again but could not. I tossed about for an hour, lighted a candle, and sat up. The door opened. Sofya Andreyevna came in and asked: 'How are you?' and she was surprised to see my light. My aversion and indignation grew. I choked and counted my pulse—97.

"I could lie there no longer and suddenly took the final decision to go away. I wrote her a letter and began to pack only what was necessary for the trip. I woke Dushan and then Sasha, and they helped me pack. I trembled at the thought that she would hear and come out—scenes, hysteria, and then there would be no getting away without an uproar.

"By six o'clock everything was somehow packed, and I went to the stable to tell them to harness. Dushan, Sasha, and Varya finished the packing. It was still night—pitch dark. I missed the path to the wing of the house, stumbled into a thicket, pricking myself, ran into the trees, fell, lost my cap and couldn't find it, made my way out with difficulty and got back to the house. I found another cap and with a lantern made my way back to the stable and saw to the harnessing. Sasha, Dushan, and Varya came out with me. I trembled, expecting to be pursued. But at last we drove off. At Shchyokino station we had to wait an hour, and I thought she would appear at any moment. However, we took our places in the railway carriage and started. My fear passed and pity for her arose in my heart, but no doubt that I had done what I had to do. Perhaps I am mistaken and am merely justifying my actions. But it seems to me that I have saved myself—not Leo Nikolayevich, but that something of which there is still a bit left in me."

XLI

To Seek, Always To Seek

On the morning of October 28 Sonya rose late, as was her custom. She went to greet her husband. He was not in his room—strange at that time of the day. An old fear gripped her. She ran to Alexandra.

"Where is papa?"

"He has gone away."

"How has he gone away? When?"

"Last night."

"Impossible! Sasha, dear . . ."

"Well, do you think I'm fooling? I'm telling you what has happened."

"Has he gone away for good?"

"Probably for good."

"Alone?"

"No, with Dushan."

"Darling, Sasha, dear . . . ! Tell me—where has he gone to?" Sonya clasped her hands imploringly. Her knees sagged and she leaned against the door.

"I don't know where he's gone," Alexandra answered. "He told me nothing, only gave me a letter for you."

"My God!" murmured Sonya. She tore open the letter and began to read:—

"My departure will grieve you. I am sorry for that, but please understand and believe that I could not act otherwise. My position in the house is becoming and has become unbearable. Apart from anything else, I can no longer live in these conditions of luxury in which I have been living, and I am doing what old men of my age commonly do: leaving this worldly life in order to live out my last days in peace and solitude.

"Please try to understand this and do not follow me if

you learn where I am. Your coming would only make your position and mine worse and would not alter my decision. I thank you for your honorable forty-eight years of life with me, and I beg you to forgive me for anything in which I have been at fault towards you, as I with all my soul forgive you for any wrong you have done me. I advise you to reconcile yourself with the new position in which my departure places you and not to have an unkindly feeling toward me. If you want to report anything to me, give it to Sasha. She will know where I am and will forward what is necessary. But she cannot tell you where I am, for she has promised me not to tell anyone."

Sonya could bear to read only the first sentence. She rushed out of the house and dashed toward the pond. Alexandra, Bulgakov, and several servants ran after her. Reaching the little platform from which the women rinsed the laundry, she slipped, fell on the planks, and rolled off into shallow water. Alexandra and Bulgakov with the aid of a servant pulled her out and with difficulty got her back to the house.

The hysterical Sonya's ravings and crude suicide attempts made the rest of that day at Yasnaya Polyana a mad experience for the whole household. She tried to jump out of the window, and again she dashed for the pond and was hauled back. A penknife, scissors, and heavy objects with which she feebly tried to injure herself were taken away from her. She had to be watched every moment. Roaming from room to room she wailed that she could not live without her husband. Her passionate outbursts of grief were a curious mingling of sentimentality and hate. Clasping to her breast her husband's pillow, a small one that she had made for him, she covered it with kisses, moaning:—

"Dear Lyovochka, where is your worn little head lying now? Do you hear me?"

And the next moment she screamed:—

"He's a beast! He couldn't have acted more cruelly! He deliberately wanted to kill me!"

In fact little serious concern for her absent husband was reflected in Sonya's grief. Her attention was centered primarily upon herself, an accepted phase of the derangement from which she suffered. She seemed now to realize the awful truth that the glory in which she had basked for years had vanished from her side, and that the world would attribute Tolstoy's flight from home to her behavior. Nor did the deception that had characterized the whole course of her nervous illness desert her at this awful moment. For she sent a servant to the station to find out what train Tolstoy had taken and dispatched a telegram to it: "Return at once. Sasha." But the servant revealed this fraud to Alexandra, who exposed it by a telegram of her own. To a chance reporter disguised as a friend, Sonya did not hesitate to show Tolstoy's farewell letter, apparently believing this to be her best defense before the world. To Alexandra, however, she declared her intention of running down her husband. If she found him, she said that would be the end of his escapes, for she would watch him day and night, even sleep at his door if necessary.

All the children, except Leo, who was abroad, were summoned in this emergency. They quickly gathered at Yasnaya Polyana and decided to send for a doctor and a nurse to keep their mother under constant observation. This new doctor, a mental specialist, found no evidence of paranoia in Sonya, but rather a psychopathic neuropsychic hysteria. Her violent agitation hardly lessened. She wrote Tolstoy a pathetic letter the day after his flight: "Lyovochka, darling, come home and save me, dear, from a second attempt at suicide. Lyovochka, friend of my whole life, I will do everything, everything you wish; I will renounce all luxury entirely; I'll be friendly with your friends; I'll cure myself; I'll be kind. Dear, dear, come back; you must *save* me. Even the Gospel says you can never, in *any circumstances,* desert your wife. My dear, darling, friend of my soul, save me, return. Come back if only to say farewell to me before we part forever." Poor Sonya's repentance was too late.

2

At last he was on the road! The great adventure had begun. But the setting was not the one he had so often imagined—of the Brahmin, bent with years, trudging his solitary way along a dusty path to some lonely wilderness refuge. Tolstoy sat gloomily in a smoky, crowded, noisy, third-class railway coach. He seemed more like some aged modern Don Quixote with Dushan, his faithful Sancho Panza, off on a hopeless quest of spiritual knight-errantry.

What a complex series of material circumstances, psychological factors, rational speculation, and moral urges had created this unique situation. On the one hand, from the time of his youth Tolstoy had indulged in dreams of abandoning civilization and living like a peasant, joining the carefree Cossacks, becoming a holy pilgrim, or entering a monastery. And after his spiritual regeneration these dreams found real substance in his desire to lead a simple life of bread-labor and service to others, which was so much at variance with his comfortable Yasnaya Polyana existence. In one form or another both the dreams and the positive plans for an entirely different life were reflected in the hopes and yearnings of his imaginary characters—Olenin, Pierre Bezukhov, Kornei Vasilyev, Saryntsov, and Father Sergei.

On the other hand, unhappy experiences of Tolstoy's married life both aided and hindered the fulfillment of his dreams and spiritual desires. They aided in the sense that he often felt he could no longer live with his wife and must go away, and always, of course, it was to go away and realize his ideal existence. Again and again he expressed this intention in his diary, and on several occasions, notably before Alexandra's birth in 1884, and at the height of Sonya's affair with Taneyev in 1897, he very nearly left home. And in the latter instance, it is significant that he never destroyed the farewell letter to his wife, as if he sensed that his determination, though unfulfilled, was unaltered. Yet these unhappy experiences also hindered him from going away, because he accepted them as a cross he must bear out of love for Sonya and duty to his family. The unpleasant incident in his study in the early hours of the morning of October 28 suddenly simplified this inhibiting complex and provided the essential impulse to action. He left home to get away from Sonya, whom love and kindness could not change, but he had left also to realize his dream of a new life. On his own moral terms it was a weakness, as he had admitted to Marya Schmidt. He had lost his spiritual struggle and regained his humanity.

How hard it had been to take that step after so many years of doubt and hesitation. And somehow Tolstoy felt that it was irrevocable—there was no returning. Conscience, however, still tugged at him. He had been on the train only a short time when he turned to the silent, faithful Dushan and said mournfully: "I wonder how Sofya Andreyevna is now? I'm sorry for her."

With an effort Tolstoy finally put these sad thoughts out of his mind. "How fine it is to be free," he declared, as though trying to cheer up his anxious companion rather than himself. Soon he began to take an interest in the passengers sitting around him. The coach was full of peasants and workers. They had long been taking an interest in him, for some had recognized him and the word had gone around that this was the great Tolstoy. Naïvely he had imagined that he could escape from Yasnaya Polyana and hide himself from Sonya in some remote place, forgetting that his face was one of the best known in Russia. Reporters and police agents were quickly on his trail, and headlines—"Leo Tolstoy Leaves Yasnaya Polyana!"—shouted their news to the world before he even had time to select that peasant hut to which he would withdraw from the world "to live out his last days in peace and solitude."

If Tolstoy's features had failed to betray him, his conversation would have given him away. For he was soon engaged in an animated discussion with a peasant, a surveyor, and a student, and the subjects of course were his favorite ones—religion, the single tax of Henry George, the use of violence, and education. Warming up to the debate, he rose to his feet in order more forcefully to drive home his points, almost shouting so that he could be heard above the customary medley of train noises. The discussion turned into a lecture as passengers from both ends of the coach left their seats and gathered around to listen to Russia's most famous man. The student assiduously took notes. This man, who a few hours before had stealthily run away from his wife to seek a peaceful retreat, now stood in a crowded third-class railway coach and expounded the eternal law, like some Biblical prophet with his massive, gray-bearded head, emphatically declaring that he did not believe in a God who created the world but in One who lived in the consciousness of people.

After an hour of this Tolstoy grew weary and was content to sit quietly and listen approvingly to the accordion playing and tuneful songs of a group of workers at the rear of the coach. He had decided to visit his sister at the Shamardino Convent. The nearest station was Kozyolsk. Although it was only some seventy miles from Yasnaya Polyana, the trip consumed more than six hours. Dr. Makovitski, who detested Russian trains, bitterly declared that this incredibly slow ride under the most uncomfortable conditions helped to kill the ailing Tolstoy. Reaching Kozyolsk late in the afternoon, they drove by cab to Optina Monastery near

Shamardino. Going to the monastery inn, he said to the monk in charge in asking for a room:—

"My being here may perhaps be disagreeable to you. I'm Leo Tolstoy, excommunicated by the Church, and I've come to talk with your elders and tomorrow will go to my sister at Shamardino."

The monk politely replied that all were welcome there, and Tolstoy was assigned a comfortable room. He had sent a telegram and a letter to Alexandra to inform her and Chertkov of his whereabouts, and after posting his diary, he went to bed, "to try to sleep," as he wrote his daughter.

3

Early next morning A. P. Sergeyenko, one of Chertkov's assistants, arrived at the monastery inn for the obvious purpose of obtaining information on Tolstoy's condition and state of mind which he would report to his employer, who had already written a letter for the press to explain the reasons that had obliged Tolstoy to leave home, and to express his own joy over this event. Sergeyenko's account of what had happened at Yasnaya Polyana after Tolstoy's departure, especially Sonya's attempt to drown herself, depressed him. And in this disturbed frame of mind he wrote Alexandra a rather bitter letter, in which he said: "The chief thing is that they [his children] should understand and try to suggest to her [Sonya] that for me—with her spying, eavesdropping, eternal reproaches, her ordering me about, her constant control over me, her feigned hatred of the man nearest and most necessary to me, together with her evident hatred of me disguised as love—life was not merely unpleasant but simply impossible. If anyone should wish to drown, it is certainly not she but I. Let her know that I desire only one thing—freedom from her, from this falsity, pretense, and the hatred which fills her whole being."

Tolstoy walked around the familiar grounds of the monastery. If only they would not require him to go to church, he thought, how pleasant it would be to live the peaceful life of these monks. He wanted very much to talk with the celebrated ascetic, Father Joseph, but as an excommunicate he felt awkward about intruding where his presence might not be desired.

In the afternoon he visited his sister Masha at Shamardino Convent. They both wept as he told her of his life Yasnaya Polyana over the last few months and why he ha felt it necessary to leave. Masha did not criticize his decisior she had long been aware of Sonya's hysterical behavio Declaring that he would not return, he asked his siste about the possibilities of renting a hut in the vicinity Shamardino. Somehow it did not occur to him how unwe come he would be in the neighborhood of these two famou religious institutions, the heads of which were already wo ried over his presence. Yet he actually hunted that day fc a desirable hut, but with no success.

The next day, while he was again visiting his siste Alexandra arrived with Varya Feokritov. The distance be tween Yasnaya Polyana and his first haven seemed to b lessening. Though he had asked his daughter not to attemp to join him until he summoned her, she had felt it neces sary to come. The detailed account she gave of events a home alarmed him even more than the recital of Sergeyenkc And when she said that her mother had guessed wher he was and threatened to pursue him, a kind of pani seized him. He decided to push on as soon as possible.

Alexandra brought her father several letters from th family which did nothing to raise his drooping spirits. Ily and Andrei wrote to condemn his desertion of their mother However wretched his life at home had been, they argued he ought to have remained and endured it. Tanya neithe approved nor disapproved his action. Only Sergei frankl supported his father's departure and even wondered why he had not taken this step long before.

Tolstoy replied in a general letter to all the children. He wrote in a kindly spirit and tried to explain why he coulc not have acted otherwise. At the same time he also an swered Sonya's letter which she had written on the day after he left home. Any lingering hope she may have cher ished that he would quickly return to her was stifled in the first sentence: "A meeting between us, and still more my return *now,* is entirely impossible." He pleaded with her to reconcile herself to his absence and try to understand his position. Her present mood and attempts to commit suicide, he said, made his return unthinkable, for she obviously still lacked control of herself, which had been the reason why he had gone away. Yet he held out hope for her: "try to direct your strength towards pacifying your soul," he wrote, "and not towards getting whatever you want, and then you will obtain what you desire. . . . Do not think," he added, "that I went away because I do not love you. I love and pity you with all my soul. But I cannot do otherwise than I am doing. . . . Farewell, dear Sonya, and may God help you! Life is not a joke, and we have no right to throw it away at our own caprice, and to measure it by length of time is also unreasonable."

That evening Tolstoy, Alexandra, and Dushan sat around the table in his room in the inn and with the aid of maps and train schedules planned their next move. He decided to go south to Novocherkassk and stay with relatives, the Denisenkos. From that point on the plans became vague. Perhaps they would try to get passports and hide out somewhere in Bulgaria. If this proved impossible, he would seek out some of his followers in the Caucasus and live with them. In the excitement of planning he had forgotten his rule—to live for the present only. He suddenly remembered it and, as though displeased with himself, he abruptly ended the discussion: they could decide tomorrow what to do.

At four o'clock the next morning, however, Tolstoy woke Alexandra. They must be off. He had already aroused Dushan. Sleep had deserted him that night, for the fear that Sonya might arrive at any moment tormented him. They were soon on their way to the Kozyolsk station, where they boarded an early morning train. The last lap of his great adventure in search of peace and solitude had begun.

4

There were no peasants and workmen in the second-class car in which Tolstoy now traveled to engage him in heartwarming discussions about religion, the land question, and education. He asked Alexandra for a newspaper and was much chagrined at reading all about his flight from home. In fact, nearly everybody on the train was reading and talking about it. His daughter overheard cynical remarks of unsuspecting passengers concerning her mother and father. In no time the news ran through the whole train that Tolstoy was on board, and Alexandra had to speak sharply in order to drive away would-be visitors from her father's compartment. A man with a red mustache walked up and down the aisle, stupidly disguised now in the uniform of a railway employee, now in civilian clothes—the ubiquitous police agent. Tolstoy's secret plan of escape seemed to have become the common property of all.

Late in the afternoon Tolstoy experienced a severe chill. Dr. Makovitski took his temperature. It was slightly over a hundred. His fever rapidly increased. Fear gripped the little group, but Tolstoy, sensing their worry, tried to cheer them up. It seemed dangerous to continue the journey. Since the train stopped at Astapovo[1] for a considerable wait, Dr. Makovitski hunted up the stationmaster and persuaded him to provide a bed for Tolstoy in his little house on the side of the railroad tracks. The sick man was at once helped to bed.

After a spell of slight convulsions, Tolstoy slept quite well and awoke the next morning, Monday, November 1, feeling much better and with a lowered temperature. He dictated a telegram to Chertkov about his illness, but declared his intention of continuing his journey. When Alexandra suggested that she inform the family, as she had promised to do if he should become seriously ill, he implored her not to. The only person he had any desire to see, he said, was Chertkov, and she at once telegraphed him to come.

Shortly after this, perhaps because his conscience troubled him over summoning Chertkov and no member of his family, Tolstoy dictated a letter to his two oldest children, Sergei and Tanya. He begged them not to reproach him, for he felt that he could not ask them to come without their mother. He had called Chertkov, he wrote, because he had devoted his life to a cause which he felt, mistakenly or not, was of importance to all people. With a premonition of the end, he thanked them for their kindness to him, offered some fatherly advice to Sergei, and asked them to try to calm their mother, for whom he felt the most sincere compassion and love.

Toward evening Tolstoy's condition grew worse; pneumonia had set in. Now thoroughly alarmed, Dr. Makovitski and Alexandra decided to call Dr. Nikitin from Moscow without seeking Tolstoy's permission. Alexandra sent a telegram to Sergei to ask him to secure the services of the Moscow physician at once.

In the course of the day Tolstoy had dictated to Alex-

[1] Now called Leo Tolstoy Station.

andra for his diary a statement on God: "God is not love, but the more love there is in man, the more is God made manifest in him, and the more truly does he exist."

Chertkov arrived with Sergeyenko on Tuesday morning. The two friends greeted each other with deep emotion. Chertkov kissed his hand and they both wept. Tolstoy plied him with questions about Yasnaya Polyana and the family. The agony of his past experiences with Sonya apparently still fresh in his mind, he asked him, according to Chertkov's account, to do everything possible to prevent her from coming to him. When Chertkov reported that Sonya had agreed not to try to see her husband against his wish, he grew calmer. What he did not report was that Sonya, in the midst of her first grief over her husband's departure, had made an effort to be reconciled with his friend and her enemy. She had sent Bulgakov to Telyatinki to ask him to call.

"Why should I go?" said this high priest of spiritual love. "Merely in order that she should humble herself before me and ask my forgiveness? . . . It is simply a trick to get me to send a telegram to Leo Nikolayevich for her." He refused to go. But Sonya was so convinced he would grant her wish that she had already indiscreetly sent a telegram to her husband to announce that she had become reconciled with Chertkov.

That evening Tolstoy's son Sergei arrived. He had set out for Astapovo at once upon receiving his sister's telegram asking him to send Dr. Nikitin. At first Sergei hesitated to enter the room, for Tolstoy was still under the delusion that the family knew nothing of his whereabouts. His father was happy to see him but obviously disturbed over his arrival. Sergei calmed his fears by saying what was partly true—that he had learned his father was at Astapovo from a conductor on the train.

Since the sick man's condition did not improve, the Zemstvo physician from a neighboring town was called in. Tolstoy hopefully asked if he would be able to resume his journey within two days. When the doctor said that it would be more like two weeks, he turned his face to the wall. He was entirely unaware that the secret he so wished to preserve was humming in all directions on the telegraph and telephone wires. Police officials demanded to know from railroad officials why Tolstoy had not been moved to a hospital. Reporters from Moscow and Petersburg wired the stationmaster for detailed reports of the sick man. And one of these reporters had already informed Sonya that her husband was dangerously ill at Astapovo. She immediately hired a special car for herself, members of the family, and her doctor and nurse. They arrived at Astapovo very late at night on Tuesday.

5

Still fearful that Sonya would come, Tolstoy had asked Alexandra to wire his sons to prevent this, "because my heart is so weak that a meeting would be fatal, though otherwise I am better." This message was handed to Sonya after she arrived. On Wednesday morning the family held a council in the special car and decided that a meeting of their mother and father might be injurious to him. So long as there was a chance of his recovery, they would allow her to see him only if he desired it. All the doctors, and there were eventually five of them in attendance, emphatically supported this position. With some complaining, Sonya agreed, for she said that she did not wish to cause her husband's death. They further decided that they would keep from their father any knowledge of the presence of the family at Astapovo, since he would guess that his wife was with them. Arrangements were made to live in the special car, which was placed on a siding. By now the stationmaster had moved out of his little house and given it up entirely to the sick man and his attendants.

Disaster nearly overtook the family's well-intentioned plans that very day. Sonya had brought with her Tolstoy's little pillow. She now pleaded with Dr. Makovitski that it should once again be placed under his head. The gentle Dushan agreed and Tanya gave it to him. Tolstoy instantly recognized the pillow and wanted to know how it got there. Unable to lie, Dushan explained that Tanya had given it to him. Disturbed but joyful, Tolstoy asked to see his beloved daughter. He eagerly put many questions to her about his sons, which she had great difficulty in answering without betraying the fact that they were only a few yards away. Then he wanted to know all about Sonya: What was she doing? How did she occupy herself?

"Perhaps you had better not talk, papa. You get excited," replied the tearful Tanya, afraid of betraying her mother's presence at Astapovo by the slightest word.

"Tell me, tell me! What can be more important to me

than that?" he asked in a sobbing voice. She mumbled something and hurriedly left the room.

Learning, perhaps from Chertkov, that Goldenweizer and Gorbunov-Posadov had arrived, Tolstoy wished to see them. Such visits taxed his waning strength, but these were old friends who loved him. After they left, however, he wrote in his diary: "Today, the 3rd, Nikitin, Tanya, and then Goldenweizer and Ivan Ivanovich [Gorbunov-Posadov]. So this is what has come of my plans! 'Do what's right, come what may!' [2] It is all for the good of others and chiefly of myself."

That night he slept badly, became delirious, and his heart action was very weak. But the doctors still had hope.

6

By Thursday the attention of the world press centered on little Astapovo. The place swarmed with reporters, smoking, drinking, bored with the hourly bulletins and the absence of any sensational news. They held up anyone coming out of Tolstoy's room for a story, or ran down members of the family for a bit of human interest. Sonya was the only one willing to talk, and she talked to them at random, in her most irresponsible manner, even declaring that Tolstoy had left home as a kind of publicity stunt to attract attention to himself. Embittered by the fact that she was not allowed to see her husband, she persuaded the unsuspecting Alexandra to let her into the anteroom so that cameramen could film her as though she were really going to see Tolstoy. Sonya, who, as Tolstoy's wife, should have been the most pitied person in the tragedy of death that was being enacted, was the most abject and pathetic. Instead of being by the side of her husband, she wandered aimlessly around the station under the guard of her sons or her nurse. At times she was escorted to the stationmaster's little house and would peer hopelessly through her husband's windows. Then the window in one of the other rooms would be opened and she would learn the latest news of his condition. Returning to the special car she gave vent to her tears. If only he could have read and answered the last letters she had written him. In them she had begged for mercy, protested her innocence in everything, and tried to explain

[2] *Fais ce que doit advienne que pourra;* a favorite saying of Tolstoy's.

away all her recent suspicions, spying, and eavesdropping as a result of "an irrational and passionate love" for him that had suddenly taken possession of her during those last months!

The tiny station restaurant labored overtime to feed the crowds and even tried to serve vegetarian meals for the Tolstoyans. The telegraph office was swamped with messages from all over the world. Government officials and police were frantically communicating with one another, wondering whether extra precautions ought not to be taken to preserve order.

Meanwhile, Tolstoy, lying in his sick room, constantly attended by doctors and nurses, with Chertkov, Alexandra, Sergei, and Tanya in the anteroom, ready for any call, was entirely ignorant of all the worldly commotion over his illness. There was something tragically ironic in his leaving his beloved Yasnaya Polyana to seek an obscure life of peace and solitude only to find himself as never before the center of attention, care, and international interest.

From Thursday to Saturday Tolstoy's condition fluctuated, inspiring alternate hope and despair among all who attended him. The pneumonia was accompanied by violent hiccoughing and severe heartburn that caused him much discomfort, and the accumulated nervous exhaustion of the past months left him no vitality to combat disease. Much of the time his mind remained clear, but there were extended periods of delirium and semiconsciousness. He kept asking for someone to write down his thoughts. Though he struggled hard to dictate, nothing came or only a jumble of words. Then he would demand to have his statement read back to him and grew agitated when this could not be done. Chertkov solved the difficulty by reading back passages from his *Circle of Reading,* which calmed him.

Once, in a delirious state, he implored Alexandra to catch his words. She could make out nothing of what he said. "Come closer," he begged, "it is so simple." She bent down and strained at the sense, but all she could understand was: "To seek, always to seek." At another time he tried to say something to Tanya. She asked him to repeat it and finally caught the words: "On Sonya . . . On Sonya much is falling. We have arranged badly . . ."

On Saturday Tanya sat by his side while one of the doctors prepared a camphor injection. Shortly after the injection he suddenly sat upright and said in a distinct voice: "But I advise you to remember one thing: there are a multitude of people in the world, but you regard only one, Leo."

During all his illness Tolstoy showed no fear of death, nor any regret over the thought that he might die. In a letter to Chertkov shortly before he left home, he had expressed the hope that he might meet his end in full possession of his faculties so as not to be deprived of the precious moments of dying which may be so beautiful. But those beautiful moments were now denied him. His mind was often clouded and clearly tormented by the memory of the recent tragic struggle with his wife and the fear that she might confront him with another hysterical outburst.

That Saturday night, when his condition was very bad, he said to his son Sergei: "I will go somewhere so that no one can interfere with me." Then he added in a loud tone of conviction: "To escape . . . I must escape!" Soon afterwards he called to Sergei and muttered some words which only Dushan could make out: "Truth . . . I love much."

On this same day the Abbot Varsonofi with a brother monk from Optina Monastery arrived at Astapovo. They were under orders from the Synod to persuade Tolstoy to die reconciled to the Church. In fact, ever since receiving the first news of his illness there had been much agitation in high ecclesiastical circles to make the most of this opportunity. The Metropolitan Anthony had telegraphed Tolstoy on November 4 from Petersburg to urge him to return to the Orthodox faith, but the attendants did not even deliver this message to the sick man. Then Anthony had wired the Bishop of Kaluga to send the ascetic, Father Joseph, of Optina to Astapovo as the man most likely to impress Tolstoy. This monk was ill, however, and Abbot Varsonofi was given the commission instead. Mindful of the duplicity of the clergy at the time of Tolstoy's illness in the Crimea, neither members of the family nor his physicians, who were fully aware of his wishes in this respect, would permit Varsonofi to enter the sickroom. The abbot was obliged to telegraph the bishop of his failure, but he added by way of justification that not even the governor of the province or high Petersburg officials had been permitted to see Tolstoy.

7

Toward midnight on Saturday Tolstoy began to sink rapidly and the doctors lost all hope. Since he was in much pain, they decided to give him a morphine injection. He objected to this but after the injection he grew quiet for several hours. The room was in semidarkness, illuminated by a single candle. Chertkov sat at the head of the bed, Sergei at the foot. The door leading to the next room had been opened. In there waited several people, among them Tanya, Alexandra, and the brothers. Doctors came and went quietly. Only the labored breathing of the dying Tolstoy could be heard in the oppressive stillness.

At about two o'clock in the morning one of the doctors suggested that Sonya be called. Chertkov at once left the room. She entered, her face frozen in grief, and for a few moments stared at the bed from a distance, as though afraid to approach. Then she swiftly went to her husband, kissed his forehead, sank on her knees and murmured: "Forgive me!" Fearful that he might wake and recognize her, a doctor led her into the next room.

The effects of the morphine wore off about three o'clock, for Tolstoy began to move about and groan. His pulse action was barely perceptible and he did not regain consciousness. His breathing became slower and softer. Sonya came in again, knelt by his bed, and uttered words of love that he could no longer hear. His breathing ceased. Complete silence reigned, suddenly broken a few moments later by the sharp voice of one of the doctors announcing: "A quarter to six." It was November 7. Dr. Makovitski, "holy Dushan," faithful to the last, went up to the bed and closed Tolstoy's sightless eyes.

Throughout cities and towns of Russia hundreds of thousands of people waited patiently before the news centers, anxiously following the frequent bulletins from Astapovo. Finally the flash came: "Tolstoy is dead!" A hush fell over the crowds. All took off their hats. Some wept softly.

Two days later the train bearing the coffin arrived at Zaseka station near Yasnaya Polyana. Several thousands of people had assembled. Many thousands more would have come if the government had not forbade the railways to supply extra trains. Stout shoulders carried the coffin all the way to the house. A lone file of silent people marched behind. In front two villagers bore a banner on poles on which was inscribed: "Leo Nikolayevich, the memory of your kindness will not die among us orphaned peasants of Yasnaya Polyana."

For hours people filed by the open coffin in the house to take their last farewell. Then the coffin was closed and carried by Tolstoy's sons to the Zakaz woods near by. All knelt bareheaded. "Eternal Memory" was sung, but no priests were present at this first public funeral in Russia without religious rites. Sonya stood with her family. She bore herself silently and with restraint. Chertkov was not present.

They buried Tolstoy in the spot he had selected, where his beloved brother Nikolai, when they were children together, had hidden the little green stick. On it was written that wonderful secret which, when known to mankind, would bring about a Golden Age on earth. Then all human misery and evil would vanish, and all men under the wide dome of heaven would be happy and love one another.

Russian Transliteration Table

(Based on the New Russian Orthography)

Nota Bene: —

1. Russian Christian names (Петр, Александр, etc.) that have common English equivalents (Peter, Alexander, etc.) retain their English form, except when they appear in the titles of books or articles.

2. The family names of a few Russian authors that have acquired fixed spellings in English (Gorky, etc.) retain their popular English spellings, except when they appear in the titles of books or articles.

А а	A a	
Б б	B b	
В в	V v	
Г г	G g	(in the genitive endings его and ого, г=v)
Д д	D d	
Е е	E e	(when initial and after ь, ъ and all vowels, except ы, — е = ye; after ы, е = ie)
Ё ё	Yo yo	(after ж and ш, ё = o)
Ж ж	Zh zh	
З з	Z z	
И и	I i	(after ь, и = yi)
Й й	I i	(the combinations ий = i and ый = y)
К к	K k	
Л л	L l	
М м	M m	
Н н	N n	
О о	O o	
П п	P p	
Р р	R r	
С с	S s	
Т т	T t	
У у	U u	
Ф ф	F f	
Х х	Kh kh	
Ц ц	Ts ts	
Ч ч	Ch ch	
Ш ш	Sh sh	
Щ щ	Shch shch	
ъ	(omitted)	
ы	y	
ь	(omitted)	
Э э	E e	
Ю ю	Yu yu	(after ы, ю = iu)
Я я	Ya ya	(after ы, я = ia)

Index

Ernest J. Simmons was born in Lawrence, Massachusetts, December 8, 1903, and educated at Harvard, where he received his Ph.D. in 1928. Although English literature and European folklore were his major interests through graduate work, a period of research in the Soviet Union, 1928–9, turned his attention to Russian literature with extraordinary significance both for himself and for the development of Russian studies in the United States. He returned to Harvard as an instructor in the English Department, 1929–36; and became assistant professor and Chairman of the Board of English Tutors, 1936–9. For 1941–6 he was associate professor of English and Russian literature at Cornell University, becoming Chairman of the Department of Slavic languages and literature in 1942. For 1946–58 Professor Simmons was Chairman of the Department of Slavic languages and has been Professor of Russian literature at the Russian Institute of Columbia University. Between 1946 and 1950 he was managing editor of *The American Slavic and East European Review*. He was also a member of the Executive Committee of the Modern Languages Association, 1953–4, and of the Board of Trustees of Sarah Lawrence College, 1956–8. Professor Simmons has done further research in the Soviet Union in 1932, 1935, 1937, 1947, and 1958, having three times been awarded the Milton grant for foreign travel. He has been on the Joint Committee on Slavic Studies of the American Council of Learned Societies and Social Science Research Council since 1947. Professor Simmons has been an associate editor of *The English Slavonic Review* and general editor of *The Columbia Slavic Studies* since 1949. His numerous books include *Pushkin* (1937), *Dostoevski: The Making of a Novelist* (1940), *Russian Fiction and Soviet Ideology: Introduction to Fedin, Leonov, and Sholokhov* (1958); he has lectured widely, contributed articles to numerous journals, and edited a variety of scholarly volumes. His *Leo Tolstoy* was originally published in 1946. Professor Simmons is married and has one son; he lives in Jaffrey Center, New Hampshire.

This book *is set on the Linotype in Granjon, a type named in compliment to Robert Granjon, but neither a copy of a classic face nor an entirely original creation. George W. Jones based his designs upon the type used by Claude Garamond (1510–61) in his beautiful French books, and more closely resembles Garamond's own than do any of the various modern types that bear his name. The book was composed, printed, and bound by* THE COLONIAL PRESS INC., *Clinton, Massachusetts. Paper manufactured by* S. D. WARREN COMPANY, *Boston. Cover design by* MILTON GLASER.

Vintage Russian Library

R-1001A *Leo Tolstoy: The Years of Development, 1828-1879* BY *Ernest J. Simmons*

R-1001B *Leo Tolstoy: The Years of Maturity, 1880-1910* BY *Ernest J. Simmons*

R-1002 *The Kremlin and World Politics: Studies in Soviet Policy and Action* BY *Philip E. Mosely* (A VINTAGE ORIGINAL)

R-1003 *Stalin: A Political Biography* BY *Isaac Deutscher*

R-1004 *How the Soviet System Works* BY *Raymond A. Bauer, Alex Inkeles, and Clyde Kluckhohn*

R-1005 *The Thief,* A NOVEL BY *Leonid Leonov*

R-1006 *The Soviets in World Affairs* BY *Louis Fischer* (Fall 1960)

R-1007 *Years of Childhood* BY *Serge Aksakov* (Fall 1960)

R-1008 *Early Joys,* A NOVEL BY *Konstantin Fedin* (Fall 1960)

R-1009 *Pan-Slavism* BY *Hans Kohn* (Fall 1960)

R-1010A *The Vintage Turgenev* (VOLUME I) *Smoke, Fathers & Sons, First Love* (Fall 1960)

R-1010B *The Vintage Turgenev* (VOLUME 2) *On the Eve, Rudin, A Quiet Spot, Diary of a Superfluous Man* (Fall 1960)

Vintage Books

-33B *Gide Journals* EDITED BY *Justin O'Brien,* VOL. II (1924–1949)

-34 *The Autobiography of Michel de Montaigne* EDITED BY *Marvin Lowenthal*

-35 *Forces in Modern British Literature* BY *William York Tindall*

-36 *Short Stories of Katherine Mansfield* EDITED BY *Elizabeth Bowen*

-37 *The American Character* BY *D. W. Brogan*

-38 *The Critical Performance* EDITED BY *Stanley Edgar Hyman*

-39 *Poetics of Music* BY *Igor Stravinsky*

-40 *The American Essays of Henry James* EDITED BY *Leon Edel*

-41 *The Future of the Novel—Essays by Henry James* EDITED BY *Leon Edel*

-42 *The Economic Basis of Politics* AND RELATED WRITINGS BY *Charles A. Beard,* COMPILED BY *William Beard*

-43 *The Coming of the French Revolution* BY *Georges Lefebvre*

K-44 *The Anatomy of Revolution* BY *Crane Brinton*

K-45 *The Good Soldier* BY *Ford Madox Ford*

K-46 *Flaubert and Madame Bovary* BY *Francis Steegmuller*

K-47 *The Classical Tradition in Poetry* BY *Gilbert Murray*

K-48 *The House in Paris* BY *Elizabeth Bowen*

K-49 *The Selected Letters of Gustave Flaubert* EDITED BY *Francis Steegmuller*

K-50 *Eleanor of Aquitaine and the Four Kings* BY *Amy Kelly*

K-51 *The Philosophy of Literary Form* BY *Kenneth Burke*

K-52 *Virgin Land* BY *Henry Nash Smith*

K-53A *The Social History of Art* BY *Arnold Hauser,* VOL. I (PREHISTORIC, ANCIENT-ORIENTAL, GREECE AND ROME, MIDDLE AGES) ILLUSTRATED

K-53B *The Social History of Art* BY *Arnold Hauser,* VOL. II (RENAISSANCE, MANNERISM, BAROQUE) ILLUSTRATED

K-53C *The Social History of Art* BY *Arnold Hauser,* VOL. III (ROCOCO, CLASSICISM, ROMANTICISM) ILLUSTRATED

K-53D *The Social History of Art* BY *Arnold Hauser,* VOL. IV (NATURALISM, IMPRESSIONISM, THE FILM AGE) ILLUSTRATED

K-54 *Some People* BY *Harold Nicolson*

K-55 *Essays* BY *Thomas Mann*

K-56 *The White Goddess* BY *Robert Graves*

K-57 *Archetypal Patterns in Poetry* BY *Maud Bodkin*

K-58 *H. L. Mencken: Prejudices—A Selection* MADE BY *James T. Farrell*

K-59 *Under the Volcano* BY *Malcolm Lowry*

K-60 *The Declaration of Independence* BY *Carl L. Becker*

K-61 *Where Angels Fear to Tread* BY *E. M. Forster*

K-62 *The Novel in France* BY *Martin Turnell*

K-63 *Confessions of Zeno* BY *Italo Svevo*

K-64 *The Natural History of Nonsense* BY *Bergen Evans*

K-65A *Great Operas* BY *Ernest Newman,* VOL. I

K-65B *Great Operas* BY *Ernest Newman,* VOL. II

K-66 *Two Legends* BY *André Gide*

K-67 *A History of Russian Literature* BY *D. S. Mirsky* EDITED BY *Francis J. Whitfield*

K-68A *Great Issues in American History,* VOL. I, 1765–1865 EDITED BY *Richard Hofstadter*

K-68B *Great Issues in American History,* VOL. II, 1864–1957 EDITED BY *Richard Hofstadter*

K-69 *The Spirit of Liberty* BY *Learned Hand* EDITED BY *Irving Dilliard*

K-70 *The Myth of the Birth of the Hero* AND OTHER WRITINGS BY *Otto Rank,* EDITED BY *Philip Freund*

K-71 *St. Mawr* AND *The Man Who Died* BY *D. H. Lawrence*

K-72 *The Road to Reunion* BY *Paul H. Buck*

K-73 *Economics and the Art of Controversy* BY *John Kenneth Galbraith*

K-74 *The Mentality of Apes* BY *Wolfgang Köhler*

K-75 *The Myth of Sisyphus* AND OTHER ESSAYS BY *Albert Camus*

K-76 *The Tree of Culture* BY *Ralph Linton*

K-77 *The Far Side of Paradise* A BIOGRAPHY OF F. SCOTT FITZGERALD BY *Arthur Mizener*

K-78 *The Folded Leaf* BY *William Maxwell*

K-79 *Stories* BY *Elizabeth Bowen*

K-80 *Seven Men and Two Others* BY *Max Beerbohm*

K-81 *The Road to Xanadu* BY *John Livingston Lowes*

K-82 *Verdi* BY *Francis Toye*

K-83 *Kings and Desperate Men* BY *Louis Kronenberger*

K-84 *The American Experience* BY *Henry Bamford Parkes*

K-85 *Poems by Wallace Stevens,* A SELECTION BY *Samuel French Morse*

K-86 *The Transposed Heads* BY *Thomas Mann*

K-87 *God's Country and Mine* BY *Jacques Barzun*

K-88 *Opera as Drama* BY *Joseph Kerman*

K-89 *William Blake* BY *Mark Schorer*

K-90 *The Power of Blackness* BY *Harry Levin*

K-91 *They Came Like Swallows* BY *William Maxwell*

K-92 *Catherine of Aragon* BY *Garrett Mattingly*

K-93 *Four Metaphysical Poets* BY *Joan Bennett*

K-94 *Alternative to Serfdom* BY *John Maurice Clark*

K-95 *The Age of Reform* BY *Richard Hofstadter*

K-96 *Lafcadio's Adventures* BY *André Gide*

K-97A *Modern French Painters* BY *R. H. Wilenski,* VOL. I

K-97B *Modern French Painters* BY *R. H. Wilenski,* VOL. II

K-98 *The Mind of The South* BY *W. J. Cash*

K-99 *The Inside Story* BY *Fritz Redlich* AND *June Bingham*

K-100 *Beethoven* BY *J. W. N. Sullivan*

K-101 *H. L. Mencken on Politics, A Carnival of Buncombe* EDITED BY *Malcolm Moos*

K-102 *The Jacksonian Persuasion* BY *Marvin Meyers*

K-103 *Domestic Manners of the Americans* BY *Mrs. Trollope* EDITED BY *Donald Smalley*

K-104 *Beyond the Mexique Bay* BY *Aldous Huxley*

K-105 *Anthropology of Folk Religion* EDITED BY *Charles M. Leslie* (Fall 1960)

K-106 *Charlemagne, From the Hammer to the Cross* BY *Richard Winston* (Fall 1960)

K-107 *Wagner as Man and Artist* BY *Ernest Newman* (Fall 1960)

K-108 *The Shape of Content* BY *Ben Shahn* (Fall 1960)

K-109 *Adventures of the Mind,* FROM The Saturday Evening Post (Fall 1960)

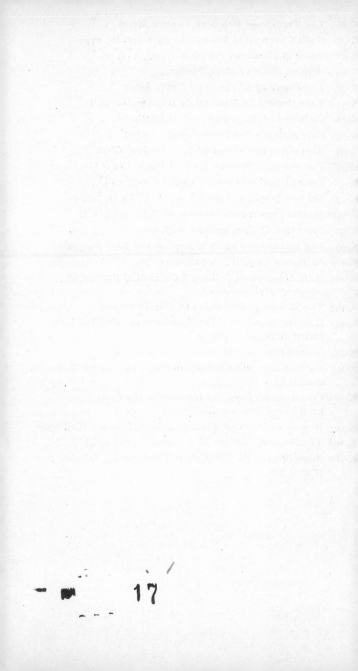

LEO TOLSTOY

by Ernest J. Simmo

"For a great many people, Mr. Simmons' biogr will be the literary event of the year. It is as co hensive a life of the man as we are likely to get.. since Tolstoy's history has a scope as wide as *Wa Peace*, it is almost as good a book as one by the M himself." —*The New Yorker*

"Far and away the most adequate biography available. It is a masterly feat, combining soun thorough scholarship with an easy and inter narrative." —*Daily Telegraph* (London)

"It is not too much to say that Simmons must b sidered among the classic biographers in Englis —*The Sketch* (Lor

Vintage Russian Library *Cover design by Milton*